AFRICAN HISTORICAL DICTIONARIES
Edited by Jon Woronoff

1. *Cameroon,* by Victor T. LeVine and Roger P. Nye. 1974. Out of print. See No. 48.
2. *The Congo,* 2nd ed., by Virginia Thompson and Richard Adloff. 1984
3. *Swaziland,* by John J. Grotpeter. 1975
4. *The Gambia,* 2nd ed., by Harry A. Gailey. 1987
5. *Botswana,* by Richard P. Stevens. 1975. Out of print. See No. 44.
6. *Somalia,* by Margaret F. Castagno. 1975
7. *Benin [Dahomey],* 2nd ed., by Samuel Decalo. 1987. Out of print. See No. 61.
8. *Burundi,* by Warren Weinstein. 1976
9. *Togo,* 2nd ed., by Samuel Decalo. 1987
10. *Lesotho,* by Gordon Haliburton. 1977
11. *Mali,* 2nd ed., by Pascal James Imperato. 1986
12. *Sierra Leone,* by Cyril Patrick Foray. 1977
13. *Chad,* 2nd ed., by Samuel Decalo. 1987
14. *Upper Volta,* by Daniel Miles McFarland. 1978
15. *Tanzania,* by Laura S. Kurtz. 1978
16. *Guinea,* 2nd ed., by Thomas O'Toole. 1987
17. *Sudan,* by John Voll. 1978. Out of print. See No. 53.
18. *Rhodesia / Zimbabwe,* by R. Kent Rasmussen. 1979. Out of print. See No. 46.
19. *Zambia,* by John J. Grotpeter. 1979
20. *Niger,* 2nd ed., by Samuel Decalo. 1989
21. *Equatorial Guinea,* 2nd ed., by Max Liniger-Goumaz. 1988
22. *Guinea-Bissau,* 2nd ed., by Richard Lobban and Joshua Forrest. 1988
23. *Senegal,* by Lucie G. Colvin. 1981. Out of print. See No. 65.
24. *Morocco,* by William Spencer. 1980
25. *Malawi,* by Cynthia A. Crosby. 1980. Out of print. See No. 54.
26. *Angola,* by Phyllis Martin. 1980. Out of print. See No. 52.
27. *The Central African Republic,* by Pierre Kalck. 1980. Out of print. See No. 51.
28. *Algeria,* by Alf Andrew Heggoy. 1981. Out of print. See No. 66.
29. *Kenya,* by Bethwell A. Ogot. 1981
30. *Gabon,* by David E. Gardinier. 1981. Out of print. See No. 58.
31. *Mauritania,* by Alfred G. Gerteiny. 1981
32. *Ethiopia,* by Chris Prouty and Eugene Rosenfeld. 1981. Out of print. See No. 56.
33. *Libya,* 2nd ed., by Ronald Bruce St John. 1991
34. *Mauritius,* by Lindsay Rivière. 1982. Out of print. See No. 49.
35. *Western Sahara,* by Tony Hodges. 1982. Out of print. See No. 55.

36. *Egypt,* by Joan Wucher King. 1984. Out of print. See No. 67.
37. *South Africa,* by Christopher Saunders. 1983
38. *Liberia,* by D. Elwood Dunn and Svend E. Holsoe. 1985
39. *Ghana,* by Daniel Miles McFarland. 1985. Out of print. See No. 63.
40. *Nigeria,* by Anthony Oyewole. 1987
41. *Ivory Coast,* by Robert J. Mundt. 1987
42. *Cape Verde,* 2nd ed., by Richard Lobban and Marilyn Halter. 1988. Out of print. See No. 62.
43. *Zaire,* by F. Scott Bobb. 1988
44. *Botswana,* by Fred Morton, Andrew Murray, and Jeff Ramsay. 1989
45. *Tunisia,* by Kenneth J. Perkins. 1989
46. *Zimbabwe,* 2nd ed., by R. Kent Rasmussen and Steven L. Rubert. 1990
47. *Mozambique,* by Mario Azevedo. 1991
48. *Cameroon,* 2nd ed., by Mark W. DeLancey and H. Mbella Mokeba. 1990
49. *Mauritius,* 2nd ed., by Sydney Selvon. 1991
50. *Madagascar,* by Maureen Covell. 1995
51. *The Central African Republic,* 2nd ed., by Pierre Kalck; translated by Thomas O'Toole. 1992
52. *Angola,* 2nd ed., by Susan H. Broadhead. 1992
53. *Sudan,* 2nd ed., by Carolyn Fluehr-Lobban, Richard A. Lobban, Jr., and John Obert Voll. 1992
54. *Malawi,* 2nd ed., by Cynthia A. Crosby. 1993
55. *Western Sahara,* 2nd ed., by Anthony Pazzanita and Tony Hodges. 1994
56. *Ethiopia and Eritrea,* 2nd ed., by Chris Prouty and Eugene Rosenfeld. 1994
57. *Namibia,* by John J. Grotpeter. 1994
58. *Gabon,* 2nd ed., by David Gardinier. 1994
59. *Comoro Islands,* by Martin Ottenheimer and Harriet Ottenheimer. 1994
60. *Rwanda,* by Learthen Dorsey. 1994
61. *Benin,* 3rd ed., by Samuel Decalo. 1995
62. *Republic of Cape Verde,* 3rd ed., by Richard Lobban and Marlene Lopes. 1995
63. *Ghana,* 2nd ed., by David Owusu-Ansah and Daniel Miles McFarland. 1995
64. *Uganda,* by M. Louise Pirouet. 1995
65. *Senegal,* 2nd ed., by Andrew F. Clark and Lucie Colvin Phillips. 1994
66. *Algeria,* 2nd ed., by Phillip Chiviges Naylor and Alf Andrew Heggoy. 1994
67. *Egypt,* by Arthur Goldschmidt, Jr. 1994

Historical Dictionary
of
NAMIBIA

by
JOHN J. GROTPETER

African Historical Dictionaries, No. 57

The Scarecrow Press, Inc.
Metuchen, N.J., & London
1994

British Library Cataloguing-in-Publication data available

Library of Congress Cataloging-in-Publication Data

Grotpeter, John J.
    Historical dictionary of Namibia / John J. Grotpeter.
        p.   cm.—(African historical dictionaries ; no. 57)
    Includes bibliographical references.
    ISBN 0-8108-2728-X (acid-free paper)
    1. Namibia—History—Dictionaries.   I. Title.   II. Series.
DT1514.G76   1994
968.81′003—dc20   94-25367

To the people of Namibia, justly proud of their recent independence, may this book be of service.

To Robert Bradford, without whose outstanding research and personal generosity this volume would be much slimmer.

In memory of Aurelia and Isadore Grotpeter, my parents, whose loving encouragement throughout their lives made this book possible.

To my wife Peggy and my daughters Jenny and Becky, for lovingly tolerating my obsession with this project.

CONTENTS

Editor's Foreword   vi

Preface   vii

Orthography   ix

Acronyms and Abbreviations   xi

Chronology   xvii

Map of Namibia   xxxii

INTRODUCTION   1

THE DICTIONARY   7

APPENDICES
   Namibian Regional Elections, November 1992   599
   1989 Constituent Assembly Election Results by District   601
   1990 National Assembly   602
   Namibian Government June 1, 1990   604
   German Rulers of South West Africa   606
   South African Administrators   606
   Election Results August 30, 1950   608

THE BIBLIOGRAPHY   609

About the Author   725

EDITOR'S FOREWORD

Namibia is not one of the largest of most important African states, but it has attracted more attention than most. The reason is obvious. It was a crucial test case for decolonization in southern Africa, and the struggle continued for years. Now that Namibia is independent, it will still attract interest as one of Africa's younger and, in some ways, more promising ventures.

While some may feel that we already know a lot about Namibia, given the extensive literature that exists, this knowledge is rather limited and skewed. We have been amply informed about the struggle for independence, the debates in the United Nations, and South Africa's role. But many other factors have been largely overlooked. There was an earlier struggle for freedom, one which influenced the more recent phase. Looking further back we must consider how the land was peopled and developed prior to colonization. These aspects are included in this extraordinary study of Namibia and make it broader and deeper than most.

This dictionary was not easy to write. While some of the information was readily available, namely that portion relating to the struggle for independence, not all of it was reliable, and the author, Dr. John Grotpeter, did much digging and sifting to understand what actually did happen. For earlier periods or lesser events, the effort had to be greater still. Nonetheless, the task was handled admirably by an unflagging author who not only read and studied but visited and observed Namibia to complete this book. Very sadly, Professor Grotpeter passed away after completing the manuscript but this book and his other historical dictionaries on Swaziland and Zambia remain a fitting tribute to his knowledge and affection for Africa.

Jon Woronoff
Series Editor

PREFACE

Writing this book has been a tremendous challenge. Despite the relatively small size of Namibia's population, there has been an enormous amount of material to draw on. Authors and scholars from South Africa, Germany, and Britain, as well as indigenous Namibians, have written at length about this fascinating country. The best of these sources have been cited in the introduction to the bibliography. I have used them in combination with my own research to prepare this book. In addition, however, I had the good fortune of meeting Dr. Robert Bradford, a political scientist at Susquehanna University in Selinsgrove, Pennsylvania. He had completed an enormous amount of research on Namibia, but was restricted by other commitments from preparing a manuscript. He generously volunteered to share with me his research data. This book is therefore the accumulation of the knowledge of many people. As must be the case, however, final responsibility for the product rests with me.

Although this book is quite large, the original manuscript was almost double the size. It has been necessary to eliminate much that I wished to include. I hope readers will understand, therefore, if material they are looking for is not included. I hope to find other ways to publish the additional material. Serious omissions will be corrected in future editions of this volume.

Aside from Bob Bradford, many others have assisted in the production of this volume. Special thanks must go to Jon Woronoff, the editor of this series, who stuck with me during trying periods when it looked like the manuscript would never be finished. Thanks also to the library staff at the St. Louis College of Pharmacy, especially Judy Longstreth, the head librarian, and David Weaver and Stephanie Reed. Their efforts to procure needed materials distinctly strengthened the book. Special recognition must also go to Professor Janice Eble, whose research assistance was invaluable.

Two student workers must be singled out. Stephanie Jannett, a 1993 graduate from our college, has been an excellent assistant and typist for a year and a half. And with great pride I must thank my daughter, Jennifer Grotpeter, a graduate of Duke University, for her outstanding work as both an editorial assistant and compiler of charts, appendices, and the map. Without these two the book might not have been completed. In addition, many students spent some time helping me organize and type the material over a period of about eight years. Among them are: Melissa Brice, Angela Robinette, Carrie Cafferty, Deanna Weekly, Sue Hopper, Beth Farmer, Kelli Burns Drury, Elaine Hinrichs Haynes, and Laurie Gaskell Hawes. The administration of the college deserves my thanks for providing me with these assistants.

ORTHOGRAPHY

The many languages of Namibia make it very difficult to produce a volume in which the spelling of the words will please everyone. While English is the official language of independent Namibia, both German and Afrikaans are used widely in the country. Thus maps may note a geographical feature in any of three languages. Is it the Elephant river or the Oliphants, the Karras Berge or the Karras Hills? Is a town named Gross Barmen or Great Barmen? Is something a Church, a Kirche, or a Kerk? In general I tried to use the form found most commonly in the literature (based usually on the original form of the name), and I have cross-referenced where necessary.

In addition, the African languages added to the problem. The use of the Khoisan languages in Namibia has introduced an entirely new set of consonants, whose forms are internationally accepted but may seem strange to the casual reader. I have used them in some instances, especially in the name of a group of African people, for whom the "click" sound is important in pronouncing their name. In other cases, however, different spellings (without resort to the "click" symbols) have become fairly standard, and these spellings have often been used. Peculiarities among the Bantu languages have also caused problems; for example, one town can be called either Rundu or Runtu, but the former is now preferred. The two official languages of Owambo do not have an *r* sound as Westerners know it, so an *l* is sometimes used in its place; still another Wambo language has an *r* that sounds similar to the *l*.

Finally, long-accepted spellings and usages have been changed in recent years. Ovamboland, for example, is now properly called Owambo. The Ovambo people are called the Wambo (or even Ambo). Herman Toivo Ja Toivo may now be referred to as Andimba Toivo Ya-Toivo in some circles, for example. I have tried to use the words Nama or Khoi wherever applicable instead

ix

of the earlier, more offensive word Hottentot. Similarly, San is usually preferred to Bushmen. Also in referring to the country I have generally used the current name, Namibia, instead of older forms such as South West Africa or German South West Africa, even when the reference is to an early period of its history.

ACRONYMS AND ABBREVIATIONS

ACN	Action Christian National or Aksie Christelik-nasionale
AG	Administrator General
AKTUR	Action Front for the Retention of Turnhalle Principles
ANC	African National Congress
ANS	Aksie Nasionale Skikking (Action for National Reconciliation)
BDP	Bevryder Demokratiese Party
CANU	Caprivi African National Union
CAP	Caprivi Alliance Party
CCN	Council of Churches in Namibia
CDA	Christian Democratic Action for Social Justice
CDM	Consolidated Diamond Mines
CSO	Central Selling Organization
DELK or DELC	German Evangelical Lutheran Church of South West Africa
DEMKOP or DEMCOP	Democratic Co-operative Party

DKG	Deutsche Kolonialgesellschaft
DTA	Democratic Turnhalle Alliance
DUF	Damara United Front
ELK or ELC	Evangelical Lutheran Church
ELKIN or ELCIN	Evangelical Lutheran Church in Namibia
ELOK or ELOC	Evangelical Lutheran Ovambo-Kavango church
ENOK	First National Development Corporation
FCN	Federal Convention of Namibia
FMS	Finnish Mission Society
GA	United Nations General Assembly
HNP	Herstigte Nasionale Party (Reconstituted National Party)
ICJ	International Court of Justice
IDC	Industrial Development Corporation
IG	Interessengemeinschaft Deutschprachiger Südwester
ISCOR	Iron and Steel Corporation of South Africa
LDP/LF	Liberated Democratic Party
LMS	London Missionary Society
LP	Labour Party

MPC	Multi-Party Conference
MUN	Mineworkers Union of Namibia
NC	National Convention of Freedom Parties
NCN	National Convention of Namibia
NIP	National Independence Party
NLO	Northern Labor Recruiting Organization
NNC	Namibia National Convention
NNF	Namibia National Front
NP	Nasionale Party (National Party)
NUDO	National Unity Democratic Organisation
NUNW	National Union of Namibian Workers
OAU	Organisation of African Unity
OMEG	Otavi Minen und Eisenbahn Gesellschaft
OPC	Ovambo People's Congress
OPO	Ovamboland People's Organisation
PLAN	People's Liberation Army of Namibia
RBD	Rehoboth Bevrydingsparty
RMS	Rhenish Mission Society
RTZ	Rio Tinto Zinc
SACU	Southern African Customs Union

SADCC	Southern African Development Coordination Conference
SADF	South African Defense Force
SAP	South African Police
SC	United Nations Security Council
S-G	Secretary-General
SWA	South West Africa
SWABC	South West Africa Broadcasting Corporation
SWAC	South West Africa Company
SWACOR	South West Africa Oil Exploration Corporation
SWADU	South West Africa Democratic Union
SWANLA	South West Africa Native Labour Association
SWANU	South West Africa National Union
SWAPA	South West Africa Progressive Association
SWAPDUF	South West Africa People's Democratic United Front
SWAPO	South West Africa People's Organization
SWAPO-D	South West Africa People's Organization— Democrats
SWAPOL	South West African Police
SWASB	South West Africa Student Body
SWATF	South West Africa Territory Force

SWP   Suidwest Partei (Southwest Party)

TCL   Tsumeb Corporation Ltd.

TGNU   Transitional Government of National Unity

UDP   United Democratic Party

UN   United Nations

UNIN   United Nations Institute for Namibia

UNITA   National Union for the Total Independence of Angola

UNSWA   United National South West Africa Party

UNSWP   United National South West Party

UNTAG   United Nations Transition Assistance Group

UPN   United Party of Namibia

VELKSWA   United Evangelical Lutheran Church of South West Africa

WMS   Wesleyan Missionary Society

WNLA   Witwatersrand Native Labour Association

CHRONOLOGY

pre-15 C	San people settle in Namibia.
1485	Portuguese explorer Diego Cao reaches the coast of Namibia and plants a stone cross.
pre-16 C	Nama and Berg Damara settle among the San.
16 C–17 C	Wambo and Herero people migrate into the territory.
1670	Dutch boat *Grundel* lands at Angra Pequena on Namibian coast.
1677	Dutch sailors aboard the *Bode* go ashore and briefly explore coastal regions.
1770–1870	Nama migrate across the Orange River to avoid colonization in the Cape.
1793	Dutch government lays claim to some Namibian coastal regions.
1830	Jonker Afrikander leads Orlams northward from the Orange River, beginning decades of conflict with the Hereros.
1858	"The Peace of Hoachanas," an historic treaty, is signed by leaders from Southern and Central Namibia and temporarily ends the second Nama-Herero conflict.
1861	Jonker Afrikander and Herero leader Tjamuaha die.

1863–1870   Further Nama-Herero Wars.

1866   Cape Colony annexes islands off southern coast. June 16.

1870   Basters settle in Rehoboth.

1876   Boers ("Thirstland Trekkers") settle in the north-eastern area of the territory.

1877–1878   Chief Maherero attempts to head off colonist intrusions by negotiating a protection treaty with the Cape Colony, but the Cape government backs off.

1878   Britain annexes Walvis Bay.

1880–1892   Renewed conflict between Namas and Hereros.

1883   A German merchant buys Lüderitz Bay.

1884   German protectorate declared over Lüderitz Bay, the coastal zone between the Orange and Kunene Rivers, Cape Frio, and Great Namaqualand.

1886–1890   Namibia's present international boundaries are established by German treaties with Portugal (1886) and Great Britain (1890).

1885–1892   Administration by the German South West Africa Colonial Society (Kolonial Gesellschaft).

1885   German protectorate declared over the Red Nation.

1885   Hereros agree to a German protectorate. October 21.

1888   Hereros renounce 1885 agreement with Germans.

1889   First German troops arrive.

1890   Germany annexes the territory; Von Francois builds fort at Windhoek.

1892–1894   German troops massacre Namas at Hornkranz, beginning two-year conflict between Germans and Hendrik Witbooi's Namas. Treaty signed September 15, 1894, by the defeated Witbooi.

1896   Germans crush Eastern Hereros.

1903–1907   Renewed Herero and Nama uprisings require huge number of German troops to subdue them.

1904   Battle of Waterberg ends German-Herero War. August 11.

1904   Hendrick Witbooi, age 80, dies leading his troops into battle against Germans. October 25.

1905   An armistice ends the genocide, after 80 percent of the Herero population have been killed. December 20.

1907   Bondelswart guerrilla leader Jacob Morenga is gunned down by Cape Colony police on behalf of the German regime, ending Nama rebellion.

1908   Diamond discovery leads to a mineral rush and a growth of settlement.

1914   Germans force Portuguese to evacuate the territory, and King Mandume destroys all Portuguese forts in an attempt to unite Owambo and preserve its independence. The Germans are also forced to withdraw. World War I begins.

1915   South Africa invades and occupies Namibia. Germans surrender at peace of Korab. July 9.

1915	Namibians try to reclaim land taken by the Germans, but South Africa imposes martial law.
1917	Mandume killed by South African troops in an invasion of Owambo.
1919	In accord with Article 22 of the Covenant of the League of Nations, "South West Africa" (SWA) mandate conferred on South Africa.
1920	"South West Africa" officially comes under South African administration as a "C Class Mandate."
1921	A civilian colonial administration replaces martial law. January 1.
1922	South Africa bombs the Namas and the Bondelswarts for refusing to pay a dog tax, killing one-sixth of the Bondelswarts.
1924–1925	The regime reinstates martial law over the Rehobothers who attempt to retain their autonomous rights.
1925	South African parliament grants a measure of political autonomy to *white* SWA—a legislative council to be chosen by an all-white electorate.
1945	South Africa asks newly created United Nations to be allowed to annex SWA.
1946	UN refuses to allow annexation of SWA, and South Africa refuses to place SWA under Trusteeship Council.
1946–1949	Traditional leaders voice popular resistance to South Africa's rule, petition UN to remove South Africa regime.

1948   National Party (NP) gains power in South Africa.
May.

1949   The new NP government amends SWA's constitution, deleting references to the mandate and giving SWA whites seats in the South African government.

1949   United Nations General Assembly requests the International Court of Justice to define the status of SWA. South Africa ceases to send reports to the UN and announces no further reports will be submitted.

1950   In an advisory opinion, the International Court of Justice (ICJ) rules that (a) the mandate is still in force, (b) the UN has succeeded to the League's supervisory powers, (c) South Africa is not competent by itself to alter the international status of SWA, though South Africa is not obliged to submit to a trustee agreement. South Africa rejects the opinion.

1953   UN General Assembly forms Committee on South West Africa to supervise mandate without South Africa's cooperation.

1958   Herman Toivo Ya Toivo and others organize the Ovamboland People's Congress, renamed the Ovamboland People's Organization (OPO) in 1959, later to dissolve into SWAPO in 1960.

1959   Riots in Windhoek as Blacks forced to leave "Old Location" and move to Katatura, an apartheid-style township near Windhoek. Thirteen killed, fifty-four injured, Arrests of Black leaders force Sam Nujoma and others into exile. December 10.

1959   SWANU formed.

1960	Ethiopia and Liberia initiate proceedings against South Africa before the ICJ on grounds it flagrantly violated the mandate. General Assembly endorses the move. November.
1961	General Assembly demands South Africa terminate the mandate and sets SWA's independence as its objective.
1962	South Africa submits preliminary objections contesting jurisdiction of the Court.
1964	After the Odendaal Commission Report, South Africa announces its plans for the fragmentation of SWA into Bantustans, and a five-year economic and social plan for the territory.
1966	ICJ in SWA case rules that Ethiopia and Liberia lack standing to obtain a judgement on the South African violations of the mandate. July.
1966	Resolution 2145 passed by UN General Assembly terminating the mandate. UNGA also assumes sovereign responsibility for SWA. August 26.
1966	SWAPO announces plan to begin armed struggle against South African occupation.
1967	UN council for SWA created to administer the territory.
1968	Security Council enters picture by adopting resolution condemning SWA terrorist trial. January.
1968	South West Africa officially renamed Namibia by General Assembly. April.
1969	Security Council formally recognizes General Assembly's termination of South Africa's Mandate and recognizes liberation struggle. March 20.

1969–1970   SWAPO's Consultative Congress meets at Tanga in Tanzania, bringing together delegates from all sections of the party.

1971   ICJ declares South Africa's presence in Namibia illegal, and other states are obliged to recognize the illegality of the occupation regime and act accordingly. June 21.

1971   National Convention of Namibia is formed with SWAPO's help, to be a united front for all anti-colonial forces. November.

1971–1972   Namibian contract workers strike, bringing economy to a halt.

1972   UN Council for Namibia denounces South Africa's decision to grant self-government to Owambo. July.

1972   UN General Assembly recognizes SWAPO as ''sole legitimate representative'' of Namibia's people. December 12.

1973   South African government establishes Owambo as self-governing territory. May 1.

1973   Owmabo Bantustan elections boycotted: 2.5 percent poll. August 1–2. First Kavango elections. August 29–30.

1974   UN Council for Namibia issues a decree to confiscate illegally exported national resources. September 27.

1974   Great Britain recognizes South African administration as unlawful. December 4.

1974   Security Council calls on South Africa for a ''solemn declaration'' on withdrawal, and proposals of

	independence to be made May 30, 1975. December 17.
1975	SWAPO withdraws from National Convention (January 17). New Namibia National Convention formed around SWAPO.
1975	Angola gains independence. August.
1975	South African forces invade Angola from Namibia. September.
1975	South Africa opens Turnhalle Constitutional Conference in Windhoek. September 1.
1976	UN Security Council calls on South Africa to transfer power to the people of Namibia and allow UN-sponsored free elections. Resolution 385.
1976	Constitutional Committee of the Turnhalle reaches an agreement on establishing an interim government and an independent Namibia by December 31, 1978, but the UN Council for Namibia rejects it. August 18–20.
1977–1979	Five Western members of the Security Council form a contact group to negotiate between South Africa and SWAPO.
1977	UN negotiations begin as Western powers, confronted by SWAPO's unity, persuade South Africa to delay implementation of the Turnhalle plan. March–June.
1977	South African prime minister and contact group meet. South Africa refuses to withdraw troops, but agrees to allow elections and suspend interim government. June 8–10.

1977	South Africa appoints an Administrator-General, M. T. Stein, to Namibia as part of strategy to establish autonomy for Namibia under South African domination (July 6), but cannot reach an agreement about the withdrawal of troops and the timing of elections. August.
1977	Democratic Turnhalle Alliance forms. November 5.
1978	Contact group submits plans to Security Council for Namibian elections: (a) UN special representative to insure free and fair elections; (b) release of political prisoners; (c) end to hostilities; (d) restriction of South African and SWAPO armies (April 10). South Africa accepts plan (April 25).
1978	South African troops attack SWAPO camp at Cassinga in southern Angola, killing 750 Namibians, mostly women and children. May 4.
1978	South Africa begins unilateral registrations in Namibia. June.
1978	SWAPO agrees to the Western plan. July 11–12.
1978	UN Security Council passes Resolution 435 (September 29). SWAPO accepts, South Africa rejects.
1978–1979	South Africa prepares way for UDI, forcing an election to an Assembly. SWAPO and most other parties boycott the elections (December 4–8, 1978). South Africa gives the "National Assembly" wide legislative powers (May 21, 1979). The UN declares it illegal.
1979	Martial law extends to 80 percent of the Namibian population. May.

1981   Emergency special session of the General As-
            sembly calls upon all states to impose compre-
            hensive sanctions against South Africa. Septem-
            ber.

1982   Contact group announces all parties to the negoti-
            ation have agreed to a set of constitutional princi-
            ples. July.

1983   South Africa dissolves "National Assembly" and
            assumes all executive functions.

1983   A G establishes a state council to draft proposals
            for an interim government until independence.
            July.

1983   South Africa organizes a Multi-Party Conference
            (MPC) consisting of six internal parties. Septem-
            ber.

1983   South Africa refuses to cooperate with the im-
            plementation of Security Council Resolution 539,
            which rejects the linking of extraneous issues with
            Namibia's independence; the resolution also af-
            firms that the electoral system to be used for the
            election of a Constituent Assembly should be
            determined before the Security Council approves
            the enabling resolution for the implementation of
            Security Council Resolution 435.

1983   Security Council demands that South Africa with-
            draw from Angola and declares that Angola is
            entitled to compensation for any material damage
            it has suffered. December.

1984   Lusaka accord: South Africa and Angola agree on
            practical measures to supervise the withdrawal of
            South African troops. February.

1984   Lusaka talks fail between South Africa and
              SWAPO because South Africa insists Cuba with-
              draw its troops from Angola.

1984   President dos Santos of Angola announces intent
              to withdraw Cuban troops within 24 hours of
              UNTAG troops in Namibia to implement Resolu-
              tion 435. November.

1985   South Africa establishes an interim government in
              Namibia despite the Security Council and Confer-
              ence of Foreign Ministers condemning the act.

1985   Because of continuing massive Soviet and Cuban
              assistance to Angola, US Congress repeals the Clark
              Amendment, which had precluded US assistance to
              any participants in the Angolan internal conflict.

1986   The US resumes assistance to UNITA (Angolan
              rebels) after a ten-year hiatus, when UNITA Presi-
              dent Savimbi visits Washington, DC.

1986   South Africa announces it is willing to implement
              Resolution 435 on August 1 if an agreement is
              reached on Cuban troops' withdrawal. Angola
              does not respond; the proposal expires.

1987   US-Angolan negotiations resume in April in Braz-
              zaville and intensify through the year to develop a
              proposal on Cuban troop withdrawal.

1988   Cuban representatives for the first time join US-
              Angolan negotiations.

1988   Delegation from South Africa, Angola, Cuba, and
              the US meet in London to launch settlement
              negotiations. The parties agree to set general prin-
              ciples, the basis of a settlement. May–July.

1988   Angola, Cuba, and South Africa agree to a cease-fire in Angola, leading to a withdrawal of South African and Cuban troops. August.

1988   Governments of Angola, Cuba, and South Africa sign the protocol of Brazzaville in the Congo, which would implement Resolution 435 on April 1. December 13.

1988   The same parties sign the Tripartite Agreement committing the parties to implement Resolution 435 and withdrawal of Cuban troops on April 1, 1989. December 22.

1989   Cuban troops begin to withdraw ahead of schedule. January.

1989   UN Security Council adopts Resolution 632, which sends UNTAG to Namibia. February.

1989   The UN plan officially begins on April 1. However, SWAPO guerrillas illegally move across the Angolan border into Namibia. Arrangements for monitoring and verification of SWAPO troop removal made. April 9–10.

1989   UN supervises registration of Namibian voters. July.

1989   Elections held for a Namibian Constituent Assembly, which will draft the Constitution and set the date for independence. SWAPO receives 57 percent of the votes, winning forty-one of seventy-two seats. November 7–11.

1989   Constituent Assembly declares its intention to base the new constitution on the principles agreed upon in 1982. November 21.

1990   The Assembly unanimously adopts a constitution guaranteeing individual rights. February 9.

1990   The Constituent Assembly declares itself the National Assembly, though it has no mandate or role until independence, and also elects SWAPO president Sam Nujoma president-elect of the Republic of Namibia. February 16.

1990   Namibia becomes independent. March 21.

1990   Namibia joins the UN. March 23.

1990   Five illegal Spanish fishing ships confiscated in Namibian waters.

1991   Two new ministries are formed: the Ministry of Fisheries and Marine Resources and the Ministry of Youth and Sport.

1991   Plans announced to introduce the Namibian dollar in 1993.

1991   Talks begin with South Africa on the status of Walvis Bay and the ''Penguin Islands.''

1991   Former South African Defence Force official, Nico Basson, reveals South Africa's efforts to discredit SWAPO prior to 1989 elections and to aid the DTA.

1991   Government begins its own newspaper, *New Era*.

1991   Team of foreign geologists, anthropologists, and paleontologists discover thirteen-million-year-old jawbone of a hominoid in the Otavi Mountains near the old Berg Aukas mine. No such Miocene epoch fossil had ever been found south of the equator. The *Otavipithecus Namibiensis* will lead to many more scientific expeditions.

1991   National census taken, beginning October 21.

1991   Approval given to 13 new "regions" based on recommendations of the Delimitation Commission. Each will have its own regional authorities, and each will elect two delegates to the upper house of parliament.

1991   SWAPO party congress in December elects a new central committee; its revised constitution is committed to political pluralism.

1991   Diamond production rises dramatically with the opening of the Elizabeth Bay mine in mid-1991.

1991   Democratic Turnhalle Alliance central committee changes the party name to the DTA of Namibia; it also became a unitary party, no longer an alliance of parties.

1992   Drought hits hard, cutting some agricultural production by two-thirds. President Nujoma declares a State of Emergency.

1992   Census results show a national population of 1.4 million.

1992   In a cabinet shuffle, Dr. Herrigel resigns in April as Minister of Finance and is replaced by Gerhard Hanekom. This is followed by several other portfolio shifts.

1992   Michelle McLean, Miss Namibia, wins the Miss Universe contest.

1992   Namibia's Frankie Fredericks wins the silver medal in the men's 100 meter race in the Olympic games in Barcelona, Spain. In other European meets he also wins world status in the 200 meters.

1992   SWAPO wins 56 of the 79 seats in the November elections held in the 13 new regions of the country. DTA of Namibia wins 20 seats.

0 km	200	400	Main Roads ———
0 miles	100	200	Main Railways ╫╫╫╫╫

INTRODUCTION

On March 21, 1990, Sam Nujoma was sworn in as the first president of an independent Namibia. This ceremony marked the end of a struggle that lasted more than two decades and a period of colonialism that laster more than a century. The new country covers a surface area of 823,145 square kilometers or 317,725 square miles. (Both figures exclude the enclave of Walvis Bay, which is claimed by both South Africa and the new leaders of Namibia. It is currently controlled by South Africa.) Namibia is almost four times the size of Great Britain, or about the same size as the area of Texas and Louisiana in the United States. Yet the total population is less than 1.5 million, making it one of the least densely populated countries in the world.

Namibia is located on the southwestern coast of Africa (thus its earlier name of South West Africa). It is separated from South Africa to the south by the Orange River, and from Angola to the north by the Kunene River. To the east of Botswana, while to the west is the vast expanse of the South Atlantic. The generally rectangular shape of the country is broken by a long, narrow arm, the Caprivi Strip, that stretches eastward from Namibia's northeast. It is about 300 kilometers wide, but generally very narrow, and it creates borders with Zambia to the north and Botswana to the south, and touches Zimbabwe.

The country is divided into at least four geographical regions. The Namib Desert runs along its entire coastline, averaging 100 kilometers in width, and features giant sand dunes in some areas. Along the eastern border is the semi-arid Kalahari Desert, which overlaps into neighboring Botswana. A mountainous central plateau, which soars to over 2000 meters above sea level less than 200 kilometers from the ocean, covers about half of the country. The northern one-third of Namibia consists of bush-covered plains. The rest of Namibia is so covered with mountains and

1

ridges that the surface looks corrugated from the air. The highest mountains are about 2500 meters above sea level.

Namibia's only perennial rivers are along its borders: the Kunene, the Okavango, the Kwando, the Zambezi, and the Orange Rivers. Interior rivers depend on rainfall, and in drought, a recurrent problem, the riverbeds are often dry. However, in rainy periods some of them flow southward into the Orange River or westward into the Atlantic Ocean. To reach the Atlantic, however, the rivers must survive the evaporating heat of the Namib Desert, so some go years without reaching the ocean and others have not done so within memory.

The climate of Namibia is generally not suitable for large-scale agriculture, although farmers are quite successful in northern areas (Owambo and Kavango) and in areas of the south where irrigation schemes have been constructed. The great central plateau is excellent for raising cattle and sheep, and both are sources of income for the country's citizens. The sheep are raised as much for their pelts as their meat, as the young karakul sheep produce the fur often called "Persian Lamb." Fishing along the coast is another source of income, as sardines and South African rock lobsters are harvested. An unusual coastal harvest is guano, which is a valuable natural product dropped by sea birds as they fly over offshore islands.

The country's most valuable natural resources today have been in the ground since the early days of the Earth. Diamonds, copper, and uranium exist in abundance, although the supply of each is finite, and Namibia's new leaders must be careful not to rely on the value of the mining industry indefinitely. They have been mined through much of the twentieth century (uranium being the most recent), and the quality of diamonds seems to be decreasing. Nevertheless, new diamond sources have been found offshore and should revitalize that industry. Natural gas fields have also been discovered in recent years, as well as deposits of coal and gold. Tin, zinc, vanadium, and manganese are among the many other products of the mining industry of Namibia.

The animals of Namibia are a special blessing. Game parks, especially the large Etosha National Park in the north, contain huge numbers of animals. With its recent independence Namibia could soon become a magnet for tourists wishing to see the last remaining large herds of animals roaming Africa. Namibian leaders are very conscious of their value, and conservation methods are diligently practiced. The spectacular scenery found in some parts of the country also lends itself to the tourist industry.

People coming to Namibia may be surprised to find only Windhoek, the capital, to be a city in the truest sense. Its population exceeds 100,000, and its busy streets, shopping malls, high-rise buildings, international-quality hotels and its university are the equal of many major cities in Africa. On the other hand, no other urban area has a population exceeding 20,000, and only a few even come close. The tenth largest community in the country has a population under 7000. A high percentage of the population is thus based in the rural areas, living in small communities or isolated clusters.

The indigenous people of Namibia are composed of a number of groups. Perhaps the earliest were the Khoisan-speaking Namas and San, who today account for only about 7 percent of Namibia's population. On the other extreme, the Wambos of northern Namibia represent about 50 percent of the entire population of the country. The Kavangos are close to 10 percent of the population, and Hereros and Damaras a little less. Mixed race people ("Coloureds" and "Basters") less than 6 percent of the population, as do assorted small groups. Namibians of European descent are estimated to number more than 80,000, but the coming of independence under African rule could have the effect of eventually lowering that total. The white population of the country is divided primarily into those speaking German, English, and Afrikaans.

The earliest inhabitants were probably the Khoi and the San, the latter perhaps being responsible for the wonderful rock art that is found throughout the country in caves and on other stone surfaces. Several centuries ago Bantu-speaking people came south from areas in Angola and possibly Zambia. These are now known as Wambos, Kavangos, Hereros, and Damaras. The Nama came in numbers from the south, especially about the beginning of the nineteenth century. Europeans began arriving from the south around the same time, although large numbers didn't enter the country until the mid-to-late nineteenth century.

Although both the Dutch and the British had laid claim to coastal areas of Namibia in earlier centuries, colonial rule really began with the arrival of the Germans in the 1880s. While their rule ended with the invasion of troops from South Africa in 1915 as part of World War I, the Germans had an effect on the country in many ways. In asserting colonial dominance they brought in an army of German soldiers who ultimately defeated the Africans (despite gallant and often successful resistance by great African leaders), with the Hereros suffering disastrous losses to German firepower. Some of the German soldiers retired to Namibia, while other settlers came from Germany to reside in the highlands, attracted by stories told by returning soldiers or German missionaries. Businessmen also came, some attracted by the prospect of mineral wealth. The Germans left their mark on the country, including striking Germanic architectural styles dotting the larger communities, not to mention German restaurants and German breweries.

While Europeans had come north from the Cape Colony throughout the nineteenth century, a much larger influx came after World War I. The Versailles Conference had created the League of Nations, and Germany was stripped of its colonial possessions. Jan Smuts, the South African representative at the Conference, had secured a leadership role and persuaded the others that the young Union of South Africa should be granted supervisory status over South West Africa under the mandate system. Thus South Africa began a colonial-style rule that lasted almost seventy years. Throughout much of that period South Africa sought ways of incorporating the territory into its system as a fifth province. This concept was rejected after World War II by the United Nations, which insisted that South West Africa/Namibia must be prepared for independence under indigenous rule. Although the International Court of Justice gave conflicting decisions on several occasions, most of the international community let it be known that South African rule of the territory would not be tolerated indefinitely. With South Africa standing firm, and no international forces prepared to invade to free the people from South African hegemony, the only hope appeared to be an uprising of the African people themselves.

Africans had been resisting foreign rule in Namibia for more than a century. Various leaders in the late nineteenth and early twentieth centuries had led their people in uprisings against Germans or South Africans. African nationalism took many forms, most of them not particularly successful, but in the late

1940s Namibians attempted to get the attention of the United Nations concerning their situation through a series of petitions presented by both Namibians and respected Europeans such as the Reverend Michael Scott. A little later, groups of young African students and workers began forming political groups to bring together those willing to sacrifice themselves for the cause of independence. The first two major groups were known as the South West Africa National Union (SWANU) and the South West Africa People's Organization (SWAPO). Thirty years later the leaders of SWAPO were sworn in as the leaders of an independent Namibia.

Between the late 1950s and the late 1980s there was a flurry of nationalist activity. Some of it took the form of political organization. Namibians took to this like a fish takes to water. It is only a slight exaggeration to say that whenever two or more Namibians got together they formed a political party. At independence there were easily fifty identifiable political parties or factions. They covered the entire political spectrum from the far right to the far left. However, South African administrators had done everything possible to discourage any organization except that which was supportive of its goals. These goals included the systematic introduction of apartheid into Namibia.

SWAPO actively opposed South African rule and sought Namibian independence. When peaceful methods failed, SWAPO undertook guerrilla activity in the late 1960s, while simultaneously working for United Nations approval of its status as the true representatives of the Namibian people. This was achieved in March 1969.

The period from 1969 to 1989 saw guerrilla activity by SWAPO being countered by the strong use of South African military force to suppress opposition. Countries in Europe and Africa provided SWAPO with both monetary and material support, but the stronger South African forces systematically forced the nationalist forces to retreat into neighboring Angola. Even there they were not safe from South African military attacks. South Africa claimed it was safeguarding its borders from a growing Communist threat. At the same time South Africa was introducing its own version of indigenous rule, through local governing bodies (initially in Owambo) and through the Turnhalle Constitutional Conference. The latter was an attempt to get all moderate to conservative politicians to join together in creating a new constitutional order for the country. SWAPO and similar groups were excluded from the Turnhalle. In addition to creating a new constitutional arrangement for the country, the conference resulted directly in the formation of the Democratic Turnhalle Alliance (DTA), a multiracial coalition of conservative factions. The DTA would dominate the "legal" political scene within Namibia for twelve years. Even when international pressures resulted in "free and fair" elections in November 1989, the DTA gained twenty-one seats in the new National Assembly.

Many factors contributed to the agreement which led to the 1989 elections, which were supervised by the United Nations. The cost of the Namibian/Angolan military activity to South Africa eventually wore down South Africa's resolve, as did some successes by Cuban forces against the South African troops. The reduction of the Soviet Union's support for both the government of Angola and its Cuban allies, coupled with behind-the-scenes efforts by President Mikhail Gorbachev made an agreement more likely. The persistence of SWAPO's freedom fighters must also be acknowledged. Finally, although the diplomatic activities of the Western powers has been frequently criticized, especially the role of the American diplomat Chester Crocker, he continued to work toward the goal of resolving the Namibian issue. With the assistance of all the above actors plus the United Nations, he was ultimately successful in getting the opposing forces to agree to military and political concessions, which in turn led directly to the holding of the 1989 elections.

With the coming of independence SWAPO is attempting to reconcile all the different groups within the population of Namibia. Some may never be entirely reconciled, but the government leaders have modified some of their earlier positions in order to establish a working relationship with the financial community of Namibia. If the government can tap some of the revenue from the sales of the country's mineral resources, it could become one of the few new countries of Africa to achieve a balanced budget early in its existence. Namibia's new constitution is, on paper, as democratic as any in the world and is filled with guarantees of basic rights to all of its citizens. If these are not violated, the Namibian experience could serve as a small-scale model for national reconciliation and change in South Africa.

THE DICTIONARY

- A -

ABRAHAMS, DR. KENNETH GODFREY (1936–) and OT-
TILIE GRETE (née SCHIMMING) (1937–). Dr. and Mrs.
Abrahams have been active in Namibian politics for more
than twenty-five years, most recently with the Namibian
Independence Party. Dr. Abrahams was born and raised in
Cape Town, South Africa, and is a Coloured medical doctor.
His wife Ottilie is a Rehoboth Baster, but was born in
Windhoek and educated there and in Cape Town. They both
have degrees from the University of Cape Town. Kenneth's
MD was earned in Stockholm, Sweden, where his wife
received an M.A. They were married in 1961 and, based on
her status as a Baster, moved to Rehoboth where she set up a
medical practice.

   Ottilie Abrahams was a founder of the SWA Student Body
in 1952; later she founded the SWA Progressive Association.
The two had joined SWAPO in Cape Town in 1960, but it
was their identification with the Yo Chi Chan, a secret
guerrilla group, that set the South African security police
against them. Their political activity led to government
attempts to deport Dr. Abrahams from Namibia in 1963. Dr.
Abrahams tried to flee the territory, but he and his associates,
including Andreas Shipanga (q.v.) were captured in
Botswana (which was still under British rule) by South
African police. Dr. Abrahams was taken back to Namibia to
be jailed in Gobabis, but was ultimately moved to Cape
Town. Finally the British, citing the lack of jurisdiction of
South African police in Botswana, obtained his release from
jail.

   The couple proceeded then to Tanzania, where they
worked in a SWAPO (q.v.) office with Sam Nujoma (q.v.).

7

They claimed he had an extravagant life style using party funds and, with several others, denounced him. Nujoma then expelled Dr. and Mrs. Abrahams and a number of others, including Shipanga, a longtime political ally of the couple. The three went next to Stockholm, Sweden, where they formed the SWAPO-Democrats (q.v.), led by Shipanga.

In August 1978, Dr. and Mrs. Abrahams returned to Namibia and set up a SWAPO-D branch there. They then split with Shipanga and joined the already existing Namibian Independence Party (q.v.). Dr. and Mrs. Abrahams became two of its most prominent leaders. Ottilie is a teacher in addition to serving as indefatigable organizer, record-keeper and publicist. Both were active campaigners for the Namibia National Front (q.v.) during the 1989 elections. Ottilie was its secretary-general, and Kenneth was its secretary for information. The two have produced an outstanding journal, *The Namibian Review*. Since independence they have altered their political activities, and Mrs. Abrahams has devoted her efforts to self-improvement schemes, such as an adult education center in the shantytowns that have been growing up in Windhoek since independence.

ACADEMY. The Academy in Windhoek consists of a central campus that houses the University of Namibia, Technikon Namibia (a technical institute), and a College for Out-of-School Training. It has an additional campus at the suburb of Khomasdal. Paid for by both the Namibian government and tuition fees, it began in 1980 with only 3 faculty members and 26 students. By 1987 it had 170 lecturers and 4200 students. Aside from the university segment, the other units emphasize vocational training and skills. Its enrollment in 1990 was 4700 students.

ACTION CHRISTIAN NATIONAL (variant; AKSIE CHRISTE-LIKNASIONALE) (ACN). One of the ten registered parties that competed in the 1989 elections, it actually was a political front for the National Party—much as AKTUR was in the 1978 elections. The ACN was founded in early 1989 after the announcement of plans to implement UN Resolution 435. Its avowed purpose was to establish a group to speak for Namibia's white community and ensure them a place in the country's future. In August 1989 the National Party was joined by the Deutsche Aktion/Deutsch Südwest Komitee, led by Dr. Hans Engelhardt. However, on October 18 Dr. Englehardt announced that his group was leaving the ACN and joining a different group, the Christian Democratic Action for Social Justice (q.v.). Thus the ACN became merely an electoral name for the National Party (q.v.). It was reasonably successful in the elections, however, winning 23,728 votes and three seats in the Assembly. Those went to its chairman, Johannes de Wet (q.v.), J. W. F. (Kosie) Pretorius, and Walter Aston. A feud soon broke out between the first two, when de Wet was being mentioned for a possible cabinet seat in a SWAPO Government. Pretorius tried and failed to force de Wet out of his assembly seat, but de Wet did not join the cabinet. Tension remains in the leadership of the ACN/National Party, but one year after independence Pretorius was still its parliamentary leader and was showing signs of cooperating on some issues with the SWAPO-led government.

ACTION FRONT FOR THE RETENTION OF TURNHALLE PRINCIPLES (AKTUR or ACTUR). Described as a non-party political body that promoted the principles announced by the Turnhalle Conference (q.v.), it was a right-wing group whose membership overlapped closely with that of the National Party. AKTUR maintained that Namibia should remain part of South Africa. At the February 1978 discussions that included the Western contact group diplomats, the South African government, and SWAPO, A. H. du Plessis and Eben Van Zijl represented AKTUR and presented its views. AKTUR took part in the December 1978 Assembly elections and its candidates won six seats and 12 percent (38,716) of the votes. At that time one of the most influential members of AKTUR was Mr. Jacques P. D. M. (Percy) Niehaus. Other victors included Petrus Diergaardt, Jacobs W. F. Pretorius (q.v.), and Eben Van Zijl (q.v.). Diergaardt was a leader of the Rehoboth Liberation Party, a member organization of AKTUR, as well as AKTUR's vice leader. As an electoral alliance, AKTUR was parallel to the Democratic Turnhalle Alliance, but considerably to its right. In a 1980 speech, AKTUR chairman Abraham du Plessis stated that his group opposed majority rule for Namibia; open housing; integration of hotels, restaurants, and schools; and elections based on universal suffrage. AKTUR questioned the legality of the 1979 Assembly when it found itself regularly outvoted. It accused South Africa of misleading it by falsely stating that the elections of 1978 would be only for a Constituent Assembly, and that new elections would be needed before it became a National Assembly. The group walked out of the Assembly in January 1979. It also strenuously opposed the arbitrary revocation of the Group Areas Act by the administrator-general, Justice M. T. Steyn. Nevertheless, AKTUR returned to the National Assembly later in 1979 and remained until it was dissolved in 1983. After that it continued to exist only on paper as a potential election front.

ACTION NATIONAL SETTLEMENT (variant: AKSIE NA-SIONALE SKIKKING) (ANS). A political group formed in February 1987, its membership consists of ''verligte'' or ''enlightened'' members of the National Party (q.v.) who created this new organization. Their goal was to work with all political groups and the business community toward a solution of the Namibian stalemate, one that would transcend party lines. Its economic position is support of free enterprise with social responsibility. The leader of the ANS has been Eben van Zijl (q.v.). Many of its members retained their NP membership while working for the ANS goals. In April 1988 the NP leader ''Kosie'' Pretorius warned them to decide, as they could not be in both the NP and the ANS. This split was especially apparent on the constitutional council, where van Zijl went along with majority proposals while the NP did not. A number of ANS principals did resign to stay with the NP, but a hard core remained. In December 1988 these, under the leadership of van Zijl, joined a new political front, the National Patriotic front of Namibia (q.v.).

ADMINISTRATOR, POST OF. South Africa's top official in Namibia, the position existed with this name from 1915 to

1977, when it was changed to administrator-general. Mr. Howard Georges was appointed on October 30, 1915, replacing military rule. (However, martial law lasted through 1920.) When Georges was appointed administrator, it was understood that the position combined the posts of military governor and chief civil secretary. Following Georges was G. R. Hofmeyr in October 1920. When martial law was abandoned two months later, Hofmeyr became the first civilian administrator. He would be succeeded by A. J. Werth, Dr. D. G. Conradie, Col. P. I. Hoogenhout (q.v.), Dr. A. J. R. van Rhijn, D. T. du P. Viljoen (q.v.), W. C. du Plessis, J. G. H. van der Wath (q.v.) and B. J. van der Walt, who left in 1977, to be replaced by an "Administrator-General" (q.v.).

ADMINISTRATOR-GENERAL. Created in July 1977 to replace the "administrator" (q.v.) in time for the Turnhalle Conference in November, the post was held first by Judge M. T. Steyn (q.v.). The creation of this top administrative position by South African Prime Minister B. J. Vorster was seen as an attempt to rebuff the five-nation contact group's negotiating position—unless the Western representatives dropped their insistence on including Walvis Bay in Namibian negotiations. When Steyn took the new post, his main task was to supervise the National Assembly elections of 1978 in a fair manner. In addition, he announced a series of steps aimed at ending apartheid in Windhoek hotels, restaurants, and theaters (but not in schools and hospitals, for example). He was succeeded by Gerrit Viljoen (q.v.) in August 1979, by Danie Hough (q.v.) in October·1980, and by W. van Niekerk (q.v.) in February 1983. Louis Pienaar (q.v.) was the last Administrator-general, replacing van Niekerk in July 1985, and remaining until independence.

AFRICA, DR. BENJAMIN J. (1938–). Medical doctor and politician, Dr. Africa was born in the Rehoboth community. He graduated from the University of Cape Town Medical School in 1964. He returned to Rehoboth where he became the first Coloured resident district surgeon there. Dr. Africa became involved in politics in the 1970s, forming the

Rehoboth Bastervereniging (q.v.) in 1971. The party was conservative and consistently opposed SWAPO (q.v.). Dr. Africa led the Baster delegation to the Turnhalle Conference (q.v.), where he was selected chairman of two major committees. When the Democratic Turnhalle Alliance (q.v.) was formed, he brought the Bastervereniging into the Alliance, of which he was named vice-president. In 1977 he was elected the Kaptein of Rehoboth, a post he held two years. He was later chosen to the Constituent Assembly, and in 1979 to the National Assembly. In July 1980 he was selected to be a member of the Council of Ministers, serving also as chairman of its Committee for Civic Affairs and Manpower, National Health, Social Welfare and Housing. In 1986 Dr. Africa expelled 26 members of his party. The same year he renamed his party the Rehoboth DTA Party (RDTAP). In the 1989 elections Dr. Africa was number 8 on the DTA electoral list and easily won a seat in the assembly.

AFRIKAANS. The language of many South Africans of Dutch descent (the "Afrikaners"), the language has traditionally been the major language of government functionaries in Namibia. It was, along with English and German, one of the territory's official languages. Under South Africa's tutelage, the administrators required that Afrikaans be the language for all education from the fifth year on. This brought on much protest. After independence, English became the official language.

AFRIKANDERS (variants: AFRIKANERS; AFRICANDERS; AFRICANERS). All of the variant spellings are used regularly in the literature. The Afrikanders were a subgroup of the Orlams (q.v.) living in South Africa late in the eighteenth century. The Orlams were Namas who had mixed with Dutch settlers and had adopted many European customs and even parts of the Dutch language. They owned horses and guns, and they were much more advanced than many other Nama people living in the northwestern Cape Colony. Several groups of the Orlams crossed the Orange River into Namibia to settle. The last group to approach the river was called the //Aicha-//ain—"the angry tribe."

According to one historian, they were given the name Afrikaner (or Afrikander) by a South African farmer and policeman named Pieter Pienaar (q.v.), who couldn't pronounce the group's name. At that point the group was led by /Hoa-/arab and his brother Titus, both sons of the previous chief, !Garuchamab. After a feud with the difficult Pienaar, Titus shot the farmer. His followers then stole Pienaar's cattle and a large supply of guns. The Afrikanders eventually crossed the Orange River, attacking some towns in their path, including Warmbad (q.v.) in 1811. The Warmbad attack was led by Jager Afrikander, brother of Titus. The Afrikanders ultimately became one of the dominant groups in the southern half of Namibia during the nineteenth century. (*See also* AFRIKANDER, JONKER; AFRIKANDER, JAN JONKER.)

AFRIKANDER, CHRISTIAN. Two prominent members of the Afrikander nation bore this name. Jager Afrikander became known by this name after he converted to Christianity. He died in 1823 and was succeeded by his son Jonker, who led his people for almost forty years. Jonker died in 1861 and was succeeded by one of his sons, also named Christian. The younger Christian led the Namas for only two years, being killed in a battle with the Hereros at Otjimbingwe in 1863. While the Afrikanders under the elder Christian had their tribal center at Windhoek, the younger Christian preferred to live in Okahandja. He was not an especially popular leader, alienating some of his people. Moreover, he had problems with the Herero leader, Maharero (q.v.), who was a close friend of Christian's brother Jan Jonker Afrikander (q.v.). Christian feared collusion between the two friends, especially when Maherero moved Christian's cattle and five thousand head of small stock to Otjimbingwe. The Hereros appeared to be organizing for a fight against their Nama masters. Christian tried to pull together a large Nama army, but failed to convince many of the other Nama chiefs. Nevertheless, he organized a small army. On June 15, 1863, he attacked Otjimbingwe, where Maherero's werf (q.v.) was. The attackers were on horseback, but the defenders' opening volley cut down several of the leaders, including Christian

Afrikander. He died on the battlefield. As his son was too young to succeed him, his brother Jan Jonker Afrikander (q.v.) became chief. (*See also* OTJIMBINGWE, BATTLE OF.)

AFRIKANDER, JAGER. *See* AFRIKANDER, CHRISTIAN.

AFRIKANDER, JAN JONKER (c. 1823–1889). The chief of the Orlam group of the Namas from 1863 to his death in 1889, he succeeded his brother Christian (q.v.) who had been killed in the battle of Otjimbingwe. Both were sons of Jonker Afrikander (q.v.). Jan had been educated by the Rhenish missionaries at Windhoek, Rev. C. Hugo Hahn and Rev. F. H. Kleinschmidt (qq.v.). Literate and knowledgeable, Jan was also both industrious and ambitious. When his brother Christian died in battle, Jan was determined to avenge the death and restore his people to their level of importance under his father Jonker Afrikander.

While attempting to organize the different Nama groups, Jan found he was too late, as Maharero (q.v.) had attacked and defeated many of the Namas in the south near Rehoboth, with the assistance of a European, C. J. Anderson (q.v.). A seven-year war took place, in which Jan Jonker's forces received other defeats at the hands of Maherero and Andersson. He was successful, however, in an attack on the Swartboois near Rehoboth. They were allies of Maherero, but he defeated them and sent them fleeing north to the vicinity of Ameib. In 1870, with both sides exhausted and beset by hunger (there had been a drought), Rev. Hahn served as mediator, and the Namas and Hereros signed a peace treaty.

The truce lasted ten years, during which Jan Jonker nevertheless threatened the Europeans who had aided Maherero, denied the Basters the right to live at Rehoboth, and forbade the Namas to hunt ostriches. Although Jan Jonker and his people were granted land rights at Windhoek, he had constant trouble with Hereros over livestock and grazing rights. In short, the "truce" was not without hostilities.

Finally in 1880 the battle resumed between the Hereros

and Jan Jonker. He was forced to flee Windhoek and take refuge in the Auas Mountains, where he fended off a Herero attack and a mutiny by his followers that led to his killing some of his own relatives. He allied himself with another Orlam leader, Moses Witbooi (q.v.), but with little gain. In 1885 he sought the aid of the Germans, ceding them land and, in 1886, accepting a protectorate. This move did not result in the military assistance against the Hereros that he anticipated, however. His alliance with the Witboois broke up, as Hendrik Witbooi (q.v.) succeeded his father, Moses. Hendrik wished to become the leader of the Namas and in August 1889 attacked Jan Jonker's remaining army—by now an undisciplined group of mercenaries, some of them criminals. In the ensuing battle Jan Jonker Afrikander was killed by one of his own sons, who had defected to the Witbooi side.

AFRIKANDER, JONKER (c. 1790–1861). Son of Jager Afrikander, he succeeded his father in 1823. Whereas Jager had settled down in peace, Jonker led his followers in many cattle raids against neighboring peoples. With the exception of a loss to the Bondelswarts he was extremely successful. His successes continued as he raided further north among the Damaras, capturing their cattle in great quantities. He became the most powerful Nama leader of his generation. He allied with the Red Nation (q.v.) for a series of battles against the Hereros and, being well-armed, stole all the Herero cattle as well. In 1840 he set up his capital at Windhoek, an area the Hereros saw as within their own domain. He settled down at Klein Windhoek. The water supply was plentiful there, and the location made it possible for Jonker to watch over both the Hereros to the north and the Namas to the south. Over the next decade his power increased, as even Herero leaders found it expedient to accept his presence in their midst. The young Maherero (q.v.) was even sent to learn marksmanship at his capital and to serve Jonker for a period.

Meanwhile, his growing forces continued to raid the cattle of all those who opposed him. In a terrible massacre at Okahandja on August 23, 1850, Jonker's forces killed many Herero men and chopped off the women's feet to remove their copper anklets. The Herero chief Tjamuaha (q.v.) in desperation allied himself with Jonker and even robbed his own people to supply Jonker with income to pay off the latter's trading debts. The Nama leader had become attracted to the traders at Walvis Bay, returning with fine silk for his wife, guns, and large quantities of brandy. Jonker began drinking heavily, and his personality changed. The 1850 massacre was not the only one of its kind. Jonker had been responsible for a number of other mass murders of Hereros. One occurred in December 1848, when he killed a wealthy Herero named Kamukamu, stole all his cattle, and used information from his victim to destroy other Herero settlements and steal their cattle. Another notorious massacre took place at Barmen, where the victims were herded into a cattle kraal which was then set on fire. They died of asphyxiation and heat.

As a result of his domination of the Hereros, Jonker was called by them "God of the World." He hoped to incorporate all the Hereros into his own Afrikander family. When he was unhappy with the Hereros he would punish Maherero, the son of Tjamuaha, the Herero chief. The young Maherero eventually escaped Windhoek and fled to the protection of missionaries. By 1860 Hereroland had given up most of its cattle to Jonker, and the people were starving. So he traveled further north of Owambo, from whence he returned with 20,000 cattle, some from Hereros who had fled north in an attempt to evade him. The trip was his downfall, however, as he contracted a disease. He died August 18, 1861. Before he died he called together his son and successor, Christian, and Maherero, soon to succeed the dying Tjamuaha, and told them to live in peace and jointly rule the Namas and Hereros.

AFRIKANERS IN NAMIBIA. Aside from isolated explorers and traders, the first large group of Afrikaners (white South Africans of Dutch descent) to enter Namibia were members of a group of Boers (farmers) in 1874 called the Thirstland Trekkers (q.v.).

After World War I a new wave of immigration began, as many Afrikaans-speakers settled in Namibia. Farmers and ranchers came, in keeping with South Africa's belief that

Namibia would someday become a fifth province. Later more Afrikaners came, many of them drawn by opportunities in mining, industry, and commerce. Most of the administrators sent from South Africa were Afrikaners. South African political parties formed branches in Namibia, including the Afrikaner parties. About 70 percent of the whites in Namibia are Afrikaans speakers.

AG8. A controversial proclamation of the Namibian government in 1980, it was a logical continuation of the Bantustan or Homelands policy (q.v.). Whereas the Development of Self-Government for Native Nations in SWA Act No. 54 of 1968 (q.v.) had provided for six self-governing homelands, Proclamation AG8 gave the "Representative Authorities" not only geographic jurisdiction but ethnic authority as well. Thus rules and regulations of these representative authorities would be binding on all members of their ethnic group, regardless of where they lived in Namibia. It was very controversial in part because it required many Namibians to obey leaders whom they neither approved of nor respected, partly because they were often seen as collaborators with South Africa.

AGRICULTURE. Certainly not the strength of Namibia's economy, agriculture is limited by extremes in rainfall. Coastal desert areas receive one inch or less a year; the south averages six inches a year; the center receives twelve inches a year; and the north averages twenty-two inches a year. But even these figures vary as great differences occur from year to year. Serious long-term droughts are frequent. Only those farmers who practice irrigation can count on an annual crop. The best farming is in the north, in the Grootfontein area, Owambo, Kavango, and the eastern part of the Caprivi Strip. In Owambo, millet is produced, along with corn, melons, pumpkins, and beans. Parts of Kavango are subtropical and produce citrus, bananas, and paw paws. Areas in central Namibia receive irrigation from the Hardap Dam and produce a variety of crops. The Grootfontein area produces maize, wheat, and beans. Other areas can also be grain producers where artesian wells are used for irrigation, especially in dry river beds. Still, most grain must be imported from South Africa and Zimbabwe.

The important agriculture in much of Namibia is stock-oriented, as pastureland is good in many areas. Meat and dairy products come from large herds of cattle. It is not by chance that many nineteenth-century wars between Hereros and Nama were based on cattle raids. But drought and disease make this production inconsistent. The raising of Karakul sheep for their pelts is a major enterprise, bringing much needed income to their producers. The product is "Persian Lamb" coats and accessories.

AHTISAARI, MARTTI (1937–). A diplomat from Finland, in 1973 he was appointed Finnish ambassador to Tanzania and accredited to Somalia, Zambia, and Mozambique. He held this post for three years and also became a member of the Senate of the UN Institute for Namibia in Lusaka. On January 1, 1977, he took office as the second UN commissioner for Namibia, a post he held until April 1, 1982. During this period he was also appointed special representative of the Secretary-General and was actively involved in diplomatic negotiations over Namibia's international status. He made frequent trips to Namibia and surrounding states to discuss diplomatic initiatives and compromises. Ahtisaari reported regularly to UN Secretary-General Kurt Waldheim, who passed on his recommendations to the Security Council. His service to the UN on Namibian issues has continued, as Secretary-General Perez de Cuellar appointed him as a special representative. He became active in independence negotiations in 1988. With the sudden death of Bernt Carllson (q.v.) in December 1988, the position of UN commissioner for Namibia became vacant. Mr. Ahtisaari was given additional duties, therefore, and placed in charge of the UN presence in Namibia in the period up to elections and independence. He was applauded by most for his success in overseeing the independence process.

AIGHAMS (variants: AIKAMS, /AI//GAMS, AI-GAMS). A Nama word meaning "The Place of Fiery Waters" (referring to local thermal springs), it is the name used prior to the change to "Windhoek" by Jonker Afrikander in 1840.

In April 1986 a meeting was held in Windhoek by delegates representing sixteen political parties, churches, and community organizations. On April 30 they proclaimed the Ai-Gams Declaration, which called for a campaign of "positive action" to bring about implementation of UN Resolution 435 (q.v.) and called for the end to compulsory military conscription into the SWA Territorial Force. While the conference was called by the Interdenominational Council of Churches in Namibia, it represented a kind of coalition of many of the groups opposed to the interior government of the country. The declaration was signed by many political parties and factions, especially SWAPO. The declaration was adopted unanimously, thus letting the government know that future political compromises must be based on fulfillment of Resolution 435.

AIR NAMIBIA. The national airline of Namibia, it took this new name on October 28, 1991. Until then it was known as Namib Air (q.v.). It is continually expanding its international flights and should soon be serving the United States and many European countries.

AKSIE CHRISTELIK NASIONALE (ACN). *See* ACTION CHRISTIAN NATIONAL.

AKSIE NASIONALE SKIKKING (ANS). *See* ACTION NATIONAL SETTLEMENT.

ALBRECHT, JOHANN CHRISTIAN (c. 1773–1815) and ABRAHAM (d. 1810). Missionaries of the London Missionary Society (LMS), these brothers were born in Germany and were trained both there and in Holland. The Netherlands Society selected them when it heard of the difficulty the LMS was having getting missionaries for southern Africa. They traveled north from Cape Town on May 22, 1805, and eight months later reached Warm Bath (Warmbad) on the north side of the Orange River. The mission was somewhat successful, and about seven hundred Africans settled in the area. A school the Albrechts opened February 3, 1806 became an attraction for the mission.

Abraham Albrecht became ill with consumption and died on the way to Cape Town, July 30, 1810. His brother continued to Cape Town, married a Dutch woman and returned with her to Warm Bath in late 1810. But the next year Jager Afrikander (q.v.) warred against other Namas again, and the Albrechts took refuge in an underground hideout for days. The attack never came, but Mrs. Albrecht was so upset that the two fled to Cape Town again. While there, they got the word that Afrikander had recently plundered the mission station at Warmbad (q.v.).

ALEXANDER, SIR JAMES (1803–1885). Acclaimed as the first scientific explorer of Namibia and as the first Englishman to penetrate Namaland and Damaraland, he made his reputation on an 1836–37 expedition. He and his company of men, sponsored by the Royal Geographical Society, crossed the Orange River into Namibia in November 1836. They reached Warmbad soon thereafter. They went north to Windhoek, and eventually west to Walvis Bay, pioneering a road for settlers later. He visited Jonker Afrikander (q.v.) at his residence north of Rehoboth, and promised to ask for more missionaries. The company then traveled south, crossing the Orange River near the end of July, and the entire group safely returned to Cape Town on September 21, 1837.

ALTE FESTE. On October 18, 1890, the foundation stone for this fortress in Windhoek was laid by Capt. Curt von Francois. The captain, his thirty-two men, their wives and African laborers constructed it based on plans drawn up by von Francois. It was made of stone, brick, and mortar, and was not finished until 1892. The Kazerne ("Barracks"), as it was originally called, was much smaller than the white structure standing on a hill on Leutwein Strasse today. Over the years sections were destroyed and others added. Until the arrival of South African troops in May 1915, the Alte Feste ("old fortress") was headquarters for German troops stationed in Namibia. It became a school dormitory later in the century, but in 1961 it was restored and reconstructed. It has become a museum to house historic relics and has been declared a national historic monument.

AMATHILA, BEN (1930–). Born in Walvis Bay, he was educated in a RMS school in Tsumeb and then entered the Augustineum in Okahandja (1954–58). He then returned to Walvis Bay to work for four years. In 1958 he joined the Ovamboland People's Organization (q.v.) and continued his political activity in Walvis Bay. His labor struggles cost him his job. He then concentrated on politics, serving as SWAPO (q.v.) organizer in Walvis Bay. He went into exile in 1966. Two years later he was named SWAPO's treasurer general. He then organized the major SWAPO congress at Tanga in 1969, where he was elected deputy secretary for education and culture. He spent later years as a SWAPO representative in Europe. He married Dr. Libertine Appolus, also a SWAPO activist. In the 1989 elections he was number 29 on SWAPO's electoral list, thus easily winning an Assembly seat. He was then named to the cabinet as minister of trade and industry.

AMATHILA, DR. LIBERTINE APPOLUS (1940–). Born in Fransfontein, her education started there, then she went to Otjiwarongo, then to the Augustineum (1955–57) and then finished secondary school in the Cape Province. She became active politically and finally left Namibia in 1962 to live in exile. She went to Tanzania, where she received a scholarship to study in Poland. She received a variety of medical degrees and diplomas in Poland, London, and Sweden. Her specialties include nutrition and public health, tropical medicine, and pediatrics. She spent several years helping in refugee camps. While in exile she married another SWAPO activist, Ben Amathila (q.v.), and they have two children. She was director of the SWAPO Women's Council during the late 1960s and early 1970s. She was appointed SWAPO's assistant secretary for health and social welfare in 1970. She has served on the Central Committee since the late 1960s. Number ten on SWAPO's electoral list, she is a member of the Assembly and was named to the cabinet as minister of local government and housing.

AMBO, AMBOLAND. See OVAMBO; OVAMBOLAND; OWAMBO.

AMRAAL, NAMA CHIEF. *See* LAMBERTS, AMRAAL.

AMRAAL HOTTENTOTS. Also known as the Gei-/Khauan, this group of Namas settled in the eastern part of Herero country, and later moved to Gobabis. They were the followers of Amraal Lamberts (q.v.).

ANDERSSON, CHARLES JOHN (KARL JOHAN) (1827–1867). Swedish-born hunter, explorer, businessman, Andersson was perhaps the most extraordinary European visitor to Namibia in the nineteenth century. He spent most of the last seventeen years of his life in the country and had an impact in many areas. He briefly attended the University of Lund (Sweden), studying zoology in keeping with his strong interest in natural history. During his lifetime he published books on Lake Ngami and the Okavango River, and others edited his notes and published his wildlife studies posthumously. His discovery of an unusual species of falcon led to its being named in his honor, the Andersson's perm.

His introduction to Africa came from a meeting in London with Sir Francis Galton (q.v.), who wanted to travel to Lake Ngami. Andersson went along as an aide, with the goal of collecting nature specimens for both knowledge and profit. Galton, Andersson, and company reached Walvis Bay from Cape Town on August 19, 1850, bringing supplies for missionaries in Hereroland. Andersson spent the rest of the year in Otjimbingwe, Barmen, and Okahandja, meeting African leaders as well as the missionaries. The next year was spent on a major expedition that took the party through northern Hereroland, into Owambo, and to the Etosha Pan— the first Europeans to "discover" it. They proceeded to within seven miles of Lake Ngami, a sight Andersson would see later but Galton would not.

In January 1852 Andersson became a partner in a hunting and trading business based at Otjimbingwe. He traded for cattle from the Africans, sent the cattle to Cape Town, and set out for Lake Ngami which he reached on July 26, 1853.

In January 1857 Andersson began a one year contract as operations manager of the Walvisch Bay Mining company, stationed at Otjimbingwe, but continued in hunting and trading on the side with an assistant, Frederick Green (q.v.).

On March 22, 1858, he took a party from Otjimbingwe on a long hunting trip to the north, sending his ivory and other items back periodically. In 1859 his expedition took him to eastern Owambo, where he visited chief Tjikongo, and then to the Okavango River area where malaria hit his party. Two servants died of it, and Andersson also fell ill. The group finally returned to Barmen in January 1860, where Andersson recovered in the care of Dr. Hugo Hahn (q.v.). In June of that year he sailed for Cape Town, and on July 25, 1860, married Sarah Jane Aitchison. They eventually had four children, one of whom later became Sir Llewellyn Andersson.

The couple returned to Otjimbingwe, where Andersson bought the Walvisch Bay Co. property, setting up workshops, a trading center, and dwellings, and acquired other land for pasturage. Business flourished for five years, and his trading post became the outfitter for other Europeans as well as providing goods for the Africans. Periodically he would send huge herds of cattle to Cape Town. In 1862 he herded 4000 head of cattle there, and returned with £5000 of merchandise.

On June 15, 1863, the Nama-Herero War broke out at Otjimbingwe, and Andersson found himself caught up in it, siding with the Hereros. He and Frederick Green encouraged them, and Andersson was even named by tribal leaders as their military chief and regent. But things began to go badly for him. A huge herd of his cattle headed for Cape Town under Green's supervision was captured by the Afrikander Namas. In June 1864 he put together a force of 3000 Hereros and others to get revenge. They reached Rehoboth quickly, and on June 22 defeated the Afrikanders at the Battle of Gamgam. Andersson was severely wounded and his leg was crippled. Dr. Hahn at Barmen again attended him. The war ruined his business, as well as his health. Late in 1864 he sold his business and land to Hahn for £600 and moved to Walvis Bay with his family. They then went to the Cape for a year, settling up with his creditors there.

Gathering more credit, he left the Cape with new employees for Otjimbingwe, reaching there in late May. He and his men spent the next year hunting and trading in northern Namibia, including to Namutoni, Ondonga, and on June 13, 1867, reached the Kunene River opposite Humbe. He was very ill, so the party turned back. But he died in Owambo about July 10, 1867. Later that year his stock at Walvis Bay was plundered by Jan Jonker Afrikander. In an obituary, Andersson was compared to Dr. David Livingstone in awakening attention to the area and in his literary and scientific work along with his discoveries.

ANGLICAN CHURCH. There are two Anglican church bodies in South Africa and Namibia: the Church of the Province of South Africa and the Church of England. The former is about four times the latter in size. The Church of England entered South Africa in the 1820s, and the Church of the Province of South Africa came into existence several decades later. Anglican Church policies in South Africa have always been more liberal on political and social matters than the general population, usually supporting integration.

Over the years a number of Anglican leaders have been expelled from Namibia, among than US-born bishop Robert Mize, Colin O'Brien Winter, Richard Wood, Rolf Friede (a German national who directed the Christian Center in Windhoek), and the Rev. Ed Morrow. The latter, vicar general of the Anglican church, was one of the signatories of a letter to the Administrator General, which protested police actions in the 1970s and the refusal of the A G to appoint a court of inquiry into allegations of police torture. Two other notable Anglican priests are the Rev. Michael Scott (q.v.), who regularly urged the UN to focus attention on Namibia, beginning about 1947, and the Reverend Theophilus Hamutumpangela, who was arrested for writing letters to the UN about the wrongs of the migrant labor system, and who was also one of the founders of the Ovamboland People's Organization, which was transformed into SWAPO (q.v.).

ANGLO AMERICAN CORPORATION. The major mining corporation in southern Africa and in Namibia, it was put together in a connection between South Africa and the United States. The link was Ernest Oppenheimer (q.v.), the son of a Jewish cigar-maker from Friedberg, Germany. He founded what was to become the dominant force in the gold-mining industry and later in diamonds as well when he took over the De Beers diamond cartel. His efforts began only fourteen years after he emigrated to South Africa. Half of the initial capital for the Anglo American Corporation came from Wall Street sources such as J. P. Morgan and Company. By 1917 Oppenheimer had become chairman of his new Anglo American Corporation of South Africa Ltd. Late in 1919 Oppenheimer went to Holland to meet with representatives of the major German diamond mining companies that had been active in Namibia prior to World War I. By purchasing their options for about R7 million he was able to form, in February 1920, the Consolidated Diamond Mines of South West Africa Ltd. (q.v.). It exercised its options and took over all the physical assets of ten former German companies in Namibia. Less than a year later he had acquired long-term rights to mining a strip of land from the mouth of the Orange River to a little north of Lüderitz Bay, the major diamond-producing area.

In 1982 the Anglo American complex of companies, acting through Gold Fields of South Africa, acquired a major interest in the Tsumeb Corporation Ltd. Through a subsidiary it owns half of Namibia's salt-mining production. In 1986 Anglo also announced that it had located bituminous coal deposits at Aranos. In 1987 Anglo American announced that it would begin to develop a small gold mining operation northwest of Windhoek at Navachab. Production commenced in November 1989, and by the end of the year had already produced 72 kg.

Perhaps the most important aspect of Anglo American investment in Namibia as independence arrived is the apparent willingness of its leaders to work with SWAPO in creating a strong economy for the new state. Its South African leadership has generally been near the forefront of the drive to improve race relations and to acknowledge Black nationalist aspirations.

ANGOLA. Namibia's neighbor to the north, Angola has significance for Namibia in several different ways. For one thing, the Wambo (or Ambo) people of northern Namibia are directly related to the people of southern Angola, where they probably originated. The Wambo are known to have lived in Namibia's present borders for about three centuries.

Furthermore, the Thirstland Trekkers (q.v.) originated in South Africa and travelled through Namibia before some settled in southern Angola. These "Angola Boers" were nineteenth-century migrants. After arriving in Angola they fought alongside the Portuguese in African wars of resistance, thus helping the Portuguese subjugate interior portions of Angola. Some of these trekkers settled in Namibia in their short-lived republic of Upingtonia (q.v.).

Another important connection is the existence of SWAPO (q.v.) guerrilla bases in southern Angola during the war of liberation. As the South African military made it difficult for SWAPO's military units to operate within Namibia, the freedom fighters increasingly crossed the border to live in the area of their Ambo brethren. Major military bases were established, especially after Angola received its independence in 1975. This only encouraged South Africa to conduct cross-border raids against SWAPO targets in Angola, both by land and air. Thousands of lives were lost, both guerrillas and civilians, in these raids.

During the period from 1975–1989 the issue of potential independence for Namibia was complicated considerably by the existence of Cuban troops in Angola, ostensibly to protect Angola from South African invasions. In the Reagan administration policy, the issue of Cuban troop withdrawal from Angola was specifically "linked" to the independence negotiations for Namibia. The breakthrough occurred only in 1988, at least in part because of the intervention of the Soviet leader Mikhail Gorbachev. On May 19, 1990, the new Namibian Government signed a border security pact with Angola that provided for the formation of a joint commission to establish security along the border. Nevertheless, the border area has continued to be a security problem, as UNITA rebels have regularly crossed into Namibia.

The construction of a major dam and hydroelectric project at the Ruacana Falls on the Kunene River, the border between the countries, will prove to be a valuable asset to both governments.

ANGULA, HELMUT K. Born in 1945, he became a SWAPO activist in 1963. He fled the country in 1966 and went to study in both Zambia and the USSR. He was appointed to the party's Central Committee and also became its Permanent Representative at the United Nations. At independence he became Deputy Minister of Mines and Energy, but in a cabinet shuffle in February, 1991, he was named Minister of Fisheries and Marine Resources.

ANGULA, NAHAS G. Born at Onyaanya in 1943, he became a member of SWAPO's Youth League while still a student. His major activity has been as a teacher, especially in Zambia. He has degrees from the University of Zambia and Columbia University in the United States. After working at the United Nations for several years, he was named the SWAPO Secretary for Education in 1981. When he returned to Namibia in 1989 he was SWAPO's head of voter registration. He was named to President Nujoma's first cabinet as Minister of Education, Culture and Sport. With a cabinet revision in February, 1991 his title became Minister of Education and Culture, with the challenge of restructuring the Namibian educational system. This includes the introduction of English as the first language.

ANGRA PEQUENA. A Portuguese name meaning "Little Bay," it was one of the earlier and most commonly used names given to what now is known as Lüderitz Bay or Lüderitzbucht (q.v.).

APARTHEID. The policy of "Separate Development" adopted officially by the South African government after the National Party came to power there in 1948, it is rooted in the entire history of race relations in South Africa. In its modern form, apartheid includes the following elements: (1) *Grand apartheid.* A policy in which land was allocated to groups of people based on their race or tribal affiliation. This was formally instituted by South Africa in Namibia after the Odendaal Commission in 1964 made its recommendations concerning Homelands Policy (q.v.). (2) *Petty apartheid.* A system of racial discrimination involving the access of people of color to amenities available to whites. Lifting of these discriminatory practices in Namibia began, at least officially, as a result of actions by the Administrator-general in the 1970s. In practice, however, many aspects of petty apartheid existed up to independence in 1990. (3) *Discriminatory employment policy.* The so-called Job Reservation system that favored whites over blacks combined with the contract labor system to create economic hardship for black Namibians. (4) *Educational restrictions.* Strict isolation of the races in schools plus a paucity of spending by the government on African schools made it difficult for Africans to achieve the necessary education for advancement. (5) *Police-state tactics and the violation of basic human rights.* While perhaps never as bad as in South Africa, these harsh practices were directed against those struggling against the existing political system.

APPOLUS, EMIL (1935–). The activities of Mr. Appolus, one of the earliest members of SWAPO (q.v.), have taken him across the world and across the Namibian political spectrum. Born in Vaalgras, he was educated in South Africa and at the University of Rochester (New York) in the United States. In his early twenties he was one of the founding members in 1958 of the Ovamboland People's Congress, and the OPO in 1959, forerunners of SWAPO. He became the publicity and information secretary of the OPO from 1959 to 1961. He also briefly served on the executive committee of SWANU in 1959. Over the next ten years he served as publisher and editor of the *South West News* in Namibia and worked as a correspondent for papers in Zambia and Johannesburg. While studying in the United States at the University of Rochester he held the title of SWAPO's publicity and information secretary (1961–67).

His early days in politics had been adventurous ones. In early 1960 he was arrested in Northern Rhodesia (later,

Zambia) and sent to South Africa and sentenced to a six-month jail term for leaving South Africa without a passport. On his release he escaped into Bechuanaland (Botswana) and then into Zambia and Tanzania where he renewed his association with Sam Nujoma (q.v.). With the formation of SWAPO, Appolus worked out of the office in Dar-es-Salaam and later set up a SWAPO office in Cairo, Egypt. At the same time he was travelling around the world to try to persuade foreign leaders to support SWAPO's cause. In 1964 he was in Botswana attempting to recruit miners going to South Africa to work under contract as potential freedom fighters. From 1968 to late 1971 Appolus worked in the United States as associate political affairs officer in the UN Council for Namibia, serving as a link between SWAPO and the UN.

By 1972 Appolus was becoming disillusioned with both SWAPO and the leadership of Nujoma. He felt that SWAPO was becoming dominated by Ovambos, and he (part Herero, part Coloured) was perceived as an outsider. In 1978 he returned to Namibia to work, first as a journalist and later as a businessman. He cooperated in the formation of the Turnhalle Conference (q.v.) and did public relations work for it. SWAPO supporters saw him as a turncoat and harassed him as he tried to speak in favor of the Conference. When Andreas Shipanga (q.v.) formed a new party, the SWAPO-Democrats, Appolus became a member. He continued to support moderate causes over the next decade, and aligned with the Multi-Party Conference (MPC) and the Transitional Government of National Unity (qq.v.). He was SWAPO-D's chief whip in the TGNU National Assembly, 1985–88. He split with Shipanga and SWAPO-D in 1988, however, claiming that Shipanga had been receiving kickbacks (R 360,000) from the Consolidated Diamond Mines from 1985–88. Appolus was then expelled from SWAPO-D for "activities prejudicial to party interests." He then formed his own group to fight for implementation of UN Resolution 435 (q.v.) and independence for Namibia, the United National Peace Action Party in August 1988. One year later he disbanded it and joined the DTA as part of the Democratic Turnhalle Party of Namibia (qq.v.).

ART. The history of the visual arts in Namibia stretches back to ancient times. The earliest rock art (q.v.) may be from about 25,000 B.C. (in the Lüderitz area). Earliest such art may be by the Wilton people, who preceded the San or Bushmen. Later rock art is attributed to the San or perhaps to the Bergdama. The best examples of this work is at Philipp's Cave (q.v.) at Amieb and the Maack Cave in the Brandberg Mountains. Most famous of all is the "White Lady of the Brandberg" (q.v.).

The honor of being Namibia's first white artist goes to Heinrich Knudsen, a nineteenth-century missionary. J. Thomas Baines (q.v.) was the first to achieve international fame, having illustrated a book on his travels through Namibia with such explorers as James Chapman and C. J. Andersson (qq.v.). Another pioneer figure was Karl E. Mayer (q.v.). Subsequent outstanding artists include H. A. Aschenborn, Axel Eriksson, Carl Ossmann, Johannes Blatt, Adolf Jentsch, Otto Schröder and Zakkie Eloff. An important organization that supports all of the arts in Namibia is the Association of Arts. The Namibia chapter of this South African organization was founded in 1947 by the wife of the administrator, P. I. Hoogenhout. It sponsors a broad range of musical activities (recitals, concerts, ballet, and opera) and operates a cultural center in Windhoek and a theater. It opened an art gallery in 1965 that houses regular exhibitions.

ART: BUSHMAN, PREHISTORIC. *See* ROCK ART.

ASIS MINES. Part of the Tsumeb mining complex in northern Namibia, Asis is actually two mines, Asis Ost ("East") and Asis West. Copper is the major product, but vanadium also exists there. The mines have been worked for about seventy years, but not continuously, depending on world ore prices.

ASSOCIATION FOR THE PRESERVATION OF THE TJAMUAHA MAHERERO ROYAL HOUSE. A tradition-oriented organization founded prior to 1970, but it then fought to protect the Herero Royal House against usurpers during the period of vacuum following the death of Chief Hosea Kutako (q.v.) in 1970. When Clemens Kapuuo (q.v.)

assumed the chieftainship, this group denounced him as a self-styled chief who would be recognized by only a minority of the Hereros. Kapuuo's association with the Democratic Turnhalle Alliance (q.v.) pushed the Association to ally with SWAPO (q.v.) instead, bringing with it a membership of 17,000 Hereros, under the leadership of Rev. Bartholemeus Karuaera. However the association has a history of fragmentation. It was associated with the SWA National United Front in the 1970s, and various other opposition groups later. It received considerable support in the 1980s from NUDO-PP (q.v.).

AUALA, BISHOP LEONARD (1909–1984). Bishop in 1963 of the Evangelical Lutheran Ovambokavango Church (formerly the Finnish Mission), he was one of Namibia's most respected spokesmen against South African rule. He usually worked in cooperation with other church leaders. A letter of protest sent by the bishop and Paulus Gowaseb to Prime Minister B. J. Vorster of South Africa in 1971 led to Vorster's calling the two to South Africa to discuss the status of Namibia. The talks were fruitless. Nevertheless Bishop Auala and his colleagues were influential behind the scenes. With a church membership of about a quarter million, Bishop Auala represented a major segment of Namibia's population. The Bishop was not afraid of taking controversial stands. In a 1978 pastoral letter issued jointly with two other church leaders, the bishop said that choosing a political party is a very personal matter, but that the people might find themselves in equally bad shape if they replace the apartheid ideology with a Marxist one. At one point in the 1970s, members of the Western Five Contact Group suggested that Bishop Auala might be the best choice to head a transitional government. On the other side, SWAPO has also acknowledged his important role in the independence struggle. In the early 1980s he was named bishop Emeritus of his church.

AUAS MOUNTAINS. The highest mountain range in Namibia, it is a chain of rugged peaks that stretch for thirty-five miles in the Windhoek District. The rail line and a highway cross the range at the Auas Pass, seven miles south of Windhoek. The highest peak in the range is Moltkeblick at 8156 feet. The range and others nearby constitute the core of Namibia's central highlands. The range is rich in a variety of flora and game.

AUCHAS. Forty-five kilometers inland from Oranjemund, this site was designated in 1989 by the Consolidated Diamond Mines as the location for a new diamond production center. It will include establishing facilities for the treatment of ore mined at Auchas and other nearby sites. Mining operations began in 1990.

AUGUSTINEUM. The oldest advanced school in Namibia, it was the result of efforts by Rev. Carl Hugo Hahn (q.v.), a noted missionary. On a trip to Germany in 1864, Hahn sought donations for an advanced school capable of training Hereros as teachers. Princess Augusta von Lippe came through as the largest donor, so the school was named for her. The Rhenish Mission first opened the school in 1866 at Otjimbingwe. In 1890 it was moved to Okahandja both because it was more centrally located and because Chief Samuel Maharero (q.v.) donated an ideal piece of land for the school. In 1901 the missionary who directed the school died, and with no suitable replacement available, teacher education ceased there until 1911. At that point Dr. Heinrich Vedder (q.v.) picked up the project at Gaub, in the Grootfontein district, and the old Augustineum buildings were used as a school for Baster children. The school closed again with the outbreak of World War I in 1914. In 1923 Dr. Vedder reopened the Augustineum in its buildings at Okahandja.

Twenty years later, in 1943, education again stopped because funds from Germany were unavailable, but the school reopened quickly, in January 1944, and average attendance doubled from 23 to 46 students. The teachers' course was a three-year curriculum covering many subjects. With support from the administrator of Namibia, P. I. Hoogenhout (q.v.) facilities were improved. In 1946 female students were finally admitted. Mr. A. I. Steinkamp became principal in 1947. When he left in 1959 enrollment had increased from 68 to 200, and the staff went from five to eleven teachers. New buildings were added, plus new curricular and extracurricular programs. In 1958 the school was raised in status to a high school, and five students passed the difficult matriculation exam. Enrollment topped the 300 mark in 1965, the same year that more classrooms and specialty rooms (science, library) were added.

Three years later a much larger Augustineum was opened in Khomasdal, a township for the "Coloureds," and a northwestern section of Windhoek. The teaching standard was raised and the curriculum was diversified. Tuition, board, and lodging became free. The Augustineum Training Centre in Windhoek offers its students a technical senior certificate course. As one of the most advanced educational institutions for Africans in the country, the Augustineum College has seen a number of activist movements grow there. In August 1973, for example, students took part in an election boycott and some of their leaders were expelled. A militant rally was held, and 250 students staged a mass walkout. Most of them were expelled and denied readmission. A week later most of the students at a nearby high school walked out in sympathy with the expelled Augustineum college students.

- B -

BAINES, JOHN THOMAS (1820–1875). An artist and mapmaker, he was the first European artist to paint scenes of what he saw in Namibia. Thomas (as he was called) was born in King's Lynn, England. In his youth he was an apprentice ornamental artist, and in 1842 he travelled to South Africa where he became a cabinet-maker's painter. By 1846 he had become a full-time artist. He soon began travelling throughout southern Africa on hunting and exploring expeditions and became a prolific painter. He returned to England from 1853 to 1855. On his return he accompanied Dr. David Livingstone on his expedition on the Zambesi River and did paintings of the Victoria Falls. His work in Namibia began in 1861 when he reached Otjimbingwe on May 18. He then travelled to Walvis Bay and back to Otjimbingwe, where he became a friend of the explorer J. C. Andersson (q.v.). His travels in the Namib Desert led him to paint an unusual plant, which was then named after him. When it was discovered that Dr. Friedrich Welwitsch had reported on it two years earlier, it was renamed Welwitschia mirabilis (q.v.), but scientists have compromised and call it Welwitschia bainesii. In 1861 Baines travelled through the land of the Hereros and went on an expedition with James Chapman (q.v.) to Lake Ngami and the Zambesi again before returning to Otjimbingwe. While there he painted pictures for a book on Namibian birds planned by Andersson. A sensitive observer, Baines did sketches, oils, and watercolors of numerous scenes of Namibia. One of the better ones is a genre scene that includes the Andersson family and now hangs in the legislative building in Windhoek. Another notable painting shows the departure of the Herero army from Otjimbingwe in June 1864. Baines stayed in Namibia until October 1864. Over the years Baines published several volumes of his diaries and sketches. One, *Explorations in South-West Africa,* was published in 1864.

BANTU AFFAIRS DEPARTMENT. Known more properly as the Department of Bantu Affairs and Development, this agency of the South African government took over the entire administration of ''Bantu Affairs'' in Namibia in April 1955. It was in charge of the vast bureaucracy that handled education, the civil service, and the general administration of all aspects of the daily lives of those Namibians not classified as Europeans. As such it was widely distrusted and despised by many of those it purported to serve. This situation continued after the Odendaal Commission Report (q.v.) of 1963, which gave the department added responsibilities in supervising the ''Homelands.'' Most aspects of apartheid legislation were in its domain. Local Bantu affairs commissioners brought the administration down to the level of everyday life.

BANTU INVESTMENT CORPORATION (BIC). A South African parastatal, it extended its operations to Namibia in 1964.

As a state-financed corporation, it has maintained a monopoly of wholesale supply and credit. In 1978 its name was changed to the First National Development Corporation (q.v.), but is popularly known by its initials in the Afrikaans language, ENOK.

BANTUSTANS. *See* HOMELANDS POLICY.

BARMEN. On October 31, 1844, the Revs. Hugo Hahn and F. H. Kleinschmidt (qq.v.) of the Rhenish Mission society founded the first German mission station at the site called Otjikango by the Hereros. The word Barmen was chosen because it was the name of the city in Germany where they had received their training. When it was founded its original name was Neu Barmen (New Barmen). It is also known as Gross Barmen (Great or Large Barmen) (q.v.). The mission station is no longer active there.

BASSINGTHWAIGHTE, JAMES FRANK (1820–1885). One of the earliest permanent European settlers in Namibia, he was born in Norfolk, England, but travelled to southern Africa in 1845. He was hired in Namibia by Peter Dixon, a trader, and worked as a blacksmith and wagon-maker. In addition to running his blacksmith's shop at Rehoboth, "Frank" assisted several visiting hunters and explorers, including Francis Galton (q.v.). He became good friends with William Latham (q.v.), in part because they each married one of Peter Dixon's daughters, the first white women to live at Walvis Bay. Together Latham and Bassingthwaighte discovered copper at what became the Matchless Mine (q.v.). He became a friend of Jonker Afrikander (q.v.), who gave Bassingthwaighte a farm near Windhoek. He then persuaded Jonker to build a road from the mine to Walvis Bay so the copper could be sold abroad. He was also involved with negotiations in 1861 with Willem Swartbooi about cattle stolen from C. J. Andersson, but his own farm was raided by Topnaars (q.v.) in December 1863, and his cattle were stolen. By the late 1870s he was paralyzed in both legs and lived near Aris. In 1881 he was living near Keetmanshoop. His children included a son, James Benjamin, who was a hunter, farmer, and cattle trader in Namibia; though his son died in 1930, the family remained prominent in Namibia.

BASSON, JAPIE. A member of the South African parliament from Namibia, he had been a member of the National Party until he broke from it to form the more liberal "National Union" on February 10, 1960. He favored allowing Coloureds the right to elect representatives to parliament and allowing Africans to gain political and economic development. On July 19, 1960, Basson formed the South West Party (q.v.) in Windhoek, as the Namibian companion to his National Union. The new party had the same basic program as the National Union, but also advocated that "South West" be allowed self-government in a federal arrangement with South Africa. The territory would have as much autonomy as possible. In the 1961 South African elections, Basson's National Union met with minimal success, so he merged it into the Union Party. He remained active in the various splits within that party, aligning himself with reformist elements.

BASSON, NICO. A former military intelligence official for the South African Defense Force, in May, 1991 he revealed that he had been part of a major disinformation campaign which was financed by R100 million of secret South African government funds. He worked from the Kalahari Sands Hotel in Windhoek, attempting to discredit SWAPO and aid the alternative parties in the period leading up to the 1989 elections. He also named Sean Cleary, a Johannesburg businessman and former South African diplomat, as a key operative. He claimed that Cleary was involved in both Namibia and Angola, as Cleary was said to be close with Jonas Savimbi, the leader of Angola's rebel group, Unita. South African President P. W. Botha had allowed the military much freedom in this effort. In addition to a series of "dirty tricks" revealed by Basson, it came to light that R65 million of the D.T.A.'s R72 million election budget came from South Africa. He also said that South Africa still hoped to influence the 1994 elections. DTA chairman Dirk Mudge acknowledged the truth of the statements. Basson said he had become disillusioned with the operations after the assassination of Anton Lubowski (q.v.), a leading white member of SWAPO.

BASTARDS. Originally "Bastaards," the term is now usually seen as "Basters" (q.v.).

BASTER COUNCIL. The Basters of Rehoboth have been a strongly independent people since their early days in Namibia. They were ruled in part by a traditional council. After South Africa assumed control of the country, the council was transformed in 1923 into an advisory body with local powers, but presided over by a South African-appointed white magistrate. Nevertheless in July 1971, the seven-member Baster Council demanded that South Africa allow the Basters themselves to supervise the development of the Rehoboth Gebiet (q.v.). Modern political parties developed and sides were taken in the mid-1970s, and the council was replaced by a revised system that provided for an elected Baster Kaptein (chief), two assistants, and a six-member Volksraad (People's Council).

BASTERS. One of the population subgroups of Namibia, it consisted of an estimated 32,000 people in 1989. (Another estimate is twice that.) The name, a variant of Bastards (originally Bastaards to the Dutch), is borne proudly by its members. Originating south of the Orange River in the northern Cape Colony, these people are generally the result of relationships between Trekboer men and Nama women in the 1840s and 1850s, although some predate this considerably. The progeny developed a pride in their mixed-race status, often speaking Afrikaans and adopting Dutch clothes and traditions as well as the family names of their fathers. However, as more Boers moved north, competition for the land became heated, and the 1865 Land Beacons Act forced the Basters to prove their ownership of the land. This not being possible, some of the Basters crossed north of the Orange River in 1867 to explore the area. A much larger group followed them in December 1868, led by Hermanus van Wyk and Rev. Johann Heidmann. This group consisted of about ninety Baster families. Two years later they settled at Rehoboth. The area had been occupied by Abraham Swartbooi (q.v.) and his followers until 1864 when they were driven out by the Afrikanders (q.v.). Swartbooi was willing to allow the Basters to rent the land for payment of one horse a year. Ownership of the area was disputed for most of the 1870s, as Jan Jonker Afrikander, van Wyk, Swartbooi, and even some white settlers laid claim. The Basters wanted to develop the land and especially the water facilities, so they attempted to get better title, especially since Jan Jonker claimed rights by conquest. Hermanus van Wyk paid 120 horses and 5 wagons to get Swartbooi to relinquish his remaining claims, and then sent notes to other Nama leaders explaining the transaction. Eventually other claims were dropped.

The Baster families settled in, developed their own constitution, improved the land, and with high birth rates greatly increased their numbers. While Rehoboth became their home, some families moved closer to Windhoek. The original Rehoboth contained 17,000 square miles, but German and South African pressures reduced this to less than a third of that today. The Basters were friendly with the Germans, supplying twenty soldiers for "Protection Troops" under Dr. Heinrich Göring in 1888. Van Wyk also refused to join the Hereros in revolt against the Germans in 1904. The Basters dropped their support of Europeans when South African invaded. The Basters resisted the attempt by South Africans to control them in the 1920s, but were defeated and ultimately accepted the authority of a white civil servant along with their own council and kaptein ("chief"). A determined people who still resist rule by outsiders, most Basters are conservative in modern political terms, and generally not supportive of SWAPO (q.v.). One Baster politician, Hans Diergaardt (q.v.), vowed a revolution if SWAPO won the election, and even threatened a declaration of independence. Basters have even purchased 250,000 acres of land toward giving themselves a corridor to the Atlantic Ocean. (*See also* REHOBOTH DISTRICT; REHOBOTH GEBIET.)

BASTERVERENIGING. *See* REHOBOTH BASTER VEREN-
IGING.

BECHUANALAND. *See* BOTSWANA.

BECHUANAS. *See* TSWANA.

BENGUELA CURRENT. The cold northward flow of the current
of the South Atlantic off the Namibian coast, it stirs up
nutrient salts from the ocean depths, beginning the great food
chain that makes the area so rich in fish and related creatures.
When a west wind blows across the current, a fog forms and
moves into the Namib Desert, bringing with it molecules of
water that are enough to satisfy some life forms in the desert.
The water's coldness can be attributed to its origins in the
Antarctic and to the ocean depths from whence it rises. The
speed of the current varies by sixteen to forty kilometers per
day, but can slow down or even reverse if there is a strong
north wind. The temperature off Namibia's coast is about ten
to twelve degrees Celsius, but varies seasonally. The current
warms as it flows northward toward the equator. The Benguela current is rich in nitrates, phosphates, oxygen, and
plankton, and also contains seaweeds and large kelps. The
fishing industry (q.v.) of Namibia relies heavily on the
current. The fish in turn attract the birds that create guano,
another profitable industry.

BERG AUKAS. A mine twelve miles east of Grootfontein that has
produced zinc, lead, and vanadium. First opened by the
Germans, who practiced open-cast mining, it was closed after
World War I. It was reopened as a shaft mine in 1958.
Originally developed by the South West Africa Company
(q.v.), its ownership now consists of Consolidated Gold Fields
Ltd. (UK), the Anglo American Corporation, and Charter
(UK). This change occurred in the mid-1970s. The Berg Aukas
Mine, adjacent to the Tsumeb Mine (q.v.), has been on a care
and maintenance basis (i.e., non-producing) since 1978. Con-
solidated Gold Fields was purchased from its stockholders in
1989 by Hanson plc., a British industrial conglomerate.

BERGDAMA (variant: BERGDAMARA). Literally the "mountain Dama," the terms are related to Dama or Damara (qq.v.).

BERSEBA. A town in south-central Namibia, it is at the foot of Mount Brukkaros, an extinct volcano. It is the center of the "Berseba Reserve," as the South African native commissioner for the area lived there. The Rhenish Mission had a station there, supervised by Rev. Samuel Hahn, who is said to have given it the Biblical name. Hahn worked among the Berseba Namas (q.v.), who had moved there early in the nineteenth century. Berseba was the site of a conference between W. C. Palgrave (q.v.) and several African leaders in late November 1876. Palgrave's goal was to convince the Africans that coordination under South African administrators could be useful to the Africans. Only a few were persuaded of that. The Berseba Reserve was the result of a treaty with the Germans and Namas in 1885, although South Africa redrew the boundaries in 1923, to include 2266 square miles.

BERSEBA NAMAS. One of five groups of Orlams (q.v.), they crossed north of the Orange River early in the nineteenth century. The eventually settled at the foot of Mount Brukkaross. Working with LMS missionaries, they centered their tribal life at the spring in what became known as Berseba. The original leader of these people was Dietrich Isaak. After his death he was succeeded by a son-in-law, Paul Goliath (q.v.). The Bersebas are related to those who settled at Bethanie and were not opposed to uniting with them. Nevertheless, the Bersebas remained distinct, and their area was declared an African reserve by South African administrators.

BERYL. A semi-precious stone found in Namibia, it is a class of stones that is in worldwide demand. The Deutsche Kolonialgesellschaft was mining for such stones in the early years of the twentieth century. It discovered a yellowish-green beryl with some radioactive properties to which the name heliodor was given. Aquamarines belong chemically and mineralogically to the same class of beryls, but have a very different tint from the heliodor.

BESSINGER, NICO (1948–). Long a member of SWAPO's executive board and its internal secretary for foreign affairs, he continues to play a major role in SWAPO (q.v.) politics. He joined SWAPO in 1972. In 1987 he and six other internal SWAPO leaders were detained by the transitional government under the terms of the Terrorism Act for withholding information. They were held for three weeks when the Supreme Court heard their appeal and ordered their release. In December 1988 the commissioner of police was required to pay R84,000 to the seven for wrongful arrest and detention. In February 1989 SWAPO reorganized its top command, unifying its internal and external wings. Bessinger was elected to its highest policy-making body, the central committee and secretariat. He was elected to the Assembly in November 1989 and is on the cabinet as minister of wildlife, conservation, and tourism.

Born in Walvis Bay and educated primarily in Namibia, he attended the University of Cape Town Architectural School from 1969 to 1972. He then studied in the US on a Fulbright scholarship, earning degrees at the University of Detroit. In 1983 he became a registered architect.

BETHANIE (variants: BETHANY; BETHANIEN). Standing at the foot of the Hanami Plateau (Schwarzrand) in the Bethany Valley, this town is 160 miles inland. Located on the Konkiep River, it is the major town in this agriculturally productive valley. It has numerous springs and large gardens. Founded as a mission station in 1814 by J. H. Schmelen (q.v.), it was abandoned five years later, but Schmelen's son-in-law, Rev. H. Kleinschmidt (q.v.), reopened the station in 1840. Schmelen's house, still standing there, is considered the oldest existing dwelling in the country. As such it is a historical landmark.

When Namas revolted against the Germans in 1904, most Namas from Bethanie did not join in, as the Germans had made it headquarters for a detachment of troops in 1894. Today there are about 2000 residents in Bethanie, which has stores and a hotel plus schools. The surrounding Bethanie District is a center for the Karakul industry.

BEUKES FAMILY. A number of members of the Beukes family have played a prominent role in Rehoboth politics over the years; recently, they have become increasingly active in Namibian politics. In 1914 Samuel Beukes fought the Germans, in 1919 he petitioned the League of Nations for Namibian independence, and in 1924 he was part of a Rehoboth Rebellion against South Africa. His nephew Hermanus Beukes was active with the Rehoboth Volksparty. Hermanus Beukes fled with Andreas Shipanga and Dr. Kenneth Abrahams (qq.v.) from Namibia into Bechuanaland (now Botswana) in 1960, fearing arrest for their activities in forming SWAPO. His son Hana fled to Oslo, Norway, but was active in promoting the cause of freedom for Namibia at the United Nations. He was smuggled out of Namibia by three young Americans. Hans's sister Martha Ford has served on SWAPO's executive board. In May 1989, the Workers Revolutionary Party (WRP) was established. Ms. Erica Beukes was elected its leader. She had started her political career in 1973 as a SWAPO Youth League leader. She later served as vice-chairman of SWAPO in Rehoboth. Her husband, Gernot Hewat Beukes, a son of Hermanus, is also a leader of the strongly left-wing WRP.

BISMARCK, OTTO VON. The noted German politician and leader, he at first resisted setting up German colonies, anticipating the need to defend them with fleets at great expense. After Adolf Lüderitz (q.v.) arrived in Namibia in 1881 to set up a trading post, he appealed to Bismarck for German protection. The chancellor resisted a number of appeals, but when faced with British interest in the area he sent a gunboat to raise the German flag, and the German colonial empire had begun. Bismarck was being pushed in this direction by German colonial societies, businessmen, and missionaries as well. In 1884 he convened the Berlin Conference, which was designed to make the partitioning of African territories an exercise that would avoid battle between Europeans. In April 1885, Bismarck sent Dr. H. Goering to be imperial commissioner for South West Africa. Four years later he sent twenty-one soldiers commanded by

Capt. Curt von Francois to the territory to reaffirm German authority. Yet Bismarck truly wanted an empire only if it did not cost much. He favored allowing German businessmen to create charter companies along the British model, to relieve the German government of all but a few responsibilities. He lost the position of chancellor in 1890, leaving colonial policy to his successors.

BLACK NOSSOB RIVER. Along with the White Nossob (q.v.), it is one of the two source-rivers of the Nossob River that flows through east-central Namibia. The Black Nossob owes its name to the black soil in its bed (versus white sand in the White Nossob). It rises in the Onjati Mountains northeast of Windhoek and meanders easterly through a well-wooded and grassy region containing much groundwater. It then dips south past the town of Gobabis (q.v.) to its union with the White Nossob at Aais. From there until it enters Botswana it is called the Nossob River (q.v.).

BLANKSWA. Literally "White South West Africa," this is one of two white racist organizations formed by young Afrikaners in the 1970s. It is reported to have a "death list" that includes SWAPO leaders and other black leaders in Namibia.

BLUE GROUND. Also called kimberlite, it is a diamondiferous rock that early miners thought would always be the source of most diamonds. Blue ground is the material in the necks of circular pipes of extinct volcanoes. Here specks of carbon were trapped in streams of molten lava, subjected to intense heat and pressure, changing their structure and making them precious diamonds. Early efforts to find more diamonds in Namibia centered on searches for the rare blue ground. Only later was it discovered that alluvial mining would be far more productive, such as the work at Oranjemund.

BLUE-WHITES. The purest and most sought-after diamonds are called blue-whites. There is money in all diamonds, but these high-quality gemstones are by far the most valuable. Namibia's proportion of blue-whites has been higher than that of any other diamond-producing area, although some fine blue-whites have been found in Angola, Liberia, Ghana, and Sierra Leone.

BOERS. *See* AFRIKANERS IN NAMIBIA; THIRSTLAND TREK.

BOESMAN COUNCIL (also: BUSHMAN ALLIANCE). The "Bushmen" (Boesman) have played a minimal political role in modern Namibia, in part because of their small numbers, but also because of their nomadic and apolitical lifestyle. (*See* SAN.) However, when the Turnhalle Conference (q.v.) was based on ethnic representation, it was necessary to find someone to fill the two seats allotted to them. These representatives were referred to as members of the Boesman Council. In 1978, led by Geelbooi Kashe (q.v.), a small "group" incorporated as a member of the Democratic Turnhalle Alliance under the name Bushman Alliance, Kashe and Martin Xaesce represented it in the assembly (1979–1983), and Kashe continued in the assembly of the TGNU (1985–1989). He remains leader of the Bushman Alliance, and as a member of the DTA won a seat in the assembly in the 1989 elections.

BOKHARA SHEEP. Bokhara, Tibet, is the home area of a fat-tailed breed of sheep, from which karakul (q.v.) sheep were developed.

BONDELSWARTS (variant: BONDELZWARTS). A society of Namas living in the southernmost part of Namibia, they are also called the Gaminus (or !GAMI-/NUN). They are thought to have crossed the Orange River from the Cape in the late eighteenth century, but formal knowledge of their early history is scant. They were nomadic peoples, following their goats and cattle from one water-hole to another, living in temporary huts. They moved when pasturage was depleted. Their governing pattern was influenced by the Dutch, to whom they considered themselves equal. They selected a chief ("Captain") and elected "Corporals" as well, subject to later replacement. There was also a council ("Rood") which had administrative and judicial functions as well. While Dutch and Germans considered them to be lazy, insolent, and hostile, an African perspective would see them as proud people who felt they were not inferior to the Europeans and need not work for them or obey them. The Bondelswarts eventually settled down in the Warmbad area. One of their noted chiefs was Jacobus Christian (q.v.). Inevitable conflicts occurred as Europeans claimed control over the area. The Bondelswarts were quick to stand up for their rights and defy the Europeans. (*See* BONDELSWART REBELLIONS.) The name Bondelswart refers to the black band that the men wore around their head when they went into battle.

BONDELSWART REBELLIONS. The Bondelswarts (q.v.) were an extremely independent group of Namas who lived in the Warmbad area. They and the Witboois were the only two Nama groups to refuse all efforts by German government agents (H. Goering and K. Buttner, qq.v.) to sign a treaty of protection with the Germans in 1885. Chief Willem Christian claimed to be on friendly terms with the Cape government. Finally Christian agreed to a treaty on August 21, 1890, with Goering, but his Bondelswarts were very upset with it, not having given their chief prior approval. The first direct fight with the Germans came in 1896. The Germans succeeded easily, with some of the Bondelswarts fleeing into the northern Cape, but they were captured, turned over to the Germans, and executed.

A more significant rebellion began in 1903. Its leaders were Jacob Marengo and Abraham Morris, along with the hereditary chief, Jacobus Christian (qq.v.). This rebellion lasted several years, and was in two parts. The first began in October 1903 when Bondelswarts living in Warmbad sought freedom from German rule. It ended a few months later, on January 27, 1904, when Governor Leutwein signed the Peace of Kalkfontein with the Bondels. It granted them a Reserve at Warmbad, but they were required to give up 300 guns. Marengo was not at all happy with this result and immediately broke the treaty. Marengo was well-educated (he was

fluent in three European and several African languages) and
an excellent military tactician and guerrilla fighter. Finally
the Germans triumphed and a treaty of peace was signed in
1906. Morris and Christian fled to the Cape. The Bondels
bitterly resented the treaty, which limited their area to
175,000 hectares, prohibited them from having a chief,
limited their stock, provided for compulsory labor, and
applied master-servant laws. The Bondels were bitter and
vowed revenge. They also kept in touch with Morris and
Christian.

When World War I broke out, the Bondelswarts saw their
chance. Morris served as a guide with the South African
Defence Force, hoping to win approval for a return to their
prior independent status. But after the Germans were defeated, South African leaders imposed a rule similar to that of
the Germans and even ruled by martial law. A brief attempt
to revolt failed. In 1918 the South Africans allowed the
Bondelswarts to have a chief again, and appointed Willam
Christian. He died in 1919 and two others followed in quick
succession. Meanwhile Jacobus Christian had left the Cape
in July 1919 with a force of fifty men in an attempt to reclaim
his leadership right. There was a battle with South African
police, and some of the fifty were captured and arrested.
Christian ultimately surrendered to a magistrate and was
fired. But he was allowed to stay.

The Rebellion of 1922 is the one that received the most
international attention, ultimately requiring the League of
Nations to appoint a commission of inquiry to get the full
story. The causes of the rebellion were numerous. Among
them:

1. Resentment that South Africa had appointed a chief, then
   Timothy Beukes, instead of acknowledging Jacobus
   Christian.
2. The gradual intrusion of white farmers into land supposedly reserved for Bondelswarts.
3. Bad relations with South African police, some of whom
   flogged the Africans.
4. The imposition of a high "dog tax," which would force
   the Bondels to enter wage labor situations. The dog was

very important to the Bondels for hunting game (which in itself made them more independent), but also for protecting their stock against jackals and other predators.

5. Restrictions on Africans retaining branding irons to identify their stock—a right held by Europeans. Bondels were angry because they were being discriminated against.

6. Poor wages when they were forced to work.

Jacobus Christian and Timothy Beukes began complaining to authorities about these problems, but it was the return of Abraham Morris from the Cape that was the catalyst of the rebellion. Police attempted to arrest Morris at Warmbad for earlier charges and for bringing weapons and stock into the country. The Bondelswarts resisted. Finally Europeans were recruited near Windhoek, and by May 25, 1922, about 400 whites were available to support the police. The Bondels set up a camp at Guruchas, for defense, but the government force was too strong. The first fight began on May 26. The white authorities used machine guns and airplanes to attack the Africans. At least one hundred Bondels died. The Bondelswarts were surrounded, but on May 29 about two hundred of the men escaped through the lines at night, including all three leaders. The women, children, and cattle were captured the next day by the South African forces. The escaped warriors were tracked by airplanes. The last fight was on June 8 at Berg Kramer, when 53 Bondels were killed, including Morris. Christian and 145 men continued to attempt to flee west, but finally surrendered on June 14, 1922.

Christian was ultimately charged with treason. The South African Supreme Court ruled against the government, ruling that South African sovereignty did not extend to "South West Africa."

BOOI, JACOBUS. Son of Jan Booi (q.v.), Jacobus succeeded Christian Afrikander as leader of the Bethanie Namas after Christian died in 1863 at the battle of Otjimbingwe (q.v.). Jacobus had a large following among the Boois and allied himself with the Afrikanders. He became the father-in-law of Jan Jonker Afrikander. Jacobus moved some of his people to Salem, in the lower Swakop Valley, trying to build a new settlement there, but it was not a success. He then returned to the Bethanie district. Jacobus and Jan Jonker Afrikander led a series of raids in 1867 and 1868. They attacked Otjimbingwe on December 14, 1867, in a day-long battle which proved to be a stand-off. They were more successful looting food and ammunition at subsequent attacks at Anawood, Salem, Heigamchab, Walvis Bay, and Rooibank. In 1868, after a stay in Bethanie to recover from an illness, Jacobus Booi joined with Jan Jonker Afrikander in plans for another attack upon the Hereros. The two forces were joined by those of Karel Ses. They hoped to subjugate the Hereros, drive all Europeans from Namibia, and avenge the death of Hendrik Ses, bother of Karel and his predecessor. The forces assembled at Rehoboth. The Hereros heard about it and moved toward the Namas, who in turn set a trap for the Hereros at a spot west of Okahandja. The Hereros were able to withstand the ambush, however, and successfully beat off all opponents. In the process the entire Booi tribe was said to have been destroyed. Jacobus Booi had slipped away, but soon died of enteric fever.

BOOI, JAN. The early leader of the Booi people, he led them into Namibia in 1815, and ultimately to settle at Bethanie, where he was subject, at least in principle, to the rule of David Christian. In fact Jan Booi was famous for conducting raids, especially against Hereros, but specific examples have been lost to history. Both Jan and Jacobus were allies of the Afrikanders, Jan being the father-in-law of Jonker Afrikander. In the 1860s the elderly Jan Booi saw Jacobus become leader of the Bethanie Nama and relished the looting raids his son undertook with Jan Jonker Afrikander. In November 1868, he saw his tribe wiped out as a result of Jacobus' attack upon the Hereros.

BOOI (TRIBE). In 1815 Jan Booi (q.v.) led his people across the Orange River into Namibia. The Boois were one of the Orlam tribes of Namas who migrated from the Cape. In order to gain grazing and water rights they had to make arrangements with the Red Nation (q.v.) already in southern Namibia. They eventually settled in the northern part of Bethanie; they are thought to have been a branch of the Bethanie Namas, the Gei-khaua. Jan Booi apparently was under the authority of David Christian of Bethanie. Jan Booi was also the father-in-law of Jonker Afrikander (q.v.), and his son Jacobus Booi (q.v.) was father-in-law of Jan Jonker Afrikander. The Booi tribe seems to have come to an end as a result of a battle with the Hereros in November, 1868. (*See* JACOBUS BOOI.)

BOTHA, J. F. A leader of the expedition known as the Thirstland Trek (q.v.).

BOTHA, GENERAL LOUIS (1862–1919). The first prime minister of the Union of South Africa, he was trained as a military man and became commander of the entire Transvaal Republican army in the Anglo-Boer War. After seeing the union take shape and receive independence, he was elected its leader. World War I broke out in 1914, and the next year he led his armed forces into German South West Africa (Namibia), conquered the Germans, and attached the territory to South Africa. In addition to his overall command during the war, he personally led the northern part of his army, based in Swakopmund (Gen. Smuts was in charge in southern Namibia). In March 1915, his forces left Swakopmund for Windhoek. He rode with his troops to Karibib, with other units heading for Okahandja and Windhoek. These were taken, plus Tsaobis, a German fortress, and Otjimbingwe. On May 13, 1915, Botha rode into Windhoek as the German flag was lowered. In 1919 General Botha was active with General Smuts in convincing the other countries to designate Namibia as a "C" class mandate under the League of Nations, but which South Africa would rule as an integral part of its territory. After a tumultuous welcome home from Paris, he developed pneumonia and soon died. His successor as prime minister was his colleague, Jan Smuts.

BOTHA, P. W. Prime minister of South Africa from 1978 to 1984 and state president from 1984 to 1989, he presided over the process of negotiating an independent status for Namibia, aided by his minister of foreign affairs, R. F. (Pik) Botha. In this process President Botha consistently fought against the SWAPO forces, favoring the Democratic Turnhalle Alliance led by Dirk Mudge. His struggle against SWAPO led to his sending troops into Angola, both to intimidate and frustrate SWAPO and to destabilize Angola. As the military costs rose, Botha had second thoughts, and before he resigned as president it was clear that he accepted a probable SWAPO electoral victory. However as the revelations from Nico Basson (q.v.) illustrate, he allowed the military a great deal of freedom and at least R100 million to use in a campaign to prevent SWAPO from winning a 2/3 majority in the 1989 parliamentary elections.

BOTSWANA. Namibia's neighbor to the east, Botswana became independent on September 30, 1966. Until then it was the British protectorate called Bechuanaland. About the size of France, Botswana has some good pasturage and farm land in its east and north, but its western regions, which border Namibia along the 20th and 21st meridians, consist mostly of the Kalahari (or Kgalagadi) Desert. Another important physical connection between the territories involves Lake Ngami, in northwestern Botswana and about 100 miles east of the Namibian border. Many European explorers and adventurers had Lake Ngami on their list to see. The path through Namibia was more inviting and accessible than one through either the Kalahari or the Okavango Swamps. Furthermore, Namibia's Caprivi Strip runs the entire length of Botswana's northern border. In May, 1992 a dispute between the two countries over Kazikili Island on the Chobe River border was resolved in an agreement.

Botswana and Namibia share people as well as geography. The nomadic San or "Bushmen" traditionally knew no boundaries and live on both sides of the border. Also a group of approximately 8000 Tswanas live in a narrow area in Namibia along its east-central border. A third shared group are the Hereros. Historians indicate that the Hereros may have first entered Namibia from Botswana. After the battle of Waterberg (q.v.) in 1904, some surviving Hereros escaped into Botswana, where some of their descendents still live. Others returned to Namibia decades later, but live apart from most other Hereros in Namibia. Still others indicated a willingness to return after Namibia gained its independence.

In recent years Botswana has had meaning for Namibia in several ways. First, as a country almost twenty-five years independent, and a full-fledged democracy with a thriving economy based heavily on mining, Botswana served as a role model for Namibia. Second, as one of the "Front Line States" (q.v.), Botswana has housed many refugees from Namibia's struggle for independence. Namibian students have studied at the University of Botswana. Finally, as a member of SADCC, Botswana is concerned about helping an independent Namibia coordinate its development with the plans of the other black-ruled states in southern Africa. One of the major projects that has been considered is that of building a rail line across Botswana and into Namibia, perhaps ending at Swakopmund. This could mean that redevelopment of port facilities there would be more viable, creating an alternative to Walvis Bay.

BOUNDARIES. Namibia's boundaries are a product not of logic or of the decisions of Africans but of decisions by Europeans in the late nineteenth century. The borders consist of the Orange River to the south, the Atlantic Ocean on the west, the Kunene and Okavango Rivers in the north, and the 20th and 21st meridians in the east. In addition, the Germans saw the Zambesi River as a possible way to traverse the width of the continent and thus insisted on acquiring the Caprivi Strip (q.v.). The precise boundaries of Namibia lie between 17 degrees and 29 degrees south latitude and 11 degrees 45 minutes and 25 degrees 15 minutes east longitude (the last figure includes the Caprivi Strip). Most of the country does not lie further than 21 degrees east longitude. (*See also* BOUNDARY DECLARATION OF 1886; BOUNDARY AGREEMENT OF 1890.)

BOUNDARY DECLARATION OF 1886. The boundary declaration of December 30, 1886, defined the northern boundary of Namibia and the southern boundary of Portuguese Angola. It used the Kunene River as the border from its mouth to the falls, then proceeded east to the Okavango River, crossed the

Kwando River to the Zambesi at the Katima Mulilo rapids, and then moved along the Zambesi River to Kazangula. Disputes between South Africa and Portugal about this border were not totally resolved until a 1926 treaty between the two countries.

BOUNDARY AGREEMENT OF 1890. The boundary agreement of July 1, 1890, was between the Germans and the British. It set the southern border as the Orange River as far as 20 degrees east longitude, then north along that longitude to its intersection with 22 degrees south latitude, east briefly to 21 degrees east longitude and north along it to 18 degrees south latitude. It then followed the 18 degrees south latitude as far as the Chobe River, and along that to its confluence with the Zambesi. It then followed the Zambesi to a spot near Kazangula.

BRANDBERG. The highest mountain in Namibia, it lies 175 kilometers due north of Swakopmund. It is also called the Daures massif. Its peak is called Königstein (King's Rock) and reaches 2579 meters (8550 feet) above sea level. Baboons, klipspringers, mountain zebra, colorful lizards, and a wide variety of unusual flora are found on the Brandberg. Perhaps its greatest fame is the result of a hiking expedition in 1918 by a German surveyor, Dr. Reinhard Maack (q.v.), who took shelter from a hot sun by sitting under a huge rock, where he discovered a wondrous example of rock art, now called "The White Lady of Brandberg" (q.v.). The origins of this unique painting are still debated. The whole Tsisab Valley in fact is filled with rock art sites, many of them dating from the Wilton culture of the Late Stone Age. One study documents over 500 sites and close to 30,000 figures. The author estimates that the Brandberg contains more than 1000 sites. The entire massif has been declared a national monument and nature reserve. The origin of the name is uncertain. It means "Burning Mountain" (not to be confused with Burnt Mountain to the north). From the distance in a certain light it does appear to have a reddish glow. Also some of the rocks have a dark, charred appearance. The Hereros knew it as Omukuruwaro ("fire mountain" or "burning mountain,'' which was translated into Brandberg by the Germans.

BRANDBERG WEST MINE. Located in the Namib Desert, this mine was opened by the South West Africa Company and produces tin and wolfram (tungsten) concentrates. Although it has now been dismantled, it was a major producer for decades. Located in the foothills of the Brandberg Mountains, an erosion of an anticline had exposed a huge schist body with irregular mineralized quartz veins of varying widths. When fully producing, about 50,000 tons of this was blasted away each month, of which 8000 tons was treated. This yielded 70 to 80 tons of tin-wolfram concentrate that contained 75 percent metal in the proportion of 60 percent tin to 40 percent wolfram.

BRENNER, DR. FRITZ. The first civilian doctor to go to Namibia in the service of the German colonial administration, he went on to be a major political activist. In 1919 he became chairman of the Deutsche Kolonial Verein of Swakopmund. On September 3, 1924, he founded a German political party, the Deutscher Bund (q.v.). It became a major force in electoral politics for the next ten years, winning the 1926 legislative assembly elections under Brenner's leadership. A strong-willed person, he vigorously defended the rights of Germans in the territory and resisted South Africa's takeover of German language schools. Ambitious and energetic, he mixed politics and medicine, and he had his hands in most aspects of German life in Windhoek until he was removed from leadership of the Bund in 1928. His political career in the territory ended finally in 1935, when he moved to Johannesburg, where he later formed a "German Club."

BREUIL, ABBÉ HENRI. A distinguished French archaeologist and expert on the Stone Age, his research and publications spanned a career of over fifty years. He was a member of the Institut de France and had honorary doctorates from both Oxford and Cambridge. In the 1940s and 1950s he and two companion researchers, Dr. E. R. Scherz and Mary E. Boyle, carried out detailed studies of Namibia's rock art. Since his many earlier studies involved such art in France and Spain, it is not surprising that he found many similarities. "The White Lady of Brandberg," for one, he attributes to European hunters or warriors, perhaps originating in Crete but with Egyptian influence. South African administrators at the time were totally unwilling to accept the possibility that "Bushmen" or other Africans could be capable of such wonderful painting. In 1955 Breuil published his theories and pictures in *White Lady of the Brandberg.* Other scholars dispute Breuil, despite his reputation, noting that the main figure is probably not even a lady and (using other rock art nearby for comparison) note that the African hunters in that area followed a widespread African practice of smearing their bodies and lower limbs with white clay or ashes.

BRITAIN. British interest in Namibia began as early as 1786, when one of its sloops, *Nautilus,* dropped anchor at Angra Pequena. It had been surveying the coast for an area that might be suitable for settling convicts. Nine years later the British occupied the Cape and sent a boat up the west coast of Africa with instructions to hoist the British flag at all potential landing areas up to Angola. For about three decades the British claimed exclusive rights to catch whales and seals off Namibia's coast. When disputes occurred in 1842 over the guano deposits on Namibia's offshore islands, the British sent a warship to restore the peace. In the 1870s Dr. W. C. Palgrave was sent to Namibia by the British to negotiate some treaties with the Africans. In signing these he saw the possibility of extending British authority over the territory, while stopping Boer migration north. With Palgrave's recommendation, the governor of the Cape suggested to Britain that it should annex Walvis Bay and surrounding regions. In 1878, the British government annexed the bay but insisted that it could not be held responsible for the rest of the territory. By the Boundary Agreement of 1890 (q.v.), Germany and Britain agreed on the borders between Namibia and adjacent British-ruled territories. Britain retained its sovereignty over adjacent South Africa until 1910, but four years later it was encouraging the young South African government to invade the German territory.

BRUKKAROS MOUNTAINS (variant: BROEKKAROSS). *See* GREAT BRUKKAROS MOUNTAINS.

BÜLOW, PRINCE BERNHARD VON (1849–1929). German statesman, he served in various diplomatic and foreign affairs positions in the late nineteenth century. On October 17, 1890, he became German chancellor. A strong imperialist, he supported the suppression of African nationalists in Namibia and sanctioned the wars against the Namas and Hereros from 1904 to 1907. While a proponent of strong military leadership, he was angered by a massacre of Herero prisoners by his soldiers. At the end of the war, he said that rebuilding the country would be his top priority. Asking the Germans for a mandate to continue his colonial mission, he won the German election in 1907. However two years later he resigned as Chancellor over a budget matter.

BUSHMAN ALLIANCE. *See* BOESMAN COUNCIL.

BUSHMAN PAINTINGS. *See* ROCK ART.

BUSHMANLAND. Loosely, the land occupied by the San (''Bushmen'') people, but the term was given more specific meaning as a result of the report of the Odendaal Commission (q.v.) to divide Namibia according to ethnic lines. Thus ''Bushmanland'' was neatly drawn out on Namibia's eastern border, south of the Kavango ''homeland.'' Tsumkwe would be its capital. The ''homeland'' consisted of 23,926 square kilometers, but South Africa decided that it would not be on of the areas scheduled for self-government. It was estimated in 1970 that as few as 30 percent of all San were living in the ''homeland.''

BUSHMEN. This is a commonly used term to denote the nomadic people who live off the land in southern Africa, primarily by hunting and gathering. Nevertheless this descriptive term is considered demeaning by many. Thus the word ''San'' (q.v.) will be used in most instances in this book. ''San'' is the name used by Namas to refer to the people called ''Bushmen'' above.

BÜTTNER, DR. KARL GOTTLIEB (1848–1893). A German missionary and language expert, he was a member of the Rhenish Mission Society. From 1872 to 1880 he was principal of the Augustineum (q.v.), the only significant educational institution for Africans in the territory at that time. He returned to Germany as a pastor from 1880–85, but returned then to Namibia. This time he was working for the German government as interpreter and intermediary for Dr. Heinrich Goering (q.v.) who was negotiating treaties of "protection" with Namibian Africans in keeping with the provisions of the Berlin Conference of 1884–85. He was directly involved in at least four of the treaties. Dr. Büttner wrote a book about Namibia and was a cotranslator of the New Testament into Otjiherero. He died in Berlin in 1893.

- C -

"C" CLASS MANDATE. Under the League of Nations arrangement for administering the former colonies of Germany (and other countries defeated in World War I), "mandates" were set up. These were subdivided into three categories, the "A," "B," and "C" class mandates. Territories in the last category were thinly populated areas, of small size, or generally remote from centers of "civilization." South West Africa and some Pacific Islands were placed in this class. (*See* LEAGUE OF NATIONS.)

CALUEQUE. The key water control works for the Ruacana Falls hydroelectric plant are located at Calueque, fifteen kilometers inside Angola. The power house is in Namibia. The project is important not only for its electrical production but for its strategic value. Control of the waters of the Kunene River is vital for the development of central Owambo in Namibia. In 1975 Portugal withdrew from Angola, leaving three African nationalist parties fighting for dominance. In August 1975 South African military forces were sent to Calueque to protect the plant from disruption, but also used this as an excuse to invade much farther into Angola, beginning thirteen and a half years of military combat in northern Namibia and the southern half (and more) of Angola. Cuban troops were brought into Angola to aid the troops of the Angolan Government.

On June 27, 1988, a series of attacks by a Cuban and Angolan force, including airplanes, killed twelve members of the South African Defense Force and damaged the dam wall, along with the water pipeline to Owambo. While South Africa claimed to have repulsed the force and inflicted many casualties, the attacks on June 27 were only part of a buildup of about 15,000 Cuban troops in southwestern Angola, near the Namibian border. (*See also* CUITO CUANAVALE.) South African leaders were forced to seriously reevaluate the reasons why they had troops in Namibia. At this point all groups involved, including South Africa, seemed more willing to seriously negotiate a cease-fire.

CÃO, DIOGO. This Portuguese explorer was the first European to arrive along the coast of Namibia. His name is also rendered as Jacobus Canus and Diego Cam. In 1482 King John the Second of Portugal sent Cão, his knight, on a journey along the West African coast to seek a new trade route to India. He reached the Congo River the same year and returned to Lisbon in 1483 with several Africans as evidence. In 1485 he made another trip south, this time reaching the Namibian coast. He constructed a commemorative stone cross (padrão, q.v.) on the desolate sandy beach, and named it Cape Cross (q.v.). His travels took him even farther south, where he is believed to have died in 1486. Cão laid the groundwork for other Portuguese explorers, notably Bartholomeu Dias (q.v.).

CAPE CROSS. Located 80 miles or 127 kilometers north of Swakopmund along the coast, this is the site where the first European, Diogo Cão (q.v.), set foot on Namibian soil in 1485. It is accessible by road. When Cão landed he erected a stone cross (padrão) and named it Cabo do Padrão. The cross had been carved in Portugal earlier, anticipating discovery of new lands en route to India, it was hoped. Germans transported the original cross to Berlin in 1893, as it had become very weather-worn. A replica was installed at Kreuskap, the original site. Today Cape Cross is noted for its huge seal population. The sea lions (Cape seals) vary in number from 10,000 to 200,000. Concession companies kill the seals for the skins, meat, and seal oil. The Cape Cross Seal Reserve is open seasonally to tourists. The cape is also a lucrative source of guano (q.v.), and the area from Cape Cross south to Swakopmund contains very valuable salt deposits. Both rock salt and granular salt is produced.

CAPRIVI. *See* CAPRIVI STRIP.

CAPRIVI, GRAF ("COUNT") GEORGE LEO VON. The successor to Prince Bismarck as imperial chancellor of Germany in 1890, he was chancellor when the British agreed in a treaty that year to concede to Germany the land area now called the Caprivi Strip (q.v.). It is now the northeastern extension of Namibia. Actually Count Caprivi's full name is very un-Germanic: Graf Georg Leo von Caprivi di Caprara di Montecuccoli. He resigned as Chancellor in 1894. Born in Charlottenburg, Germany, in 1831, he was an officer in the Franco-Prussian War of 1870. He died in 1899.

CAPRIVI AFRICAN NATIONAL UNION (CANU). Organized in the eastern part of the Caprivi Strip in 1962 by Bredan K. Simbwaye, it was independent at first from SWAPO but received support and encouragement from groups in Zambia. It even opened offices in Lusaka, Zambia. It petitioned the United Nations for assistance in obtaining the withdrawal of South African authorities from Caprivi. The South African government in turn launched strong repressive measures against CANU, banned the movement, and arrested its leaders. Seeing little hope of success independently, Simbwaye and his followers joined SWAPO in October 1964, but he disappeared soon after. Reports indicated that he may have been killed by South Africans. Its vice-president, Albert Mishake Muyongo, became acting vice-president of SWAPO eventually. However, a dispute continued on whether CANU had given up its identity when joining SWAPO or retained the right to act on its own. In 1980 Muyongo was expelled from SWAPO for having resurrected CANU as a splinter organization. In August, 1985, Muyongo led a number of members of CANU's executive into a new party with Patrick Limbo, formerly a leader of the Caprivi Alliance Party. With this merger they formed the United Democratic Party (q.v.), and Muyongo was appointed a vice-president of the Democratic Turnhalle Alliance.

CAPRIVI AFRICAN NATIONAL UNION-NPF. When Mishake Muyongo disbanded CANU in 1985 while forming the United Democratic Party (*see* CAPRIVI AFRICAN NATIONAL UNION), a group of young CANU executive members, led by Siseho Simasiku, revived CANU. They led it to membership in the Caprivi 2nd Tier Representative Authority, and later on the Constitutional Council. From April 1987 until September 1988, CANU-NPF joined with the Caprivi Alliance Party in a Namibia Unity Front. In December 1988, CANU-NPF joined with SWANU and Action National Settlement in forming the National Patriotic Front for the 1989 elections. SWANU got the NPF's only Assembly seat. CANU-NPF favors a unitary Namibia, but one which would recognize the traditional roles of Mafwe and Basubia chiefs. CANU-NPF split in April 1989, resulting in a new faction (*see* CAPRIVI AFRICAN NATIONAL UNION-UDF).

CAPRIVI AFRICAN NATIONAL UNION-UDF. The Caprivi African National Union-NPF split in April 1989, when its leader, Siseho Simesika, expelled its vice-president, George Mutwa, and several other leaders. Fourteen branches met and declared the expulsion illegal. They then named Mutwa president and in September 1989 joined the United Democratic Front for the election. The UDF won four seats in the Assembly, none of which went to CANU-UDF members. The differences between this group and CANU-NPF appear to be based on personal disagreements more than serious policy differences.

CAPRIVI ALLIANCE PARTY-UDF. When Patrick Limbo of the Caprivi Alliance Party joined with Mishake Muyongo of CANU to form the United Democratic Party (q.v.) in 1985, some dissident members of CAP revived the organization.

Their principal leader was Gabriel Siseho, who became its president. Some who had joined the UDP even returned to CAP. This party broke its alliance with the DTA in April 1987, briefly joined with CANU in a Namibia United Front until September 1988, and in May 1988 joined the United Democratic Front. In the 1989 elections the UDF won four seats, one of which went to Siseho.

CAPRIVI COUNCIL (later: CAPRIVI ALLIANCE PARTY). Not originally a party as such, it consisted of eight members of the Caprivi Legislative Council who represented the area at the Turnhalle Conference. Its leader was Chief Richard Mamili. The Caprivi Alliance Party was established in November 1977 and became a founding organization of the Democratic Turnhalle Alliance (DTA). The extent of its support in the Caprivi Strip remained very questionable. It received a greater semblance of legitimacy in 1985 when A. M. Muyongo (q.v.) split from his well-established Caprivi African National Union and merged with some Caprivi Alliance Party leaders to create a new party, the United Democratic Party (q.v.). This was also affiliated with the DTA, and Muyongo was named a vice-president of the DTA. However, other members of the Caprivi Alliance Party did not join Muyongo and kept the identity alive.

CAPRIVI STRIP (variant: CAPRIVI ZIPFEL). A quirk of history, this strangely shaped area becomes a long handle attached to the rest of Namibia and extending deep into the center of southern Africa. Parts of it border Angola, Zambia, Botswana, and Zimbabwe. The people living in the Caprivi are related much more directly to Africans in those countries than to other Namibians. The Caprivi Strip was actually the result of an Anglo-German agreement of July 1, 1890, that involved territory in Africa and Heligoland. Graf G. L. Caprivi was the German chancellor at the time. Britain conceded it so that Germany would have free access to the Zambesi River, and thus perhaps to the Indian Ocean. The agreement was based on an inadequate knowledge of the Zambesi, which cannot be travelled completely from the Victoria Falls to the Indian Ocean. The Okavango River cuts through the western Caprivi

Strip, while the Kwando River cuts through in the center and changes its flow to the east as the Linyanti River. At that point it forms the southern border of the Strip, and the Zambesi eventually becomes its northern border.

The strip is 300 miles long and 73 miles wide at its widest point. When a 1968 act of the South African Parliament designated the eastern Caprivi for some autonomy, Katima Mulilo was established as its capital. The western section of the Caprivi is centered at Rundu. It contains 2269 square miles, whereas the Eastern Caprivi contains 4453 square miles. Much of the Strip is only 20 miles wide, especially in the western section as far east as the Kwando/Linyanti River. The Western Caprivi is lightly populated, mostly by San, while the Eastern Caprivi has a population of 30,000 Masubia and Mafwe (qq.v.). The Eastern Caprivi received more rainfall than any other part of Namibia, to the point where much of it is little more than a floodplain. In the decade prior to Namibian independence, the South African government militarized the Caprivi, notably with an airbase at Katima Mulilo. From here attacks could reach many countries, and indeed Zambia was a victim.

CAPRIVI ZIPFEL. *See* CAPRIVI STRIP.

CAPTAIN. A word used loosely to mean the leader of a group of Africans. Often it is spelled in a Germanic form as Kaptein. Its use has the same connotation as chief, except that the captain may be an elected leader. It has been used especially by Namas in the southern half of the country and by Rehoboth Basters.

CARLSSON, BERNT (d. 1988). Appointed UN commissioner for Namibia, beginning July 1987. From 1983 he acted as the special emissary of the late Swedish prime minister Olof Palme to Africa and the Middle East. He was Sweden's under-secretary of state for Nordic affairs until his appointment as commissioner for Namibia. His appointment had been renewed for 1989 by the General Assembly, when he died in an airline tragedy over Lockerbie, Scotland, December 21, 1988.

CASSINGA. A SWAPO base 150 miles inside Angola, it was the target of a major attack by South African forces in early May 1978. About six hundred people were killed, mostly (according to SWAPO) unarmed men, women, and children who were refugees from northern Namibia. SWAPO refers to it as the Cassinga Massacre. South Africa claims it merely destroyed a "terrorist camp" and a People's Liberation Army (q.v.) base. Many saw the attack as an attempt by South Africa to get SWAPO to back out of negotiations then being mediated by Western nations.

CASTLES. No African country other than Namibia has miniature Germanic castles high on the hillsides overlooking the major city. The most famous of Namibia's "castles" are Schwerinsburg, Heynitzburg, and Sanderburg, all the product of a German architect, Willi Sander (q.v.). Those three are all within eyesight of each other overlooking Windhoek. Their equal is Duwisib Castle, built in 1908 on the edge of the Namib Desert on a large karakul farm.

CATTLE. An export item for Namibia today, they have long been a source of conflict in the country. In the eighteenth century people at the Cape of Good Hope (Cape Town) were aware of the huge herds of cattle belonging to the Herero nation. For example, one of the purposes of the exploratory trip of Namibia by Sebastiaan van Reenen (q.v.) was to see if the Hereros would trade their cattle for export to the Cape. The history of Namibia in the nineteenth century is replete with wars over cattle, usually between the Namas and the Hereros. Often cattle owned by Europeans were stolen, however. Various traders from the Cape came north to participate in cattle purchases for export, among them F. J. Green and C. J. Andersson (qq.v.). Cattle can be raised in a large area of the central highlands, especially the grassy region north of Windhoek. Rinderpest (q.v.), an animal disease that affects cattle especially, had disastrous effects on the Herero herds in 1896 and 1897. In 1921 a livestock census counted 528,912 cattle in Namibia. Unfortunately, the country has periodic problems with drought, most recently in the early 1980s. The country's cattle total in 1979 was 2.5 million head, but five years later it was only 1.3 million. In 1981 437,000 cattle were marketed but only 267,000 were sold in 1983. This figure rose to about 350,000 a year in the late 1980s. Much of this is in the form of meat cuts exported to South Africa. The rest is transported by road or rail or on the hoof to three large abattoirs in South Africa, where up to 80 percent of all carcasses come from Namibia. The country fills about 12 percent of South Africa's total meat demand. Cattle farming today is practiced on 51 percent of the farmland in the country, and contributed 68.3 percent of the total agricultural revenue. In January, 1991 Namibia began to export cattle to the European Community under the terms of the beef export quota of the Lome' Convention. Namibia was allocated a quota of 60,000 tons in the 1991–1995 period. It will require the slaughter of at least 60,000 head of cattle each year, a number easily attained, as 334,000 head were marketed in 1991. With the drought of the early 1990s, many cattle owners sped up the marketing of their cattle.

CENTRAL PLATEAU. A geographic term that covers about half of Namibia. It is a savannah area that extends 1000 to 2000 meters above sea level and stretches from the Namib Desert on the west to the Kalahari Desert on the east. It is bordered by the Etosha Pan on the north. While the area is rather compact, there are "legs" off the plateau that extend to the northwest and southwest. Parts of the plateau are excellent for either cattle grazing or sheep pastures. Its mountain ranges contain major mineral deposits. Such cities as Windhoek and Grootfontein and the mining town of Tsumeb are major population centers.

CHAPMAN, JAMES, JR. (1831–1872). Author of *Travels in the Interior of South Africa* (1868), Chapman was an industrious lad already at the age of nineteen, as he was a trader in southeast Africa. He proved that travel was possible from the Indian Ocean (at Natal) across to Lake Ngami and then to the Atlantic coast at Walvis Bay. While this never became an actual trade route, he promoted an awareness of the interior of southern Africa. Not just an adventurer, he made serious observations on the people and the flora and fauna. One of his traveling companions to Lake Ngami on one occasion was the great artist, Thomas Baines. In one of his trips across Namibia in the 1860s he refused to help C. J. Andersson (q.v.) in a move to lead the Hereros against Nama cattle rustlers. In 1863 he settled down on a farm on the Swakop River, raising cattle himself. He took several trips to Lake Ngami, and at least one on the Zambesi River and to Victoria Falls. His farming was interrupted by the Nama-Herero War, so he sent his wife and sons to Cape Town in 1864 and soon followed them. In 1870 he hunted and traded in most of northern Namibia, reaching the Kunene River. In 1871 he went to the Diamond Fields of Kimberley, South Africa, where he died the next year.

CHARLOTTENTAL. Located just north of the town of Lüderitz (q.v.) along the Atlantic coast of Namibia, it was one of the sites where diamonds were found in abundance during the early stages of the diamond rush early in the twentieth century. It was also the site of a conflict between South African and German troops on September 29, 1914, one of the first such skirmishes in World War I. Troopships carrying men of the South African Defense Force had sailed on September 14 for the German-held ports of Lüderitz and Swakopmund.

CHOBE RIVER. Also known as the Kwando or Mashi or Linyanti River, it flows in a southeastern direction through parts of Angola until it touches Zambia. It then serves as the Zambian-Angolan border for 138 miles until it dips into Namibia's Caprivi Strip (q.v.). It then turns northeast and becomes the southern border of the Caprivi Strip until it joins the Zambesi River just east of Kazangula. While this is the normal flow, under flood conditions on the Zambesi the Chobe-Linyanti River receives this overflow and runs ''backward'' in a southwest direction, emptying into the Okavango Swamps of northern Botswana.

CHRISTIAN, DAVID. Leader of the Namas at Bethanie in the mid-nineteenth century, he was part of a period of change in the country. As leader he wanted his people to be educated in the Dutch language, rejecting his own Nama tongue for the schools, despite the well-intentioned work by German missionaries to produce a written Nama language, with grammar, literature (usually biblical), and even translation dictionaries. Although Bethanie is about 220 kilometers east of the Atlantic coast, Christian and his people claimed the intervening land and traded with settlers at Lüderitz and provided storage places at Aus for other traders to use.

Having claimed all land to the Atlantic, it should not be surprising that he "sold" part of that coast to businessmen. This land later became the site of the rich Pomona Diamond fields. No one, and certainly not David Christian, seemed to be aware of the possibility of large sources of diamonds under the sand. Although sometimes warlike in relations with other Africans, in 1858 Christian and Paul Goliath agreed to promote mutual support and protection. They subscribed to the previous treaty called the peace at Hoachanas (q.v.). He also negotiated with the Hereros, helping to alleviate some of the "cold war" that existed between Namas and Herero leaders.

CHRISTIAN, JACOBUS. The hereditary chief of the Bondelswarts (q.v.) at the beginning of the twentieth century, he took part in battles against the Germans a few years later and in defeat fled with some supporters into the Cape in 1906. When South Africa defeated the Germans in 1915, he and his followers requested permission to return, but were denied. Instead the administration selected Timothy Beukes as the chief of the Bondelswarts. He returned illegally in 1919 and was arrested, although he was then allowed to settle in the Warmbad district. His presence and activities undermined Beukes, but the two worked together, along with Abraham Morris (q.v.) and others to stage the Bondelswarts Rebellion (q.v.) of 1922. The rebellion was put down by South Africa with brutal force, and some of the Bondelswarts' leaders were killed. Christian and Beukes were among those captured. They were convicted on a charge of high treason. Although they were sentenced to five years in prison, they were released after one year. Christian was then appointed "Government Headman" of the bondelswarts. He received a subsidy of forty-eight rands per year and agreed to cooperate in all ways with the administration. He kept his word.

CHRISTIAN, JOHANNES. The son of Jacobus Christian (q.v.), the hereditary chief of the Bondelswarts, he became one of the military leaders of his people in the battle against the Germans in June 1905. For the next year Christian and his allies kept up a valiant fight against the Germans, catching them off guard. Finally on August 6, 1906, Christian and about fifty followers attacked a German post at Alurisfontein. While beaten off, Christian and his men forced three German columns to trail them for almost two weeks before they were caught and defeated by the Germans. Many survived, however, until they were again found by the Germans on August 30. This time only Christian and a few followers survived. They had covered more than 500 miles in the three weeks since Alurisfontein. While the Bondelswarts were decimated, eight Germans also died and seventeen were wounded. On October 25, Christian let the German Commander Deimling know he was prepared to negotiate. The peace conference occurred at Ukamas on December 21, 1906, where a definitive peace was signed. While agreeing to turn in their guns (they did do on December 23), the Bondelswarts refused to settle down at Keetmanshoop. Johannes Christian and his father Jacobus were among those who crossed the Orange River into the Cape to live.

CHRISTIAN DEMOCRATIC ACTION FOR SOCIAL JUSTICE (CDA). One of the political groups with a high profile throughout the 1980s, its prominence was due primarily to its active and vocal leader, Peter Kalangula. Supported primarily by Wambos, it was formed in February 1982 by members of the National Democratic Party who had become disillusioned with the Democratic Turnhalle Alliance. Kalangula had been president of the DTA, a figurehead position. At one point Kalangula tried and failed to merge his group with Justus Garoeb's Damara Council (q.v.). He did obtain the support of a prominent German-speaking politician, Werner Neef, thus getting financial backing from some parties in Germany. Even more significantly, he began to receive aid from the South African Defence Force and encouragement from South African officials who saw him as potentially drawing Wambo support from SWAPO. After this connection became obvious, however, the reverse effect occurred and his popularity waned. Kalangula meanwhile had been named chairman of the Owambo Executive Council, the top Wambo position in the Second Tier government of the Owambo Legislative Assembly. In September 1989 the CDA became one of the parties to register and file its slate of candidates for the November election for the Constituent Assembly. In the election, however, it received only 2495 votes, and thus received no seats in the assembly.

CHRISTIAN DEMOCRATIC PARTY (CDP). Not to be confused with the Namibia Christian Democratic Party (q.v.), this group was formed in March 1989. It was a merger between the Progressive People's Party, the Namibia Volksparty, and members of Andrew Kloppers' Christian Democratic Union who refused to let the CDU die when Kloppers disbanded it in 1988. The CDP affiliated with the DTA for the 1989 elections. Its leader Piet Junius won a DTA seat in the Assembly in those elections. The CDP was the major Coloured group in the DTA at independence.

CHRISTIAN DEMOCRATIC UNION (CDU). A small political movement founded in 1982 as a merger between A. F. Kloppers' Labour Party and the Democratic People's Party of Joey Julius. The CDU then joined the DTA, and participated in the Transitional Government of National Unity. It was also the opposition party in the Coloured Second Tier authority from 1980 to 1988. Later in 1988 Kloppers merged with a revitalized Labour Party and disbanded the CDU. (*See* CHRISTIAN DEMOCRATIC PARTY.)

CHRISTUSKIRCHE. One of the most prominent landmarks in Windhoek, sitting upon a hill, this neo-romantic style Lutheran church was built by the government architect, Gottlieb Redecker. Inaugurated on October 16, 1910, it was constructed of local limestone. Marble from Carrara was used for the portal, while the wonderful organ was built in

Ludwigsburg, Germany. A painting by P. P. Rubens was copied by Klara Berkowski and is used as the alter-piece. The church tower is 132 feet high. The stained glass window was the gift of Kaiser Wilhelm, and the Bible was donated by the Kaiserin. Nearby is the statue of a German soldier, ''Der Reiter von Südwest,'' in front of the Alte Feste (q.v.).

CHURCHES. Christian churches have been prominent in the history of Namibia, and frequent entries in this book refer to much of the activity by groups such as the Rhenish Mission Society, the Finnish Mission Society, the Wesleyan Methodist Mission Society, the Roman Catholic Missions, the Dutch Reformed Church, the Anglican Church, and more recently the African-run Evangelical Lutheran Ovambokavango Church (formerly Finnish Mission), and the Evangelical Lutheran Church (formerly Rhenish Mission). All of these churches have played a role in the educational and economic advancement of the Namibian people, and in many ways to their political advancement, despite the fact that early missionaries were more likely to assist the European travelers and officials at the expense of the Africans they served. Since the 1960s most churches in Namibia have worked steadfastly for the political advancement of Namibia, often at great cost. The destruction of church property in mysterious explosions occurred more than once. Moreover, the actions of church officials encouraged the World Council of Churches to contribute its resources to assist the Africans, especially to aid the efforts of SWAPO. Now Black church leaders are playing a prominent role in the emerging Namibia.

In 1989 the largest single religious organization was the United Evangelical Lutheran Church, with about 57 percent of the Namibian population belonging to it. This is actually a federation of the Evangelical Lutheran Church in Namibia (ELCIN), formerly the Evangelical Lutheran Ovambokavango Church, the Evangelical Lutheran Church (ELC), and the German Evangelical Lutheran Church (DELK), the main church of the German-speaking Namibians. Churches active in Namibia in addition to those mentioned earlier are the African Methodist Episcopal (AME), which broke from the Rhenish Mission Society in 1947; the Oruuano Church, founded in 1955 by Hereros breaking from the Rhenish Mission; the United Congregational Church; the Pentecostal Church; the Baptist Church; the Hebrew Congregation; the Full Evangelical Church of God; and the Apostolic Faith Mission. The Council of Churches in Namibia (CCN) is an umbrella group for seven of the churches. There are also three theological training institutions in the country.

COETZEE (variant: COETSE), JACOBUS (c. 1730–c. 1804). The first European known to have entered Namibia, this farmer and hunter was born in South Africa. Farming there at the Piquetberg, he received permission from the government to go elephant hunting further north. He left his farm in mid-July 1760 with two wagons and a dozen Nama servants. Getting only two elephants, he decided to go all the way to the Groot River (the Orange). He and his party crossed it at Goodhouse Drift and paralleled the Houm River to Warmbad and a little beyond. He encountered Bondelswarts living there and also heard stories about the Hereros. He returned home in October, and his report led to a larger expedition the next year led by Hendrik Hop (q.v.). Coetzee served as guide and scout on this trip into Namibia. When the rest of the Hop expedition returned across the Orange River in early 1762, Coetzee stayed in Namibia a little longer.

COHEN, SIMON (SAM) (1890–). An incredibly energetic and far-sighted pioneer businessman, Cohen dominated commerce in Namibia for more than fifty years. He created a financial, commercial, industrial, and agricultural empire, while becoming also a philanthropist. He became known as "the uncrowned king of South West Africa." Born in Russia, July 26, 1890, he was taken by his parents to Britain at the age of nine months. His father, Meyer Cohen, was a shopkeeper who went to South Africa during the Anglo-Boer War and then sent for his family in 1902. Meyer Cohen moved to Namibia in 1905, setting up a general merchant business in Swakopmund. Sam joined him in 1906 on his sixteenth birthday. The family business expanded to include Windhoek also. From 1912 to 1914 Sam ran an export business from London, shopping merchandise to retailers in

Namibia. Two years later he returned to open a store, "S. Cohen." In his first four years he opened five branches around the country. He married Sophia Kantor of Johannesburg in 1920, the same year he became the distributor for an American automobile firm, Willys-Overland. He built "Overland House" on Kaiserstrasse. He soon became the country's major distributor of gasoline and of Dunlop Tires. In 1928 he bought the rights to be distributor for Caterpillar Tractors and for General Motors products in 1933. He persuaded the administrator to buy not only his cars and trucks but also road-building machinery to construct roads and dams. He also sold equipment to the Consolidated Diamond Mines. By 1938 he handled 68 percent of all motor vehicle business in the country. The next year he added radios and electrical appliances to his business empire. In the 1940s he opened a furniture business and also invested heavily in the karakul sheep industry. He was also active politically; during the 1930s he served for eight years as a Windhoek municipal councillor, and served as chairman of the council's Financial Committee.

In 1951 he added truck assembly to his businesses, but sold off his farming interests (up to 400,000 acres with over 10,000 karakul sheep and five Angus cattle). He also bought interest in the fishing industry, owning rock lobster canning factories in Walvis Bay and Lüderitz. To house all of his businesses he constructed a much-heralded headquarters building in Windhoek in the mid-1950s.

COLMANSKOP. *See* KOLMANSKOP.

COLOUREDS. A population group that originated at the Cape as a result of the sexual unions of European sailors, settlers, and adventurers with African women, often Namas. Their mixed-race children had further cross-race relations with several groups, resulting in a diverse mix. The language of most became the Dutch-derived Afrikaans. Some of the Coloureds organized into groups in the nineteenth century under strong leaders. They moved north in the Cape Province to escape harassment and to get land of their own. Eventually groups crossed into Namibia. Others came individually at a later date to fill skilled and semi-skilled jobs in Namibia. A South West Africa Coloured Council was formed and political parties formed there. There were an estimated 52,000 Coloureds in Namibia in 1989, mostly in urban areas, but also in Walvis Bay where they are fisherman and in southern districts where they are stock farmers. While technically the Basters (q.v.) of Namibia have a similar background to the Coloureds, they have a unique history and immigration pattern. They insist on being considered separate from the Coloureds because of their uniqueness. There are about 32,000 Basters in Namibia.

COMMISSION OF INQUIRY INTO SWA. *See* ODENDAAL COMMISSION.

COMMITTEE ON SOUTH WEST AFRICA. Established in 1953 by the UN General Assembly, it was a seven-member group for the purpose of examining all information of the territory within the scope of the old League of Nations Mandate. It also was to examine all petitions and reports from the territory, to report to the General Assembly on conditions there, and to continue negotiations with South Africa. In 1954 the committee established rules of procedure for receiving and considering petitions from Namibia. Petitions began pouring in to the committee, both written and oral. They came from such men as the Rev. Michael Scott, the Rev. Samuel Witbooi, Hosea Kutako, Herman Toivo Ja Toivo, and the Rev. Markus Kooper (qq.v.). The committee began issuing annual reports in 1954. In 1960 the General Assembly instructed it to visit the territory, but the South African Government refused visas to its members. Its 1961 report included detailed proposals from SWAPO and SWANU (qq.v.) and other petitioners, and made a list of recommendations, including that the Security Council act in ensuring peace and security, and that a UN presence be immediately established in the territory. It called for preparations for a constitutional convention, a popular referendum, an educational system, and economic and agricultural organizations. The General Assembly met in 1961 and reviewed the report, noted the deteriorating situation, decided a new approach was needed, and thus dissolved the committee. In its place it created a Special Committee for South West Africa (q.v.).

CONSOLIDATED DIAMOND MINES OF SOUTH WEST AFRICA, LTD. (CDM). Controlling 99 percent of Namibia's diamond production today, CDM was formed in February 1920 with a total share capital of R9 million. It is a subsidiary of De Beers, which in turn is one of the three components of the Anglo American Corp. (qq.v.). CDM was formed by Sir Ernest Oppenheimer (q.v.) who exercised options he had purchased and took over all the assets of ten German diamond producing companies. At first the world diamond market was poor, flooded with Russian output, but CDM declared its first dividend in 1925. However, over the next several years CDM discovered fantastically rich marine terraces just south of the mouth of the Orange River and subsequently to the north as well. The town of Oranjemund (q.v.) was founded primarily for CDM employees. Life is self-contained there, including vegetable and fruit production. CDM also controls coastal diamond concessions to 240 miles north of Oranjemund. It is the richest area of diamond gem production in the world. CDM has created a revolution in diamond mining operations. Its production process is highly mechanized. In 1973 it had 300 large earth movers and over 5000 workers. Production peaked at 2 million carats in 1977 (twice that of 1976), leading to accusations that CDM was trying to drain the reserves before Namibia would become independent under African rule. Production dropped to 1.5 million carats in 1980 and then further for several years. It was at 1.02 million carats in 1987 but fell again to 938,000 carats in 1988 as the average recovery grade declined and there was a smaller average size of stones. Nevertheless, its after-tax profits in 1988 rose to R115 mn. Despite the vacillations in the diamond market, there will always be a demand for them. Thus CDM is investing hundreds of millions in new mines at Auchas, Elizabeth Bay, Chameis, and at offshore locations. Despite problems with diamond smuggling, 1991 was a banner year, with the production of 1.19 million carats. This is up from a low of

748,000 carats in 1990. The mine at Elizabeth Bay and the offshore mining account for much of the increase.

CDM made another commitment to the emerging Namibia when it shifted its diamond sorting and valuation processes to Windhoek. The company also opened (and paid for) Namibia's first genuine technical high school—oriented toward mining—in 1979. The De Beers lease on diamonds in Namibia lasts until the year 2010, and the De Beers organization has been cultivating good relations with SWAPO in the last decade or more. On the other hand SWAPO has not threatened to nationalize CDM either. It only says that the mining companies will have to pay higher taxes and plow more of their profits back into the economy. Not coincidentally, in early November 1989 CDM and the Mineworkers Union of Namibia ended a two-month wage dispute. The company agreed to an across-the-board wage increase of 18 percent. The union's general secretary, Ben Ulenga, and the general secretary of the National Union of Namibian workers, John Otto, both hold SWAPO seats in the 1989 Constituent Assembly.

CONSTITUENT ASSEMBLY. The name originally given to the Assembly elected December 4–8, 1978. In May 1979 it was renamed the National Assembly (q.v.) and given broad powers of internal legislation. The DTA had a majority in this Assembly, perhaps because SWAPO (q.v.) and many other African parties had boycotted the election.

The same name has been given to the Assembly elected November 7–11, 1989. SWAPO won forty-one of the seventy-two seats in this Assembly, the first job of which was to write a constitution for an independent Namibia and then to prepare the country for independence.

CONSTITUTION. South Africa administered Namibia under a mandate of December 17, 1920. Rule over the territory was based on: the Act of the Union No. 42 of 1925, amended by Act of the Union #22 of 1927 and Act of the Union No. 38 of 1931. These provided for the appointment of an administrator and the establishment of an Executive Committee, an

Advisory Council, and a Legislative Assembly. Six members of the latter were to be appointed by the administrator and the rest elected. A major amendment in 1949 made all 18 Assembly seats elected, with none appointed. Additional powers were given to the Assembly.

Reacting to international demands for Namibian independence, South Africa called for a constitutional conference to begin in 1975. Known commonly as the Turnhalle Conference (q.v.), its dominant figure was Dirk Mudge (q.v.), who brought together the key participants and led their development of new constitutional arrangements. It provided for an elected Constituent Assembly (later called the National Assembly), an Executive Council (''Minister's Council'') and for the selection of Second Tier (regional or ethnic authorities) and a Third Tier of local authorities.

Both the Minister's Council and the National Assembly dissolved January 18, 1983, and a Multi-Party Conference (MPC) agreed to lead the country beginning in November 1983. SWAPO and several other major political parties refused to participate. In March 1985 the MPC petitioned the state president of South Africa, P. W. Botha, to introduce a transitional government in Namibia. As a result then of Proclamation R 101 of 1985, on June 17, 1985 Mr. Botha instituted the Transitional Government of National Unity (q.v.). A Constitutional Council under Mr. Justice Victor Hiemstra was appointed November 27, 1985, to consider a new constitution. A draft bill for such a constitution was accepted by majority vote in the National Assembly on July 8, 1987. However, this action became moot as international negotiations produced a settlement of the Angola/Cuba/ Namibia issues in 1988, and in November 1989 a new Constituent Assembly (q.v.) was elected. Its main task was to draw up a constitution for an independent Namibia.

On February 9, 1990, the Constituent Assembly adopted the country's draft constitution by a unanimous vote. It was the result of considerable compromising by the various parties in the Assembly. It is considered to be one of the most democratic constitutions in Africa. It states that Namibia shall be a multi-party secular republic, with an executive president serving a maximum of two five-year terms, a two-chamber Parliament (a National Assembly and a House of Review), and an independent judiciary. Fundamental rights will be entrenched. Initially the Constituent Assembly will serve as the first National Assembly, holding a five-year term. A proportional representation system, similar but not necessarily identical to that used to select the Constituent Assembly, will be used to select future National Assemblies. The House of Review will consist of two members selected by each regional council (still to be set up), which will replace the current eleven ethnic second-tier authorities. The House of Review will have the power to refer back legislation that the Assembly has approved. The executive president will need 50 percent of the popular vote to be elected. He/she will have the power to appoint a prime minister and a list of other typical executive appointments. The president can be impeached by a two-thirds majority, the same needed to amend the constitution. The president can declare a state of emergency and rule by decree, but such decrees would be invalid if the Assembly has not approved them after seven days.

The Constitution also lists a range of "fundamental rights and freedoms" which the courts must enforce. Discrimination of all kinds is forbidden, but the right to maintain and promote any culture, language, or religion is guaranteed, along with the right to participate in "peaceful political activity." There is also a fundamental right of all Namibians to free and compulsory education. The constitution states that the economic order of the country "is to be based on the principles of a mixed economy with the objective of securing economic growth, prosperity and a life of human dignity for all Namibians."

CONTACT GROUP. The five Western states (US, UK, France, Canada, and West Germany) who came together in the late 1970s to try to improve chances for a peaceful resolution of Namibia's independence. For example, in April 1977 representatives of the five states intervened with South Africa's Prime Minister Vorster to stop him from declaring the Turnhalle Conference to be an "interim government." In April 1978, the group released a package plan (q.v.) for an equitable solution of the Namibian conflict. Despite various setbacks and divisions among the five, they all continued to work on it, together and individually for more than another decade, until terms of a settlement were reached.

CONTRACT LABOR SYSTEM. *See* LABOR, AFRICAN.

COOPER, REV. MARCUS. *See* KOOPER, MARCUS.

COPPER. Traditionally one of the major mineral products of Namibia, copper has been produced at a rate of 45,000 to 50,000 tons per year from 1970 to 1990. However a combination of weaker reserves at Tsumeb (q.v.) and lower world prices and demand now threaten the copper mines of Namibia. The existence of copper in Namibia was known to Europeans as early as the eighteenth century, as early encounters with Namas and Bergdamas exposed them to copper beads and bangles. The Bergdama were familiar with copper smelting, which they presumably learned before they migrated to Namibia. They traded their copper jewelry to the Namas. In 1851, Sir Francis Galton (q.v.) encountered copper in the Otavi Mountains. The Wambos smelted copper at Ondangwa.

In 1854 a trader named Aaron, probably Aaron De Pass, opened a concession for copper. He transferred his concession rights to three companies at the Cape, having been unsuccessful at finding copper himself. The Walvisch Bay Mining Company was the only one of the three that proceeded beyond prospecting. Also about 1854 a prospector named Fielding secured copper concessions from the chief at Bethanie and likewise the next year from the leader at Warmbad. Another prospector, named Van Reenen, scoured the area near Baker's Cove and prospected near Bethanie for a while in 1855. The Great Namaqualand Mining Company prospected along the coast briefly in late 1854 and early 1855. It was followed, with equal lack of success, by the Phoenix Mining Company in 1856. A successful discovery was finally made in 1856 north of Rehoboth and a mine was opened. It was run by Stead and Todd based on a concession from the chiefs at Rehoboth and Hoachanas. For a period the work at the mine was very active, but that came to an end when they realized the difficulty in transporting the ore. Also the African leaders argued with each other about the royalty payments. The managers of the mine, Todd and Goodman, were told to stop all work there on May 21, 1858.

A number of other companies worked to discover copper in the 1860s, but none had significant success. DePass, Spence and Co. (q.v.) briefly worked the Ebonie Mine near Walvis Bay. The Pomona Mine near Bethanie closed in 1863. Also the Pomona Mining company worked a copper deposit at Naub, but small profits forced its closure around 1870.

The Tsumeb deposits were first reported in 1857, and described as surface outcrops of almost pure copper ore in a wonderful hue of blue-green. The first major European company to exploit the copper was the South West Africa Company (q.v.), a British-owned company that began in 1892. (It survives today as a subsidiary of Gold Fields of South Africa, Ltd.) This company did not discover the real value of the deposits until it sent out an expedition in 1901. It then transferred its mineral rights to the Otavi Minen-und-Eisenbahn-Gesellschaft, a company that had been registered in Germany in 1888. The Otavi company then built a rail line linking Tsumeb with Swakopmund with a narrow-gauge railway, which was completed in 1906. In the 1907–08 fiscal year, 16,800 tons of cooper-lead ore was shipped. (Copper is usually found in conjunction with lead ore.) Six years later, 1913–1914, the total had increased to 50,070 tons of copper-lead ores.

Meanwhile, production began at the Groot Otavi and Bubus Mines, the Khan Mine and elsewhere. The Khan and Ida Mines were not in the Otavi area but nearer Swakopmund, while the Sinclair Mine was even further south in the Lüderitz Bay district and the Otyisongati Mine was thirty miles east of Okahandja. Various other mines have existed. The Oamites copper and silver mine closed early in 1985 and the similar Klein Aub Mine did likewise in 1987. The Otjihase copper/pyrite mine had closed in 1977 but was reopened by Tsumeb and JCI of South Africa in 1981. Tsumeb owns 70 percent of the output and JCI the other 30 percent. While Tsumeb reserves were expected to hold up into the 21st century, in mid-1991 the announcement was made that the Tsumeb copper/lead mine could close as early as 1994 or 1995. The Kombat Mine, 64 km south of Tsumeb in the Otavi Mts., began production in 1962 and presumably will continue production for several more decades. Also it is anticipated that a large porphyry copper and molybdenum deposit near Haib, 7 km north of the Orange River, could begin operation in late 1992.

CORNELIUS, CAPTAIN. Leader of one group of Namas early in the twentieth century, he at first remained loyal to the Germans while other Namas were revolting. But in April 1905 General von Trotha took command of the German forces and, for some inexplicable reason, placed a bounty on the head of all Nama leaders, including Captain (''Chief'') Cornelius. In his case it was 3000 marks. This heavy-handed move pushed Cornelius into active opposition to the Germans. In a fast series of raids his men overran six German outposts, frightening other local German commanders. Von Trotha concentrated his forces against Cornelius, who usually evaded contact. In June 1905 he joined forces with others, including a Bondelswart leader, Johannes Christian (q.v.). General von Trotha then sent his son to negotiate with Cornelius, who liked the younger von Trotha, having ridden with him in the Herero campaign. Unfortunately, while the lieutenant was with Cornelius, a German patrol attacked the latter's camp. Although Cornelius tried to protect his young friend, a follower of Cornelius shot and killed von Trotha, thinking he had set up this ambush. The Germans broke off negotiations and attacked Cornelius' forces in a series of battles in June and July. Usually the Africans escaped, but were forced into southern Namibia. In August Cornelius joined forces with Jacob Marengo (q.v.). For the next three months, with a force of less than four hundred poorly armed men, they fought off the German forces, killing or wounding 125 Germans. Cornelius and Marengo and their followers eventually secured themselves in the Karras hills and von Trotha shifted his forces to other rebels. The Germans finally offered settlement terms to these opponents and other Nama groups came forth as well. The last major surrender came on March 2, 1906, when Captain Cornelius led his followers, now only 86 men and 36 women and children, to surrender to the Germans. They had been on the run for 23 months. Marengo, however, did not surrender.

COUNCIL FOR NAMIBIA. *See* UNITED NATIONS COUNCIL FOR NAMIBIA.

CROCKER, CHESTER. The American assistant secretary of state for African affairs from 1981 to 1989 under President Ronald Reagan, he made it a point very early to attack the issue of South Africa's control over Namibia. From June to September 1981, Crocker established proposals for Namibian independence. His proposals included: a bill of rights, an independent judiciary, a format for general elections, and a constituent assembly that would ensure fair representation for Namibia's different ethnic groups. He added in 1982 the further provision that South African Defence Forces be withdrawn from Namibia simultaneous to Cuban troops returning home from Angola. His greatest achievement came from having stayed with the Namibian issue, however frustrating. Thus in 1988 his talks with South Africa, Cuba, Angola, and the UNITA leaders led to a political break-through resulting in Namibia's independence in 1990.

CUNENE RIVER. *See* KUNENE RIVER.

CUITO CUANEVALE. A town in southern Angola, it took on great significance as the battle for its control seems to have been a turning point in South Africa's military struggle in Angola and, by extension, in Namibia as well. Not important in itself, the town was along a critical Cuban supply route needed to fight the UNITA rebel forces in Angola. South Africa was determined to win it, and Cuba was determined to defend it. South Africa and UNITA first tried to take it in 1986, but failed, losing about a hundred soldiers in the process. Namibian battalions were also brought in, along with white South African mechanized units. Soviet and Cuban fighter planes, tanks, helicopters, and ground-to-air missiles faced the South Africans. Battles and deaths in November and December 1987 brought home the horrors of the war to white families in South Africa. In early 1988 the South African Air force reportedly lost forty jet planes. Yet the SA Defense Force began an armoured assault on March 23, 1988, and met Cuban forces head on. Meanwhile, Chester Crocker (q.v.) was trying to get the various sides to negotiate a peace. As South African casualties mounted and their inability to beat the Cubans became obvious, South African public and governmental opinion turned away from a military solution. A treaty was signed late in 1988, one which paved the way for Namibian independence. This outcome seemed highly unlikely prior to the battles over Cuito Cuanevale.

CUVELAI RIVER (variant: GUVELAI). One of the more important rivers in Owambo, it rises in the highlands of southern Angola and crosses southward into Namibia. It ultimately drains into Oponono Lake. On occasion it will flood and cover Owambo's pans or depressions (''oshanas'') before draining into the Etosha Pan (q.v.). When its flood overflow large parts of Owambo, it is more properly called the Cuvelai System.

- D -

DAMARA (variants: BERGDAMA; BERGDAMARA; DAMA). There is considerable confusion about this term, as the variants above (only a few of many) might indicate. Evidently many of the early Khoisan-speaking peoples of Namibia (Nama and San) used the word Dama to refer to ''Black'' Africans who entered the territory. This included the Hereros (q.v.) and the Bergdamas (q.v.), two groups with very different traditions. In order to differentiate the two groups, the Namas later added to the word. Thus ''Chow Dama'' (meaning ''the dirty Dama'') was used for the ''Bergdama,'' and Gomacha Dama (meaning ''Damas rich in cattle'') was used for the Hereros.

Actually the word ''Damas'' is itself incorrect, although

commonly used. "Dama" is singular; "Daman" is the correct plural; "Damas" is one Dama woman; "Damab" is one Dama man. "Damara" means two Dama women, while "Damagu" means several Dama men. "Damagua" is another common variant for the latter.

Nevertheless, the common "Damas" will be used here as the plural. Likewise this entry will not deal with the Hereros (q.v.), but only the "Bergdamas," or "mountain" Damas.

Recent archaeological research indicates that Damas have been in Namibia for centuries. In the early years they were hunters and gatherers, had some goats, occasionally had small agricultural plots, and were skilled workers and traders in iron and copper products—perhaps skills brought from their home area of Africa. Their physical characteristics resemble more closely the people of West and Central Africa than those to their south, such as Namas and San.

The Damas had no central authority figure like a chief, but did have important local elders who cared for the "sacred fire." They tended to live in family or hunting bands. Eleven regional subgroups of the Damas have been identified. They were spread over a wide area, overlapping the Namas in the territory's south and south-central areas, and all the way north to the Herero country. (*See* DAMARALAND.) It was not uncommon for the Damas to fall into a kind of serfdom to the Namas or the Hereros. While in the service of Namas, they picked up the language and made it theirs as well. As Nama political strength weakened, some Damas fled to freedom in the mountains (thus "Berg" Dama or even "Klip Kaffir"). There is evidence, however, that their link with the mountains goes back hundreds of years, to homes in the Auos and Erongo Mountains, where goat-herding was reputedly common.

German missionaries worked among them in the nineteenth century (as early as 1860), and the Damas began to settle down in places like Rehoboth, Otjimbingwe, and Omaruru. A Herero chief even gave them the Okombahe Reserve, which was later recognized as theirs by the German administration in the 1890s. When the Hereros and Namas revolted a few years later, the Damas generally remained loyal to the Germans. In 1951 there were 76,000 Damara in Namibia, and the projection for 1989 was 97,000.

DAMARA COUNCIL (DC). Formed in August 1971 as an interim administrative body with South Africa's approval at the time when Damaraland was being placed on a path toward self-rule, it has nevertheless played a more directly political role than was first envisaged. Based in Khorixas, its leader has been Mr. Justus Garoëb (q.v.) who was elected senior headman of the council in 1971. As Garoëb led the council to oppose South Africa's plans for the territory, however, the Damara United Front (q.v.) replaced it in official favor. Despite appeals by Dirk Mudge (q.v.), the council refused to participate in the 1975 Turnhalle Conference (where the DUF ultimately replaced it). Instead it took part in the Okahandja Summit Conference, which then renamed its confederation of political groups the Namibia National Council (q.v.). Garoëb was its vice-chairman and the leading figure at the conference. It demanded independence for a unified Namibia and opposed the Turnhalle Conference. The Damara Council has also been part of at least two other political federations, the Namibia National Convention and the Namibia National Front (qq.v.), both of which it later left.

When the Damara Representative Authority was formed in 1977, the Damara Council was abolished by officials, but three years later it was re-formed as a political party to compete in the Damara Second Tier elections, which it won in both 1980 and 1982. It controlled that body until 1989.

The Damara Council continued to be active at the national level also. In November 1983 it participated in the discussions at the first Multi-Party Conference (q.v.), where its delegation argued that the United Nations Security Council Resolution 435 remained the only basis for Namibia's independence, while deploring the Security Council's inability to enforce its decision. However it broke with the MPC in 1984.

When the MPC regime took power in 1985, the Damara Council vigorously opposed it. On the day that the MPC inauguration occurred, police used tear gas to break up a demonstration by members of a number of factions, including the Damara Council.

In February 1989, Garoëb and the DC took the lead in

forming the United Democratic Front of Namibia (q.v.), an alliance of parties that would compete in the Assembly elections. The UDF won four seats, one of which is held by Garoëb. The DC continues to take the middle ground between SWAPO on its left and the DTA on its right.

DAMARA EXECUTIVE COMMITTEE (DEC). A Damara-based organization opposed to both the South African government and the "authority" of the appointed Damara chief, it formed as a result of dissension within the Damara Tribal Executive Committee in 1958. Based in the urban centers, especially Okahandja, Otjimbingwe, and Karabib, its leaders have included J. Gawanab, O. Kharuchab, M. Kheib, and P. Gowaseb (q.v.). The committee worked closely and agreed politically with the elected Damara Council (q.v.) until the early 1980s. Dirk Mudge conducted lengthy talks with the committee, trying to persuade it to participate in the Turnhalle Conference, but in July 1975 its leaders declined, condemning the conference as a fraud. At one point the committee belonged to the National Convention of Freedom Parties, but in 1975 it joined the rival Namibia National Convention (q.v.). It also joined the Okahandja Summit, the only organization to belong to both the NNC and the Summit. (For more on its principles, see DAMARA COUNCIL, with which it often spoke out in concert.)

In 1978 it left its other alliances to become a founding member of the Namibia People's Liberation Front (NPLF) (q.v.), and that membership continues. From 1980 to 1982 the DEC held an elected seat in the Damara Second Tier Representative Authority. Led by its long-time president, Josephat Gawanab, it followed the NPLF into another alliance, the Federal Convention of Namibia (q.v.), in 1989. No DEC members won an Assembly seat, however. Gawanab and the DEC continue to oppose the involvement of Damara Paramount Chief Justus Garoëb in electoral politics.

DAMARA UNITED FRONT (DUF). Regardless of its rhetoric during "Homeland" elections, this organization appears to have been created with the encouragement and assistance of several South African government organizations, perhaps even the Bureau of State Security (BOSS), in order to ensure the implementation of the "Homelands" scheme in Namibia. It was established in October 1974 under the leadership of Engelhardt H. L. Christy, and consisted primarily of Damara teachers. Its head office was in Khorixas, and its motto was "Unity is Power." Its leaders broke away from the Damara Council (q.v.), which opposed South Africa's policies. Christy and his supporters, on the other hand, acknowledged South Africa's sovereignty and preferred to work within the system for changes. Favoring the creation of a Damara Representative Council, it participated in such elections when they occurred. Likewise it supported and participated in the Turnhalle Conference (q.v.). Dirk Mudge, an organizer of the Turnhalle, recruited Christy after the Damara Council refused to participate. Christy brought a delegation of twenty-six Damaras to the conference. In April 1976 it changed its name to the South West Africa Peoples' Democratic United Front (SWAPDUF) (q.v.). Later it affiliated with the Democratic Turnhalle Alliance (q.v.), and was also known as Damara-DTA.

DAMARALAND. While the term obviously refers to the land inhabited by the Damaras (q.v.), it has more precise usages. In the early days of European exploration of Namibia, the term "Damaraland" referred to all of the territory from the Atlantic Ocean to the Kalahari, and north of Namaqualand but south of Ovamboland. Windhoek would have been about the geographic center. In modern days the Odendaal Commission (q.v.) in the early 1960s recommended the creation of a "Damaraland" reserve that would cover the area from Sessfontein in the north to Okombake and Otjohorongo in the south. This 4.8 million hectare tract included what was then 223 European farms, plus most of the Kaokoveld and Game Reserve Number 2. Its administrative center would be at Welwitschia, which later changed its name or Khorixas (q.v.). This Odendaal "Damaraland" was put on the first level toward self-rule by the formation of the Damara Representative Council, an interim administrative body, in 1972. It was also the first "homeland" to hold elections.

In the more traditional use of the word, Damaraland is the

home area of the Damaras or Bergdamas (qq.v.) and the Hereros who came later. This region contains three sub-regions: the Otavi highlands in the north, the Damara plain to the south, and the Khomas highlands. It is a mountainous region, and even the plateaus are well above sea level. It is a relatively arid country, although the Windhoek area in the center can get some good rainfall annually. The area is considered today to be especially good for raising cattle, goats, and karakul (q.v.) sheep. The country's hilly areas have also been noted for valuable resources (tin, copper, etc.). Most of Namibia's rivers begin in these highlands and flow westward, such as the Swakop, Kuiseb, Omaruru, and Ugab rivers. Others, such as the Black and White Nossab Rivers (qq.v.), flow into the Kalahari Desert to the east. The Windhoek Valley is its only significant valley.

DAURES MASSIF. *See* BRANDBERG.

DE BEERS COMPANY. De Beers was the richest of the diamond mines near the Vaal River in South Africa, where diamonds were found in the early 1870s. It was owned by Cecil Rhodes. Another early fortune seeker was Barnett Isaacs, better known as Barney Barnato. By 1880 he was becoming very wealthy as a result of his diamond mining decisions. After a period of fierce competition, Rhodes forced Barnato to accept a merger in 1888, and the De Beers Consolidated Mines came into being, with its headquarters in Kimberley. It has produced about 80 percent of South Africa and Namibia's diamonds, and controls nearly 80 percent of the world's diamond sales. Germans did most of the early diamond mining in Namibia (*see* DIAMONDS). After World War I, in February 1920, the Anglo American Corporation (so-named in large part because of a large loan from the prominent American banker, J. P. Morgan) bought into the mining industry by buying virtually all of the German diamond interests for only R7 million (*see* DIAMOND BOARD OF SOUTH WEST AFRICA). Anglo American's strong leader, Ernest Oppenheimer (q.v.) placed all of these holdings under a single subsidiary, Consolidated Diamond Mines (CDM) (q.v.), an offshoot of De Beers, which has held that monopoly ever since. The determined Oppenheimer added to his power by becoming Board Chairman of De Beers in 1929, following the American stock market crash.

Meanwhile CDM's discovery of diamonds south of the Orange River in 1925 led to major exploration in the whole area and along the coast by CDM. Thus the vast mining complex at Oranjemund (q.v.) was established. De Beers also helped the Marine Diamond Corporation with loans, and it began to recover diamonds from the seabed off the Namibian coast. De Beers ultimately took over that whole operation.

CDM operates mining projects for De Beers. In 1974 it contributed 40 percent to the total profits of the De Beers group, of which it is a fully owned subsidiary. Meanwhile both are part of the Oppenheimer family's larger Anglo American Corporation. When De Beers became involved in newer diamond mines (and other minerals) in Botswana and South African in the 1970s and 1980s, CDM's portion of De Beers profits dipped to 17 percent, still a large figure considering that it represents only 10.5 percent of the carats mined by De Beers. The reason is that Namibia's diamonds are of exceptional gem quality. Not all of its efforts have met with equal success, however, as the search for oil near Keetmanshoop by De Beers Oil Holdings was unsuccessful.

Since 1933, when Oppenheimer formed the Diamond Trading Company (now the Central Selling Organization), De Beers has controlled the world trade in diamonds, maintaining the price per carat at a level decided by itself. The CSO's decrees are absolute; even the former Soviet Union channeled its diamonds through the CSO. Critical to its success has been control of all major sources of diamonds, especially those in southern Africa.

De Beers was the object of criticism in the report of the Thirion Commission (q.v.) in 1986. Justice Thirion claimed that De Beers, through CDM, had violated its "Halbscheid Agreement" with the South African government, which had granted monopoly diamond mining rights on the Namibian coastal strip. The violation consisted of mining very heavily the most valuable diamonds in hopes of exhausting them before political changes took place. The less valuable diamonds might be uneconomical to mine by themselves if they were all that was left after independence.

DEIMLING, BERTHOLD VON (1853–1917). German military commander, he was born at Karlsruhe in Baden. He was sent to Namibia in 1904 to help quell the Herero revolt. Then a major, he was sent to Waterberg (q.v.) with four companies of mounted infantry and six guns. The battle of Waterberg took place on August 11, 1904. The German forces were positioned around the Hereros, with each segment commanded by a different officer. Deimling led the largest force and was to attack the Hereros along the base of the mountain from the west. His force met minimal opposition and suffered no losses while taking Waterberg. Other segments of the German forces were facing much more opposition in their areas. While the major battle had been won by the Germans, bands of Hereros continued to roam their region, raiding German cattle. At the end of August, German forces were stationed in heavily armed camps along the edge of the desert to intercept the Hereros. Deimling was in charge of a camp at Epukiro (q.v.).

Two months later the Namas began a series of uprisings further south in Namibia, and Deimling, now a colonel, was sent to command the German forces. He had six companies and one and a half batteries at his disposal. Two months later his forces included 4300 men and 2800 horses, some newly sent from Germany. In his first battle Deimling surprised Hendrik Witbooi (q.v.) at Naris, and after a brief battle, the Namas fled, leaving many casualties. While the Germans pursued the Namas, the Africans succeeded in avoiding further battle. General von Trotha (q.v.), meanwhile, felt the Germans did not have the forces to defeat the Namas. Deimling disagreed, arguing that a series of attacks could succeed. He followed up his beliefs by attacking Witbooi's forces in the Auob valley on January 2, 1905. The battle lasted three days, before the Namas retreated into the Kalahari. Deimling's victory claim was weakened by the escape of most of the Namas, and by the death of twenty-two German soldiers. Fifty more were wounded or missing.

Deimling then attacked the Namas led by Marengo (q.v.),

encamped in the Karras hills. The engagement lasted two weeks, and again ended up with the Africans scattering from the area. Deimling claimed victory, but seemed to underestimate the strength of indigenous forces in a guerrilla setting. Von Trotha realized that an antiguerrilla action would be hard for the Germans to sustain, so he went south and put himself in charge. Deimling, nursing an arm injury, was sent back to Berlin in March 1905. He was rewarded with a nobleman's title and reappointment to the general staff.

In late 1905 von Trotha was also called back to Berlin, and Deimling was eventually appointed commander-in-chief of German forces in Namibia. (He actually replaced Colonel Dame.) Deimling had convinced the Kaiser and others in Berlin that he had the answers to the problems facing German forces in Namibia since he had left. After conferring with Colonel Dame and Governor Lindequist, Deimling officially assumed command on July 6, 1906. He had three parts to his plan to deal with the Namas, especially the Bondelswarts of Johannes Christian (qq.v.). First, the vulnerable German cattle and horses (frequently attacked and sold by the Africans) would be either moved to safety in the north or, if needed, kept in a few very securely guarded locations. Second, a kind of zone defense would be set up. The southern area was divided into a number of zones, each with its German forces in flying squads. When an African band struck somewhere and fled, it would be pursued by the forces in that zone, but only to the edge of that zone, where the next German troops took over the chase. Thirdly, Deimling gave clear indication of a willingness to negotiate an end to the battles.

His tactics bore fruit quickly. On August 6, 1906, Johannes Christian and about fifty men attacked a German outpost. A flying squad of Germans took off in pursuit. Three weeks later, the Bondels were exhausted after covering 500 miles and fighting three battles against four different flying squads, each picking up pursuit when the Africans entered their zone. German forces were still fresh and their losses were moderate, but the Bondelswart raiders were almost annihilated. Other attacking Africans met the same successful tactics, and by October the Africans were willing to negotiate. Deimling offered generous terms, and preliminary negotiations began

November 16, 1906. A definitive peace was signed at Ukamas on December 21. Ironically, Governor Lindequist was in Berlin at the time, and neither he nor the Colonial Office had been consulted about the terms. Deimling felt that secret negotiations would be more successful. The governor objected to the generosity of the terms, but ultimately the Kaiser chose to accept Deimling's judgement, and the treaty became a fait accompli. The Germans officially declared the territory "pacified" on March 31, 1907. Meanwhile, Deimling had been promoted to major general and returned to Germany. There he wrote his memoirs, published as *Südwestafrika, Land und Leute* in 1907.

DEMOCRATIC CO-OPERATIVE PARTY (DEMKOP or DEMCOP). A political party founded in 1970 by Johannes Jefta Nangutuuala, it was then called the Democratic Co-operation of Developments. Two years later it took its now familiar name. (It is also called the Demokratiese Kiiperatiewe Party.) Nangutuuala's deputy leader was Andreas Nunkwawo, a teacher. The party leader had played a major role in the nationwide strike of African workers against South African control of Namibia. On January 10, 1972, he led a mass meeting of 3500 strikers at Oluna-Ondangwa. His strike committee issued an impressive statement of the workers' demands and grievances, most of which denounced the system of contract labor (*see* LABOR, AFRICAN). DEMKOP, like SWAPO, was a modernizing party, receiving its support mostly from the educated classes in Owambo (e.g., teachers, traders, clerks, nurses).

DEMKOP had a detailed party program. It said that political parties were necessary for the proper political development of the country, yet it promised to cooperate with South Africa and with traditional chiefs and headmen if they agreed to help the people progress politically. Democracy, it said, requires free speech and the popular franchise. Separate development was denounced as a policy of hatred, denying human rights to Blacks. It opposed Communism, but said that South African policy could be promoting it by maintaining economic inequality among the races of southern Africa.

Despite the moderate and rational party program, when the second Owambo Legislative Council was being elected in 1973, Nangutuuala was not allowed to present his party in the elections. With DEMKOP and SWAPO both boycotting the vote, only 5 percent of the people of Owambo voted. However, Nangutuuala won a seat in a 1975 by-election as an independent. Until then DEMKOP had participated in the alliance of parties called the Namibia National Convention (NNC) (q.v.). SWAPO denounced Nangutuuala's running for office in the discredited Legislative Council, so DEMKOP quit the NNC.

Meanwhile, the 1973 boycotts resulted in the arrest of both Nangutuuala and Nunkwawo (along with some SWAPO leaders). They were convicted of holding illegal meetings, and both fined and flogged in public. This brought international attention to the DEMKOP leaders. Support came from both religious authorities and international jurists. In April 1976, Nangutuuala and five supporters were reportedly kidnapped in southern Angola. DEMKOP soon disintegrated.

DEMOCRATIC TURNHALLE ALLIANCE. (Now known as DTA of Namibia.) One of the most significant political groupings in Namibia after its formation in 1977, it underwent some structural change in November 1991. It also officially changed its name to "DTA of Namibia." Previously an alliance of twelve ethnically-based political parties, factions, and groups that functioned as a single party, it has formally become a unitary party. It is a right-of-center organization, although it sees itself as the "moderate" alternative to the "radical" SWAPO and "reactionary" whites in Namibia. The origins of the DTA were in the Turnhalle Constitutional Conference (q.v.) that began in 1975. While the conference was a multiracial gathering, it did not include most of the politically active Africans, especially members of SWAPO. White politicians were very active in the conference, notably members of the South West Africa National Party. A split developed in that group between the hard-line right wing, and the "moderate" multi-racialists led by Dirk Mudge (q.v.) on the issue of continuing certain apartheid laws in a new constitution. Mudge finally split from the National Party, and created a new white group, the Republican Party (q.v.). South Africa favored and encouraged this development as the only hope for the kind of progress that would alleviate international diplomatic pressure from the West. Mudge was committed to cooperate with Black participants in the Turnhalle, and on November 5, 1977, a federated coalition was formed, the Democratic Turnhalle Alliance.

Actually the possibility of such a group had been rumored for at least six months prior to that date. Mudge, who was to become its chairman, had been working closely at the conference with Chief Clemens Kapuuo (q.v.) of the National Unity Democratic Organization. Chief Kapuuo became the first president of the DTA. For him the organization replaced his federated National Convention of Namibia (q.v.). Other groups joining were the National Democratic Party, the Labour Party of South West Africa, the South West Africa Peoples Damara United Front, the Rehoboth Bastervereniging, and members of the Turnhalle Conference who were called the Caprivi Alliance, the Tswana Alliance, the Bushman Alliance, the Kavango Alliance, and the Nama Alliance (qq.v.). Each of the "Alliance" groups consisted of members of their ethnic group who agreed to sit at the conference. they had few true constituents.

Since all of the members of the DTA had been at the Turnhalle Conference, it is not surprising that a key part of the DTA Constitution was acceptance of the "South West Africa Constitution" that had been drafted at the conference. However it did not favor transfer of some functions of the second-tier regional governments to the first-tier central government.

Among the less controversial aspects of the DTA Constitution are recognition of the rule of law and the freedom and human dignity of the individual and rejection of all discrimination on the grounds of race and color. On the other hand, it makes reference to different language and population groups which will have the right "to assert themselves in moral and material spheres." It also states that it will strive toward the country's economic independence, "but recognizes the economic interdependence of countries." This appears to be an opening to acceptance of a neo-colonial relationship with South Africa. Further entrenchment of white economic dominance is hinted at in the provision for maintaining "the principles of acquisition of property rights without discrimination merely on the grounds of race or colour."

The DTA claims that human rights can only be safeguarded by means of a system of government that prevents any one group from dominating the others and a strict application of democratic principles. (The concern about one group being dominant clearly is aimed at the Wambo people in whom SWAPO has its foundation.) The democratic principles mentioned appear to include equality before the law; freedom of religion, conscience, movement, expression, the press, property, and political participation; and freedom from arrest without recourse to the courts. To protect these rights the DTA advocated a constitutional court to advise lawmakers on whether proposed laws are compatible with human rights, and an ombudsman who would investigate all complaints of violation of these rights resulting from administrative practice or action.

The DTA also claims to work toward certain economic and social goals, such as general improvement of living conditions, equal pay for equal work, an economic system based on free enterprise, compulsory education based on equal standards, provision of adequate housing, encouragement of foreign investment, and establishment of trade relations with friendly countries.

Regardless of whether DTA's political, constitutional, economic, and social objectives were sincere or designed to gain Western favor, the alliance began functioning as a political unit. The December 1978 election was the first target for the DTA. With SWAPO and most other popular parties boycotting the election, it is not surprising that the DTA candidates won 268,130 of the 326,264 votes cast. This gave DTA members forty-one of the fifty seats in the Constituent Assembly. Mudge was named chairman of the Council of Ministers. Mudge's leadership held the DTA together; the Black leadership of the DTA was constantly changing. Chief Kapuuo (q.v.) was assassinated in 1978. After Kapuuo's death, he was replaced by Pastor C. T. Ndjoba (q.v.). He in turn was replaced by Rev. Peter Kalangula (q.v.), who resigned in frustration and disagreement with Mudge and South African policies in early 1982. Ben Africa (q.v.) became acting president for a short time in 1982 before being replaced by Kuaima Riruako (q.v.), the Herero "Paramount Chief."

The DTA served as ruling party during the existence of the Constituent Assembly (soon renamed National Assembly). A large building in central Windhoek served as its headquarters. It had seemingly unlimited financial resources available, presumably from the South African government, which secretly helped it purchase two Windhoek newspapers.

The DTA instigated a mass resignation from the Council of Ministers in 1983 over a dispute with the AG, Danie Hough. Both the Council and the National Assembly were then dissolved. The DTA began to seek the writing of a new Constitution, one that would exclude the ethnic Second Tier governments. In November 1983, it joined in the formation of a Multi-Party Conference (q.v.) with several other centrist parties. This led to the formation eventually of the Transitional Government of National Unity (q.v.) or TGNU in June 1985. The DTA was the dominant member of the TGNU, holding twenty-two Assembly seats and three ministerial posts. Simultaneously it had six seats on the Constitutional Council that was drafting a new constitution, one that would rule an independent Namibia without UN-supervised elections. The DTA regularly rejected SWAPO's claim to be the sole and authentic representative of Namibians. DTA leaders asserted that it and the other internal parties must be treated equally with SWAPO. The council was concluding work on a new constitution just about the time that world events caught up with it.

It became clear that a settlement of Namibian independence was imminent and that a Constituent Assembly would be elected in 1989 to write a constitution and then become a National Assembly. The DTA began reorganizing for the 1989 elections. Dirk Mudge remained the party's chairman and unifying force. The president was still Kuaima Riruako, and Mishake Muyongo was named senior vice-president. Five other vice-presidents represented some of the other alliance member groups. Over the years some of the alliance parties underwent reorganization or name change. Thus the DTA in 1989 consisted of: Bushman Alliance, Christian Democratic Party, Democratic Turnhalle Party of Namibia, National Democratic Party, National Democratic Unity Party, National Unity Democratic Organization, Rehoboth DTA Party, Republican Party, Seoposengwe, SWA People's Democratic United Front, United Democratic Party, and the United Party of Namibia. Most of their leaders had at least fifteen years' experience in Namibian politics.

The DTA did well in the Constituent Assembly elections. It won 191,532 votes (28.6 percent), and twenty-one seats in the seventy-two-member Assembly, the second largest bloc. While it only won 4.3 percent of the votes in the Owambo District, it got 36 percent in Windhoek, 41.8 percent in the Kavango district, 25.5 percent in Swakopmund district, and 53 percent in the Caprivi.

Negotiations on the new constitution went smoothly as SWAPO's proposals were countered by DTA's plan from the TGNU Constitutional Council. The result was a compromise. At independence the DTA became the opposition in the National Assembly. Six months later Mudge noted with pleasure that SWAPO was abiding by the constitution and remained committed to multiparty democracy. Meanwhile the Namibia National Front (q.v.) appeared to be ready to merge with the DTA, as several other small groups also considered the same move for the purpose of regional or local elections. After the elections the DTA President, Kuaima Riruako, split with the party over his low status on the electoral list. Vice-President Mishake Muyongo was named as acting president, and formally confirmed as President in November, 1991. Another leading figure of the DTA, Jaritendu Kozonguisi (q.v.) resigned his seat in the National Assembly because of disagreements with the DTA leadership over his role. Another DTA MP also resigned, as Barney Barnes left both the Assembly and the DTA in March, 1992, supposedly for a combination of policy and business reasons.

All of this came after revelations by Nico Basson (q.v.) in

mid-1991 that he had helped implement a South African government scheme to help the DTA and other parties opposed to SWAPO in the run up to the 1989 elections. R65 million found its way to the DTA election budget, it was revealed (and chairman Dirk Mudge ultimately acknowledged). This merely confirmed what many observers had suspected, however. It also did not prevent the DTA from continuing to use funds from unknown sources to buy Namibian newspapers. In August, 1991 it bought the oldest daily paper, the German *Allgemeine Zeitung,* and later a German weekly, the *Namibia Nachrichtung.* It also purchased the previously independent John Meinert printing press, giving it control of both presses in Namibia that could print daily newspapers.

In late 1992 there were elections in Namibia's thirteen new regional areas. Of the 79 constituencies, the DTA won 20 seats to SWAPO's 56. Its greatest strength was in the Hardap region (4 of 6 seats), the Liambezi (Caprivi) region (4 of 6), the Omaheke region (5 of 6), the Khomas region (3 of 9), and the Otjozondjupa region (2 of 6). In general it did better in urban areas with large concentrations of whites, and in areas where the African population had traditionally opposed SWAPO. Many of the DTA candidates—and many of its winners—were not white (usually Herero, Caprivians, Rehoboth Basters, and Coloureds).

DEMOCRATIC TURNHALLE PARTY OF NAMIBIA (DTPN). Originally known as the Nama Alliance (1975) and the Democratic Turnhalle Party (1979), this Nama-based party got this name in 1980. It is a member of the Democratic Turnhalle Alliance. Its leader, Kaptein Daniel Luipert (q.v.) is one of the DTA's Vice-Presidents. The DTPN held a majority of the seats in the Nama Second Tier Government from 1980 to its dissolution in 1989. It also held two seats in the Assembly of the TGNU from 1985 to 1989. Its program has been essentially that of the DTA. In the 1989 Assembly elections Luipert was fourth on the electoral list of the DTA and easily won a seat, and Jeremiah Jagger also was selected.

DE PASS, SPENCE & CO. Founded originally as a Cape Town shipping company by members of the De Pass family, it was originally called the A. & E. De Pass Company. (Later Captain John Spence became a partner.) In its early days it controlled many of the coastal vessels in South Africa. As early as 1849 it was shipping salted fish to Madagascar from Namibia by way of Cape Town. The De Pass brothers also set up fisheries at Sandwich Harbor and worked the guano (q.v.) deposits on islands off the Namibian coast. In 1856 the firm set up a fishing and sealing industry on the coast. Oil and dried fish were produced and shipped to Cape Town. They also set up a ship-repair yard at Angra Pequeña. De Pass was the dominant commercial firm in Namibia in the nineteenth century. From its stores at Angra Pequeña and the Naub, its traders moved regularly into the interior.

In 1850 the high price of copper led De Pass to explore in Namibia for copper. It formed a firm called the Pomona Mining Company. While copper was never found, years later the De Pass land concession would be valuable for the diamonds discovered there. The concession, De Pass claimed, came from an agreement in September 1863 with the Bethanie chief, David Christian. It authorized rights to the coast (and fifty-five miles inland) from Angra Pequeña to Baker's Cove. It also received rights, it claimed, to fishing interests along the coast and guano collecting on the offshore islands. (In the long run, far more important were the Pomona mining rights, as fabulous wealth came from the diamonds found in the Pomona area.)

Problems developed in 1883 when a German business-man, Adolf Lüderitz, claimed that he also had purchased rights around Angra Pequeña from the local chief, in this case, Josef Frederick. Daniel De Pass complained to the colonial government at the Cape when Lüderitz went so far as to build a fort and mount a cannon.

Conflicting British and German claims resulted in a long legal conflict plus a series of negotiations. British authorities even sent a warship to protect the interests of De Pass, Spence & Co., and the Germans countered with a gunboat.

Although Britain accepted Germany's "protection" rights to the Namibian coast in 1884, a joint Anglo-German Commission continued to negotiate the resolution of the rights of British citizens, especially the De Pass Company. A settlement finally came in July 1886, by which time the bankrupt Captain Spence had sold out his interests to the De Pass brothers. The settlement accepted De Pass's land titles to Sandwich Harbor and fishing rights along the coast, and to collect guano at Hottentot Bay. Rights to some islets would end, however, on June 30, 1895. On the other hand, full rights to the Pomona land were granted in perpetuity. Nevertheless De Pass was not totally satisfied with the outcome and complained without success to the British Foreign Office. After diamonds were discovered in the Pomona area and off the coast, the De Pass rights became far more important than ever imagined by the company that had been more interested in guano.

DEUTSCHER BUND (variant: DEUTSCHE BUND). A political party established September 3, 1924, among the territory's German-speaking people (then about 11,000). Dr. Fritz Brenner (q.v.) was the moving force of the party, especially following a meeting of German individuals and corporations, and representing most of the German cultural, religious, and economic societies. The Bund was supported by both the German Colonial Society and the Foreign Office in Berlin. Two years after its formation, the Bund won the elections for the territorial Legislative Assembly, under Brenner's leadership. The purpose of the party was to maintain a separate identity for Germans in Namibia (so as not to get absorbed by the Afrikaners), to promote German immigration to the territory (while screening out the lower class), and to influence the territory's political and economic development. The Germans vigorously opposed any attempt by South Africa to incorporate the territory as a fifth province. The Germans also resented Jan Smuts sending his "voting cattle" (poor Boer immigrants) into the territory in order to expand the non-German voting lists. Fear of German power led to the formation of the United National South West Africa Party (q.v.) by non-Germans, which won the July 3, 1929 Legislative Assembly elections. The Bund only won four of the twelve elected seats, but blamed its loss on South Africa's long waiting period before German immigrants became nationalized (voting) citizens.

The Bund then changed tactics and began to seek non-

German support, especially from British subjects. The Depression of the 1930s required cooperation between the United National South West Africa Party and the Bund, especially on economic issues. The resulting conference brought some mutual understanding, and even the adoption of German as a third official language, April 27, 1932. That same year the National Sozialistische Deutsche Arbeiterpartei (NSDAP) was formed in Windhoek. This Nazi party was banned in 1934, and some of its followers joined the Bund, thereby casting suspicion on the whole organization. In 1937 the Deutscher Bund and two other German parties were banned. It was replaced by a newly formed Deutscher Südwest Bund, which called itself a cultural organization. But it also took a political stand against the incorporation of the territory into South Africa. Thus it was also declared a foreign political organization, and aliens were forbidden to join it. The UNSWA Party did this because it was a proponent of incorporation, and also feared the possibility that Germany would try to reclaim its old African colonies.

DEUTSCHE KOLONIAL GESELLSCHAFT. An emigration society formed in November 1891. Not to be confused with the Deutsche Kolonialgesellschaft für Südwestafrika (q.v.), it was formed to encourage settlers to go to Namibia. The first site selected was Skein Windhoek, in the vicinity of the quarters of the Schutztruppe. Only a few settlers were successfully recruited, however, and in 1895 a new company, the Siedelungsgesellschaft für Deutsche-Süd-west Afrika, was founded for the same purpose. It was larger and more successful.

DEUTSCHE KOLONIALGESELLSCHAFT FÜR SÜDWEST-AFRIKA (DKG). The first in the field of all the land and mining companies, the DKG was founded in April 1885 with a capital of £15,000 in order to take over the concessions owned by Adolph Lüderitz (q.v.). It was granted mining rights over the entire area controlled by Germany (about 25 percent of Namibia), and was given administrative rights under the sovereignty of the German empire. Its only limits were the rights of the Africans and concessions previously granted to individuals or other associations. However, it lost its monopoly of mining rights in 1889, and three years later was relieved of the administrative task. By agreements made in 1908 and 1910 the company transferred to the government all of its properties except mine districts near Swakopmund and Lüderitz Bay. It retained a coastal strip also, so long as it continued large-scale mining and diamond extraction. While few profits were made prior to 1905, dividends to stockholders increased dramatically from 1906 to 1911, primarily because of its diamond holdings. It held 80 percent of the capital of the Deutsche Diamanten-Gesellschaft and significant interests in several other companies. It had its own banking departments also to handle its monetary dealings.

The company was founded with the encouragement of the German Chancellor Otto von Bismarck with the aid of a number of German financial leaders. The intention was to eventually grant it a charter, but the DKG refused any charter because it was too understaffed and underfinanced to handle all of the administration involved, or even properly exploit the region's mineral resources. By December 1889 the DKG's resources were only about 84,000 marks. In 1890 it was reported that its meat curing and canning facility had closed in failure. An attempt at that time by a group of British financiers to purchase its holdings was meeting major opposition in Germany, and early in 1891 it reached the end of its finances, and a new attempt was made to create a financial syndicate to replace it. With the creation of the South West Africa Company (q.v.) in August 1892, some of the pressure was removed from the DKG. In 1894, it was successful in selling 113 square kilometers to a company called the Kaoko-Land und Miner Gesellschaft, and periodically thereafter sold other parts of its concession to obtain working capital. Otherwise it remained essentially inactive at this time. It withdrew from a sheep-raising project and sold its guano fields. Nevertheless in 1903 it still controlled several major companies, the Kaoko Company, the Otavi Company, and the South African Territories Company. Between then the DKG controlled about one-third of Namibia, some of which would be transferred back to the government in 1908 and 1910. But the discovery of diamonds in 1908 in DKG territory near Lüderitz Bay substantially changed its whole financial picture. It joined with the German government to form the Diamanten-Regie (q.v.) to create a monopoly over the mining and sale of these diamonds.

In 1920, the Consolidated Diamond Mines of South West Africa Ltd. (q.v.) bought out all the German mining properties, including the DKG.

DEVELOPMENT OF SELF-GOVERNMENT FOR NATIVE NATIONS IN SWA ACT NO. 54 OF 1968. This act provided for the setting up of Homelands or ''Bantustans'' in Namibia after the model in South Africa itself. Each would have a legislative assembly constituted on a tribal basis. The ''nations'' would be Ovamboland, Damaraland, Hereroland, Kaokoland, Okavangoland, and Eastern Caprivi. South Africa's state president could set up legislative and executive councils in each, which would have the power to pass laws on specified matters subject to agreement by the state president. These matters were generally limited to subjects such as education, welfare services, water supplies, roads, sanitation, labor, collection of taxes, and the registration of Africans. In fact the act was a sham, as the president could amend or repeal the laws and make new laws by proclamation alone. He could also replace any tribal government. The act made no provisions for ultimate independence. Ovamboland was the first ''Homeland'' to be selected for self-rule under this plan.

The 1968 Act was amended by Act No. 20 of 1973, which was approved by South Africa's Parliament March 30, 1973. It redefined the boundaries of the areas not set aside for Africans, excluded certain matters from the powers of the legislative councils, and, among other matters, dealt with the powers of chiefs and headmen, official languages of certain areas, the establishment of a High Court, and certain financial matters.

DE VRIES, JOHANNES LUKAS (1938–). Along with his colleague, Bishop L. Auala (q.v.), one of the most influential churchmen in Namibia in the 1970s. He has been described by Sam Nujoma, the leader of SWAPO, as ''a freedom-fighter like us.'' Dr. de Vries was chosen in 1967 as the first

Black head of the Evangelical Lutheran Ovambokavango Church (q.v.). His title of Präses is the equivalent of Bishop. He also served as president of the federated body, the United Evangelical Lutheran Church of South West Africa (q.v.). In 1973, de Vries and Bishop Auala headed a delegation to South Africa protesting the imposition of a South Africa-like apartheid system on Namibia.

Dr. de Vries is a Baster (q.v.), born in Rehoboth. His training at the Paulineum at Otjimbingwe led to further studies in West Germany. His doctorate in theology was earned at the University of Brussels. He wrote a thesis on "Mission and Colonialism in South West Africa." He believed that non-violent opposition as preached by the churches would succeed ultimately. A church cannot remain inactive and thus neutral toward a state that is oppressive. He and Dr. Auala led the opposition of "non-politicians," and pledged to continue until Namibia was free and self-governing.

DE WET, JOHANNES (JANNIE) MARTHUS (1927–). One of the most prominent white political figures in Namibia since the 1960s, De Wet was commissioner-general for the indigenous peoples of SWA from May 1970 until September 1977. He was born in South Africa, but his family moved to Namibia the next year. He was raised at Outjo, 250 miles north of Windhoek. He attended secondary School in South Africa, and received a BS in Agriculture from Witwatersrand University. He returned to farm in Namibia and became very active in various cattle-breeding and agricultural organizations in the 1950s. He joined South Africa's Parliament in 1964 as MP for the Namib constituency of SWA, and later represented Karas as MP in the Legislative Assembly (1964–70).

His appointment as commissioner-general in 1970 meant living at Oshakati, the new capital of Owambo. Problems quickly developed. Chief Councillor Ushona Shiimi (q.v.) was mysteriously killed in 1971, and his successor, Fileman Elfias (q.v.) was assassinated in 1975. In late 1971 there was a major labor disturbance as 13,000 Wambo workers struck, and there were clashes with the police. De Wet flew to Cape

Town for military reinforcements. A more passive form of resistance occurred in 1973 when Wambos had a very low turn out for Legislative Council elections. De Wet chose to believe that it was a form of silent support for the Owambo government and that the people favored a one-party system. In October 1974, De Wet got into trouble with his Pretoria superiors by revealing the existence of a South African plan to create (and give independence to) a Greater Ovamboland, a region that would include Wambos across the Angolan border as well. It would have created a buffer, South Africa felt, between Angola and the rest of Namibia. Despite a life spent mostly in Namibia, De Wet was apparently too naive to understand fully the feelings of the indigenous peoples he was supposed to represent. Nevertheless, in one key speech at a conference in 1970 he showed an understanding that not all Wambos were still tied to traditional leaders, and that some way had to be found to accommodate these new political aspirations. His superiors in Pretoria were either not listening or chose not to hear.

He was elected to the National Assembly, serving from 1979 to 1982. He was also minister for agriculture in the white Second Tier Authority from 1980 to 1987. He had a similar post in the Transitional Government of National Unity 1987 to 1988. He took a public stand against educational desegregation in 1987 and generally has represented a very conservative white position on issues. (Curiously, however, after the 1989 elections there were rumors that SWAPO might name him to the position of minister of agriculture. This did not happen.)

As a longtime member of the National Party and its vice-chairman in 1987, De Wet was active in the formation of the Action Christian National (q.v.) alliance for the 1989 elections. He was its chairman, under J. (Kosie) Pretorius. The alliance won three seats in the Assembly, and De Wet and Pretorius hold two of them. A split developed between them in January 1990, and Pretorius tried to have De Wet evicted from his Assembly seat. The Assembly Chairman, Hage Geingob, refused to do it, however, saying that it was not in his power and that the two should resolve their own disputes through negotiation.

DIAMANTEN-REGIE-GESELLSCHAFT DES SÜDWESTAF-
RIKANISCHEN SCHUTZGEBIETS. Founded in Berlin in
early 1909 by the German government (imitating the attempt
by De Beers [q.v.] to control the world diamond market), this
purely German association was designed to monopolize the
diamond market in Namibia. All diamonds produced were to
be brought to it, which would sell the diamonds under
controlled conditions (both quantity and time). The goal was
to keep diamonds out of English control. Proceeds of the
diamond sales were distributed among the companies, after
deducting taxes, royalties, and commissions. German bankers were the chief shareholders. The diamond producers were
not pleased with the prices they received; in 1913 they
secured from the government a share in the company's
operation. Prices the next year rose by 15 percent. However,
a squabble broke out over conditions of that year's sales, and
the German government intervened, taking over the shares of
the bankers. It then declared that from the beginning of 1914,
the government would decide how many diamonds would be
sold each year and the quota of each producer. Thus the
Regie ceased to exist in its original form. After setting policy
for 1914, the government reorganized the Regie, giving
producers four of the eight seats on its board. This reconstituted Regie was recognized as authoritative by the various
diamond industries of the world at a joint meeting in London
in July 1914. In 1921, the Regie was replaced by the
Diamond Board of South West Africa (q.v.).

DIAMOND BOARD OF SOUTH WEST AFRICA. Formed in
1921 after the Union of South Africa took over the administration of Namibia under the League of Nations mandate, it
became the successor to the older Diamanten-Regie (q.v.).
Its functions included distributing the quotas for diamond
sales, setting up the delivery to those buying the diamonds,
and collecting the receipts. In short it held the monopoly (and
responsibility) for selling all the diamonds produced. The
law required all diamonds to be delivered to the Diamond
Board. This board consisted of three members: two representatives of the producers and one of the administration. The
latter had effective control of the board's actions. The

administration, however, agreed in February 1920, to grant its exclusive rights in the Sperrgebiet (q.v.) to the Oppenheimer's Consolidated Diamond Mines of South West Africa Ltd. (q.v.), with profits to be divided between the CDM and the administration. Board functions have been adjusted by proclamation in 1932 and 1939. The latter proclamation provides that the board continues as a statutory corporate person, with three or five members. If three, one is a representative of the Administrator General; if five, two are his or her representatives.

DIAMONDS. Among Namibia's most valuable assets, diamonds have been a major source of revenue in the country only since the early part of the twentieth century. Diamonds were discovered in neighboring areas of South Africa in the 1860s, so it was obvious why the De Beers Company (q.v.) would have explored parts of Namibia for gems from the 1890s into the twentieth century. But their attempts focussed on the wrong areas. The major discovery came in 1908 at the hands of a German railway builder, August Stauch (q.v.). He told his workers at a site near Lüderitzbucht to watch for unusual stones. When one found a ''pretty stone'' and showed it to him, Stauch realized what he had. He quit his job, staked his claims, and produced a good supply of the gems. When he revealed his find in Swakopmund on June 20, 1908, a diamond rush began. The land near the southwestern coast of the territory became inundated with miners, but Stauch led the way in major claims. In 1909 the Deutsche Kolonialgesellschaft für Südwestafrika made major discoveries in the Bogenfels area. From 1908 to 1914 about 5 million carats of diamonds were mined amidst the sands of the desert. The value topped R17 million.

World War I briefly interrupted mining, but South Africa's victory over the Germans there in 1915 allowed work to resume. Nine companies were soon involved. Among the diamond-seekers to come in was Sir Ernest Oppenheimer, who united the smaller producers in 1920 by creating the Consolidated Diamond Mines of South West Africa Ltd. (q.v.). He obtained mining rights from January 1, 1921, for a period of fifty years (and later added another twenty years), to a 30-mile wide strip from the mouth of the Orange River north to a little north of Lüderitz Bay, about 120 miles. All gems produced had to be brought to the Diamond Board of South West Africa for sale. From 1926 to 1928 fantastic discoveries were made near the mouth of the Orange River, and the town of Oranjemund eventually arose. The gems there surpassed all of the earlier discoveries in both size and quality. Still today Namibia produces a much finer gem than other sources, and only 4 percent of its diamonds are "merely industrial quality," compared to 80 percent at most mines.

Huge earth-moving machines process millions of tons of sand to uncover the gravels in which the gems lay. The largest found there was 246 carats. In 1977 Oranjemund itself produced 2 million carats, and the CDM produced 22 percent of De Beers net profit. For each of those 2 million carats, over 100 tons of sand had to be removed. A depressed market in the 1980s (partly produced by large new supplies being discovered in neighboring Botswana) reduced CDM production for De Beers to 1 million carats. (A carat is 0.2 grams.)

Geologists believe that the coastal diamonds were carried down the Orange River about 2 million years ago from the highland diamond region (near Kimberley, for example) to the river delta. The diamonds were then swept north and onshore onto the bedrock by the north-flowing Benguela Current along the coast. Massive quantities of sand and gravel flowed down the river in later millennia, and were dumped on top of the diamond-bearing deposits just above the bedrock.

Diamond mining had reached a low in 1990 of 748,000 carats but CDM opened its new mine at Elizabeth Bay in 1991 and also began offshore production, swelling the total dramatically to 1.19 million carats. With other mines to be opened at Auchas and Chameis, the near-term prospect for replacing areas with depleted reserves is extremely promising. In 1991, the value of diamonds exported from Namibia was $442 million, almost 40 percent of the country's total export value.

DIAS, BARTHOLOMEU (variants: BARTHOLOMEW; BARTOLOMUS DIAZ) (c. 1450–1500). Portuguese navigator and gentleman of the king's court who discovered the Cape of Good Hope in 1488, and in so doing traveled further south than any known European explored until then. In 1486 he had been selected by Dom Joao (John) II of Portugal to command a fleet which should follow the path of previous sailors (Diogo Cão, q.v.) and find a sea route around Africa to the Orient and perhaps also locate the legendary lands of Prester John. In December 1487 he sailed along the Namibian coast past the southernmost point of Diogo Cão. He reached what is now Walvis Bay on December 8, Spencer Bay on December 21, Hottentot Bay on December 23, and Lüderitzbucht on Christmas Eve. He called the latter Angra des Voltas ("Bay of Tacking"), because of the large number of tacks needed to enter it.

Dias had three ships, two of them being hundred-ton caravels and one a larger provision ship, the latter commanded by his brothers. There were also six Africans on the trip who had been previously taken to Portugal. They were brought along in the hope of opening doors to trade in gold, silver, and spices. It is thought that as many as three of the Africans were left near Lüderitzbucht.

Dias stayed at Lüderitzbucht for five days because of the bad weather but then continued south, passing the mouth of the Orange River on New Year's Eve. About five weeks later he rounded the Cape of Good Hope and went as far as the mouth of the Bushman River before heading back toward Portugal. He discovered Table Bay on the way back around the Cape. Again he stopped at Lüderitzbucht, this time naming it Golfo de San Cristovão when he landed on July 25, 1488. At nearby Dias Point he erected his third cross (padrão, q.v.) in southern Africa, and dedicated it to St. James (Santiago). He reached Lisbon in December 1488 after an absence of sixteen and a half months, but is not known to have received public acclaim for his feat. Of his later life we know little. He served as commander of Elmina Castle on the Guinea Coast about a decade after his return to Lisbon. He perished at sea on May 24, 1500, when his ship was one of four to disappear in a violent storm near Tristan da Cunha Island; he had been en route with a fleet of thirteen ships under the command of Pedro Cabral, who discovered Brazil later in 1500.

DIAS CROSS. When Bartholomeu Dias (q.v.) landed at Lüderitzbucht for the second time, July 25, 1488, he erected a cross (padrão, q.v.) at what is now called Dias Point. By 1786 the cross had seriously deteriorated, according to a report by Captain T. B. Thompson. Remnants of it are claimed by museums in Cape Town, Berlin, Auckland, Lisbon, and Windhoek. A Capt. Owen is noted as finding it in the sand in 1825 and perhaps with breaking it into the fragments. Parts of it were only found in 1953 by Professor and Mrs. Eric Axelson and Dr. C. Lemmer. It is these (including one piece with an inscription) that are in the Windhoek Museum. German administrators placed a wooden cross at Dia Point, and the South African authorities replaced it with a granite cross in 1929.

DIERGAARDT, JOHANNES G. A. ("HANS")(1927–). An active political figure in Namibia for over four decades, Diergaardt is a Baster born in Rehoboth, and is a farmer and a businessman. In 1947 he joined the Rehoboth Burgervereniging, the beginning of a long career of fighting for Rehoboth sovereignty. As founder of the Rehoboth Taxpayers Association he served as an elected member of the Rehoboth Advisory Council from 1959 until 1977. In 1968 he founded the Rehoboth Volkspartei and represented it at the National Convention (q.v.) when it was formed in November 1971. He was elected its chairman at that initial meeting. The National Convention split into two parts in 1975, and the Volkspartei split with it. Diergaardt, along with D. J. Izaaks (q.v.) formed the Rehoboth Liberation Party (RLP) and also became part of the new National Convention of Namibia. The RLP won two seats in the Baster Council in 1975 and Diergaardt was one of its representatives at the Turnhalle Conference until the party withdrew from it in 1976. In 1979 he was elected kaptein of Rehoboth, a post he still holds.

In 1978 he was elected to the National Assembly, but he walked out of it in 1980. In 1979 he was also elected president of the Liberated Democratic Party (LDP) (q.v.). He represented the Liberation Front at the Multi-Party Conference (q.v.) in 1983, and when a new Namibian Government of National Unity was formed in June 1985, he was named to the cabinet as minister of local government and civil affairs (1985–1988) and as minister of agriculture and nature conservation (1988–1989).

In late 1988 Hans Diergaardt became the founder and president of the Federal Convention of Namibia (q.v.), in hopes of putting together a successful electoral alliance of traditionally oriented Africans. The FCN stood for a federal Namibia, in which diversity would be recognized and traditional authority and local autonomy protected. Late in the election campaign he threatened to lead Rehoboth in a secession from Namibia; linked (he said) with allies to the west he could even procure access to the ocean.

The FCN only won one seat in the 1989 Assembly elections, and Diergaardt received it. However he then backed out of it "for personal reasons," and the seat was filled by Mburumba Kerina (q.v.), who was then chosen deputy speaker of the Assembly. Meanwhile, he maintains his position as chairman (Kaptein) of Rehoboth and has strong support there. He and his council declared a Unilateral Declaration of Independence from Namibia on March 19, 1990, in direct opposition to the unitary constitution of Namibia. He even threatened to take the issue to the International Court of Justice. Diergaardt contended that the Rehoboth Basters had settled on land granted to them by Nama leaders before Germans colonized the country. Thus they have an independent status and can not be forced into a unitary system of Namibian government. In September of 1990 Prime Minister Hage Geingob helped to defuse the situation by convincing Diergaardt and a group of followers to vacate government owned property that they had been "occupying." It avoided a confrontation between the police and armed Basters.

While this solved the immediate crisis, it did not end Diergaardt's attempt to win independence for the Basters. In April, 1992 from his home in Rehoboth, he was still maintaining the position that Basterland should be independent, and cited the changes in eastern Europe as precedents for a separate Baster state based on a combination of historical tradition and ethnicity. In the regional elections in 1992, all three Rehoboth-area seats (in the Hardap region) were won by members of the DTA.

DIERGAARDT, RAYMOND REGINALD ("REGGIE")
(1957–). One of Namibia's younger and most promising
political figures, he was born in Kalkveld, educated in
Rehoboth, and received a teacher's diploma from a college in
Port Elizabeth, South Africa, in 1978. That same year he
returned to Namibia and became an organizer for the Labour
Party (q.v.). At the age of twenty-three he was elected to the
Executive Committee of the Coloured Second Tier Govern-
ment. He was its chairman when it was disbanded in 1989.
He was elected secretary general of the Labour Party in 1984,
and became its leader in 1988. He also served on the TGNU
Constitutional Council from 1985 to 1987.

In 1989 he became a founding member of an election
alliance, the United Democratic Front (UDF) (q.v.), and was
selected its national chairman (third in command). The
alliance won four seats in the Assembly, and "Reggie"
Diergaardt received one of them. In the Assembly he became
the UDF deputy leader. Despite this opposition position,
Diergaardt was selected by the president to be Deputy
Minister of Trade and Industry.

On February 19, 1991 there was a restructuring of government ministries, and Diergaardt was made Deputy Minister
of the newly created Ministry of Youth and Sport.

DIXON, PETER. A trader from South Africa, he lived more than
thirty years in Namibia in the middle of the nineteenth
century. The missionaries at Warmbad had relayed a request
from Jonker Afrikander for traders to come to the territory.
Two families responded, leaving Cape Town together in
October 1843, the Thomas Morris family and the Peter
Dixon family. Dixon had two sons and two daughters (a third
son was born and later died of illness in Namibia). The
women in this entourage were the first white women settlers
in Namibia. The two Dixon girls both married traders
(William Latham and J. F. Bassingthwaighte) and remained
in the country.

The Dixon and Morris families settled at Sandfontein,
building a store there and a cattle post on the Swakop River.
They traded salt, meat, and livestock to the guano (q.v.) ships
operating along the coast. The cattle were lifted onto the

ships by slings, after having been towed on rafts up to the ships. Thus livestock was exported first to St. Helena and then to the Cape itself. When they had difficulty meeting their quota of cattle to St. Helena, the partnership with the Lawton firm broke up. Nevertheless the Dixon and Morris families continued the trade in livestock to the Cape.

By 1846 illness struck the Dixon family, and Peter and his daughter Rebecca spent nine months in Cape Town so he could recover. When the two returned, the family travelled to Gobabis (April 1847), where they helped the ill family of the missionary, J. Tindall. However, Mrs. Dixon and all her five children became ill also, and the third son died. The rest eventually recovered, but tragedy struck again in 1850 when their home at Sandfontein was damaged by Namas while the family was trading elsewhere in the territory.

In early 1861 Dixon was actively assisting such noted explorers as James Chapman and Thomas Baines (qq.v.). He was an important resource for all whites moving into or through Namibia. His sons and sons-in-law also settled their own homesteads in Namibia. Peter Dixon was still alive and travelling in 1877.

DOBRA MISSION SCHOOL. One of the first few secondary schools for Africans in Namibia (*see also* AUGUSTI-NEUM), it is located 16 kilometers from Windhoek. It provided free board and tuition for these students until the government began to subsidize and control all such education. It is a Catholic school.

DOG TAX. A factor in the resistance by the Bondelswarts (q.v.) in the twentieth century, it was a colonial tax designed to limit their ability to hunt with packs of dogs. This hunting gave them a degree of freedom from the need to become wage-laborers. Thus the dog tax, which became prohibitively high in 1921, combined with a drought, pushed the Bondelswarts to the edge of starvation, and a brief rebellion took place. The administration attacked, leaving 100 Bondelswarts dead, and 468 wounded or prisoners of war.

DORSLAND TREKKERS. *See* THIRSTLAND TREKKERS.

DROUGHT. Any country whose borders are marked by one major desert on the east (the Kalahari) and another on the west (the Namib) is bound to experience periodic bouts with drought. This becomes especially critical if the population lives off wild game or such livestock as cattle and sheep. Thus Namibia's history (and indeed political climate) has been affected by periodic droughts. For example, in 1829 and 1830 drought hit the northern part of the country, while rain fell sufficiently in the areas south of the Swakop River. When the Hereros brought their cattle south into Nama territory, conflict inevitably developed. Likewise in the 1860s and 1870s, rain was sparse in Hereroland, and Maherero's large cattle herds lacked grazing areas. Again they invaded Nama territory, and only the intervention of missionaries kept the conflict from becoming disastrous.

Most of Namibia's rivers (q.v.) flow sporadically, as little as once or twice a decade. Some have sub-surface streams, however, that can be easily reached with a little digging. A terrible drought returned to Namibia in the 1970s and 1980s. It not only hurt agriculture but also the game parks (and thus tourism). The Etosha Game Park in the north did not suffer as badly as others, such as the Dann Viljoen or the Namib-Naukluft parks.

While the drought somewhat alleviated in the mid and late 1980s, it returned in 1989. Good rains came in late 1991, allowing an excellent harvest, but 1992 was again a drought year, and President Sam Nujoma declared a state of emergency. He encouraged communal farmers to lessen the pressure on grazing land by selling their cattle for slaughter. Cereal imports had to be doubled, and international donors were called on for relief. By mid-1992 it was estimated that rainfall had reached its lowest level ever recorded.

DUMENI, BISHOP KLEOPAS. Head of the Evangelical Lutheran Church in Namibia (formerly the Evangelical Lutheran Ovambo Kavango Church), the Bishop has been active in protesting the actions of the South African government. One study showed that Wambos saw him as being among the most respected people in Owambo. He joined with other church leaders in the country in protesting torture and other abuses of power. These abuses came primarily from the police and the military, the latter threatened the bishop himself while he was conducting a worship service. He became the bishop in 1979, succeeding Bishop Leonard Auala (q.v.). In 1986 he was a delegate to the /Ai//gams Conference, but did not sign its concluding declaration.

DUMINY, CAPTAIN. Captain of the Dutch ship *Meermin* (q.v.), which was sent in 1793 up the Namibian coastline to annex part of it. Duminy proclaimed Dutch sovereignty over Walvis Bay, Halifax Island, and Angra Pequena. The ship landed at Walvis Bay on January 23, 1793, but Duminy waited until February 26 to issue the formal act of occupation. Also on the *Meermin* was Sebastiaan van Reenen (q.v.).

DUNEDIN STAR. One of history's more dramatic shipwreck and rescue dramas occurred on November 29, 1942, when the *Dunedin Star*'s bottom tore open off the Skeleton Coast (or Kaokoveld Coast) of northern Namibia. The ship was likely a munitions carrier, though it has also been described as a 13,000-ton British liner. There were twenty-one passengers and eighty-five crewmen aboard.

In the two months that followed the accident, rescue crews from all over southern Africa and Britain attempted to rescue people and salvage the ship. Due to inclement weather and unpassable sand, many of the rescue missions by land, sea, and air failed, leaving the rescuers in need of rescue. All of the people were saved by December 24, 1942, and attempts to salvage ships and planes ended by February 5, 1943. Only two people died in the incident and its aftermath.

DUNES, SAND. Like massive living sculpture, the dunes of Namibia are very imposing. Not all of the Namib Desert consists of dunes, which in fact are usually found in strips, as winds drift the sand into high mounds. Between Swakopmund and Lüderitz, the world's tallest dunes reach as high as 300 meters or 350 yards.

Any stone or bush can be the point around which a dune is formed, as winds deposit the sand around it. Namibian dunes are found in four types. (1) Kalahari dunes are longitudinal, running north to south, parallel to the prevailing wind. They are usually straight and elongated, with a sharp crest. They are often fixed by vegetation and acacia trees and have a grass cover. They range from ten to thirty feet high. Their reddish hue comes from a thin film of iron oxide coating each grain of sand. (2) Shrub-coppice dunes are along the coast and in arid inland areas. A plant becomes the stabilizing agent for the sand in these small dunes. The plant extends its roots and survives at the top of the evergrowing mound of sand trapped by its stems and leaves. (3) Crescent-shaped "Barchan" dunes occur where sand is scarce. These transitory dunes can move up to about ten miles a year. Facing the northeast, they can be found along the Skeleton Coast (q.v.) south to Lüderitz. Their color ranges from black magnetite to a maroon layer of garnet and magnetite. (4) The spectacular Star Dunes are sharply crested sand mountains found between Lüderitz and Swakopmund. They are stationary, but multidirectional winds shift the sand back and forth into star shapes. Their color ranges from yellow-gold to rose, maroon or even brick-red. At up to 350 feet, they are the world's tallest dunes.

DU PLESSIS, ABRAHAM HERMANUS (1914–). Born in the Cape Province of South Africa, A. H. du Plessis was active in both South African and Namibian politics for five decades. Educated at the University of South Africa, he went to live in Namibia in 1934. There he became active in their branch of South Africa's National Party after it organized in the late 1930s, becoming its general secretary in Windhoek in 1945. When elections for the new Legislative Assembly of South West Africa were held on August 30, 1950, du Plessis ran in the Usakos electoral division, beating his opponent by a margin of 707 to 471. He was then selected a member of the Assembly's Executive Committee, and later its chairman. He was elected to the South African Parliament as the member from Windhoek in 1969, rising to cabinet status as deputy minister of finance and economic affairs and later as minister of public works and community development. All along, of course, he remained active as leader of the National Party at home. In September 1974, it was announced that du Plessis was prepared to talk with Black leaders about the territory's future. Du Plessis stated that ''all options would be open.''

When the Turnhalle Constitutional Conference (q.v.) began to take shape, South Africa's Prime Minister J. B. Vorster ordered du Plessis (in November 1975) to give up his cabinet post in order to return home to lead the National Party delegation. Vorster wanted Dirk Mudge out of the leadership post because Vorster considered Mudge to be too sympathetic towards Blacks. Du Plessis later also resigned his seat in Parliament. Mudge and du Plessis then became foes in their party and Mudge eventually resigned to form his own party. Du Plessis and Eben van Zijl (q.v.) became the party's strongest leaders. Long a supporter of continued white leadership of Namibia and separate development based on ethnicity, du Plessis continued his fight during the Turnhalle Conference, where he was a major policy spokesman. After Mudge broke from the National Party, du Plessis and van Zijl formed a new political body called the Action Front for the Retention of Tumballe Principles (AKTUR) (q.v.). The two represented AKTUR at ''proximity talks'' in New York in February 1978. In December of that year, AKTUR took part in Assembly elections and won six seats. Van Zijl took one of those seats and, as a younger man, continued in active governing positions. Du Plessis remained an ardent opponent of majority rule for Namibia. He served as National Party leader from 1968 to 1981.

DUTCH EAST INDIA COMPANY. The charter company that first began to settle the Cape area of South Africa when it established a refreshment station there in 1652 under Jan van Riebeeck, it also began to explore the coast of Namibia. Technically it was called Vereenigde Nederlandsche Ge-Octroyeerde Oost-Indische Compagnie (VOC). In order to supply fresh water, vegetables, and meat for ships sailing around the Cape, it set up gardens and farms and also began trade with the local ''Hottentots.'' It also began to explore along the coast of Namibia, notably with the ships *Grundel* (q.v.) in 1670 and *Bode* in 1677. Both captains had difficulties with the indigenous Namibians, which discouraged further explorations there by the company for many years. Other countries did not feel equally constrained, and the Dutch government ultimately felt it had to declare its rights in the area. It did this in 1793 when the Dutch ship *Meermin* (q.v.) embarked for Namibia, its captain under orders to annex part of the Namibian coast. He declared Dutch sovereignty over Walvis Bay, Halifax Island, and Angra Pequena (qq.v.).

A former employee of the company, H. J. Wikar, spent several years on Namibia's border, and his writings provide some of the earliest accounts (1779) we have of the peoples who would settle the southern half of Namibia. Wikar was soon followed by Robert J. Gordon, a captain in the service of the VOC, who commanded the troops at the Cape. He crossed the Orange River briefly, and indeed gave it that name in honor of the royal house of the Netherlands, the House of Orange.

DUWISIB CASTLE. One of the lovely "castles" that grace Namibia, it was designed like the others by architect Willi Sander (q.v.). It is located 70 kilometers from Maltahohe on the edge of the Namib Desert. Today it is part of a 130,000-acre karakul farm. It was built by Baron Hans Heinrich von Wolff in 1908. His wife was an American heiress who paid for its construction. The castle's name is derived from a Nama word meaning "the white chalk place without water." The sandstone castle's beautiful furnishings were imported from Germany and required twenty ox-wagons to bring them from the port. They included paintings, valuable porcelain, and numerous antiques. The baron also had a collection of rare engravings and prints. When World War I began in 1914, the baron and baroness fled the castle for South America, leaving most of their valuables in their home. He later died in the war in Europe, and his wife sold the castle to a wealthy Swede in 1918. In the late 1920s the castle and farm were sold again, to the Thorer Organization. It has since been bought by the Department of Agriculture and Nature Conservations, and a caravan and camping site have been added nearby, along with a restaurant.

- E -

EASTERN CAPRIVI. That portion of the Caprivi Strip (q.v.) that lies east of the Kwando (also called Mashi or Linyanti) River which cuts through Caprivi from north to south. As the Kwando is also the border between Angola and Zambia, it bisects Caprivi where the strip widens considerably. The population of the Eastern Caprivi area consists of two primary groups, the Masubia and the Mafwe peoples (about 88 percent of the total) plus smaller groups of Mayeyi, Mutotela, Mashi, and Mbukushu peoples, many of whom are becoming integrated into the Mafwe group. There are also about 100 white farm families. The total population of the Eastern Caprivi is now over 35,000. Most of them are farmers but some also raise cattle and also live by hunting, gathering, and fishing in the rivers that totally surround the region. The people of the Eastern Caprivi are not related at all to other Namibians, but are ethnically tied to those in western Zambia and northeastern Botswana. South Africa declared Eastern Caprivi to be a separate "homeland," with its own Legislative Council, and a capital at Katima Mulibo (q.v.). In modern politics the area has been organized by the Caprivi African National Union (q.v.), some of whose members in early 1984 called for negotiations with South Africa to create a separate Republic of Itenge (q.v.).

EASTERN HERERO. The Namibian people known as the Herero (q.v.) were found to live in nine subgroups in the 1890s, just prior to their major conflicts with the Germans. The largest group lived near Okahandja and was led by Samuel Maharero (q.v.). Two other groups were nearby, and a fourth resided near Mount Waterberg. The "Eastern Herero" were five smaller groups led by Nikodemus, Tjetjoo, Kakimena, Ombundju, and Mambo. Nikodemus especially resented the fact that he was passed over after the death of Maherero for leadership of the Hereros in favor of Samuel Maharero. He blamed this injustice on German influence. General Leutwein finally demanded in 1894 that Nikodemus recognize Samuel Maherero's position as permanent chief, and in turn confirmed Nikodemus status as independent subchief of the eastern Herero. Samuel Maherero soon signed away the rights to the land of the Eastern Hereros (which he had no authority to do), and Germans began confiscating Herero cattle. The Eastern Herero groups thus rose up against the Germans in the War of the Boundary in March 1896. Within several weeks the Germans had won, and both Nikodemus and Kakimena were shot by a German firing squad in Okahandja. Many of the Eastern Hereros then fled into Botswana, where some are still found today. Others have returned to eastern Namibia, especially to the southern part of the Epukiro Reserve.

ECONOMY. Outstanding works on Namibia's economy have been written by Wolfgang Thomas, the most succinct being *Namibia, Political and Economic Prospects,* Robert Rotberg, editor. He notes the following principal sections of the Namibian economy: (1) *Agriculture* (q.v.), both for subsistence and wage employment. Nevertheless, the bulk of Namibia's basic food products are imported from South Africa. (2) *The fishing industry* (q.v.) in the South Atlantic. Once a major source of income and employment, the pelagic fish were overharvested in the mid-1970s and both the catches and the processing thereof declined by as much as 75 percent. Quotas have resulted in a rebound. (3) *Mining* (q.v.), the principal source of foreign exchange. It consists mainly of diamond mining (despite a slumping world market currently) and uranium mining at Rössing. Lesser production of copper, lead, and zinc also exists. (4) *Industry (q.v.) and construction.* Less than 10 percent of Namibia's GNP is accounted for by this sector, notably because the small population provides such a small potential market. Thus again Namibia finds itself closely integrated with the South African economy in this sector. (5) *Tourism* may continue to grow after independence, but was low while fighting continued in the country.

While Namibia's trade balance regularly shows a surplus (thanks mainly to diamonds and uranium), government revenues do not meet expenses, and the South African government had to subsidize the budget heavily (as much as 50 percent). In addition, seventy years under South African domination has left much of the Namibian economy dependent on that of South Africa, both for imports and exports. Still the economy is fairly stable. The country does not rely on export of migrant labor, it has great mineral wealth, a strong balance of payments, and a dynamic entrepreneurial class (many of whom, however, are whites who may flee a Black-ruled Namibia). One of the economy's biggest weaknesses is that it relies so heavily on exploitation of its finite mineral resources and has neglected to expand secondary industries.

EDUCATION. The first educational institutions in Namibia were for Black students, sponsored primarily by Finnish and Anglican missionaries as early as the 1870s. The early missionaries built schools and churches and, as elsewhere in Africa, combined elementary education with religious prose-lytizing, especially among the Wambo. Missionaries re-tained a significant role in African education until 1970, when the Bantu Education Amendment Act phased out most of the mission schools. The African school with the largest and most prestigious history is the Augustineum (q.v.), which was the result of the efforts of the German missionary Hugo Hahn (q.v.), who began his drive for the school in 1864. Its location has changed several times, as has its precise purpose. Many of the country's Black teachers were educated there.

Education for white students began soon after large num-bers of Europeans moved into the territory. Schools were built not only in the towns but also in the countryside, with adjacent hostels to house the students. Many of the rural schools have their own vegetable gardens (worked by the students) and raise their own meat, but they also have sporting fields, swimming pools, and movie projectors. Compulsory education for white and "Brown" students was in force by 1906, but not for Blacks.

When South Africans replaced Germans in the country, Coloured schools followed the Afrikaans-medium syllabus, but Blacks received their own separate one. Schools for Africans were aimed at vocational education with teacher training as the highest goal. In 1948 240 schools for "Natives" existed in the territory, enrolling 22,000 pupils. There were 504 certificated teachers (some of whom had only a primary education) and 154 "unqualified" teachers.

With the implementation of the Odendaal Commission Report (q.v.) of 1962, the South African government spent considerably more on "Bantu" education, building many schools throughout the country. In the northern part of the country, territorial authorities controlled education. They opened a showcase high school and technical college among the Ovambos in Oshakati in August 1971. A boycott by students, part of the broader political unrest of the time, closed it a few days after its formal opening. Teaching in all "Bantu" schools was in the vernacular for the first four years, and then in Afrikaans. This was part of the reason for the protests. By 1970, there were 130,000 students enrolled in the schools, of whom 108,000 were Africans. However, a disproportionately large amount of money for education was spent on the 22,000 white students. One estimate from 1978 said that if the same amount were expended on the other students as on whites, the cost would be R200 million a year, a twelve-fold increase. Nevertheless, contemporary political groups in Namibia are calling for a reformed educational system with free universal education and a mix of both government and private schools. The government statistics claim that there have been significant gains in the field of education. They show an increase of teachers from 3836 in 1970 to 11,945 in 1987, while the number of pupils has increased from 134,355 to 364,000. The government also points to its new Academy for Tertiary Education in Windhoek, now the University of Namibia. This institution includes university courses, technical education, teacher training, and evening classes for self-improvement. For those Namibians living temporarily in Lusaka, Zambia, the United Nations Institute for Namibia was a very important facility, providing a wide range of education for people who planned to return home to an independent, African-ruled Namibia. The institute had close ties with SWAPO (q.v.).

EICHA-AIS HOTTENTOTS. *See* //AICHA-//AIN.

EIK HAMS. *See* AIKAMS.

EIS-GAOB. The name given by the Zwartbooi Hottentots (q.v.) to August 18, 1864, a day when about thirty women and children plus an unknown number of men were killed in an attack on their wagon train by the followers of Jan Jonker Afrikander. The wagon train was travelling from Rehoboth to Otjimbingwe when it was attacked near the Kuiseb River. The travellers were accompanied by the Rev. F. H. Kleinschmidt. The greatest loss of life came when the long dry grass was set aflame by Hendrik Ses. The twenty-five circled wagons were quickly ablaze, and those in the circle suffocated. The name comes from the intention (*eis*) in the hearts (*gaob*) of the attackers to destroy the whole tribe.

ELECTIONS. Elections have been held in Namibia for years. Local elections among whites produced mayors and councils. Elections in African "homelands" produced local African leaders and legislators. White "South Westers" even elected (after 1949) representatives to the South African Parliament. On September 20, 1978, however, South African Prime Minister John Vorster announced that Namibia would soon have nationwide multiracial elections. Administrator-General Steyn announced that December 4 to 8 would be the period for elections to choose a fifty-member constituent assembly. Two of the major black political organizations, SWAPO and the Namibia National Front (NNF) (qq.v.) declared they would not participate and urged a black boycott. The major competitors, therefore, were the Democratic Turnhalle Alliance (q.v.), a coalition of eleven political groups (some extremely small); AKTUR (q.v.), a right-wing white coalition; and several other parties. While conservatives won more than 60 percent of the white vote, the DTA was declared the winner of forty-one of the fifty seats in the constituent assembly. AKTUR received six seats, and the other three were given to the Herstigte Nasionale Party, the Liberation Front, and the Namibia Christian Democratic Party. Of the 326,264 votes, officials announced that the DTA had 268,130, AKTUR had 38,716, the NCDP 9073, HNP 5781, and LF 4864. Officials claimed that 77.84

percent of the registered voters voted, and 93 percent of those eligible to register were on the lists. These official figures were challenged by SWAPO and others, however, who contended that, for example, white employers herded their black employees to the polls and watched while they voted. The presence of South African soldiers also limited the free choice, SWAPO said.

The most important elections in Namibia's history occurred in November, 1989 and in November, 1992. The first was for a Constituent Assembly (which became the National Assembly at independence), and the second was for seats in 13 new regional authorities and in local areas, such as cities and towns. The 1989 elections were critical as the constitution would be drawn up and affirmed by the new Constituent Assembly. SWAPO won 41 of the 72 seats in this Assembly (57.3 percent of the voters), clearly a majority but short of the two-thirds needed to totally control the shape of the new constitution. The DTA won 28.6 percent of the votes, and 21 of the seats; other groups won the remaining 10 seats.

In the 1992 regional elections, SWAPO won a total of 56 seats, the DTA won 20, and the UDF won the remaining 3. SWAPO had a majority of nine of the regions, DTA controlled three. The Kunene region was divided, with the UDF and SWAPO each having two seats and the DTA one. (See the Appendix for results of the 1989 and 1992 elections.)

ELEPHANT RIVER (variant: OLIFANTS). This lengthy river flows generally north to south in eastern Namibia, parallel to and east of the Auob River, with which it merges before it flows into northern Botswana. The Elephant River rises in the Auas Mountains east of Windhoek, and in the upper course it generally has supplies of ground water. Its valley is not broad, and in the lower reaches is more like a dune valley. Some San people live near the river, and, in some of its southern stretches, traces of human settlements estimated to be 25,000 years old have been found. Older traces have been found along the Auob River. Along the river near Okangondo, a fierce battle occurred between Nama and Herero forces on October 28, 1880. The victorious Nama took thousands of Herero cattle and killed 230 men.

ELF AQUITAINE. Along with Langer Heinrich (q.v.), this is one of the newer uranium mines in Namibia.

ELFIAS, PAULUS. Declared chief of the Ndonga branch of the Ovambo people, he was not accepted by all of Ndonga. Many did not accept him as the rightful successor to Chief Martin Ashikoto, who had been deposed and banished by the South African government on charges of criminal acts. When the South Africans established an Ovamboland government in 1968, Elfias was also named councillor in charge of justice in the Executive Council. When he died in 1970, Paulus Elfias was succeeded as chief by Philemon Elfias (q.v.).

ELFIAS, PHILEMON (variant: FILEMON) (1932–1975). Controversial successor to Paulus Elfias (q.v.) as chief of the Ndonga tribe of the Ovambo nation, he was never accepted by many of his people. Most of his schooling was at Oniipa (formerly Onamugundo when it was the great chief Kambonde's village early in the twentieth century). The village is due north of the Etosha Pan. Elfias did not finish his education (Standard IV) until he was about twenty years old. In 1970 he was chosen chief of the Ndonga. South Africa instituted an elected Ovamboland government in 1968, and the first chief councillor of the Ovambo Executive Council was Ushona Shiima. When Shiima died in an automobile accident in late 1971, Phileman Elfias was selected to be his successor. Chief Elfias was considered by many to be arbitrary and unjust in his meting out of punishment, especially when dealing with persons suspected to belonging to SWAPO; he was also accused of being a puppet of South Africa and a traitor to his people. A particularly controversial position espoused by Elfias was his proposal that a separate Ovamboland be formed, based on the union of the Ovambo "homeland" with the Ovambos of southern Angola. When Ovamboland became a self-governing territory in 1973, Elfias' title changed from chief councillor to chief minister. He was assassinated in a liquor store on August 16, 1975. His killer was never found, but thousands of Ovambos presumably had motives. SWAPO was widely suspected as being involved, so hundreds of political activists were rounded up for questioning, including nine SWAPO and NNC leaders. Seven men were tried in 1976 for "complicity," but no single assassin was ever discovered.

ELIZABETH BAY (ELIZABETHBUCHT). Located about twenty miles south of Lüderitz, this town once was a thriving center of the early twentieth-century diamond-mining industry, and it apparently soon will be again. The small bay on the coast after which the town was named had been called Golfo de São Estevão by the Portuguese explorer Bartholomeu Dias (q.v.), as he had reached it on the feast of St. Stephen (December 26) in 1487. Germans first reached the area in 1884, but the diamond boom came over a quarter of a century later. Diamonds were found deep in the sand there, and the Germans built the town nearby. It thrived for a decade or more, but the area was gradually abandoned in the mid-1920s, and Elizabeth Bay became a ghost town. Its buildings remained remarkably well-preserved, however, and there was thought of restoring it as a tourist site. CDM became interested in the Elizabeth Bay area for mining again in the 1980s, and late in the decade announced plans to develop a new mine there. Once mining would begin in 1991, it was planned to produce about 250,000 carats a year there, from the treatment of about four million tons of ore. Reserves were expected to last at least ten years. Production began at Elizabeth Bay in June, 1991, although formal ceremonies were held by President Nujoma two months later. The mine produces primarily small, gem quality diamonds.

In addition to diamonds, an extensive bed of rock salt that contains a high percentage of sodium chloride exists in the area, several miles from the coast.

EMERGENCY REGULATION R16 OF 1939. As a result of the outbreak of World War II in Europe, this emergency regulation was passed providing for the arrest and detention without charge or trial of anyone "in the interest of the State or in that person's own interest." Internment camps were set up at several locations, and about two thousand individuals were detained for varying periods. Most of the detainees were men of German ancestry from Namibia who had not been naturalized in their new home. Some were specifically pro-German in sentiment. Later, about two thousand Germans from other parts of Africa were added to the camps.

EMERGENCY REGULATION R17 OF 1972. Passed on February 4, 1972, it was a government reaction to strikes by Black contract workers two months earlier. The regulation imposed a state of emergency, which severely restricted the rights of the people to gather collectively or to organize politically. However, church services were still acceptable as meeting spots, although even these could be interrupted by the military. Many SWAPO leaders were banned or otherwise detained under this regulation.

ENGLISH LANGUAGE. While the official language of the country and understood by a wide range of the population, English is the native language of only 7 percent of the white population of Namibia. Afrikaans is ten times more common among whites and has been the teaching medium for Africans since the territory's early years.

EPUKIRO. Located on the Epukiro River (q.v.) in eastern Namibia, it is the site of a mission station placed there by the Roman Catholic Missionary Society in 1903. The name means "the country where one gets lost" in Herero. It is 58 miles (93 kilometers) north of Gobabis and is at an altitude of 4595 feet. The mission station and school were designed to support a settlement of people who had crossed the border from Botswana. Later it also served the Epukiro Reserve that was set up for Hereros in 1923. During the 1904 German-Herero War, a heavily armed German camp was set up at Epukiro under the command of Major B. von Deimling (q.v.). Today roads link Epukiro with Gobabis and other population centers.

EPUKIRO RIVER. Located in the northeastern quadrant of Namibia, it flows eastward into the Kalahari Desert. It lies south of the Eiseb River and north of the Black Nossob River and joins the Botletle River in Botswana, north of Lake Ngami. Some Nama groups live nearby; there is a stretch of good farming country, suitable for both stock and agriculture. The town of Epukiro (q.v.) is located on its banks.

EPUPA FALLS. A natural phenomenon on the Kunene (or Cunene) River between Angola and Namibia, the Epupa Falls occur 80 miles (129 kilometers) downstream (west) from the Ruacana Falls (q.v.). The Epupa Falls have a 118-foot (36-meter) vertical drop, roaring through a slim chasm barely 6 meters (20 feet) wide. The Kunene then flows into the Baynes Mountains. The area has rock outcroppings interspersed with vegetation and baobab trees populated by baboons. Palm trees and crocodiles are common near the banks of the many cataracts. "Epupa" is a Herero word referring to the foam produced by the falls. As Namibia experienced rising electricity demand after independence, it began to look at the Epupa Falls as a source of hydroelectric power to supplement the Ruacana Falls station. In late 1991 the cabinet approved a feasibility study and an environmental impact study of the project, with the hope of beginning construction in the mid-1990s. The new plant could potentially generate 450 mw annually, almost twice the capacity of 240 mw now produced at Ruacana. Its potential annual energy output of 1750 gwh would alone equal the total annual output in 1991 of Swawek, the Namibia power utility. The facility could take seven years to build, but would then be able to sell surplus capacity to South Africa and other neighbors. A dam with a storage capacity of 5000 mn cubic meters would be constructed on the Kunene River.

ERIKSSON, AXEL WILHELM (1846–1901). One of the most important pioneers in Namibia, this hunter and trader became known as the Merchant Prince of all the country north of the Orange River and south of the Kunene River (thus all of Namibia). His partner in trade, Anders Ohlsson, testified to a commission that their business turnover in Great Namaqualand, Damaraland, and Ovamboland amounted to £200,000 per annum in the late nineteenth century. Born at Vanesborg, Sweden, Axel was apprenticed as a nineteen-year-old to C. J. Andersson (q.v.) on a three-year contract. In late 1865 or early 1866, he reached Cape Town, where he joined with

Andersson and T. C. Een in exploring Africa's interior. In May 1866, the three of them reached Walvis Bay by boat, and then went by land to Otjimbingwe. Een and Eriksson were sent by Anderson to Ovambo. They departed on September 22, 1866. During October Eriksson was mauled by a leopard. However, the next year he went with Andersson to patrol the northern border along the Kunene River. After Andersson's death that year, Eriksson proceeded north to the Kunene River. He spent several years hunting elephants; he had great success on an expedition in 1870 and had a very successful elephant hunt in 1877 along the Okavango River.

Eriksson married, and his son Axel Francis Eriksson became a prominent artist in Namibia. In 1871 A. W. Eriksson joined in a partnership with Anders Ohlsson, a Swedish brewer and businessman in Cape Town. Eriksson was successful in running a trading company with its offices in Omaruru, and stores at both Omaruru and Walvis Bay. A. W. Eriksson and Company was a flourishing business in the 1870s, and many traders and hunters worked for it. He led or set up numerous expeditions to northern Namibia or to Lake Ngami. By 1878 about forty Europeans were in his employ plus an untold number of Africans. Although he and his family lived at Omaruru, he traveled north to Okahandja to witness one of W. C. Palgrave's (q.v.) meetings with the Hereros. The same year Eriksson was with the Thirstland Trekkers (q.v.) and witnessed their plight. Along with Jan Hofmeyr, Eriksson was responsible for alerting the Cape Colony to their difficulties, which resulted in public donations. Financial problems developed for Eriksson himself after the second Nama-Herero War began in August 1880. Many of the hunters and traders were unable to pay their debts, and Eriksson's Company lost money. Nevertheless, he gave many of them assistance to travel to Cape Town.

Throughout the 1880s Eriksson continued to lead expeditions around Namibia and into Botswana (to Lake Ngami) and Angola. Occasionally he led punitive raids against Africans who robbed or killed Europeans. In the late 1880s Eriksson dissolved his partnership with Ohlsson and moved from Omaruru to a cattle farm near Namutoni. He also became involved with an unsuccessful exploration team seeking minerals in Botswana. In 1892–93 he returned to Sweden and England for a visit. After his return he spent a great deal of time in Ovamboland, where he and his companions were well-received by African leaders. In 1897 he worked with Africans to show them how to inoculate their cattle against rinderpest (q.v.), which had devastated many herds. Africans near the Etosha Pan called him ''Karuwapa'' (''The Pale-Faced One''). He was always interested in zoology, and even called new species to the attention of the scientific community. He had three brothers who also spent many years as hunters and traders in Namibia and Angola, but his activities exceeded the others by far. He died near Grootfontein on May 30, 1901, having been one of the most important of all the early European traders, explorers, and pioneers in Namibia. The expeditions he sponsored were among the very first (for Europeans) into Ovamboland, northern Kaokoveld, and the upper reaches of the Okavango River.

ERONGO MOUNTAINS. One of the most striking ranges in Namibia, the view from Etiro in the Karabib district is that of the back of a dragon and the steep escarpment provides a dramatic vista. The range of volcanic rock and granite covers an area of about thirty miles (forty-eight kilometers) in diameter in the Omaruru district, south west of the town of Omaruru and north of Usakos. Boksberg (7830 feet) and Kransberg are its tallest peaks. The Erongo Mountains are in the shape of a ring with steep sides and an interior plateau with hills. Several passes cut across the ring. Because the inner plateau is lower than the ring, it resembles a volcano. There is little rainfall, so vegetation is sparse and waterholes scarce. Nevertheless, leopards, kudu, and zebra have inhabited the area, and when the missionary, Johannes Roth, explored the mountains in 1850, he was repeatedly molested by rhinocerosi. Ethnologists have reported the Erongo Mountains as being inhabited by Berg-Damas (q.v.). The mountains and the area to the south near Ameib were the sites of the discovery of tin in 1910. It exists in both alluvial deposits and in reefs of pegmatite and quartz. Tin exporting began in 1911, and the first tin-mining company was the

Erongo Zinn-Gesellschaft, formed in December 1910. The caves and overhangs of the mountains also contain many fine examples of rock paintings. The well-known Philipp's Cave (q.v.) with its "White Elephant" is on the "Ameib" farm in the Erongos.

EROS AIRPORT. Windhoek's "old" airport, it once had the name J. G. Strijbm Airport, but that name was transferred to the new one built in the mid-1960s. The name was then changed to Eros, a reference to the nearby Eros Mountains (q.v.). Namibia's first scheduled air service began on August 5, 1931, when a small plane carried mail and one passenger from Windhoek to several towns to the north. In January 1952 a new era in its aviation history began when South African Airways had its first direct flight between Johannesberg and Windhoek. Flights to Europe began the next year. However, despite a new terminal and control buildings built in the late 1950s, the original airport left much to be desired. Its location between the mountains made it susceptible to sudden wind changes and strong drafts. Also, its best runways were too short for the newer, larger aircraft. Thus a new airport was completed and the old name was transferred. The Eros Airport continues to schedule flight services within the country and is available for charter services and private planes.

EROS MOUNTAINS. Along with the Otjihavera Mountains, the Eros are the eroded edges of the Neudam Plateau. They are on the eastern side of the Windhoek Valley, a six- to nine-mile-wide depression that stretches from the Aus Mountains to the Swakop River near Okahandja. The name "Eros" has nothing to do with the god of love, but comes from the Nama term for a bush that grows there which bears very sour but visually attractive red or yellow plum-like fruit. The height of the Eros range averages about 6000 feet (1830 meters).

ESTORFF, GENERAL LUDWIG VON (1859–1943). Born in Hanover, Germany, he entered the army and was sent to Namibia in 1894 as a captain in the Schutztruppe. He was involved in a number of battles against the African peoples, and was honored by the Germans for his bravery combined with self-restraint. He was nicknamed "der alte Romer" (the old Roman). He became a friend of the Boers during the second Anglo-Boer War and, representing General Leut-wein, concluded a treaty with the Boers which granted them the right to religious and educational freedoms. He wrote a book on the Anglo-Boer War, published in 1902, and later a book of recollections in 1912. During the war with the Hereros, Estorff (now a major) was successful (on February 24, 1903) in forcing the Hereros away from the vicinity of Omaruru in a skirmish that the German press played up as the Battle of Otjihinamaparero, thus securing Western Herero-land for the German forces. In August 1904 he led a force of 500 German soldiers that held the eastern arc of the circle surrounding Waterberg, in one of the critical battles of the war. Following the Battle of Waterberg, his force set up a camp at Okatawbaka. At the beginning of 1906 Estorff was commander of the German troops in southern Namibia near the Orange River. In late February his task was to stop the Nama nationalist Jacob Marengo (q.v.). He thought he had Marengo surrounded at Kumkum on March 13, but the Nama fighter and his men neatly escaped the trap. By December, however, von Estorff (promoted to lieutenant colonel) con-ducted the talks with Bondels leaders that led to a peaceful settlement to the Nama-German conflict. On March 31, 1907, the German government declared the territory to be pacified and reduced the German forces to 4000 men, under von Estorff's command. He remained commander-in-chief in Namibia until 1911.

ETEMBA. The name of a farm owned by a German, Walter Kahn, it is the site of numerous unique rock engravings in the nearby hills and mountains. Kahn turned it into a profitable rest camp with attractions for tourists. It is located twenty-five miles west of Omaruru in the Erongo Mountains. The name is a Herero word for "Resting Place," as oxwagons had used it as a stopping point in travel between Swa-kopmund and Omaruru.

The battle of Etemba was an important event in Herero

history, probably occurring in the early nineteenth century, but far to the east of the Etemba farm. Vedder reports it to be in the Sandveld, perhaps even in Botswana's Kalahari Desert. Hereros, Namas, and Boers all had allowed their cattle to wander east across the border in the area of Ghanzi. Tswanas took for themselves some of these cattle, and Hereros raided the Tswanas' herds in return. War between the two groups continued for weeks, with many dying on both sides. Ndebele warriors joined on the side of the Tswanas, and their superior assegais and shields slowed the Hereros. A Herero attack was stalled in the quagmires and bogs near Lake Ngami, but they killed the Tswana leader and felt they were the victors. While the Hereros gained new grazing ground, they lost some of their best warriors, and the Pyrrhic victory is remembered in Herero proverbs. Maherero's father fought in the Battle of Etemba as a young man.

ETOSHA NATIONAL PARK. After the discovery of Etosha Pan (q.v.) in 1851 by Sir Francis Galton and Charles John Andersson, more and more Europeans found their way to the Pan and its tremendous population of game animals and birds. It became a hunter's paradise. In 1907 German Governor Friedrich von Lindequist proclaimed a game reserve covering 104,800 square kilometers. This was later reduced to 57,920 square kilometers, and reduced even further by the Odendaal Commission Report (q.v.) to its present 22,270 square kilometers, of which the Etosha Pan itself occupies about 6000 square kilometers. Before the Odendaal Commission excised the Kaokoveld area, Etosha was the largest game park in the world, and probably the only one that was a complete ecological unit. With the elimination of Kaokoveld, however, major paths of game migration have been cut. (Parts of the Kaokoveld have been made into a separate reserve, and the others areas are adjacent to great scenic conservation areas.) Despite these cuts, the park's remaining 8,598 square miles makes it larger than the American state of New Jersey.

The variety of birds and game in the park is enormous. Elephants, lions, leopards, cheetah, kudu, springbok, gemsbok, giraffe, zebra, black-faced impala, elands, rhino, hyena, jackals, dik-dik are just a few of the mammals. The birds include ostriches, bustards, flamingo, pelicans, shrike, spoonbills, and countless others. Rainfall, to aid the vegetation as well as to provide vital fluids, averages only eighteen inches a year. But some years are very bad, so the government has drilled fifty-five wells, mostly in the drier west, in the last thirty years. Conscious of the tourists—an estimated fifty thousand a year—the government has provided modern facilities since opening it formally to tourists in 1958. A wire game fence five hundred miles long and eight and a half feet high surrounds the park. A great amount of conservation work goes on within these boundaries, and rare animals have been imported from other parts of Namibia to make it easier to ensure the survival of rare species. The human species is also cared for. A picturesque old German fort, Fort Namutoni (q.v.), has become a modern rest stop complete with a restaurant and swimming pool. The main administrative camp is Okaukuejo. Travellers can stay at their luxurious rondavels (circular bungalows) and watch animals drinking at the spring. Halali, located halfway between the other two, is a modern camp, begun in 1967. All are on the southern segment of the Etosha Pan. The park is closed during the rainy season (generally November to April) because of the muddy roads and malarial mosquitoes. Low humidity and moderate temperatures make it attractive the rest of the year. Easiest access to the park is through organized tour groups starting in Windhoek or Swakopmund.

ETOSHA PAN. Located in northern Namibia, just south of Ovamboland, the Etosha Pan is a very large but shallow depression estimated to cover from 1800 to 2300 square miles (or about 6000 square kilometers). It is about 80 miles (128 kilometers) long and 45 miles (72 kilometers) wide. Its origins are uncertain, but many believe that the Kunene River (q.v.), now to the north of Etosha, formerly flowed into the Pan instead of into the Atlantic Ocean. When the Kunene bed shifted (or alternatively, when major geographical and climatic changes hit Africa), perhaps twelve million years ago, the great lake that had existed began to dry up, having been denied its tributaries. Thus the bed of the great Pan is clay saturated with highly alkaline mineral salts. From its salty surface it received its name, as "Etosha" means "big white place." Yet the Pan is not always dry. There is an average annual rainfall of 18 inches (451 mm) and some waters reach the Pan from the Cuvelai system, with its origins in southern Angola. The rainy season is November to April. The Pan attracts a tremendous assortment of birds and mammals, so many in fact that the surrounding Etosha National Park (q.v.) is considered one of the finest in the world. Literally millions of flamingo visit the Pan yearly, in addition to pelicans, ostriches, elephants, lions, gemsbok, eland, kudu, springbok, and so on. All but small parts of the northern edge of the Etosha Pan are contained in the Etosha National Park. Aside from the Ovambo people who have visited from the north, Heikom "Bushmen" have also lived in the vicinity of the Pan. The Pan and park are tremendous tourist attractions. The first Europeans to see the Pan were the explorers Sir Francis Galton and Charles John Andersson (qq.v.) in 1851.

EUNDA. Depending on the source, one will find the Ovambo people classified in either seven or eight distinct tribes. When eight are named, one of them is the Eunda tribe, and in any case the smallest of them all by far (1 percent of the Ndonga, for example). Other times they are listed as combined with another small group as the Kolonkadhi-Eunda (q.v.).

EVANGELICAL LUTHERAN CHURCH (ELK). The independent, Black-run successor to the German-founded Rhenish Mission Society (q.v.), its membership probably numbers more than 150,000. The Rhenish missionaries had functioned primarily in central and southern Namibia, and in fact had encouraged the Finnish Mission Society to assist in the territory by proselytizing in the north. For years the RMS had refused to train Black pastors, causing a degree of racial tension. As early as 1926 Black church assistants had formed the Nama Onderwysers in Evangelistebond. A number of separatist movements started in the next decades, including one founded by Hosea Kutako (q.v.). After much pressure from Germany to decolonize itself, the RMS gave its church local autonomy in 1957 as the Evangelise Lutherse Kerk (ELK). In 1967 it became fully independent. The first non-white head of the church was Prases (equivalent to Bishop) Dr. Johannes Lukas de Vries, who took over in 1967. A similar independence drive within the Finnish Church produced the Evangelical Lutheran Ovambokavango Church (ELOK) (q.v.). The two churches are linked in a confederal manner in the United Evangelical Lutheran Church of Southwest Africa (VELKSWA). The two churches have frequently spoken out in public against apartheid and all forms of social injustice.

EVANGELICAL LUTHERAN OVAMBOKAVANGO CHURCH (ELOK). The autonomous, independent, Black-run product of a century of work by the Finnish Missionary Society (FMS) (q.v.), this church became an outspoken opponent of apartheid and a supporter of Namibian independence. Finnish missionaries began their work in Namibia on July 9, 1870, working exclusively in Ovamboland. In 1923 they began training native ministers. The first seven were ordained in 1925, and there were thirty-one working as ministers by 1942. The creation of the autonomous, independent Ovambokavango Church (ELOK) occurred in 1954. In 1960 the synod chose its first Black bishop, Dr. Leonard Auala (q.v.). Gradually white missionaries were replaced by Africans. In 1972 only four of ninety-seven ministers were European. An estimate indicated that ELOK has over 300,000 members, making it the largest church in the country. Bishop Auala frequently spoke out against South African rule of Namibia. He was active in linking ELOK with the Evangelical Lutheran Church (ELK) in a confederal church body, the United Evangelical Church of South West Africa (VELKSWA), which bitterly condemned the system of apartheid and called for Namibian independence. The most significant act of retribution, blamed on South Africa by most Africans, was the destruction of the ELOK presses at Onipa. At 3 AM on May 11, 1973, a dynamite charge blew up two large printing presses. The fire destroyed two thousand Bibles and many church and school books. It seemed aimed at silencing the church paper, Omukwetu, which had been publishing pages of political news and comments. The church rebuilt its publishing enterprise, but it was again mysteriously blown up in 1980. In June 1982 it was re-opened, only to be blown up later in the year by a South African anti-aircraft shell. A nurses' home run by ELOK was destroyed on April 23, 1982, also bombed from the air by a South African military plane.

EXPORTS. In the nineteenth century, livestock sold by Africans were the only exports. Early in the twentieth century, diamonds were discovered and became a major source of revenue. The fishing industry grew, expanding in quantity of catches, as well as through the development of processing plants. Sardines, rock lobsters, fish meal, and fish oil became significant until overfishing hit the industry in the 1970s. Karakul pelts ("Persian lamb") became major export items in the 1930s and have continued to earn income. Other mining besides diamond has brought export income, includ-ing tin, copper, zinc, and lead, but the most important source of export earnings for the foreseeable future is uranium.

EXTERMINATION ORDER. The famous "Schrecklichkeit" or-der was issued on October 2, 1904, by German General Lothar von Trotha. A seasoned colonial fighter, von Trotha already had a reputation for ferocity from his work in East Africa. He explained that "His Majesty the Emperor . . . expected that I would crush the uprising with any means necessary and then inform him of the reasons for the uprising." He explained to Gen. Leutwein, "I know the tribes of Africa. They are all alike. They only respond to force. It was and is my policy to use force with terrorism and even brutality. I shall annihilate the revolt-ing tribes with streams of blood and streams of gold." He told his superiors, "I believe that the Herero must be destroyed as a nation." It should not be surprising, therefore, that von Trotha's "Extermination Order" during the Herero-German War, read in part:

Hereros are no longer German subjects. . . . All the Hereros must leave the land. If the people do not do this, then I will force them to do it with the great guns. Any Herero found within the German borders with or without a gun, with or without cattle, will be shot. I shall no longer receive any women or children. I will drive them back to their people or I will shoot them. This is my decision for the Herero people. The Great General of the Mighty Kaiser.

Other German leaders, both in Namibia and Germany, objected to the order, saying it was unChristian, not feasible, economically senseless, and would give the Germans a bad reputation among civilized people. Pressured from both sides, the Kaiser decided in December (having put the decision off as long as possible) to order von Trotha to rescind the order. The general reluctantly did, but said the surrendering Hereros would be chained, used for forced labor, branded, and shot if they failed to reveal where weapons were hidden.

- F -

FAHLGRAS, BATTLE OF (variant: VAALGRAS). A German supply train was travelling through southern Namibia at the height of conflict with the Namas when it was attacked by a group of warriors on October 29, 1905. The leader of the attacking Namas was the great chief, Hendrik Witbooi (q.v.). He was mortally wounded in the raid, and though dragged to safety by his men, the old leader quickly died from loss of blood. Peace between the Germans and the Witboois came about a month later. The raid occurred at a place called Fahlgras, about 100 kilometers northeast of Keetmanshoop.

FARMING. *See* AGRICULTURE.

FEDERAL COLOURED PEOPLE'S PARTY OF SWA (FCPP). Originally known as the South West Africa Coloured People's Organization (q.v.) when it was founded in 1959, it took this new name in 1973. Its leader was Andrew Kloppers, Sr. It won the election for the Coloured Council in 1974, and then was renamed the Labour Party (q.v.) in August 1975.

FEDERAL CONVENTION OF NAMIBIA. An election alliance formed in Rehoboth late in 1988, it was an attempt by some of its organizers to bring back the concept of the earlier National Convention (q.v.). For a brief time it was even known as the Second National Convention. The alliance consisted of five groups: (1) Democratic Action for Namas, (2) Liberated Democratic Party (q.v.), (3) NUDO Progressive Party (q.v.), (4) National Progressive Party, and (5) Namibia People's Liberation Front (q.v.). The last named is itself an alliance of six smaller groups: (1) Bondelswarts Council, (2) Damara Executive Committee, (3) Damara Christian Democratic Party, (4) Riemvasmaak United Party, (5) United Liberation Movement, and (6) Voice of the People.

The programme of the FCN is called a Christian-based platform, and supports a federal system. It insists that the central government must recognize the diversity of all of the country's ethnic groups and respect their languages, traditions and local autonomy. Its economic policy favors free enterprise within a mixed economy.

The alliance's top leaders in the election period were: president Hans Diergaardt and first vice-president Patrick Limbo. In the November 1989 elections, the FCN received a total of 10,452 votes, placing it sixth of the ten competing groups. Almost half of its votes came from Rehoboth. Only one seat in the Assembly was earned by the FCN. Hans Diergaardt took this seat, but when he resigned for personal reasons, Mburumba Kerina took his place.

FEDERAL PARTY. 1. The abbreviated name of the "Federal Coloured People's Party," the principal Coloured party until it changed its name in August 1975 to the Labour Party of South West Africa (q.v.).

2. The party later bearing this name was known as the United South West African Party from 1927 until 1971 when it became the South West Africa branch of South Africa's United Party. In October 1975 it became the Federal Party in order to emphasize the need to divorce itself from South African politics. The party had urged federal arrangement within Namibia, based on regional legislatures and a single National Assembly. It had proposed that whites control the National Assembly for a time, gradually giving Africans

greater representation and ultimately control of the Assembly as Africans achieved educational and economic advancement. The Federal Party was the opposition party in the all-white Parliament, receiving 30 percent of the votes in 1974. In April 1976 Bryan O'Linn called for a boycott of elections to choose a delegate to the South African Parliament. He urged whites to concentrate on making changes within Namibia, instead of paying allegiance to South African rule. O'Linn had been a member of the party but had resigned because its outlook was too narrow. He rejoined in 1975 and became its leader the next year.

Under O'Linn's leadership the Federal Party opened its membership to all racial groups, thus losing some of its more conservative members. In 1977 he entered into an alliance, the Namibian National Front (NNF) (q.v.), which represented many of Namibia's ethnic groups. This "moderate" grouping sought an orderly, multiracial, liberal, and capitalist solution to the Namibia question—an alternative to both SWAPO and the right-wing white groups. However, O'Linn took the Federal Party out of the NNF by mid-1979 because some of the Black parties, especially the SWANU representatives, did not accept a non-racial approach, preferring a kind of reverse discrimination. There were also personality clashes with some of the SWANU leaders who followed Maoist theories.

When the Federal Party boycotted the December 1978 elections, it lost a great number of its white supporters, who had favored participation in the National Assembly elections. In the mid 1980s the party still existed, but its membership was not large. O'Linn remained its leader, and John Kirkpatrick its chairman (the second in charge). The party leadership did not wish to be part of any elections that did not lead directly to a Namibian settlement, and would only try to rebuild the party when internationally supervised elections occur. Thus the party remained relatively inactive, meeting about twice a year to keep its organization intact. In 1984 the Federal Party decided not to participate in the Multi-Party Conference (q.v.). It also did not take part in the 1989 elections.

FEDERATED TRIBES. Six separate Nama tribes that entered into a loose federation in the eighteenth century under the leadership of the Red Nation (q.v.). The other five were the Franzmannschen Hottentots (q.v.), the Feldschuhträgers (q.v.), the Zwartboois (q.v.), the Groot-doden (q.v.), and the Kara-oan.

FELDSCHUTRÄGERS (variants: VELSKOENDRAERS, VELDSCHOENDRAGERS). A group of Namas who are elsewhere referred to by Dr. Vedder as //Hawoben, they live in an area south of Keetsmanshoop, generally east of the Karras Hills. There is an area southwest of Keetsmannshoop today called Feldschuhhorn. The unusual German name for the group means literally, "wearers of field shoes." They are given credit for having introduced to the territory a new idea, that of giving their feet better protection by attaching a thin skin to protect the foot. This group was the first to join the Red Nation (q.v.) as one of the six "federated tribes" and to recognize their own chief to be subordinate to the leader of the Red Nation. According to Dr. Vedder's map, in the mid-nineteenth century the Feldschuhträgers were to be found somewhat north of their present location—north of keetsmanshoop and east of Berseba. In fact they drifted further north in the 1850s when, under the leadership of Chief Hendrik Zes (q.v.) they periodically raided the Hereros. In March 1857, however, he led his men in an unsuccessful raid against the Hereros, in which many of his men were killed. The survivors fled south without the cattle they had sought. In 1860 Zes led his bands against white settlers and their cattle posts. However over 250 head were stolen from him in a retaliatory raid by Willem Swartbooi. Zes was eager to gain cattle, and joined with Christian Afrikander (q.v.), hoping to raid the Hereros. However Zes and his followers were evidently not with Christian in the 1863 raid on Otjimbingwe where many of the attackers, including Christian Afrikander, were killed. Zes continued to raid for cattle, including an 1864 attack on 1600 head of Charles Andersson's cattle being herded to the Cape by Frederick Green. The successful raid led to a counterattack by Andersson in June 1864. Finally on September 3, 1865, Zes and Jan Jonker Afrikander led another attack on Otjimbingwe, in which Zes was killed by the successful Herero defenders.

By the 1870s the Namas were petitioning the British government for protection from the encroaching Europeans. Paul Links was leader of the Feldschuhträgers in 1878 when officials at the Cape attempted to set up meetings with Nama groups. The Africans themselves were not always at peace with each other. A leadership dispute between Moses Witbooi and Paul Visser, for example, led to an attack by Hendrik Witbooi on January 23, 1888, on the village of Arisemab, then the leader of the Feldschuhträgers, who had supported Visser. Arisemab's son was killed, and while he was only wounded, the captain ("chief") committed suicide. Visser retaliated and drove Hendrik Witbooi in retreat and, ultimately killed Moses Witbooi. By 1894 Hendrik Witbooi was looking for aid against Leutwein and the Germans. Chief Hans Hendrick of the Feldschuhträgers turned down Witbooi's request, but allowed a small number of his followers to join him. Ten years later, however, Hans Hendrick openly joined Witbooi, the Red Nation, and other Nama in rebelling against the Germans, an enterprise that ultimately failed. As a result of the German victory, the tribal leadership system of the defeated tribes was abolished, and the movable and immovable tribal possessions were confiscated.

FINGER OF GOD. Translation of the Nama word Mukurob (q.v.), a notable Namibian landmark. It collapsed in December 1988.

FINLAND. Because of the work of the Finnish Mission Church (q.v.) in Namibia, there has been an interest in Namibia's future that is greater than one would have anticipated in this Scandinavian country. Volunteers and funds have come from Finland (from the government and from private individuals and groups) to aid in such important areas as health and education. It may be of some significance that the former UN commissioner for Namibia, Mr. Martti Ahtisaari (q.v.), a specialist at the UN on Namibia, is from Finland.

FINNISH MISSION CHURCH. When the German missionary Reverend Hugo Hahn (q.v.) realized in the 1860s that his Rhenish Mission Society would be unable to effectively proselytize the entire territory of South West Africa, he invited his Lutheran co-religionists in Finland to join him. Thus in mid-1868 the Finnish Mission Society agreed to send seven Finnish missionaries and three Christian craftsmen to work in this new mission field. They reached Walvis Bay in early 1869, and proceeded to the Rhenish mission station at Barmen. Since there were various military conflicts between Africans occurring at that time, it was decided that the ten Finns should stay for a while with Hahn at Otjimbingwe, before proceeding to their destination, Ovamboland. The battles persisted, so they stayed there for a year, learning the Herero language and gaining insights into local customs and missionary techniques. They entered Ovambo in 1870, establishing their first station on July 9 at Omandongo. Opposition from tribal leaders made acceptance come slowly, with initial conversions only twelve years later. An important member of the mission was Mertti Rautanen, who translated the Bible into the Oshindonga language. By 1890 there were only five missionaries and twenty-one African converts. The relationship became warmer, however, as attitudes on both sides changed (the early Finns had been very puritanical), and church influence grew. By 1910 there were fifteen missionaries and lay workers (including five women doctors) and two thousand Christians among the Ndonga Ovambos alone. Important new areas were opened when the women doctors began to arrive in 1908. The first hospital was built in 1911, and in 1913 a teacher training center was opened at Oniipa. About two new primary schools were established each year for the next four decades, so that by 1959 there were 350 teachers and 12,800 pupils in schools run by the mission church. Missionaries also taught the useful trades, such as carpentry and bricklaying, and made great efforts to improve agricultural methods and introduce new crops. A social revolution began as well, as the corps of women doctors inspired Ovambo women to strive for self-improvement, even equality with the men. Polygamy eventually disappeared. The Mission Society received its own printing press at Oniipa in 1901 and became involved in printing its own religious literature as well as some secular items. A monthly church paper, *Omukuetu* ("One of Us") has since become a fortnightly with a circulation of 10,000 copies.

In 1926 the church expanded eastward into the Kavango area, but an even more significant move occurred three years earlier when the church began to train African ministers. By 1972, out of ninety-seven ministers only four were whites. This naturally led to greater autonomy for the African ministers, and in 1954 the Finnish Mission Church was transformed into the autonomous and independent Evangelical Lutheran Ovambokavango Church (ELOK) (q.v.). Its leader was an African, Bishop Leonard Auala (q.v.), and it has a membership of at least 300,000. Longterm effects of the Finnish Mission Church include certainly its work and training in the fields of medicine, education, agriculture, and the trades. In addition, it has had subtler and perhaps more substantial effects. It seems to have emphasized broader nationality, so that Ovambos are less likely to see themselves as Ndonga or Kwanyama, but as Ovambos. The early training of ministers has imparted a degree of self-confidence that has made the Ovambo people the leaders of Namibia in pushing for political autonomy. It is probably not an accident that many of SWAPO's leaders are Ovambos, and that its membership is strongest in areas touched by the Finnish Mission Church. Bishop Auala has been an outspoken advocate for an independent Namibia under African leadership.

FIRE, SACRED. A very important aspect of the traditional way of life for many Namibian peoples, there have been both similarities and differences in the role played by the fire in the rituals of the tribes. Cattle are extremely important to the Hereros, and the man designated by inheritance and ritual as priest of the sacred fire is also keeper of the sacred herd. Thus in Herero villages, the sacred fire is near the cattle kraals. It is the responsibility of the priest's principal wife to keep the sacred fire burning. If it dies out, the traditionalists believe that disaster will befall the family, as the fire is a sacred inheritance from the ancestors. At night the wife looks after the coals, and the next morning her oldest daughter can assist her by kindling the coals to a bright flame. That is the signal for the day to begin (e.g., milking the cows, etc.).

The sacred fire was also the center of all important meetings and rituals. Marriages, funerals, council meetings, the naming of newborns, purification ceremonies, all these events occurred by the sacred ancestral fire. If the family moved to a new location, it carefully took the fire with it, and if the fire should become extinguished it could be restarted only with a whirling stick used by an ancestor to kindle his fire (these sticks were also carefully preserved). As a new village site was selected, the location of the new sacred fire was the first decision. A flaming brand lit from the old fire or its coals was the basis of the new one. Among the Ovambo the fire was located near the place where the chief slept, and was tended also by his principal wife or her daughter. It was not allowed to flame and only green wood from certain trees could be used to keep it going. District chiefs received coals from the central fire to start the fire in their own werfs (q.v.). The only food that could be cooked on the sacred fire was the last meal of men going off to war. The fire brought a blessing because it was thought to be a gift from their God, Kalunga.

Bushmen also have a sacred fire, but without a "chief" the head of the family is responsible for it. Only after he builds the fire can the building of huts begin. The family head has inherited the fire from his ancestors, and in turn he leaves it to his eldest son. Since all able-bodied men are hunting and the women are gathering, the care of the fire is left to the elderly who stay at the dwellings. Family health and success in hunting are owed to this fire. Only the family head may light this fire, using the words of a special prayer to their God, but again the principal wife must tend the embers so it shall flame again in the morning. If it should die out for any reason, only the family head could reignite it—even if it meant calling him home from the hunt. If the hunt has been good, the fire ("God's fire") receives the praise, but a poor hunt means the fire has been offended, perhaps because someone has broken the laws of the hunt. The best solution is then for the family head to replace it with a new fire. In any case, "God's fire" lasts only for one year. At the end of the rainy season a ceremony involves covering the glowing embers of the old fire one evening and beginning a new one the next morning, thus also beginning a new year.

FIRST NATIONAL DEVELOPMENT CORPORATION (ENOK). Known as the Bantu Investment Corporation (q.v.) until its name was changed in 1978, it is a state financial corporation that, through its subsidiaries, has maintained a monopoly of wholesale supply and credit. This has greatly limited the attempt of Africans to become independent in the small business area. ENOK (the letters are derived from its name in Afrikaans) also controls, directly or through associated agencies, industrial sites and marketing outlets. Defenders of ENOK point to successes such as an agricultural scheme begun in 1979 near Rundu in the extreme north near the Angolan border. There a 1235 acre (500 hactare) peanut and maize plantation has been very successful. Its manager says that its major value could be in demonstrating to local farmers new production methods that would help free Namibia from South African imports. Nevertheless, many Africans have seen ENOK as a way of preventing their economic advancement. In November, 1990 Namibia's Minister of Agriculture, Gerhard Hanekom, announced that the agriculture ministry would be assuming ownership of ENOK's farms and cattle ranches in the northern part of the country. However ENOK would continue administering them temporarily, pending the execution of a plan to convert them into agricultural development centers.

In mid-1992 the government announced that it was in the process of structuring two new agencies to take over the principal functions carried out by ENOK, an agricultural development corporation and an industrial development corporation. ENOK had continued to function since independence, but has been hampered by its image as a remnant of South African colonialism. If it is restructured out of existence, its principal commercial assets could be either sold or transferred to a holding company.

FISH RIVER (variants: GREAT FISH RIVER; OUB RIVER). It is a periodic river, originating northwest of Gibeon in the

Nauchas Highlands, that flows south for 475 miles (704 kilometers) until it joins the Orange River just east of Sendlings Drift. Its two major tributaries are the Lion and Konkiep rivers. While it appears to be dry, semi-permanent surface water comes through the sandy base much of the year. This results in pools that are home to the only freshwater fish in the country (thus its name). The Berseba Valley drained by the river is large, but relatively low rainfall leaves it with little runoff to maintain a steady flow; the river flows mostly in February and March. The Hardap Dam (q.v.) was built in 1962 for irrigation purposes and is thirteen miles (twenty-one kilometers) from Mariental. In its course, the river passes several major towns, notably Mariental, Gibeon, and Seeheim. It also passes through the spectacular Fish River Canyon (q.v.) for about forty miles (sixty-four kilometers). The hot springs called Ai-Ais are located thirty miles north of its confluence with the Orange River. With their high magnesium sulfate content, the springs are visited for medicinal purposes. The Fish River is the longest river flowing entirely within Namibia. It flooded in February and March 1988, causing extensive damage to Ai-Ais. Various Nama groups, notably the Witboois and the "Groot-doden" or //O-gein traditionally made their home in the Fish River Valley after coming north into Namibia. Scientists have found evidence of human settlements near the river that could date back 25,000 years.

FISH RIVER CANYON (variant: GRAND CANYON OF THE FISH RIVER). The second largest river canyon in the world, behind only the Grand Canyon of the Colorado River in the United States, this spectacularly beautiful gorge through which the Fish River twists for forty miles (sixty-four kilometers) is one of the scenic marvels in southern Africa. The gorge has a maximum depth of two thousand feet (six hundred meters), and on its floor the temperature rises to 113°F (45°C) during the day. Sporadic pools of water are precious for the canyon's fauna, which includes zebra, baboons, and several varieties of buck; a wide variety of Namibia's flora is also found there. Hot sulphurous springs also bubble up from the floor. The river itself flows intermittently, coming down in flood typically in February and March. The ravine itself is 161 kilometers long and up to 27 kilometers wide. A road runs along the eastern edge of the canyon for 58 kilometers and leads to a series of good viewing sites. A 90-kilometer hiking road along the bed of the canyon ends at Ai-Ais, a hot springs resort. Hiking is permitted only from May through August, and permits are needed for this very strenuous trail that takes up to four days to complete. The canyon, located in extreme southern Namibia, figured prominently in the Nama wars of resistance against the Germans that began in 1903. Soldiers' graves and military debris can be seen at various points along the river and in the valleys, and the Kara-oan Namas, one of the federated tribes, and the Franztmannschen Nama lived near Gochas. Anthropologists have found evidence that humans may have lived along the Fish River as long as 25,000 years ago.

FISHING INDUSTRY. Commercial fishing has been a major industry in Namibia. Since virtually no commercial fishing occurs along the country's rivers, the industry is limited to its Atlantic coast. A Portuguese mapmaker in 1489 called the Walvis Bay area Praia dos Sardinha (Sardine Coast). A century later other Portuguese sailors called it Bahia dos Baleas (Bay of Whales). Dutch and English sailors also named it after the many whales nearby. Whalers and sealers were found off the coast throughout the sixteenth and seventeenth centuries, and both industries thrived in the early nineteenth century. In 1856 the firm of De Pass, Spence and Company set up a coastal fishing and sealing industry to export oil and dried fish to Cape Town. Barry Munnik of Cape Town established a fishery there in 1859, exporting dried fish to Cape Town and Mauritius. A decision in 1898 to build a jetty at Walvis Bay by the Cape Government made this area competitive with the Germans at Swakopmund.

In 1922 four rock lobster factories were established at Lüderitz (where most of the territory's rock lobsters are found). The South African government recognized the possibilities of the new industry and encouraged its development by refraining from direct taxation. European markets were soon found, notably in France, but the worldwide depression of the 1930s hit the industry hard. A boom followed, however, and when World War II created a need for new, available foodstuffs, the rock lobster industry greatly expanded. Frozen lobster tails came into great demand. Six and a half million pounds were sold in 1948. Conservation rules at that time prevented overharvesting, and sales remained steady for a decade. All processors sold their frozen tails through the South African Frozen Rock Lobster Packers (Proprietary) Limited. A huge new market was found in the United States after the war. Fish meal also became an important product, as the total weight of the fish catch each year was about twenty million pounds. Only a third of that weight was sold as lobster tails. During the boom a fleet of forty-eight boats kept six factories busy. Overexploitation finally hit the industry, however, and by 1971 the catch was 40 percent short of even its lower quota. The lobster industry continues at much lower levels, as foreign fishing fleets are no longer dominating the area.

Whaling has been common off the coast for centuries, and in 1923 the whaling station at Walvis Bay was reopened. In that year, 296 whales were caught, but by 1930 the development of large factory ships and the consequent overharvesting of the whales devastated the population of the giant mammals, and the station was again closed.

In 1924 the South West Africa Cold Storage and Stock Farmers Limited began building cold-storage rooms, abattoirs, and a fish-canning plant at Walvis Bay, anticipating profitability in a frozen meat and fish exporting market. The plant was inadequate, however, and was only used experimentally until the project was abandoned. There were unsuccessful attempts to revive it until the Ovenstone family (*see* OVENSTONE INVESTMENTS) founded the Walvis Bay Canning Company in 1943, again in the wartime response to the need for foodstuffs, for the purpose of salting and canning snoek. Five years later the Ovenstones took a giant step by beginning the new pilchard industry. It was to be based on an abundant little fish, the *Sardinops ocellata,* the common pilchard. The factory they had bought became the largest canning unit on the coast, a far cry from its desolate failures in 1925. Enormous catches fed a huge market, the fleet grew from six boats to twenty-four, and the plant was expanded to cover four acres. Only government quotas prevented the Ovenstones from expanding. No one company was allowed more than twenty boats. In 1959 the Walvis Bay Canning Company alone was exporting forty million cans of sardines, plus producing 8000 tons of fishmeal in 100-pound bags and about half a million gallons of fish oil, and this was only one of six licensed pilchard factories. By 1970 the value of the industry doubled to about R34 million. Again overfishing caught up with the industry, and severe government quotas were established. In addition, a new emphasis on anchovies developed. The 1969 catch was 676,000 tons of pilchards and 180,000 tons of anchovies. Overexploitation and imposed quotas led the pilchard totals to drop to 28,000 tons in 1979 and 59,260 in 1988. Anchovies increased to 183,428 tons in 1983 and dropped to 13,685 in 1984, again due to overexploitation and imposed quotas. The catch of anchovies has been unstable since then, reaching 377,276 tons in 1987 and 114,784 in 1988. Anchovies are also used for fish meal, a high-protein product important in cattle, sheep, pig, and poultry feeds. The USA is the largest market for it. Another byproduct, fish oil, is used in the production of such diverse articles as linoleum, pressed board, and varnishes.

The government has moved to protect its 200 mile exclusive economic zone (EEZ) by restricting the number of foreign vessels engaged in deep sea fishing off its shore, especially those operating illegally. Unregistered trawlers have been identified, and several Spanish-owned ships were captured and detained in 1990. Some previous agreements with South African concession owners must be honored until 1994, but Namibian fleet owners and individuals have been promised top priority at that time. This is especially true of inshore pelagic fishing. This resource has recovered well from the overfishing, notably the pilchard and the Cape horse mackerel.

FLORA. Among the more interesting of the plants and trees found in Namibia are the kokerbaum and camel thorn trees, and the desert plant *Welwitschia Mirabilis*. The Moringo Ovalifolia is a tree found only in Namibia. Palms, wild figs, wild dates, different species of acacia, buffalo thorn, tambotie, and mopane are among the other trees found in the country. Cactus grows in the desert areas, as do many varieties of small plants and shrubs that need little water. Some have beautiful flowers, such as "The Morning Star," with its yellow blossoms and "The South West Edelweiss," with its tiny red, white, and green flower.

FOOD AND CANNING WORKER'S UNION. One of the earlier significant unions in Namibia, its origins are in South Africa. Based in the Cape, the union sent its president, Frank Marquard, in 1949 to Lüderitz to organize the fish canning workers in that center of the fish canning industry. It was basically a union for the Coloured workers there. In 1952 Ray Alexander was also sent, and a branch of the union was established. It immediately moved to try to get better wages and conditions, but just after an agreement had been negotiated, the police attacked and broke up the branch meeting. They forced the members to disband the branch, and Ray Alexander was banned. He was ordered to resign immediately from the union. Ties with the Cape Union were forbidden.

FORBIDDEN AREA. *See SPERRGEBIET.*

FORD, MARTHA. The daughter of Hermanus Beukes, a politician whose family (q.v.) had been active in Rehoboth local politics, Mrs. Ford was also active in the Rehoboth Volkspartei (q.v.). In 1974–75, she and Dr. Stellmacher led other pro-SWAPO members of that group to split off and join the Namibia National Convention (q.v.). In November 1976 the Volkspartei announced its intention to merge into SWAPO. Meanwhile Mrs. Ford became chairman of the SWAPO Women's Movement and a member of the SWAPO Executive. She became a major force in organizing and leading SWAPO women, and urged better representation of women in its decision making. In 1979 she was detained for a period by South Africa.

FORSYTH, CHARLES CODRINGTON. Captain of Her Majesty's steam frigate *Victorious,* Forsyth stepped ashore on Penguin Island (q.v.) on May 5, 1866, and declared British sovereignty over all the islands, rocks, and inlets along the Namibian coast.

FORT NAMUTONI. Now the eastern-most tourist camp in the Etosha National Park (q.v.), it began when the German government decided in May 1901 to establish a police station on the southeastern portion of the Etosha Pan. A fountain called Klein Namutoni flows nearby. A reed building was sufficient for the small contingent stationed there at first, but after several minor conflicts with the Ovambos, it was decided to place a larger garrison there. A considerably strengthened fort was needed to fend off attacks and to make it self-sufficient, thus near the end of 1902 a fort was completed that resembled an old castle, including four towers. On January 28, 1904, during an uprising against European colonists, a force of about five hundred Ovambos under King Nehale of the Eastern Ondonga attacked and surrounded the fort. It was such a surprise that only seven soldiers had been stationed there that particular night. The man in charge was Sergeant Bruno Lassmann, a sanitation sergeant. The Germans fired in return until their ammunition was exhausted after a week, then escaped from the fort during a nighttime lull in the fighting. The Ovambos destroyed the fort, but it was rebuilt in a somewhat larger version in 1907. The current fort, as renovated by the government in the 1950s to become an Etosha rest camp, has facilities such as a swimming pool, restaurant, and gift shop. Yet its gleaming white walls and towers set behind a grove of palm trees give the impression of a functioning outpost of some foreign legion. On February 15, 1950, it was proclaimed a National Monument, and the restoration followed.

FORT WILHELM (variant: WILHELMFESTE). Founded in 1889 at a spot called Tsoabis by Captain Kurt von Francois (q.v.), it was about 80 miles (129 kilometers) west of Windhoek and 40 miles south of Karibib. Described once as "the Gibraltar of Hereroland," its location was chosen for its position at a key road junction as well as its excellent defensive advantages. Plentiful water supply and pastureland added to its appeal to the German soldiers.

FRANCOIS, MAJOR CURT (variant: KURT) VON (1853–1931). German military officer and a founder of modern Windhoek. Although born in Luxembourg, he joined the Prussian army. Prior to his Namibia assignment he had accompanied the explorers von Wissman and Grenfell on trips through the Belgian Congo, and in 1887 he explored Togoland on the west coast of Africa. He was surveying the border to Togoland when the German government decided to send a small military force to Namibia to help pacify the Africans. A group of heavily armed volunteers was sent, under the guise of a scientific expedition. Its leader then was Lieut. Hugo von Francois, but shortly after, his brother Curt, a captain at the time, was instructed to leave his Togoland work to serve as commander. The small force landed at Walvis Bay on June 24, 1889, prepared to assert German authority in the territory. His civilian predecessor. Dr. H. E. Goering, had let the Africans defy his authority. His special charge was to defeat Hendrick Witbooi (q.v.). The contingent went first to Otjimbingwe (q.v.), where it arrived on July 8. The Hereros were peaceful, and the soldiers settled down in buildings of the Deutsche Kolonialgesellschaft (q.v.). A principal opponent of the Germans, trader and concessionaire Robert Lewis (q.v.) was in South Africa at the time, but two of his assistants tried to incite the Hereros against the troops, without much success. Since Lewis would not return to Namibia for several weeks, Captain von Francois took his troops to Omaruru, where they received a friendly welcome, and then to Usakos (July 20). An incorrect rumor that Lewis was returning with a military force sent the Germans quickly to Otjimbingwe where they arrived on August 5. Von Francois requested that the German warship at Walvis Bay send a division of marines and a cannon to discourage the Hereros from joining with Lewis. Meanwhile he feared the anti-German sentiment among some Hereros (especially Maherero) and took his troops suddenly out of

Otjimbingwe, without informing the Herero leaders, a very undiplomatic act. A confrontation almost ensued as the Hereros tried to turn the wagons back, and von Francois responded by ordering his soldiers to guard the supply wagons with fixed bayonets. The Germans then travelled twenty miles west to Tsoabis, where von Francois ordered the building of Wihelmsfeste (Fort Wilhelm, q.v.) at a very defendable site. Von Francois tried to halt the spread of ammunition to the Hereros by searching all wagons for contraband, a practice that Herero leaders quickly denounced. Nevertheless, they also proposed a conference with von Francois to clear up difficulties, but he rejected it. The Hereros thus became much more hostile, especially after the German troops aggressively searched a wagon belonging to Lewis, their friend. The German government notified von Francois that the fifty extra soldiers would be sent, but that they should not be used against Hereros, only against white agitators. While waiting for the reinforcements, von Francois travelled to Lake Ngami and then to Rehoboth, where he was joined by his brother Hugo, commanding the new men.

In mid-May 1890, Curt von Francois and Dr. Goering, recently appointed German imperial commissioner for South West Africa, held a meeting with sixty Herero chiefs, trying to soothe relations. Their success was evidenced by the chiefs asking the German soldiers to protect them against the cattle-raiding Hendrick Witbooi, even allowing the Germans to build a fort at Windhoek. Maherero also agreed to renew his treaty with the Germans. An unfortunate accident involving one of von Francois' camels and the Herero sacred fire led directly to the death of Maherero, who was replaced by his son Samuel Maharero. Von Francois meanwhile took his troops to Windhoek, the former capital of Jonker Afrikander (q.v.), where on October 18, 1890, he laid the foundation stone for a fort (the Alte Feste, q.v.), the first European building there. He thus literally founded the modern Windhoek. Since his headquarters were there, and the climate and soil were very attractive to Europeans, German colonists began to arrive within two years and settled near Windhoek. This established it firmly as a German colony. Von Francois also requested and received funds to improve the harbor at

Swakopmund in order to free the Germans of foreign control at Walvis Bay. He also urged Germany to send more troops as the only way to subjugate the Africans; he argued that the settlers and concessionaires should be allowed to acquire greater economic rewards. The number of troops did gradually increase, but the settlers also formed protective societies in areas where military influence was weak.

By mid-1891 von Francois had decided to break African power by splitting the Namas and Hereros and fighting them separately. This position was urged by another of Curt's brothers, Major Alfred Von Francois. Hendrick Witbooi's Namas were the most dangerous, and thus to be the first foe. Meanwhile Curt von Francois had been given a new position of authority. In May 1891, the position of German imperial commissioner and that of troop commander were united, under the title "Landeshauptmann." Curt von Francois was given the title first on a temporary basis, and then permanently. In early 1891 he had visited most of the Herero leaders, so now as Landeshauptmann he visited the Namas in late 1891 and early 1892. He also concerned himself with the future of German settlers and with the harbor at Swakopmund.

After unsuccessful attempts to negotiate peace with Hendrick Witbooi, the Landeshauptmann began planning in July 1982 to attack Witbooi's capital at Hoornkranz (q.v.), perhaps even with Herero assistance. But the Nama-Herero Peace Treaty of November 1892 was a threat to his plan and to German interests in general. He thus requested several hundred additional German soldiers, who arrived in March 1893 at Walvis Bay. Military action against Hoornkranz began three weeks later, troops leaving the Windhoek fort on April 8. Three days later the Landeshauptmann and his two hundred German soldiers reached Hoornkranz. The attack began on the morning of April 12, and German military superiority quickly showed: 150 Witboois were killed, but only one German. However, of the Nama dead, seventy-eight were women and children, as the German strategy failed to prevent Hendrik and most of his men from fleeing into the mountains. The massacre at Hoornkranz of women and children brought a great deal of criticism against von Francois in Germany.

The military situation did not improve for the next year. Witbooi's forces repeatedly escaped von Francois, even after more troops and cannons were sent. There were several other attacks on Hoornkranz and many others at temporary Witbooi encampments, but the Namas always escaped with few losses. In fact Witbooi sent patrols to harass Germans in the countryside and even Windhoek itself. At one point they stole 120 horses the Landeshauptmann was in the process of purchasing. In August more soldiers arrived by sea, being met by von Francois who had been promoted to major. His military tactics continued to fail, however, although the Witboois suffered one setback in a battle in the Dorisi-bikloof. Generally they moved into southern Nama country, followed by the Germans. The failures of von Francois were being criticized severely in the German press, so the chancellor sent Major Theodore von Leutwein, an instructor in military tactics, to advise von Francois. He arrived in Windhoek in mid-January 1894. Success still eluded them, and von Francois decided to go on leave, beginning April 5, 1894. Von Leutwein (q.v.) took over the title of Landeshauptmann. Major Von Francois spent several years travelling in Africa, but did not resume his position in Namibia.

FRANKE, VICTOR (1866–1936). Noted German military leader in many campaigns in Namibia, he was born in Silesia at Zuchmantel of a farm family. His full name was Erich Victor Karl August Franke. He served in Prussia for five years before joining the Schutztruppe in 1896, arriving in Swakopmund in July. He was then named district officer for Swakopmund and Otjimbingwe, which required frequent dangerous trips across the Namib Desert. His courage and leadership helped his men survive several life-threatening ordeals. In early 1898 he took part in military activity against the Topnaar (q.v.) Hottentots led by David Swartbooi. It too involved a treacherous long journey, and Franke's "Schimmel" or white horse was the only animal to survive the trip of Otjimbingwe to Fransfontein. He won the coveted Iron Cross for his leadership in battles against the Topnaars, notably at the battle of Grootberg. In February 1899 he was named commander of the northern districts, succeeding Hauptmann von Estorff (q.v.), and moved his headquarters from Otjim-bingwe to Outjo. Totally against the wishes of the German government he made a trip of Ovamboland, the first German official to do so, in an attempt to persuade the Ndonga and Kwanyama chiefs to accept German protection. While there were no written agreements, Franke succeeded in establish-ing such good relations that he was awarded the Hohenzollen Order. In 1908 he took part in finalizing treaties giving the Ovambos the protection of the Germans in return for rights to recruit the Ovambos for contract labor further south.

In 1901, after settling the remaining Topnaars at Sesfon-tein, Oberleutnant Franke was given command of the Second Company, stationed at Omaruru, the fort of the north. Two years later he was promoted to Hauptmann (captain). On December 25, 1903, General Leutwein ordered Franke and his Second Company to head south to deal with the Bon-delswarts, leaving the north with only a few German soldiers. Reaching Gibeon, Franke got the news that the Hereros had revolted at Okahandja, and on January 15, 1904 started his men on a 900-kilometer, nineteen-and-a-half day march. At one point he saved a lieutenant from the flooding Swakop River, for which he won the Rettungsmedaille, the medal he would always be proudest of. Reaching Okahandja on January 26, he led his men against the Hereros the following day and gave the Hereros their first defeat. After four days and one minor battle, the force moved to Omaruru, which they reached on the morning of February 4. Three or four thousand Hereros were there, but a bold Franke did his own scouting on his white horse and survived a barrage of bullets, strengthening the growing legend of his invulnerability. The battle raged all day, until Franke organized his men for one last charge. With Franke at the head of the charge on his horse, the Hereros fled, breaking the nearly three-week siege of Omaruru. In Germany he was awarded the Pour le Merite, the highest military award.

Franke returned to northern Namibia in 1906, an area he greatly enjoyed, and spent several years exploring. At the Kaiser's request he was recalled to Germany in 1909 and promoted to major, but returned to Africa in 1911. When World War I broke out and South African troops invaded

Namibia, Major Franke again led troops in battle, including an important support role at Sandfontein where the South Africans were beaten. When Colonel von Heyderbreck died in an accident, Franke was named his successor as senior officer. Franke had been leading a successful punitive raid on the Portuguese at Naulilu, where he was wounded in November 1914. Recovered within two months, Franke was promoted on January 24, 1915, to Oberstleutnant and commander of the Schutztruppe. Despite overwhelming South African forces, Franke used delaying tactics and strategic withdrawal to avoid defeat for seven months. Defeat finally was due more to the maneuverings of Governor Seitz than military tactics. Franke and his 4373 men surrendered. After ultimately being released on parole, he lived until 1919 near Karibib. Many Germans made him the scapegoat for the defeat. He returned to Germany in April 1919.

FRANZFONTEIN (variant: FRANSFONTEIN). An African reserve in the Outjo district with an administrative center of the same name. The reserve covers 223 square miles (578 square kilometers) in the southern part of Kaokoland. The strong fountain there provides a good water supply for orchards, gardens, and pasturelands in the area. The Huab and Awahuao Rivers are in the area. Citrus fruits, grapes, and tobacco have been grown there. The Otavi Mountains extend as far as Franzfontein. The Zwartboois (q.v.), a Nama subgroup, migrated to the area of Franzfontein after an agreement with Chief Maherero on March 3, 1882. By 1890 their settlement was thriving, and in 1891 the Rhenish missionary, Riechmann, established a mission station. Uprisings against the Germans occurred in both 1896 and 1898. In 1906 a German proclamation set aside the area of the Zwartboois, an act that the South African government later affirmed. By 1963 the population was 813, with some Bergdama people along with the Zwartbooi Namas. There was also an African primary school, shops, and a hostel. It is also the site of a petrified forest (q.v.).

FRANZMANNSCHEN HOTTENTOTS (variants: FRANSMAN; FRANSCHMANNSCHE). One of the smaller Nama groups referred to as the "federated tribes" that allied with the Red Nation (q.v.) in the nineteenth century, they lived in the Gochas area in southeastern Namibia and along the Fish River (q.v.). Although they once had bowed to German power, they were the first to join with the Witboois in rebellion against the Germans in 1904. Their greatest impact on Namibian history came when under the leadership of Simon Koper (q.v.), and in fact they came to be known by some as Simon Koper's Leute ("people").

FREDERICKS, CHIEF JOSEF (variant: JOSEPH) (d. 1893). The Name chief of Bethanie (or Bethany) in the 1880s, he "sold" the area at Angra Pequena to the German merchant, F. A. Lüderitz on May 1, 1883. Since tribal laws do not allow for their land to be surrendered permanently, perhaps Fredericks did not intend for it to be a sale. The area with a radius of eight square kilometers was later named Lüderitz (q.v.). A German flag was hoisted and business with the Namas quickly commenced. In a later "sale," Lüderitz acquired the desert land from the Orange River north to the 26 latitude and 32 kilometers inland, also from Chief Fredericks. The agent for Lüderitz in both deals was Heinrich Vogelsang (q.v.). The purchase price for the first 25 square miles was 2500 marks (£100 in gold), 200 rifles, and miscellaneous toys that included many lead soldiers. He raised his price further for the "useless" desert in the second deal, where of course diamonds were later found in abundance. For this the chief received £500 and 60 guns. Later he protested to no avail that he had not agreed to the land deal as interpreted by the Rhenish Mission Society's J. H. Bam who had been the translator during the negotiations. Chief Fredericks was the first African leader to sign a protection treaty with Bismarck's representative, Dr. Gustav Nachtigal, which he did on October 28, 1884. The chief's cottage where it was signed is today a protected historic site. In November 1886 Fredericks agreed to German rights to administer justice in his territory. Having learned his lesson in 1890, he only rented land to the Germans, north of present day Maltahohe. Chief Fredericks died October 20, 1893.

FREDERICKS, FRANKIE. A world-class sprinter from Namibia, he won his country's first Olympic medal in the 1992 Olympic Games in Barcelona, Spain. He won the silver medal in the men's 100 meter dash, with a time of 10.02 seconds, just .06 seconds behind the gold medal winner. He also ran in the 200 meter race, but did not place in the top three. He reversed that in a meet in Italy in July, 1992, when he came in first in the 200 meter race but lost in the 100 meter by .01 seconds. In the 1991 World Championship he was second in the 200 meter race.

FREWER, WILLI. One of the most prominent influences on music in Namibia, Frewer had been a music teacher in Windhoek in the late 1930s. Hans Müller (q.v.), the founder of the Windhoeker Musikfreunde (orchestra) and various singing groups, left the territory at the beginning of World War II and handed his conducting baton to Frewer. He prepared the orchestra and mixed choir for a performance of Schubert's *Stabat Mater* on Good Friday, 1940. That was the last concert for seven years, as Frewer and a number of his musical colleagues spent the rest of the war in an internment camp. He was released in 1946, and in early 1947 founded the Windhoek Music Society. With a goal of becoming a true symphony orchestra, it prepared a full classical program for a 1948 concert, including Beethoven's fourth Piano Concerto that featured Frewer as soloist. By 1952 the orchestra called itself the Windhoek Symphony Orchestra. Frewer was still active as the conductor almost two decades later.

FRIEDRICH, L. W. One of the great pioneers of Namibia's karakul industry (q.v.), in 1931 he gathered five thousand pelts from fifty farmers and took them to Leipzig in Germany to set up an auction for their sale. This was not a great success, but he repeated the process the next year with 35,000 karakul pelts. The success that time led directly to annual auctions in London and later in New York.

FRONT LINE STATES. During the protracted war for majority rule in Zimbabwe, five independent African states interceded on the international level for the African freedom fighters, and often provided material assistance or bases of operation. These five were Angola, Mozambique, Zambia, Botswana, and Tanzania. All of them either border Zimbabwe or are only separated from it by one of the other five. Once Zimbabwe gained independence under Robert Mugabe, it was added to the list of Front Line States in the struggle for African rule in Namibia. While they all support SWAPO (q.v.) and its leaders, their vulnerability to South Africa made them lean more toward diplomacy and peacemaking rather than military activity. They especially urged SWAPO's Sam Nujoma (q.v.) to accept compromise peace proposals, such as one in July 1978. Nevertheless the same "Front Line States" remained militant in their rhetoric at the United Nations. They will be among the closest allies of Namibia now that it is independent.

- G -

GALTON, SIR FRANCIS (1822–1911). British scientist and world traveller, he was a cousin of Charles Darwin. After hearing of the work of David Livingstone, he decided to follow after him in exploring southern Africa. His travels took him to Namibia in 1850–51. He reached Walvis Bay on August 19, 1850, accompanied by the noted explorer Charles Andersson (q.v.). His travels took him to Otjimbingwe by the end of November, then to Barmen where they met Rev. C. H. Hahn (q.v.), then to the Erongo Mountains, and further by wagon to Okahandja. He travelled to Rehoboth with the hope of meeting with Jonker Afrikander about several matters. The chief returned with him to Windhoek, where Jonker and other African leaders discussed the principal issues. One was the problem of Jonker's warriors raiding and killing Hereros. Galton urged Jonker and Oasib, another Nama leader, to accept a code of governance for the area. (Indeed, Jonker refrained from raiding for at least a year after.) A truce was also arranged between Oasib and Jonker concerning jurisdictional authority. Finally Galton persuaded Jonker to relax his restrictions on Europeans crossing through Namibia. (Galton had earlier been warned that he could not complete his travel plans because of Jonker.) Jonker reluctantly and temporarily agreed to this. After concluding a treaty with Jonker, Galton returned to Okahandja, and on March 3 his party (including Andersson) travelled north to Ovambo territory, where they were promised passage. Returning for their guides, the men reached the Etosha Pan on May 30, 1851, and visited the village of Nangoro. Galton was the first white explorer to reach Ovamboland from the south. The party they returned to Okahandja.

Galton visited Rehoboth, and then he and his party pushed northeast to Gobabis, which they reached September 14. They proceeded further to Rietfontein, where they hunted before returning to Gobabis on October 22. Galton and Andersson trekked to Walvis Bay via Barmen and Otjimbingwe, reaching it by December 4. They sailed on January 16, 1852, and eventually Galton returned to England. Galton had travelled further north and east then any European traveller entering Namibia from the south, pioneering the way for Andersson's trip to Lake Ngami two years later, and others who would follow. His books on his journeys were widely read by the English. Galton was later to make his fame in areas such as eugenics, heredity, and psychology. While in Namibia he studied the physiological condition called steatopygia (a pattern of fat distribution) among the Nama, measuring the size discreetly from a distance using a sextant, so as not to embarrass either the African women or the missionary hosts.

GAMSBERG (variant: GANSBERG). The tallest peak in the Hakos Mountains in the Rehoboth District, it is 2335 meters high and a conspicuous table-topped landmark. It is the location of a Stone Age settlement. Gamsberg is a spectacular sight on the road from Windhoek toward the Namib-Naukluft Park, as one travels through the Gamsberg Pass. It has a surface of quartzite that gleams in the sun. From a historical point of view, the Gamsberg is interesting as a stronghold of Jan Jonker Afrikander (q.v.), who used it as a safe refuge. He and his followers would come down periodically and raid cattle and quickly return to the safety of their hideouts. A few years later, in the late 1880s, Hendrik Witbooi (q.v.) was forced to use the Gamsberg and adopt the same tactics for survival.

GARIEP RIVER (variant: GARIB). *See* ORANGE RIVER.

GAROËB, JUSTUS (1942–). The brother of Moses Garoëb, a senior SWAPO official, he has been one of the more active Black politicians outside the SWAPO camp. Born in Omaruru, he matriculated at the Augustineum in Okahandja and then attended the University of Zululand with the intention of entering medical school. Financial pressures led him to return to Namibia after only a year, however. An articulate man, he was elected senior headman of the Damara Advisory Council in 1971 at its formation and became its chairman in 1972. The government tried to persuade him to participate in the Turnhalle Conference (q.v.) in 1975, but he refused unless conditions were met, such as the inclusion of UN observers. Thus other Damaras, led by Engelhard Christie were co-opted to appear at the Turnhalle. (He later defeated Christie in the Second Tier election.) Countering the Turnhalle Conference, Garoëb helped organize the Okahandja Summit or Conference in 1975, which demanded Namibian independence under UN supervision. He was the meeting's vice-chairman and its leading figure. In January 1976 he and several other Okahandja participants took part in the Dakar (Senegal) Conference on Human Rights in Namibia. The same Okahandja participants organized more formally as the Namibian National Front (NNF) (q.v.), with Garoëb as its President, but it eventually disintegrated as a coalition. Garoëb converted the Damara Council into a political party in 1980 and led it to success in elections for the Damara Second Tier Representative Authority. He has been courted by both SWAPO and by Dirk Mudge (q.v.), but has retained an independent status. He led his party at both the 1984 Lusaka Conference and the 1986 /Ai//Gams Conference. He has continued to demand UN-supervised elections. Preparing for the elections of 1989 he formed the United Democratic Front of Namibia (UDF) (q.v.), an alliance in which his Damara Council is the strongest party. The

UDF won four seats in the Assembly, and Garoëb was the first one on the electoral list.

GAROËB, MOSES M. Appointed Secretary General of SWAPO at the December, 1991 party congress, he has long been a major SWAPO leader. In 1970 he was appointed SWAPO's Administrative Secretary, third in the party hierarchy. In exile with Sam Nujoma and others during the 1970s and 1980s, he was one of the party's principal spokesmen. For example, in June, 1981 he bitterly rejected the proposal of the Reagan Administration to link the withdrawal of Cuban troops from Angola with a settlement of the Namibian issues. In November, 1989 he was elected to the Constituent Assembly on the SWAPO electoral list. He is the brother of Justus Garoëb (q.v.), the leader of the United Democratic Front of Namibia.

GCIRIKU. One of the five autonomous subgroups of the Kavango (q.v.) people of northeastern Namibia.

GEBIET. See REHOBOTH GEBIET.

GEI-/KHAUAN. See AMRAAL HOTTENTOTS.

GEIKOUS HOTTENTOTS. See RED NATION.

GEINGOB, HAGE GOTTFRIED (1941–). The first prime minister of Namibia, Geingob was born in Otjiwarongo. He was educated at the Augustineum Secondary Teachers' Training College and taught primary school for one year at Tsumeb. He left the country in 1962 on a scholarship sponsored by SWAPO. After two years of work in Botswana he left for the US. In 1966 he completed American secondary education in Philadelphia at the Temple University High School, and then went to Fordham University in New York. He received a BA in political science there in 1970, and later a masters' degree from the New School for Social Research. For much of this time (1964–71) he was also SWAPO deputy chief representative in the Americas and at the United Nations. He had been a member of SWAPO's Central Committee since 1969.

In 1972 he was hired by the office of the UN commissioner for Namibia. In July 1975, he was appointed first director of the UN Institute for Namibia (q.v.) in Lusaka, Zambia, which he developed from nothing. A dynamic leader, he remained its director until he returned to Namibia, June 18, 1989, as SWAPO's election director. He has been quoted as saying about the UNIN, "We don't train terrorists; we train future administrators." Geingob was very highly placed (number seven) on SWAPO's 1989 election list and easily secured a seat in the Assembly. His leadership, intelligence, and political skills made him an obvious choice as prime minister.

GEMS. Namibia is noted for its abundance of precious stones. Diamonds (q.v.) in the south are the most significant, but great mountain ranges in central Namibia are home to many. Beryls, aquamarines, heliodors, tourmalines, and the more recently discovered amethysts are also in abundance. Garnets, various members of the quartz group (such as chalcedony, citrine, rose quartz, jasper, silex, agate, and carndian) are likewise important, while lesser ornamental gemstones are also to be found, such as fluorites, feldspar, sodalite, dumortierite, azurite, ceruzite, and diptase. Shops in Windhoek carry large supplies of most of the country's gemstones.

GENERAL ASSEMBLY (GA). The most representative of all the UN organizations, because all member states have representation there, the General Assembly's considerations of the Namibia issue fall into four time periods:
1946–1950. The first full session of the GA in 1946 considered the status of South West Africa because South Africa proposed incorporating it into itself. Its representative claimed that the people had been consulted and the majority favored incorporation. This claim was effectively refuted, however, by Rev. Michael Scott (q.v.) who had served in the territory and assured the UN that the Africans were not adequately informed about the issues and only one side of the story was given. The General Assembly decided that the people of Namibia were not yet ready to make such an important decision and turned down the South African

proposal. It recommended further that the territory be placed under the international trusteeship system. In 1948, South Africa told the General Assembly that, while giving up on incorporation, it would allow the people of South West Africa to elect members to the South African Parliament. The new National Party Government in South Africa also informed the United Nations in 1949 that it would not send additional reports (it had only sent one) on the status of the territory to the UN. The General Assembly expressed regrets at this, and urged South Africa to continue to send reports. The General Assembly also requested opinions from the International Court of Justice (ICJ) on the status of South West Africa.

1950–1966. In 1950 the GA accepted the ICJ's judgement that it should not go beyond the supervision used under the mandate system. It did, however, establish a five-member Ad Hoc Committee on South West Africa to confer with South Africa on procedural matters concerning the court's ruling. South Africa informed the committee that it believed the court's opinion to be only advisory, and the government would not accept it. Proposals and counterproposals were presented by each side and rejected by the other. By 1953 it was clear no agreement could be reached, and the Ad Hoc Committee so reported to the General Assembly. Thus that year the GA created a new seven-member Committee on South West Africa (q.v.). At the same time, the GA began responding to numerous petitions from representatives of the territory, among them Rev. Scott, Hosea Kutako, and Herman Toivo Ja Toivo (qq.v.). Because it could not adequately deal with the hundreds of petitions and questions, the GA asked the committee for a report on its recommendations. In general, the GA endorsed the recommendations of the committee over the years, such as in 1957 requesting the consideration again of the International Court of Justice. The GA repeatedly tried to persuade South Africa to negotiate with the committee. In 1960 the GA requested the committee to go to the territory, with or without South Africa's permission, to investigate the situation and to determine what steps could be taken to bring the inhabitants to self-government and eventually independence. The committee reported back that South Africa had refused entrance and had threatened physical action to prevent it from crossing the border. But the committee did report the responses of groups like SWAPO and SWANU, and that the Security Council should consider actions to force implementation of UN decisions. The complete report was filled with other specific recommendations. The GA considered the report, decided new approaches were needed, and dissolved the committee in 1961. (Another GA-appointed committee, the Good Offices Committee, was equally unsuccessful.) The same year the GA appointed a Special Committee on South West Africa to visit the territory by May 1, 1962, evacuate all South African military forces there, release all political prisoners, prepare for general elections to a Legislative Assembly, etc. The committee eventually reported back that the government of South Africa had no intention of instituting any reforms and that the local Africans wanted the UN to assume administration of the territory and prepare them for independence. The Special Committee was then dissolved (1962) and replaced by the Decolonization Committee, which continued in the footsteps of its predecessors until the establishment of the Council for South West Africa (q.v.) in 1967. The General Assembly reviewed its reports and regularly approved them.

1966–1975. In 1966 the International Court of Justice handed down its infamous ''non-decision'' on South Africa in Namibia, and the General Assembly responded by passing Resolution 2145, which terminated South Africa's mandate and took to itself the obligation of administering the territory to independence. This led to the creation in 1967 of the United Nations Council for South West Africa, which was renamed UN Council for Namibia in 1968 (qq.v.). The Western powers refused to join these councils, claiming that the councils were powerless, but others said the councils were weak because the Western states did not participate. Meanwhile, the General Assembly appealed without success for the Security Council to assist in the establishment of UN authority in Namibia. It did get the Security Council to act in regard to South Africa's ''treason trial,'' which included some Namibians. The GA also appealed to its members in 1967 to put economic pressure on South Africa. Various UN agencies soon began to exercise their own sanctions against South Africa, while the GA also emphasized positive steps to aid the territory by encouraging cooperation with the activities of the Council for Namibia. The name Namibia was formally recognized by the General Assembly in 1968, one small step of defiance to show South Africa that it had assumed authority there. This was followed in 1970 by the creation of a United Nations Fund for Namibia to provide education and training programs for Namibians. In 1971 the GA called on South Africa to withdraw from Namibia in keeping with the 1970 advisory opinion from the World Court. Also, the General Assembly renewed the request that all countries refrain from economic and other relations with South Africa. The following year it instructed the Council for Namibia to represent the interests of Namibians in international organization and at appropriate conferences. The same council would later be enlarged and a full-time Commissioner for Namibia appointed. In 1972 SWAPO was invited by the General Assembly to participate in an observer capacity in discussions on Namibia. The next year SWAPO was recognized by it as "the authentic representative of the Namibian people." A SWAPO office in New York was budgeted in 1974, and two years later SWAPO was designated as "the sole and authentic representative" and was invited to be an observer in the work of the General Assembly and all international conferences organized under the GA's auspices.

1975–1990. Angolan independence from Portugal and the subsequent infusion of South African and Cuban troops into the region brought a whole new set of needs and responses. The GA urged the Security Council to take action against South Africa and especially to institute an arms embargo. In 1976 resolutions emphasized the need for free elections supervised by the UN and that SWAPO must be a part of all independence talks. The GA also supported the need for armed struggle, led by SWAPO, if freedom were to be achieved. A 1977 resolution denounced South Africa's claims over Walvis Bay. The GA also demanded that all Namibian political prisoners be released by South Africa and all Namibian exiles be allowed to return home safely. Other resolutions were related to South African treatment of prisoners of war and the Universal Declaration of Human Rights. Subsequent years saw resolutions denouncing South Africa's unilateral holdings of elections inside Namibia, claiming instead that the UN had jurisdiction. The 1981 General Assembly condemned the South African decision to establish compulsory military training for Namibians. A 1982 resolution rejected the concept of linkage between the issue of Namibian independence and removal of Cuban forces from Angola. In March 1990 it voted to accept Namibia as a member of the UN.

GENEVA CONFERENCE, 1981. The only public negotiating conference to include both SWAPO and the South African Government (which was represented by Brand Fourie, director-general for foreign affairs, and later ambassador to the United States). In the long process of negotiations for the independence of Namibia, UN Security Council Resolution No. 435 has been a central focus. In late 1980, South Africa agreed to a "pre-implementation meeting" where a number of issues could be discussed, including the neutrality of the UN and the protection of minority rights in a Namibian constitution. The dates were set for January 7–14, 1981. This was only a week before the inauguration of Ronald Reagan as president of the United States. Many observers claim that South Africa never intended to come to an agreement at this meeting in Geneva, Switzerland, but agreed to it only as a delaying mechanism. The government, this version goes, knew that the newly elected Reagan would pursue policies much more sympathetic toward South African whites than had the much more liberal Jimmy Carter. The planning for the conference would eat up the last months of the Carter presidency. Included in the South African delegation was a reluctant Dirk Mudge (q.v.), leader of the Democratic Turnhalle Alliance (DTA) (q.v.), and representatives of some of Namibia's pro-South African ethnic factions. The UN delegation included SWAPO (q.v.) leaders, notably Sam Nujoma (q.v.). The "middle parties" (between SWAPO and DTA) were not at the conference, as they would have to be part of South Africa's delegation. Surprisingly, Fourie let the

meant that the next few years were dominated by the creation of new companies and the granting of mining concessions.

In May 1912, native commissioners were appointed. These German officials were given extensive control and supervisory powers in regard to the Africans under their jurisdiction and were expected to care for their physical needs. They also were to regulate African service contracts, however, to the benefit of the mining companies and German farmers. How the German administration might have worked out cannot be determined. In two years World War I broke out, and on August 7, 1914, the government of the Union of South Africa notified London that it was willing to use its Defence Force against the Germans. Despite objections from its own generals, South African soldiers boarded troopships on September 14, 1914, and sailed for South West Africa. A series of battles ensued, especially in the southern part of the country, but by May 20, 1915, South Africa's General Botha reached Windhoek, and on July 9 the Germans surrendered at Khorab. On the same day Botha placed the country under martial law. German rule had ended, about thirty-one years after it began.

GERMANS IN SOUTH WEST AFRICA/NAMIBIA. Aside from German administrators and military men, German influence in South West Africa/Namibia was the result of three groups: missionaries, settlers, and businessmen (some of whom were also settlers). The first German missionary to cross the Orange River was Heinrich Schmelen (q.v.) who erected a house in Bethanie in 1814. He traveled extensively in the lower half of the territory. In 1840 the London Missionary Society transferred its activities to the Rhenish Missionary Society (q.v.) in Barmen, which then sent an outstanding man, Rev. Carl Hugo Hahn (q.v.), who arrived with Rev. F. H. Kleinschmidt near the end of 1842. Within ten years the Rhenish Mission Society had established a network of mission stations in the southern two-thirds of the territory which became recognized centers for the tribal leaders. Mission stations and the missionaries who staffed them would play important roles in political events at least through the end of the period of German rule.

While Adolf Lüderitz would be the catalyst for German political involvement in the region, he died young and no major settlement survived him, despite the town named after him. Various commercial groups tried to encourage Germans to immigrate to the territory. But groups like the Deutsche Kolonialgesellschaft (q.v.) and the Siedlungsgesellschaft für Deutsch-Südwestafrika had minimal success in attracting German migration to Klein Windhoek. The Siedlungsgesellschaft was well-financed and offered free land plus 2000 marks. On June 16, 1892, a boat left Hamburg with Albert Nitze, a pensioned official, his son Albert Nitze, Jr., and Mr. and Mrs. Richard Stosz. A few others soon joined them. By February 24, 1894, there were thirty-four German families in the Windhoek area. German soldiers being discharged from duty in the territory were also allotted land.

After peace was established with Hendrik Witbooi in 1894, it became easier to attract settlers, who arrived at the ports of Swakopmund and Lüderitzbicht. Pioneers settled at Karibib, halfway from Swakopmund to Windhoek, and at Okahandja. A few went to more distant places such as Grootfontein, Gibeon, and Keetmanshoop. Farms were bought and developed. Samuel Maharero was not at all reluctant to sell land to eager German settlers. Traders came, as did mineral prospectors, until the Nama and Herero wars of 1903–1905. After peace was established, tribal lands were expropriated by the government and sold to farmers with heavy subsidies. Hundreds of Germans came each year, and many Schutztruppe soldiers stayed on after completing their military obligation. Soon there were 10,000 Germans settling there. Government programs encouraged all forms of enterprise. Mines began in the north, even before the discovery of diamonds in the south in 1908. Windhoek grew quickly. After World War I, however, the next wave of immigration was Afrikaans-speakers from South Africa. They would overwhelm the Germans in number, 70 percent to 23 percent of the whites in Namibia in 1980. Still the German influence remains very strong today. German-style castles on the hillsides of Windhoek startle the unprepared visitor. Street names like Kaiser Strasse and Göring Strasse, beer gardens, and Germanic architecture are reminders in the major cities of the period of German rule. The German language is spoken by many residents, including some Africans. German-created choral societies, symphony orchestras, and theater groups are remnants of the German heritage. As Namibia gains its independence, it is clear that whites of German ancestry are far more likely to stay in the country than their South African counterparts. Having been in the country for almost a century, most of the German-speakers look on themselves today as Namibians. German companies are again investing heavily in Namibia, and German tourists are coming in large numbers.

GERMAN SOUTH WEST AFRICA. Anglicized form of Deutsche Südwestafrika, the official name of Namibia from 1884 to 1915, when it was under German rule (q.v.).

GERMANIUM (ATOMIC No. 32). Discovered in 1886 by a German chemist, Clemens Winkler, this metallic element was at one time produced in Namibia as a byproduct of the ore production at the Tsumeb Mine (q.v.). Lower prices in the past decade or so have brought about the closing of the germanium separation plant. The mineral is very important today in the semiconductor industry, so it could be more important in Namibia's future.

GETZEN, ERIC WILLIAM. *See* KERINA, MBURUMBA.

GIBEON. Founded as a mission station in 1862, it was the chief village of the Witboois and headquarters of their chief, Hendrik Witbooi. His great-grandson and namesake is a vice-president of SWAPO and still spends time at Gibeon. Gibeon remained free of foreign rule until 1894, when the Germans defeated the Namas in the mountains and took Gibeon under their protection. Gibeon is located in the south-central part of the country, near the main north-south road, about 40 kilometers south of Mariental, and 300 kilometers southeast of Windhoek. Before being settled by Kido Witbooi and his followers, the area had been known by other Africans as Goregu-ra-as ("the spot where the zebras drink"), and Khacha-tsus ("the spot where the fighters had a hard time''), but Kido gave it the name of Gibeon. A RMS missionary named Knauer spent time there during the early 1860s and helped Witbooi negotiate with rival Africans. The village was destroyed in an attack in late 1864, and again in mid-1865, with Oasib (q.v.) the principal enemy. Peace was finally negotiated at a conference, and the treaty was signed December 19, 1867. Decades later, however, Hendrik Witbooi (q.v.) would lead his people in battle against neighboring groups, and especially the Hereros. While a truce was signed in 1892 with the Hereros, German soldiers tried to overcome Witbooi, who regularly outsmarted and outfought them. Superior German equipment finally won in 1894 and a treaty was signed. Gibeon also had a place in World War I, as forces from the Union of South Africa defeated a German force at Gibeon April 26–27, 1915.

GOBABIS. A town in east-central Namibia, it is located 229 kilometers due east of Windhoek and 113 kilometers west of the Botswana border. It sits alongside the Black Nossob River (q.v.) in the center of a large farming district. Although considered to be in the Kalahari region, the land consists of rich, grassy plains interspersed with hills. Many white farmers have large farms nearby, and the town serves as a commercial center. It has a number of large schools. Governed by a municipal council, Gobabis is the principal town in the Gobabis district. It gets its water supply from the Daan Viljoen Dam on the Black Nossob River, which also is the site of an electric power station. Good cattle pasturage is nearby, so Gobabis is noted for dairy products; butter is produced at its large creamery. A railroad line has linked it with Windhoek since 1930. The town also has a prison, which housed many SWAPO detainees for over a decade, some in solitary confinement. There were 5,528 residents during the 1981 census, and the estimate for 1988 was 6,500 residents.

Gobabis was the site of a Mbanderu (Eastern Herero) settlement in the eighteenth and early nineteenth centuries, but the Orlam group had moved in by the mid-century mark, under their leader Amraal Lamberts (q.v.). Hereros claimed the land, but by the 1880s the principal inhabitants were

Witbooi Namas. In 1896 both groups rebelled against the Germans, who set up a garrison in Gobabis. Europeans traveled through the area frequently on their way to Lake Ngami in Botswana. Sir Francis Galton (q.v.) was one of the first and informed others of the path. German Rehnish missionaries had a station there from 1856 to 1865, and again a decade later. A Catholic mission was set up in 1907.

GOERING, DR. HEINRICH ERNST (1839–1913). The first German imperial commissioner for Südwest Afrika, he resided there from 1885 to 1890. Born at Emmerich, Germany, on October 31, 1839, he studied law at the University of Heidelberg. He practiced law until 1873, but then joined the High Court at Metz. In 1885 he changed careers, entering the German foreign service. His distinguished record led to his immediate appointment as a resident commissioner in Namibia. His assignment was to set up a German administrative authority over the area. He was given lawmaking and judicial authority, but no German troops to support him, as troops would be too expensive in this distant outpost. Commercial interests and settlers were expected to create their own militia as needed. Goering set up his headquarters at a Rhenish Mission station at Otjimbingwe. He soon concluded "protective treaties" with African leaders at Warmbad, Keepmanshoop, Berseba, Hoachanas, Rehoboth, Omaruru, and Okahandja. In 1886 he also signed a treaty with the Boers at Upingtonia. The rights of the inhabitants were formally recognized in these treaties, but the Germans promised "protection," a difficult promise to fulfill without troops. He was unable to protect the Hereros when they were attacked by the Namas. Maherero had signed the treaty with Goering, even granting an economic concession to the Germans, which he later renounced when gold was reportedly found and a flood of English miners came to Otjimbingwe. Nevertheless Goering returned to Germany in 1887 to report the discovery (a hoax, it turned out) and German economic interests increased dramatically. But on October 30, 1888, Maherero and his counsellors met with Goering at Okahandja. The African ridiculed German "protection" and all treaties with the Germans. Goering them moved his headquarters to Walvis Bay. From that post he reestablished contact with other African leaders, including Hermanus van Wyck and Jan Jonker Afrikander (q.v.), and he sent arms to the Basters when Hendrik Witbooi (q.v.) renewed his raids. German Chancellor Bismarck finally agreed to send a small contingent of twenty to thirty German soldiers to Namibia, in part to help capture Robert Lewis (q.v.), who had instigated the Herero renunciations. This force, under Captain Curt von Francois (q.v.), landed at Walvis Bay on June 24, 1889, while Goering was back in Berlin reporting to Bismarck. He arrived back in Walvis Bay on March 15, 1890. In an attempt to regain control he issued orders designed to limit both the liquor trade and the weapons trade by requiring permits in both cases. He then visited the Hereros at Okahandja and found Kamaherero had done an about-face. The meeting on May 20, 1890, was very cordial. The Herero leader reinstated the German treaty, and specifically asked for German protection from Hendrik Witbooi. Goering then sent an ultimatum to Witbooi, warning him to stop his frequent raiding and plundering. Unless he turned to peace, Witbooi would have to face the Germans. But Witbooi flatly refused to cease hostilities, and said he was unwilling to accept German protection. He also ridiculed the Herero leader for his German alliance. Goering then signed a protection treaty with Jan Hendriks of the Velskoendraers and with Willem Christian of the Bondelswarts of Warmbad. That was Goering's last official act in Namibia, as he soon left for Cape Town, en route to Germany. He served for a while as resident minister in Haiti, but spent his later years in Munich, where he died December 7, 1913. A major street in Windhoek is named for him. His son Hermann Goering became a notorious Nazi official.

GOLD. Gold has played a role in Namibia's history, despite the fact that production is small (only 172 kilograms in 1987). It is found in two locations, east of the Etosha Pan and about midway on a lien between Uis and Outjo. Yet it was rumors of gold in abundance (and copper) that brought the Van Reenen (q.v.) brothers to Namibia aboard the *Meermin* in 1793. They annexed part of the Namibian coast in the name of the Dutch. Likewise in 1887 a gold discovery hoax by six Australian miners-adventurers had an impact. The hoax led Dr. Goering (q.v.) to seek to bring Maherero under German "protection," and to establish the first semblance of political administration over the territory. Also it brought the first contingent of German officers who would lead the first protectorate troops.

In 1984, a gold mine was located at Navachab, northwest of Windhoek. The Anglo American Corporation announced that it showed promise and might be developed. This would be Namibia's first "primary" gold mine, meaning one where gold was not merely a byproduct of other mining operations. Mine construction began in 1988 at the site, about fifteen kilometers from Karibib. Mining began in November 1989, producing 72 kilograms in its first two months. Enough reserves exist for at least thirteen years of production, and about two hundred workers would be needed, mostly local residents. Mining rights belong to the Erongo Mining and Exploration Company, of which Anglo American owns a 53 percent share, and Consolidated Diamond Mines owns 33 percent. In 1987 about 172 kilograms of gold was produced at Tsumeb as a byproduct of copper production. Total gold production in 1989 rose to 342 kg, with the beginning of production at Navachab late in the year. The formal "opening" of the mine by President Sam Nujoma took place in June, 1990. Just three months later it was announced that the mine had already produced its first ton of gold. Eventually it should produce two tons of gold annually, from about 840,000 tons of ore.

GOLIATH, PAUL. Leader of a group of Orlam (q.v.) Namas who first arrived in southern Namibia in the early nineteenth century. Dietrich Izaak had led the people across the Orange River to settle in the Karras Mountains, but when he died he was succeeded by Goliath, his son-in-law. Settling in 1850 at the foot of Mount Brukkaross, Goliath established the group's center at the spring in what became known as Berseba (q.v.). European influences began in October 1850, when the Rhenish missionary, Samuel Hahn, arrived at Berseba. Goliath's people were called the Hei-khaua. Hei means "light brown," referring to the color of the clothes worn by their leaders, while khaua (meaning "broken up") refers to the split among the several branches of the Orlams who had once been united.

In 1857, Goliath was described as an old man and a relatively weak chief. Yet he was very concerned about peace among the Nama groups and the Hereros. He met with his ally David Christian (q.v.) to agree on terms for acceptance of a peace with both Jonker Afrikander and the Hereros. They concluded that peace would only work if a police force could be established to protect both Herero cattle from the other people and the Nama groups from the Herero warriors. Other leaders failed to join these two, and the proposed peace conference at Hoachanas did not occur at that time. The process began anew late in 1857, however, and many African leaders met at Hoachanas in December, including Christian and Goliath. Negotiations continued until the treaty was signed on January 9, 1858.

GORDON, CAPTAIN (COLONEL) ROBERT JACOB (1741–1795). The man who named the Orange River (after the Dutch royal family), Gordon was of mixed Scottish and Dutch extraction. As a captain in the service of the Dutch East India Company, he was named commander of the troops at the Cape in 1780. In July 1777, Gordon had travelled north to the Groot River, which he renamed the "Orange," and also travelled upriver (east) many miles, drawing a map as he went. Until then it was not known for certain whether the Groot River reached the ocean. Gordon repeated the trip with naturalist William Paterson in July and August 1779.

GORGES, SIR EDMOND HOWARD LACAM (1872–1924). The first South African civilian administrator of Namibia, "Howard" Gorges held that position from 1915 to 1920. In 1907 he became secretary to Prime Minister Louis Botha and clerk to the Executive Council. Following the defeat of the Germans in early 1915, he was added to Botha's staff to examine the conditions existing in the conquered territory, to draw up a plan for its future administration, and to serve as advisor to the military authorities in all matters concerning the civilian population. In June 1915, he submitted the report and began duties as chief civil secretary. Military rule was abolished (but not martial law) on October 30, 1915, and Gorges was named administrator, a position that combined the posts of chief civil secretary and military governor. He was noted as an extremely competent administrator, and was knighted (KCMG) in 1919. In October 1920, he was replaced as administrator by G. R. Hofmeyr and was chairman of the Board of Trade and Industries when he died in Cape Town, November 18, 1924.

GOWASEB, PAULUS. Moderator of the Evangelical Lutheran Church (formerly the Rhenish Mission), Pastor Gowaseb was also active politically as a leader of the Damara Tribal Executive Committee. His church, known as ELK, includes many of the country's ethnic groups, under the leadership of Dr. J. L. de Vries (q.v.). The elderly Pastor Gowaseb was more active in the 1960s and early 1970s. In 1971 he and Bishop Leonard Auala of the Evangelical Lutheran Ovambokavango Church (q.v.) cosigned an open letter to the South African prime minister. In it they condemned both South Africa's stand on the subject of Namibian independence and on its treatment of Blacks. Similarly he was one of a number of Namibian church leaders who cosigned a letter of protest to the territory's administrator-general (AG). In it they condemned both police investigations and the AG's failure to look into charges of torture by the police.

GRASPLATZ. A few kilometers east of Lüderitz, it was the site of the first engagement between German and South African forces in World War I. A force of 1824 men sailed from Cape Town on September 15, 1914. Four days later they occupied Lüderitz. The German forces moved inland, leaving a rearguard at Grasplatz. It was badly beaten and dispersed by the South Africans.

GREAT BARMEN. *See* GROSS BARMEN.

GREAT BRUKKAROS MOUNTAIN. A very conspicuous landmark in the Berseba Valley, it rises 1800 feet (550 meters). It

was once a volcanic pipe, and the results of circum-
denudation have left it a solitary mountain surrounded by
wide plains. Paul Goliath (q.v.) chose the base of it for his
settlement, Berseba (q.v.), in 1850. The mountain had also
been known as Geitsequbub.

GREAT FISH RIVER CANYON. *See* FISH RIVER CANYON.

GREAT NAMAQUALAND (variant: GREAT NAMALAND).
The term formerly used by South Africans to refer to the
southern half of Namibia, since it was inhabited by Namas
(or the older term, Namaquas). ''Little Namaqualand'' was
that part of the northern Cape Province in which many
Namas lived. The Orange River was the dividing line
between Little and Great Namaqualand. The eastern and
western borders are understood to have been the two deserts,
the Kalahari and the Namib. The northern boundary is
roughly a line corresponding to the Tropic of Capricorn.
Great Namaqualand was declared to be a German protectorate on October 18, 1884.
    The area is composed of table-mountains or plateaus,
between which are wide plains interrupted by numerous
valleys, which are deep gorges with very rough and steep
sides. The area is divided into three parts by the Bethany and
Berseba Valleys. Each of the three parts have somewhat
different characteristics. The longest and most important
river in Great Namaqualand is the Fish River (q.v.). Annual
rainfall increases as one travels north, and the climate is
warmer than in other parts of Namibia.

GREAT RIVER. Early name for the Orange River (q.v.).

GREEN, FREDERICK JOSEPH (1829–1876). The most significant of the three Green brothers (the others were Charles and
Henry) for Namibian history, this Canadian-born hunter,
trader and explorer also took an active part in the battles
between the Hereros and Namas. He and his family came to
South Africa in the 1840s and soon became involved in
hunting and trading. His travels took him through many
uncharted areas of today's Botswana, Namibia, and Angola.

His traveling companions ranged from Swedish naturalist J. A. Wahlberg to explorer C. J. Hahn (q.v.) and J. Roth. In terms of hunting alone his results were extraordinary. he is said to have killed more than a thousand elephants in less than a quarter of a century in southern Africa. He wrote articles on some of his adventures that were published in southern African magazines.

Green's earliest travels took him to Lake Ngami in Botswana, but in 1854 he travelled through Herero country to Walvis Bay, only the second European (after C. J. Andersson) to make that westward trek. That same year he met Andersson in Cape Town, which began a working relationship that spanned two decades.

Green's regular route to Lake Ngami was from Cape Town to Walvis Bay by ship and then eastward across Namibia. He was with Wahlberg on one of these trips when the latter was killed by an elephant. In 1857 Green stopped to visit Andersson at Otjimbingwe. He then went north to hunt in Owambo, where he and his hunting partner, George Bonfield, encountered the missionaries Hahn and Roth. The four went to visit Chief Nangoro in Ondonga (July 1857). When relations deteriorated with the Africans, the four started to leave Ondonga and were attacked by as many as 800 Ovambo warriors. Green was well-armed, however, and managed to keep the Ovambos at bay. When the party returned to central Namibia, it had put together much new material on the people and places of northern Namibia, notably the Ovambos, the San, and the Etosha Pan (qq.v.). Green spent the next seven years on a number of trips from Cape Town to Lake Ngami, with occasional detours further north. In 1864 he also married the daughter of a hunter and trader named Stewardson.

Green's friendship with Andersson led him to assist the Hereros against the Namas in the first war between those groups. Indeed, in March 1864, he successfully led a band of 1400 Hereros from Otjimbingwe into battle against the Namas of Jonker Afrikander (q.v.) at Witvlei. They captured 3000 head of cattle, more smaller animals, plus other valuable supplies, which they brought back to Otjimbingwe.

Green then began a trip south to Cape Town with about

1400 head of cattle and numerous sheep and goats. As they neared Rehoboth the same Namas he just defeated took revenge and ambushed the caravan. Green made it safely to Rehoboth, but the animals were lost. Andersson sent Green back to Otjimbingwe to recruit a Herero force, which the two then led south toward Rehoboth for revenge. There they won the Battle of Gamgam against the Namas, although Andersson was seriously wounded.

Green and his family then spent several years in the north among the Ovambos to avoid the Nama-Herero battles. They collected much ivory there for trade. Their daughter Mary was the first white girl born in Owambo, in 1865. Eventually they made their way south to Otjimbingwe and later to Walvis Bay, at both of which they survived Nama attacks on the community. Green sent his daughter to school in Cape Town in 1871, and the whole family spent some time there over the next few years. By 1874, however, he was again working with the Hereros, this time urging the Cape governor to protect the Hereros from the Thirstland Trekkers.

In April 1876, he left Walvis Bay on a hunt with William Chapman, but Green died at Haigamkab of an abscessed liver on May 4, 1876. W. C. Palgrave (q.v.) buried him, and Chapman brought Green's family to Omaruru. Green's wife was also very courageous. In one incident in 1877 she intervened to rescue a man of mixed race who was being beaten to death by twenty Hereros, saving his life.

GRIQUAS. Said to be the forebears of the Basters (q.v.) of South Africa and Namibia, these people were apparently related to the Namas. The early Griquas lived near St. Helena's Bay in South Africa, and were known as the Charigariqua (a name easily adjusted to Griqua over many years of oral use). The colony near Cape Town was forced to disband and scatter. Griqua women associated with South African white men, producing a mixed race group called "Basters" by many. This occurred in South Africa, notably in the Karee Mountains south of the Orange River. It has been written by Dr. H. Vedder (q.v.) that some of these people later moved north of the Orange River, finally ending in Rehoboth. Many Griquas in the late nineteenth century wished to flee South African control to the freedom of Namibia. A large settlement of Griquas in South Africa is south of Botswana, east of southern Namibia.

GROOT-DODEN ("Great Deaths"). One of the eight separate groups of Namas who crossed into Namibia from the Cape Colony in the early nineteenth century, the Groot-Dodens were also called //O-gein. They settled in the Hornkranz area, their pastures being on the upper course of the Fish River (q.v.). Along with five other Nama groups, they formed a loose federation under the leadership of the Red Nation (q.v.). In the 1880s they ceased to exist as a separate group, in part because of the many battles against the Hereros. In one notable case, Maharero had made a camp to the south of Aris. The Groot-Dodens bravely attacked his camp twice, but he destroyed their village in retaliation, and the small tribe scattered.

GROOTE RIVER. Meaning Great River, it was an early Dutch name for what became known as the Orange River (q.v.).

GROOTBERG. A conspicuous, 1613-meter high mountain in the Outjo District, 84 kilometers east of Fransfontein, it was the site of a major battle in 1898. Swartbooi Namas led by Samuel Swartbooi living in the Kaokoveld rebelled against the Germans in 1897. Capt. Ludwig von Estorff and a company of cavalry were sent from Outjo to Fransfontein to negotiate with the Namas. But at a night camp, the Swartbooi stole all the German horses and mules who were grazing away from the camp. German reinforcements plus artillery were sent from several sites, and a battle between the Namas and Germans was fought at Grootberg on March 13, 1898. The Namas were defeated, and the clan was disarmed and sent to Windhoek.

GROOTFONTEIN. A large and important town in north-central Namibia, it has a long history. Hereros had called it Otjivanda ("the place of the leopards"), while the San called it Gei-/ous ("the big spring"). Germans followed the latter name, thus today's "Grootfontein." Sir Francis Galton (q.v.) visited the area, having heard of mineral deposits nearby. He was followed later by geologists. Today major mines at Tsumeb and Otavi are to the north and west. Galton and Charles Andersson (q.v.) also stopped there on their hunting trips north and east, as it had an abundant water supply for their animals. The area was not permanently settled, however, until 1884, when W. W. Jordan (q.v.) established his Republic of Upingtonia there. When he died two years later the republic collapsed, but in 1892 the German government granted a concession for it to the Deutsche Kolonial-gesellschaft für Südwest Afrika. German settlers began arriving the next year, and in 1896 troops were stationed there. A rail line reached the settlement in 1908, the same year as did Catholic missionaries. The Rhenish missionaries came two years later. Part of the attraction of Grootfontein is an ample water supply from the fountain, plus rainfall of about twenty-four inches a year. Good soil is suitable for both agriculture and grazing, and game is abundant nearby. Moreover, it is now also near major mines, such as Tsumeb, only about forty kilometers away. Thus Grootfontein was a logical site for the headquarters of SWANLA, the South West Africa Native Labor Association, which recruited workers for migrant labor in mines as well as other work sites throughout the territory.

The town had an estimated population of 13,000 in 1991 but that does not include thousands of Hereros living on its outskirts. It is a major commercial center, and has hospitals and schools. In the 1970s as South Africa built a fighting force against SWAPO, it created both an army base and a military airport at Grootfontein. Its location on both a rail line and a road to the Caprivi gives it a strategic location. With independence bringing demilitarization to the area, one might expect to see the town emerging as a growing commercial area again.

GROSS BARMEN (variant: GREAT BARMEN). Originally called Otjikango, Gross Barmen is north of Windhoek and about twenty-four kilometers southeast of Okahandja. It is on the banks of the Swakop River. The first European to settle there was Carl Hugo Hahn (q.v.), a Rhenish missionary, who set up a mission station there in 1844. Hahn's primary mission was to work among the Herero, but in the sixty years the mission station existed there, Rhenish missionaries crossed the lives of many of the major African leaders, such as Jan Jonker Afrikander, Hendrik Witbooi, and Maherero, plus European explorers like Francis Galton and Charles John Andersson (qq.v.). The ruins of the church, the mission house, and a military post can still be seen today. Old forgotten graves are scattered in the grass. But the area has a new life today. One of the area's attractions has always been its warm mineral springs. Thus it is now a luxurious resort, less than a hundred kilometers from Windhoek. A glass-enclosed thermal hall houses the thermal bath fed by the hot spring for those seeking medical relief. Others use the outdoor swimming pool, tennis courts, and other facilities. Palm trees surrounding the area date back to the mission period. The resort cost over R3 million to build in 1977.

GRUNDEL. Sent out from Table Bay (Cape Town) in 1670 by the Dutch East India Company (q.v.), its orders were to sail as far north as the tropics, to survey all landing places, and to determine how far north the "Hottentots" (Namas) lived. The ship's captain was G. R. Muys. He was also to watch for places where food or wood could be procured from the indigenous people. Items were taken for barter and gifts as well, some of which might be bartered for slaves, the captain was instructed.

The ship sailed in March 1670, and was besieged by fog. It reached Namibia on April 14 in a terrible storm, and landed at Angra Pequena (Lüderitzbucht) twelve days later. On May 1, it reached Sandwich Harbour. The captain and two others disembarked there and saw five Namas. This led to an encounter with a larger group who physically threatened the Dutchmen, even wounding one in the chest. The sailors fled to the ship ahead of the Africans and the *Grundel* renewed its trip northward. By May 4, they had seen no new bay or river mouth, and also decided that the land was still that of the "Hottentots" (rather than black Africans), so they turned southward again. They reached Table Bay on May 26.

GUANO; GUANO INDUSTRY. Literally seabird manure, guano has been known for centuries as an excellent fertilizer. It has become a major coastal industry. The cold Benguela Current (q.v.) is rich in nitrogenous plankton. These attract surface-feeding fish, which in turn attract huge flocks of seabirds. The birds eat fish several times their weight daily. Since the birds have made their homes on the Penguin Islands, off the southern Namibian coast, these islands have become thickly layered with guano. The Dutch used the guano already in the seventeenth century, but it was two centuries later before they would heavily "mine" guano. The guano covered some of the islands (few of which are very large) to a thickness of about one hundred feet, with small peaks and valleys creating a kind of snowy landscape. This was the sight that greeted Benjamin Morrell, an American sealing captain in 1828. He saw the guano-covered island called Ichabo, about a half mile offshore, forty kilometers north of Lüderitz. Guano mining soon began. The British claimed all the islands in the 1860s, but today South Africa claims them, and its government supervises the guano trade. However, an enterprising German carpenter, Adolf Winter, built a large wooden platform in the water in 1932. It eventually attracted a bird population that deposits an annual slab of four inches of guano. Many similar platforms followed, in Namibian territorial waters, some of them near Swakopmund. Thousands of tons of guano are sold yearly. It is rich in nitrogen and phosphorus, but low in potassium.

GUANO ISLANDS. Another name for the Penguin Islands (q.v.), because guano is found there in great quantity and has become a major industry. The islands are claimed by South Africa, despite their location off the coast of Namibia.

GUINAS. See LAKE GUINAS.

GURIRAB, THEO-BEN (1938–). Born and educated in Usakas, Gurirab received a teacher's diploma from the Augustineum College in 1960. He went to the USA, where he earned a BA in political science and an MA in international relations (1969, 1971) from Temple University. A forceful and dynamic spokesman for SWAPO in his role as its representative at the United Nations beginning in 1972, he was a significant leader of SWAPO's external wing. For many years he served as Sam Nujoma's principal advisor during diplomatic negotiations, and as a party spokesman. As a Damara, he is also an important symbol that not all of SWAPO's leadership is Wambo. In January 1986, he was appointed SWAPO's secretary of foreign affairs. He returned to Namibia in 1989, a couple of months prior to the election. Highly placed (number nine) in SWAPO's electoral list, he easily won a seat in the Assembly. With his education and experience, his appointment as Namibia's minister of foreign affairs surprised nobody.

GURUCHAS. The hill that was the site of the death of Abraham Morris (q.v.) and a hundred or more other men, women, and children of the Bondelswarts (q.v.) who were massacred there by government troops, May 29, 1922. The hill is located on the small reserve for the Bondelswarts, which is located northwest of Warmbad in the extreme southern part of Namibia.

GURUMANAS. A site, located west of Rehoboth in central Namibia, where considerable tension and conflict occurred between the Hereros and the Namas in the 1880s. The area was noted for its exceptional grazing land, so Maharero stretched his "borders" to include the area at Gurumanas. He established a cattle post there in 1880, stocked with 1500 fine cattle, several thousand sheep and some horses. The Namas living in a nearby werf (village) resented the condescending attitude of the Hereros, and tempers were short. A fight broke out in August 1880. When the Hereros invaded the Nama village and fired into the huts, Nama warriors encircled the Hereros and killed at least thirty of Maharero's best herdsmen. The stock was taken by the Namas who fled in all directions. This event set off a renewal of the larger Nama-Herero conflict. It began the so-called Second Nama-Herero War.

Despite this resounding loss of men and stock, Maharero continued to claim Gurumanas as his territory and visited it in 1883 to emphasize his claim to it, setting up a camp there. Henry Carew, a hunter and a trader, had a house at Gurumanas, which was used as a church and school by the missionary Friedrich Eich who was with Maharero. Although the entourage returned to Okahandja, the Herero camp was maintained at Gurumanas.

- H -

HABICHT. A German gunboat, its men played an important part in the German suppression of the Herero revolt in 1904. When the revolt began in January, the *Habicht* was in port in Cape Town. On January 14 it was ordered by the German high command to proceed quickly to Swakopmund. It arrived four days later, and its crew quickly worked to restore the rail line and some locomotives which were out of commission. By early February the line was open from Swakopmund to Okahandja. The restoration of the railroad and its reopening of German communication to the interior forced Samuel Maharero to change his strategy against the Germans. In tribute to the crew of the *Habicht* a memorial was erected to them in Swakopmund.

HAHN, REV. CARL HUGO (1818–1895). Born in Riga, Latvia, on October 18, 1818, he became a member of the Rhenish Mission Society in 1838. He completed his training and was ordained three years later; he was then sent to South Africa. He would spend over a half century in southern Africa, mostly in Namibia, and become a trader as well as a missionary, and at the same time an expert on the Hereros. Along with a colleague, F. H. Kleinschmidt (q.v.), Rev. Hahn began his work at Eikhams in October 1842, and visited both Okahandja and Hoachanas the next near. He married Sara Hone in 1843. The next year Hahn and Kleinschmidt were replaced at Eikhams by other missionaries, at the request of Jan Jonker Afrikander (q.v.). They moved on to Okahandja to set up a mission among the Hereros. When drought soon forced the Hereros to move on, Jonker advised the missionaries to travel a little south to the hot springs at Otjikango. They did this and set up a mission in October 1844 named after Barmen, the German city that was headquarters of the

Rhenish Mission Society. The mission was variously called Neu-Barmen (New Barmen), Gross Barmen (q.v.), Great Barmen, or simply Barmen. The mission station remained active until 1890.

Hahn had originally introduced himself to Jonker in 1842 and offered his services to the Namas. Jonker accepted but two years later, as indicated above, suggested that Hahn leave. However Hahn was to spend much time over the next decades serving as an intermediary between the Namas and the Hereros when friction occurred between them. Hahn served unofficially as the mediator at a meeting between Nama and Herero chiefs in September 1870. That meeting ended the first Nama-Herero War. War broke out again ten years later, and in 1882 the Cape Government called Hahn out of retirement to negotiate a settlement to this second Nama-Herero War, which he did. However, this truce was also soon broke.

Hahn was also a skilled linguist, and in 1857 wrote the first Herero grammar. In 1873 his translation of the Bible into Herero was published.

On several occasions Hahn took a leave and spent a couple of years preaching in Germany and raising money for his missions. On one return to Namibia in January 1864, he brought a group of mission colonists along with a great quantity of equipment and supplies. From 1855 to 1873 Hahn had his mission at Otjimbingwe. There he began a training school for Herero teachers, the Augustineum (q.v.), in 1866. It later moved to Okahandja. Hahn resigned from the RMS in 1872 and left Okahandja early the next year. However, he remained a Lutheran pastor in Cape Town until 1884. After visiting both Germany and the United States (where a daughter lived), he returned to live with a son in South Africa. He died in Cape Town on November 24, 1895.

HAINYEKO, TOBIAS. Commander in chief of SWAPO's armed forces in the late 1960s, he was based in Zambia. He became the first SWAPO senior commander to be killed in action, dying in the eastern Caprivi region on May 18, 1968.

HAKAFIA. According to Wambo tradition, it was at this lake or pan in north-central Namibia that the Wambo people split into the several subdivisions that are known today. It is believed that this occurred in the sixteenth century, when various leaders moved away from Hakafia to establish their people elsewhere. Only Omundonga and his followers stayed at Hakafia, and the Ndonga tribe emerged.

HAMAAMBO, DIMO (variant: AMAAMBO). An important member of SWAPO's Politburo, he served as field commander of PLAN (SWAPO's military arm) from 1968 until independence. In June 1990 Lt. Gen. Hamaambo was named army commander, and late in the year was named chief of defense.

HAMAKUAMBI. A sixteenth-century leader of the Wambo people, he took his followers, whose descendants are called the Kwambi, from the lake called Hakafia (q.v.). They travelled west a little and settled in their current home region. The Kwambi are one of the seven subdivisions of the Wambo people. They took their name from Hamakuambi.

HAMAKARI RIVERBED. An important battlefield in the Herero-German war of 1904, specifically in the Battle of Waterberg. This battle took place on August 11. At first the German troops, under Lieutenant Colonel von Mueller, were outnumbered and outfought, and they pleaded for assistance from other army battalions nearby. But German military equipment made the difference, and late in the day the Hereros retreated. Twelve Germans died, and thirty-three were wounded. Since many Hereros had camped along the Hamakari, it became the site of a vindictive attack of slaughter and destruction under the leadership of General von Trotha himself.

HAMUNGANDJERA. A sixteenth-century leader of the Ovambos in northern Namibia, he led his people first to a lake or pan called Hakafia (q.v.). He then chose to split his people, to be called the Ngandjera, from the other groups of Ovambos. They traveled about 125 kilometers due west, where many of their descendants still live today. Hamungandjera was recognized as the group's first chief.

HAMUTENYA, HIDIPO (1939–). A prominent leader of SWAPO, he was born in Onengali, Namibia. He received a BA from Lincoln University in Pennsylvania, where he was active in African students' organizations. He then studied for an MA at McGill University in the early 1970s. At the same time he was SWAPO's deputy representative to the UN, presenting petitions to that body from Namibia. In 1975 he was a founder and assistant director of the UN Institute for Namibia (q.v.). He had emerged as a strong and eloquent spokesman for SWAPO; he is its information secretary and a member of its Political Bureau and its Central Committee. Some consider him the most powerful member of SWAPO's external leadership and the architect of its policies.

HAMUTUMPANGELA, REV. THEOPHILUS. An Anglican priest and a pioneer African nationalist in Namibia, he became actively involved in politics in 1954. He was upset about the persecution and robbery of African contract workers by police as they prepared to come home at the expiration of their contracts. He gathered evidence on these crimes and sent numerous protest letters to the UN, requesting its protection for the Africans against this treatment. In 1955 he was arrested by the police and put on trial. A huge crowd of Africans showed up at the court to support their hero and champion. The trial judge saw Hamutumpangela's support and, instead of trying him, requested that the Anglican Church transfer him outside his home region to Windhoek. The church did this, but Hamutumpangela was not silenced. There he met frequently with other nationalists, including Sam Nujoma (q.v.). Later he became one of the founding members of the Ovamboland Peoples Organization (OPO), the predecessor of SWAPO. In 1958 he was sent back to Owambo, but by then he was very ill.

HARASEB, JOSEPH "MAX" (1942–). Born in Windhoek, his occupations have included teaching and farming. He was a founder and vice-president of the Damara United Front, which later became the South West Africa People's Democratic United Front (SWAPDUF) (q.v.). He was a participant in the Turnhalle Conference 1975–77. In December 1978 he was elected to Namibia's National Assembly as a member of SWAPDUF, which had become in 1977 an affiliate of the Democratic Turnhalle Alliance (q.v.). In 1989, he was elected to the Constituent Assembly with the DTA. He is one of the DTA's vice-presidents.

HARDAP DAM AND RECREATION PARK. A major dam and irrigation settlement on the upper Fish River in the Gibeon district, it was built in 1961–62 at a cost of R6 million and is one of the largest storage dams in southern Africa. It is located 24 kilometers north of Mariental and 306 kilometers southeast of Windhoek. The dam is 866 meters long and 39.2 meters high and has four sluice gates. The lake has a capacity of 323 million cubic meters and covers an area of 25 square kilometers. It extends for 30 kilometers up the Fish River. It produces enough water to irrigate over 2000 hectares of land plus supply water for the city of Mariental. A recreation resort has been built along the shores. On the southern side of the dam is a game reserve. In 1978, during the period of guerrilla warfare, SWAPO refugees captured by South African forces at Kassinga in Angola were placed in a detention camp near the Hardap Dam.

HARTUNG, CHARLES A. A founder and leader of the National Independence Party (q.v.), a party of Coloureds who opposed South African policies. He was elected in 1975 to one of the two seats his party held out of six seats in the South west Africa Coloured Council. As such, he was leader of the opposition, and in July 1978 he initiated a motion in the council calling for the dissolution of all ethnic councils in Namibia, even the White Legislative Assembly. He took a hard-line position at the Turnhalle Conference (q.v.) and affiliated his party with the National Convention of Namibia.

HEI-KHAUAS. A group of the Nama peoples who live at Berseba (q.v.) in south-central Namibia, near the Fish River. Their northern neighbors are the Witbooi Nama. They were the only Nama tribe not driven into rebellion against the Germans, and thus escaped the universal confiscation of land and cattle that all other Namas and Hereros experienced.

HEIKOM (variants: HAIKUM; HEIKUM, and HEI//OM). A highly acculturated group of San ("Bushmen") who live between the Ovambo in the north and the white-owned farms further south; some live near the Etosha Pan. Although they once had their own language, today they speak either Nama of Ovambo. A nomadic people, they once roamed the arid region in small bands or families, living on the game. The name Hei//om means "men who sleep in the bush," thus the common term "Bushmen." Today many have settled on farms or live among Nama families.

HELIGOLAND TREATY. This treaty, signed July 1, 1890, transferred the Caprivi Strip (q.v.) to Germany as part of a broader deal with Great Britain. Another part of the treaty transferred Heligoland, a small island and naval base in the North Sea, to Germany in exchange for Germany's giving up Uganda to the British. Among the other provisions of the treaty was the drawing of boundaries between Namibia and adjacent British territory, especially today's Botswana and Zambia. The treaty did not set the southern borders of Walvis Bay, but provided for future negotiations on it and, if needed, arbitration. The main point of the transfer of the Caprivi Strip to Germany was that Germany wanted access to the Zambesi River and thereby to its East African possessions.

HENTIES BAY. A seaside summer resort area seventy-two kilometers north of Swakopmund, about halfway from there to Cape Cross, it lies at the mouth of the Omaruru River, which provides fresh water for the residents. It was named after Major Hentie van der Merwe of Otjiwarongo, among the first to popularize it as a resort. Henties Bay has been identified by some as a possible location for a new major port for an independent Namibia, replacing Walvis Bay, which is under South African control.

HERERO. A Bantu people, the Herero migrated to Namibia, perhaps in the mid-sixteenth century, from south-central Africa. Their previous home may have been near Lake Victoria, and they seem to be related to the Sotho groups of southern Africa. They call themselves "Ovaherero," which is plural for "Umherero" (a Herero man). People speaking Khoisan languages call them Damara, and many whites in Namibia adopted that word when referring to the Herero. The Herero are, like the Sotho, cattle-raising people to whom their herds mean everything. The cattle indicate wealth and are important to tribal customs and rituals. Thus the men spend their time with the cattle while the women do subsistence agriculture. Physically the Herero tend to be darker in pigmentation than are the many Namibians of Nama origin and certainly more so than the Sam with whom they share the Kalahari today. Herero men and women are tall and regal-looking. The clothing of the Herero women is striking. As German missionaries brought their wives to the territory in the nineteenth century, the Herero women copied their Victorian style of dress. The high bodice, small waist and floorlength dress plus a turban-like hat all in bright colors makes a remarkable sight for tourists, as the costume is worn even in Windhoek in the warmer months of the year.

The first wave of Hereros crossing into Namibia came across to the Kaokoveld area. But many of these drifted south, looking for better cattle pasture. Others stayed in the Kaoko area and are called the Tjimba (q.v.). Others who migrated south were called Damaras by the Khoi-speaking peoples. The Herero name was not lost by those living in the center of the territory and further east. Politically the Herero had several great leaders, notably Tjamuaha, Maherero, and Samuel Maharero (qq.v.). Maherero was also known as Kamaherero. While the Herero fought the Name in numerous Herero Wars (q.v.) in the nineteenth century, they lived in peace with the early white missionaries. The first such missionary to reach them was J. Heinrich Schmelen (q.v.) of the London Missionary Society, who reached Okahandja in 1814. While conflicts with Namas filled much of the nineteenth century, it was a war with the Germans from 1904 to 1907 that decimated the Herero. Indiscriminate slaughter of Hereros by the Germans at the end reduced the 80,000 Hereros in 1904 to as few as 15,000 after the war. Some others made it safely into Botswana, where they still live. Today there may be 94,000 Hereros in Namibia. That would include the "true Herero" plus small groups called the Tjimba, the Himba, and the Mbanderu (qq.v.).

HERERO CHIEF'S COUNCIL (variant: HERERO COUNCIL OF HEADMEN). While not formally a political party, the Herero Chief's Council played an antigovernment political role for many years, leading internal campaigns against the South African government and submitting numerous petitions to the United Nations for a referendum. When a group of Hereros formed the South West Africa National Union (SWANU) in May 1959, they received strong support from the Herero Chief's Council. However, in 1964 the Council's 95-year-old leader Chief Hosea Kutako and his protege and successor Clemens Kapuuo (qq.v.) participated in the formation of the National Unity Democratic Organization (q.v.). Chief Kutako died in 1970 at the age of 100, and Kapuuo was elected his successor, but not without a challenge by the Society for the Preservation of the Royal House of Tjamuaha/Maharero. The Herero Chief's Council continued as an entity separate from NUDO, although it shared the same leader, Kapuuo, until his assassination in 1978. His ultimate successor in both roles was Kuaimo Riruako (q.v.) the nephew of Chief Hosea Kutako. In 1971 the Chief's Council joined the National Convention of Freedom Parties. When some groups rebelled in February 1975 to form the Namibia National Convention, the Chief's Council, led by its secretary, Johannes Karuaihe, stayed with Kapuuo in the reorganized National Convention of Namibia. The Herero Chief's Council was an active participant body in the Turnhalle Conference; through NUDO it has given support to the Democratic Turnhalle Alliance.

HERERO WARS. Herero conflicts can be divided into two major categories: those with the Namas and those with the Germans. Conflicts with the Namas can be organized into four separate "Wars." Up until the mid-1820s, different groups of Africans generally lived peaceably in the large territory. But in the decade from 1815 to 1825 an increasing number of Namas, especially the Orlams (q.v.), moved into the southern half, forcing others to push further north. Simultaneously the Herero were drifting south looking for more pastureland for their cattle. This was especially true after the drought of 1829–30. The two groups clashed in central Namibia. The Hereros were generally a stronger group, and the Namas had to give way to them. This changed when they turned to a strong Orlam leader, Jonker Afrikander (q.v.) for aid. In taking up the fight he became the Nama leader de facto. While conflicts were generally of the "cattle raid" type, Jonker was the relentless aggressor and the Herero were put on the defensive. Casualties were not great, but a peace was signed in 1842 to end the twelve-year conflict.

During the four years of peace Jonker was besieged by European traders offering all kinds of goods, including guns. It was suggested to him by traders that he could afford them if he acquired more Herero cattle. His raids therefore resumed in 1846, and the Hereros fought back. This war was much more costly, especially for the poorly armed Hereros, and the second twelve-year conflict ended in 1858 with a peace treaty signed at Hoachanas (q.v.). The peace was urged by both missionaries and other Nama leaders. The treaty was aimed at punishing those who stole Herero cattle and at preventing Herero from taking over Nama land. Jonker was, however the dominant warrior in the country; he lived in a large camp at Windhoek before it became a European town.

When Jonker died in 1861, there was no other strong Nama leader. This time it was the Herero who acquired European guns—from Charles Andersson (q.v.)—and they began their own "Freedom War." This third war lasted from 1863 until 1870. While the Hereros did win a major battle or two, it soon became another war of raiding parties. A peace treaty was signed at Okahandja in 1870, but the Hereros were clearly the winners. One important aspect of the third war was the participation of some white officers at the head of Herero units. This peace lasted a full decade, during which time Maherero (q.v.) was the most respected and powerful Namibian leader. He was frequently called upon to help conciliate conflicts between other groups, including the Europeans. He requested aid from the Cape Government in this peacekeeping, and W. Coates Palgrave (q.v.) was sent to help. Despite Palgrave's presence, a small border conflict sparked a new battle with the Namas, and Palgrave withdrew in distress.

This final war lasted for twelve years (1880–1892). It was one of the bloodiest of all, involving almost a battle royal among three strong African leaders and their armies: Maherero, Jan Jonker Afrikander, and Hendrik Witbooi (qq.v.). It also featured the intrusion of German administrators, military men, and missionaries, all of whom sought to resolve the conflicts. Maherero lost his heir, Wilhelm, in a successful Herero attack on Jan Jonker Afrikander's warriors at Barmen. Another Herero victory, this time against Hendrik Witbooi, occurred in 1885 (*see* OSONA, BATTLE OF). Witbooi surprised the Hereros in a dawn attack in April 1888, but again the Hereros were able to withstand the Namas, ultimately pursuing them and capturing many of their possessions. Later the same year Jan Jonker Afrikander, with few remaining supporters, fled to Hereroland to escape Hendrik Witbooi, who pursued him and killed him en route. Maherero died in 1890 (his son Samuel Maharero succeeded him), ending the fourth Herero War.

Conflicts with the Germans began in 1904. The German forces had been busy fighting a group of Namas, the Bondelswarts (q.v.), then the Hereros took advantage of the absence of German soldiers in central Namibia. Samuel Maharero, bitter at the treatment the Hereros had received from German traders and settlers, especially the loss of Herero pasture land to large groups of settlers, called for an attack upon German outposts and on German farmers. In January 1904 the Hereros killed 123 German settlers, farmers, and traders. Samuel Maharero specifically ordered that women, children, Boers, Englishmen, and missionaries be spared. Okahandja's fort was besieged also, but a force of Germans under Captain Victor Franke (q.v.) was able to get back to save the fortress while the Hereros fled into the mountains. Franke's forces flushed them from there as well, and the Hereros fled into the veld. Franke then led his forces against an army of several thousand Hereros at Omaruru. Again he managed to occupy the fort and the Hereros fled into the veld. Some raids by Herero forces took place at outposts near Windhoek, but no major battle was waged there.

In February and March of 1904 a large supply of German reinforcements arrived, including 1576 men, 1000 horses, 6 machine guns, and 10 artillery pieces. There were now 2500 Germans available to fight 10,000 Hereros, but the firepower advantage went heavily to the Germans. Nevertheless German attempts to pursue and destroy the Hereros in March and April were very unsuccessful, as the new German troops were inexperienced at countering guerrilla warfare, and the big artillery pieces made troop travel too slow. By the end of April 1904, Herero troops were moving around the countryside almost at will. However, between May 20 and June 17 more German reinforcements arrived, including more than 2300 men and 2000 horses. More would soon arrive, bringing the total to about 20,000 Germans. On June 16 General von Trotha (q.v.) an extremely tough-minded soldier, arrived to take charge of the German forces. Two months of planning and distribution of manpower led to the decisive Battle of Waterberg (q.v.) on August 11. There the Hereros suffered a devastating defeat, and during subsequent months the German forces relentlessly pursued the remnants of the Herero forces and their families. Von Trotha instructed that the Herero should be annihilated. The results came close to fulfilling that instruction.

HEREROLAND. Until the creation of tribal "homelands" by South Africa in the 1960s, no well-defined Hereroland existed. Yet it is known where Hereros lived. The first wave of Herero immigrants moved in from today's Botswana in the sixteenth century and ultimately settled in the Kaokoveld, the far northwest of Namibia. Today most of the people there are still considered to be Herero. Some later moved south with their cattle to better land. In the nineteenth century, most of the Hereros lived south of the Ugab River and north of the Swakop River and the White Nossob River. The Herero people stretched across most of Namibia from the Namib Desert on the west to the Kalahari Desert on the east. A related tribe, the Mbanderu (q.v.) lived in eastern Namibia near Gobabis. When the Homelands Policy (q.v.)

was implemented in the 1960s, a Hereroland Homeland was set up by the government. The areas involved are called Hereroland West and Hereroland East and are adjacent. The western boundary is east of Grootfontein and the Waterberg Park, an important site in the German victory over the Hereros. On the east the territory stretches through the Kalahari Desert to the border with Botswana. A subpart of the Hereroland East, not contiguous with the rest, lies along the Botswana border southeast of Gobabis.

HERSTIGTE NASIONALE PARTY (HNP). The extreme right of Namibia's political spectrum, the HNP in Namibia is a branch of the party formed in South Africa by Dr. Albert Hertzog in late 1969. Its leader in Namibia has been a Windhoek lawyer, Sarel Becker. The party attracts little support to its meetings, but claims to have the support of many Afrikaner farmers. In the December 4, 1978, elections for the National Assembly the HNP received 5,781 votes and elected one representative, Becker. Its speakers have denounced the Multi-Party Conference, the Administrator-General, and the Constitutional Council; the party has called for the banning of SWAPO. It has also supported the inclusion of Namibia as a fifth province of South Africa. It claims to have picked up support from voters who previously supported the National Party. The HNP was heard from frequently in the run-up to the 1989 election, but did not run a slate of candidates.

HEYNITZBURG. A wonderful "German castle" built in 1914 on a hillside in Windhoek, it was designed by the architect Willi Sander (q.v.) under the commission of German Fieldmarshal Graf von Schwerin. The team was also responsible for building another nearby castle, called Schwerinsburg. Heynitzburg was named in honor of von Schwerin's wife, whose maiden name was von Heynitz. The couple eventually chose Heynitzburg as their home. It is the most enchanting of the Windhoek castles, with a crenellated tower and turrets, arched doorways and windows, pillars, and panelling. In more recent years it had been the home of a mayor of Windhoek and businessman, Jack Levinson, and his wife

Olga, author of some of the best historical studies of Namibia.

HIEMSTRA, VICTOR. A liberal Afrikaner and former supreme Court Judge in south Africa, Hiemstra was appointed chairman of the Constitution Council in 1985 to compile a constitution for Namibia. Its first meeting was January 13, 1986. The guidelines Hiemstra issued called for adherence to the proposals drawn up by the Western "contact group" in 1981–82, which included protection of minority rights and precluded the expropriation of private property. He also suggested that the West German constitution might serve as a model. Finally a draft constitution was approved on July 6, 1987. It provides for a unitary state with protection of individual rights but not guarantees for minority group rights and provides for a Westminster-style democracy.

HIMBA. A Herero clan who live in Kaokoland and are separated from the rest of the Herero nation. They are nomadic people who are cattle herders and many have retained a traditional lifestyle and appearance. Their language is the same as the other Hereros, and they are nominally under the Herero tribal rule. However, most of them ignore modern government and education.

HIRSKORN, DR. HANS. A German sent from Berlin in the 1930s to organize and lead a Nazi movement in Namibia. The Nazi front was called the Deutsche Südwest Bund. He was accompanied by propaganda and sabotage specialists. German residents put on Nazi uniforms, waved swastikas, and held torchlight processions. Hirskorn recruited some Hereros to his cause as well. German children in the territory were sent to Germany for political indoctrination. Hirskorn called on the Germans to renounce South African citizenship in exchange for dual German-South African identification. He had many allies in South Africa also; he was a leader in trying to get South Africa, with all its mineral wealth, in the Nazi camp. Hirskorn's activities might have been triumphantly successful except for the stand ultimately taken by South African prime minister Jan Smuts. In April 1939,

Smuts took over the South West African police and sent three hundred armed troops to Windhoek. They occupied the public buildings. Smuts claimed the territory was being used by the Nazis as a base.

HOACHANAS (variant: HOAGANAS). A village in the Rehoboth District, it lies about 150 kilometers southwest of Windhoek. In the nineteenth century various groups of Namas lived in the area, but eventually it became home to members of the so-called Red Nation (q.v.). In 1853 the first missionary came to live there with them. In 1858 Hoachanas became important as the site of the Peace Treaty of Hoachanas, which brought an end to the Second Herero War. Jonker Afrikander signed for the Orlams (Namas). The treaty was designed to protect Herero cattle on one hand, and the Namas from Herero encroachment on the other. In addition to Jonker Afrikander, it was signed by all the Nama-speaking chiefs (except those of the Bondelswarts, who had not been involved in the fighting) and by Maherero, two sons of Tjamuaha, and Andries van Rooi, a leader of the Griquas. It has been described as a kind of Namibian Magna Carta, and even through it was soon broken it is seen as the beginning of a tradition of negotiation among Namibian leaders.

However, by the 1890s wars among the Africans forced the Red Nation from Hoachanas. Hendrick Witbooi (q.v.) claimed it for his people. By 1905 Simon Koper (q.v.) was the leader of the Namas at both Hoachanas and Gochas, but he was not usually in the area. He was busily engaged in guerrilla activity against the Germans. When the Homelands Policy (q.v.) was put into effect in the late 1960s, the Namas living at Hoachanas, under the leadership of M. Mattheus Kooper, refused to leave for a home in the designated Nama Homeland area.

HOBA METEORITE. The largest known meteorite in earth, it is located on a farm, Hoba West, 19 kilometers west of Grootfontein. It is believed to have struck the earth about 30,000 years ago. Its content is 83 percent iron, 16 percent nickel, with small parts of carbon, copper, and cobalt. The date of its discovery is uncertain, but it was early in the twentieth century. Scientists first analyzed it in 1929. It is believed to weigh 54,422 kilograms. The rectangular shape measures 2.95 meters by 2.84 meters, and it varies between 0.8 and 1.2 meters in thickness.

HOFMEYR, GYSBERT REITZ (1871–1942). The second South African administrator of Namibia, he succeeded Sir Howard Gorges (q.v.) in that position on October 10, 1920. At that time the territory was still under martial law (which ended on the last day of 1920). Thus he was the first civilian administrator. He served until March 31, 1926. During that period he was responsible for government actions regarding both the Bondelswarts rebellion of 1922 and the Rehoboth uprising of 1925. While holding the position of administrator for South West Africa, he regularly attended meetings sponsored by the League of Nations to report on the mandate.

HOMELANDS POLICY. The general structure of government of the ten "homelands" set up by the Report of the Odendaal Commission (q.v.) was provided for in the Development of Self-Government for Native Nations in South West Africa Act (No. 54 of 1968) (q.v.). This act echoed the "Bantustan" or "homelands" concept used in South Africa, in that ten Black or mixed-race groups of Namibians were classified as separate nations. Each was allocated an area as their homeland, and those in the group not living within its boundaries would be forced to move there. Each homeland was to have a Legislative Council to pass laws on a restricted range of subjects, while an Executive Council had corresponding executive powers. Foreign affairs, defense, and police matters were outside the jurisdiction of the homeland government. Even Legislative Council decisions (laws) could be vetoed, amended, or repealed by the South African state president.

By 1976 three homelands were self-governing under this act: Ovamboland, Kavango, and Caprivi. Other homelands received various forms of advisory tribal authorities, short of self-government. Meanwhile the powers of the white Legislative Assembly (established in 1925) were transferred almost entirely to the South African Parliament, thereby all but integrating Namibia into the South African legislative and administrative system. The various Legislative Councils and Advisory Councils thus established became the "Second Tiers" of government in the 1980s.

HOOGENHOUT, COL. PETRUS IMKER (1884–1970). Educator, author, civil servant, Col. Hoogenhout served as South Africa's administrator for South West Africa from 1943 to 1951. His father, Casper Peter Hoogenhout, was the most famous Dutch-born South African poet and author of Afrikaans literature in the nineteenth century. Like his father, Imker championed the use of the Afrikaans language, and he wrote many song lyrics, essays, and academic texts in Afrikaans. Educated at the University of Stellenbosch, Imker became a teacher in 1905, but soon worked his way up the ranks of education administration. By 1929 he was in government, serving in the Hertzog Cabinet from 1929 to 1937. Other posts followed, but in 1943 he was appointed to succeed D. G. Conradie as administrator of South West Africa. In his reports to the people in the South West African Annual he repeatedly emphasized the ways in which his government was building better schools, hospitals and housing for the "Non-Europeans." In 1951 he resigned in order to accept appointment as South African ambassador to the Netherlands, a post he held until his retirement in 1956. His length of service in Namibia assured he would be honored in various ways. For example, a primary school for the children of white farmers and mining personnel at Otjosundu mine was named Imkerhof in his honor.

HOORNKRANZ (variants: HORNKRANTZ, HORNKRANZ, HOORNKRANS). A village in the Rehoboth District, it is located about seventy-five kilometers northwest of Rehoboth itself. It became famous in the 1880s as the headquarters of the great leader Hendrick Witbooi (q.v.). The location was an excellent site for his raids on the Herero people and their cattle. He was also well-positioned to attack southern Nama peoples who failed to recognize his authority. The German commander, Curt von Francois (q.v.), decided to punish Witbooi for his raids. In a predawn attack on Hoornkranz on April 12, 1893, he led the German forces in what has been called the Hoornkranz Massacre. Hendrik Witbooi and his soldiers escaped, but 150 Witboois were killed, including 86 women, children, and old men. This included Hendrik's youngest son, a twelve-year-old. The town was burned. Seventy-nine women and children were taken captive. While the German force returned to Windhoek in a victorious mood, the massacre was condemned in the German Reichstag and in the South African English-language press. Witbooi and his forces had fled to the Naukluft Mountains, from which they retaliated with raids on German targets. A daring raid captured most of the German horses and immobilized the German troops. Subsequent raids were even more successful. The embarrassments involved in the Hoornkranz Massacre and its aftermath led directly to the sending of Major Theodor Leutwein (q.v.) to eventually replace Von Francois.

HOP, HENDRIK. Among the first whites to explore Namibia, Hop was a farmer and a captain in the local militia at Stellenbosch in the mid-eighteenth century. Inspired by the reports of Jacobus Coetzee (q.v.) about the land across the Gariep River (now the Orange River), he requested the permission of the Cape governor to put together an expedition to explore the area beyond the river. He received approval on June 30, 1761. He gathered volunteers, while the government supplied tools, weapons, a boat, three wagons each with ten oxen, and presents for the Nama peoples in southern Namibia. Coetzee became the guide for the eighty-five-man expedition, which included a surveyor, a botanist, and a surgeon who was also an expert in minerals. There were seventeen Europeans and sixty-eight Baster helpers and servants. Hop's goals were to draw a map, collect plants, explore for minerals, investigate the fauna, and search for unknown civilizations. They crossed the Orange River on September 29, 1761, and proceeded to Warmbad six days later. They went on to the Great Karras Mountains. On November 22 they reached their farthest position, the dry Xamob River. Small parties explored briefly in different directions to find out more about the Hereros and others. On

December 7 the expedition headed south again, stopping several times en route. They reached Cape Town finally on April 27, 1762. Hop's diary aroused a great deal of interest in the territory, and the expedition resulted in a map, information on giraffes in Namibia, and samples of copper ore.

HOTTENTOTS. A name given by early Dutch settlers to the first African people they encountered in South Africa. They spoke a Khoisan language filled with "click" sounds that were unfamiliar to European linguists and seemed like gibberish to the Dutch ears. Some said it sounded like the chatter of a parrot, not like a recognizable (to them) speech pattern. In Frisian or Low German the word "Hüttentüt" means "a quack." The people called themselves Khoikhoi, meaning "men of men," that is, the best of all men. A major subgroup of the Khoikhoi are the Nama, some of whom lived in the northern Cape Province while others were in southern Namibia. (*See* NAMA for much more information on these people and their place in Namibia's history.)

HOUGH, DANIE. The administrator-general of Namibia from September 1980 to February 1, 1983. Hough had been a provincial councillor in Natal. Replacing the experienced and high-placed Gerrit Viljoen (a real force in the National Party), his appointment was seen as an effort to downgrade the importance of the position of administrator-general. He was replaced two-and-a-half years later by Dr. Willie Van Niekerk after the National Assembly had been dissolved and the administrator-general became a powerful governor again. Perhaps Hough's greatest international exposure was as the head of one of the teams at the Geneva conference on Namibia in January 1981. He led a delegation of thirteen representatives of the "internal parties," primarily the Democratic Turnhalle Alliance and its allies. At the conference he called on the UN representatives to give a "full rethink" of Resolution 435 (q.v.) and he asserted that the neutrality of the United Nations was very much at question.

HUKWEVELD. In the western half of the Caprivi Strip, between the Okavango and Kwando Rivers, Hukweveld is a very dry area with few pans. River courses contain water only in the rainy season, and are between 400 and 800 yards broad. Some contain dry woods, while others are covered with grass. The ridges between the river courses are covered with deep red sand, overgrown by dry woods. San people live in the Hukweveld, attracted in part by the abundance of all species of game.

- I -

IDATAL (translation: IDA VALLEY). Located about eighty kilometers south of Lüderitz and perhaps ten kilometers from the coast, this valley near the former town of Pomona (q.v.) was the site of some of the more spectacular diamond deposits in Namibia. Finds in the Ida Valley have been recorded as large as 200 carats per cubic meter. These areas were naturally worked first, and the Ida Valley was pretty well finished as a production site by 1920. A principal land holder was the Pomona Diamenten-Gesellschaft. The valley was named by August Stauch after his wife Ida. Stauch made the first major diamond discoveries in Namibia in 1907 and began the diamond rush.

IMBILI, TARA (variant: IIMBILI) (1932–). Born at Onduktu, he is a member of the Ndonga tribe of the Wambo people. His studies led him to a diploma in nursing at a South African hospital, and from 1956 to 1960 he was director of a medical clinic at Oranjemund. He began to study law through South African correspondence courses while working as a clerk during the early 1970s for the Owambo government's Department of Economic Affairs. He also served for a year as private secretary for Chief F. S. Elfias (q.v.). In 1973 he became secretary-general of the Ovamboland Independent Party, having also served in the Owambo Legislative Council. He also became active in the National Democratic Party (NDP) (q.v.). After Chief Elfias was assassinated in August 1975, the Third Legislative Council nominated a new cabinet, and Imbili was made minister of justice. He himself survived a December 1975 assassination attempt. He retained his justice post in the new cabinet that was appointed April 1, 1977. When the Turnhalle Constitutional Conference was held, he was appointed to represent the Ndonga. He later was chosen to the Council of Ministers and served as chairman of its Agricultural Committee. In 1980 he was chosen president of the National Democratic Party, but he resigned from the party in 1985.

He had been chosen vice-chairman of the Democratic Turnhalle Alliance in 1982. The next year he became part of the Multi-Party Conference as well.

Imbili reemerged on the national scene in early 1989 when he and Paul Helmuth created the Namibian National Democratic Party. However, a few months later Imbili broke with Helmuth and resigned from the party. He has since joined SWAPO.

IMPORTS. Namibia's greatest quantity of imports by far comes from South Africa. The highest value is in the category that includes machinery, vehicles, metals, and metal manufactures. Mining equipment, farm implements, steel pipes, and sheet iron are also in this category. Second in value is in the category that includes textiles, apparel, fibers, and yarns. Third comes foodstuffs, including sugar, tea, potatoes, jams, and canned fruit. Another valuable import category includes waxes, resins, oils, paints, and varnishes. Further down the line comes rubber, leather, tobacco, wood, glassware, and cement.

INCORPORATION. The question of the incorporation of Namibia into South Africa first surfaced in the early years of South Africa's mandate over the territory. While South Africa assumed that the mandate allowed it administrative and legislative powers over the territory, it received objections from the Permanent Mandates Commission (q.v.) when it applied its ''race laws'' such as the Colour Bar Act of 1926 to Namibia. The commission was wary of signs that South Africa might try to incorporate the territory as a fifth province, a subject much discussed in South Africa. The first serious call for such a move was raised by the United National South West Party (q.v.) in Namibia during the campaign preceding the 1934 Legislative Assembly elections. The UNSWP was terrified at the unexpected rise of Nazism in Namibia in July 1933; the banning of the Nazi party in 1934 and the deportation of its leader had not effectively curbed Nazi activities. (The Germans had reorganized as the Economic League, an apparently non-Nazi party.) Thus the UNSWP campaigned almost exclusively on a platform calling for annexation by South Africa. The Weimar Republic in Germany had hoped for the return of its colonies, with Germany as the mandatory power, but the Nazi's open advocacy of a return of the territory to Germany as a colony resulted in the UNSWP making an appeal to South Africa to annex South West. Meanwhile South Africa had been gradually integrating a number of the common services. For example, in the area of customs, a 1921 Act provided that Namibia should be regarded as part of South Africa. Namibian railways had been taken over by South Africa's Railways Administration on August 1, 1915, and a proposal for integrating the systems was passed as Act No. 20 of 1922. Police in the two areas were integrated after June 1, 1939. Four months later the South Africa Defence Act was applied to Namibia. Taxes in Namibia remained separate, however, and lower than those in South Africa. If incorporation took place, residents of Namibia would have had little to gain financially, and much to lose. In 1947, South Africa arranged for a plebiscite in Namibia to test Black sentiment concerning incorporation. The white Legislative Assembly had expressed itself in favor of it on May 8, 1946. This so-called "Plebiscite of 1947" was a farce, and its results were rigged; for example, in Ovamboland they showed 129,760 Ovambos in favor and *no one* against! The SWA Affairs Amendment Act of 1949 (in South Africa) provided for ten whites from the territory to be elected to South Africa's Parliament, and two senators to be also selected. One of the latter had to be selected because of his "thorough acquaintance with the reasonable wants and needs of the Coloured races." On April 1, 1955, the transfer was made of the administration of "Native Affairs" from the SWA administrator to the South African government's minister of native affairs. Other examples of gradual de facto incorporation by South Africa are the application of South African laws—such as the Terrorism Act and the Suppression of Communism Act—to Namibia. The Terrorism Act was even backdated to 1962 to facilitate prosecution of thirty-seven Namibians already in jail at the time. In 1968 the SA Departments of Bantu Education and Bantu Affairs had their administrative functions extended to cover Namibia. And of course the Odendaal Commission Report (q.v.) was an attempt to apply South Africa's "homeland" policies to Namibia.

INDUSTRY. The most important industries of Namibia, past or present, are: fishing (notably rock lobsters, plus canning pilchards and making fish meal); mining (diamonds, uranium, and base metals); cattle (in the northern half of the country); sheep and goats (in the southern half), with karakul sheep being the source of "Persian lamb" pelts; and to a lesser extent, farming, brewing, and winemaking. (*See* the individual entries for more details.)

INSTITUTE FOR NAMIBIA. *See* UNITED NATIONS INSTITUTE FOR NAMIBIA.

INTERESSENGEMEINSCHAFT DEUTSCHPRÄCHIGER SÜDWESTER (IG). Its original purposes were to serve as an "interest group" (rather than a political party) dedicated to promoting and maintaining German culture and to protect the interests of Namibia's Germans and German-speakers during the process of deciding upon the future of Namibia.

While it was originally neutral in political matters, it found the Democratic Turnhalle Alliance (q.v.) much to its liking in the 1978 election. It finally became an ally of the Republican Party (q.v.) within the DTA. This led to a split within the IG, and many of its National Party members defected. A few years later the IG found itself also opposing the DTA on various matters. On September 9, 1983, the IG formally decided to loosen the ties with the Republican Party and the DTA.

It again became an independent agent in the negotiations. Its leaders were at both the Geneva and Lusaka Conferences, and on various occasions from 1981 to 1987 they had bilateral talks with SWAPO. (It is not surprising therefore that German names appear in SWAPO's first cabinet, notably Otto Herrigel as minister of finance.) During the period leading to the 1989 Assembly elections there was talk of the IG joining the UDF alliance, but it decided not to do so because, its leaders said, its members belong to many different political parties. After leadership changes in the last few years, the president of the IG is Konrad van Marees. Dr. Herbert Halenke, one of its founders, is honorary president.

INTERNATIONAL COURT OF JUSTICE (ICJ). The successor to the Permanent Court of International Justice, which was created in 1920 and discontinued after World War II, ICJ (instituted by the UN in 1945) is almost identical to its predecessor. Both are often called "the World Court." It is open automatically to members of the United Nations, but can be open to nonmembers if certain conditions are fulfilled. The Court has fifteen judges serving nine-year, staggered terms; all are competent in international law, and they represent all of the major legal systems of the world. The court first met in April 1946 at the Hague. The ICJ became involved with the Namibian question in 1950, when it was asked to give an advisory opinion concerning South Africa's international obligations toward the territory and the United Nations. South Africa had contended that its obligations were owed only to the now defunct League of Nations.

When the National Party came to power in 1948, it refused to continue sending annual reports on the territory to the United Nations. In its July 11, 1950, advisory opinion, the court concluded that South Africa continued to have international obligations under the League of Nations' Covenant, and that South Africa was not competent to modify the international status of Namibia without the United Nations' consent. Yet it also added that while the UN charter contains provisions by which Namibia could be brought under the trusteeship system, the charter does not require South Africa to switch the territory from a mandate to a trust territory. The General Assembly accepted this opinion, but South Africa did not.

The ICJ issued further advisory opinions on related issues.

On June 7, 1955, it delivered an advisory opinion to the General Assembly that a two-thirds majority vote in the General Assembly on Namibian issues would be compatible with the court's 1950 advisory opinion. South Africa had contended that the League of Nations required a unanimous vote, and thus a two-thirds vote constituted a greater degree of supervision than in the original mandate. On June 1, 1956, the ICJ handed down still another advisory opinion regarding Namibia. The question this time dealt with the legality of granting oral hearings to petitioners. The Permanent Mandates Commission had not allowed oral testimony from petitioners, but the General Assembly contended that South Africa's refusal to provide information to the Committee on South West Africa made it necessary to have oral hearings. Again the ICJ advised that this was compatible with its 1950 decision. It also reaffirmed that it recognized the General Assembly as the replacement body for the Council of the League in matters of supervising mandates and trusts. The court ruled by an 8–5 vote that the grant of oral petitioners was consistent with its 1950 opinion, in light of South Africa's failure to cooperate with the supervisory rules.

ICJ advisory opinions have no binding effect on any country. Thus Ethiopia and Liberia asked the court to give a binding judgement on South Africa's obligations and alleged breaches under the mandate. These two countries raised the issue because they were the only other African countries that had been members of the League of Nations, and thus the only Africans who could presume to have the right by legal practice to raise this issue before the ICJ. The two countries filed their applications with the ICJ on November 4, 1960. The next year Liberia submitted its position: the original mandate still exists and South Africa still has duties and obligations thereunder, that the UN is not the proper supervisory body, that South Africa is violating the League of Nations covenant and its mandate provisions. In arguments lasting from October 2 to 22, 1962, South Africa contended: the mandate has lapsed, thus there is no case; even if that is rejected, Liberia and Ethiopia have no proper standing in this case and thus cannot legally raise the issue. They have no material interests in the matter, nor do any of their nationals.

The court delivered its opinion on this question on December 21, 1962 by 8–7 majority vote. It rejected South Africa's objections and stated that the case should proceed. Written pleadings were filed over a two-year period, and oral hearings began on March 15, 1965. The petitioners argued not only that South Africa had duties such as submitting reports to the UN, but that the policy of apartheid was in conflict with mandate provisions regarding the promotion of the well-being of all the inhabitants. Meanwhile South Africa produced fourteen "expert witnesses" to testify in the case, all of whom were cross-examined. One of South Africa's major answers to the charge that racial discrimination inherently violates the well-being of Namibians was that its treatment of different ethnic groups was based on the uneven development of the different tribes and groups who happen to live in close proximity. A policy of separate development will solve these inequalities, it contended.

The ultimate decision was clearly affected by the composition of the court. While its normal membership would be fifteen, each party in a case is allowed to add one judge to represent its views. But seventeen judges did not cast votes in this case; fourteen did. One judge, Sir Muhammad Khan of Pakistan, was eliminated from the case on the first day by President Sir Percy Spender of Australia, because his name had been suggested by Ethiopia and Liberia as their nominee prior to the time he was officially chosen to a nine-year term. A second judge, Bustamante Y Rivero of Peru, who had voted against South Africa in 1962, was too ill to participate in this case, and Judge Badawi of the United Arab Republic (who also voted against South Africa in 1962) died on August 5, 1965. Thus a vote that would most likely have been 10–7 against South Africa became 7–7. The rules provide for the president to cast a deciding vote in a case of a tie. Thus Sir Percy Spender cast a second vote for South Africa, resulting in an 8–7 result.

The final opinion of the court handed down July 18, 1966 dealt with one issue. Ignoring most substantive questions concerning apartheid, and reversing its own 1962 opinion, the ICJ majority decided that there was no case because Ethiopia and Liberia had no real interests at stake and thus were not entitled to file the case. Mere membership in the League was not sufficient. This "nondecision" thus allowed South Africa to continue on with its previous practices, despite considerable worldwide protest. This did not end the ICJ involvement in the Namibian issue, however. On October 27, 1966, the UN General Assembly terminated the mandate, claiming that South Africa had failed to meet its obligations. It then decided that Namibian matters would become the direct responsibility of the United Nations, ultimately creating the United Nations Council for Namibia to administer the territory until independence. In January 1970 the Security Council passed Resolution 276, which stated that South Africa's continued presence in Namibia is illegal. In order to remove any legal doubts about its subsequent actions, the Security Council resolved on July 29, 1970, to ask the ICJ for an advisory opinion on this question: What are the legal consequences for states of the continued presence of South Africa in Namibia, notwithstanding Resolution 276? By the time of the court's opinion, delivered on June 21, 1971, the composition of the ICJ had changed considerably, and was not strongly hostile to the South African position. A 13–2 majority ruled that the continued presence of South Africa in Namibia was illegal and that South Africa was obliged to immediately withdraw its administration. It ruled that members of the UN had an obligation to recognize the illegality of South Africa's presence. Finally, it ruled that the UN had inherited the supervisory functions of the League of Nations in the case of Namibia, and thus the General Assembly was entitled to revoke the mandate. While this decision would appear to end the matter, it must be recalled that as an advisory opinion it has no binding effects on UN members. Subsequent ICJ rulings since 1971 have not contradicted that opinion.

IPELEGENG DEMOCRATIC PARTY (IDP) (variant: EP-ILENGE PARTY). In 1980 a number of members of the Tswana-based Seoposengwe Party (q.v.) were bitter with the choice by its leaders of those who were to serve on the Second Tier Tswana Authority. They especially were displeased with the dominance of Paramount Chief Constance

Kgosiemang. In February 1981 they created the Ipelegeng Democratic Party. ("Ipelegeng" in Setswana means "carry yourself.") Among its founders are Leader H. Gates Mootseng, Deputy Leader Moitsepi Masaka and National Chairman Anton Monageng. The party's program involves for the most part Tswana tribal matters. It adamantly opposes the involvement of the paramount chief in modern political groups. It considered joining an alliance at election time in 1989, but ultimately did not.

IPUMBU, CHIEF. An Ovambo chief of the Kwambi, Ipumbu has been variously called a despot who disdained his subjects and was rebellious against the white resident commissioner, or a courageous symbol of Black resistance following the death of Chief Mandume (q.v.). The latter view holds that in 1932 South Africa used a weak pretext to depose him, claiming he had fired rifle shots at the Finnish mission while pursuing a young woman. He ignored the fine imposed by the native commissioner for Ovamboland, Mr. "Cocky" Hahn, who had been resisted by Ipumbu previously. Hahn then called for a column of armored cars plus five airplanes. The attack destroyed Ipumbu's headquarters, despite the lack of resistance. Ipumbu had fled the area, but was tracked down after several days. After his surrender he was dismissed as chief by the white authorities and banished from his home region; he lived his final years at Oshikango.

IRON AND STEEL INDUSTRIAL CORPORATION OF SOUTH AFRICA (ISCOR). A South African parastatal, it produced low grade tin through a subsidiary at the Uis Tin Mines. It also owns the Rosh Pinah mine that supplies zinc to a South African refinery in which it has a one-third interest and which supplies ISCOR's steelworks.

ITENGE, REPUBLIC OF. The proposed name for an Eastern Caprivi nation, to be split off from Namibia. The idea comes from leaders of the Caprivi African National Union (q.v.). While CANU leaders urged South Africa to accept such a secession, DTA representatives derided it as "CANU's dream."

ITHANA, PENDUKENI IIVULA KAULINGE (1952–). A longtime member of the ruling elite of SWAPO, she has been a member of its Central Committee at least ten years. Ithana fled Namibia in 1974 after having been active in the SWAPO Youth League. While in Zambia she studied public administration and management at the UN Institute for Namibia. Ithana has been the Secretary of SWAPO's Women's Council but also a military commander during the years of revolution. Elected to the Assembly in 1989, she was number fifteen on SWAPO's electoral list. In the Constituent Assembly she was selected to the twenty-one member standing committee that hammered out the details of the new constitution for Namibia. One of her concerns on this committee was guaranteeing equality for women. She has been named to the cabinet as deputy minister for wildlife conservation and tourism. In a cabinet shuffle in February, 1991 she was promoted to Minister of Youth and Sport, a new ministry.

IZAAK, JACOBUS (variant: ISAAK). An important nineteenth-century chief, he was a senior judge and assistant chief under Chief Paul Goliath of Berseba, who died April 15, 1869. Izaak then became his successor. Vedder describes him as being energetic, impulsive, and domineering, but reasonable after his temper subsided. In 1872 he became concerned about his borders with Maherero (q.v.). A confrontation almost occurred when Izaak visited the border area where Maherero seemed to be on the verge of encroachment. Negotiations at Okahandja cooled matters, but Izaak returned to Berseba furious. Always eager to argue for his rights, Izaak was a principal spokesman at a meeting of Namibian chiefs with W. C. Palgrave (q.v.) in Berseba on November 22, 1876. He argued that white resident magistrates were not needed in Namibia, as they would only undermine the authority of the chiefs, who were ruling satisfactorily without the aid of outsiders. This position was proven to be too optimistic, however, when Berseba was attacked by Hereros on August 30, 1880. Izaak and his family escaped to the south, but many of his people were slaughtered during this battle in the larger Herero-Nama conflict. A Nama force led by Izaak and Andries Lambert was successful against a Herero force at Khoa-gaos on September 12, 1880. After a series of other defeats, Maherero called back his commandos, but Izaak traveled to the various Nama communities, calling on them to unite and attack Maherero. He must be taught to respect boundaries, he said. A surprise attack by the Hereros routed the Namas, however, and Izaak and his men fled back to Berseba. He was now prepared to negotiate peace with Maherero, and represented both Berseba and Bethanie at a conference at Rehoboth in June 1882 that resulted finally in an agreement. The peace of Rehoboth did not settle the boundary problem, as this was left to a commission. Since Maherero himself was not present at the signing, nor were several important Nama leaders, the treaty meant little. Izaak returned to Berseba in an angry mood. When the Germans came into the territory, Izaak was at first unresponsive, but on January 29, 1885, he agreed to a Protection and Friendship Treaty with the German representative. The treaty was signed July 28, 1885.

IZAAKS, DAVID JACOBUS ("DAP") (1933–). Along with Hans Diergaardt (q.v.), Izaaks was a leader of the Rehoboth Liberation Party (RLP) that they formed in 1974 after breaking away from the Rehoboth Volkspartei. The RLP remained active in the National Convention of Freedom Parties (q.v.) of which Izaaks served as Chairman. From 1975 to 1977 he was a member of the Turnhalle Conference. Known as a moderate, Izaaks tried to steer his Baster followers between the anti-SWAPO and pro-SWAPO extremes. From 1984 to 1989 Izaaks served as speaker of the Rehoboth Volksraad. He was also a member of the TGNU from 1985 to 1989.

When the Liberated Democratic Party was formed in 1979 in a merger of his RLP and the Rehoboth Democratic Party, Izaaks became a leading member of it. He is currently its vice-chairman.

- J -

JA TOIVO, H. A. TOIVO. *See* YA-TOIVO, H. A. TOIVO.

JAGGER, JEREMIAH, W. (variant: JAGER) (1933–). Born in Rehoboth, Jagger has a teacher's diploma. He was a leading member of SWANU from 1959 to 1967. That year he left SWANU and was a co-founder and president of the Voice of the People (q.v.), a town-oriented political organization composed primarily of Namas and Damaras. He split with K. Conradie in 1975 on the issue of the Turnhalle Conference, which Jagger attended (1975–77) and Conradie did not. Jagger was expelled from the Voice of the People in 1975 and joined the Democratic Turnhalle Alliance. He was elected to the 1979–83 National Assembly. In 1984 he was one of the founders of Democratic Action for Namas, but the next year rejoined the Democratic Turnhalle Party of Namibia (q.v.), and was chosen one of its two members in the TGNU. In 1989 he won a DTA seat in the National Assembly.

JANONI. In the Ovambo tale of their beginning, Kalunga (their supreme being) created a man and a woman. The man (in one version of the tale) is named Noni. He and the woman had three sons and a daughter. The woman was named Janoni. She became the ancestral mother of the Ovambos.

JENTSCH, ADOLPH (1888–1977). One of the most influential of the Namibian painters, his work has influenced many younger artists. Born in Dresden, Germany, in 1888, he studied there before moving on to Paris, London, and Italy. He won several awards in Germany and later in South Africa. He came to Namibia and settled in 1936. His beautiful landscapes made use of an unusual vision of space, and portrayed the country almost spiritually, capturing a sense of timelessness. He specialized in watercolors, although he first worked in oil.

JOHANNES, AXEL (1946–). SWAPO administrative secretary inside Namibia during much of the 1970s, he was repeatedly arrested and tortured, but never formally charged with a crime. He joined SWAPO early in its history, and became secretary of its Youth League in 1966. During every police crackdown on SWAPO, Johannes was arrested and tortured. He was in solitary confinement for five months in 1974 under the Terrorism Act, and again after his arrest in August 1975, following the murder of Philemon Elifas (q.v.). In March 1976 he was sentenced to a year in prison for failing to give evidence in a trial of SWAPO members. In 1977 he was rearrested for failing to respond to a subpoena. On April 14, 1978, he was arrested under the Terrorism Act for questioning concerning the assassination of Chief Clemens Kapuuo (q.v.). Details of the torture he received then have been published. Finally he signed a "confession." Without having been tried, he spent five months in jail and was released in September 1978, only to be detained again from December until February 1979. En route to his parents' home in Owambo, he was again stopped by police and assaulted. He was arrested in April 1979 along with all other SWAPO leaders. In 1980 he was briefly held under house arrest in his Katatura home, but was permitted to leave Namibia for London in December 1980. He is currently a member of SWAPO's Central Committee and assigned to the office of the president.

JONKER, JAN. *See* AFRIKANDER, JAN JONKER.

JORDAN, WILLIAM WORTHINGTON (variant: WILLEM JORDAAN) (1849–1886). A unique and remarkable individual, he described himself as a trader, but might well be called a guide and real-estate promoter. Born at Wynberg in the Cape, his father was English and his mother was "Cape Coloured." He was in Bechuanaland (now Botswana) in late 1877 or early 1878 where he first met the group called the Thirstland Trekkers (q.v.). Later in 1878 he encountered the same group south of the Okavango River, and also in 1879 when he was trading and hunting at the Etosha Pan. He was able to help them in several ways, including medical services, and recorded their history as "Journal of the Trek Boers" in *The Cape Quarterly Review* (1881). He felt this group of South African pioneers could be the core of a "civilized" settler community in Namibia. After going off with Finnish missionaries for a few months, he met the Boers again in Kaokoland in 1880, and became their guide and friend. He told them that Angola was the answer to their quest, leading them to the highlands north of the Kunene River. He intervened with Portuguese authorities on their behalf. He also arranged to get wagons brought to their settlement in the Humpata area in 1881. He returned to the Cape for awhile, but, concerned about the Trekkers, he came back to Humpata in 1882 and found some of them to be unhappy. His next two years were spent variously guiding hunting parties and even bringing Jesuit missionaries to the new college at Huila. In January 1884, he arranged to purchase the Rehoboth territory from Chief Petrus Zwartbooi, head of the Zwartbooi Nama, but the deal fell through when the Germans declared it to be under their protective rule. Jordan then bought land south and southwest of the Etosha Pan from Chief Kambonde Ka Mpingana of the Ondongo people in Ovamboland. The price was twenty-five muskets, a salted horse, and a keg of brandy. He named the area the Republic of Upingtonia (q.v.) and laid out three hundred farms for the Trek Boers. He then led a small group of them there from Humpata. His deal with Kambonde also included mineral rights to this area, which includes the Otavi copper district. This angered Maharero and other Hereros who claimed the Otavi area as their own. Kambonde was even urged to kill Jordan to discourage whites from occupying the whole region. In March 1886, Kambonde revoked the sale, and on June 30, men working for Nehale (Kambonde's brother) killed Jordan, who was travelling from Grootfontein to see Kambonde and had camped at Omandonga in Ondonga. While this murder ended the Republic of Upingtonia, it did not end the problem of the concessions. Jordan had sent his sale document to Cape Town, where it was auctioned after his death. A syndicate of seven men bought it, and after the Germans acknowledged its validity, the South West Africa Company was formed in London to exploit it.

JOSEPH, MAXTON (variant: MAXTON JOSEPH MUTON-GULUME). One of the earliest members of SWAPO, having worked with Herman Toivo, Andreas Shipanga and the others in its formative years in Cape Town. In the mid-1960s Joseph, an Ovambo, set up a SWAPO office in Francistown, Botswana. He had a Land Rover which he used to transport

Ovambo mine workers into Zambia at the Kazungula crossing. These were potential freedom fighters. British authorities put an end to this, so an office was opened in Lusaka, Zambia, linked to the Francistown base. The Organization of African Unity set up a camp for the potential guerrillas, providing weapons and training. Joseph remained active in diverting potential guerrillas to these offices and camps. A member of SWAPO's Central Committee, he returned to Namibia in 1989 in preparation for Namibian independence. In its first cabinet Joseph is minister of transport.

JUNIUS, PETRUS M. ("PIET") (1941–). A teacher and a farmer, he was born in Rehoboth and in 1971 helped fund the Rehoboth Baster Association. He represented the Basters at the Turnhalle Conference (1975–77) as a member of the Rehoboth delegation. When the DTA was formed in 1977 he was a founder, as the Rehoboth Baster Association became a part of the DTA. He was elected to the 1979–83 National Assembly, and was vice-chairman of the DTA from 1985–89. In 1986 he was expelled from the RBA, so he formed the Progressive People's Party in September of that year. From 1985 to 1989 he was a member of the cabinet of the TGNU. When his PPP merged with the Christian Democratic Union in March 1989, he was the founding leader of the resulting Christian Democratic Party, which he affiliated with the DTA. Number seven on the DTA electoral list in 1989, he easily secured a seat in the National Assembly.

- K -

KAHITJENE. A distinguished nineteenth-century Herero chief, he was a rival of Tjamuaha (q.v.) and an enemy of Jonker Afrikander (q.v.), who was notorious for raiding the cattle of both Herero leaders. In December 1842, Jonker agreed to stop the raids, but this was not a lasting peace. Jonker even gave him a few guns as a gift. Late in 1844, however, a new source of trouble came. Oasib (q.v.), a Nama leader, visited Kahitjene's village, presumably in peace. After the Herero leader courteously provided Oasib and his men with milk, the Namas turned on their hosts and attacked them. Oasib's men took all the cattle at that village, killing those who resisted. This disillusioned Kahitjene about Jonker's ability to protect him.

In December 1848, Jonker Afrikander again began attacking the Hereros. One of the first he killed was Kamukamu, Kahitjene's half-brother, who had just revealed (unawares) where all the Herero cattle kraals were. Jonker went on a series of raids, killing sixty Herero defenders and stealing the cattle. Kahitjene was obliged to take revenge, but his attack on Jonker was not much of a success. The brother of the Herero leader was killed, as were some of his best warriors, and he lost many cattle as well. Kahitjene then turned to several weaker victims, among them Hekununa and Mungundu, and regained some land and cattle.

In mid-1850, Kahitjene then moved his people to Okahandja where the pastures were better, near Tjamuaha's village. Kahitjene lived in constant fear of an attack by Jonker. On August 23 he and his people left Okahandja to seek refuge with Rev. C. H. Hahn at Barmen. But they were only briefly on the trail when Jonker and 350 warriors (with 150 guns) attacked the travellers. A massacre took place, and even the women and children were not spared. Kahitjene and about 20 warriors escaped back to Rev. Kolbe's mission station at Okahandja. They took sanctuary in the church and were not harmed. When Jonker pretended to leave, the Hereros left the church. Again the Namas attacked. The Herero leader wounded one of them with an arrow and the distraction was enough to permit his escape. This time he fled at night to Barmen, but Jonker anticipated that move and followed. A messenger from Rev. Kolbe to Rev. Hahn saved the Herero chief, who fled to one of his outposts, considerably to the north near the Omatako River.

When Kahitjene's uncle, Mungunda, died, he inherited control of the estate, but a dispute arose when he took many of the cattle to his northern outposts. Mungunda's sons were furious, attacked one of the outposts, and killed one of Katjihene's sons in early 1851. In mid-March he and a few of his remaining men, plus his nephew and heir, Mauto, went to visit the graves of those recently killed. He was aware of the danger involved, but went in mourning. Mungunda's sons and their warriors attacked, killing both the old chief and his heir. Tjamuaha expropriated his remaining cattle.

KAISER STREET, WINDHOEK. Known by the Germans as Kaiserstrasse, this is the main street of Windhoek and is lined with both late-twentieth-century multistoried buildings and quaint Germanic store fronts from eighty years earlier. It is the bustling heart of the capital city. After independence it might be renamed Independence Street.

KAISER WILHELM MOUNTAIN. One of the largest mountains near Windhoek, it is 1997 meters high and is located about 8 kilometers southwest of the heart of the capital. The mountain was a good point for refuge when Hereros faced their enemies. Maherero (q.v.) was known to flee there to avoid the Namas, and at one point in August 1850 he defeated Namas there. On January 28, 1904, Hereros who had attacked Okahandja in a revolt against the Germans were themselves attacked by a German relief column led by Captain Victor Franke (q.v.). The Hereros fled to this mountain, but Franke's troops flushed them from their refuge and forced them into the open.

The mountain was named by two German missionaries, Diehl and Irle, who were the first Europeans to climb it. In 1871 they climbed it in celebration of the formation of the German empire. For that reason they named it after their new emperor.

KALAHARI DESERT. One of Africa's great deserts, it stretches along much of the eastern border of Namibia, but even more of it lies within the boundaries of Botswana, where a favorite spelling is Kgalagadi. The name means "salt pans." While the Kalahari has its share of sand dunes, most of it can be better described as a dry and waterless region, sometimes covered with a layer of red sand. Nevertheless, there are areas where water is more plentiful, shrubs grow, and grazing of livestock is possible. The San people have survived there for many centuries, hunting game animals and gathering veldkost (q.v.). Among the rivers that cross Namibia's portion of the Kalahari are the Elephant, the Nossob, the Rietfontein, the Epikuro, the Eiseb, and the Auob. Gobabis is the largest town, but there are areas heavily populated by Tswanas, Eastern Hereros, and San.

In the early twentieth century, the Kalahari had significance as Africans battled the Germans. Nama leaders like Hendrik Witbooi and Simon Koper (qq.v.) used it as a refuge for their guerrilla attacks, knowing that the Germans were not likely to pursue them there. Unfortunately Hereros were not as fortunate, as many perished in the desert sands fleeing the Germans after the Battle of Waterberg (q.v.) in 1904.

Rocky hills sometimes protrude from the desert floor, with areas near Namibia's eastern border reaching 1200 meters above sea level (compared to a low of 200 meters). The Kalahari is home to many game animals, some of them in the Kalahari Gemsbok National Park in western Botswana. The northern Kalahari is well-watered, with the Okavango River creating swamplands and lakes. Lake Ngami, further south, is now increasingly dry. Most of these areas are in Botswana, not Namibia, but there are many Africans who have traditionally cared little for international boundaries. San, Herero, and Tswana are among the people who cross them at will, and in the nineteenth century many European explorers crossed through Namibia to reach Lake Ngami.

KALANGULA, REV. PETER T. (1926–). A major Wambo political figure who has remained outside SWAPO, Rev. Kalangula was born in Omafo in the Kwanyama tribal area of Owambo. He was educated at the St. Mary's Anglican Mission School, and later taught school for two years before entering the civil service, where he worked as a clerk in the Native Affairs Department from 1948 to 1965. In 1966 he went to a theological school in South Africa and was ordained an Anglican deacon in 1969. A dispute with bishop Colin Winter (q.v.) led him to found the Owambo Independent (Anglican) Church in 1971. (However, in 1979 he was ordained a priest of the Church of England in South Africa.)

Kalangula's leadership in the church dispute led many to encourage him to become active politically. He was named to the Owambo Legislative Council in 1973 as a member of the Owambo Independence Party, which later became the National Democratic Party (NDP) (q.v.). He was a delegate to the Turnhalle Conference, where he was active on the committees. When the Democratic Turnhalle Alliance was formed, the NDP became part of it. Meanwhile Kalangula was serving as minister of works and later also minister of education on Owambo. In 1978, he was elected to the National Assembly, but relinquished that seat in 1981 to spend more of his time in Owambo government.

With the death of Rev. Cornelius Ndjoba (q.v.) in 1980, Kalangula replaced the pastor as chairman of the Owambo Executive Committee and as president of the DTA. The next year he also became president of the NDP. He soon became frustrated with DTA, condemning its ethnic policies as unworkable. He felt the alliance should be converted into a single united party. He also was disturbed that DTA leaders did not try to hasten changes in Namibia, and he repeatedly charged that the South African Defence Force and the South African police were guilty of violence and intimidation in Owambo. In February 1982, he resigned from the DTA, taking with him other NDP members and even a member of the Republican Party. He then founded a new party, the Christian Democratic Action for Social Justice (CDA) (q.v.). He led the CDA as the majority party in the Owambo Legislative Assembly up until Assembly was disbanded in 1989. His actions as chairman of the Assembly's Executive Committee included "localization" of the Owambo civil service wherever possible and the adoption of English as the teaching medium in schools.

In the mid to late 1980s, there were various reports that Kalangula was trying to unite the CDA with other groups, such as the People's Consultative Conference in 1986, the TGNU in 1987, and the United Democratic Front in 1989. But none of these mergers came to fruition. Ultimately he ran the CDA in the 1989 elections as an independent political party and lost terribly. Its electoral list attracted only 2495 voters, the second lowest total; it won no seats in the new National Assembly.

KALKFONTEIN, PEACE OF. An agreement was concluded at Kalkfontein on January 27, 1904. The German governor, T.

von Leutwein (q.v.), settled a dispute with the Bondelswarts by agreeing to grant them the Warmbad Reserve in exchange for their turning in three hundred guns. This action freed German troops from the south to move north against the Hereros. It did not stop Jacob Marengo (q.v.), however, from resuming his anti-German raids. Kalkfontein was re-named Karasburg (q.v.) in 1939.

KALUNGA. The Wambo name for their Supreme Spirit, who has the form of a man but moves among them invisibly. To him are attributed all good and evil that humans experience. Famine is sent by Kalunga, as is a bountiful harvest. A spirit doctor can try to rid a person of sickness or evil spirits, but if he fails he says that only Kalunga can decide whether the person is to be cured. Kalunga also created the first man and woman. All Wambo tribes believe in him. Kalunga's concerns are with the whole universe. He is not a lawgiver, as morality stems from tribal customs, yet he expects people to abide by these community mores. While he is omnipresent and omniscient, he lives in the sacred fire (*see* FIRE, SACRED), which must not be extinguished because the welfare of the community depends on it.

KAMAHERERO. *See* MAHERERO.

KAMBUNGO. According to Wambo tradition, Kambungo was one of several sixteenth-century leaders who brought his people south into today's Namibia. He settled his people near a lake or pan to a site called Hakafia, from which other leaders took their followers to still further sites.

KAMEETA, REV. ZEPHANIA (1945–). The head of the Paulineum College at Otjimbingwe from 1975 to 1977, he was one of the political figures arrested and detained by the South African police in 1975 after the assassination of Chief Elfias (q.v.). He had been prominent in the founding of the Namibia National Convention (q.v.) in 1974. He is considered to be a leading exponent of Black liberation theology in Namibia. He was named a deputy bishop of the Evangelical Lutheran Church in 1985. Meanwhile, he was also an officer of internal SWAPO, and in the 1989 elections he was chosen to the new Assembly, having been number thirteen on the SWAPO electoral list.

KAOKOLAND. The word Kaoko means "a place of silence." The difference between the two works "Kaokoland" and "Kaokoveld" (q.v.) are probably more semantic than real. Both refer to the same general area of northwestern Namibia. "Kaokoland" is a more recent usage than the other and is obviously an Anglicized version, as there is little real difference between land and veld. The latter is perhaps more a descriptive term used by geographers rather than historians or politicians. This leads to the second and more significant difference. In referring to the different sections of the country as "homelands," South Africa has used the term "Kaokoland."

As a homeland, Kaokoland is certainly the least homogeneous. Its residents include the Himba (a Herero clan), Nama subgroups, Damara, and San. Most of these people took refuge in this barren rock country because they were not welcome elsewhere and found tranquility there. The underdeveloped character of the area is demonstrated by South Africa's decision not to create a "tribal government" in the area. It set up a bare minimum administrative center at Ohopoho, a tiny community at the intersection of two dirt paths in the eastern part of Kaokoland, only thirty kilometers from Owambo. The total area of Kaokoland is about 23,000 square miles.

The area of "official" Kaokoland extends from the Atlantic Ocean to Owambo, and from the Kunene River on the north to the Hoanib River on the south as its stretches from west to east in an arc. The Etosha National Park abuts its southeast segment. The town of Sesfontein (q.v.) is almost at its southernmost point.

KAOKOVELD. As explained in the previous entry, it is difficult to define precisely what the word means. Loosely it is the same region as that called Kaokoland, but perhaps minus the Skeleton Coast segment of the Namib Desert that marks its western boundary. Some prefer to limit the word to the more accessible and better watered savanna region in the southern part of the Kaokoland homeland.

The rivers in the Kaokoveld tend to be dry most of the time, except for the Kunene on the northern border, and the best sources of water are the various strong springs that are scattered through the area, such as at Sesfontein and Kaoko-Otavi, among others.

The total population of Kaokoveld is probably under 20,000, mostly Himba, Tjimba (both of Herero background), Damara, Nama, and San (qq.v.). Most of them live as hunters and gatherers, mixed sometimes with a little agriculture. There is some very productive agriculture, however, in the southern section, especially around Sesfontein (q.v.), where there are strong springs and better rainfall. The mountainous north (there are perhaps twenty separate mountain ranges in Kaokoveld) is rocky and barren, with the exception of some lush valleys. Some of the mountains contain excellent iron ore reserves that can be mined in the future.

Parts of the Kaokoveld were formerly part of the Etosha National Park, but have since been removed from it, including the most scenic sections. Fortunately, endangered species like the rhino and black-faced impala were removed to safety.

KAPELWA, RICHARD. A longtime SWAPO activist in the Caprivi, he is head of the party's Katima Mulilo regional center. His rise to party influence accelerated in January 1986, when a SWAPO Politburo meeting in Luanda promoted him from interim secretary of defence to be advisor to Sam Nujoma (q.v.). In the 1989 Assembly elections he was number thirty-one on SWAPO's electoral list, and thus procured a seat in the Assembly. He was then named to the cabinet as minister of works, transport, and communications. In a cabinet shuffle on April 10, 1992, Kapelwa traded portfolios with the minister of lands, resettlement, and rehabilitation, Marco Hausiku.

KAPTEIN (variant: CAPTAIN). A word used equivalently to Chief, it is especially used today by the Basters at Rehoboth, but has been applied in the literature to other African leaders.

KAPUUO, CLEMENS (1923–1978). One of the most important figures in Namibian politics in the 1960s and 1970s, he was born at Ozondjona in the Okahandja district. His basic education was at an Anglican mission school in Windhoek, but he then went to Johannesburg to take a program to become a teacher. His activism was demonstrated as early as 1950 when he was elected president of the SWA Teachers' Association. He served in that role for three years.

A cousin of the late Herero chief, Samuel Maharero (q.v.), he held a high place in Herero traditional circles. In 1947 he was an interpreter for Chief Hosea Kutako (q.v.), and thus was involved in the latter's petitions to the United Nations. He also served on the Chief's Council for well over a decade. In 1958 the leaders of the twelve Herero Reserves decided that they needed a deputy paramount chief serving under the eighty-eight-year-old Kutako, so that South Africa would not be able to appoint a successor if he died. The choice of Kapuuo as Kutako's successor was confirmed unanimously by the headmen of all the Reserves in March 1960. (Kutako did not die until 1970.)

Kapuuo's involvement in modern politics certainly began when working with Kutako on the appeals to the UN, but he has also been implicated in the Windhoek Old Location riots of December 1959. He corresponded with Mburumba Kerina (q.v.) about the failure of the West to help liberate Namibia. He also admitted to having helped in the drafting of SWANU's constitution. As the presiding leader of the Herero Chief's Council he strongly supported SWANU. However he eventually became unhappy with the party, most of whose leaders were in self-exile in Europe. In 1964 Kapuuo reorganized the Chief's Council and on September 25 created a new political party, the National Unity Democratic Organization (q.v.), known as NUDO. Its leadership was virtually identical to the new Chief's Council, and Kapuuo was its leader.

Meanwhile Kapuuo had resigned his teaching position and had opened a small grocery store in Katatura. When Chief Kutako died on July 26, 1970, Kapuuo immediately became the Herero paramount chief. However, the South African administrators chose not to accept him for a long time, designating instead a Herero whom they had brought back from Botswana. The reason was clear, as Kapuuo was an outspoken political activist. When the International Court gave Namibia a favorable ruling in 1971 he quickly endorsed it, arguing that South Africa did not have the right to impose its rule or to implement the Report of the Odendaal Commission (q.v.). Late in 1971 he joined with other traditional leaders in calling for a meeting with Namibian whites and in calling for freedom of speech and movement and equal work opportunities.

As a result, Kapuuo's home was regularly searched by police, and his own travel rights were limited. He was allowed (with no advance warning) a three-hour meeting with UN Secretary-General Kurt Waldheim in March 1972. He presented Waldheim with a petition requesting that the UN immediately take over Namibia's rule.

Meanwhile, Kapuuo was part of a movement to bring together Namibians who had created separate political groups. The National Convention of Freedom Parties (q.v.) met in Rehoboth in November 1971. It appointed a committee to draw up a New Namibian constitution, and Kapuuo chaired that committee. He specifically invited whites and all parties not at Rehoboth to join in the movement. While he encouraged UN involvement in Namibia, when he visited the UN in New York in 1973 he denounced its choice of SWAPO as the sole representative of Namibians.

The National Convention of Freedom Parties split up in February 1975, as some groups were opposed to Kapuuo. He then forged a new alliance immediately, called the National Convention (of Namibia) (q.v.), not to be confused with the Namibia National Convention (q.v.). Kapuuo's NCN lasted into the Turnhalle Conference, as many groups represented there joined it. In fact at the Turnhalle Kapuuo made a detailed constitutional proposal under the sponsorship of the NCN. (For some of the proposal's details, *see* NATIONAL CONVENTION OF NAMIBIA.)

Kapuuo was an extremely vocal and active leader at the Turnhalle, and could almost be called charismatic in his ability to attract followers. When the conference was over, Dirk Mudge (q.v.) and Chief Kapuuo formed the Democratic

Turnhalle Alliance. Kapuuo was its president and Mudge was chairman. The NCN ceased to exist, as most of the member groups joined the DTA.

While both SWAPO and Chief Kapuuo were struggling to get independence for Namibia, their tactics were totally different and each side bitterly worked against the other. Kapuuo was smeared, probably unjustly, as the white man's puppet. SWAPO is accused of having killed Kapuuo's bodyguard in 1978; on March 27, 1978, Kapuuo was assassinated behind his shop in Katutura. SWAPO denied having killed him. Supporters of SWAPO and South Africans are other suspects.

!KARA-GAI-KHOIN (variant: KARA-GEI-KHOI). A name used by those Nama peoples who were later referred to as Franzmannschen Hottentots (q.v.). The name means "the very tall people."

KARAKUL SHEEP. The breeding of karakul sheep and the sale of their pelts is a major commercial enterprise in Namibia. This can be seen by the value of karakul pelt exports reaching R35 million in 1988. (However, prices were much better in the 1970s, when R47 million was earned in 1979.) Since 1965 karakul pelts from Namibia have been marketed under the name Swakara: "Swa" for South West Africa, combined with "kara" from the sheeps' name (q.v.).

Karakul sheep came originally from the Uzbekistan region (formerly part of the USSR), near the border of Afghanistan. For many centuries the pelts have been sent from Turkestan to Europe on old caravan routes run by Persian traders. Thus the pelts were often called "Persian lamb," or sometimes "astrakhan." The word "karakul" is derived from a language in central Asia that says "kara-gyull," which means "black rose." An alternative story, however, says that the name means "black lake," and refers to the Great Kara Kul, a lake in Tadzhikistan where the sheep were also commonly found.

A German businessman visited Bokhara in 1902 and decided that there was a potential for raising these sheep in German colonies. A few sheep were sent to Germany in 1903 to see if they could be bred outside Asia. That experiment was a success, so the same businessman, Paul A. Thorer (q.v.) brought 23 rams and 255 ewes to Namibia in 1909. (Reportedly a small group of 12 sheep were imported in 1907 by the governor.) Another large shipment came four years later. The sheep did better in Namibia than in Germany, as they thrive on a semi-arid climate, such as central and southern Namibia. They feed on short grass and various bushes. If the grass to too sweet it causes undesirable traits in the fur.

The good karakul comes from the pelts of lambs that are killed twenty-four to forty-eight hours after birth. It is then that the curl is the tightest. Some farmers say anything after twenty-four hours is automatically less desirable. The best pelts have a rich, silky luster or sheen. The texture is like velvet and designers can do more with the best pelts. Originally black pelts were bred, but dyes can now be applied. Also other shades, including brown and blue-gray, have some popularity. The carcasses of the lambs are not generally eaten, as whites do not like the meat's taste. Some Africans consider it to be a favorite delicacy, however. The farmers typically crush the carcasses into bonemeal to feed other animals or use it as manure.

Older karakul sheep, including those previously used as breeders, have a straight and less lustrous hair that can be used for carpets or blankets. Some of the wool can be used for fine worsteds.

The growth of the karakul industry can be seen in the number produced and sold in the territory. In 1936 the figure was 814,561. By 1950 it had reached 2,607,327 pelts. During the 1930s, diamond sales were low, and the karakul exports were the highest values export industry. The raising of karakul sheep is not limited to Namibia, as nearby areas of South Africa also produce the sheep, but in smaller quantities than Namibia. Pelts in Namibia have been generally marketed through cooperatives, the largest being the Boeremakelaars Koöperatief Beperk. They are collected, packed and shipped to London. There one of two big auctions houses, Eastwood and Holt Ltd. or Hudson Bay and Annings Ltd. sell the pelts. The government's Karakul Board controls breeding and sales in Namibia and charges an export fee.

KARASBURG. With a population estimated at 4000 (3484 in 1981), it ranks eleventh among the communities of Namibia in population. Its name had been Kalkfontein but was changed in 1939. The principal town in the Warmbad district of southern Namibia, it is located on the main rail line going north to Windhoek. It is situated on the southern fringe of the Karas Mountains, about 123 kilometers from the eastern border with South Africa along the rail line from Upington, and about 100 kilometers due north of the Orange River. Karasburg has been the major commercial center for a large rural area, with karakul pelts a major commodity of the region.

KARAS MOUNTAINS, GREAT AND LITTLE (variant: KAR-RAS). Two ranges separated by a valley generally about 30 kilometers wide, they are located in south-central Namibia. They are south and southeast of Keetmanshoop. Both receive plentiful rainfall, as a number of streams begin in these mountains. The Great Karas range is further east than the Small Karas, and is considerably longer (100 kilometers to 40 kilometers), wider (30 kilometers to 12 kilometers) and taller (2,167 meters to 1500 meters for the tallest eminences). Great Karas is actually two great ridges topped with quartzite, while Little Karas is a plateau with a steep drop on the west side. Most game animals have vanished from both ranges, although some smaller antelopes still live there.

The Karas (referred to some places as the Karras Hills) played an important role in Nama insurgency movements against the Germans early in the twentieth century. The Bondelswarts, led by Chief Willem Christian, used the Karas heights as a refuge. Jacob Marengo (q.v.) also frequently used them and had his base of operations against the Germans in the Karas Mountains as of September 1904. From this location he could make swift raids and harass the German soldiers. Captain Cornelius (q.v.) joined his forces with Marengo in the mountains in July 1905. It took a year to a year and a half before the German forces could successfully eliminate the African resistance groups in the Karas Mountains.

KARIBIB. Meaning literally "the watering place beside the plain," this town is situated along the line of rail and the main trunk road between Swakopmund and Windhoek. It is 184 kilometers (121 miles) northeast of the former and 192 kilometers (117 meters) northwest of the latter. With a population estimated to be about 2000 in 1988, it is among the country's twenty largest towns. The area originally was a farm owned by the German trader Otto Hälbich, who was the son of a nineteenth-century German missionary. The Rhenish mission station there was not actually constructed until 1902. It took on more importance when the rail line was built, as Karibib was located about halfway between the two ends of the line. In 1906 railway workshops were established there to do repair work. The plentiful water supply nearby was another reason for the trains to stop at Karibib, which soon became a thriving village. One report mentions that Karibib was briefly called the capital of "South West." During World War I, German troops fought to defend Karibib, but it was ultimately taken by the South African forces.

KARRAS HILLS. *See* KARAS MOUNTAINS.

KARSTVELD. Also referred to as the Karst region or district, it is a large semicircular land tract lying between Damaraland and Owambo. It is a wide plain that slopes gently toward the Etosha Pan. Parts of it are now within the boundaries of the Etosha National Park, while both Tsumeb and Grootfontein are in the eastern part of the Karstveld. The area stops just north of Otjiwarongo. On the west it abuts Kaokoveld (q.v.). Like the European plateau called the "Karst," after which it was named, Namibia's Karst region consists of limestone and dolomite hills. Cattle find excellent grazing in its wide valleys, which made it a popular region for Herero chiefs to send their surplus cattle.

KASHE, GEELBOOI (variant: KAESJE) (1931–). A leader of the Bushmen Alliance Group in the 1970s, and a participant at the Turnhalle Conference, he followed through and worked with the DTA in the December 1978 Assembly elections. He was elected to the Assembly and then appointed to Namibia's Council of Ministers.

Born near Gobabis in 1931, he received no formal education. Married and the father of seven children, he worked in his younger years as a laborer, as a police officer, and as an administrative assistant. Later he became involved with "Bushman" politics, serving as translator for the Bushman Representative to the South African prime minister's Advisory Council. He was then appointed in 1975 as a delegate to the Turnhalle Conference.

He has been a member of the DTA Head Committee since 1983 and served in the TGNU. His continuing involvement in the Democratic Turnhalle Alliance led to his placement as number twelve on the DTA electoral list in the 1989 elections. As a result, he was given one of the DTA's seats in the Constituent Assembly and ultimately Namibia's first truly National Assembly.

KASSINGA. *See* CASSINGA.

KATATURA. *See* KATUTURA.

KATHU. According to Wambo tradition, Kathu was the son of Nangombe Ya Mungundu (q.v.) and the brother of Nangombe. The brothers traveled from the north and east into the Ndonga area to today's Owambo. There they split up. While Nangombe and his successors stayed in Owambo, Kathu travelled on with his followers and herds of cattle, first into the Kaokoveld, where some stayed and became known as the Himbas (q.v.), and then further south.

KATIMA MULILO. The capital of the Eastern Caprivi and its only significant town, it is situated on the Namibian bank of the Zambezi River. It is one of the country's more attractive and colorful towns and could become a magnet for tourists. Tiger fishing, motor boating on the river, and watching game close-up are among its attractions. It is located directly across the Zambezi from the Zambian town called Shisheke. During the period of SWAPO guerrilla activity, the South

African Defence Force used the town as an air base from which to conduct operations into Zambia. In 1978 guerrilla forces fired a deadly artillery bombardment of Katima Mulilo. South African forces retaliated by crossing the Zambezi in pursuit of the guerrillas. South Africa regularly used the town to raid SWAPO bases in Zambia.

KATJAVIVI, PETER HITJITEVI (1941–). An increasingly important member of the SWAPO hierarchy, he is becoming one of the most visible Hereros in a party dominated by Wambos. Born in Okahandja, he was educated first at a Lutheran mission school there, then at the Herero school in Windhoek, and finally at the Augustineum College in Okahandja. He then worked briefly as a law clerk in Windhoek before being awarded a scholarship to Stanford University in the United States. He tried to escape the country in 1962 to travel to the US, but was arrested by Rhodesian police en route to Tanganyika. After a series of detentions, including a period of forced labor, he was freed by a British resident commissioner in Bechuanaland (now Botswana). When he arrived in Dar es Salaam in December 1962, it was too late to take the American scholarship. Instead he was given a grant to study at a college in Nigeria for two years. Afterwards, he returned to Dar es Salaam to study history and law; he also became deeply involved in SWAPO. President Nujoma made him an executive assistant in 1967 and assigned him to run the London office in 1968. He also attended the International Court sessions on Namibia in 1971 and appeared with Nujoma before the UN Security Council the same year.

He has been a valuable member of SWAPO. At one point he was its minister for economics and justice and in the late 1970s he was secretary for information and publicity. In the latter capacity he was heavily involved in writing and editing an excellent SWAPO publication, *To Be Born a Nation*. He later wrote another fine treatment of Namibian politics, *A History of Resistance in Namibia*, published in 1988. This was a revised version of his doctoral dissertation; he has returned from England, where he had earned a doctorate at St. Anthony's College of Oxford University. His education, world contacts, and job experience made him an obvious choice to run for office. In the 1989 elections he was number twenty-four of the SWAPO's electoral list, easily winning him a seat in the National Assembly. He may end up more active in SWAPO than in the government, however.

KATJIUONGUA, MOSES KATJIKURU (1942–). Born in Windhoek, Katjiuongua is the son of a man who was a counsellor to the then Herero Chief, Hosea Kutako (q.v.). His education was truly international; he has studied in Botswana, Sweden, East Germany, and Canada. He has a BS in political science from the University of Stockholm (1980), as well as an MA from the same school. He later earned an MA in public administration from Carleton University in Ottawa, Canada.

The college degrees came, however, long after he had begun to make contributions to Namibia's political development. At the age of seventeen, in 1959, he left Namibia with two colleagues and travelled through Botswana to Tanzania and ultimately Cairo. He studied journalism for a year and a half in East Germany and then returned to Cairo to work in SWANU's office there. He travelled over the next few years to several foreign capitals, usually in conjunction with a leftist conference. His itinerary included Tanzania in 1963, Bejing in 1964, Tanzania again in 1965, and Havana, Cuba, in 1966. By this time he was on SWANU's External Council and editor of the *Windhoek Review*. He then moved to Stockholm, Sweden, for more education, while continuing his SWAPO work, and finally to Canada for his second MA.

In 1982 Katjiuongua returned to Namibia and was elected president of SWANU. When he agreed to lead SWANU into the Multi-Party Conference (q.v.) in 1983, he triggered a major conflict within the party. While he was out of the country, dissidents within SWANU called a party congress and deposed him from all offices. After his return a later congress reversed this, but many members then broke away to form what became known as SWANU-P and later as SWANU-NNF. He was then re-elected president of SWANU in 1984. In the Transitional Government of National Unity he served as minister of manpower, national health, and welfare from 1985 to 1989.

When plans were formulated for an election in 1989 to a Constituent Assembly, Katjiuongua teamed SWANU with two other groups, CANU and ANS (qq.v.) in an election alliance called the National Patriotic Front of Namibia. (Thus his faction is sometimes referred to as SWANU-NPF.) He was elected chairman of the National Patriotic Front (q.v.). In the elections the NPF won only one seat in the Assembly, and Katjiuongua was the designated recipient. He is thus now a member of the National Assembly of Namibia. Since independence there has been talk about the possibility of reuniting the two factions of SWANU. In Namibia's new National Assembly he proposed the creation of a commission to investigate the fact that many individuals detained by SWAPO during the war of independence were never accounted for. The government agreed to do so in July, 1990.

KATUTURA (variant: KATATURA). A large township five to seven kilometers northwest of the business center of Windhoek, it was built by the South African-appointed administration beginning in August 1958. It was built to be a "black" township, designed to ease the overcrowding in Windhoek, according to the administration. Africans saw it as a step toward bringing apartheid to Namibia. This perception was reinforced by the fact that a separate community, Khomasdal (q.v.), was being built for Windhoek's Coloured population, and by the fact that Katutura itself was subdivided into zones for the various tribal groups.

Katutura originally was to have 2630 four-room "cottages," plus 222 three-room apartments, 264 two-room units, and bachelor flats for seasonal workers. They were to be built of concrete and brick. Shops, government buildings, a post office, bank, library, and a beer hall were all part of the plan, plus spaces for churches. While South Africa praised the new township, Namibians saw themselves being forced from their homes near the heart of Windhoek in the "Old Location." Riots broke out in the Windhoek Old Location (q.v.) in December 1959 to protest the forced eviction.

Ironically the word "Katutura," from the Herero language, means "place where we do not stay." This is opposite the government's original intent to call it "Katututura" meaning "he does not move from here." Because of the large concentration of Blacks in Katutura, it was obviously the center of political demonstrations and strikes prior to serious independence negotiations. It was also the scene of regular "sweeps" by police units. Ironically, after independence, notably in 1991, the residents of Katutura complain that their new police force is not efficient enough in dealing with a rising rate of violent crimes. These are mainly armed robberies by gangs of unemployed youths in the older black townships. The new police force has a lack of adequately trained personnel.

KAUKAUVELD. An 83,000-square-mile section of the Omaheke or Sandveld region, it is part of the Kalahari Desert and stretches from east of Grootfontein (in northern Namibia) to the Botswana border. It is covered with a thick layer of sand, yet has an abundance of thick bush, huge baobab trees, and marulu trees. Palm trees grow in the north. (Trees are generally thicker in the north near the Okavango swamps in Botswana.) Animals are also numerous in the north. There are numerous lime-pans, ensuring a plentiful and reliable water supply. Settlers were not permitted in the area, so its population consists mostly of San. The major settlement in the area is Tsumkwe (q.v.).

KAULUMA, REV. JAMES HAMUPANDA. Born in Ongula in Owambo, he became the first Namibian to be appointed Bishop of Namibia by the Anglican Church. He was consecrated in London on January 15, 1978. He received a BA from the University of Toronto, and an MA from New York University. He continued his studies, working toward an MA in divinity and a Ph.D. in history. As Bishop he became involved somewhat in politics as well. When a conference was held in Geneva, Switzerland, in January 1981 to discuss a resolution of the question of Namibia's independence, bishop Kauluma and other Namibian church leaders travelled there also to work behind the scenes.

KAURA, N. KATUUTIRE (1941–). A member of Namibia's National Assembly chosen in 1989, he first became involved in politics in 1959 when he joined SWANU. He was its UN representative from 1961 to 1971. He joined NUDO in 1975 and is still active as its chairman.

Kaura received a bachelor's degree in history at Long Island University in 1971; a master of science degree, also from LIU, in 1971; a master of education degree from Columbia University in 1976; and then continued for two more years at Columbia as a Ph.D. candidate. However, he returned to Windhoek in 1978 and was elected to the National Assembly that same year. He (and NUDO) were also affiliated with the DTA. He became an outspoken critic of SWAPO, calling its members "Russian stooges" and "racist murderers." He also denounced the United Nations for its support of SWAPO. He represented the DTA in the Multi-Party Conference (q.v.) and in the Transitional government of National Unity. In the latter he served as deputy minister of finance and governmental affairs, working under its minister, Dirk Mudge (q.v.). He was given a high placement (number thirteen) on the DTA electoral list in 1989 and was elected to the Assembly, where he again will work closely with Mudge from the opposition benches. At a DTA central committee meeting in November, 1991, Kaura was confirmed as Vice President of the DTA of Namibia. In June, 1992 he gained added importance in the National Assembly when the party gave him the responsibility in its shadow cabinet as chief spokesman on matters of Home Affairs, Justice, and Lands, all very important issues.

KAVANGO NATIONAL COUNCIL (variant: KAVANGO AL-LIANCE). The political organization of this "self-governing homeland" was represented at the Turnhalle Conference (q.v.) by five delegates. Their leader was Chief Alfons Majavero. When it affiliated later with the Democratic Turnhalle Alliance it took a new name, the Kavango Alliance. Later it was reorganized as the National Democratic Unity Party (q.v.) but remained a part of the DTA under Chief Majavero in the 1978 Assembly elections. Three of its supporters were chosen to the National Assembly: Hendrik Muremi, Rudolf Nekwaya, and Gerhard Shakadya. Gelasius Sivhute served on the Council of Ministers. All would be considered "conservative" politicians. Chief Majavero was number eleven on the DTA electoral list in 1989, and thus was awarded a seat in the Constituent Assembly—and therefore in independent Namibia's first legislature.

KAVANGOLAND. An artificial creation of South African administrators who attempted to divide Namibia into distinct ethnic-based units, its form is intimately related to the Okavango River, from which it gets its name. The Okavango begins in Angola and flows south until it reaches—and becomes—the Angolan/Namibia border. It then flows east and is the northern border of both Namibia and Kavangoland. When the river turns south again, slicing through the Caprivi Strip, it forms the principal eastern border of Kavangoland. The central area of the Strip, between the Kavango and the Kwando River (also cutting through roughly north to south), is a game reserve often called Western Caprivi. It is listed on other maps as Kavangoland #2. Essentially, Kavangoland is the northeastern sector of Namibia, minus the eastern part of the Caprivi Strip. Kavangoland is bordered on the west by Owambo, on the southeast by Botswana. The southern border does not reach as far as the mining areas around Tsumeb and Grootfontein.

Kavangoland has a hot climate with plentiful rainfall, the highest in Namibia. More than two hundred varieties of trees and shrubs cover its landscape. Tall grass is common. Under these circumstances Kavangoland has ample potential to become a major agricultural area for Namibia. Cattle can also be raised there, and the timber industry has potential also. Many of the Kavango people are talented sculptors in wood, and their products are sold to tourists. The people of Kavangoland are dealt with separately under the entry "Kavangos" (q.v.).

After the report of the Odendaal Commission (q.v.), South Africa began preparing Namibian peoples for so-called "self-government." Thus, a Kavango Legislative Assembly was begun in 1970, and "self-governing" status was granted Kavangoland in 1973. The administrative capital of the Homeland was Rundu (q.v.). All this is subject to change since Namibia has gained independence.

KAVANGOS. While Kavangoland is also inhabited by groups of the San people, most of its population can be generally called Kavangos. The Kavango group is actually an offshoot of the Wambo peoples, having separated from them centuries ago and settled along the Okavango River, itself named by the Wambo people. The "Kavangos" are actually five federated subgroups. From west to east along the river they are (with alternate spellings): the Kwangali (Kuangali), Mbunza, Sambya (Sambju), Gciriku (Keiriku), and the Mbukushu. Like their Wambo cousins, the Kavangos are a matrilineal society who have lived in small-scale kingship states. They smelted iron before most of their neighbors and engaged in trade. The Kwangali and Mbunza speak the same language, but it differs considerably from those of the other three groups farther east.

KEETMANSHOOP. One of the more populous towns in Namibia (based on a 1991 population estimate of 15,000), it has been referred to as "the economic capital of southern Namibia." As center of the karakul farming district, it has also been called "Queen of the arid south." It is certainly the hub of southern Namibia, as major roads go in all directions. The port at Lüderitz is 363 kilometers (227 miles) to the west, Windhoek is 502 kilometers (321 miles) north, Nakob at the country's eastern border is 352 kilometers (220 miles) away, and the Orange River crossing at Noordoewer/Vioolsdrif (South Africa) is 331 kilometers (208 miles) to the south. The first documented settlement of the area began about 1784 when Guilliam Visagie (q.v.) and his family lived there. The next white visitors were members of the expedition led by Willem van Reenen (q.v.) in November, 1791. They called it Modderfontein. In 1810 the Red Nation (q.v.) of Namas lived there under Chief Tseib. They called it Nu Goeis, Nama for "black mud." Later white visitors translated that into Swartmodder. It kept that name until the Rhenish Mission Society set up a mission station there in 1866 under Rev. J. G. Schröder. He changed the name to Keetmanshoop ("Keetman's hope") after Johann Keetman, a businessman from Elberfeld in the German Rhineland. He was not only chairman of the Rhenish Missionary Society but also a major benefactor of foreign missions. His donation made this station possible. The first church there dates back to 1869. Early wagon tracks were cut into the rocks and can be seen at several places nearby.

Development of the area quickly expanded after the Germans made it the site of its southern military headquarters in 1894. The largest German military arsenal was established there, and the Germans established rail connections both the Windhoek and to the port of Lüderitz. (An airport came much later.) Since 1909 it has had a Town Council. As the commercial center of the area it has two hotels. Not far from the town is an experimental farm that shows visitors the latest in karakul farming, and also nearby is the Gariganus Nature Reserve that features the koker baum (q.v.) or quiver trees. There are dams both north and south of the city to enhance the water supply, but artesian wells are also found.

The Keetmanshoop administrative district covers 51,092 square kilometers. Among its major rivers are the Fish River in the west (through the Great Fish River Canyon) and the Löwen River, a tributary of the Fish. The Karas Mountains are also in the district, along with Kalahari sand-dunes in the eastern part. The district is semi-arid and vegetation is sparse.

KERINA, MBURUMBA (1928–). A seemingly ubiquitous political activist, he has covered the spectrum of Namibian politics for more than thirty years. He is a member of the 1990 National Assembly. He was born in Tsumeb with the name Eric William Getzen. In 1953 he left the country on a passport to study medicine at Lincoln University in Pennsylvania. He did not complete his medical studies, however, as he got wrapped up in Namibia political affairs. Beginning in 1956 he began to appear before the UN as a petitioner for the Herero Chief's Council, until Chief Kutako decided to replace Kerina (who had by now assumed this name) and Rev. Michael Scott with a Herero, Fanuel Kozonguizi (q.v.). The latter then became Kerina's rival.

Working from New York, Kerina encouraged his friends at home to be active politically. For example, it was H. Toivo

Ya Toivo's tape that was smuggled to Kerina that got Ya Toivo into trouble with South African police. He is also reported to have influenced the Old Location riots in 1959. Kerina also encouraged young Sam Nujoma to convert the Ovamboland People's Organization to a more truly national organization to compete with Kozonguizi's SWANU. Kerina is credited with suggesting the name South West Africa People's Organization to Nujoma. He was named chairman of SWAPO and Nujoma president. Kerina is also said to have later suggested the name Namibia for the country. He was very conscious of avoiding too much emphasis on one ethnic group or another, as his father was Wambo and his mother Herero.

Although he worked for SWAPO at the UN from 1960 to 1963, he ran into personal conflicts with its leaders and was expelled from SWAPO in 1963. He also served with the Liberian delegation to the UN for a period; he is said to have had some responsibility for urging that nation to take the Namibian question to the World Court.

An attempt by Kerina to return to Namibia in 1964 failed. He was finally expelled from neighboring Bechuanaland (Botswana) that year and travelled to Tanzania. He repaired his split with the Herero Chief's Council, suggested the creation of the National Unity Democratic Organization (NUDO), and became its chairman until he again had conflicts with the Chief's Council in 1966. He returned to New York and founded the SWA National United Front (q.v.) as an attempt to unite Namibian political groups. It was only slightly more successful than similar attempts by him earlier.

Kerina did finally complete his education, receiving a doctorate in politics at the Padjadjoran State University in Indonesia (although there is no record that he spent any significant time there). This enabled him to teach African-American studies at Brooklyn College (part of the City University of New York) for ten years. He married an American woman and they have three children.

While his exact movements are unclear, it has been reported that he returned to Namibia in the mid-1970s to encourage other politicians to join the Turnhalle Conference.

He did come home in 1976 and for a time became Director of Information for PROSWA (the Pro South West Africa/ Namibia Foundation), a group some saw as a propaganda attempt to undermine the positions of SWAPO.

Kerina returned to New York in 1979 and tried his hand at the business world with much fanfare but little obvious success. Taking advantage of increasing world interest in Namibia and his many New York contacts, he put together a book, *Namibia, the Making of a Nation*, published in 1981. It is a jumble of information that sheds no new light on his country's history.

Kerina formed other political groups in the 1980s, such as the Namibia National Democratic Coalition, which gained the support of both the NUDO-PP and the Association for the Preservation of the Tjamauaha/Maherero Royal House, both Herero-based organizations. In the merger Kerina became president of the National Unity Democratic Organization-Progressive Party (NUDO-PP) in 1989. In 1988 he also helped to found the Federal Convention of Namibia (FCN), an alliance of parties designed to succeed the old National Convention. In the 1989 Assembly elections the FCN earned only one seat, which was bestowed on Hans Diergaardt. When he chose to resign that seat soon thereafter for personal reasons, Kerina was next in line, and thus joined the first Assembly of independent Namibia. At very least he earned the honor for sheer persistence. The Assembly then elected him its deputy speaker.

KGALAGADI. *See* KALAHARI.

KGOSIEMANG, CONSTANCE. A Tswana chief from eastern Namibia, Chief Kgosiemang became a supporter of the Democratic Turnhalle Alliance, and by 1978 had formed the Seoposengwe Party, which affiliated with the DTA. The Chief became its chairman. In the November 1989 elections for the Constituent Assembly that would write Namibia's independence constitution, Chief Kgosiemang was placed tenth on the DTA electoral list. With the DTA winning twenty-one seats the chief received a place in the Assembly, and thus also in Namibia's legislature at independence.

//KHAN-/GOAN. Meaning literally "children of the tribe of the //Khauben," this group of Namas is better known as the Zwartboois (q.v.).

KHAN RIVER. One of Namibia's many "periodic" rivers, it begins southeast of Omaruru and flows southwest to where it joins the Swakop River in west-central Namibia. The Khan is a major tributary of the Swakop. Near where they merge is one of the country's better collection of *Welwitschia mirabilis* (q.v.) plants. Near the southern end of the Khan, a little east of Swakopmund, are deposits of cassiterite ore (from which tin is processed) and copper.

//KHAUBEN. *See* RED NATION.

KHOI-KHOIN. Meaning literally "Men of men," that is, the best of all people, this is the name by which the people who Europeans called "Hottentots" (q.v.) knew themselves. The largest settlements of these people living in Africa today are in Namibia, where they are called Namas (q.v.). However, the Namas are only one of many "tribes" of these people who once inhabited much of western South Africa as well. Some of the Namas today also are the result of intermarriage with other peoples. The Khoi-khoin, contrary to some beliefs, are not alien to Africa, and do share some characteristics with the more typical Bantu peoples. However, they migrated to southern Africa much earlier than the Bantu (e.g., Herero, Wambo). They share this fact with the San, along with certain physical traits. The so-called "Khoisan" (q.v.) also seem to have some substantial physical differences from most Bantu, along with notable linguistic distinctions.

In South Africa these people were generally the first to meet the Dutch who landed at the Cape. There were at least three significant results: first, many of them became servants (even slaves) to the Dutch; second, the Dutch men had relations with these women, a major source of the group known as "Coloured"; and third, European diseases for which the Africans had no natural antibodies devastated the African population.

KHOISAN. A word apparently coined in 1928 by L. Schultze in his *Zur Kenntnis des Körpers der Hottentten und Buschmänner,* it is a term used to link the Khoi-khoin and San (qq.v.) peoples. The two groups, known by Europeans more commonly as "Hottentots" and "Bushmen," preceded most Bantu peoples into southern Africa by many centuries, even millennia. The Khoi-khoin and San also share some distinctive physical differences from the Bantu. Even more distinctive, however, are the "click" sounds in the Khoisan languages: consonants not found in other languages, except where some southern African peoples have picked them up from the Khoisan people who preceded them. There are at least four separate subgroups of San; and there were many subgroups of Khoi-khoin, but only the Nama exist in Namibia in significant numbers today.

On the other hand, the two groups have some physical differences as well as significant cultural differences. For example, most Khoi-khoin were originally cattle-owners, while the San (incidentally, the name was given them by the Khoi-khoin) traditionally lived by hunting and gathering.

KHOMAS HIGHLANDS. Lying to the north and west of Windhoek, these highlands or hills constitute one side of the 6- to 9-mile-wide Windhoek Valley. The Kuiseb River (q.v.) begins in the Khomas highlands, and at one point there is a canyon 650 feet deep, with almost vertical sides. At one point earlier in the century the highlands teemed with great game animals, and the so-called Berg Damara peoples lived in the more inaccessible parts of the highlands. The rugged tableland covers an area of about 4480 square kilometers, and the highest elevation reaches 2000 meters. The area is now one of the best places in Namibia to raise cattle and sheep. As travellers move west through the highlands the view becomes ever more dramatic and beautiful, until they suddenly reach the Namib Desert. Beyond that lies the Atlantic Ocean.

KHOMASDAL. Part of South Africa's attempt to introduce apartheid into Namibia, the settlement called Khomasdal was begun in 1960 as a residential area for Windhoek's

Coloured population. Originally 457 houses were built plus a number of apartment blocks. At least four churches, shops, and a hotel were built. The Khomasdal township was built about three to four kilometers northwest of Windhoek's central business district and a little south of the Katutura (q.v.) area built for Black Africans.

KHORAB, PEACE OF. *See* KORAB, PEACE OF.

KHORIXAS. A word that means "water-bush," it is the new name for a town once known as Welwitschia (q.v.). Its name comes from the fact that subterranean water is often found close to the land surface near this bush. Khorixas is the capital of what was called Damaraland by the South African administrators who created a "homeland" there. The town had an estimated population of 6500 in 1988. It is located about 120 kilometers west of Outjo, and 26 kilometers by road southwest of Fransfontein.

The town is in the center of a very interesting area for tourists, with the Petrified Forest (q.v.), Twyfelfontein (q.v.), and the Burnt Mountain all within 40 kilometers or so. A rest camp with furnished bungalows, a swimming pool, a restaurant, and a small store are there.

/KHOWESIN. One of five Orlam tribes to leave the Cape Colony in the nineteenth century, they followed their leader, Kido Witbooi (q.v.). They left from Pella on the south bank of the Orange and spent some years in a nomadic existence in the Fish River area. They finally settled at what became known later as Gibeon (q.v.). The word "/Khowesin" is said to mean "Queen Bees."

KIMBERLITE. The name for diamondiferous rock that is known more commonly as blue ground (q.v.).

KLEIN AUB MINE. A copper and silver mine near Rehoboth, it opened in 1966 under the ownership of South Africa's Goncor and the Federal Voldsbeleggings Ltd. At the peak of production in 1981 it produced 5900 tons of copper and 13,000 kilograms of silver. An estimate that year indicated reserves for eight more years. It then had a little over 1000 workers, most of whom were indigenous Africans. In 1985 it was purchased by South Africa's Metrorex. In March 1987 the black workers (now only 500) went on strike for compensation and severance pay prior to being fired, but the management refused to negotiate. The owners then closed it in April, claiming it was no longer financially viable.

KLEIN BARMEN. Located near Barmen (q.v.), southwest of Okahandja, it has been the site of three historic battles. The first took place in 1851, when the cattle post of a wealthy Herero cattle-owner was attacked by armed followers of Tjamuaha (q.v.) plus a number of Afrikanders. The dwellings were surrounded by the attackers at dawn. Resistance was not possible. Instead of shooting or clubbing the Herero victims, the raiders put them into a cattle kraal, sealed off the entrance, and set it ablaze. Everyone in the kraal suffocated. A second battle also occurred near the hot springs, and is called the Battle of Klein Barmen. It took place on December 11, 1880. A group of Namas under Jan Jonker Afrikander (q.v.) attacked the Hereros there and took all their cattle. The third battle involved Germans and Hereros and took place March 4, 1904. A company of 100 German soldiers was nearing Klein Barmen when they were ambushed by Herero warriors. German sources said that six Germans were killed before the fighting ended, and they estimated that ten Hereros may have been killed.

KLEIN WINDHOEK. A lovely garden suburb a few kilometers east of the heart of Windhoek, it was settled in 1840 by Jonker Afrikander (q.v.) and about 800 of his followers. Rhenish missionaries came and called it Elberfeld, but the name didn't last. In 1837 the area had been visited by the British explorer, Sir James Alexander, and in 1840 the Rhenish Mission built the first house there. Roman Catholic missionaries landed in 1896. They bought the RMS land in 1899 and converted it into a little Eden, with palms and fruit trees, along with grape vines imported from both Germany and France. Their first vintage was 1904. Wine is still produced there today. Water for the gardens was pumped from a very steady bore-hole, but originally a spring took care of all the water needs. The famous "castles" (q.v.) of Windhoek are in the hills that separate Windhoek from Klein Windhoek. The Gobabis Road is the main link between the city and its loveliest suburb.

KLEINSCHMIDT, REV. FRANS HEINRICH (1812–1864). An RMS missionary in Namibia for over twenty years, he was born in Westphalia, Prussia. After completing his training for the missions he went to South Africa with Rev. C. H. Hahn (q.v.) in 1841. The two visited with the venerable Rev. J. H. Schmelen (q.v.) in South Africa and then went into Namibia. They arrived at Klein Windhoek in October 1842, where Jonker Afrikander welcomed them. Their stay there was only two years when they were replaced by Wesleyan missionaries. Hahn and Kleinschmidt tried to set up at Okahandja, but when that didn't work out they moved to Otjikango, which they renamed Barmen after the town in Germany where the RMS had its seminary. This was to be the first mission among the Hereros.

Kleinschmidt left Hahn at Barmen and moved south to Rehoboth, where he worked among the Zwartbooi Namas (q.v.) then living there. It was he who gave the town its biblical name. With the RMS working among both Hereros and Namas there was a degree of peace between the two groups for a period. Kleinschmidt worked at Rehoboth beginning in May 1845. He took several trips to South Africa. On one he married a daughter of Rev. Schmelen. Occasionally he had an assistant at Rehoboth, for example, Rev. Vollmer in 1851–52.

In 1861 Kleinschmidt relieved another missionary at Otjimbingwe and set up his home there. From this location he supervised the missions at Okahandja and Rehoboth, as well as Windhoek when necessary. At Jonker Afrikander's dying request he came to the chief's deathbed in Okahandja in August 1861, and was present when he died.

Rev. Kleinschmidt spent time at both Okahandja and Otjimbingwe. He was living at the latter when Namas attacked June 15, 1863. He was unsuccessful at negotiating a peace between the Namas and Hereros at that time, in part because of the intervention of the explorer C. J. Andersson (q.v.). Ironically the missionary helped the wounded explorer near Rehoboth a year later.

When the Zwartboois left Rehoboth to move closer to their Herero allies in July 1864, Kleinschmidt and his family went along. In their migration, however, they were attacked by the forces of Jan Jonker Afrikander, and all their possessions were either burned or stolen. The Kleinschmidts managed to escape into the Khomas Highlands, however, and made their way to Otjimbingwe on July 31. Hahn cared for the family there, but Rev. Kleinschmidt was suffering from exhaustion and died at Hahn's home, September 2, 1864. His sons stayed in the territory in business capacities.

KLIPKAFFERS. Another name for the people better known as Bergdamaras or Bergdamas (q.v.). In either case, the Berg or Klip refers to the fact that they moved their homes into relatively inaccessible mountainous regions, instead of living in the open plains.

KLOPPERS, ANDREAS J. F., SR. (c. 1921–1989). Born in Genadedal (SA), Kloppers was educated to be a teacher and ultimately rose to be a principal. He had emigrated from South Africa in 1946, a very militant activist in the Teachers League of South Africa. He was a founder (in 1947) and secretary general of the SWA Coloured Teachers' Association, a position he held until 1963. Although seemingly nonpolitical, in fact it had a nationwide network of PTAs. In the late 1940s he worked closely with such activists as Clemens Kapuuo and Rev. Michael Scott (qq.v.), agitating for independence.

Kloppers' wife started St. Andrew's, Namibia's first private nonracial school, in Windhoek in 1956, and Kloppers became principal from 1957 to 1966. Blacks and Coloureds studied together, despite government attempts to close the school. In 1960 it was finally recognized by the government.

Kloppers began the South West African Coloured Organization (SWACO) in April 1959, and through it achieved the creation of Khomasdal (q.v.), where Coloureds were allowed to own property for the first time. The first Coloured Council was started by the government in 1962, and Kloppers was appointed its first chairman. He held the post until 1974. He eventually became frustrated with his inability to get the government to respond to the Council's requests. In 1972 he founded (and became president of) the SWA Non-European Unity Movement (q.v.), an alliance of groups that tried to pressure South Africa to respond to the demands of the people.

Meanwhile, SWACO changed its name to the Federal Coloured People's Party (FCPP) in 1973, and when the Coloured Council had its first elections the next year, the "Federal Party" won. The FCPP changed its name in 1975 to the Labour Party (q.v.).

In 1973 Kloppers was named to the Prime Minister's Advisory Council, and two years later became part of the Turnhalle Conference. There he worked again with his old friend, Clemens Kapuuo (q.v.), and initiated the so-called "Black Caucus" that was responsible for getting the government to abolish the Mixed Marriages Act and the Immorality Act.

In 1978 Kloppers became increasingly militant, even giving speeches where he used the SWAPO slogan "One Namibia, One Nation." He had been a member of the DTA, but his advocacy was angering its leaders. Realizing that he was being pushed out of the leadership of the Labour Party, he resigned from both the Labour Party and the DTA in October 1978. He then created a new group, the Liberal Party (q.v.). He was defeated by a DTA-supported candidate for his seat on the Coloured Council in 1978.

When he resigned from the DTA he announced he would affiliate his Liberal Party with an election front called the Action Front for the Retention of Turnhalle Principles (q.v.). In this alliance he won a seat in the 1979–83 National Assembly. However, he strongly differed with some of this group's positions, and he resigned from it in 1979. He held his seat as an independent.

In 1982 Kloppers merged his Liberal Party with the Democratic People's Party, and he became president of the Christian Democratic Union that resulted. That party then joined the DTA in 1983, and the aging Coloured leader joined the Multi-Party Conference as well. He served as a delegate of the DTA at the 1984 talks in Lusaka, Zambia. Meanwhile, he was also trying to restore relations between his CDU and the Labour Party. He moved the CDU from the DTA in 1987 and the next year rejoined the Labour Party, along with most of his executive committee. He was named its second national chairman. Kloppers did not live to see an independent Namibia, however, dying in a road accident in 1989. His followers took part in the election as part of the United Democratic Front.

His son A. J. Kloppers, Jr., is following closely in his father's footsteps.

KOEVOET. The word means literally "crowbar" in Afrikaans and was officially a counterinsurgency unit of the South African Police in Namibia. Designated Police Unit K, it was commanded by Brigadier Hans Dreyer out of offices at Oshakati. The unit consisted of elite black Namibian troops under South African or Namibian white officers. Its task was to hunt PLAN guerrillas, and the unit claimed a "kill" percentage as high as 60 percent. The unit's tactics were notoriously ruthless and brutal. In its role as a death squad, it was considered responsible for the killings of a number of high-level SWAPO supporters, for bombing the ELOK Church press at Oniipa in November 1980, and for an attack at a mission in Odipa.

Sometimes unit members would wear PLAN uniforms and commit atrocities against villages, killing large numbers. In one case in Oshikutu in March 1982, they robbed the local store, shot eight villagers at point blank range, and began shooting up the whole village. Some of the survivors, however, knew some of the men as members of Koevoet. For the most part the atrocities occurred in northern Namibia areas among the Wambo people from whom SWAPO received the greatest support. In one incident in April 1989, after UNTAG had already entered Namibia, eighteen members of PLAN were executed by Koevoet. By then KOEVOET was supposed to be under the South West African Police, but clearly the 3000 members of Koevoet were out of control. By mid-July, barely four months before the Assembly elections, at least 2000 members of Koevoet were reportedly terrorizing parts of the north, despite having been commanded to return to their base two months earlier.

On August 18, 1989, responding to UN pressure, A-G Louis Pienaar announced that Koevoet would definitely be confined to barracks. By the end of October, UNTAG could announce that it was satisfied that Koevoet had been demobilized, and that its weapons had been handed over to the UN. Yet during the election campaign SWAPO accused ex-Koevoet members of disrupting its meetings disguised as DTA vigilantes. In early 1990 accusations continued that ex-members of Koevoet were roaming northern Namibia seeking vengeance, although UNTAG thought the roving terrorists could be UNITA (q.v.) soldiers crossing over from Angola.

KOKER BAUM (variants: KOKER TREE; KOKERBOOM; KOKERBOOM TREE). Also known as the quiver tree, it is technically known as the *Aloe dichotoma*. It is especially hardy in southern Namibia or Great Namaland. It has "fingers," actually forked branches of its stem, that point skyward. The thick-stemmed tree, which grows up to twelve feet, casts a strangely decorative silhouette on the skyline. It is a true desert tree, capable of living without almost any water. Unique to Namibia, it belongs to the same family as the lily, and was named by Francis Masson in 1776, but it had been described by Simon van der Stel (q.v.) a century earlier. Legend says that the koker baum lives two hundred years. The tree is protected by law.

KOLMANSKOP. Now a sand-smothered ghost town best visible from the air, this was the home of the great diamond rush that began with the discovery of diamonds by August Stauch (q.v.) and his workers in 1908. Stauch was working as a railway supervisor on a line to Lüderitzbucht, four miles to the northwest, when one of his workers brought him the first diamond discovered in Namibia. The town grew rapidly to include a two-story casino (with a theater), shops, a school for children of mine workers, and a post office, plus houses. It became a pleasant comfortable village, especially as its mine became for a while an outstanding producer of diamonds. In the first six years five million carats of diamonds were mined there. Thirty years later the lode was exhausted and the village soon lost its citizens to newer mining centers.

The origin of the name is in question; several stories exist. Perhaps the most reliable is that a transport rider named Coleman was forced to abandon his two wagons there in 1905 when they were buried in a sand storm.

A road goes to Kolmanskop for curious tourists, who are allowed to visit only on weekends and with a permit from Consolidated Diamond Mines Ltd., which still owns diamond rights there. The good news is that tourist-conscious individuals are trying to restore some of the buildings to their early condition, even to the point of establishing overnight accommodations in the quaint village that has been dormant for half a century.

KOLOLO (variant: MAKOLOLO). A Sotho-speaking people who played an important role in the Eastern Caprivi in the mid-nineteenth century. Originally from the area of today's Orange Free State, these people fled north during the Mfecane that was caused by the actions of Zulu leader Shaka. As they travelled north they cut a swath through Botswana, led by their chief, Sebituane. Their force powered through the Eastern Caprivi and crossed the Zambezi at Kazangula in the early 1830s. They had great influence over Zambia's Lozi (or Barotse). The Kololo domain extended from western Zambia south through the Caprivi and into northeastern Botswana. Their cattle raids penetrated southern Zambia and even parts of Zimbabwe; however the Ndebele there were enemies and fierce opponents. Sebituane's son Sekeletu eventually became chief, only to see his people virtually die out due to malaria and revenge-seeking Lozi. The tribal capital was on the Zambezi just across from the Eastern Caprivi.

KOLONKHADHI-EUNDA (variants: NKOLONKATI; ONKO-LONKATHI). Two of the eight main tribes of the Wambo people, they are actually two of three groups (the other is the Mbalantu) that split from the Ndonga tribe of Wambos. In 1970 there were an estimated 9,700 members of this combined group, only 2.83 percent of all Wambos. Because of the sparse population, these people did not have need for a traditional chief. Political power rested in the hands of several headmen of autonomous clan groups. While the hyphen indicates two separate groups, they are often discussed as one.

KOLONIALE BERGBAUGESELLSCHAFT. A company founded by August Stauch (q.v.) and two partners to prospect for diamonds. Their discovery of major sites in late 1908 and 1909 made Stauch a millionaire. In 1919 he sold his diamond interests to Ernest Oppenheimer, who was putting together what is known today as Consolidated Diamond Mines (q.v.). The holdings of the Koloniale Bergbaugesellschaft were among the most valuable in the area prior to 1920, averaging production of over 300,000 carats a year from 1912 to 1914. At the end of 1919 it also took over management of the Diamanten-Pacht Gesellschaft, in return for half the profits. The claims of the Diamantfelderverwertungsgesellschaft in the Conception Bay area were also worked by Stauch's company.

KOMBAT MINE. Run by the Tsumeb Corporation (q.v.), this copper, lead, and zinc mine was brought into production in 1962. It appears to have a rich supply of reserves. It lies 62 kilometers south of Tsumeb itself. Its production was halted totally in November 1988 when major flooding occurred at the mine and seven miners were killed in the accident. The incident occurred in a newly developed area at a depth of 530 kilometers. Prior to the accident Kombat had been open for 397 days without a disabling injury. Several months passed before it resumed normal mining.

The current mine at Kombat is not the first mining to occur there. Germans had a 4-level, 120-meter deep mine at Kombat prior to World War I. Production was stopped by the war. (At that point the mine was known as Asis.) The Tsumeb Corporation began prospecting there from 1953 to 1960, first restarting the old German shaft and then drilling two deeper ones of its own. The mine and milling plant were opened in 1962 and production began. Kombat is a complete mining camp, with Tsumeb building all necessary buildings and facilities.

KÖNIGSTEIN. The highest peak in Namibia at 2586 meters, the "King's Rock" (or alternately, "King's Monument") is located in the middle of the Brandberg (q.v.). It was on his descent from climbing Königstein that Dr. Reinhard Maack discovered the famous rock painting, "The White Lady of the Brandberg" (q.v.) in 1918.

KONKIEP RIVER (variants: KONKIB; KONKIP). Cutting a major trench from north to south in southern Namibia, this river separates the Tsaris and Tiras Mountains from the Huib Plateau on the east. Further to the east and parallel to the Konkiep is the Fish River, which it joins a little north of the Orange River. The Konkiep drains the Bethanie Valley, while the Fish River drains the Berseba Valley. Both rivers have flood plains that are not very fertile but are suitable for settlements and roads. Archaeologists have found signs of some of the earliest settlements in Namibia—perhaps 25,000 years old—along these rivers.

KOOPER, REV. MARCUS (variant: COOPER) (1918–). Born at Hoachanas of a Nama family, he was educated to be a teacher. He taught in mission schools from 1942 to 1946, and again from 1949 to 1952. He was ordained by the African Methodist Episcopal Church several years later and appointed to a church at Hoachanas.

In the late 1950s Rev. Kooper made a name for himself far from Namibia. He had been fighting government attempts to move his Nama community away from the white farming area to a new location 180 miles away. He vigorously led his people to fight the removal order in 1957 and 1958 and even appealed to the United Nations. His actions resulted in his being called by the SWA government to court. The High Court finally ruled in June 1958 that all the Namas were living in Hoachanas illegally. In January 1959 Kooper and his family were forcibly removed to the new area without any possessions.

He returned to Hoachanas in November and stayed until

April 1960. Meanwhile, his case had been argued at the UN by F. J. Kozonguizi (q.v.). Finally he appeared in person at the UN in September 1960. The international pressure on SWA authorities resulted in Hoachanas being listed as a "Temporary Reserve." During his stay in New York he also spoke for a Nama organization called South West Africa United National Independence Organization (q.v.), a group that tried to unite Namas in opposition to the Government of the territory.

KOPER, SIMON (variants: KOOPER; KOPPER) (d. 1913). Leader of the Franzmannchen Namas for at least the last decades of the nineteenth century and the first decade of the twentieth, he made his capital first at Haruchas and later at Gochas. He was among the chiefs met by W. C. Palgrave (q.v.) in November 1876, when Palgrave called a conference to discuss the establishment of a protectorate over the Nama territory (southern Namibia). Nothing came out of that conference, but in the 1880s Dr. Heinrich Goering (q.v.), representing Germany, was more successful in getting chiefs to sign protective treaties. Koper was one of the last hold-outs, asking for a treaty only in 1894.

Ten years later, however, Koper and his followers were among the first to throw in their lot with Hendrik Witbooi in rebelling against the Germans in October 1904. Two years later many of the Namas had been defeated and Witbooi was dead, but Koper, leader of the Gochas and Hoachanas Namas, continued to fight on with a band of followers. Based in the Kalahari Desert, they conducted unexpected raids against the Germans. The Germans declared the region "pacified" in March 1907 because Koper was unlikely to affect peaceful settlement. He was finally defeated in 1908 by a force led by German Captain Friedrich von Erckert. Koper and his followers fled into British Bechuanaland (Botswana) and in 1909 signed a treaty that allowed him and his people to settle there. He also received an annual grant of £100 from the Colonial Office until he died in 1913.

KORAB, PEACE OF (variant: KHORAB). The last stand of the German army in Namibia in World War I occurred at Korab.

German forces had been forced to retreat to the northeast quadrant of the country to a farm called Korab in a rich grazing area. It was in the midst of the Otavi-Tsumeb-Grootfontein triangle. The advancing South African forces under Gen. Louis Botha (q.v.) were divided into three columns: the central force and two flanking columns. The German commander Franke found his retreat being cut off, especially when the northwestern flank was defeated. He hoped to flee to East Africa via the Caprivi, but finally decided that no more blood need be shed. On July 9, 1915, the German commander handed Namibia over to General Botha at the signing of "The Peace of Korab."

KORANAS. One of three subgroups of the so-called "Hotten-tots" (q.v.), they generally lived south of the Orange River. (A second subgroup, the Namas are a very important part of Namibia today. The third group is best known as the Girquas.) The Koranas were nomadic and were known to raid southern Namibia in the late eighteenth century, especially under an aggressive leader named Eiseb. His raiders even went as far north as the Kuiseb River valley, where they stole the cattle of the Hereros. When Eiseb and his men were confronted by the Afrikanders (q.v.) early in the nineteenth century, however, there was a different result, as the latter had guns. The Koranas thus fled back across the Orange after losing several men to bullets.

KORNELIUS OF BETHANIE. *See* CORNELIUS, CAPTAIN.

KOUCHANAS. The site of an important battle between guerrilla leader Jacob Marengo (q.v.) and the Germans, August 30, 1904. The Germans suffered a serious defeat there, with their leader and two others killed and the rest of the thirty-man detachment taking flight. The site is in the southeastern part of the country, fifty or more kilometers northeast of Kar-asburg. The area is sometimes referred to as "Freyer's Farm," after the Boer who lived there at the time of the battle, or Schambockberge (q.v.) after the nearby Sambock Hills whence the guerrillas came.

KOWESES HOTTENTOTS. An early reference to the Witboois (q.v.).

KOZONGUIZI, FANUEL JARIRETUNDU (1932–). One of the earliest of the Namibian nationalist politicians, he is also a member of Namibia's first Assembly as an independent state. Born in Windhoek, he graduated from a high school in Warmbad. His university career included Fort Hare College and Rhodes College (both in South Africa). He received a BA in history and psychology from the latter in 1956. He also studied at the University of Cape Town, and read law in London in the late 1960s. He was called to the English bar in 1970 and was appointed a member of the Inner Temple.

As a student at Fort Hare he was active in politics, influenced by the recent (1952) Defiance Campaign in South Africa. He and M. Kerina and Z. Ngavirue (qq.v.) were leaders in the formation of the SWA Student Body (q.v.), and later formed the SWA Progressive Association (q.v.). He joined the African National Congress Youth League in 1954, and was a leader of its Fort Hare branch. He moved to Cape Town as an ANC Organizer in 1958, where he joined H. A. Toivo Ya-Toivo and a dozen other early SWAPO leaders in forming the Ovamboland People's Congress in 1958. It was modelled after the ANC.

In 1958 the Herero Chief's Council also appointed him to be its Permanent UN Petitioner in New York, replacing Rev. Michael Scott (q.v.). He left Namibia illegally in 1958 and served as Chief Kutako's spokesman until 1966. The Chief's Council was also trying to form a Herero-based political party (to parallel the Wambo-based SWAPO), and Kozonguizi became a founder and president of it, the South West Africa National Union, in November 1959. After a disagreement with other SWANU leaders, he resigned in 1966. Inbetween 1959 and 1966 he spent part of his time in New York, occasionally trying to find ways for SWAPO and SWANU to work together, and the rest of the time travelling to organize chapters in other countries. SWANU was more active abroad than in Namibia. For example, he gained its membership in the Afro-Asian People's Solidarity Organization and the All-African People's Conference.

He then went to London for his law studies and returned to Namibia in 1976 as legal advisor to Chief Clemens Kapuuo and the Herero delegates to the Turnhalle Conference. At its conclusion he joined Kapuuo in the Democratic Turnhalle Alliance in various capacities. He accepted a position in the office of the administrator-general in 1980 as head of the Division of Interstate Relations; he served in other important administrative capacities in subsequent years. He was certainly the highest ranking Black Namibian in the colonial government. When the TGNU was formed he was appointed minister of posts and telecommunications (1985–88) and minister of information (1988–89).

He became a member of the National Unity Democratic Organization (NUDO), which had been founded by Chief Kapuuo, and through that association was a member of the DTA alliance. In the 1989 elections he was third on the DTA electoral list, evidence of his importance to its leadership. In the National Assembly he was the DTA spokesman on justice issues. By late 1991 he was in dispute with the other party leaders and a few months later resigned his seat in the Assembly. He was soon appointed by the Government as Namibia's first full-time ombudsman, a post he assumed in May, 1992.

KRAMPE, FRITZ (1912–1966). Born near Berlin, this exceptional wildlife artist studied at the Berlin Academy of Fine Arts. He painted until World War II, then served in both Poland and France before being captured at Tobruk, North Africa, in 1941. He spent more than five years in a prisoner-of-war camp. After the war his travels took him to Cape Town in 1950 and to Windhoek the following year, where he settled.

While he painted some fine portraits and even murals, he is best remembered for his exceptional wildlife art. He especially loved the Etosha Game Park.

KROHNE, ALBERT (1932–). Born in Aroab, he received a teaching certificate at the Augustineum Training College in

1950. He was a teacher from 1958 to 1962, a principal or vice-principal from 1963 to 1974. He started a chapter of SWANU in Keetmanshoop in 1962. Since 1974 he has worked for the Council of Churches in Namibia and has been an active politician.

In 1974 Krohne and Charlie Hartung were the founders of the National Independence Party (NIP), which was renamed the Namibia Independence Party (q.v.) in 1981. Primarily a party of the Coloureds, it won three of the six seats in the Coloured Council in 1974, and Krohne won one of those. He retained the seat until NIP withdrew from the Council in 1980. He was a representative of the Coloureds at the Turnhalle Conference (1975–77), but withdrew in 1977 with other NIP members in frustration at the conference's work. He then led NIP into the Namibia National Front (q.v.) and was a member of its Central Committee until it folded in 1980. When Hartung retired as president of NIP in 1982, Krohne was selected its new president. He attended the /Ai//gams conference in Windhoek in 1986 as leader of the NIP delegation (*see* AIGHAMS). He then became a founder of the Namibia Nationhood Programme.

The old Namibia National front was reconstituted for the 1989 elections, and Krohne led NIP into it. He became the vice-president of the NNF. It only gained one seat in the National Assembly, and Krohne was second on the electoral list.

KRÖNLEIN, JOHANN GEORG (1826–1892). Born near Würzburg in Bavaria, he originally set out to enter business, but after a while he joined·the RMS seminary at Barmen. His first assignment was to replace J. S. (Samuel) Hahn at Berseba in 1851, working among Paul Goliath's Namas. He was said to have been very successful there, and Berseba was described as a model community under his influence. He moved to Gibeon to settle among Kido Witbooi's people in 1862, and the same year established a mission at Keetman-shoop.

Meanwhile Krönlein had become an authority on the Nama language. He and H. H. Kreft translated a catechism into Nama and in 1857 completed a comprehensive Nama dictionary. He also produced a Bible history and a reader in Nama. By 1862 he had translated the entire New Testament in the language. He spent two years (1865–67) in Germany to supervise the printing of his translations, because no one there could print this language because of its linguistic peculiarities.

When he returned he was made supervisor of all the RMS missions among the Namas. His reputation led to his being called upon to help negotiate a peace between Namas and Hereros at Okahandja in September 1870. Similarly he negotiated with W. C. Palgrave (q.v.) at Berseba in 1876. Even after he retired to South Africa because of poor health in 1877 he was called back to try to facilitate peace between the Namas and Hereros. He returned in 1882 to lay the foundation for a peace treaty to be signed (by some at least) at Rehoboth in June of that year. He then returned to the Cape, where he continued to teach young RMS missionaries until he died ten years later.

Sometimes overlooked was another contribution that came from his understanding of the Nama language and his deep appreciation for their culture. In the late 1850s he was requested by Sir George Grey to collect Nama literature for the Grey collection in the Cape library. Krönlein recorded twenty-four Nama fables, twelve riddles, thirty-two proverbs and sayings, and twelve songs, all in the native language as recorded by him directly from the people. Some of these were the basis of W. H. Bleek's *Reynard the Fox in South Africa; or Hottentot Fables and Tales,* which was published in 1864. The importance of this material is that it forced some individuals, at least, to reevaluate the Namas. Previously considered by many to be the most primitive of South Africa's indigenous peoples, the Namas showed in their literature a breadth and scope of sophistication and literary tradition that had been unappreciated until Krönlein's work was available.

KUBANGO RIVER. The name by which the Okavango River (q.v.) is known in Angola prior to its entry into northeastern Namibia.

KUDU GASFIELD. One of the most important recent discoveries in Namibia is the existence of this large gas field off the coast of Namibia. Bids were requested in April 1989 for the development of a new well about 213 kilometers southwest of Lüderitz, just inside Namibia's territory. The first exploration well had been drilled by Chevron in 1984 and produced 98 percent methane gas. SWACOR (South West African Oil Exploration Corporation) granted the drilling rights in July 1989 to a French firm, Forinter. It was expected that the well would be dug to a depth of about 5000 meters. Results were so successful that a third well was proposed in 1988. Kudu's reserves were then estimated at two trillion cubic feet of gas, much larger than South Africa's Mossel Bay fields. These figures were revised upward dramatically in early 1991 when it was estimated that the Kudu field may have a minimum size of 5 trillion cubic feet and the reservoir could even be as large as 50 trillion cubic feet. The huge supply could be sold in the South African market as well as solving many of Namibia's energy questions, but there are problems regarding the cost of piping the gas to shore for liquefaction. On November 1, 1991 oil companies submitted bids on a number of concessions, including the Kudu gasfield. The assumption is that Royal Dutch Shell is the high bidder.

KUHANGUA, JACOB. One of the earliest leaders of modern African nationalism in Namibia, he was among those who met in Cape Town in 1958 to help found the Ovamboland People's Congress. The next year Kuhangua and Sam Nujoma were the co-founders of the Ovamboland People's Organization in Windhoek. The two were among those Namibians who then went into exile abroad. When SWAPO was organized in April 1960, the first list of its leaders show Kuhangua as the party's Secretary General. A list later that year has him as assistant secretary-general. As such he and other SWAPO leaders appeared before the UN in November 1960, appealing for UN intervention in their country.

In December 1965 Kuhangua was the party's secretary-general and based in Dar es Salaam, Tanzania. A fight occurred there one day between him and Louis Nelengani, then SWAPO's vice-president. Nelengani stabbed Kuhangua during the fight, leaving him paralyzed from the waist down as a result. Nelengani was expelled from SWAPO, while Kuhangua eventually returned to live in Owambo, still confined to a chair.

KUISEB RIVER (variants: !KHUISEB; KOOISIP; KUISIP; KUIZEB). One of the more substantial rivers in Namibia, it dies out in the Namib Desert shortly before it would have reached the seacoast at Walvis Bay. It flows underground in some areas where the bed appears dry at the surface. Some of this underground water has been tapped for use in mines and to satisfy the urban demand at Walvis Bay. The river rises in the Khomas Highlands west of Windhoek and meanders through a steep-sided valley. At Hudaub (also called Devil's Cave), there is a spectacular canyon 650 feet deep, with sides that are almost vertical.

From its beginnings in the Khomas Highlands the Kuiseb flows on a south-southwest diagonal for about half its length, and then heads almost due west before cutting along a northwest diagonal as if aiming for Walvis Bay. But it dies in the desert about twenty kilometers short of the bay. One report says it last reached the sea in 1934 when rain had been very heavy.

Some contend that the Kuiseb River has been the traditional dividing line between the land of the Namas (to the south) and the Hereros. However, relatively few Hereros travelled as far south as the southernmost stretches of the river.

KUMMERNAIS. The site of the first conflict between South African and German forces in World War I, it is near where the Ham River meets the Orange River, in extreme southeastern Namibia. Forces led by General Van Deventer overcame the Germans there on August 23, 1914.

KUNENE HYDRO-ELECTRIC SCHEME. See RUACANA FALLS AND HYDRO-ELECTRIC SCHEME.

KUNENE RIVER (variant: CUNENE). Composing the western segment of Namibia's northern border with Angola, this river is one of the country's few continuous flowing rivers. It begins in Angola and flows southward until it reaches the Ruacana Falls (q.v.) and then turns west. It is here that it becomes Namibia's border. Downstream it empties into the Atlantic Ocean. The river is not suitable for navigation as it contains too many cataracts, not only the Ruacana Falls but also the Epupa Falls (q.v.), to mention just the two largest ones.

Curiously the name of the river comes from a misunderstanding. Wambos call it "Omulonga," which merely means "stream," and the Hereros similarly call it "Omuronga." However the Hereros have words for the two land areas on the opposing sides of a river. The word Kaoko (q.v.) from "okaoko" means the small or left side, while "okunene" means the wide or right side. By the latter they actually referred to southern Angola. Presumably some European pointed toward the river (from the Namibia side) and asked what that was called. The Herero person would have said "okunene," referring to the opposite shore, not the river.

The Kunene has tremendous potential for Namibia, not only for supplying power but also as the source of irrigation schemes. It has an estimated annual flow of four to five billion cubic meters of water. It is typically highest in April and lowest in October. The flow in October is only 3 to 4 percent of the flow in April. Storage dams could create a more constant flow.

For the more adventurous, boating on the Kunene provides spectacular scenic views, especially in the midst of the Baynes Mountains, although one must know where to expect the frequent falls and treacherous rapids. The river may be 300 feet wide at times and then be forced through a 10-foot-wide crevice. Crocodiles and hippos are also common in some stretches of the river. As the river pushes toward the Atlantic it loses volume due to evaporation along the Namib Desert area, and it also has difficulty pushing through a perennial sand bar, which has been created at its mouth by the function of ocean waves.

There are specialists who feel the Kunene may have flowed at one time (millions of years ago) due south into Etosha, creating the giant lake, but then other forces shifted it to a westward course to the Atlantic. The Etosha then began to shrink in size.

!KUNG (variant: KHUNG). The Kung are one of four different groups of San (q.v.), the others being the Heikam (q.v.), the Naron, and the Mbarakwengo (q.v.). Each of the four has its own distinct language, although they each use the distinctive "click" sounds that go with the Khoisan languages. They are nomadic peoples but generally live within the Kungveld (q.v.) in northeastern Namibia. During the guerrilla campaign of SWAPO against the South African-led government, !Kung were recruited into special tracking and hunting units of the South African Defence Force. Proud of their tracking abilities they would lead the South African troops on six-week patrols that resembled their old hunting parties. However recently anthropologists warn against creating a myth about the "Bushmen," pointing out, for example, that many of them abandoned the nomadic life a long time ago, and that their "primitive" image is a way of romanticizing them, continuing to reflect a colonial mentality.

KUNGVELD. A descriptive term for the part of the Kalahari Desert in northeastern Namibia, the name refers to the !Kung San who are among its inhabitants. One source says that it stretches from the Shadum River to the Okavango River. It is a stoneless sandveld which is crossed by many river-beds. In them are sand-pans that contain some surface water from permanent springs. The main river in the area is the Omuramba Omatako (q.v.).

KUPFERBERG, PEACE OF. A dispute over the rights to grant mining concessions in the upper Kuiseb Valley caused problems for Reid, manager of field operations of the Matchless copper mine. He succeeded in getting Jonker Afrikander, Oasib, and Willem Swartbooi (qq.v.), the disputants, to come together at Kupferberg. A huge crowd gathered, as each of the leaders brought bodyguards, councillors, and other supporters. Two missionaries present (F. H. Kleinschmidt and Vollmar) persuaded the leaders to negotiate quietly. This resulted in an agreement on November 24,

1855, by which Oasib's authority was recognized but Jonker held on to his rights. The precise questions of boundaries and the division of mineral concessions income was settled at a smaller conference between Oasib and Jonker at Hugo Hahn's house at Barmen on April 22, 1858. Royalties would be evenly divided, and the Kuiseb River was set as the southern border of Jonker's land.

KUTAKO, CHIEF HOSEA (1870–1970). Perhaps Namibia's greatest national patriot, his life was devoted to opposing foreign rule of his country. Born at Okahurimehi in the Okahandja district, Kutako's father was an RMS clergyman at Omburo and a member of an aristocratic Herero family. Kutako received a good mission school education.

During the 1904 Herero uprising against the Germans, Kutako was twice wounded in battle. He did not follow others into exile, but was briefly detained and then fled into the mountains of Namibia. In 1906 he became a school-teacher at Omaruru, but two years later began working in the mines at Tsumeb.

When South Africa defeated the Germans they looked for a leader of the Hereros, and in 1917 appointed Kutako the Herero Chief. Samuel Maharero agreed to that in 1920 from his position in exile. Kutako was not a compliant leader, however, and in 1925 he was imprisoned briefly for refusing to allow Hereros to be pushed off their land. Similarly in 1946 he fought the attempt to resettle returning South African soldiers in his areas and move Hereros to northern Namibia.

In 1946 South Africa also asked him to accept the incorporation of Namibia into South Africa. Not only did he refuse, but he began petitioning the UN to remove the South African mandate and assume control itself. His petitions continued for fifteen years. One of his chosen intermediaries in this process was Fanuel J. Kozonguizi (q.v.). He also worked closely with Rev. Michael Scott and Mburumba Kerina on these matters (qq.v.).

Chief Kutako recognized the need for modern political organization. The Herero Chief's Council (q.v.), which he founded in 1945, was highly active in modern politics under his leadership, but the chief also encouraged such Hererobased groups as SWANU and the National Unity Democratic Organization (NUDO) (qq.v.). Despite his advancing years (he was 90 years old in 1960), he was both actually and symbolically the leader of African nationalism in Namibia until groups like SWAPO emerged as strong opponents of South African rule. As he became older he turned over some of his activities to his designated successor, Clemens Kapuuo (q.v.).

Chief Kutako died in 1970, at the age of 100. His funeral attracted at least seven thousand mourners. It can be truthfully said that his leadership inspired more than one generation of Namibian nationalists, and not just Hereros.

KWALUUDHI (variants: UKUALUDZI; UKUALUTHI). One of the eight kindred tribes of Owambo (q.v.). An estimate around 1970 indicated there were about 16,600 members of this group, 4.85 percent of all Wambos. They retained rule by a traditional chief after it had been abandoned by four of the other groups. The Kwaluudhi people live west of the original Wambo home area near Hakafia (q.v.), having broken away from another of the groups, the Ngandjera, who now live to their south. Another group, the Mbalantu, live further to their northeast.

When South African established a modern government system for Owambo, it established a Legislative Council (the Kwaluudhi were allotted three members), and a community authority system for each of the groups.

KWAMBI (variants: KUAMBI; UKUAMBI). The third largest of the eight related groups that make up the Wambo nation. A 1970 estimate indicated about 39,600 members of the Kwambi group, 11.55 percent of all Wambos.

Like several of the other groups, the Kwambi have maintained the rule by a traditional chief. However, in 1932 the South African authorities used a weak pretext to depose the then Chief (or King) Ipumbu (q.v.). His son, S. F. Iipumbu, was chosen to succeed him. He was selected to the newly established Executive Council in the late 1960s and held that post until 1973.

Traditionally the Kwambi have been excellent potters. The most suitable clay for making pots is found in their area, and Kwambi women developed a reputation for their artistry. Their products became a profitable trade item.

KWANDO RIVER. Elsewhere known variously as the Mashi, Chobe, or Linyanti River, it originates in Angola and flows in a southeastern direction until it touches Zambia. It then serves as the Zambian-Angolan border for 138 miles until it dips through the Caprivi Strip of Namibia (in this last stretch it is called the Mashi). It then turns east as the Linyanti River while it serves as the southern border of the Caprivi, separating it from Botswana. It eventually joins the Zambezi River just west of Kazangula. Tswanas prefer to call the Linyanti River the Chobe River.

KWANGALI (variant: KUANGALI). One of the five autonomous political subgroups of the Kavango people, the Kwangali, like the others, are a matrilineal society with hereditary chiefs. They live in the extreme north of the country, along the Okavango River, east of Owambo. Historically they were once part of the Greater Wambo nation.

KWANYAMA (variant: KUANJAMA). The largest and most political-minded of the eight subgroups of the Wambo nation, an estimate around 1970 gave a population of 132,400, 38.65 percent of the Wambos. This is significant for contemporary politics as well, as the Kwanyamas exercise great influence in SWAPO, a heavily Wambo political organization. Among the more influential of these is Hidipo Hamutenya (q.v.), minister of information and broadcasting.

The Kwanyama live on both sides of the Namibia/Angola border, and as a result SWAPO guerrillas of that origin found ready sanctuary among their fellow tribesmen across the Kunene.

Until 1917 the Kwanyama were ruled by a strong chief, with Mandume (q.v.) being the last to rule; South African forces killed him in 1917. Thus was destroyed the last truly independent chief among the Wambos. Nevertheless, strong headmen have remained a constant in Kwanyama traditional government, with leadership being passed on to chosen relatives as successors. After Mandume the South African administrators set up a tribal council of eight senior headmen and divided the area into eight districts. Each of these was further subdivided into wards ruled by sub-headmen. The large population made such organized rule necessary.

When South Africa set up a separate Owambo government in the late 1960s, Rev. Cornelius Ndjoba (q.v.) became a member of its Executive Council, and was the minister of education. When Chief Elfias was assassinated, Ndjoba was named his successor as the Council's chief minister. He also headed its constitutional committee. In 1977 he was named Kwanyama senior-headman.

In the Legislative Council each Wambo subgroup received only three seats, despite the numerical dominance of Kwanyamas. That region also had the most competitive elections, as several parties were organized to contest for the seats. The political awareness of Kwanyamas was also seen in the area of labor relations, as they were usually the strike leaders and the most willing to strike against the foreign-owned mining companies. It is not at all surprising, therefore, that many early founders of SWAPO came from the Kwanyama group.

- L -

LABOR, AFRICAN. At the beginning of the twentieth century, German policy towards Africans in Namibia could be best described as colonialist, but with the discovery of diamonds a new need arose. A supply of workers would be needed for mines. Ordinance No. 82 of 1907 was aimed at forcing Africans to become dependent on wages from whites. It barred Africans from gaining title to land and (with the exception of the Rehoboth Basters) from owning cattle or horses. "Vagrancy" was also punished. Only a job from a white employer could make an African reasonably secure from prosecution.

Work on the farms was generally done by Namas, Hereros, Damaras, Basters, and some San. Arrangements for feeding and housing farm workers tended to be poor, and historically those farmers who made better provisions found workers more readily. Still, farmers found the competition for workers difficult as a result of the higher salaries available at the mines.

Most mining and railroad work was done by Wambos, who left their northern homes after their harvests to work for wages. Contracts were therefore generally only for half a year at a time. The Wambos (including many from southern Angola) experienced both a material and a spiritual transformation by their employment in the south. A returning worker found many of his values different from his fellow villagers, and these new values affected the traditional societies. It is not surprising that modern political parties ultimately emerged first among the Wambos (*see* SWAPO).

When the South Africans took over the territory, Owambo was seen as a labor reserve for the whole region. The Southern Labor Recruiting Organization (SLO) was founded in 1925 to recruit for the diamond mines, while the Northern Labor Recruiting Organization (NLO), also formed in 1925, recruited for mining interests in the North. They were merged in 1943 as the South West African Native Labour Association (Pty.) Ltd (SWANLA), with Grootfontein its base. SWANLA had the sole right to recruit workers in the north under contracts until 1972. Major strikes and protests that year as a result of low salaries and poor working conditions led to a change by which responsibility for recruitment was switched to the governments of Owambo and Kavango.

SWANLA contracts were generally for a full year, but eighteen months became common. Recruits were checked medically at Ondangwa, and separated into three classes: those suited for heavy work, especially mining; those suited for surface work and industry; and those suited for farms and general work. The number of contracted recruits in 1942 was only about 7,600, but this rose to more than 18,000 in 1952 (half of them from Angola). The figure jumped to almost 35,000 by 1962 and over 40,000 from Owambo alone in 1975. In 1990 the National Union of Namibian Workers (NUNW) claims a membership of 40,000.

Generally wages for a single wage-earner were well below

the official poverty line for a family of five. While the 1972 strike led to a doubling and tripling of wages for Africans, inflationary spirals in the economy kept most Africans below the poverty line. Employers claimed that payment "in kind" (food and accommodations, however meager) provided a satisfactory supplement to low wages. (White workers were not required to accept payment in kind, however.) Wages for skilled workers, tradesmen, and teachers were generally better, but even in these cases two or more had to earn wages to enable the family to top the poverty line.

A series of laws gave employers coercive rights over their African laborers. The Mines and Works Act of 1917, the Masters and Servants Act of 1920, and the Natives (Urban Areas) Act of 1924 enabled employers to dismiss workers or withhold wages for almost any reason, while making it impossible for workers to resist or protest the abuses of the system. The Industrial and Commercial Workers Union had branches in Windhoek and Walvis Bay briefly in 1920s, but most labor resistance was unorganized or at least unplanned. For example, about two thousand Ovambo workers struck at Tsumeb in 1948 when a white foreman shot a worker to death. While the Food and Canning Workers Union was founded among Coloured workers at Lüderitz in 1949, police arrested Wambo workers who tried to form a union around the same time and banned all meetings. Three large strikes of contract laborers in 1952 and 1953 resulted in the firm suppression of all trade unionism. Strikes became illegal.

Nevertheless, large-scale labor unrest in Windhoek and Walvis Bay in December 1971 quickly spread around the country. For example, 13,500 striking Wambos were sent home immediately, but took their discontent north with them and began to organize with the aid of Johannes Nangutuuala. In January 1972 3,500 workers met at Oluna near Ondangwa and elected Nangutuuala as their strike chairman. The strike committee produced a detailed resolution that stated workers' grievances. While not addressing these grievances directly, a new labor agreement between the South African and Owambo governments was signed on January 20, 1972. It resolved some of the problems but ignored others. It specifically put Owambo leaders in charge of recruiting and distributing workers, an arrangement no less subject to abuse than previous practices. In 1973 a Labour Co-ordinating Advisory Committee was founded, aimed at improving labor conditions in Namibia. As indicated, wages have risen, but so have living costs. One estimate had unemployment of Africans as high as 27.7 percent in 1981, with population shifts from north to south and toward larger towns adding to the problem daily.

Since the development of modern labor unions in Namibia there have been a number of strikes. One of the largest of these began July 26, 1987, at Tsumeb, a center of activity by the Mineworkers Union of Namibia (MUN). Workers struck for higher wages and better working conditions, but management refused to negotiate. Four thousand workers—two-thirds of the nation's work force—were dismissed en masse. When the company began hiring again, only about a third of the dismissed workers were rehired, while new workers were brought in.

In 1987 Professor Nic Wiehahn, part of the team that recommended labor reforms in South Africa, was appointed head of a similar Namibian commission to review industrial relations, including the position of migratory laborers. Its findings, submitted in April 1989 just as the independence process was starting, should be implemented quickly under the new government.

Unionization of African workers was the most important development of the 1980s. The Mineworkers Union of Namibia (MUN) claims a membership of more than 9000, and represents most of the country's miners. The Namibia Food and Allied Workers Union (NAFAU), the Metal and Allied Namibian Workers Union (MANWU), and the Namibia Public Workers Union (NAPWU), plus the MUN, are the major affiliates of the National Union of Namibian Workers (NUNW), which claims a membership of more than 40,000.

Since many SWAPO members are trade unionists, it is likely that the influence of organized labor will increase under the new government. John Ya-Otto (q.v.) is a member of the Assembly, a long-standing leader with SWAPO, and the general secretary of the NUNW. Ben Ulenga (q.v.) holds the same position in the MUN and is an equally respected SWAPO activist of long standing. The MUN has been considered to be an arm of SWAPO since its creation.

LABOR PARTY OF SOUTH WEST AFRICA. Known as the Federal Coloured People's Party until August 1975, it changed its name at that time after the Labour Party in South Africa won control of the South African Coloured Representative Council. The Party's founder, Mr. Andreas L. F. Kloppers, had formed the South West Africa Coloured Teachers Association in the 1950s. His party won three of the six elected seats in the South West Africa Coloured Council early in 1975, thus allowing it to dominate the Coloured seats at the Turnhalle Conference as well. Although Kloppers and his party have been considered by many to be pro-apartheid, the designation is misleading. The party pursued a policy of cooperation, but with persistent pressure for government concessions (only to be disappointed by unfulfilled promises). The frustration peaked in August 1975, when Kloppers (chairman) and other members of the Coloured Council suspended its meetings and called for cabinet-level talks, while calling the council a useless instrument that was usually ignored. The party also urged that SWAPO be included in the Turnhalle Conference. As the conference proceeded, the Labour Party adopted a tougher, anti-government line. When the Democratic Turnhalle Alliance (DTA) was formed in 1977, the Labour Party became a member of this coalition. A leadership struggle in July 1978 resulted in Kloppers being ousted as chairman. Kloppers then formed the Liberal Party and in December 1978 was elected to the National Assembly.

The 1978 leadership struggle gave Labour Party leadership to Joey Julius, who became a member of the Ministers' Council from 1980 to 1983. The Labour Party also had two seats in the 1979–83 National Assembly. In 1980 the party also won a majority in the Second Tier Coloured Representative Authority, which it retained until the CRA was disbanded in 1989 when independence approached.

In 1981 L. J. "Barney" Barnes was elected by the LP Congress to replace Julius. This caused another split as Julius and his supporters left to form the Democratic People's Party (q.v.). In 1984 Barnes was replaced as leader by Dawid Bezuidenhout. The LP then joined the Multi-Party Conference, and later held eight seats in the TGNU National Assembly. Bezuidenhout served for a time as minister of transport in the TGNU.

Meanwhile "Reggie" Diergaardt was becoming an increasingly important member of the LP, and was elected its leader in 1987. Bezuidenhout is deputy national chairman, and Harry Booysen is the national chairman.

In 1988 Andrew Kloppers, Sr. (q.v.), rejoined the Labour Party, merging his Christian Democratic Union with it, but he died in an accident the next year. The LP joined the United Democratic Front for the 1989 elections, and Diergaardt gained one of its four seats in the Assembly.

The party's 1988 program called for Namibia to be an independent, nonracial, democratic, and unitary state. It called for a universal franchise and a system of proportional representation.

LAKE GUINAS. The larger of the two major lakes in the country (*see* LAKE OTJIKOTO), it is a crater lake that exposes underground water. Guinas adds a beautiful touch of color to the surrounding terrain. If one descends the rocky sides to the water's edge, one sees an unusual assortment of cave fish. Said to reach a depth of two hundred meters, the water is used to irrigate nearby farmlands. Guinas is a little to the northwest of Lake Otjikoto, and both are situated to the east of Etosha National Park and west of Tsumeb, in north-central Namibia.

LAKE NGAMI. Not located in Namibia at all but nearby in north-central Botswana, this once healthy lake became quite dry in the twentieth century except for a decade beginning in 1953 when waters from the Okavango River to the north again filled it. African hunters who first saw it around 1750 described it as "a lake with waves that throw hippos ashore, roaring like thunder." Word reached London of this legendary lake, and on August 1, 1849, Dr. David Livingstone and two companions were the first Europeans to see it. This visit was well-publicized, and others soon sought it, in part because of the valuable elephant tusks available in abundance nearby. It was explored by the Swedish explorer, Charles John Andersson (q.v.), whose party reached its west edge in July 1853. Andersson's book on Lake Ngami brought great waves of European hunters and explorers to the lake. Ngami's significance for Namibia is that most of its early visitors came to it through Namibia, and their contact sometimes led to hostility. At minimum this travel through the territory opened up large areas to European visitors and, ultimately, the Herero survivors fled their arid land into Botswana, in the hope (vain for most of them) of finding water and peace near Lake Ngami. Later an elaborate proposal by a Professor Schwartz would have diverted the waters of the Chobe and Kunene Rivers to help refill Lake Ngami.

LAKE OTJIKOTO. On May 26, 1851, Sir Francis Galton (q.v.) was the first European to see this beautiful crater lake, located in northern Namibia between the Etosha National Park and the town of Tsumeb. Its water has been used both for the town and for agricultural projects near Tsumeb (q.v.). Otjikoto is southeast of Lake Guinas, Namibia's other major lake. Otjikoto was formed when the roof of a huge dolomitic cave collapsed, and is about 820 feet by 650 feet, with a depth of about 600 feet. The water level varies according to rainfall but is generally about 120 feet deep, although Galton measured it as 180 feet in depth. The clear green waters are home to several species of fish, two rare mouth-breeding species among them, the *Tilapia guinasana* and the *Haplochromis philander.* Since both species are also found in Lake Guinas (q.v.), one might hypothesize that they are joined by an underground passage. The Wambo and Ovahimba people maintain that no one who swims in the lake will survive. When Galton, Charles Andersson, and others swam in it and emerged alive, the Africans suspected them of sorcery. Since then, however, at least one man dived in and vanished completely. Also a German soldier accidentally fell into the lake during World War I and drowned; Africans claim that his ghost still haunts Otjikoto today.

LAMBERTS, AMRAAL (d. 1864). Amraal (a contraction of "Admiral") was a man of part Nama, part European descent who was born in Clanwilliam, South Africa, and was a slave in Worcester. An honest and wise man, he led a group of followers (called Gei-khaua) into Namibia in 1815. They went first to Bethanie and later to Gobabis. They were part of the group referred to collectively as the Orlams (q.v.). Amraal's followers were related to the group led by Paul Goliath (q.v.), but the two groups had split in a dispute about where to settle. A man of peace, Amraal ruled his people at Gobabis until about 1864 when he died at about the age of ninety. His succession was complicated when his sixty-year-old heir, Lambert Lamberts, died of smallpox fifteen days after Amraal, the same day as Lamberts' son and heir Willem. A year later the tribe chose Andries Lambert as its chief.

LANDESHAUPTMANN. German title created for the newly created position that combined the role of commander of the troops with the duties of the former German Imperial Commissioner. The change took place in May 1891. Captain Curt Von Francois (q.v.) was the first to hold the title. He was succeeded by Theodore Von Leutwein (q.v.). The title can be translated literally as "Captain of the land." The two leadership positions were divided again when General Von Trotha was given the military command in October 1904. In the following year Leutwein was replaced in the civil government by Friedrich Von Lindequist.

LANGER HEINRICH. The site of a uranium mine and pilot plant, it is located about thirty kilometers south of Rössing. It had great potential, but a drop in the world spot market prices has caused the opening of the mine along with the expansion of the Rössing mine to appear overly optimistic.

LANGUAGES. The languages of Namibia can be categorized in three groups: the Bantu languages, spoken heavily in the northern and central regions, the Khoisan languages, found generally in the south and east, and European-based languages, spoken by whites and Blacks alike. Most Namibians of all ethnic groups are familiar with more than one language. Figures on primary languages indicate that about 65 percent of whites speak Afrikaans, 25 percent speak German, and 10 percent speak English. Nevertheless, English, for example, is understood by a high percentage of whites and many Blacks, even though it is not their primary language. Afrikaans is also the language of two other ethnic groups, the Coloureds and the Basters. Khoisan languages, recognizable by their distinctive "clicks," are spoken by Damaras, Namas, and the San. The Bantu languages are those of the Wambos, Hereros, Subia, Lozi, and Tswanas. Afrikaans became the dominant language of the government and of the educational system after the establishment of the League of Nations Mandate. After independence in 1990, English has become the official language.

LATHAM, WILLIAM. A trader and farmer in Namibia for at least two decades in the middle of the nineteenth century, he came from England and arrived at Walvis Bay in 1845. He was hired by Peter Dixon (q.v.) as a bookkeeper and general assistant, and later married Dixon's daughter. Mrs. Latham and her sister (who married James Frank Bassingthwaighte, q.v.) were the first white women to live at Walvis Bay, in the 1850s. Mr. Latham and Bassingthwaighte discovered the Matchless Mine. Latham served also as manager of a fishery at Walvis Bay in 1860, and he and his wife survived a shipwreck early the next year. He became an acquaintance of the noted explorers, James Chapman and C. J. Andersson (qq.v.), the latter even sending Latham as part of a delegation to Willem Swartbooi (q.v.) in Rehoboth to try to recover some stolen cattle. Latham himself had cattle stolen from him in April 1862, but Andersson sent armed Hereros with Latham's brother-in-law to recover them. Latham did not get involved in the battle between the Namas and the Hereros, living near the Bassingthwaightes on the road to Otjimbingwe, sixteen miles from the Matchless Mine. Despite his neutrality, however, one band of warriors burned down his house while he was away.

LEAD. Found in both central and southern Namibia, this important metal ranked fifth in value of sales in 1981 for Namibia, after uranium, diamonds, copper, and silver. It is thought that Namibia has larger reserves of lead than South Africa. The value of lead produced in Namibia rose from R15 million in 1970 to R32.7 million in 1980, and its value has increased throughout the 1980s. Revenue from sales of lead increased from R33 million in 1985 to R78 million in 1990. However this was due wholly to price increases, as the quantity of lead refined in 1990 was actually over three tons less than in 1985. All the lead is now refined before export. It is produced at the following mines: Tsumeb, Rosh Pinah, Kombat, and Berg Aukas. Kombat flooded in November 1988, but production has resumed. Tsumeb is now primarily a lead-producing mine, although zinc and germanium were formerly very important there as well.

LEAGUE OF NATIONS. Founded as a result of the Versailles Peace Conference of 1919 that ended World War I, the League of Nations was an attempt by the victors in that war to settle world affairs and lay the foundation for world peace. A major actor in its development was Jan C. Smuts (q.v.), a delegate from South Africa. His pamphlet, *The League of Nations: A Practical Suggestion,* was published on December 15, 1918, just as the delegates were gathering in Paris, and many of its ideas found their way into the League Covenant. The major decision of the conference affecting Namibia was the decision to divide the colonies of the vanquished among the victors, who were to administer these "mandates" (q.v.) in behalf of the League until the territories were sufficiently developed to govern themselves. Article 22 of the Covenant describes the principle that the well-being and development of the inhabitants was primary as "a sacred trust of civilization." South West Africa was awarded to South Africa as a "C" class mandate, indicative that it was a thinly populated area, rather remote, with "primitive" peoples. A "C" mandate could be administered as an integral part of the ruling country, as it would have little hope of true independence and self-sufficiency. However, the ruling country was obligated "to promote to the utmost the material and moral well-being and the social progress of the inhabitants of the territory." Smuts told a group in 1921, however, that the mandate "was nothing else but annexa-tion." And in 1925 he said that the mandate "gives the Union such complete sovereignty, not only administrative but legislative, that we need not ask for anything more." In fact, however, it was necessary for South Africa and other ruling countries to report regularly to the Permanent Man-dates Commission (q.v.) of the League, but neither the commission nor the League had any power to enforce any rulings. It was hoped that the commission's vigilance and occasional criticism would be sufficient to check abuses. Curiously (in light of current problems with the United Nations), South Africa, under the influence of Smuts, fa-vored applying international sanctions against countries that threatened world peace, at least in the case of Italy's invasion of Ethiopia.

For all practical purposes the League ceased to exist after the beginning of World War II in 1939, but it was not formally dissolved until the final Assembly met in 1946, with South Africa in attendance. By this time the United Nations (q.v.) existed, and had transformed the old "man-dates" into similar "trust territories." South Africa main-tained that its mandatory obligations ceased with the demise of the League of Nations and refused to accept the UN trusteeship arrangement as being legal, saying that it had never entered into such an agreement with the UN.

LEGISLATIVE ASSEMBLY. The official designation of the legislative body in South West Africa as provided for by a 1925 South African law that allowed limited self-administration for the territory. The original assembly con-sisted of twelve elected members, plus six appointed by the administration. Four of the eighteen were chosen for the Executive, which advised the administrator much like a cabinet. Later legislation made all eighteen elected. The Assembly at first had the power to legislate on all matters relating to the territory, with the exception of justice, posts and telegraphs, defense, immigration, railways and harbors, excise, and currency. Later the administration of police was also withdrawn from its authority and returned to the govern-ment of South Africa, as was "native affairs." All members of the Legislative Assembly were to be white, elected by white voters who were South African citizens. The Assembly served for five years before new elections.

Prior to this Legislative Assembly, one had been created on April 16, 1910, when the territory was under German rule, but this was soon eliminated when the Germans were defeated by South Africa. A new Legislative Assembly building was opened formally on May 14, 1964, replacing the old "Tintenpalast" (q.v.).

LEUTWEIN, THEODORE GOTTHILF VON (1849–1921). This soldier and top administrator of Namibia was born May 9, 1849, in Strumpfelbronn, Baden, Germany. He studied law nearby at Freiburg im Breisgau. At the age of 20 he was commissioned in the German army. Sixteen years later (1885) he was a captain and company commander. He lectured at the Neisse military college from 1887 to 1892 and was promoted to major in 1893. The German government was not especially pleased with some of the military forays of its chief administrator in Namibia, Curt von Francois (q.v.), and desired a report on conditions there. Problems with the African peoples were retarding development of the colony. Late in 1893 Leutwein was sent to make a report and (it appears) to succeed von Francois. He arrived at the port that would become Swakopmund on January 1, 1894. He noted at the time that, contrary to von Francois' official claims, and the granting of commercial concessions, the Germans controlled very little land outside Windhoek. Moreover, troop strength was not sufficient to maintain control.

In a couple of months Leutwein was named to succeed von Francois (who did not leave Namibia until April 24, 1894), and was Germany's top leader there for eleven years. (He later wrote a significant memoir, *Elf Jahre Gouverneur in Deutsch-Südwestafrika,* published in 1906.) He was given the title *Landeshauptmann* in 1895 and governor in 1898.

Leutwein's career in the territory might be divided into three phases. The first involved asserting German control over the African peoples inhabiting the territory. His initial attack was against the followers of Hendrik Witbooi (q.v.), a prominent Nama leader. He first had the German troops merely track and limit the range of the Namas, while he tried an exchange of letters with Witbooi. The latter expressed an interest in ending warfare with the Germans. But when a large force of German reinforcements arrived in July along with more modern rifles, Leutwein planned an attack. This began on August 27, 1894, in the Naukluft Mountains, west of Hornkrans. By mid-September the defeated Namas were ready to sign a protection agreement. Witbooi agreed to live peacefully in Gibeon with a salary or pension from the government. He would also supply the Germans with armed men to fight other African groups, a condition that he fulfilled.

This persuaded Leutwein to continue with his stated approach of "divide and rule." He next took on the Hereros, a nation of about 80,000 Africans divided into seven or eight tribes that were very competitive with each other. The largest of these was led by Samuel Maharero (q.v.). The land of the Herero nation was very desirable for current and future German settlers, so it had to be pacified. Leutwein used Samuel Maharero's weak claim as "paramount chief" to get him to agree to a boundary between Herero land and that of the Germans to the south. The fact that Samuel did not have the right to alienate this land and the fact that the boundary gave away land of some of his Herero competitors was seemingly irrelevant. The deal also gave Germans the right to confiscate cattle found south of the line and sell them to new settlers. Thus thousands of cattle were confiscated, forcing a confrontation between Leutwein and the Herero leaders. He again used the policy of "divide and rule," coming to peaceful agreement with the western Hereros of Samuel Maharero, but going to battle with eastern Hereros under Nikodemus in May 1896. The German victory opened up new lands for German settlers and solidified Samuel's claim as "paramount chief." An uprising occurred in 1897 in which Namas at Gobabis allied with eastern Hereros, and Leutwein's policies paid off. Hendrik Witbooi sent armed troops and Samuel Maharero supported the Germans against the Mbanderus. The German victory with its African allies pointed toward a possibility of peace and new settlement.

The second aspect of Leutwein's service in Namibia involved the peaceful settlement and expansion of the colony. An early setback was the outbreak of rinderpest (a cattle plague) in 1897. Because oxwagon transport became impossible, the port at Swakopmund was developed to handle freight. Likewise the port at Lüderitzbucht (q.v.) was developed, and towns grew at both places. Ultimately Leutwein arranged for train tracks to be laid and service started between Swakopmund and Windhoek, a route still used today, with some adjustments for drifting sand dunes and shifting river beds.

Pioneers settled new towns, such as Karibib, and at locations such as Okahandja, Grootfontein, Keetmanshoop, and Gibeon. Samuel Maharero was especially eager to ''sell'' land to German settlers. To avoid potential trouble, Leutwein tried to ban the sale of firearms or alcohol to Africans. He was also concerned with the shortage of German women immigrants (in 1903 only 712 of 4682 white immigrants). To stem the increase of interracial sex, he promoted the immigration of women by creating places for them in government and community services. He even set up a German school. Starting with eleven children, it occupied a room of his own house, which he placed at the disposal of the teacher.

The third and final phase of Leutwein's career in Namibia began with the rebellion of a Nama tribe, the Bondelswarts (q.v.), in 1903. Major von Leutwein personally led the Schutztruppe to Warmbad to reestablish order. The Bondels signed a peace treaty at Kalkfontein in 1904 rather than face defeat. But by taking most of the soldiers to Warmbad he had left few among the Hereros. And in January 1904 a Herero uprising (fostered by a wide range of grievances) resulted in the death of 123 German farmers, traders and settlers. Okahandja was besieged and Captain Victor Franke (q.v.) was sent by Leutwein to break the siege. After signing the treaty with the Namas, Leutwein brought the troops to Okahandja to establish a defense zone and to plan a counter attack. Always preferring diplomacy to battle, Leutwein wanted to arrange a peaceful settlement rather than a test of strength. The German leadership in Berlin disagreed, however, preferring a harsh attack on the Hereros. They sent General Lothar von Trotha (q.v.) to the territory to replace Leutwein as military commander on June 11, 1904. Leutwein remained as civil administrator, and saw von Trotha defeat the Hereros at Waterberg (q.v.) and exterminate many of the fleeing Hereros. Seeing this and the demotion of Leutwein, his friend and protector, Hendrik Witbooi declared war against the Germans on October 1, 1904. The dejected Leutwein soon returned to Germany and resigned from the colonial service in 1905.

LEVINSON, JACK AND OLGA. A remarkable couple, they were among the country's wealthiest property-owners, and lived in one of the country's "castles" built by the German architect, Willi Sander (q.v.). Jack Levinson was mayor of Windhoek from 1963 to 1965 and publicly expressed his concern for the territory's future. He supported peaceful change quickly, so that people of all races could live together without discrimination or recrimination. All minorities must be protected if the confidence of investors and white residents was to be retained, he believed. His business interests included serving as a director of Lithium Mines.

Olga, Jack's wife, died in 1989. She was the author of several excellent books (including *Call Me Master, The Ageless Land,* and *Adolph Jentsch*) and many articles. Her *Story of Namibia,* published in 1978, is an enlarged and updated version of *South West Africa* (1976). While barely over 150 pages, it is perhaps the most informative and comprehensive introduction available. Born in South Africa, she received a BA degree from the University of Witwatersrand. Moving to Namibia in 1943, she immersed herself in its history and fine arts. She had an outstanding collection of art by every significant artist painting her adopted country from Thomas Baines on. She served as president of the territory's Association of Arts for eighteen years, and as chairman of Opera and Ballet for the South West African Performing Arts Council.

LEWIS, ROBERT (c. 1841–1894). British-born hunter, trader, mine manager, agent, and concessionaire, he arrived in Cape

Town with his parents at the age of ten. In 1858 the teenager travelled to Herero territory to begin a career hunting elephants and selling the ivory. By 1868 he was managing the Ebonie Mine near Walvis Bay for De Pass, Spence and Co. His fluency in Seherero gave him influence among the Herero leaders, who called him KaRobbie (Chief Robbie). For the next twenty years he had a variety of business interests among the Herero, and had a store in Walvis Bay for some time. In 1877 he received a concession for twenty-one years from Maherero for the Ebonie Mine. In 1883 he also obtained a concession to the Otavi Mine for thirty years.

Lewis's close relations with Maherero (Lewis was even a member of the Herero Council) allowed him to assist W. C. Palgrave (q.v.) in dealings with Herero chiefs in 1876. He unsuccessfully represented Maherero in an attempt in 1883 to frighten away the Boers at the Republic of Upingtonia (q.v.). Throughout the 1880s KaRobbie was Maherero's closest advisor on foreign affairs, as Lewis lived as a trader in Otjimbingwe. Maherero even told the Germans in 1888 that Lewis had his power of attorney to exercise authority and control over his territory. The same year Lewis came to Okahandja with a staff of fifteen, as a representative of the Kimberley Damaraland Syndicate. His influence with Maherero was extremely strong, and he may also have been backed by Cecil Rhodes, but German strength grew, and in 1889 the Germans confiscated eight of Lewis's loads of machinery and one of trade goods designated for Otjimbingwe. Seeing their growing strength, he ceded most of his concession rights to a company planning to work Otavi's copper. Lewis then began trading in eastern Namibia and in Botswana, where he hunted and sold guns to Namas. In late 1894 he was killed by a leopard he had wounded at Rietfontein. He left a widow and five children in Hereroland, where he had been raising cattle.

LIBERAL PARTY. Represented in the 1979–83 National Assembly by its leader, Andreas J. F. Kloppers, Sr. (q.v.), it was formed after Kloppers lost a leadership struggle with L. J. Barnes for control of the Labour Party of South West Africa (q.v.) in July 1978. Kloppers, a longtime political activist in the Coloured community, has always worked to develop communication with the territory's white leadership, while simultaneously working to meet his people's needs. At first his party worked in an alliance with the Action Front for the Retention of Turnhalle Principles (q.v.) in an effort to win a Liberal Party seat in the National Assembly. He won a seat, but soon found that the Action Front was far too conservative for him. In June 1979 he announced that he would break from that alliance. That immediately accomplished one thing, as Klopper's son Andy rejoined his father, serving as secretary general of the Liberal Party. In 1982 the two Kloppers merged their party with the Democratic People's Party of Joey Julius, with the result named the Christian Democratic Union. Kloppers, Sr., became its president.

In 1988 Kloppers, Sr., merged the CDU with the Labour Party, and the next year he died in an automobile accident. His son Andy then declared the Liberal Party to be reconstituted in August 1989 and said it would join the Federal Convention of Namibia for the coming elections. Kloppers did not get a seat in the Assembly. The new Liberal Party's deputy chairman is Frans Ferris, and the secretary-general is Aubrey Groenemeyer.

LIBERATED DEMOCRATIC PARTY (LDP/LF). Few political groups have been known by so many different names and have had such a complex parentage as this one. Part of the problem involves splits and mergers. The other involves different languages. Because its support has always been among the Rehoboth Basters, its name is sometimes given in Afrikaans and sometimes in English.

Its origins go back to 1975 when Johannes ("Hans") Diergaardt (q.v.) and D. J. Izaaks (q.v.) broke away from the Rehoboth Volkspartei (q.v.) and formed the Rehoboth Liberation Party ("Rehoboth Bevrydingsparty" or RBD). This new group supported an older alliance, the National Convention of Freedom Parties (q.v.), a conservative coalition, at a time when the leaders of the Volkspartei had switched to a new coalition, the Namibia National Convention (q.v.). Izaaks was chosen the alliance's chairman. During elections for the Baster Raad in April 1975, the Rehoboth Liberation

Party won two of the seven seats. It also sent two delegates in 1975 as part of the Rehoboth representation to the Turnhalle Conference, although it withdrew them in 1976.

When Assembly elections were announced in 1978, the party assumed the name Liberation Front, in order to be open to more than just Rehobothers. However it only won one seat, which was held by Hans Diergaardt. He and his party pulled out of the Assembly after only one year, in 1980. It did retain its alliance with the National Convention of Namibia (the new name of the National Convention of Freedom Parties). The party's position was somewhere between the pro-SWAPO Volkspartei and the anti-SWAPO Rehoboth Baster Vereniging. The latter party lost several key members in 1977 who broke away to form the Rehoboth Democratic Party over clashes with Dr. Africa. They had held seats in the Raad (council). In 1979 they merged with Diergaardt's group to form the Liberated Democratic Party (Bevryder Demokratiese Party, BDP), which is also sometimes written as "Democratic Liberation Party." The group is popularly called the "Free Democrats" or "Bevryders." For its initials it may be referred to as LDP/LF or LF/LDP or (in Afrikaans) BDP. Under any name, its president is Hans Diergaardt. Its vice-president is Karel Freigang (or Freygang) of the old Rehoboth Democratic Party. In 1979 the LDP/LF defeated Dr. Africa'a party in the Raad elections and again in 1984. Hans Diergaardt won election as Baster Kaptein (Chief). When the Multi-Party Conference was created in November 1983, Diergaardt joined as a founder along with other centrist politicians. He accused SWAPO of being more interested in breaking up centrist movements than in negotiating peace. However, as proven in 1990, Diergaardt's major concern is that a truly centralized Namibia under SWAPO would spell the end of Rehoboth's special status with its own elected leaders.

When the Transitional Government of National Unity was formed, the LDP/LF held two ministerial positions. Diergaardt was minister of local government and civil affairs, and Hendrik January was a deputy minister for agriculture and nature conservation. The party was also represented in the Constitutional Council from 1985 to 1987. A party split occurred in 1988, however, and several leading members resigned. They were Dr. Lukas de Vries, Samuel Cloete, and Pieter Diergaardt.

In late 1988 the party participated with other parties in trying to bring back an old coalition. The result was finally the formation of a new alliance, the Federal Convention of Namibia (q.v.), which became an electoral alliance for the 1989 elections. The FCN only won 10,452 votes, almost half of them in Rehoboth. It received one seat in the Assembly, which went to Hans Diergaardt. However, he soon resigned "temporarily" for health reasons, and Mburumba Kerina (q.v.) of the NUDO Progressive Party took the seat.

In the period leading up to independence, Diergaardt has continued to assert the right of Rehoboth to self-government. On March 19, 1990, two days before independence, he proclaimed (as its kaptein) that Rehoboth was declaring its independence. He has also indicated that the Basters would try to buy farms between Rehoboth and Walvis Bay to give it access to the sea. The future of the LDP/LF is uncertain, but it can be expected to remain controversial.

LIBERATION FRONT (LF). *See* NAMIBIA PEOPLE'S LIBER-ATION FRONT *and* LIBERATED DEMOCRATIC PARTY.

LIBERATION MOVEMENT. *See* LIBERATED DEMO-CRATIC PARTY.

LINDEQUIST, FRIEDRICH VON (1862–1945). A man who rose from the ranks to become colonial governor of South West Africa from 1905 to 1907. Born in Wosteritz, Germany, he became a judge in Namibia from 1894 to 1899, and consul-general in Cape Town from 1900 to 1903. When the Hereros were ruthlessly defeated by General von Trotha (q.v.), Lindequist was chosen to replace him in late 1905. He is remembered for being kindly, tactful, and wise, a perfect choice to settle the rebellion after the merciless policies of von Trotha. Lindequist had served as a local authority and administrative troubleshooter for Major T. Leutwein (q.v.). Thus his knowledge of the region made him a logical choice to rebuild the land after the war. One of his tasks was to persuade bands of fugitive Hereros to voluntarily surrender. Three camps for Herero prisoners were assigned to Rhenish missionaries to assure good treatment. Thus at least 12,000 Hereros survived the aftermath of the rebellion to return to some semblance of livelihood. Von Lindequist's capital, following Leutwein's example, was Windhoek, still a young city. He called for reconstructing the territory into a German stronghold that all Germans could look up to. Things were not yet totally peaceful, however. While many Nama had surrendered, Marengo (q.v.) and his bands created havoc for German settlers as well as for the army until mid-1906. Other groups also were active until almost the end of 1906, when the tactics of Commander-in-Chief Colonel von Deimling proved victorious.

One of his early development measures was to assist farmers by developing bore-holes to exploit water resources. His name is also linked with the introduction of karakul sheep, the basis for a major commercial venture for Namibia. The first herd arrived in 1907 when he enthusiastically accepted the proposal from the director of sheep breeding in Germany. A much larger herd arrived in 1909, again after his encouragement. In 1907, with great foresight he proclaimed the northwestern part of the territory to be a protected game reserve, laying the foundation for another important industry today. His last official duty in Namibia was the laying of the cornerstone of the landmark Christ Church in Windhoek. He was called back to Germany in 1907 to serve as state under-secretary in the German Colonial Office, a post he resigned four years later after disagreeing with the German-French treaty on Morocco. During World War I he held an administrative post dealing with health questions. However, he became vice-president of the Deutsche Kolonial-gesellschaft (q.v.), which had major interests in Namibia, and for two decades was involved in a number of business-oriented organizations.

LINYANTI. A village in the Singalamwe district of the Caprivi Strip, where sixty-three Africans were killed by South African troops in 1968 during forced removal of the village's

population. It had been the capital or principal village of the
Makololo under Chief Sebituane in the mid-nineteenth century. Sebituane maintained his influence throughout most of
southern and western Zambia from this location, just north of
the Linyanti River. Dr. David Livingstone met Sebituane at
this village in 1851, two weeks before the chief died.
Livingstone and his party stayed there another month after
Sebituane's death, and the doctor's wife gave birth there.

LINYANTI RIVER. The southern border of the Eastern Caprivi
Strip, separating Namibia from Botswana, the river is also
known variously as the Chobe, Mashi, or Kwando River.
Beginning in Angola where it is the Kwando or Cuando
River, it flows southeasterly until it touches Zambia. It then
serves as the Angolan-Zambian border for 130 miles until it
dips into the Caprivi Strip of Namibia. It then turns east and
becomes the southern border of the Caprivi until it joins the
Zambezi River just west of Kazangula. During its Caprivi
phase it is called either the Chobe or the Linyanti. The
Makololo people chose to live in the unhealthy, swampy area
north of the Linyanti in the mid-nineteenth century because
they saw the river as the best defensive barrier against the
Matabele of Chief Mzilikazi. The river bed is broad and
shallow, but in the rainy season it overflows its banks,
creating islands, streams, and shallows. The Savuti Channel
is an offshoot of the Linyanti that finally dies in the Savuti
Marsh. It remained dry from the mid-1850s until 1957 when
the Savuti began to flood again. The Linyanti also occasionally receives overflow from the Okavango River in years of
exceptions flooding by way of the Magwegquana Spillway,
along the Magwegquana Fault. It is said that the Linyanti-
Chobe River sometimes reverses itself, flowing westward.
This is an illusion that occurs when the Zambezi is at its
height or even flooding. The waters of the Linyanti cannot
merge with the Zambezi, and indeed the latter's flood waters
push their way westward along the course of the Linyanti-
Chobe.

LITTLE NAMAQUALAND. Namaqualand was a term given by
early South African settlers to the area occupied by the Nama

people. They distinguished between the area south of the Orange River, called Little Namaqualand, and the area in southern Namibia, which was called Great Namaqualand. Most of the early European travellers into Namibia came through Little Namaqualand, where they acquired provisions and, often, guides. The guides were especially useful as they spoke a language similar to the people in Great Namaqualand, which made travel in Namibia much easier.

LOBSTER, SOUTH AFRICAN ROCK. A prominent part of the fishing industry (q.v.), these crustaceans thrive on a particular form of plankton. This plankton is found in the Benguela Current, an icy current that flows up the coast from Antarctica to Angola, where it heads out to sea and dissipates. The sweet, firm, white-fleshed tail is eaten by humans, while the rest is ground up into meal for animal feed. This variety of lobster has no large claws like the American variety. At maturity it may weight from one-and-one-quarter pounds up to four pounds, but the tail is less than a quarter of this weight. This lobster was not discovered until the late nineteenth century, and exports to Europe and North America did not begin until the 1930s. In 1988, 1,751 metric tons of rock lobster were caught. Over 96 percent of the catch was exported whole to Japan, where they are a highlight at marriage ceremonies.

LONDON MISSIONARY SOCIETY (LMS). Founded in London in 1795 as "The Missionary Society," it was originally an interdenominational organization that included Anglican, Presbyterian, and Congregationalist missionaries. The first two soon established separate mission societies and only the Congregationalists remained. The activities of the LMS in Namibia are dominated by the careers of J. Christian Albrecht and J. Heinrich Schmelen (qq.v.), but the work of other missionaries such as Robert Moffat and David Livingstone in other parts of central and southern Africa made the LMS synonymous with inspirational missionary work. LMS work in Namibia originated when J. Christian Albrecht, his brother Abraham, and Johannes Seidenfaden left Cape Town May 22, 1805, with Namaland as their destination. They crossed the Orange River into Namibia and opened a school at Warmbad (or Warm Bath) on February 3, 1806. Despite the barren and dry character of the soil in the area, the LMS required the missionaries to make it self-supporting, an order they protested. The mission station attracted visits by seven hundred Namas in 1807, and seemed somewhat successful. But Abraham Albrecht died of lung disease in 1810, and the mission station was sacked and burned by a force led by Jager Afrikander in 1811. The attack was because Namas at the mission had allied themselves with Hans Dreyer, with whom Jager was at war. Christian Albrecht was in Cape Town at the time of the attack, so he did not return to Warmbad; instead he went to Pella, a few miles south of the Orange River, inside the Cape Colony, where he was joined by some of the Warmbad Namas. Coming from Cape Town with Albrecht were several new LMS missionaries, notably Heinrich Schmelen and John Ebner. Schmelen entered Namibia in 1814, travelling as far north as Okahandja. The Namas invited him to settle at Bethanie, 55 miles north of the Orange River, which he did in 1815, travelling from Pella with about 150 Orlam Namas. He became an expert on the Nama language, and even took a Nama bride. The latter act was criticized by whites in the Cape and in London and was perceived as being unscrupulous behavior. This situation, plus slow communication with London, presented problems for the LMS. In addition, the Bethanie station had to be abandoned in 1822, and a combination of drought, locusts, and trouble among the Namas hindered several attempts to reestablish it. Schmelen stayed in Namibia, however, working in the areas near Walvis Bay and near Rehoboth.

His last mission station was founded at Komaggas in 1829. Although he persuaded the Rhenish Missionary Society to take it over in 1838 (formally in 1840), he remained there until his death ten years later. Other LMS mission stations meanwhile were also transferred to the Rhenish missionaries, one of whom married Schmelen's daughter.

LORELEI. The site of both diamond and copper discoveries, it is on the north bank of the Orange River about 160 miles south of Aus. The first discoveries were in 1924, when Moisha

Kahan came across a copper deposit. The extremely difficult mountainous terrain was conquered, as Kahan had a road built to the copper deposit, which he had called Lorelei after a famous rocky point on the Rhine River in his native Germany. When copper prices plummeted in 1930, Kahan stopped production. Years later some excellent quality gem diamonds were discovered in the Lorelei area, averaging 1.8 carats in size. Most of the companies working in the area now are South African parastatals, or companies owned by South Africans. For a period in the 1960s a company called Lorelei (or Loreley) Copper Mines was able to reopen production of copper at Lorelei.

LÖWEN RIVER (variant: LION RIVER). A tributary of the Fish River in southern Namibia, it begins in two branches east of Keetmanshoop and flows in a southwesterly direction, in the valley north of the Little Karas mountains, until it reaches the Fish River, halfway between Seeheim and the Fish River Canyon. The Naute Dam is on this river. The name ''Lion River'' is used by Professor Vedder in both his text and maps. He has it starting near the Karas Mountains also, but flowing due south past Warmbad before joining the Orange River. This description fits the river that is called the Hom River today.

LUBOWSKI, ANTON (1953–1989). The most prominent white member of SWAPO until he was assassinated two months before the 1989 elections, he was born in Lüderitz. His education was at Stellenbosch and Cape Town University. He had both a BA and an LLB degree. He was also a member of the Windhoek Bar. At one time he also had been an officer in the South African Defence Force.

His first involvement with SWAPO came when he assisted its delegation at the 1981 Geneva Conference. He stirred great controversy when he joined SWAPO in 1984. He won the confidence of SWAPO's activists and later was named SWAPO's deputy head of finance and administration. He was also active in labor activities and was treasurer of the National Union of Namibia Workers (q.v.). His activities for SWAPO in Windhoek got him arrested and detained on six occasions, but they also won for him the Bruno Kreisky Prize for Achievements in Human Rights. He had frequently represented Namibians who had been accused of terrorism merely because of their support for SWAPO. He spoke out against human rights atrocities, and condemned the brutal activities of Koevoet (q.v.). He spoke frequently at meetings in South Africa against conscription, and at meetings of the Detainees Parents Support Committee.

Lubowski was committed to a peaceful partnership between Namibia's Blacks and whites, and hoped to be a bridge between them. In the year before his assassination he began a project to draft laws for Namibia and noted laws that must be repealed at independence. Some thought he might be named minister of justice.

Lubowski was killed at his own home by a man firing an AK47 rifle. A white man carrying an Irish passport who had just entered the country on September 10, two days before Lubowski's murder, was held for questioning.

The death of Lubowski led directly to the revelations by Nico Basson (q.v.) concerning the policies of South Africa that aimed at weakening SWAPO in the 1989 elections.

LÜDERITZ, F. A. E. (ADOLF) (1834–1886). Born Franz Adolf Edward Lüderitz in Bremen, Germany, he was trained to be a tobacco merchant. He applied the knowledge in North America from 1854 to 1859. He came to West Africa in 1878 after inheriting his father's tobacco company in Hamburg and based himself in Lagos, Nigeria. Looking for less congested areas of Africa, he sent an expedition under another merchant, Heinrich Vogelsang (q.v.) on the small ship *Tully* to explore the interior of South West Africa from the bay called Angra Pequeña. He hoped to establish a trading zone there. The young Vogelsang landed April 10, 1883, and virtually founded the town of Lüderitzbucht (q.v.). With the aid of a Rhenish missionary, Vogelsang "purchased" Angra Pequeña and twenty-five square miles around it from Josef Fredericks (q.v.), Orlam chief of Bethanie, for 2500 German marks, 200 rifles, and a collection of toys including small lead soldiers. This purchase was important because Lüderitz had requested German protection for the area in 1882 but chancellor Bismarck promised it only if Lüderitz acquired a harbor and had clear title to the area to be protected. In August 1883 Lüderitz brought 1000 square miles of Namib coastal desert to the north of the bay from the same chief. Calling the area Lüderitzland, he asked Bismarck for protection. This was granted on April 24, 1884, after Bismarck had attempted to clarify Britain's claims in the area.

Lüderitz meanwhile set up a profitable trade with the local Africans, especially the Namas. He then concluded treaties with Nama chiefs around Walvis Bay, Windhoek, Fransfontein, and Sesfontein, effectively giving him control of the entire Namib Desert. Unfortunately for him, two prospecting expeditions, including botanists and geologists, did not have encouraging results to report to Lüderitz, and the expense of the expeditions plus other ventures caused him financial problems. He lost about £100,000, a third of which was tied up in drilling tools lost at sea when the *Tully* sank in the bay. Nearly bankrupt, in April 1885 he sold his mineral rights to a new German company, the Deutsche Kolonialgesellschaft für Südwestafrika (q.v.). Ironically his prospectors had searched for copper, not knowing about the diamonds along the coast. In 1886 he personally began to explore the area along the north bank of the Orange River for possible settlements. At Nabasdrift he and a companion ignored warnings and set off in canvas boats to ride the river to the sea. They were never seen again after embarking on October 22, 1886, and were presumed drowned. The German government honored him for laying the foundation for the German empire in South West Africa by changing the name of the bay and town to Lüderitzbucht (q.v.).

LÜDERITZ. Principal town of the magisterial district of the same name, it was formerly known as Lüderitzbucht (q.v.). It is a port on a bay about 298 kilometers north of the Orange River. The district extends south to the South African border, including the coastal town of Oranjemund. The district is relatively dry, and includes large areas of Namib Desert and its dunes. Its 58,719 square kilometers include about 20 percent farm land but 69 percent reserved diamond area. The town itself was a settlement began by F. A. E. Lüderitz (q.v.) as part of the broader region he claimed for Germany as Lüderitzland (q.v.).

The German chancellor, Otto von Bismarck (q.v.), formally placed the area under German protection on April 24, 1884, but the German flag was not hoisted at Lüderitzbucht until August 6, 1884. By this time a great deal of commerce had been going on for several decades, especially in the fishing, sealing, and ship-repair industries. For the first quarter century after its founding, it remained a relatively quiet trading port but in April 1908 a diamond was discovered only ten miles away. It suddenly became a boom town, filled with fortune seekers and edged with prospecting tents. The drinking establishments had diamond scales for those who wanted to pay in stones. The lucky prospectors built Wagnerian villas in the hills overlooking the bay. Charming German architecture from that era still makes it a place to be seen, although the few thousand inhabitants today are a fraction of its boom size. The diamonds petered out and the diamond industry established itself 150 miles to the south. Nevertheless, it was a battleground during World War I. The Germans built a defensive system to protect it from the east, only to find themselves surrounded as South African troops under General Mackenzie were landed on the coast in September 1914.

The economy turned around after the war when an Italian fishing man named Napoli discovered the lobsters there and saw the potential for a great industry. Great quantities of "South African Rock Lobsters" (q.v.) were exported from Lüderitz. The canning industry that also developed not only helped the economy but gave birth to the first African trade unions and political organizations in Namibia. The Industrial and Commercial Workers' Union and the Universal Negro Improvement Association had branches in Lüderitz in the 1920s. In 1949 a new and stronger union, the Food and Canning Workers Union, was founded in Lüderitz, then the center of fish canning. The canning industry has spread: in 1965 a factory to process sardines for the fish meal industry was opened in Lüderitz.

The town has a unique water supply, as all of the water it uses is reclaimed from the sea by boiling under low pressure and condensing the steam. The harbor at Lüderitz is formed mainly of two islands, called Shark and Seal Islands, and it handled 233 vessels in 1979–80, less than half of that of

Walvis Bay. A rail line extended from Keetmanshoop to Lüderitz. It is considered today to be a quaint resort town with good beaches. 4,748 resided in Lüderitz in 1981, and the 1988 estimate was 6,000.

LÜDERITZ BAY. *See* LÜDERITZBUCHT.

LÜDERITZBUCHT (translation: LÜDERITZ BAY). One of the more important landing spots for ships reaching Namibia, especially prior to the twentieth century, the bay is located about 150 miles north of the South African border. The first European to reach it was Bartholomew Dias (q.v.), who called it Angra das Voltas (Bay of the Tacks, because of the many tacks needed to get out of it), who stayed five days there in December 1487. On his return to Portugal in July 1488 he entered the bay again and set up a stone cross marker, renaming the area Golfo de São Cristovão. Dutch ships landed there almost two centuries later, and the bay meanwhile became known as Angra Pequeña (q.v.) or "Little Bay." The Namas living there were not receptive to the Dutch, and there were confrontations. It was 1787 before a major landing occurred, and British Captain T. B. Thompson found the Dias Cross in deteriorating condition. In 1793 the southern Namibian coast was proclaimed to be Dutch territory, but in 1795 a British ship hoisted its flag at the bay. A great deal more commercial activity took place in the nineteenth century, especially as guano (q.v.) deposits on the offshore islands were worked and as whaling and sealing activities flourished. DePass, Spence and Co. (q.v.) set up a fishing and sealing industry on the coast in 1856 and a ship repair yard at Angra Pequeña. But the first major European settlement was begun by a German merchant, F. A. E. Lüderitz (q.v.) in 1883. The bay was renamed Lüderitzbucht in his honor. Both the municipality that developed there and the bay itself eventually had their name abbreviated to Lüderitz (q.v.).

LÜDERITZLAND. A name given in 1883 by Adolf Lüderitz to two tracts of Namibian land he acquired that year. The first was the bay called Angra Pequeña (q.v.) and twenty-five square miles around it; the second was a strip of coast fifty miles long and twenty miles wide to the north of the bay. Lüderitz petitioned the German chancellor, Otto von Bismarck, for German "protection" of Lüderitzland. the chancellor hesitated, as the question of British rights and influence was unanswered, but in 1884 he finally agreed to grant protection. Bismarck saw British royal chartered companies as being models and precedents for German activity in Africa, and Lüderitz, a businessman, fit the mold.

LUIPERT, DANIËL (1937–). Born in Fransfontein, Luipert studied at the Augustineum Training College in Okahandjo, graduating in 1961. He also spent two years at the University of the North in South Africa, where he earned a teacher's diploma in 1964. He then returned to teach at the Augustineum for three years; he was assistant inspector of schools at Keetmanshoop from 1968 to 1974.

Luipert was the leader of the Nama delegation to the 1957–77 Turnhalle Conference and also served on its Constitutional Committee. When the Nama Representative Authority was set up in 1978, he was named a member of its Executive Committee, a post he held for two years.

After the Turnhalle Conference ended in 1977 his Nama Alliance party affiliated with the DTA. Two years later his group took a new name, the Democratic Turnhalle party, but added "of Namibia" in 1980 to avoid confusion with the DTA. The group he now leads is referred to as the DTPN. He was elected to the 1979–83 National Assembly, and in 1980 became a member of its Ministers Council.

Luipert has been a member of the Executive Council and/or chairman of the Nama Second Tier Representative Authority throughout its existence (1980–89). He served with the Multi-Party Conference in 1984, representing the DTA. In 1986 he was appointed Kaptein (Chief) of his Fransfontein Swartboois. As a vice-president of the DTA, Luipert was placed fourth on its 1989 electoral list, and easily secured a seat in the National Assembly.

LUTHERAN CHURCH. Represented originally in Namibia by the Rhenish Mission society from Germany and later by the Finnish Mission Society (qq.v.), both Evangelical Lutheran

Mission groups, the Lutheran Church in Namibia today is strongest in the form of two African-run churches, the Evangelical Lutheran Church in Namibia (ELCIN) and the Evangelical Lutheran Church (ELC).

- M -

MAACK, DR. REINHARDT, and MAACK CAVE. A surveyor by trade (although he later became a geologist), he traveled to the Brandberg in 1917 with Alfred Hofmann, a mapmaker. After climbing Königstein, the highest peak in Namibia, Maack slept one night in a cave in the Tsisab Valley. The next morning he found that the walls contained some remarkable rock art, notably the renowned "White Lady of Brandberg" (q.v.). His sketch was reproduced in a book on Namibia's rock art and the world of archaeology soon discovered it. The cave is now called Maack Cave.

MACBRIDE, SEAN (1904–). The first UN commissioner for Namibia. His education was split between Ireland and Paris. He worked as a journalist before being called to the Irish Bar in 1937. In 1946 he founded the Republican Party in Ireland. He served as a member of the Irish Parliament ("Dail Eireann") from 1947 to 1958. From 1963 to 1971 he was secretary general of the International Commission of Jurists, and from 1961 to 1974 he was chairman of the Amnesty International Executive. He won the Nobel Peace Prize in 1974. From the late 1960s he took on a number of posts at the international level, including some involving the United Nations. When he became the UN commissioner for Namibia on the first day of 1974, he also received the rank of assistant secretary-general of the United Nations. From the 1940s to the 1970s he authored numerous books and articles, many dealing with his favorite topics, human rights and international law.

With this background he brought tremendous prestige and validity to his role as the first UN commissioner for Namibia, a post he held for three terms. He was succeeded on February 1, 1977, by Martti Ahtisaari (q.v.).

MAFWE (variant: MAFUE). Originally from Angola and Zambia, the Mafwe are one of the two largest groups of people living in the Caprivi Strip. These Bantu-speaking people live in the Eastern Caprivi. They are woodsmen, but farm where they have open spaces. They have traditionally preferred situating their villages deep in the forests of the Eastern Caprivi.

MAFWEVELD (variant: MAFUEVELD). Home of the Mafwe people (q.v.), it lies between the Kwando and Zambesi Rivers in the eastern part of the Caprivi Strip. While it has several dry river beds, it is also full of forested areas, ranging from baobab and mopane trees to date palms. The ground is generally sandy and red in color.

MAHANGU. The staple food in the diet of most of the people in northern Namibia, especially the Wambo. This important grain is a fast maturing kind of millet (q.v.).

MAHARERO. See MAHERERO.

MAHARERO, FREDERICK. The son of Samuel Maharero and his successor as chief of the Hereros, he was involved in the 1904 uprising against the Germans. On January 12, 1904, many farms around Windhoek were attacked by his forces. The attacks continued for several days. When the war ended he and his father fled into exile in Botswana. He returned to Namibia in 1923 accompanying his father's body for burial. In the 1940s he was active in petitioning the United Nations to oppose the incorporation of Namibia into South Africa. His intermediary in this was Rev. Michael Scott (q.v.).

MAHARERO, SAMUEL (variant: SAMUEL MAHERERO) (1856–1923). The son of Maherero and the brother of Wilhelm Maharero (qq.v.), he was not his father's favorite. Reputedly a heavy drinker, he was also receptive to German "deals" to his benefit, while his father favored the Cape or British. Despite being older than Wilhelm, he saw his brother chosen as heir apparent, but when Wilhelm died in a battle in December 1880, Samuel was the next choice. The choice was disputed later and instigated a major split among the Hereros. Eastern Hereros claimed the chieftainship should belong to Nikodemus Kavikunua, the oldest son of Maherero's oldest sister. Nikodemus (q.v.) had been proven to be a successful military leader. Nevertheless, Samuel became the designated heir at his father's death on October 7, 1890. As such he led his people in defending against the invading Witboois in 1891–92. This war ended with a peace treaty signed in November 1892 at the suggestion of Hendrik Witbooi (q.v.). This noted Nama leader wanted the two groups to be united against Germany.

With Samuel's claim to the chieftainship in question, the German General Leutwein interceded on his behalf and intimidated other Herero groups to accept Samuel as paramount chief. Samuel then allowed the Germans to station troops at Okahandja, and on December 6, 1894, signed a treaty with the Germans in which he ceded to Germans a large territory inhabited by the Eastern Hereros for use by German settlers. To the cattle-owning Hereros, their livelihood was being given away, and many of them saw their cattle taken by the Germans when they strayed into the ceded territory. Some of these Eastern Hereros revolted in 1896, but since Samuel did not support them, the Germans easily crushed the revolt. Nikodemus was one of the defeated leaders, and he and Kahimemua Nguvauva were executed by a firing squad at Okahandja on June 11, 1896, with Samuel Maharero's full support.

In 1904, however, Samuel had an amazing change of heart. As the Germans were defeating the Namas who had risen against them, the Hereros saw a chance to start their own uprising. It began in January 1904 when Samuel ordered his warriors to attack all German men (and to spare all others); 123 Germans were killed, and the Hereros encircled the fortress at Okahandja. Only reinforcements led by Captain Victor Franke (q.v.) saved the German garrison. The Hereros fled to the Kaiser Wilhelm Mountain, but Franke's forces again proved victorious as the Hereros fled. Samuel Maharero led his people to the Waterberg mountains for protection, where both pastures and water were abundant. There were about 60,000 Hereros there. The Germans encircled the area with troops (*see* WATERBERG, BATTLE OF). The main battle occurred on August 11, 1904. Some Hereros escaped under cover of night. Samuel Maherero and about 1500 of his followers escaped to Botswana, where they were given permission to live. Samuel died there at Serowe in 1923, but his son and successor Frederick Maharero (q.v.) returned his body to Namibia, where it was buried alongside his father and grandfather.

MAHARERO, WILHELM. The son and heir of the great Maherero (q.v.), he was also the brother of Samuel Maharero (q.v.). The two brothers were among the first pupils at the Augustineum (q.v.) built by the Rhenish Mission at Otjimbingwe in 1866. He has been described as "an able man of excellent character" by Dr. Vedder, and as the founder of a Christian community at Okahandja. However he was also evidently strong-willed, and freely disagreed with others, even his legendary father. Wilhelm was one of the few Hereros to see value in the diplomatic missions of Dr. W. C. Palgrave (q.v.), and Wilhelm and Samuel both accompanied Palgrave to Cape Town in 1879–80. Unfortunately the heir-apparent met a premature death in December 1880. Jan Jonker Afrikander (q.v.) had attacked and taken Barmen, en route to Okahandja. After his success, however, he was caught unaware by a force of 800 Hereros who attacked at dawn under the leadership of Wilhelm Maharero. Most of the Namas fled in shock, and Wilhelm's wing of the attackers tried to cut off the escape route. However, a shot from ambush mortally wounded the leader. Wilhelm was carried to the Barmen Mission where he died that night, his wife Magdalena at his side. He was buried next to the church at Okahandja. His brother Samuel later succeeded their father.

MAHERERO (variant: KAMAHERERO; MAHARERO) (1829?–1890). A legendary figure among the Hereros, he was a leader of his people for half a century, from 1840 to his death in 1890. His name means "person reminiscent of times long past." As a youth, Maherero, son of Tjamuaha, traveled from Okahandja to Windhoek where he learned how to use guns from Jonker Afrikander. The Namas would later regret this education. Jonker taunted the youth by calling him "Tjamuaha's calf." The young man was also physically tortured by Jonker, who tied him to a wagon wheel for several days. The Hereros tolerated this in order to keep peace with the Namas and to allow the Hereros to build large cattle herds.

When Jonker and his people broke the treaty and began raiding Herero cattle again, Maherero came back to lead his father's warriors. After Tjamuaha died in 1861, Maherero succeeded him, and in his first battle Maherero beat Christian Afrikander (who had succeeded his father, Jonker) at Otjimbingwe in 1863. These battles continued for seven years, and the Namas and Hereros did not sign a peace treaty until 1870. The Hereros were able to proclaim their freedom from Nama domination. (While there were quite a few Herero tribes, Maherero took precedence over all other chiefs.) The peace lasted until 1880, and during this time Maherero developed good relations with RMS missionaries, even sending his own sons to a mission school.

Maherero was vehemently opposed to European settlers in his territory, and thus repeatedly requested the Cape government, through Commissioner W. C. Palgrave (q.v.), to put the Hereros under British protection. Such a treaty was signed in 1876 by Maherero and other Herero leaders. He also refused to let the Thirstland Trekkers (q.v.), a large group of Boer pioneers, from settling in Hereroland.

War with the Namas began again in 1880. Jan Jonker Afrikander broke the armistice and was successful in several raids. In December 1880 he was surprised by a force led by Wilhelm Maharero, the son and chosen successor of Maherero. In the battle Wilhelm was shot from ambush and died. His brother Samuel would be the future successor to Maherero. Despite the death of Wilhelm, the Hereros had routed the Namas at the battle of Otjikongo (near Okahandja), and Jan Jonker's subsequent attacks on the Herero were more like pesky raids than major attacks. Still, Herero cattle were not safe.

A new foe emerged for Maherero from among the Namas, Hendrik Witbooi (q.v.). In June 1884 he was so well armed that, bolstered by some of Jan Jonker's supporters, he was able to initiate a campaign against the Hereros. Maherero meanwhile had been trying to stake a claim to land south of Windhoek, areas that the Namas claimed. The inevitable clash occurred, but it proved to be a standoff, and the two sides agreed to a peace agreement. But one year later Witbooi attacked Okahandja itself. This battle was won by the Hereros, who intercepted the Namas at Osona, south of Okahandja on October 14, 1885. The Namas were utterly defeated, and Hendrik Witbooi barely escaped. He tried to attack Okahandja again in 1886, but again Maherero's men routed the Namas. Meanwhile in 1884 the Germans had established their influence in Namibia and Dr. H. Goering visited Maherero and tried to convince him to accept German "protection." The Herero leader declined at the time. However, after the battle of Osona, Dr. Goering came to help the wounded Hereros and so impressed Maherero that he signed the treaty with the Germans, on October 21, 1885. After the 1886 battle of Okahandja Maherero and Witbooi clashed twice in 1887 at Otjimbingwe. Disillusioned by Goering's lack of ability to control the Nama's aggressiveness, Maherero declared the "protection treaty" null and void in 1888. He initially turned to a longtime British agent, Robert Lewis (q.v.), who lived at Okahandja, and granted him authority in the territory and forced Goering and his men to leave Herero territory. In July 1889 a new German initiative took place with the arrival of Captain Curt von Francois with a token force of soldiers. The German established a fort and laid the groundwork for a system to weaken Witbooi. He then went to Maherero, who agreed to restore the treaty with the Germans. He hoped this would bring peace to his people. The elderly Herero leader knew he would not live much longer, and in a most unusual governmental transition allowed his wife, the mother of Samuel, to poison him with goat meat that would result in certain death. He died of this meal on October 5, 1890, and was buried next to his father, Tjamuaha.

MAIEI (variant: MAYEYI). A small group of Bantu-speaking Africans who live in the Eastern Caprivi Strip on the Upper Linyanti River. They make their homes in forested areas.

MAIZE. While an important grain for Namibia, production has usually been low, with the yield per acre one of the lowest in the world. A grain very sensitive to adequate rainfall or appropriate irrigation, it has done well in parts of the Kavango valley and in irrigated areas near Mariental and the Hardap dam. Traditionally most of the maize has been imported from Zimbabwe and South Africa. Since independence, however, there has been a serious attempt to become self-sufficient. The 1990/91 crop season produced a record, with the tonnage up 1/3 over the previous year. It equalled 80% of the demand. Plantings in 91/92 were increased significantly, but the drought cut production by 75%, resulting in massive imports.

MAJAVERO, CHIEF ALFONS. Chief councillor of the Kavango after replacing Chief Ninus Shashipapo, he was the leader of the Kavango Council (or Alliance) delegation of the Turnhalle Conference (q.v.). He was elected to the first National Assembly (1979–83). In 1984 he was the founding president of the National Democratic Unity Party (q.v.), which Chief Majavero then affiliated with the DTA. Majavero had the eleventh spot on the DTA slate for the 1989 elections and became a member of the Constituent Assembly and thus of the first National Assembly of an independent Namibia in 1990.

MALTAHÖHE. A town of about 2000 people, it is situated on the Hudup River in south-central Namibia. At an altitude of 1400 meters, it has annual rainfall of 165 meters. The town, and its district of the same name, were named after Frau Malta von Burgsdorff, wife of its founder, the commander of the garrison at Gibeon, Hauptmann von Burgsdorff. The town lies 120 kilometers west of Mariental, and 400 kilometers east of Walvis Bay, with both of which it is linked by direct roads. While founded in 1900, no village management board was set up until 1945. Maltahöhe is the center of a fairly prosperous district, to which karakul sheep bring good income when the prices are high. Thus it has shops, churches, hotel facilities, and police and postal services. On July 7, 1905, a battle occurred about 20 kilometers east of Maltahöhe between German soldiers and a force of Witboois.

MANDATE SYSTEM. The arrangement under the League of Nations (q.v.) by which the League would dispose of the African and Arabian territories of Germany and Turkey after World War I. It was the system under which German South West Africa was placed. That territory was called a "C-class Mandate" (q.v.), and attached to the Union of South Africa for the sake of administration. The mandate system was supervised by the League's Permanent Mandate Commission (q.v.).

MANDUME, CHIEF. One of the last truly independent chiefs of the Wambo peoples, he was head of the Kwanyamas (q.v.) from 1911 to 1917. Attempting to unite the separate Wambo kingdoms in 1915, he attacked the Portuguese forts in southern Angola, destroying them. (Wambos are found on both sides of the present Angola-Namibian border.) In mid-1915 the Portuguese put together an army of about 1200 men and attacked the Kwanyama, killing as many as 5000 warriors or 6 percent of all Kwanyamas. The Portuguese took no prisoners. Mandume, just twenty-one years old, crossed into Namibia to seek German protection, only to find out he was now dealing with South Africa. Major S. M. Pritchard was the leader of an expedition that went to Owambo to work with the chiefs in the north. Mandume urged protection for his people. Pritchard first tried to serve as a mediator with the Portuguese, but found that they saw the fleeing Kwanyamas as rebellious killers. Ultimately Mandume signed a declaration of allegiance to South Africa in exchange for protection for his people. But when the Angola-Namibia border was negotiated by Pritchard, the boundary placed two of every three Kwanyama in Angola. Mandume was told to forget his people who ended up in Angola. He couldn't do this, and crossed the border illegally and frequently. In 1917 the South African administrator demanded that Mandume come to Windhoek to explain his defiance, but the young leader refused, citing tribal tradition that chiefs could not leave their territory. This was the only excuse South Africa needed to send a large force to attack Mandume. (Portuguese leaders in Angola agreed to provide back-up strength at the Angolan border to assist South Africa if needed.) The large South

African force attacked Mandume and defeated him on February 6, 1917. Over a hundred Kwanyamas were killed or wounded, and Mandume was one of them, losing his life to a maxim gun after having pledged to fight until "my last bullet is spent." His memory lives on in Kwanyama Praise Poems.

MARENGO, JACOB (variant: JAKOB MORENGA, MARENGA). Almost a legendary leader of the Namas, he epitomizes "African Nationalism" in his battles against the Germans early in the twentieth century. Little is known about his youth, although it is known that his father was a Nama and his mother a Herero, an unusual combination for the mid-nineteenth century when the two groups were frequently fighting. His birthdate is also not known, but a fair estimate would be 1860, give or take up to ten years. (This is based on the fact that he had a mature son in 1906 who could succeed him as guerrilla leader.) Marengo received some education at a Christian mission, and could speak English, German, and Afrikaans fluently. Around the turn of the century he worked in the copper mines in the northern Cape Colony.

When the Bondelswarts rose up against the Germans in late 1903, Marengo returned to Namibia. Several German leaders called him the "Headman" of the Bondelswarts, especially those living in the Karras Mountains of southeastern Namibia. When the uprising ended in the Peace Treaty of Kalkfontein, Marengo was declared an outlaw, and a reward of 1000 Marks was promised to his captor. Marengo meanwhile was secure in the mountains in July 1904, from whence he and his followers raided the countryside, disarming all the white farmers. This also provided him with arms, ammunitions and food. A thirty-man German detachment was sent to stop him, but on August 30, 1904, at a battle in the Schambock Mountains the German officer and two other soldiers were killed, and the rest fled. This was the first of many victories for Marengo. He retreated into the Karras Mountains when the Germans sent larger forces against him. He proved a master of guerrilla warfare and defeated the Germans in one skirmish after another. In October Marengo instituted a surprise attack at Wasserfall and captured the horse of an entire German mounted company, virtually immobilizing them. Beginning with only eleven men in July 1904, his activities attracted other Africans, and his forces numbered about four hundred near the end of the year. They included both Namas and Hereros.

In October 1904 Hendrick Witbooi revolted against the Germans in the center of Namibia, so Marengo was ignored for awhile. But Marengo did not ignore the Germans. In a battle at Warmbad in November 1904, Marengo's attack on the German garrison killed or wounded 40 percent of the officers and a fourth of the other soldiers. In the spring of 1905 the German commander-in-chief, Colonel Deimling moved on the Karras Mountains to get Marengo, with three detachments of German troops. On March 10, 1905, Marengo surprised the first detachment and swiftly defeated it near Aub. Marengo's other units had failed to follow his plan, however, and the remaining German detachments counterattacked. Marengo was wounded and his men withdrew. It was only a temporary setback, however, and between June and November 1905 Marengo's men conducted many more attacks. In a battle near Narus on June 19, forty-nine Germans were either killed or wounded; and October 24 at Hartebeestmund the Germans were ambushed by Marengo, with more loss of German officers (about 25 percent) and soldiers (20 percent). German staff members acknowledge him as a master of both strategy and tactics. Moreover, when he took prisoners he provided medical care, something the Germans did not do. A major German offensive in March 1906 forced Marengo and his followers to cross into the Cape Colony, just ten kilometers across the border. The German troops violated the frontier, however, and attacked the Marengo camp, killing twenty-three. The wounded Marengo escaped.

When Germans crossed the border again to attack his new camp, Marengo barely escaped. Two days later, May 7, 1906, Marengo, his son Petrus, and six others surrendered to the British Cape Police, who moved them to Prieska, 300 kilometers away from Namibia. There Marengo became a cause celebre, as journalists, officials and the population as a whole hurried to see this famous guerrilla leader. The Germans, meanwhile, were pleased that he was out of

Namibia, but they preferred that he be killed. Marengo had asked the British for political asylum, so they could not hold him indefinitely. He was finally given his freedom in early June 1907, under condition that he stay in touch with the police at Upington. He fled this area, however, and the Germans and British seemed to work together to recapture or eliminate him.

Back in southern Namibia Marengo attracted warriors quickly, and the Germans countered with a major commitment that included twelve companies of soldiers, mountain artillery, and four machine guns. Marengo crossed again into the Cape and told a British officer that he would never surrender to the Germans, but perhaps to an appropriate English officer. Three days later, on September 20, 1907, an Englishman, Major Elliott pursued Marengo and caught him near Eenzamheid, 100 kilometers north of Upington. Marengo was not given a chance to surrender, and the Englishman and a German officer shot down Marengo, his brother, and two of his nephews.

MARIENTAL (variant: **MARIENTHAL**). One of the major towns on the main road and rail line north from the Orange River, it is 232 kilometers north of Keetmanshoop and 274 kilometers south of Windhoek. Its population in 1988 was estimated at 6500, putting it in the mid-level of Namibia's larger towns. It is the educational and administrative center of the near south districts. Karakul sheep are bred commercially in the area, and over 2000 hectares of land are irrigated by the Hardap Dam (q.v.), with vegetables a major crop. Mariental was founded in 1912 as a rail center.

In 1978 the South African forces established a detention camp or prison near Mariental for about 1500 prisoners of the battles with SWAPO in Angola, especially the infamous Kassinga raid.

"MARTIN LUTHER." One of the world's more unusual national monuments, this is actually a heavy steam tractor that was imported from German in 1896 with the intention of pulling loads of supplies from Swakopmund across the Namib Desert to central Namibia. but in an inauspicious beginning it almost didn't even reach Swakopmund from its landing place at Walvis Bay. The project was under the leadership of Lieut. Edmund Troost of the German Schutztruppe. The heavy engine moved slowly across the desert sand, only making it with the ingenuity and hard work of many people. It took three months to travel the 30 kilometers to Swakopmund, and in the process used up large quantities of precious water that was hauled long distances. The "steam ox" eventually made a few successful runs, but in fact failed to meet its expectations. The Germans decided to install a narrow gauge railroad instead, and while Troost returned to Germany for a new engine for the railway, the steam tractor was caught in a rare flood of the Swakop River and became stuck in the desert. It was left there in the sand and nicknamed "Martin Luther" because of the theologian's famous statement of defiance in 1521, "Here I stand, may God help me, I can go no further."

MASHI RIVER (variant: MASCHI). The name of the Kwando River when it crosses into the Caprivi Strip and heads south. When it merges with the east-flowing Linyanti River (also called the Chobe) it gives up its name. It is the "Mashi" for over 100 kilometers.

MASTERS AND SERVANTS LAW (1920). Along with the Mines and Works Proclamation of 1917, this law served as a means for white employers to control their Black employees for over fifty years. Blacks working outside their "tribal reserves" had to register with the state, work under a service contract, and could work only so long as their employers needed them. Farm or contract workers were subject to heavy fines and imprisonment for "desertion" and were then required to go back to the employer to complete the contract. The only way to become free of your contract was by complaining of maltreatment to the police, but this was rarely feasible, and farmers were known to hunt down any of their laborers who were absent. Stockherders could be forced by the farmers to account for every animal they watched, and to compensate the owner for any that were said to be missing. The law was repealed in 1975.

MASUBIA (variant: SUBIA). One of the major groups of Africans in the Eastern Caprivi, they are nevertheless one of the smaller population groups in Namibia. They live in a wooded area, and traditionally lived by means of hunting and fishing. Their home area is part of the Zambezi River floodplain. Today many of these people cultivate the soil and raise cattle, but when the waters rise they leave their dry season villages and drive their herds to their second homes on higher ground. This is often scores of miles away. The Masubia peoples are related to others living across the Zambesi River in Zambia, as they came under rule of the Lozi (Barotse) as early as the seventeenth century. They were occupied by Lozi leaders, sent to represent the Lozi king. They paid the Lozi tribute in the form of grain, fish, meat, skins, ivory, or honey. The attempt by the Masubia to revolt in 1865–66 was ruthlessly suppressed by Sipopa, the Lozi King. He tried to placate them later by giving them minor government positions. Even today the Masubia are mostly Lozi-speaking.

MATCHLESS MINE. One of the oldest mines in Namibia, it was discovered in the 1850s by J. F. Bassingthwaighte and William Latham (qq.v.). Located a little west of Windhoek, it was producing copper for the Walwich Bay Mining Company in 1855, and the ore was carried to Walvis Bay on ox-wagons. Run more recently by the Tsumeb Corp., its ownership has included American Metal Climax Inc., the Newmont Mining Corp., and the South West Africa Company among others. It has not been in continuous operation for the 135 years since its discovery, and the Tsumeb corporation has opened and closed it depending on world market prices for copper. In 1982 it delivered 123,000 tons of ore. The same year it was estimated that Matchless had total reserves of about 2,200,000 tons. Yet Tsumeb shut it down whenever copper prices dropped.

MATJILA, ANDREW NICK (1932–   ). Born in Pretoria and educated to be a primary school teacher, this is Namibia's true Renaissance man. Not only is he the vice-chairman of the Executive Committee of the DTA and a member of the National Assembly, but he speaks sixteen African languages, has published two books of Lozi poems and a Tswana reader, has arranged and recorded traditional music, conducted church music, ran a weightlifting club, and opened a golf course. He taught in Katima Mulilo from 1964 to 1971, when he was promoted to school inspector (until 1975). He has also been active in teachers' associations.

His career in government began in 1976 when he went to work for the Caprivi administration. He developed an expertise there in tribal law and customs. In 1980 his work continued on the Government Service Commission, but he took a fulltime position as school inspector for the Department of National Education. He came to the attention of the DTA during the Turnhalle Conference (1975–77) where he was an interpreter. In 1981 he attended the Geneva Conference as a DTA delegate, and continued as an advisor to the DTA secretary. He became a fulltime member of the Government Service Commission in 1982, and has served on the board of the Academy (q.v.) and of the First National Development Corporation (q.v.). In the Transitional Government of National Unity he was minister of national education and the cabinet chairman. In the 1989 Assembly elections he was on the DTA electoral list and won a seat. He was the DTA's choice for chairman of the Constituent Assembly, but was defeated by SWAPO's Hage Geingob. Matjila is active in the Seoposengwe Party (q.v.).

MAXUILILI, EMMANUEL GOTTLIEB NATHANIEL (variants: MAXUIRIRI; IMMANUEL GOTTLIEB "MAXUILILI"; NATHANIEL) (1927–). Born in Tsumeb, he has been a leading member of SWAPO for many years. Maxuilili served as acting president of the organization for about thirty years, while Sam Nujoma was outside the country. His early years included employment as a policeman for the South African railways and later as a lay preacher. He combined the toughness of the former and the appearance and speaking ability of the latter. In the late 1950s and early 1960s he was one of SWAPO's best organizers. In 1967 he was one of the thirty-seven Namibians arrested by South Africa and brought to trial under a newly passed Terrorism Act. With little evidence to convict him, the court freed him in 1968 after a long trial, with only a four-year suspended sentence. However he was restricted indefinitely to the municipal district of Walvis Bay and had to report twice a day to police. In 1972 he was served a five-year order confining him to his home near Walvis Bay, prohibiting him from attending political allies. Also he could not be quoted in any publication. When Dr. Alfred Escher, a UN representative, visited Namibia in 1972 on a fact-finding mission, he specifically traveled to Walvis Bay to meet with Maxuilili. In 1977 his banning order was extended to 1982. When he was eventually released, Maxuilili again resumed functioning as Acting President of SWAPO inside Namibia. With Nujoma back in Namibia, he continues to serve SWAPO as a member of its Central Committee. In the 1989 elections he won a seat in Namibia's Assembly.

MAYEYI. *See* MAIEI.

MBALANTU (variant: OMBALANTU). One of the smaller of the seven tribes among the Wambo nation, their language is not written, but is closely related to others that are, such as the Ndonga from whom they split off. The name itself means "people of the ruling house." Their home territory is in the extreme north-central part of Namibia, close to the Angola border. Population estimates ranged from about 13,000 in 1957 to 17,600 in 1960 to 24,000 in 1970. The Mbalantu have had no actual chief for over a century, but have a hereditary leader for each of the fourteen clans. South African officials established a four-man council of headmen in 1915, as South Africa attempted to create a system of indirect rule. When South Africa created a Legislative Council for Ovamboland in 1973, the Mbalantu were allowed to select three representatives.

MBANDERU. A people related to the Hereros, they are said to have migrated south from Angola in the area between Owambo and Kaokoveld seeking better pasture land for their cattle. The Mbanderu get their name from a word meaning "to fight." They are literally "fighters of former times." Yet when the Mbanderu reached Namibia they found the Herero already occupying the good pasturage. The Herero attacked the Mbanderu for their large cattle herds, killing many of the immigrants. The survivors moved considerably to the east, but they were attacked there in the middle of the nineteenth century by Jonker Afrikander, who further devastated the group. Known eventually as the East Hereros, the remaining Mbanderu were led by two notable chiefs, Nikodemus and Kahimemua, both of whom were killed by a German firing squad in 1897. Many of their followers fled into Botswana, where they lived for about sixty years. In October 1960, Munjuka the Second, grandson of Kahimemua, responded to pleas by Mbanderu living in Namibia to come home. He did so and was installed as chief of their part of the Epukiro Reserve. He also established a political party, the Mbanderu Council. In the late 1970s Chief Munjuka led the Council into membership in the Namibia National Front (NNF), a group that rejected the results of the Turnhalle Conference (q.v.), but was not prepared to accept SWAPO leadership. This issue split the Mbanderu, however, as some did support SWAPO. However in November 1988 Munjuka announced that the Mbanderu Council was now formally aligned with SWAPO.

MBANDERU COUNCIL. *See* MBANDERU.

MBARAKWENGO (variant: MBARAGWENCO). One of the four subgroups of the San (or "Bushmen"), each of which has its own "click" language. The other San are the !Kung (q.v.), the Heikom (q.v.), and the Naron. They live in a very dry and inhospitable part of the Western Caprivi Strip.

MBUKUSHU. Living in the Western Caprivi Strip, the Mbukushu comprise one of the five groups who make up the Kavango peoples. In fact all of them were originally Wambos, but they joined together and moved east of the other seven groups that are still considered Wambos today.

MBUNZA. One of five Wambo tribes that joined together early in Wambo history to form the Kavango people today. They settled east of Owambo, near the Okavango River. When a Kavango "homeland" was formed in 1970, each of the five groups was set up autonomously under hereditary chiefs, while also having representatives in the Legislative Council.

MEERMIN (variant: *MERMIN*). A Dutch ship that was sent in 1793 to annex part of the Namibian coast. Following orders the *Meermin* was landed at Walvis Bay on January 23, 1793, and a little over a month later Captain Duminy proclaimed Dutch sovereignty over Angra Pequeña, Walvis Bay, and Halifax Island. Also on board the *Meermin* was Sebastian van Reenen (q.v.), who was seeking mineral wealth.

MERORO, DAVID H. (1917–   ). One of the most influential leaders of SWAPO, he was number three on the SWAPO electoral list in the 1989 elections for the Assembly. However due to illness he was not assigned a seat in the cabinet. Born in Keetmanshoop, he was educated at mission schools there and in Windhoek. He worked as a government clerk for a few years while getting further education at night. This was part of his participation in the African Improvement Society, a Windhoek organization that established adult education and literacy classes. He struck out on his own in 1952, establishing a general store in Windhoek, which soon expanded into a very profitable business. He became active politically in 1962 when he joined SWAPO. By 1964 he was appointed national chairman; a soft-spoken man, he was able to avoid government retaliation and, unlike other SWAPO leaders, stayed in Namibia. However in 1972 he and Chief Clemens Kapuuo (q.v.) pushed through barriers to reach UN Secretary Kurt Waldheim to try to convince him to investigate the problems faced by Namibian contract laborers at Katutura. As the longtime chairman of "internal SWAPO" Merero represented it in coalitions such as the National Convention of Freedom Parties (q.v.) in 1971. In January 1974 he and many other SWAPO members were arrested en route to a meeting. He was tortured and held for five months in solitary confinement. In 1975, with waves of arrests sweeping Namibia, Merero fled into exile. He returned home in 1989 with other self-exiled SWAPO leaders. He has been the most prominent Herero in SWAPO until his illness. In 1989 he was still listed as SWAPO's national chairman.

METHODIST CHURCH IN NAMIBIA. The origins of Methodists in Namibia can be traced to the work of the Wesleyan Missionary Society (q.v.). Reverends Threlfall and Cook began their work in 1825, but illness hindered their plans. Others followed but in 1851 and 1867 the Wesleyans turned over their work to the Rhenish Missionary Society (q.v.). Methodists did not return until 1916, when Rev. C. C. Harris began his work in Windhoek.

METJE, HERMANN (1870–1939). At his death one of Namibia's most successful businessmen, Metje was born April 18, 1870, in the village of Greene in Brunswick, Germany. As a youth Hermann was apprenticed as a joiner and carpenter. In 1895 he started a joinery shop. With business not good in Hanover, he followed the example of a friend and moved to South Africa. Arriving in 1900, Hermann opened a carpentry and joinery shop in Cape Town. His family followed later in the year.

In 1906 he abandoned Cape Town and traveled to Lüderitzbucht in Namibia, bringing with him goods for trading purposes. Hermann found trade excellent there, and began to import in a large way. He continued as a carpenter and joiner, however, and again became a building contractor. He added a partner in the architect Ziegler, creating what is today one of Namibia's major businesses, Metje and Ziegler Limited. In 1934 he bought a farm which he built up to be a model for cattle and karakul ranching.

Hermann became ill in 1939 and went to Germany for treatment, but died shortly after his ship landed in Hamburg. His ashes were returned to Namibia in 1949. However his children built the company in even more directions, and by 1956 it was in such diverse products as iron and steel, paints, machine tools, household goods and appliances, furniture and carpets, sporting equipment, automobiles, tires, oil, and farm implements.

MIFIMA, SOLOMON (d. 1988). One of the founders of the Ovambo People's Congress in 1958, he saw the organization become the Ovambo People's Organization and then South

West Africa People's Organization (SWAPO) (q.v.). He remained active in it for about twenty years.

MILLET. Known locally as *mahangu,* it is one of the traditional crops of Namibia, and is a dietary staple, especially in the north. Namibians have used a hardy, fast maturing millet (durra), which can be stamped and eaten as a dry porridge. Subsistence farmers have produced 45,000–60,000 tons a year, but it was not a commercial crop until after independence. The government has undertaken pilot projects to upgrade the production of the farmers, including experimentation with higher yielding strains imported from Kenya and Zimbabwe. There were significant production gains in the 1990/91 crop year, and greatly increased planting for 1991/92. Unfortunately the drought devastated that crop and major cereal imports were needed.

MINES AND WORKS PROCLAMATION (1917). When combined with the 1920 Masters and Servants Law (q.v.), used to control farm workers, and the Natives (Urban Areas) Proclamation (q.v.) of 1924, this act placed serious restrictions on the rights of Africans to travel where they wanted and work for whom they wanted. It required registering with the state for employment in the mines and then accepting the contract tendered. This led to many other personal restrictions as well. Changes in the contract labor system in 1972 and the amendment of the Mines and Works Law in 1975 were minimal steps in the direction of labor reform.

MINERAL EXPLORATION AND PROSPECTING. African peoples were working mineral deposits in Namibia long before Europeans arrived. Copper was found in the Otavi area, and iron was worked by the Ondonga people, for example. Rumors of mineral wealth attracted a party led by Willem Van Reenen (q.v.) to enter Namibia in 1791, and he brought back reports about Africans working with copper. Other Europeans followed, but the influx picked up in 1850 when world copper prices soared. The Pomona Mining Company was formed that year by DePass, Spence and Co.

(q.v.). Pomona bought a mining concession from the local chief, but no copper was found. This became more important almost sixty years later when diamonds were found in the concession area. The value of these gems for Namibia is well-known. (*See* CONSOLIDATED DIAMOND MINES LTD.; DIAMONDS; MINING INDUSTRY; and STAUCH, AUGUST.) Among other important mineral finds were zinc, lead, copper, vanadium, and uranium (qq.v.).

MINEWORKERS UNION OF NAMIBIA (MUN). Organized in November 1986 and led by a veteran SWAPO member, Ben Ulenga (q.v.), it has quickly become one of the more prominent forces in Namibia's economy. For example in November 1989, Consolidated Diamond Mines agreed to pay an across the board increase of 18 percent to its workers. In early 1988 MUN claimed a membership of 9000. Later that year it negotiated bargaining agreements with both CDM and Rössing. In 1990 Ulenga announced that membership was up to 12,600, over 60% of those employed in Namibia's mines, in 22 branches. Its secretary-general, Ben Ulenga was elected to the Assembly, and its president is Asser Kapere. MUN announced during the 1989 elections that it supports SWAPO, which did not surprise anyone because of the overlapping membership among its top leaders. At the union's fourth congress in April, 1990, Ulenga and Kapere were reelected to their union posts. Three months later the MUN signed its first recognition with the Tsumeb Corporation (q.v.).

MINING INDUSTRY. The most important productive sector of Namibia's economy, it typically accounts for at least 75 percent of the country's total exports by value. It is also the country's biggest private sector employer and the largest source of corporate tax revenue. Despite frequent talk by SWAPO in the 1970s and early 1980s that it would nationalize the mines, it was clear that after independence SWAPO would work out a rapprochement with the major mining companies. More than 13,000 Namibians were employed in mines in 1988, down from a peak of 21,000 in 1977. A major critique of the mining industry was contained in the report of the Thirion Commission (q.v.) of 1986. (*See also* CONSOLIDATED DIAMOND MINES; MINEWORKERS UNION OF NAMIBIA; RÖSSING URANIUM MINE; TSUMEB CORPORATION; and separate listings for all the major commodities mined.) The value of diamonds exported in 198 was R654,000,000, up 51 percent from 1987. Export of all other minerals was R889,000,000 in 1988, down only R2,000,000 from 1987. Uranium accounts for over half those export totals. The high value of diamond production may have peaked, however. It is estimated that output will begin a serious decline in about 1996, after which most diamond mining will occur offshore in the seabed. On the other hand, new coal mines and gold mines have just been opened, raising the prospects of new forms of mining to replace lost production of diamonds.

MISHRA, BRAJESH. The United Nations commissioner for Namibia from 1981 to July 1987, when he was replaced by the ill-fated Bernt Carlsson (q.v.). A diplomat from India, he was strongly anticolonialist, and was not supportive of the proposals and activities of the "Western 5" who were seeking to find compromise formulas for Namibia's independence.

MISSIONS AND MISSIONARIES. The important role of Christian mission societies and their missionaries is treated thoroughly in this book, among the major ones are the Rhenish Missionary Society, the Finnish Missionary Society, the London Missionary Society, and the Wesleyan Methodist Missionary Society (qq.v.). Prominent individuals include Johann and Abraham Albrecht, Edward Cook, Heinrich Schmelen, Carl Hugo Hahn, F. H. Kleinschmidt, Henrich Vedder (qq.v.), and many more.

MODDERFONTEIN. The original name for the town now called Keetmanshoop. After "Modderfontein" it was named "Swartmodder" for a while, but was named after a wealthy textile factory owner, Mr. Keetman, who donated money for a mission station to be built there.

MOLKTEBLICK. The second highest point in Namibia, after Brandberg, it rises 2483 meters in the Auas Mountains south of Windhoek.

MONTECUCCOLI, COUNT CAPRIVI DE. *See* CAPRIVI, COUNT.

MORENGA, JACOB. *See* MARENGO, JACOB.

MORRELL, BENJAMIN. The discoverer of the huge guano (q.v.) deposits, this American sealing captain was in his schooner, *Antarctica* in 1828 when he noticed the peaks and valleys of what appeared to be a small, snow-covered mountain. It was in fact the small island of Ichabo, about a half mile off the Namibian coastline at Wreck Point. The island was covered with guano fifteen to twenty meters deep. The "mining" of Namibia's guano deposits became an important industry.

MORRIS, ABRAHAM. The grandson of a Scottish missionary and his Nama wife, Morris experienced much animosity from the white farmers of southern Namibia around the beginning of the twentieth century and became a prominent fighter for African nationalism. Originally an ally of Jacob Marengo (q.v.), Morris had broken with him for a while. When Marengo was wounded in 1905 in fighting the Germans, Morris and two Nama chiefs, Johannes Christian and Cornelius (qq.v.), rejoined the war on Marengo's side. They fought a successful guerrilla war in the rugged land near the Lower Fish River. They ambushed one nine-man German patrol that was tracking Morris and Christian and killed all nine. A series of battles with the Germans in May 1905, at De Villierputz, Tsumab, and Nukas left the Germans exhausted, frustrated and with another twenty or more dead. Morris, Christian, and Marengo were running the German army in circles. Morris was particularly adept at cutting off German supplies that came in from the Cape Colony at Raman's Drift. Thus his Bondelswarts were kept supplied at the expense of the Germans. In 1906, however, the tide of war turned toward the Germans, especially after Colonel Deimling took over in July. Abraham's brother, Edward Morris, was killed in a battle, Johannes Christian signed a treaty with the Germans, and both Morris and Christian fled with their followers into the Cape Province of South Africa. He reached the French mission station at Pella, embraced the Roman Catholic faith, and claimed the protection of the missionaries. He stayed at Pella about ten years. In the 1915 campaign he served with South African troops in Namibia against the Germans, serving as head scout of the southern army of Gen. Louis Botha. The Germans showed their fear of him by fixing a price on his head. Morris's duties included sneaking into the heart of a German-occupied town (such as Warmbad) and determining the strength of their forces. Morris expected to be rewarded by being allowed to return to Namibia in 1919 after the war, but only Chief Christian and fifty followers were accepted back. Finally Morris returned in 1922 without formal permission. The arrest of Morris by South African officials was a major incident leading to the Bondelswart Rebellion in 1922 (q.v.). The major battles occurred in May 1922, but Morris was killed on June 8 at Berg Kramer, along with fifty-two others. Chief Christian surrendered six days later.

MORROW, REV. EDWARD. The vicar-general of the Anglican church in Namibia when, in May 1978, he and five other prominent clerics signed a letter protesting police tortures inflicted on Africans, and the failure of the Administrator-General to investigate several well-documented cases. Two months after the letter was sent, Rev. Morrow and another signatory, Father H. Hunke, a Roman Catholic priest from Germany, were given deportation orders. Rev. Morrow returned to his home in South Africa.

MOUNTAINS. The mountains of Namibia are not extremely steep. (Although the Great Spitskop [1742 meters] near Usakos in the Namib Desert is called the Matterhorn of Namibia, and Königstein in the Brandberg rises to 2600 meters.) The mountains generally rise in rows parallel to the coastline, relatively close to the sea. From the air southern Namibia looks corrugated. Windhoek is only 250 kilometers from the coast, but its altitude is 1654 meters, and nearby heights reach 2100 meters. Among the major mountains or mountain chains in addition to the above are the Great Karras Mountains; the Great Brukharos Mountains; the Naukloof, Auas and Erongo Mountains; and the Baynes, Zebra and Hartmann Mountains, to mention a few.

MÖWE BAY. Located on the northwestern coast of Namibia, this site has been suggested as a possible new harbor and fishing port for the country. Its location would be convenient for exporting millions of tons of low-grade iron ore in the region, but its main justification would be its benefit to the fishing industry. Situated about 20 percent of the way down the Namibian coast, it is far from the older European cities such as Swakopmund and Windhoek. It is 200 miles north of Walvis Bay, for example. On the other hand, it could help the northern third of the country if more access roads were built. Sesfontein is a major town less than 100 kilometers away.

MUDGE, DIRK FREDERICK (1928–   ). The most powerful white politician in Namibia at independence, Dirk Mudge was the founder of the Democratic Turnhalle Alliance. He was born at Otjiwarongo; his father was a farmer who had moved to Namibia in the early 1920s from the northern Cape Province. After his education at Otjiwarongo and Windhoek, Dirk earned a bachelor of commerce degree at the University of Stellenbosch in 1947. He married Stienie Jacobs in 1951 and they have five children. After college he became an accountant, and in 1952 began to raise cattle as well.

He entered politics in 1961, as an elected member of the Legislative Assembly in Windhoek. He served on its Executive Committee from 1965 to 1977. A member of the ruling National Party, he was its vice-chairman from 1970 to 1977. That was the same year he broke from the National Party and formed the white Republican Party, which became the basis for the interracial Democratic Turnhalle Alliance (DTA).

As early as 1972 Mudge began to break with the white supremacist views of the National Party by meeting with the Herero paramount chief, the late Clemens Kapuuo (q.v.). When the National Party (urged on by South Africa) organized the Turnhalle Constitutional Conference in 1975,

Mudge took a leading role. He was not only a representative of the white ethnic group, but was heavily responsible for recruiting many of the representatives of the other ethnic groups that were there. Where there were no legitimately elected representatives, he found people to attend. During the meeting he was a mediator between the other white delegates and the various Black groups. Many of the latter followed him into the DTA a few years later. A moderate pragmatist (some would say realist), he pushed for a government that would be changed from the apartheid-based system. More matters of national concern should be dealt with by the central government in which all races would be represented. That meant more integration at all levels of society. On this he split with his colleagues in the National Party, especially A. H. Du Plessis and Eben Van Zijl (qq.v.).

He thus left the NP on September 28, 1977, and took a number of its verligte ("enlisted") members with him into his new, all-white Republican Party. Within the next two months he had formed the multiracial DTA, with Mudge as its chairman and Chief Clemens Kapuuo as its president. The Republican Party and all of the ethnic parties that joined the DTA were partners in this political alliance. In the December 4, 1978, elections to the National Assembly, not only was Mudge elected as one of the fifty members but DTA member parties won a majority of the seats. Thus Mudge was selected by the Assembly to serve on the Council of Ministers. He then became its chairman (1980–83). In that capacity Namibia's ideological left saw him as a South African puppet, while the ideological right saw him as being far too liberal. Examples of the latter idea can be found in the DTA Manifesto of 1978 when it said that the DTA "undertakes to open all public amenities for everybody in Namibia," "believes that everyone should live and work where they prefer," and "believes that every individual should have an equal opportunity of competing for available work," among its many provisions. Mudge was clearly a believer in integration, not separation. In his position as chairman of the DTA and chairman of the Namibia Government Council of Ministers, Mudge regularly urged South Africa to grant Namibia independence.

During all this period he was a strong opponent of SWAPO, seeing it as antidemocratic, prosocialist or even Communist, and dominated by one group, the Wambos. In 1982 he urged South Africa to grant Namibia independence in 1983. Instead a Multi-Party Conference (q.v.) was held on November 12, 1983. The DTA and Mudge played the major roles in organizing it. However, most of the more popular black parties, including SWAPO, did not join the MPC. It gained some degree of recognition when its leaders met with both the UN Secretary-General Javier Perez de Cuellar and US Secretary of State George Schultz.

The work of the Multi-Party Conference led to South Africa officially transferring many governmental powers (in effect, ''internal self-government'') to a Transitional Government of National Unity (TGNU) on June 17, 1985. Mudge became one of the eight cabinet ministers in the TGNU, serving as minister of finance and governmental affairs. The goal of this government was to achieve internationally recognized independence for Namibia.

In September 1986 Mudge became Chairman of the TGNU Cabinet. he also urged a new constitutional council headed by Judge Victor Hiemstra (q.v.) to speed up work on drafting a new constitution so that a national referendum could take place by mid-1987. As chairman of the cabinet and minister of finance, Mudge was attempting to prepare Namibia for independence by loosening Namibia's economic dependence on South Africa. Also his budgetary priorities were the more liberal social issues, such as education, housing, employment opportunities, and upgrading the Katutura (q.v.) Township. During this same period in the all-white ''second tier'' Legislative Assembly, Mudge's Republican Party was in the minority to the dominant National Party. Mudge was the Official opposition leader in that relatively inactive assembly.

By 1988 the prospects of full independence were realizable. When agreements were reached among all parties and elections promised, Mudge's stature in the white community increased. He was clearly the only white to have positioned himself to gain significant electoral support. In the 1989 elections the DTA won 191,000 votes or 28.6 percent of those cast. It won twenty-one seats in the Assembly, and Mudge, of course, filled one of them. He remains the chairman of the DTA of Namibia, and is the de facto leader of the opposition in the National Assembly.

MUESHIHANGE, PETER (variant: MWESHIHANGE). One of the initial activists who formed the OPC in Cape Town in 1958, in 1970 at a conference in Tanzania he was named acting secretary for foreign affairs of SWAPO. In the 1989 elections for the Constituent Assembly he was sixth on the SWAPO list of candidates and was easily elected to a seat in the Assembly. He has since been named minister of defence in Namibia's first cabinet at independence.

MUKUROB. An awe-inspiring rock formation thirty-four meters high, this tower of sandstone was one of the most memorable sights in the country. It resembled a huge gnarled finger pointing upward, isolated from all of its surrounding rock. The Nama word that is its name translated to "Finger of God." All else around it eroded to dust over the centuries, and it was puzzling how it survived, for it was once part of a nearby plateau. It was located in southern Namibia, about halfway between Hardap Dam (to the north) and Keetmanshoop (to its south), east of the main road. Unfortunately this tourist attraction and landmark collapsed in December 1988. Strong winds raged through the area on December 7, and probably caused its collapse. It broke at the narrow neck, toppled over, and smashed into thousands of pieces. The formation was twenty-three kilometers from Asab, northeast of Keetmanshoop, and weighed about 834 tons. While the upper section consisted of hard sandstone, the "neck" was made of a kind of shale rock that was easily eroded.

MÜLLER, HANS (1880–1955). The father of music in Namibia, he came to the area with the German Schutztruppe but stayed on and became a resident. He was the founder and moving force behind the *Männergesangverein* (Male Choral Society) formed in 1907, which became the *Windhoeker Liedertafel* (Windhoek Glee Club) in 1910. He also founded the *Gesellschaft der Musikfreude* (Society of Music Lovers).

Müller served with the German Consular Corps, and had to return to Germany in 1939. He later returned to Namibia, and was active as a choral conductor in Namibia almost until his death in 1955.

MULTI-PARTY CONFERENCE (MPC). Originally formed as an "All Party Political Conference" on September 14, 1983, the MPC would become a center-right coalition in Namibia. Its original members were the eleven ethnic parties of the DTA plus the SWAPO-Democrats, SWANU, the Damara Council, the Rehoboth Liberation Front, the Namibia Christian Democratic Party, the Mbanderu Council, and the Progressive Party. Aside from the DTA and perhaps the Damara Council, the remaining groups each had very limited support. The MPC pledged to work for self-government without interference by the UN or SWAPO.

While the September 14 meeting may be seen as the earliest gathering of the parties, the term Multi-Party Conference was first applied to a meeting of the groups on November 12, 1983, almost two months later. A member party was the SWA National Party, represented by Eben Van Zijl (q.v.). The MPC representatives continued to meet in Windhoek until February 24, 1984, when the MPC issued its "Declaration of Basic Principles." The MPC clearly had the support of South African Prime Minister P. W. Botha, who had met with it in January 1984, conveying his government's view on major issues. Leaders of the MPC then traveled to the United States, where they met with UN Secretary General Javier Perez de Cuellar, and US Secretary of State George Schultz. They could talk to Schultz about their "Bill of Fundamental Rights and Objectives," which greatly resembled key sections of the American Bill of Rights. Leaders of the MPC invited SWAPO to join it, while boldly predicting that it would defeat SWAPO in a "free and fair election." Some MPC leaders such as Kuaima Riruako denounced SWAPO as "a tool of the Russians."

An important step occurred when an MPC mission went to Cape Town in April 1985. It returned on April 18 with a pledge from South Africa to allow a transitional government with "muscles and teeth." A South African legal team worked with the MPC in laying the groundwork for legislation to authorize the new government. This would become the Transitional Government of National Unity (q.v.). This was essentially a form of internal self-government, but without control of foreign affairs, defense, etc. This power was handed over to the MPC (and the TGNU) in a ceremony on June 17, 1985. By this time the MPC was considerably smaller than its first meetings. The only parties in the MPC by 1985 were the DTA (and its eleven ethnic parties), SWANU, SWAPO-D, the SWA National Party, the Labour Party, and the Rehoboth Free Democratic Party. During the entire period of rule by the TGNU it was understood that the MPC still existed as the functional basis for the TGNU, although the two were relatively congruent. With the setting up of elections in 1989 new coalitions took shape and the MPC ceased to exist.

MUYONGO, ALBERT MISHEK (1940–   ). Vice-president of the Democratic Turnhalle Alliance at independence in 1990 and one of its representatives in the National Assembly, Muyongo has been an active politician for more than twenty-five years. Born into the Mafwe Royal House at Linyanti in the Caprivi Strip, he was once first in line for the chieftainship. He received his education at Roman Catholic mission schools at Katimo Mulilo in the Caprivi, and in Zimbabwe. He attended colleges in South Africa and then taught for several years. In March 1964 he helped form the Caprivi African National Union (CANU) and became its first vice-president. He was co-leader of a protest march at Katima Mulilo five months later, at which police killed two and wounded many more. He avoided arrest and escaped into Zambia. Seeing the need for a broad national political front, he negotiated a merger with SWAPO in November 1964 and served two years as SWAPO's representative in Zambia. In 1966 he was selected SWAPO's Secretary for Education, and at a party congress four years later he was promoted to vice-president. However, the exact nature of the CANU-SWAPO merger was never clearly resolved between the parties, as CANU leaders thought it would still have its own identity. When Muyongo revived CANU's identity in 1980 he was expelled from SWAPO. He returned to Namibia in June 1985, broke with CANU later that year, and created the Caprivi-based United Democratic Party, becoming its leader. He claimed support of 80 percent of the Caprivians; however, CANU leaders responded by saying he had no real support. In 1987 he was appointed a vice-president of the DTA, in which he continued to work for greater attention to the problems in the Caprivi Strip. During the 1989 election campaign he challenged SWAPO's Sam Nujoma to a televised debate. As DTA's senior vice-president he is expected to continue as a major spokesman for it in the Assembly. With the resignation of DTA President Chief Kuaima Riruako (q.v.), a DTA congress in March, 1990 named Muyongo as acting president. At a meeting of the DTA of Namibia central committee in November, 1991 he was confirmed as President of the party. In an attempt to create more cooperation with the DTA, in June, 1992 the Government elected Muyongo to the Security Commission, a body mandated by the constitution to recommend senior appointments such as the country's Police Chief and Army Commander.

- N -

NACHTIGAL, DR. GUSTAV. A German explorer in Africa who in the mid-1880s was the German Consul-General for the west coast of Africa. In August 1884 Chancellor Bismarck instructed Nachtigal to go to Namibia and annex all the territories near Walvis Bay where German businesses had received mining concessions, and to conclude treaties with African tribal leaders there, placing them under German "protection." However, the Africans would retain control over their subjects.

Nachtigal's boat, *Möwe,* landed at Angra Pequeña on October 7. Dr. Nachtigal heard that the top Nama chiefs were meeting at Bethanie, under instructions from Adolf Lüderitz (q.v.). He went to Bethanie, but the chiefs weren't there. Nevertheless he negotiated with Chief Josef Fredericks a treaty of "friendship and protection," October 28, 1884. In addition the Africans promised to allow free entry to German merchants and settlers. Less than a month later he also concluded a treaty with Chief Haibib of the Topnaar Namas. He appointed Heinrich Vogelsang as temporary German consul for the area of Bethanie and Lüderitz. Nachtigal also concluded a treaty with Hermanus van Wyk of the Rehoboth Basters. He was not successful with Maherero, so in 1885 Bismarck sent Dr. H. E. Goering to pursue further treaties.

NAMA. One of several groups of people known collectively as Khoi-Khoin (q.v.) or disparagingly as Hottentots, they comprise a very significant percentage of the indigenous people living in the southern third of Namibia. An estimate for 1989 indicates there are about 62,000 Nama living in Namibia, making it the third largest African group. (Wambos were projected at 641,000 and Kavangos at 120,000.)

The Namas have been in southern Africa for many centuries, but their original home area is not known. Their lighter skin tone is not like that of West and Central Africans, for example, and both in their language and their tendency to steatopygia they show similarities to the San. As the Khoi-Khoin entered southern Africa along the western side, some of them stayed in the region of Namibia, while others travelled well into South Africa, as far as the Cape itself. These were the first Africans seen by Dutch sailors who landed there. Some Namas crossed south of the Orange River, where they mixed with other people, including even the Dutch, and adopted their clothes, language, and even their names. Members of this latter group recrossed the Orange River into Namibia, generally in the early nineteenth century, and are often called the Orlams (q.v.).

Thus there are two major divisions of Nama in Namibia, the so-called ''pure'' Nama and the Orlams. Each group is further subdivided. (Each subdivision is discussed under its name elsewhere in this book.) The ''pure'' Namas who never left Namibia are divided into eight subgroups. The Topnaars (q.v.) remained independent and generally lived around Walvis Bay and as far north as Okahandja. Likewise remaining independent were the Bondelswarts (q.v.), who lived near the Orange River and who once had their capital at Warmbad.

The other six groups of "pure" Nama formed an alliance. Its leaders were the //Khauben or Gei-Khaun, better known as the Red Nation (q.v.) or Rode Natie. One of their great leaders was //Oaseb or Oasib (q.v.). Some of this group lived near Hoachanas, but in fact the warlike Red Nation has been virtually destroyed. A second ally was the Franzmännschen (q.v.), who lived near Gochas and along the Fish River. These were later led by Simon Koper (q.v.). A third ally was the !Kara-!oan, who lived along the Chamob River. A fourth, the /Hawoben, were better known as the Feldschuhträgers (q.v.). The fifth allied group, known as the Zwartbois (q.v.), lived in Rehoboth until 1870 when they moved north to Fransfontein. The sixth of the federated tribes, commonly called the Groot-doden or //O-gein, lived in the upper parts of the Fish River.

The word "Orlam" is of uncertain derivation, but one source calls it a Malay word for "foreigner." Some of the Orlams mixed with other South Africans prior to their reentry into Namibia. Five different groups of Orlams crossed the Orange. The first were the /Khowesin, but are best known as the Witbois (q.v.) after the man who led the emigration. Many of them settled in Gibeon. The second Orlam group were the Gei-/Khauon, led by Amraal Lamberts. They first settled in Naosannabis, but later went to Gobabis. The third were the =Kari-/Khauan, who settled in Berseba. The fourth group, known as !Aman, settled in Bethanie. The last Orlam group to cross the Orange River were called //Aicha-//ain, or the "angry tribe," better known as the Afrikanders (q.v.).

Nama tradition had the clan headed by a ruling family from which the Chief (sometimes called the Kaptein) would be elected. His authority was not unlimited, as his council played an important role in advising him, and the consent of the whole tribe was needed. Nevertheless, a few very powerful leaders dominated their followers. The Namas tended to establish central villages which became their permanent homes (Gibeon, Bethanie, Berseba, Warmbad), and they responded well to RMS missionaries who worked among them.

The history of the Namas can be found throughout this

book, especially under the names of such key figures as Kido Witbooi, Hendrik Witbooi, Jonker Afrikander, Jan Jonker Afrikander, Jacob Marengo, and Simon Koper, to name a few. The Namas fought two major foes, the Hereros (*see* HERERO WARS) and the German Schutztruppe (colonial army). Sometimes the battles were initiated by the Namas (those fought by Jonker Afrikander and //Oaseb, for example), and other times they were battles of resistance and defense (those fought by H. Witbooi, J. Marengo, and the Bondelswarts, for example). In any case, the Nama have survived to play a significant role in modern Namibia.

NAMA ALLIANCE PARTY. Formed by delegates to the Turnhalle Conference in 1975, it affiliated with the Democratic Turnhalle Alliance in 1977. Among its founders were Daniel Luipert (q.v.), Moses Jacobs, and Ernst Kuhlmann. It is now known as the Democratic Turnhalle Party of Namibia (q.v.).

NAMA CHIEFS' COUNCIL (variant: COUNCIL OF NAMA CHIEFS). The traditional authorities that represented the loosely knit Nama peoples periodically met in this council to discuss common concerns. Its leader in the 1960s was David Witbooi. Although each of the Nama chiefs retained his own autonomy, they have cooperated with each other since the war against Germany in the late nineteenth century. The Nama chiefs have also worked closely with the Herero chiefs since that same period. Thus in the 1960s the two groups were united in petitions they sent to the United Nations, for example.

However, in the 1970s some splits occurred around the time of the Turnhalle Conference. Some of them chose to work with the Democratic Turnhalle Alliance, while others preferred SWAPO.

NAMALAND. Logically this should mean all the land traditionally occupied by the Namas (roughly the southern one-third of Namibia), an area equivalent to the meaning of the older term "Great Namaqualand." However under South Africa's application of the plan of the Odendaal Commission (q.v.), the area designated as Namaland (a "Homeland") was very much smaller. The area covered about equal distances on both sides of the Fish River, but was limited to a region only 100 kilometers wide and 150 kilometers long. The town of Gibeon was within its border, but the "Homeland" did not reach as far north as either Maltahöhe or Mariental, nor as far south as Keetmanshoop.

NAMAQUA. An eighteenth- and nineteenth-century term for the people now correctly called Nama (q.v.). The word is etymologically incorrect, as the suffix "qua" is merely a masculine plural denoting "people."

NAMAQUALAND. Based on the incorrect term "Namaqua" (q.v.), it naturally refers to the lands in which they live. However, a greater explanation is needed, since it is found so frequently in eighteenth- and nineteenth-century literature from southern Africa. Writers wishing to refer to the home areas of the body of people they preferred to call "Hottentots" (q.v.), but otherwise called Namaquas, used the word "Namaqualand." Most of these writers entered South Africa at the Cape, and looking northward saw Namaqualand as a vast territory in the northern Cape and beyond. Thus they would refer to Little Namaqualand when meaning the area up to the Orange River, and Great Namaqualand when referring to the area beyond, essentially the lower third of Namibia today. Adventurous explorers penetrated these areas and wrote about their daring exploits and adventures in "the land of the Namaquas."

NAMIB. Various sources give slightly different meanings of the word, but in any case it refers in some way to the great desert that dominates the country's western coast. In the Nama (Khoikhoi) language, "!Namib" means either "shield" or "enclosure." Certainly the barren coastal area provided a shield against all but the most persistent approachers from the sea. Curiously if the "!" click sound did not precede it, the word Namib would mean "mirage."

NAMIB AIR. Namibia's first scheduled air service was begun on August 1, 1931, by South West African Airways Ltd. Other companies followed. In 1946 three of them, Oryx Aviation, Namib Air, and South West Air Transport united to form South West Airways. This company became a fundamental part of the territory's infrastructure. In 1977 it changed its name to Namib Air. On May 14, 1987, Namib Air became the national airline company of the country; it is owned by the government and operated as a state-owned enterprise. Its offices are at Eros Airport in Windhoek. It owns and maintains its aircraft. Namib Air offers both chartered and scheduled flights, as well as arranging tours to other parts of southern Africa, including Malawi and Victoria Falls. Besides linking the various cities and towns of Namibia, it is increasingly extending flights to other countries, especially with the coming of independence. Cooperation began with Air Botswana in April 1989, for example. In August 1989 Namib Air began operating fifteen flights a week from Windhoek to Cape Town and Johannesburg. In April 1990 Namib Air made its biggest leap forward, however. It took over the twice-weekly Windhoek–Frankfurt, Germany, flights using a Boeing 747-SP that it leased from South African Airways. Flights to Zambia, Zimbabwe, and Botswana began in November, 1990, and in July, 1992 there was service added to London. The airline is actually a subsidiary of a government-owned transportation corporation called TransNamib. On October 28, 1991 the airline was officially renamed Air Namibia (q.v.).

NAMIB DESERT. The Namib (q.v.), called by some "the world's oldest desert," is a region that stretches from Mossamedes in Angola to the St. Helena Bay in South Africa's northwestern Cape Province. Its width varies from fifteen to eighty-five miles inland from the coast, but averages thirty-five to forty miles in much of Namibia. However, the semi-arid region that extends between the starkest parts of the Namib and the great plateau region that extends down the center of the country (about sixty to eighty miles inland) could be labelled another segment of the Namib.

Along the coast the desert provides virtually a "shield" (an English translation of the Nama word "Namib") from outside visitors. There are only two capes, Cape Frio and

Cape Cross, and comparatively few bays, considering the distance of 1770 kilometers from Angola's Bay of Elephants to the Orange River. Walvis Bay is the only good, natural harbor. Otherwise the coast is unfriendly to navigation.

The ocean plays a vital part in the development and continuity of the desert. It was caused by the permanent South Atlantic anticyclone, which creates a counter-clockwise circulation of the air and the waters. This results in southeasterly trade winds, which blow away from the coast, and the north/northwest flowing Benguela Current (q.v.), which brings cold sub-Antarctic water in contact with the coast.

Rainfall is minimal in most of the desert, but morning mists and fog drift over it and provide the moisture needed for the little but hardy vegetation that survives even in the worst of the desert. For example, the southern Namib sand dunes are stationary, as a light cover of vegetation holds them in place. The dunes a little further north shift regularly, however, by as many as five feet after a stormy day. Among the other desert vegetation are the "Bushman's candle," the kokerbaum, the *Welwitschia mirabilis,* the naras (qq.v.), and the dainty little Morning Star and South West Edelweiss. Once out of the worst of the desert, moving toward the plateau region, acacia trees, grasses, and shrub become somewhat more common.

Isolated mountain chains, massifs, and hills (koppies or kopjes) are plentiful in the Namib. The highest elevation in the country is the Brandberg, a massif near the Ugab River. East of Swakopmund are the Rössing Mountains; east of Lüderitz are the Chaukaib and Kubub Mountains; further south are the Klinghardt Mountains.

Except for the Kunene River in the extreme north and the Orange River in the extreme south, the rivers that enter the Namib from the east are generally not successful in reaching the coast except when the rainfall is exceptional on the plateau. Most are therefore intermittent streams. These include the Kuiseb, Swakop, Omaruru, Ugab, Huab, Uniab, Hoanib, and Hoarusib Rivers. From the Kuiseb south to the Orange, no river ever successfully reaches the sea. Neverthe-less, the dry water beds do support vegetation in some areas.

The Omaruru River reaches the sea every year, and even when the surface is dry one can find good quantities of water year round by digging two or three feet deep in the river bed. Thus ground water (found in the subsurface layers of sand and rock that rest on impervious rock) can be found regularly, even when surface water is not apparent.

Animal life in the Namib depends upon the extremities of the weather. After good rainy seasons the shrub and grass areas will support a variety of animals, especially gemsbok, springbok, and mountain zebra. Ostriches are also found there.

Relatively few indigenous Africans live in the Namib, although some San and Nama families do. Major coastal towns that are within the Namib boundaries are Walvis Bay, Lüderitz, and Swakopmund.

NAMIB-NAUKLUFT PARK. Even larger than the Etosha National Park, this park was created by the consolidation in 1978 of the Namib Desert Park, the Naukluft Mountain Zebra Park, part of Diamond Area 2, and some state land. The Namib Desert Research Station is located in it, as is the Sossusvlei (q.v.), the Kuiseb Canyon, the Welwitschia Plain, and the lagoon at Sandwich Harbour. The park consists of 2.3 million hectares (23,000 square kilometers) and contains thousands of animals. It comprises grasslands, granite mountains, and towering sand dunes. There are two camping areas for visitors. The park is located east, southeast, and south of the Swakopmund-Walvis Bay area.

NAMIBIA. The territory has been known by many names over the years. An early one was "Transgariep," as the Orange River was once known as the Gariep River. Under German rule it became "Deutsche Südwest-Afrika." After South Africa took over in 1915 it became South West Africa, or, for many, "South West." In 1969 the General Assembly of the United Nations passed a resolution that proclaimed "that in accordance with the desire of its people, South West Africa shall henceforth be known as Namibia." The Security Council endorsed the name change. It is claimed that the UN took this action on the insistence of Mburumba Kerina (q.v.), who is said to have invented the word. The root of the word obviously refers to the great Namib Desert (q.v.) that dominates the territory's coastline.

NAMIBIA CHRISTIAN DEMOCRATIC PARTY (NCDP). A small party founded in 1978 by Johannes ("Hans") Röhr—who has remained its leader since the beginning—it did not compete for seats in the 1989 Assembly elections. The party's secretary-treasurer is Wolfgang Adam, and its honorary president is Chief Johannes Shihepo. The party has consistently taken positions against both extremes. It is strongly based on Christian views and is both antiracist and anticommunist. Röhr has spoken out strongly against all forms of human rights violations, both those practiced by the South African army and police and those reportedly practiced by elements in SWAPO. The party consistently supported independence under the provisions of UN Resolution 435.

The NCDP participated in the 1978 Assembly elections and Röhr won its only seat. It also won a seat in the Kavango Second Tier Representative Authority, which it held from 1980 to 1989. Röhr attended both the Geneva and Lusaka conferences for the party, and briefly joined the MPC until he resigned in protest. The party attended the /Ai//gams conference in 1986 and signed its declaration.

NAMIBIA INDEPENDENCE PARTY (NIP). Originally the National Independence Party when it was founded in 1974 in Keetmanshoop, its leaders then were Charles Hartung and Albert Krohne (q.v.). Behind the scenes, however, its most active and vital members were Dr. Kenneth Abrahams and his wife Ottilie (Schimming) Abrahams (q.v.). The party favors a unitary state, although in earlier days it proposed federal elements. The party is strongly in favor of a multiparty and multiracial Namibia, yet opposed SWAPO for several reasons. Some involved personalities, while others involved principles (such as opposition to violence). It favors a mildly socialistic approach to national wealth, but also supports free enterprise.

The party began—and to some extent remains—a party of Coloureds. It won three of the six elected seats in the 1974 elections of the Coloured Council. Its membership has been open to all racial groups since 1975. It took part in the Turnhalle Conference (1975–77), but withdrew in opposition to the conference's proposed constitution. In 1977 it joined the Namibia National Front (q.v.), and three years later withdrew from the Coloured Council.

The NIP concentrated during the 1980s on self-support projects among the people; it has aided a variety of educational and cultural projects. It participated in the 1986 /Ai//gams Conference in Windhoek, and in 1988 it joined the revived Namibia National Front (q.v.) for the elections the next year. Krohne was chosen the NNF vice-president and Mrs. Abrahams its secretary-general. It won only one seat, however, and no NIP member received it.

NAMIBIA NATIONAL CONVENTION (NNC). A coalition of political groups formed when the National Convention (q.v.) split in February 1975. The groundwork had been laid in December 1974 when SWAPO resigned from the National Convention (NC). When the NC met at Okahandja in February 1975, younger and more radical members managed to replace Clemens Kapuuo as the organization's leader and changed the name to the Namibia National Convention (NNC). (Kapuuo took the remnants of the NC and created the National Convention of Namibia, the NCN.)

The executive of the NNC was elected on February 23, 1975. Rev. Zephania Kameeta (q.v.) was chair. The executive also included a SWANU supporter, Jephta Tjongoro, as president, and other SWAPO, SWANU, and Rehoboth Volkspartei activists. Other groups that were members included the Damara Tribal Executive, various Nama and Herero traditionalists, and the Namibia African People's Democratic Organization (NAPDO).

From the beginning this organization opposed the proposed talks that ultimately became the Turnhalle Conference. It would have boycotted the conference even if political parties had been allowed to participate. The NNC proclaimed its goal to be "one man, one vote in an undivided country," without any "federation" or "multi-nationalism" or any other system that would emphasize ethnic differences.

The NNC folded in November 1976 when it was announced that NAPDO and the Rehoboth Volkspartei and others would merge with SWAPO, which then withdrew from the NNC. The remaining members then regrouped in the Namibia National Front (q.v.).

NAMIBIA NATIONAL COUNCIL. The name taken by the group of political factions that met at the Okahandja National Unity Conference (q.v.) in 1975. The latter is also often called the Okahandja Summit. This coalition opposed the Turnhalle Conference and favored a unitary state for Namibia, with elections to be held under UN supervision. This group abandoned its efforts after it failed to get international recognition.

NAMIBIA NATIONAL FRONT (NNF). Formed in 1977 out of the remnants of its predecessor, the Namibia National Convention (q.v.), it saw itself as a middle-of-the-road alternative to the DTA on the right and SWAPO on its left. Like the DTA it was an alliance of many other parties, most of which had a strong ethnic base. At various times in its three-year existence its membership included SWANU (led by Gerson Veii), the Mbanderu Council, the National Independence Party, the Damara Executive Committee and Damara Council, the Bondelswarts council, the Voice of the People, the Rehoboth Volkspartei, and the Federal Party led by Bryan O'Linn (qq.v.). While SWAPO-D considered joining and claimed to believe in the principles of the NNF, it never formally joined, as it demanded more members on the ruling council than its membership would justify.

The NNF saw itself as a centrist bloc, and it called for independence under UN Resolution 435. It sought internationally supervised elections and bitterly fought the 1978 Assembly elections promoted by South Africa. It called for a nonracial approach to government, emphasizing national unity instead. The president was Justus Garoëb (q.v.), the vice-president was Gerson Veii, and Bryan O'Linn was secretary-general (q.v.). The Federal Party's John Kirkpatrick was another of its leaders. Nevertheless, the NNF disintegrated due to internal friction over a variety of issues.

The Bondelswarts and the Voice of the People left in 1978, and the Federal Party left in 1979. The next year the NNF ceased to function as an alliance.

The spirit of the NNF as a centrist alliance remained, however, and on February 24, 1989, it was revived. The member organizations this time were SWANU (q.v.), the Namibia Independence Party (q.v.), the new Rehoboth Volkspartei (q.v.), the United Namibia People's Party, and the Mmabatho People's Party. Like the old NNF the new group desired a unitary Namibia under UN-supervised elections, and a constitution guaranteeing fundamental human rights. It proposed an impeachable executive president, a parliament elected every five years, and an independent judiciary. The country should be divided into regional districts that would not be based on ethnic divisions.

At the time of the elections the President of the new NNF was Vekuii Rukoro, and its Vice-President was Albert Krohne of the Namibia Independence Party. Secretary-General was Ottilie Abrahams of the NIP. Rukoro's faction of SWANU and NIP were its strongest parties. In the 1989 elections the NNF received 5344 votes, about 30% of them in Windhoek. Its one Assembly seat went to Rukoro. When the NNF central committee voted in mid-1990 to merge with the DTA in opposition to the Government, Rukoro and faction walked out of the alliance. The rift was healed, however, and in late October, 1991 the NNF disbanded and merged with Rukoro's SWANU. He then announced that SWANU might ally itself with SWAPO in future election campaigns, as they were both ''progressive'' parties.

NAMIBIA PEOPLE'S LIBERATION FRONT (NPLF). Literally an alliance within an alliance, the NPLF was founded in June 1978. It brought together the Voice of the People, the Damara Executive Committee, and the Bondelswarts Council as their leaders broke away from the Namibia National Front (which lasted from 1977 to 1980 in its first life). Later the Damara Christian Democratic Party and the Riemvasmaak United Party also joined the NPLF. All are small organizations. The leader and life president of the NPLF is Kephes Conradie, head of Voice of the People.

The party joined the DTA for a brief period in 1982, but Conradie walked out of it when DTA leaders suggested that the NPLF merge with several other small ethnic-oriented parties. When it attempted to join the Multi-Party Conference in 1985 it was refused membership. It did join an electoral alliance, the Federal Convention of Namibia (FCN) in 1989, but received no Assembly seat as the FCN only won one seat.

Despite its ethnic base, the NPLF supported a unitary system for an independent Namibia, opposing ethnic and racial division and discrimination. It has argued for free basic education, while retaining the right to study in the mother tongue. Its economic policies can be described as essentially capitalist yet with social welfare safeguarded and labor unions encouraged.

NAMIBIAN DOLLAR. At the end of January, 1991 the Minister of Finance, Dr. Otto Herrigel, confirmed plans for a Namibian currency unit, the Namibian dollar (N$). He asserted that it was a move toward monetary independence from South Africa, and that the currency would probably come into use in 1993. At a press conference in Windhoek on June 25, 1992, the new Minister of Finance, Mr. Gerhard Hanekom, announced that the currency would be introduced in the latter part of 1993. The banknotes would come in N$10, N$50 and N$100 bills that would be printed by Sweden's Tumba Bruk. The 19th century chief, Hendrik Witbooi, will be featured on one side of the bills. Hanekom said that the N$ would be at parity with the South African Rand, at least at the beginning, and both would serve as acceptable currencies. However if the Rand were to lose too much value against the principal world currencies. Namibia could leave the Common Monetary Area as Botswana had done.

NAMUTONI, FORT. See FORT NAMUTONI.

NANGOMBE YA MANGUNDU. According to Wambo legend, this person lived near the upper sections of the Zambezi River, presumably in eastern Angola or western Zambia. Two sons, Nangombe and Kathu (q.v.) travelled southwest into what is today northern Namibia. In the Ndonga area they split up, and Nangombe began the Wambo nation while Kathu moved on and began the Herero nation. Tradition is reportedly not clear as to whether Nangombe Ya Mangundu was the father or mother of the two. Curiously, the Herero do not have this story in their traditions.

NARAS (variants: !NARAS; NARRA). A round, lumpy green fruit found in the Namib Desert, it is eaten by Namas, San, and others who live off the veldkost of field food. Some animals also eat it. The fruit of the spiny and thorny but leafless shrub does not much resemble the pumpkin to which it is related. The plant's taproot can grow about forty feet in order to reach subsurface water, enabling the naras to grow even in sand dunes. Few other plants can survive such an environment. San and others who eat the naras find in them both moisture and food, and even roast the seeds as a delicacy. Others collect the seeds and export them through Walvis Bay, as they can be a substitute for almonds in baking and candies. Called "The Wonder of the Waste," the naras (or !naras as the Namas call it) is found nowhere else in the world, yet it is plentiful in the Kuiseb River valley.

The green fruit is about the size of an adult fist. One can make a hole in it, mash the inside into a pulp, and drink the liquid, preferably boiling it first. The pulp can then be removed and made into a kind of bread, and the husk can be saved to make flasks or even musical instruments. Nothing goes to waste in the desert.

NATIONAL ASSEMBLY. There are actually three separate National Assemblies that must be dealt with.

The first was actually elected as a Constituent Assembly (q.v.) in December 1978. SWAPO and most of the other parties with mass support boycotted the elections. As a result the Democratic Turnhalle Alliance and its associated parties won an overwhelming majority. On May 21, 1979, it was renamed the National Assembly and was given broad legislative powers. It lasted from 1979 until it was dissolved on January 19, 1983, in part because the DTA was greatly weakened by dissension and defections. This left the administrator-general as the all-powerful governor.

The second National Assembly developed out of another South African initiative, the Multi-Party Conference (MPC), an alliance of moderate to conservative parties, most of them very small. The DTA was again active here, along with SWAPO-D, SWANU, the National Party, and others. The MPC led to an announcement in April 1985 that self-government as a transition to independence would be granted. The new Transitional Government of National Unity (TGNU) was led by the parties in the MPC. These groups were all said to be "not happy with UN Resolution 435." The TGNU formally took power on June 17, 1985. A National Assembly of sixty-two members was provided for, along with a cabinet of eight ministers and eight deputy ministers. A sixteen-member Constitutional Council, drawn from the Assembly, was selected to write an independence constitution for Namibia. This Assembly ruled until the 1989 elections.

The third Assembly was a result of complex international negotiations. Elections were held in November 1989 for a seventy-two-member Constituent Assembly to write a Constitution in keeping with UN Resolution 435. Once the constitution was complete this Assembly voted for itself to serve as Namibia's first independent National Assembly.

NATIONAL CONVENTION (NC). Also known as the National Convention of Freedom Parties, this coalition represented the major political groups that were opposed to South African policies for Namibia. Formed at Rehoboth in November 1971, it represented the largest Black political groups in the country. The meeting was chaired by Hans Diergaardt, then of the Rehoboth Volkspartei. Other groups that joined were SWAPO (led by its international leader, David Meroro), SWANU, NUDO, DEMKOP, NAPDO, the Herero Chief's Council, and the Damara Tribal Executive.

This coalition was strongly opposed to the plan of South Africa to create ethnic "Homelands" in Namibia, preferring that the UN take it over in preparation for independence as a united territory. Letters were sent to the UN in 1973, and a delegation led by Chief Kapuuo arrived there in November 1973 to seek recognition of the group as representing the

Namibian people. However, the strength of SWAPO's external wing was already well established at the UN, and Kapuuo failed. A similar visit by Gerson Veii of SWANU in 1974 was also unsuccessful. Attempts by Kapuuo to get Sam Nujoma of SWAPO's external wing to join the NC were rejected by Nujoma.

The SWAPO internal wing left the coalition in December 1974 under pressure from Nujoma, and the NC split entirely two months later. At a meeting in Okahandja in late February 1975, Kapuuo was ousted as leader of the NC. The rebels, including SWAPO (internal wing), SWANU, NAPDO, the Damara Tribal Executive, the Rehoboth Volkspartei, and others, reformed as the Namibia National Convention (q.v.). Kapuuo pulled together his remaining supporters under the name National Convention of Namibia (NCN) (q.v.).

NATIONAL CONVENTION OF NAMIBIA (NCN). A coalition of Namibian political parties and factions led by Chief Clemens Kapuuo after he was deposed as leader of the National Convention (q.v.) in February 1975. Besides Kapuuo's own NUDO, the member groups of the NCN included the Herero Chief's Council, the Damara United Front, the Rehoboth Liberation Movement, the National Independence Party, and a faction of Tswanas.

A statement issued by several of its leaders on March 10, 1975, was strongly critical of South Africa's "illegal occupation and colonial rule," and proclaimed the necessity of ridding the country of all racial discrimination. Yet the NCN was notably different from the rival NNC by its willingness to become involved in talks with South Africa concerning a new constitution. Thus Kapuuo and his associates took part in the Turnhalle Conference, where he developed and introduced a detailed constitutional proposal under the NCN's sponsorship. Other groups at the Turnhalle followed Kapuuo's lead and joined his NCN.

At the conclusion of the Turnhalle Conference in 1977, Dirk Mudge of the Republican Party (qq.v.) and Chief Kapuuo created the Democratic Turnhalle Alliance (q.v.). Most of the NCN member groups then joined the DTA, and the NCN ceased to exist.

NATIONAL DEMOCRATIC PARTY (NDP). Once among the strongest political groups in Owambo the NDP merged into the DTA of the Namibia when it became a unitary party in November, 1991. It grew out of the Owambo Independence Party (q.v.) that was founded in 1973. But when that party became inactive a year later, the National Democratic Party (NDP) was formed by many of the members of the OIP in order to win seats in an enlarged Owambo Legislative Assembly. Among its founders were Rev. Cornelius Ndjoba (q.v.) and Chief Gabriel Kautuima. Ndjoba was elected its president. The NDP won all the seats in the Assembly.

The NDP, led by Ndjoba, attended the Turnhalle Conference (1975–77), and joined the DTA when it was created in 1977. Ndjoba became the DTA's second president in 1978 after his predecessor, Chief Clemens Kapuuo (q.v.), was assassinated. Two years later Peter Kalangula (q.v.) replaced Ndjoba as president of both the DTA and the NDP. However, in 1982 Kalangula broke with the DTA and left it. He then created a new party, Christian Democratic Action for Social Justice (q.v.) and most of the NDP members joined him in it.

Those who remained in the NDP elected Tara Imbili (q.v.) as their president in 1982, but he resigned in 1985. Meanwhile the party slipped to being the opposition group in the Owambo Legislative Assembly, which was now led by Kalangula. The NDP remained in the DTA and held two seats in the Assembly of the TGNU and one on the Constitutional Council. The party's president is Chief Gabriel Kautuima, but more active is its DTA representative, Headman Gottlieb Dan. The NDP campaigned as part of the DTA in the 1989 Assembly elections, and Dan was sixth on the DTA electoral list and easily won a seat in the Assembly.

NATIONAL DEMOCRATIC UNITY PARTY (NDUP). A party representing the country's Kavango population, its origins go back to the Kavango National Council (q.v.), an alliance of Kavango traditional leaders who attended the Turnhalle Conference, 1975–77. At the conference the group became known as the Kavango Alliance and became a fledgling political party. When the DTA formed in 1977, the Kavango Alliance joined it. In April 1984, the year after one member of the KA broke away to form the Namibia National Independence Party, the KA reconstituted itself as the National Democratic Unity Party. It continued to affiliate with the DTA, and received two seats in the Assembly of the TGNU and one on the Constitutional Council. In the 1989 Assembly elections, the founder and President, Chief Majavero was in the eleventh spot on the DTA electoral list and won a seat in the first National Assembly of independent Namibia. When the DTA of Namibia became a unitary party in November, 1991 the NDUP lost its individual identity along with the other ethnic-based parties in the alliance.

NATIONAL INDEPENDENCE PARTY (NIP). Founded in 1974 among the Coloureds in Keetmanshoop, it changed its name in 1981 to the Namibia Independence Party (q.v.).

NATIONAL PARTY [OF SOUTH WEST AFRICA] (NP). The dominant party among Namibia's white population for more than forty years, it originated in Mariental in July 1924. Frikkie Jooste founded the party, using the slogan "South Africa First." Three years later it merged with the Union Party (q.v.) to become the United National South West Party (q.v.). Both had lost the 1926 Legislative Assembly elections to the Deutscher Bund in Südwestafrika (q.v.). The merger was tenuous, however, and in 1939 it broke up in a move parallel to that occurring in South Africa.

Thus the National Party (NP) reemerged in 1939, and the next year lost to the United National South West Party (UNSWP) in the Legislative Assembly elections. Prior to 1950 it only held three of the eighteen seats in the Assembly. The two parties agreed only on a central issue, the full incorporation of Namibia into South Africa.

In 1948 the National Party of South Africa won control there, and the next year its leaders announced that white South West Africans would be given direct representation in the South African Parliament, with elections to occur in 1950. The UNSWP had alienated the German-speakers before and during World War II, so 1950 was the first year these voters were able to counterattack. They chose the National Party as their vehicle. Furthermore, since 1948 an influx of NP supporters came from South Africa to work in the Territorial Government Service, which also swelled the number of NP voters.

Thus the 1950 election dramatically changed the makeup of the Legislative Assembly, with NP seats increasing from three to sixteen of the eighteen. (The two others were finally won in 1966.) Also for the first time the territory's whites elected representatives to South Africa's Parliament. The NP won all six House of Assembly seats, and all four Senators (two elected, two appointed) were also NP members.

For almost a quarter of a century after the 1950 elections the NP remained static, closely linked to its South African counterpart, and regularly dominating white electoral politics in Namibia. The NP of SWA was also one of five branches in the Federal Council of South Africa's NP, having equal standing with the four provinces of South Africa. Policies at election time were dominated by the assumption that the territory should continue to work closely with South Africa, as it was expected to soon become the republic's "fifth province." One of its major figures during part of this period was A. H. du Plessis (q.v.), who was the NP leader from 1968 to 1981.

In 1973 South African Prime Minister John Vorster announced that Namibia would choose its own future. The NP in Namibia had to adjust its own party program to the changing official policies of South Africa. In 1974 the Legislative Assembly, dominated by the NP, passed a resolution inviting all groups to participate in a constitutional conference. Du Plessis was serving in South Africa's Parliament, but younger leaders like Dirk Mudge (q.v.), the party's leader in the Assembly, and Eben Van Zijl (q.v.) were appointed to lead the NP in organizing what would be called the Turnhalle Conference (q.v.). Within the NP Mudge was regarded as centrist or even left-wing, in contrast to the conservative stance of both du Plessis and Van Zijl.

When the Turnhalle Conference began, a large number of Africans were present, with Chief Clemens Kapuuo most prominent, in large part because of the negotiating skills and moderate tone of Mudge. This won his support within the NP, and especially among Germans. However, du Plessis returned to lead the NP delegation, a move seen as a victory by Van Zijl over Mudge. A deep split within the party surfaced in 1976. The power struggle continued for more than a year, with rumors persisting that Mudge might form a multiracial alliance with Chief Kapuuo (ultimately the Democratic Turnhalle Alliance, q.v.). Du Plessis and Van Zijl succeeded in retaining control of the party, and insisted on retaining certain aspects of apartheid in the newly formed constitution that emerged from the Turnhalle. At a party congress held in September 1977, Mudge led a walkout of eighty members, and on October 5 he announced the formation of his new Republican Party (q.v.). The next month the formation of the DTA was also announced. About the same time the NP was announcing that it was cutting its formal links with South Africa's NP, perhaps because even its conservative leadership had accepted a constitution that the Southern African NP could not begin to consider in 1977.

When South Africa announced elections would be held in late 1978 for a Namibian Constituent Assembly, the NP leaders formed an election front, AKTUR (q.v.), which was its own ad-hoc multiracial alliance. It won almost 12 percent of the votes and six seats in the Assembly. The NP delegates walked out, however, in January 1979 when it was announced that this "Constituent Assembly" would now become a "National Assembly." The NP felt that South Africa tricked it into participating. In any case the delegates returned a few months later, and remained until it was disbanded in 1983. Meanwhile Van Zijl retired briefly from the NP (1981–83) when he was passed over for a new NP leader to replace du Plessis.

With the new constitution, a White Second Tier Representative Authority was organized in 1980. The National Party continued to dominate this group until it was disbanded in 1989, easily defeating Mudge's Republican Party. In 1984 the NP joined the Multi-Party Conference, and the next year also joined the TGNU and took part in the Constitutional Council from 1985 to 1987. However, a split developed in the NP over these constitutional matters as the party's more liberal wing (surprisingly now led by Van Zijl) defected from the party and the Constitutional Council on the issue of desegregation of education. Van Zijl had been a deputy leader. When he resigned to form Action National Settlement (q.v.), the NP leadership consisted of Jacobus (''Kosie'') Pretorius (q.v.) as leader, and ''Jannie'' de Wet (q.v.) as vice-chairman. When the Constitutional Council submitted its draft document in mid-1987 the NP was one of two groups to oppose it and submit a dissenting document. This called for a system of ''group councils,'' in essence perpetuating the Second Tier ethnic divisions in the country, especially in matters such as education, social services, health, and land.

When the 1989 elections were scheduled, NP leaders founded an alliance with a small German group, Deutsche Aktion, and called it the Action Christian National (ACN) or Aksie Christelik Nasional (q.v.). This group, formed in early 1989, was led by Jan de Wet of the NP. One month before the election the Deutsche Aktion group withdrew from the ACN. In the election the ACN received 23,728 votes, the fourth highest total of the ten contesting groups. It won three Assembly seats, which went to de Wet, Pretorius, and Walther Aston. In January 1990, a split occurred between Pretorius and de Wet. The former tried to get the Assembly's chairman to remove de Wet as an ACN delegate. De Wet claimed that Pretorius had no right to request this. The Assembly chairman, Hage Geingob, declared he had neither the power nor the duty to remove de Wet, and suggested the two resolve their dispute in the spirit of national reconciliation.

NATIONAL PATRIOTIC FRONT (NPF). Formed in February 1989 for the elections coming nine months later, this alliance consists of the Action National Settlement (led by Eben van Zijl), the segment of SWANU led by Moses Katjiuongua, and the segment of the Caprivi African National Union led by Siseho Simasiku. High in its program is a Bill of Fundamental Rights in the constitution and enforced by an independent judiciary. It advocates a multiparty democracy, decentralization of government in regional and local governments *not* based on ethnicity, and a mixed economic system. Its chairman is Katjiuongua, and the other two leaders are both classed as vice-chairmen. During the election campaign the NPF challenged the impartiality of both the administrator-general and the UN special representative.

When the election was complete, the NPF had won 10,693 votes, with substantial numbers in Hereroland, Kaokoland, and Windhoek. It received one seat in the Assembly, which went to Katjiuongua.

NATIONAL SOZIALISTISCHE DEUTSCHE ARBEITERPARTEI. Building on the political involvement generated in the German-speaking community (about 6000) in the 1920s by the Deutscher Bund (q.v.), this "National Socialist German Workers' Party" was formed in 1932 in Windhoek. These Nazis had considerable support from their counterparts in Germany. While they came to the fore in 1932, captured German documents indicated that their leader in Namibia, K. Schröder, was already active in organizing his party in 1930. Leaflets, pamphlets, propaganda signs and swastika symbols were surfacing in Windhoek and Lüderitz. A new "Führer," Dr. Schwietering, emerged in the party. One of the major issues for which it fought was opposition to South Africa's negating the mandate and incorporating the country as a fifth province of South Africa. This position appealed to Germans who feared further dilution of their ethnic identity. Some openly advocated the return of the territory to Germany.

As the economy of the territory deteriorated in the early 1930s, the Nazis found support among younger Germans, who joined groups like the Hitler Jugend ("Youth") or Deutsche Mädchen ("Girls"). A few young men even went to Germany and joined the army or air force of the Reich. The Nazi Party was banned in 1934 by the South African administrators, and leaders such as Major H. Weigel and Capt. Erich von Lossnitzer were deported. This did not stop the activity, however, and many of the faithful worked through the Deutscher Bund. When that was banned in 1937 with two other German parties, they created the "Deutscher Südwest Bund" as a cultural organization that took political positions. It was led by Dr. Hans Hirskorn, who was reportedly sent from Berlin with both propagandists and sabotage experts. Torchlight parades, brown uniforms, and swastikas became more common, especially when children of German families returned from educational visits to Germany. Moreover, they also received support from similar elements in South Africa, especially a right-wing group called the Ossewa Brandweg. Hitler evidently saw "South West" as a ripe opportunity in the heart of mineral-rich southern Africa. Ultimately Hitler's activities were checked by the countermoves of South Africa's Jan Smuts. On April 18, 1939, he sent police and troops to Windhoek to occupy all public buildings, charging that the area had been used by the National Socialists "as a base for intrigue, and for undermining our liberties and seducing our citizens." All Nazi leaders there were arrested and interned.

NATIONAL UNION OF NAMIBIAN WORKERS (NUNW). Originally created by SWAPO in the early 1960s in Dar es Salaam, Tanzania, it was revived inside Namibia in 1976. However, it was forced to work underground until it could be legally revived in 1986. It functions as the labor arm of SWAPO, and its general secretary at the time of independence, John Ya Otto (q.v.), is a long-time SWAPO activist and leader. It has offices in Katutura, and serves as a union federation. Its member unions include the Namibian Food and Allied Workers Union, the Namibian National Teachers Union, the Namibian Public Workers Union, the Namibian Transport and Allied Workers Union, the Metal and Allied Namibian Workers Union, and the Mineworkers Union of Namibia. This represents about 40,000 workers, or 20 percent of those in formal sector employment (non-agriculture).

In mid-1987 security police harassed the NUNW, raiding its offices and the home of its national treasurer, Anton Lubowski (q.v.). However, with SWAPO winning control of the government in the 1989 elections, and both Ya Otto and Ben Ulenga of the Mineworkers Union of Namibia winning seats in the Assembly, the NUNW will only grow more influential in the near future. In 1992 the NUNW, led by its General Secretary, Bernard Esau, fought with the Assembly to strengthen the new Labour Act in order to protect the interests of Namibian workers. It was not totally happy with the results, but Esau conceded that the group's main positions had been written into the law.

NATIONAL UNITY DEMOCRATIC ORGANIZATION (NUDO). Formed September 25, 1964, it was one of the oldest of the Namibian Black nationalist parties still existing at independence. It was founded under the auspices of the Herero Chief's Council (q.v.) which had earlier been involved with forming SWANU but had since turned against it. Mburumba Kerina (q.v.) had conceived of NUDO, recommended its formation to the Herero Chief's Council (HCC), and became NUDO's first chairman. The active leader of the HCC at that point was Chief Clemens Kapuuo (q.v.), who was NUDO's co-founder. When Kerina had a disagreement with the HCC in 1966, he left the chairmanship and Kapuuo took over.

NUDO was represented in New York, as were SWAPO and SWANU, as it considered itself a truly national liberation movement like the others. Although its base was then (and still is) heavily Herero, it sought broader support. Under Kapuuo's leadership NUDO was active in forming the National Convention (q.v.) in 1971 with SWAPO and other groups. That group opposed the application of apartheid to Namibia and sought a constitution for an independent Namibia. NUDO also opposed SWAPO, which was insisting that it was the only true representative of Namibia's people. The National Convention broke up. Other groups like the NCN and the NNC also failed to unify the various nationalist groups.

In 1975 Kapuuo eschewed SWAPO's violence and agreed to talk with South Africa about a new constitution. Thus NUDO joined the Turnhalle Conference, where Kapuuo took a leading, activist role. When the conference ended, the Democratic Turnhalle Alliance was formed, and Kapuuo led NUDO into it. He even became the DTA's first president. Six months later Kapuuo was assassinated by unknown killers, although most people blamed SWAPO. With his death there was considerable rivalry, especially over who would be selected Herero's top chief. Kuaimo Riruako (q.v.) eventually won out, but not without creating enemies, who accused him of being authoritarian. He also became president of NUDO, spurring a breakaway movement led by Johannes Karuaihe, which created the National Unity Democratic Organization Progressive Party (q.v.) or NUDO-PP.

Riruako continued NUDO's affiliation with the DTA, and NUDO representatives thus participated in the 1979–83 National Assembly, the Multi-Party Conference, and the Transitional Government of National Unity, as well as in the Constitutional Council. While Riruako was active in all this and was even the president of DTA's Executive Committee, a rising star in NUDO has been its Chairman, N. Katuutire Kaura (q.v.). He held thirteenth place on the DTA electoral list for the 1989 Assembly, and thus won a seat. On the other hand Riruako was only given the third position, despite being DTA's President, and in a fit of pique withdrew his name totally from the list. In March 1990 Riruako resigned from the DTA executive committee (and thus the presidency of DTA). When the DTA of Namibia was reorganized as a unitary party in November, 1991, NUDO merged its identity with the others and ceased to exist separately. Kaura continued as Vice-President of the DTA, assuring the continuing influence of the old NUDO elements.

NATIONAL UNITY DEMOCRATIC ORGANIZATION PRO-GRESSIVE PARTY (NUDO-PP). A centrist party, it opposed both SWAPO's policy of violence as a means of gaining independence and the DTA approach of collaboration with South African plans. It was founded in 1981 by Johannes Karuaihe, who broke away from the National Unity Democratic Organization. He had been very close to the Herero Chief Clemens Kapuuo, and after the latter was assassinated Karuaihe was angry at the dominating manner of the new Herero Chief, Kuaima Riruako (q.v.). NUDO-PP has remained supportive of the Association for the Preservation of the Tjamuaha/Maherero Royal House.

Karuaihe died in 1983, and he was succeeded by Rehabiam Uazukuani, who served as president until 1988. In 1984 NUDO-PP became part of Mburumba Kerina's Namibia National Democratic Coalition, but that became defunct. In 1986 the party signed the /Ai//gam Declaration. In 1988 it also worked with the Liberated Democratic Party in reorganizing the old National Convention.

In 1988 the party sought younger leadership, and Mburumba Kerina (q.v.) was elected its president. As elections approached in 1989 he linked the party with the Federal Convention of Namibia (FCN) alliance. "Hans" Diergaardt won the only FCN seat in the Assembly, but when he resigned for personal reasons Kerina was selected to replace him. Kerina, one of the earliest of Namibia's active nationalists, was subsequently elected deputy speaker of the Assembly.

NATIVE ADMINISTRATION ACT OF 1927. *See* NATIVE (URBAN AREAS) ACT OF 1923.

NATIVE ADMINISTRATION PROCLAMATION No. 11 (1922). Generally known as the Pass Law, it regulated the movement of "Natives," who with some exceptions could not enter or leave certain limited areas without a permit. They had to exhibit this "pass" on demand of the police, and if they didn't they could be arrested. A curfew regulation the same year allowed local authorities to make additional rules regarding certain hours when "Natives" were not allowed in the public areas of a town.

NATIVE ADMINISTRATION PROCLAMATION (1928). This act of the South African government gave it the power to appoint and dismiss tribal leaders (chiefs or headmen) in the "Reserves." This gave it effective control over all aspects of African life, and institutionalized in theory—if not always in practice—the idea that all African leaders were now collaborationists.

NATIVE RESERVES COMMISSION (1920–22). In 1920 the administrator of South West Africa decided it was necessary to investigate the availability of African labor in the territory. He thus appointed a two-man commission to investigate that subject, but added to their assignment the investigation of the administration of "Native locations and reserves," their size and conditions therein, in order to supply white settlers with an adequate number of workers. Later in 1920, however, he added three more members, including the commissioner for Native affairs, the head of the land branch, and the surveyor-general. The larger commission was also instructed to "establish certainty to the whites as the permanent places of abode of the Natives'' and to ''tighten up Native Administration to prevent vagrancy and idleness.''

The commission reported in 1922 and recommended segregation as a general principle and thus to remove Native settlements from areas that were essentially European (''black islands''). It also recommended that whites should be prevented from renting land to Natives, and the need to provide more natural living conditions for the Natives and facilities for better, more efficient control over the Reserves. The Germans had first begun this concept of Native Reserves, and this commission recommended that those Native Reserves be maintained. It also added new Reserves that had not been part of the German plan. In total the Commission recommended a mere 11 percent (five million hectares) of the south and central sections of the land for African Reserves. Only a small fraction had good ground water, with the exception of the Rehoboth Gebiet (q.v.).

Worse yet, however the actual Proclamation of 1923 reduced the amount for Africans to only two million hectares. Additional land was designated in the Kaokoveld and the Sandveld, arid and rocky areas that no whites wanted. In the Epikuro Reserve one had to drill 800 feet down to find water for a well in some areas. The average depth for all wells dug in 1925 was 241 feet. Fewer than half the wells dug found any water at all.

NATIVE (URBAN AREAS) ACT OF 1923. By imposing residential segregation, this act (plus the Native Administration Act of 1927) had the effect of preventing Blacks from owning shops or businesses except in the locations or townships to which they were restricted.

NAUKLUFT MOUNTAINS. A range of mountains just east of the great dunes of the Namib Desert, they are about 160 kilometers inland. They are southwest of Rehoboth and northwest of Maltahöhe. The highest point of the dolomitic massif is called Friedensberg (1973 meters). The word ''Naukluft'' means ''narrow gorge.'' The many ravines in the mountains are the home of natural springs, some of which feed the desert pans (vlei) via underground routes. Part of the range was incorporated into the Naukluft Mountain Zebra Park, which has since been merged into the Namib-Naukluft Park.

During the German attacks on Hendrik Witbooi and his followers in the 1890s, the Naukluft Mountains became a place for the Witboois to hide, as well as a battleground as the Germans pursued the Witboois there.

NAVACHAB. An important new Namibian gold mine that produced its first ore late in 1989, it was formally opened by President Nujoma in June, 1990. (*See* GOLD.)

NDJAMBI KARUNGA. The traditional Supreme Being of the Hereros.

Ndjambi lives in a Heaven and is omnipresent. He is noted for outstanding kindness, and all humans are dependent on him for his blessings. In death one is taken by Ndjambi. He is not feared but venerated. He is seen as the giver of rain. Along with belief in Ndjambi Karunga, Hereros also traditionally followed a kind of ancestor devotion.

NDJOBA, REV. CORNELIUS TUHAFENI (variant: KOR-NELIUS) (1930–1983). Born in the Kwanyama area of Owambo into a family of tribal chiefs, Ndjoba received a teacher's certificate from Oniipa Training College in 1952. He became a school principal for several years at Eenhana Boys' School. In 1957 he began seminary studies at Oshigambo and Elim. In 1968 the Ovambokavango Church ordained him as a pastor.

He also began his political career in 1968, as he was appointed to Owambo's first Legislative Council. In 1972 he was appointed to the Executive Council, to serve as councillor in charge of education and culture. He was by far the most educated member of this council, most of whom were traditional chiefs or headmen with limited education. On May 30, 1977, Reverend Ndjoba was also installed as senior headman of the Kwanyama people. Meanwhile, he had also made it to the top of the Executive Council. In 1975 Chief Minister Philemon Elfias (q.v.) was assassinated. Ndjoba was elected to replace him as head of the government of the Owambo homeland. In this capacity he had the bitter opposition of both SWAPO and the modernizing elites of the area, who saw him as a puppet of South Africa. He in turn had been strongly critical of SWAPO for years, denouncing their violence and radicalism. He contended that his approach was a better way to get an independent Owambo. He called SWAPO a communist organization that only wanted to kill.

In 1974 Ndjoba and others active in the Owambo government founded the National Democratic Party (q.v.), which had been preceded by a minimally successful Owambo Independence Party. Ndjoba was elected president of the NDP and it won all the seats in the 1974 Owambo Legislative Council elections. The next year the Turnhalle Conference (q.v.) began, and Ndjoba was a key participant. When the Democratic Turnhalle Alliance was founded in 1977, Ndjoba brought the NDP into that alliance and was named vice-president. When the DTA President, Chief Clemens Kapuuo, was assassinated in 1978, Ndjoba succeeded him as DTA president, a largely ceremonial office.

In 1980 Ndjoba was replaced as chairman of the Owambo Executive Council and as president of the DTA by Peter Kalangula (q.v.). In early 1981 he also lost the presidency of NDP to Kalangula. He reputedly remained a supporter of the DTA and was a headman at Elenja until his death in 1983. He was killed when he stopped on a land-mine, planted by SWAPO supporters, it has been suggested.

NDONGA (variant: ONDONGA). One of the largest of the Wambo subgroups, the Ndonga had been larger than the Kwanyama (q.v.), but have been surpassed by them in the last fifty years or so. (However, older censuses were notoriously inaccurate.) A figure in the early 1970s gave the Ndonga about 28 percent of all Wambos, or two out of seven. The Ndonga are located furthest to the east of the other Wambo and subgroups and are southeast of the Kwanyama. The Ndonga are among those who have maintained a traditional chieftainship, with succession following a matrilineal pattern. One of their strongest leaders in the nineteenth century was Shikongo. The chief today rules over fifty-one wards, each of which has a headman. The chief is aided by nine senior headmen. Controversy swirled around the chieftainship in the 1960s and 1970s, as South Africa began to play an increasing role in chieftainship matters. Thus the legitimacy of Chiefs Paulus Elfias and Philemon Elfias (qq.v.) was seriously questioned, by many Ndongas. It is not surprising, therefore, that the latter was assassinated in 1975.

NEHALE. A Wambo chief. On January 28, 1904, Nehale and a force of five hundred fighters attacked Fort Namutoni. This was the only military encounter between the German Schutztruppe and the Wambos. The leader of an eastern group of Ndonga (q.v.), Chief Nehale instituted a surprise attack. The small group of German defenders used nightfall to mask their escape from the encirclement. (*See also* FORT NAMUTONI.)

NEW ERA. Launched in early July, 1991, this government-owned newspaper began with a print run of 50,000 copies. The weekly publication is funded by the Ministry of Information and Broadcasting. It was acknowledged by Minister Hidipo Hamutenya that it would be in friendly competition with the other newspapers, providing a government-sanctioned view of issues of interest to Namibians.

NGAMI. *See* LAKE NGAMI.

NGANDJERA. One of the subgroups of the Wambo nation. A statistic of the early 1970s indicates a little over 7 percent of all Wambos belong to this group, or about one in fourteen. Historically it is claimed that they are named after their first leader, Hamungandjera, who led them from their first Namibian home near Hakafia (q.v.). They travelled a little west before settling down south of the Mbalantu. The Ngandjera are among those Wambos who maintained the practice of following the autonomous authority of a hereditary chief. Among their more recent chiefs were Shaanika Ipinge, maternal uncle of his successor, Ushona Shiimi (q.v.), who became chief when Ipinge died in 1948. Shiimi died in an automobile accident in 1971, and his successor was Munkundi.

NGAVIRUE, DR. ZEDEKIA. One of the earliest of Namibia's modern political activists, Dr. Ngavirue was a founding member of the South West Africa Student Body (q.v.)— along with F. J. Kozonguizi and M. Kerina (qq.v.)—while they were students at Fort Hare College in 1952. In 1959 he was named chairman of a committee that was working to form a truly national party. It eventually formed the South West Africa National Union (SWANU). In 1961 he left Namibia to work at the UN on behalf of SWANU.

Ngavirue then continued his education. He graduated in economics, sociology, and political science at the Universities of Stockholm and Uppsala in Sweden. He then went on to Oxford University, where he gained a Ph.D. in 1973. His thesis was entitled: *Political Parties and Interest Groups in S.W.A.—A Study of a Plural Society.* While remaining a member of SWANU's external council, he accepted an academic position as senior lecturer at the University of Papua, New Guinea. In July 1978 he returned to Namibia for six months so he could update his thesis.

Dr. Ngavirue has settled again in Namibia, accepting the position of chairman of Rössing Uranium Ltd., which was attempting to establish that it would be prepared to work with a Black Government of Namibia. At independence he was named chairman of the country's National Planning Commission. His title was later changed to Director General of the Commission.

NIEHAUS, JAQUES PERCY (c. 1910–   ). One of the most conservative of Namibia's white politicians, he was the leader of the United National South West Party (q.v.) for almost twenty years. However in 1974 he was ousted from its leadership when a younger and more liberal party group selected Brian O'Linn (q.v.) to succeed him. Advocate Niehaus reemerged later, however, after O'Linn had changed the party's name to the Federal Party (q.v.). Some of Niehaus's supporters joined him in reorganizing themselves as the South West Africa Action Group. As the December 1978 Assembly elections approached, this group joined with members of the National Party and others in an ad hoc

alliance referred to as AKTUR (q.v.). Niehaus won one of
AKTUR's seats in the Assembly that opened in 1979.

NISBETT'S BATH (variant: NISBET). An early name for the
town now known as Warmbad (q.v.). An early mission
station there had been closed by the LMS in 1811. In 1835
the Wesleyan Mission Society was able to reopen it, due to
funds provided by Josiah Nisbett, an official of the East India
Civil Service at Madras. The warm springs there are the
reason for the second half of the name.

NORTHERN LABOUR RECRUITING ORGANIZATION
(NLO). *See* LABOR, AFRICAN.

NORTHERN RAILWAY. Also known as the State Railway, it
was built between 1897 and 1902, primarily to connect the
port of Swakopmund with the capital, Windhoek. Its length
was 238 miles in total, with Karibib (121 miles from
Swakopmund) as the virtual halfway point. It originally had
a gauge of two feet, but it was soon obvious that the Cape
gauge of three-and-a-half feet, which was used on the
railways south from Windhoek, would be a much better
width. Thus in 1911 it was broadened from Karibib to
Windhoek at a cost of £550,000. The rest of the route, to the
port, was soon abandoned, as the Otavi Railway (q.v.) made
it unnecessary.

NORTH-SOUTH RAILWAY. Begun in March 1910, this railway
linked Windhoek to Keetmanshoop, a distance of 317 miles.
Work began from each end toward the middle and was
contracted separately. The three-and-a-half-foot Cape gauge
was used, meaning it was compatible with South Africa's
railways. Not only was the link between two commercial
centers justifiable on economic grounds, but the German
government knew it would be useful in moving troops and
supplies if another Nama uprising occurred in southern
Namibia. Also, it would provide a link between the Northern
Railway and the Southern Railway (qq.v.). The track was
single when first built, except at stations, and one tunnel was

built, a fifty-yard segment through the Aus Mountains, ten miles south of Windhoek.

NOSSOB RIVER (variant: NOSOB). While an intermittent river, it is the longest one in the country's southeast quadrant. Its major sources, the White Nossob and Black Nossob (qq.v.) begin in the mountains north and east of Windhoek and flow to the southeast where they merge at Aais. A little below their confluence the Nossob River Valley is two miles wide and has steep sides. In normal rainy seasons the river can flow heavily and give enough water for numerous farms to use for irrigation. At Aranos the river shifts to a much more southeasterly course. It eventually cuts into Botswana, at the north edge of the Kalahari Gemsbok Park.

NUJOMA, SHAFILSHONA SAMUEL ("SAM") (1929–). The first president of independent Namibia, Nujoma was also among the early nationalist political organizers in his country. Born May 12, 1929, he was the first-born of eight children of a farmer and his wife, Daniel Utoma Nujoma and Helvi Mpingena Kondombola. His birthplace apparently was Ongandjera, a town in northwestern Namibia, about seventy kilometers southwest of Oshakati and about the same distance by road from the Angolan border. (A usually accurate source gives his birthplace as Okahao.) As a youth he assisted his father with the cattle and received some education at the Finnish Mission Primary School. However this was interrupted when he was sent to live with an aunt at Walvis Bay in 1943. Six years later he moved in with an uncle in Windhoek's Old Location. Here he attended night classes at St. Barnabas Anglican Mission and studied English for the first time. In 1955 he was given his first paying job, working for South African Railways. He was employed in several capacities in his two years on that job. The important aspect of this, however, was that he periodically got to Cape Town, where he became friends with Herman Andimba Toivo Ya-Toivo (q.v.) and several other political activists who were organizing the Ovamboland People's Congress (q.v.). He was also a labor union organizer, which got him fired from the railway in 1957. He then worked for several months in Windhoek's municipal offices as a clerk. In August 1957 he began a two-year job as a clerk in a Windhoek wholesale store. He spent much of his spare time following liberation struggles in Ghana, Zambia, and Tanzania.

Inspired by Ya-Toivo, in 1959 Nujoma and Jacob Kuhangua (q.v.) began the Windhoek branch of the Ovamboland People's Organization. He became president of the OPO later that same year. He also joined the first national political group, SWANU, after it was formed in May 1959. Four months later he and others from the OPO were added to SWANU's Executive Committee. About the same time there was considerable anger among Windhoek's Blacks about being forced to move from the "Old Location" in the city to a more distant new town, Katutura (q.v.). Many of the newly active politicians, including Nujoma, led the protests. Violence broke out on December 10, 1959. Nujoma was among those arrested on December 12, but he was released a week later.

OPO leaders decided that some of them must escape the country and get to the UN in New York to plead the case for Namibia. Nujoma was among them, and he left Windhoek on February 29, 1960. Assisted by many people he made his way into Botswana, then Zimbabwe, Zambia, and Tanzania. Julius Nyerere (later the first president of Tanzania) got him a passport (until that point all travel was based on subterfuge). This allowed him into Sudan, then to Liberia, Ghana, and (with the aid of Kwame Nkrumah) to New York. He appeared before the UN with SWANU's leader, F. J. Kozonguizi (q.v.) in June 1960. While he was en route, on April 19, 1960, the OPO was renamed SWAPO, and Nujoma was named its president.

Nujoma stayed in New York until December, and then began his return to Tanzania (still Tanganyika at the time), and in March 1961 he established SWAPO's provisional headquarters in Dar es Salaam. He spent the next five years organizing the Namibians who had joined him in exile and lobbying world capitals for support for SWAPO. He achieved a major victory in 1964 when the Organization of African Unity instructed its Liberation Committee to recognize SWAPO as the appropriate recipient of its aid. On March 20, 1966, Nujoma and his colleague Lucas Pohamba (q.v.) defied the ruling by the International Court of Justice and flew into Windhoek. However they were arrested when they arrived and deported the next day.

SWAPO then committed itself to an armed struggle against South African administration of the territory. Obtaining some weapons from Algeria, Nujoma had his followers begin the attacks in Owambo and Kavango, where they had the most support. He procured further aid from Egypt, Tanzania, and Algeria, among others. He says the armed struggle really began in August 1966. There was a reorganization of his guerrillas in February 1968. He also travelled frequently to friendly countries, establishing diplomatic missions in Sweden, Finland, and Britain, plus his African allies. Meanwhile he restructured SWAPO, creating a number of supportive offices, at the Tanga Consultative Congress in Tanzania, December 26, 1969 to January 2, 1970. It was the most widely representative of all SWAPO meetings up until then, and it reelected Nujoma as president. He also reorganized the People's Liberation Army of Namibia (PLAN) in 1973. At a meeting near Lusaka, Zambia, in July 1976, there was a further reorganization of SWAPO.

Meanwhile his world travels continued. In 1968 he accepted the Lenin Peace Prize. In 1971 he gave evidence before the UN Security Council. He attended the Namibia Conference in Brussels, Belgium, in 1972, and the OAU Summit Conference in Morocco the same year. In 1973 he attended the Non-Aligned Conference in Algeria. Few African countries were not visited by him in the next decade, as he lobbied for aid and support. Part of his purpose was to counter the effect of the Turnhalle Constitutional Conference (1975–77). He also visited Cuba in 1976. In 1978 he received the November Medal Prize. The next year he gained for SWAPO recognition at the UN as the sole representative of the Namibian people. Also in 1979 SWAPO was granted official member status of the Non-Aligned Movement.

The 1980s were devoted both to supervision of the guerrilla movement, based in Angola, and frequent international negotiations on a solution to the Namibian question.

The negotiations involved the Western Five, the Front Line States, the UN, and eventually South Africa itself. A major but nonproductive conference met in Geneva in January 1981. Talks held in Lusaka, Zambia, in 1984 were more successful in finding grounds for agreement among some of Namibia's many factions.

One of the more significant developments in the final years of negotiations was the apparent softening of Nujoma's leftist rhetoric. During the 1960s and 1970s, when most of his military and economic support came from either Eastern Bloc nations or the more radical African states, Nujoma's speeches were filled with typical Marxist language and concepts. Nevertheless he had reassured Chester Crocker, the American diplomat, in 1982 that Namibia under his rule would adopt a policy of "true non-alignment" between East and West. Whites were welcome to stay, no foreign bases would be allowed in Namibia, and his country would cooperate with the West, especially in economic matters. SWAPO did continue, however, in its policy of calling for the nationalization of all natural resources, thus threatening foreign mining companies.

As negotiations wound down, however, and independence seemed feasible, Nujoma's speeches were much more conciliatory, especially toward the major mining companies. He also appeased the white agricultural and business interests. Six of the SWAPO seats in the new Assembly at independence are held by whites, and a half-dozen major cabinet and non-cabinet posts went to whites.

Nujoma returned in triumph to Namibia on September 14, 1989, less than two months before the Assembly elections. Confident of success, he agreed to release hundreds of prisoners held by SWAPO (although his detractors say that there are hundreds more who are unaccounted for). He was number one on the SWAPO electoral list. After a SWAPO majority was elected and a constitution was written, the Constituent Assembly became a National Assembly. On February 16, 1990, the NA elected him as head-of-state-designate. He then relinquished his Assembly seat to another SWAPO member. During the next month he finalized his cabinet choices. With the coming of independence on March

21, 1990, he was sworn in as president by the UN Secretary General, Javier Perez de Cuellar.

Nujoma is married to Kovambo Theoplidine Katjimuina. He has three sons and a daughter.

/NU-SAN. A subgroup of the San, they live in the southern Kalahari. They have especially been found in the sections of the Gobabis, Gibeon, and Aroab districts to the east of the Elephant (Olifants) and Auob Rivers. Their northern limit is generally about the Tropic of Capricorn.

- O -

OASIB (variant: //OASEB) (c. 1820–1867). A major nineteenth-century Nama chief, he was the most prominent of the leaders of the //Khauben or Red Nation (q.v.). His father died in 1830, when he was too young to serve as chief, so for ten years his sister, Games (q.v.), served as the tribe's leader. He was a very militant young man, always eager to raid the Hereros. At one point in 1844 he tried to get Jonker Afrikander (q.v.) to join him in attacks, but the latter refused. Oasib then went on his own. One notable attack was on the Herero nobleman, Kahitjene (q.v.). The arrogant young Oasib was also furious with all the Orlam chiefs, because they refused to join him in attacking Hereros. In about 1846 or 1847 he attacked the Mbanderus in the east, and brought home great spoils. Later one of his bands attacked an outpost of the noted Herero chief, Tjamuaha. Eventually, in late 1849 Jonker decided it was better to sign an alliance with Oasib; he then took advantage of Oasib, who began seeking allies against Jonker. Failing in this, he resumed raiding Hereros, but he was thwarted by another Nama leader, Willem Swartbooi.

Sir Francis Galton (q.v.) tried to set up a peace treaty with all the groups in 1851. Oasib was one of the major chiefs he negotiated with, but Oasib essentially disregarded the peace treaty that others had signed. He did, however, allow a missionary named Vollmar to work among his people at Hoachanas. The Nama leader sometimes used Vollmar to translate in negotiations, such as with Europeans who wanted mining concessions in his area. Vollmar also persuaded Oasib to agree to a peace signed at Kupferberg (q.v.) in 1855. Other chiefs involved were Willem Swartbooi and Jonker Afrikander. Three years later, on January 9, 1858, an even broader peace was signed at Hoachanas (q.v.). It was designed to bring peace between all Namas, but also to safeguard Herero cattle from attack by the Namas. Oasib joined the others in agreeing to this, and indeed gave evidence of settling down peacefully.

In the 1860s there were several opportunities to go to war, but Oasib seemed to be affected by the reasoning and guidance of Rev. Vollmar and usually avoided conflict. However, he inadvertently ran into trouble when he granted Kido Witbooi the right to settle at Gibeon. When Witbooi refused his request to supply warriors to help Christian Afrikander against the Hereros, Oasib mounted a large force to punish Witbooi. He allied with Hendrik Zes, of the Feldschuhträgers, and Amiab, a leader of the Groot-doden. On December 3, 1864, they attacked Gibeon and plundered it. Kido tried to negotiate, but Oasib said, "Whoever wants to live in my country must be my servant." Since no peace was established, Oasib attacked Gibeon again in July 1865, but in the process he also had his own richest werf raided and looted. Tiring of war, Oasib proposed peace to Kido Witbooi, but was refused. On September 25, 1866, Oasib again attacked Gibeon and brutalized its inhabitants. (Kido and most of the warriors were away at the time.) He left with many wagons filled with spoils. Witbooi pursued him for several months to gain retribution, and finally did so in a bloody battle several months into 1867. Oasib returned to Hoachanas. He heard there that Rev. Vollmar had recently died and said, "That is a very bad sign for us." He soon fell ill himself, and died in mid-1867.

ODENDAAL COMMISSION, REPORT OF. The basis of South Africa's "Homelands Policy" (q.v.) in Namibia, this 550-page document was published in early 1964. Its beginning was in September 1962, when the South African government appointed a Commission of Inquiry into South West Africa.

Its chairman was Frans Hendrik Odendaal, the administrator of the Transvaal at that time. The other four members were Drs. H. J. van Eck and P. J. Quin, and Professors H. W. Snyman and J. P. van S. Bruwer. The committee was told to look into ways of "promoting the material and moral welfare and the social welfare and social progress of the inhabitants" and to submit a report suggesting a plan of implementation "for the accelerated development of the various non-white groups of South West Africa," based on the development of Native territories.

The commission worked for over a year. With South Africa's 1951–55 Tomlinson Commission (the basis for the Bantustans) as an example, the Odendaal Plan recommended that 40 percent of the land should be placed in Reserves for 89 percent of the population. Another 43 percent was set aside for exclusively white use. Ten homelands were designated in the report: Owambo, Damaraland, Hereroland, Namaland, Kavango, East Caprivi, Kaokoland, Bushmanland, Tswanaland, and the Rehoboth Gebiet. In the years following the report, implementation slowly began, with Representative Authorities and Legislative Councils established on an ethnic basis, following the principle of divide and rule.

//O-GEIN (variant: OGEIS). The original Nama name for those people also called the Groot-doden (q.v.).

OHOPOHO (variant: OPUWO). A small village in northwestern Namibia, it was designated by South Africa to be the administrative center for the Kaokoland area. One map indicated that it is the intersecting point of five "tracks," which are a standard below the worst roads. Evidently some of them have been improved to allow administrators better access.

OKAHANDJA. One of the oldest towns in Namibia, it was the dwelling place of major Herero chiefs, such as Tjamuaha, Maherero, and Samuel Maharero. Its central location (71 km north of Windhoek) and its location on both the north-south highway and the rail line has attracted both settlers and businesses. For example a R4 million factory to produce power and telecommunication cables was added to its fast growing industrial area in 1992. It was estimated in 1991 that it had a population of 12,000, ranking it tenth in the country.

Okahandja's name relates to its placement on the Okahandja River, a tributary of the Swakop River. While not a major river, as it passes the town it is much wider than the Swakop. Thus its Herero name means "the small wide one." The river flows only in times of good rainfall.

The first European interest in the area was a visit by Heinrich Schmelen (q.v.) of the RMS in 1827. The RMS did not set up a mission station there, as they had established one in 1844 only twenty-six kilometers to the southwest at Barmen. Rev. C. H. Hahn (q.v.) was there for many years. The RMS finally established a house there in 1872, and a church in 1876. Meanwhile the town experienced numerous conflicts (see OKAHANDJA, BATTLES OF), as Jonker Afrikander's Namas regularly raided the area and tried to dominate it militarily. A number of noted Herero chiefs are buried at the site of the old Herero Chief's kraal in Okahandja, and on Maherero Day each August thousands of Hereros come to pay their respects to the memories of the great chiefs.

Whites began to settle in the area in 1884, when a German garrison was stationed at Okahandja. German pioneers established farms nearby (the pasture land there is very rich) and businesses in the town itself. As a result, when the Hereros rose up against the Germans in 1904, Okahandja was the flash-point. The events began on the morning of January 12, and the resultant siege of the German fort (where as many German residents went as could get there) lasted until the intervention of Captain Victor Franke (q.v.) on January 28.

The German government established experimental tobacco farms in Okahandja around 1910, with the emphasis on pipe-tobacco. World War I interrupted their endeavors, as the South Africans came through on their way to victory over the Germans in 1915. The Germans also established an excellent school for Africans, the Augustineum (q.v.). It was open sporadically (1890–1901, 1911–14, 1923–68). In 1968 it was moved to Windhoek. Okahandja is a lovely community, and has been called the "garden town" of Namibia, as public and private gardens abound. A large nursery ships plants throughout the country.

OKAHANDJA, BATTLES OF. As a favorite spot of Herero leaders, the Okahandja area has always attracted a large population. Likewise a number of battles have occurred at or near Okahandja (q.v.). One notable such battle took place in August 1850, and the victims were the followers of Chief Kahitjene (q.v.). The battle at Omukaru (q.v.) in 1868 was just across from Okahandja.

For most people, however, the most memorable recent battle occurred in January 1904. At that time there were 159 whites living there and more than a thousand Hereros either in or near the town. On the night of January 10–11 a large force of Hereros rode through town and camped a few miles outside. The German district leader was alarmed and wired Windhoek for aid. Twenty soldiers under Bergrat Duft came from Windhoek and quickly reached the German fortress. The whites of Okahandja feared an attack. On the morning of January 12, mounted Hereros raided and looted the town, burned a few buildings, and killed a few German citizens who had not gone to the fort. The Hereros held the town until January 28. They also destroyed the railroad bridge and cut all telegraph wires, although Duft did get one message to Swakopmund before they were cut. The fortress was completely cut off from help from January 12 to 15. One relief column arrived on January 15 from Swakopmund. It consisted of a hundred men led by Lieutenant Zülow. While they reached the fort, ambushes along the railway cost German casualties in later days. The siege was finally ended on January 28, 1904, when the Second Company, led by Capt. Victor Franke (q.v.) were successful in driving off the Herero warriors near Okahandja. Fifteen Germans had died.

OKAHANDJA NATIONAL UNITY CONFERENCE (variant: OKAHANDJA SUMMIT). Convened in late 1975 by political groups opposed to the Turnhalle Conference then going on, it was a sequel to a similar conference held in Okahandja in December 1975 under the leadership of Rev. Zephania

Kameeta (q.v.). The 1975 conference called on South Africa to stop carrying out its "dangerous Bantustan schemes" in Namibia. It also proposed a constitution for a "truly non-racial democratic independent government." It demanded independence for Namibia under UN supervision, called for the return of political exiles, and recommended that SWAPO and SWANU unite against South Africa. The ten groups at the conference represented mainly Damara and Nama groups and factions, along with some Herero groups. Among the most prominent were the Damara Council (whose leader, Justus Garoëb, became the meeting's vice-chairman and leading figure), the Damara Tribal Executive, and the Voice of the People (whose leader, K. H. Conradie, became its secretary-general). Garoëb and several other conference participants then traveled to Dakar, Senegal, in January 1976, to attend a conference on human rights in Namibia. The conference groups also formed a coalition called the Namibia National Council, which lasted longer under a different name, the Namibia National Front (q.v.).

OKAHARUI. A site about fifty kilometers northeast of Oka-handja, it was the scene of a significant Herero victory over German troops, April 3, 1904. Major Glasenapp was leading a couple of marine companies, a company of colonial troops, artillery, and supply wagons, totalling 230 men. The line was two-and-a-half kilometers long. Everyone was exhausted because of a month of constant travel. Hereros attacked the main body from three sides, and cut part of the rear guard off from the rest. Most of the German losses resulted from Herero gunfire from a cover of heavy bush. Eventually Glasenapp was able to counterattack the Hereros, who fled after a three-hour battle. Thirty-three Germans were killed and seventeen others seriously wounded. Precise Herero losses are not known.

OKATANA. The old name for what is now called Oshakati (q.v.), it had been a mere hamlet with a few mud-and-daub thatched huts and some kraals and stockades for livestock in extreme north-central Namibia (about fifty kilometers south of the Angola border). Then things changed, as it became the terminus of a very expensive canal system stretching south from the Kunene River. A 475-bed hospital was opened in 1966, following shortly after the movement of the headquarters of the commissioner general for the northern territories from Ondangwa. With a whole new settlement taking form it was decided that a new name was needed. Oshakati means "the center."

OKAVANGO RIVER. Unlike most of the other rivers of Namibia, the Okavango is constantly flowing. It is also extremely wide. It rises in Angola and flows southeast to almost the 18 degree latitude, where it turns due east for 250 kilometers. It then turns southeast again, cutting through the Western Caprivi Strip and into Botswana. There it eventually creates an immense inland delta. Its total length is about 1100 kilometers. (A spectacular picture book about the river is called *Okavango,* by Peter Johnson and Anthony Bannister.) In Angola it is called the Cubango River. Before it turns due east it becomes the Angolan/Namibian border, and continues as such for about 355 kilometers (200 miles). Since its runoff is lost in the Okavango Swamp of northern Botswana, judicious use of irrigation could be very useful for parts of northeastern Namibia.

Along its course a number of omurambas (q.v.) empty into it in the rainy season. The largest of these is the Omuramba Omatako (q.v.). The explorer, C. J. Andersson (q.v.), reached the Okavango by following the dry watercourse of the Omuramba Omatako. He later wrote a book called *The Okavango.*

OKURUUO. The center of an oruzo community or werf (q.v.) among the Hereros, it is the sacred fireplace where the holy fire burns. (*See* FIRE, SACRED.)

OLD LOCATION. *See* WINDHOEK "OLD LOCATION."

OLIFANTS RIVER. *See* ELEPHANT RIVER.

O'LINN, BRYAN (1927–). One of the most respected white politicians in Namibia, he was appointed a permanent judge of the Namibian Supreme Court on November 30, 1989, his sixty-second birthday. O'Linn was born in Brandfort, South Africa, but his family moved to Namibia when he was only a year old. He served with the South African Police from 1946 to 1952, in lieu of military service, and also earned two degrees by correspondence from the University of South Africa. In 1960 he received an LLB from the University of Natal. Meanwhile he also made a name for himself in sports. In 1956 he was the country's wrestling champion, attended the Olympic trials in Johannesburg, and was narrowly beaten by M. Kenny of the Transvaal, thus missing a spot on South Africa's 1956 Olympic team.

He was already active in politics, being a member of the United National South West Party from 1955 to 1970. When it merged with South Africa's United Party in 1970 he was opposed to that move, but returned to join it in 1973 and 1974, when he lost in the general election while running for the Windhoek West seat in the Legislative Assembly. In 1975 he led a faction that broke from the United Party to form the Federal Party (q.v.). He was its leader until he retired from party politics in 1983. His retirement was due in part to the virtual disintegration of the party after he transformed it into a multiracial party in 1977. At that same time he helped form the Namibia National Front (NNF) (q.v.) and served as its secretary-general.

He has had a very diverse career. As an advocate he frequently defended in the courts Africans who were charged with violating Namibia's apartheid-like laws in the 1960s and 1970s. This helped him win the respect of the African nationalists, and probably played a role in his elevation to the Supreme Court in 1989. He is also a writer. He wrote a book on Namibia in Afrikaans in 1974, on the future of South West Africa. (Despite his Irish surname he is from an Afrikaner family.) In 1985 he also wrote *The Priority for Namibia Today: An Honourable Peace.* In 1982 he was interviewed by the American diplomat, Henry Kissinger, who was attempting to study American policy in the region and possible future directions for it. O'Linn let it be known clearly in the 1980s that he would not be involved in any elections that were not directly tied to UN Resolution 435 and internationally supervised. To that purpose he founded a study and contact group in Windhoek in November 1986 called Namibia Peace Plan 435. He was its first chairman, but resigned in 1989 when he was appointed chairman of the Commission for the Prevention and Combatting of Intimidation and Election Malpractices, usually called the O'Linn Commission. It was given quasi-judicial status and the power to investigate any election practices that seemed illicit or unethical during the November 1989 Assembly elections. When the commission's task was complete, he was appointed a permanent judge on Namibia's Supreme Court.

OMAHEKE. The waterless parts of the Kalahari Desert, also called the Sandveld. It is the eastern part of the desert, where it has been described as having "lifeless, shifting sands." While the term's use is timeless, it occurs most in the literature on Namibia in conjunction with the German-Herero war of 1904. After the important battle at the Waterberg (q.v.), thousands of Herero men, women and children, plus their cattle, attempted to escape the pursuing Germans by the only available route: into the Omaheke, with hope of reaching Lake Ngami in Botswana. Only a little over a thousand of them made it. Tens of thousands of Hereros reportedly perished in the Omaheke in August and September 1904. The Germans did not follow them into the Omaheke.

OMARURU. Traditionally an important Herero town, largely because of an abundance of water and good pasturage, Omaruru attracted German settlers at the turn of the twentieth century for the same reasons. Its name comes from Herero words that mean bitter, sour milk. Hereros discovered that their cows gave that kind of milk if they ate certain bushes nearby. Omaruru is located only about seventy kilometers north of Karibib and the line of rail between Windhoek and Swakopmund. As a district capital of the Omaruru district, it has a number of businesses and schools. It has excellent water service from an underground supply in the Omaruru River.

The first recorded settlers at Omaruru were Hereros under

Chief Tjiseseta, who moved his followers there in the mid-nineteenth century. In 1870 the RMS set up a mission station there with Rev. F. W. Viehe. Traders soon followed, including Axel Eriksson, and Commissioner W. C. Palgrave (q.v.) visited in 1876. As German settlers moved in, a garrison of German troops were stationed there from 1889 on. But the area was shared with the Hereros, who lived under a prominent chief. When the Herero uprising against the Germans began in January 1904, the German barracks were under siege by the Hereros from January 15 to February 2. On that date Major Victor Franke (q.v.) came to its rescue, as he did earlier to Okahandja. The Franke-Turm monument there commemorates that day. Eleven years later South African troops led by General Botha beat the Germans there in one of the last battles of the southern African theatre of World War I. The South Africans, marching north, defeated the Germans at Omaruru on June 17, 1915.

OMARURU RIVER. While one of Namibia's intermittent streams, subject to rainfall, it does reach the sea every year. It also has an enormous amount of ground water, which can be obtained at all times by digging two or three feet into the river bed. The river rises in the Etjo Mountains in north-central Namibia, southeast of Kalkfeld. The river flows southwest to the town of Omaruru, then west for about sixty kilometers before again heading southwest to meet the ocean at Henties Bay (q.v.), north of Swakopmund. The river's importance includes its springs, its abundance of ground water, and its rich alluvial deposits. Water flows above ground at places like Okombahe and Kawab, where there are springs. The riverbed varies in width from 80 to 350 yards. Its banks are heavy with trees and bushes. At the town of Omaruru the riverbed is very fertile and has produced as many as two maize crops in a season.

OMATAKO RIVER. *See* OMURAMBA OMATAKO.

OMUKWETU. Established in 1941 by the Finnish missionaries, this religious magazine has been published in the language of the Wambos. In the 1970s it was published every two weeks, with an edition of 10,000 copies. It grew to have considerable influence in Owambo, and its persistent reporting angered South African administrators. The religious leadership was using *Omukwetu*'s columns for commenting on social, economic and political matters. Twice the church printing press at Oniipa (q.v.) was bombed in an effort to stop its work, but both times the printing was soon continued. The first bombing took place May 11, 1973, with South Africa the presumed culprit. A similar bombing occurred in November 1980, and again there were highly suspicious South African activities prior to the bombing. Both times South African leaders denied any responsibility for the bombings. In each case publication continued, although in 1973 it was printed on a simple duplicating machine for many months.

OMUNDONGO. The founder and first paramount chief of the Ndonga people (q.v.), he governed his people at the original site in Owambo. Some regard his people as the mother-group of all the Wambo chieftainships.

OMUNGANDJERA. Referred to in a Wambo legend as one of their three ancestors (with Kantene and Amangundu). He is considered the father of the Ngandjera (q.v.), whose earliest known leader was Hamungandjera (q.v.).

OMURAMBA. Refers to any wide, shallow, normally dry water course, which will normally contain water only after heavy local storms. Even after storms they might flow for only a few kilometers. The largest omuramba is called the Omuramba Omatako (q.v.). (For a similar water course, *see* OSHANA.)

OMURAMBA OMATAKO. An intermittent stream that only flows with enough rainfall, it rises in the northeast of the Central Highlands and flows for four hundred miles in a northeasterly direction into the Okavango River (q.v.). To be more specific, however, it has two sources. One begins on the west side of the Waterberg, dips south around it and them flows northeast. The other branch begins about thirty kilometers east of Kalkfeld and also dips south before heading northeast. The latter has the more regular flow. The two merge about forty kilometers east of the northern edge of the Waterberg Plateau Park. The Omuramba Omatako has its confluence with the Okavango about 140 kilometers below Rundu, although the last 100 kilometers or so is blocked in part by sand. While many parts of the intercourse are dry, pools of water can be found regularly just beneath the surface. People as different as Rev. C. H. Hahn and German soldiers fighting the Herero in 1904 found life-saving water beneath the dry riverbed. The explorer C. J. Andersson used the watercourse as a guide for traveling east, knowing it would keep him out of Owambo. Its banks are lined with thick growth of thorn bush, making it easy to follow. The Omuramba Omatako is also sometimes called the Chuob River.

ONDANGWA (variant: ONDANGUA). One of the larger towns in Owambo, it had an estimated population of 1500 in 1988. It is located thirty-five kilometers southeast of Oshakati and about sixty kilometers due south of the Angolan border. If one excepts the Caprivi Strip, Ondangwa is about in the center of Namibia from east to west. Prior to the Odendaal Plan, which resulted in Oshakati becoming the capital of Owambo, Ondangwa was more important. A Native commissioner lived there as an official advisor to the Wambo Councils of Headmen. A recruiting officer for the SWA Native Laborers Association (q.v.) was stationed there. Medical examinations of the recruits was easy, as a government regional medical officer of health was posted there. Other officials stationed at Ondangwa then were the organizer of Native education, a district surgeon, a postmaster, and a rodent inspector.

Finnish missionaries had been the first Europeans to settle at or near Ondangwa. They arrived in 1870, guided by the hunter Frederick Green (q.v.), and Ondangwa became the center of their religious activities. A century later it had been made a fortified town by the South African military, with extremely limited access. Security fences surrounded it, as it was a major base of the South African Defence Force, which also had built there one of the two major military airports in northern Namibia.

ONDEKAREMBA. Twenty-six miles east of Windhoek on the road to Gobabis, it is the site of Namibia's major international airport, known at least until independence as the J. G. Strydom Airport. In addition the rail line between Windhoek and Gobabis also goes through the community. The Windhoek-Ondekaremba branch was opened officially in a ceremony on May 15, 1924.

ONDONGA. The land of the Ndonga (q.v.). It is also a common variant of Ndonga.

ONGANDJIRA MOUNTAIN, BATTLE OF. The mountain, a very prominent peak east of Okahandja, rises quickly from the floor of the Otjisasu Valley. During the German-Herero War of 1904, Major Leutwein led a force of almost a thousand from Okahandja to track down and fight the Hereros in early April 1904. The battle occurred on either April 8 or 9 (sources differ), when the German force neared Mount Ongandjira and came under heavy fire. The Germans dismounted quickly and spread out but the Hereros, under Samuel Maharero, were already attacking the left flank en masse, hoping to overwhelm it and move along the line. German machine guns and artillery arrived to foil them, however. Courageous Herero warriors charged right at the German guns twice as their women cheered them on. But the machine guns won out and the Hereros left the scene. Germans estimated a hundred Hereros were killed, while fourteen Germans died and twelve were wounded.

ONGULUMBASHE (variant: OMGULUMBASHE). The site of the first battle of Namibia's twenty-two-year guerrilla war, it was in extreme northwestern Owambo. Events began there in 1965 when a group of six guerrilla-trained SWAPO men established a base. They were soon joined by other small groups of fighters. The idea was to establish a Vietnam-style guerrilla force in the rural countryside. About fifty men were based there, but South African authorities found out about the camp and launched an attack on August 26, 1966, the first armed encounter between SWAPO and South African forces. The latter claimed that they had destroyed the guerrillas during the battle, but a reliable SWAPO leader says that only two SWAPO fighters were killed. The rest either retreated or were captured.

ONGWEDIVA (variant: ONGUEDIVA). Under the Homeland system, a new capital was planted at Ongwediva, near Oshakati. The site of the Owambo Legislative Assembly, it also became a major educational center. In the 1970s the Ongwediva High School was one of only two such institutions in Owambo that went to the matriculation standard. The earliest institution there was a Finnish technical school that once educated H. A. Toivo Ya Toivo. In addition it now has the Ongwediva Teachers' Training and Technical College. Classes were suspended at the high school in the early 1970s when hundreds of students demonstrated publicly to protest the idea that Namibia should remain under South African control.

ONIIPA. For many years the headquarters of ELOC, the Evangelical Lutheran Ovambokavango Church (now the Evangelical Lutheran Church in Namibia), it began as a mission station of the Finnish Mission Society (q.v.). The FMS founded its first teachers' training college at Oniipa in 1913, and its graduates served many Owambo schools in succeeding decades. ELOC established a publishing business there. An explosion (of which South African authorities were generally accused) at 3 AM on May 11, 1973, destroyed not only the two large printing presses that produced the controversial newspaper, *Omukwetu* (q.v.), but also 2000 Bibles and additional church and school books. The publication facilities were rebuilt and reopened in 1975, but five years later another explosion of equally suspicious origin took place there. Oniipa is just to the east of Ondangwa (q.v.) in extreme north-central Namibia.

OPERATION PROTEA. The largest single South African military operation since World War II took place in August and September 1981, when South African tanks and armored vehicles preceded three columns of about 11,000 South African troops into southern Angola, ostensibly to destroy

SWAPO guerrilla bases in northern Namibia. The attack was accompanied by aerial bombing, massed tank assaults, and artillery barrages. The Angolan towns of Xangongo, N'giva, Cahoma, and Chibemba were destroyed, causing about 1000 Angolan and Namibian deaths, mostly civilian. An area two hundred miles wide and one hundred deep was devastated by the fighting.

South Africa at first denied that any major military operation was underway, but later announced the capture of 38 prisoners and 4000 tons of war material, including tanks, rocket launchers, and other types of equipment. It also claimed to have killed several Soviet military advisors and some civilians in N'giva; a Russian sergeant-major was taken prisoner. When the UN Security Council tried to pass a resolution condemning the invasion, the USA vetoed it.

South Africa's invasion, by its own admission, did not fulfill its objectives. SWAPO's command and logistics networks were seriously disturbed by the invasion, which damaged but did not destroy SWAPO's ability to carry out attacks inside Namibia.

During the operation a smaller South African incursion into Angola took place 100 kilometers further east, in an effort to resupply the UNITA (q.v.) forces of Jonas Savimbi, which opposed the government of Angola. It hoped to create a UNITA-controlled buffer zone in southeastern Angola, which would deny SWAPO use of that region as a staging area for raids into Namibia.

While some raids by the South African Defence Force occurred in July, preceding the invasion, the main force entered August 23, 1981. South African Air Force planes bombed up to 150 kilometers inside Angola. SWAPO claimed that 3000 mercenaries from Europe, Israel, and Latin America participated in the invasion. South Africa reported that 41 percent of its invasion force consisted of the newly established SWA Territorial Force. It also claimed to have lost only ten soldiers, one helicopter, and a number of armored vehicles.

In addition to the reported 1000 Angolan and Namibian deaths, 80,000 people were reportedly displaced from their homes. Angola claimed that South Africa's goal was to push

Angola and SWAPO forces out of the area so as to create a buffer zone along most of the border region across southern Angola. It would then have been policed by the UNITA forces.

OPPENHEIMER, SIR ERNEST (1880–1957). Born in Friedberg (Hesse), Germany, he traveled to South Africa in 1902 representing a diamond trading company. He settled at Kimberley, the center of diamond mining. Diamonds were discovered in Namibia six years later, but he was not involved. However he became interested in that area through his involvement in World War I. He organized the labor force that built a railroad from Upington (South Africa) to the Namibia border that made the South African military invasion possible. He also raised and equipped the Kimberley Regiment, which fought against the Germans in the war. He was honored in England by being knighted in 1921.

More important in Namibia's future, however, was his founding of the Anglo American Corporation (q.v.) in South Africa, and the Consolidated Diamond Mines of South West Africa, Ltd. (q.v.). The latter was formed in February 1920, and merged the holdings and activities of ten German diamond mining companies.

Ernest Oppenheimer's only surviving son, Harry Oppenheimer, succeeded him in leading his extensive mining and industrial empire. Ernest died in Johannesburg in 1957.

OPUWO. *See* OHOPOHO.

ORANGE RIVER. One of the major rivers of Africa, the largest river system in South Africa, the Orange River begins in the Drakensberg mountains of Lesotho, and flows westward until it reaches the Atlantic Ocean at Oranjemund (q.v.). Its total length is 1360 kilometers, and for its final twisting and turning 500 or so kilometers it creates the entire southern border of Namibia. In an unusual departure from the norm, the border is the northern bank of the Orange, not the center of the river.

Early sources call the river "Gariep," which is merely the Khoi word for "river." Early European pioneers called it

Grootrivier (the Great River). It received its current name from Robert Jacob Gordon, a Dutch soldier of Scottish background. He commanded a garrison at the Cape in the late eighteenth century, and visited the river in both 1777 and 1779. On the second visit he named it in honor of Prince William V of Orange.

The river is very deep, but generally not navigable because of falls and rapids. Its steep banks hinder its use for irrigation. On the other hand, those same banks make the construction of dams easier. The mouth of the river is often closed by a sandbar, as the flow is too weak to keep a channel open. The width of the mouth is 4 kilometer, and a wave-created sandbar closes it (as it also does the Kunene River) except when flood waters destroy the sand bar. Waves soon re-form the bar, however, leaving a narrow channel opening. Part of the problem is that rainfall is minimal in the last 200 kilometers of the river. At the mouth the annual rainfall is only 50 meters. Evaporation is great in this stretch, as it moves along the Namib Desert. It also has a limited number of active tributaries. The Fish River (q.v.) could be important, but the Hardap Dam on it restricts the flow. The mean annual runoff at the mouth is 12,000,000,000 cubic meters, but this fluctuates widely by seasons. There are two major dams on the Orange, but both the Hendrik Verwoerd Dam and the P. K. le Roux Dam are South Africa's. On the positive side, the Orange River is the only major river in southern Africa that is not infected by the dangerous disease bilharzia, which is caused by a parasite hosted by a small snail. In other rivers this disease can infect people who drink or bathe in the river.

ORANJEMUND. A town at the heart of today's diamond-mining in Namibia, it is located on the north bank of the Orange River, just eight kilometers from its mouth. Diamonds were discovered there in 1928, and it soon became the headquarters of Consolidated Diamond Mines, Ltd. (q.v.), which holds all the mining concessions in that area. It is in an area where people cannot travel unless they have permission from CDM. Security is very tight. It is thus exclusively a mining town, but its facilities and even its parks have been beautifully laid out by CDM or its workers. A road north to Lüderitz is used and controlled by the mining company, and a bridge southward across the Orange River's mouth allows communications with South Africa. It was opened in February 1965. Company farms provide the town with food, and the river's water is processed for drinking. Otherwise the surrounding area is desert. Yet the company has provided every conceivable recreational facility for their workers there.

Many tons of sand must be removed from the diamondiferous gravel in order to uncover the gems. Then mechanical shovels send the gravel to a treatment and recovery plant where the gems are found by screening the gravel. The value of the diamonds mined there has been estimated at $1 million a day. About a million carats of alluvial diamonds are produced there each year. Recent discoveries indicate that diamonds will be found off the coast near Oranjemund, and natural gas fields have also been found in the nearby waters of the South Atlantic.

ORDINANCE NO. 82 (1907). A German ordinance issued by the governor on August 18, 1907, it restricted the rights of indigenous Namibians with the goal of making them dependent on employment by Europeans. Its first clause prohibited natives from acquiring rights over or title to land except with the approval of the governor. The second clause barred all but the Rehoboth Basters from owning cattle or riding animals. Later clauses made the indigenous Namibians liable to penalties as vagrants unless they carried identifying passes. That left them little choice except European employment.

It further provided that without benefit of trial a servant could be accused of wrongful behavior by his master and sentenced to any of several punishments, from corporal punishment to imprisonment in irons.

ORIGINAL PEOPLES PARTY OF NAMIBIA (OPPN). A party based among the San people, it was founded in 1980 by Theophilus Soroseb in opposition to the Boesman Council (q.v.). It belonged to the DTA briefly in 1980–81. Its program calls for a more productive and developed San community, with improved social, economic, and educational conditions. In 1989 it joined the United Democratic Front (q.v.) for the elections later that year, and Soroseb was rewarded with a seat in the National Assembly as a result. He is also the Deputy National Chairman of the UDF.

ORLAM (variant: OORLAM). This term is seldom used today except in its historical context. It refers to people who were basically Namas, but who often had mixed blood infused by relations with Dutchmen in the Cape Colony. They had lived and worked there among the Dutch until the early nineteenth century, when large numbers of them migrated into Namibia. The name "Orlam" is of questionable origin. One version is that it comes from a Dutch phrase, "Oorlandse mense," or "the overland men," foreigners. Another version traces the word back to the Malay language (Malays had been imported to the Cape Colony as servants). In that language there is a term for old and trusted servants "Orang lami." In this interpretation the Orlams used this term to describe themselves as being better than the "pure" Namas who worked in the area. Indeed their mixture with the Dutch gave the Orlams some linguistic and educational advantages over their "pure" Nama brothers and sisters. They had often been given greater leadership roles and responsibilities and had even acquired horses and firearms. As a result when they crossed the Orange River they had certain real advantages over the Namas who already lived in the territory.

The Orlams came in five separate groups (it would be inaccurate to call them tribes if that word implied a great deal of familial homogeneity). They fled South Africa for varying reasons. Since the stories of these groups are told elsewhere in this volume, it is only necessary here to identify the groups and principal leaders.

1. Khowesin, led by Kido Witbooi. They later were usually just called the Witboois. Among their strong leaders were Moses and Hendrik Witbooi. The great-grandson of the latter is a minister in Namibia's first independent government.

2. Gei-Khauan, who ultimately settled in Gobabis. Once

referred to as the Amraal Namas or "Hottentots," they were the followers of Amraal Lamberts.

3. /Kari-/Khauan, who were originally led by Dietrich Isaak. He was succeeded by Paul Goliath, his son-in-law. As they lived in Berseba, they are often referred to as the Berseba Namas.

4. !Aman are related to those at Berseba, but settled in Bethanie under the leadership of Jan Boois.

5. //Aicha-//ain, the "angry tribe." One of their leaders was called Afrikander by his Dutch master. His successors made names for themselves and their people, as they penetrated deep into the heart of Namibia and frequently came into conflict with the Hereros. Their best known leaders were Jonker Afrikander and his son Jan Jonker Afrikander.

All of the Orlam groups were either originally accompanied by missionaries or allowed them to settle in their villages. However the story of Namibia in the nineteenth century (until the Germans arrived in the last couple of decades) was generally that of the feuding between the Orlams, the "pure" Namas (led by the Red Nation), and the Hereros. (*See* names of individual groups.)

OSHAKATI. The second largest town in the country, it had an estimated population in 1991 of 40,000. It is one of the country's younger towns, but is Owambo's main regional center and administrative seat. Its growth was governed by an orderly development plan. In 1966 a 475-bed hospital was completed there. A good water supply was assured by channeling water to it in a cement-lined canal from the Kunene River.

Originally the town was a small hamlet called Okatama. When administrators decided to expand and develop it the place was renamed Oshakati, which means "the center." The headquarters of South Africa's commissionary-general for the Northern Territories was transferred there from Ondangwa, and an office of the Corporation for Economic Development was established there also. The hospital complex required housing for its employees and staff. A factory and other industries were also established.

OSHANAS. Not to be confused with an omuramba (q.v.), which is essentially a river bed that is dry except when the rains come, the oshana is a depression, similar to a dry lake bed, that fills only when the rains come. It can fill from the rainfall itself or from rivers that overflow into it. Oshanas are found primarily in northern Namibia, especially in Owambo. Several oshanas may link up when the rains are very heavy and become a giant pool that eventually feeds into a river.

OSHIKANGO. A South African administrative center in extreme northern Owambo. it is located just south of the Angolan border on the main road north from Ondangwa. While the Native commissioner was stationed at Ondangwa, he had an assistant commissioner on the border at Oshikango. A police post was also set up there. When the guerrilla war began in 1966, SWAPO launched its first military attack against that police post.

OSONA. A small agricultural community immediately south of Okahandja on the rail line from Windhoek, it has been especially important three times in Namibian history. The first two involved intra-African battles (*see* OSONA, BATTLES OF). The third time was during the German-Herero conflict in 1904. A railway bridge over the Swakop River at Osona was a key target. When the Hereros destroyed it, German reinforcements and their equipment had a much harder time reaching Okahandja, where the Herero rebellion began.

OSONA, BATTLES OF. Two major battles occurred at Osona. 1. After Nama forces under Jan Jonker Afrikander and Moses Witbooi had individually been bested in battle by Maherero's warriors in December 1880, Witbooi was determined to defeat the Hereros (qq.v.). After almost a year of preparation—and with Maherero fully aware of the impending attack—Witbooi led a very large force of Namas to Okahandja in November 1881. The missionary/historian Dr. H. Vedder calls the resulting battle, which occurred at Osoma on November 22 and 23, 1881, "the greatest battle which had yet been fought in South West Africa, . . . that is, the greatest from the point of view of the number of combatants on both sides.'' In addition to Witbooi and his men, Jan Jonker Afrikander had a large force of Namas at the battle scene, while Maherero had accumulated a very large force of Hereros. The Hereros won the two-day battle, and Witbooi lost all his wagons, horses, and ammunition, plus a large number of warriors. He returned to Gibeon a defeated man.

2. The son of Moses Witbooi, Hendrik Witbooi (q.v.) took over leadership of these Namas (although his father was still alive). Historians feel he was trying to prove his right to leadership when he brought his men to Okahandja to fight the Hereros in mid-1884. A battle ensued, but without much enthusiasm on either side, and after three days the two sides agreed to sign a peace treaty. But neither side appeared to be too serious about it. In October 1885 Hendrik informed Maherero that he was coming near Okahandja with a large group of his followers, but that he was coming in peace and the Hereros need not fear. (Later Hendrik swore to everyone that he was indeed without warlike intent. Others seem to feel he was using subterfuge.) The Nama forces reached Osona where they set up camp on October 14, 1885. The Namas were on one side of the Swakop River, but had to pass through the Herero camp to get supplies of water. Maherero and Witbooi even sat down together for tea and coffee. Whether the impending battle took place by accident or by contrivance on the part of either side cannot be reliably determined, but the proximity of two armed, hostile groups could only result in battle. Banter at the waterhole led to a skirmish between Hereros and Namas. This quickly developed into a major battle. Again the Namas were totally defeated. Two of Hendrik's sons were among the many killed. The Namas lost 130 horses and all their draught oxen, wagons, and ammunition to the Hereros. Hendrik barely escaped. In letters to Maherero he accused him of duplicity and vowed to get even. However, his attack on Okahandja in 1886 was also driven back.

OTAVI. A mining town along the road and railway to the north, it is situated at the point where both divide: one rail line continues a northeasterly course to Tsumeb, while the other heads due east to Grootfontein. The name is attributed to Nandavetu, a Herero who found the large spring (*see* OTA-VIFONTEIN) spouting nearby and thought it similar to those at Kaoko Otavi. A cattle farmer, Nandavetu was reminded of the way a calf jerks milk from his mother's udder. This is called tava in the Herero language, so Otavi was named. (Technically it should by Outavi.) Copper has been mined at Otavi for centuries, especially by the San who lived near the Etosha Pan. Wambo smiths also mined and worked the copper long before the first Europeans discovered the rich deposits.

The Germans established a police post at Otavi in 1900, and it was besieged by Hereros from January 17–22, 1904, before relief arrived. While it was declared an urban area in 1936, it did not grow dramatically until after World War II. The excellent water sources (Otavifontein), the Tsumeb Corp., and the good agricultural potential (maize, for example) attracted settlers to the area. A grain mill and meat-canning factory were built. (*See also* OTAVI MINEN-UND EISENBAHNGESELLSCHAFT.) The last battle between German and South African armies occurred a few kilometers north of Otavi, and the peace treaty at Korab (q.v.) was signed just two kilometers north of Otavi.

OTAVI EXPLORING SYNDICATE LTD. Established in London in 1909 with a capital of £63,000, it purchased prospecting rights for the Otavi-Tsumeb area from the Otavi Minen-und Eisenbahn Gesellschaft. It went on to ship considerable quantities of copper ore from the mines it developed. Lead was another byproduct, and from 1910 to 1912 it exported 2,616 tons of lead. Its exports were carried by the Otavi Railway (q.v.).

OTAVI MINEN-UND EISENBAHNGESELLSCHAFT (OMEG). An offshoot of the South West Africa Company (q.v.), it was formed in 1888 in Germany with the goal of working the mines at Otavi (q.v.) and building a rail line southwest to the coast. It was originally capitalized at £200,000. The line was completed from Swakopmund to Otavi in 1906. OMEG held rights (from the government) to more than 23,000 square miles in Owambo. which it had acquired in a deal by which it surrendered additional rail concessions. However, it retained the right to manage the Otavi Railway, which at first earned 75 percent of its income. The rest came from copper mining. OMEG was probably the most profitable of all of Namibia's early copper mining companies. The dividends it paid its investors in 1912 to 1914 were 30 percent, 40 percent, and 45 percent per ordinary share. It continued to profit from both the railway and the copper mining, especially the Tsumeb mine (q.v.), until World War II, although there were years when mining was shut down because of world market conditions. After World War II the Tsumeb Corporation Ltd. (q.v.) was allowed to purchase mining rights from the South African government, which had expropriated them from OMEG during the war.

OTAVI MOUNTAINS (variant: OTAVI HIGHLANDS). A system of ancient dolomite folded mountains, which have been sliced into a number of ridges, mostly parallel, separated by flat valleys. These are in northeastern Namibia, from the town of Otavi north and east toward Grootfontein to Tsumeb. The major ridge extends from Otavi and on the north side of the Otavi-Grootfontein Railway. Its highest part is "Nageib Peak," 7000 feet above sea level (2148 meters). The ridges often have prominent escarpments leading down to deep, fertile valleys. The plains are dotted with numerous hills or koppies that are remnants of some of the ridges. The Otavi Valley is one of the most prominent of the valleys, and separates the Southern Otavi Ridge from the southern Otavi Range. Rainfall in the Otavi Mountains is quite good. Copper mines are prominent in the mountains, as extensive deposits have been known there for centuries. The mountains were traditionally inhabited by a group of Damas (q.v.), who were thereby called Bergdamas (mountain Damas). They lived freely in the hills much longer than most Namibians, and thus retained their traditions for a much longer time than others who interacted with Europeans earlier. The flora of the area is subtropical. Because of population growth, relatively few animals still roam the region.

OTAVI RAILWAY. Begun in 1903, but delayed by the Herero War in 1904, this rail line was finally completed in August 1906. The main line is from Swakopmund to Tsumeb and is 356.25 miles long. Branch lines were added from Otavi to Grootfontein (59.5 miles), and from Ongoati to Karibib on the Northern Railway (q.v.) (12.5 miles). The main line and these two branches cost about £1 million to build. The government purchased it in 1910 for £1.25 million, but allowed the Otavi Company to continue to run it. This company owned the mines at Otavi and Tsumeb. The South Africans changed the line to the Cape gauge after 1915, laying the new tracks alongside the original line, which retreating Germans had destroyed early in 1915. Two small branch lines and three small private lines were built over the years to link mining enterprises, etc., to the Otavi Railway. The original motivation for building the line was to bring the copper ore south to the port at Swakopmund. Along the route are several major towns, especially Omaruru, Kalkfeld, and Otjiwarongo.

A major controversy around the construction of the railway involved the Hereros. In granting the construction right, the German government gave the company the right to a wide strip of land on each side of the right of way. This cut right through excellent Herero pastures. They objected, and some chiefs demanded that no villages could be forcibly removed. The governor felt that it would be a moot point, as ultimately any Hereros would move away from the tracks. Some believe that Herero anger over the rail line and their loss of land may have been a trigger for the 1904 Herero revolt against the Germans.

OTAVIFONTEIN. The strongest fountain known in all of Namibia, its flow has been measured at 3,636,800 liters a day. It is located eight km east of the town of Otavi, on the road to Grootfontein. For centuries it has been known by travelers, African and European alike, as a welcome source of fresh water. In the final days of the Namibian phase of World War I, South African troops defeated the Germans at Otavifontein on July 1, 1915. This was just eight days before the final German surrender.

OTJIHASE MINE. A copper mine near Windhoek, it was originally developed by Johannesburg Consolidated Investments and Minerts (also South African); it also produced zinc and silver. When world copper prices dropped, it was closed by its owners in 1978, two years after production began amidst predictions that it would become Namibia's largest base metal mine. Two thousand Africans had been employed in 1976–77. About R60 million had been invested in it.

The mine was reopened in December 1980 after the Tsumeb Corporation (q.v.) purchased a 70 percent share. Tsumeb received a tax deduction from the government to encourage it to revive production there. Its production of ore rose to 769,000 tons in 1982, which contained 15,000 tons of copper and 4000 kilograms of silver. Ore reserves at that time were estimated to be thirteen years.

Otjihase has not been without labor problems. In April 1983 all Black workers struck over the introduction of a new work rule and the attitude of their supervisor. The management revoked the rule, but would not suspend the superintendent. After the strike, 112 workers did not return to their jobs.

The mine continues to thrive. In 1988 it produced almost 25 percent of Tsumeb's total copper smelter feed. Otjihase also produced 227,000 tons of iron pyrites in 1988, which it sold to Rössing Uranium for use in the solvent extraction process. However, in 1989 production of pyrites dropped to 196,500 tons. This could increase again, as the dropping of sanctions against Namibian products should trigger a growth at Rössing, with a corresponding need for more pyrites.

OTJIHINAMAPARERO. Located about fifty kilometers northeast of Omaruru, it was the site of a battle between German troops and Herero warriors on February 25, 1904. The Germans were led by then Major Ludwig von Estorff (q.v.), who had come from the garrison at Okahandja with three companies. About fifty Hereros died, and ten Germans were killed or wounded. The press in Germany, desperate for victories to applaud, played it as a major victory. Estorff's report indicated that the battle persisted for ten hours. He received a congratulatory telegram from the Kaiser.

OTJIKANGO. *See* BARMEN.

OTJIKANGO, BATTLE OF. This battle occurred as part of the renewal of hostilities between Hereros and Namas again in 1880. Maherero, reacting to the killing of some Herero herdsmen by Namas, had all Namas living in Okahandja massacred on August 23, 1880, exactly thirty years after Namas had massacred Hereros at the same location. Maherero then ordered all Namas in Herero country killed. In a fierce battle on December 11 and 12 a large force of Namas under Jan Jonker Afrikander were convincingly defeated at Otjikango, near Okahandja. The Nama leader survived along with a small force of warriors, but his power was now broken. Nama leadership shifted to the Witboois at Gibeon (qq.v.).

OTJIKOTO, LAKE. *See* LAKE OTJIKOTO.

OTJIMBINGWE (variant: OTJIMBINGUE). One of the larger towns in Namibia, its population was estimated at about 3000 in 1988. It is sixty-four kilometers southeast of Karibib. It is southwest of Okahandja and northwest of Windhoek. While it was traditionally a popular area for Hereros to live, it did not receive white settlers until after a RMS missionary, Johannes Rath, established a mission station there in 1849. It gained a modicum of fame when the first German administrator, Dr. Heinrich Goering, was headquartered there in 1885. In 1891, Captain Curt van Francois (q.v.) could move his troops to a new capital at Windhoek. Two important battles took place there, one in 1863 (*see* OTJIMBINGWE, BATTLE OF) in which Hereros defeated Namas led by Christian Afrikander, and the other in 1915 (*see* OTJIM-BINGWE, SIEGE OF) when South African troops surrounded the town. Among the town's more important landmarks today is the Paulineum, the Evangelical Lutheran theological seminary.

OTJIMBINGWE, BATTLE OF. An important confrontation between major Herero and Nama armies, it took place on June 15, 1863. Christian Afrikander (q.v.), son and successor of Jonker Afrikander, gathered a very large force of Nama warriors from several villages to try to subdue the rebellious Hereros under their new chief, Maherero (q.v.). Jonker had treated all Hereros as his inferiors, and had even called them his "dogs." Christian Afrikander led a much larger force than Maherero, but the Hereros used the buildings of the new mission station at Otjimbingwe very effectively as shields. An attempt by the Namas to burn the mission house, where Herero women and children huddled, was foiled by Herero marksmen. (The Hereros had about a hundred rifles, ironically many of them a gift from Jonker Afrikander.) Nama horsemen then led a charge on Maherero's werf, expecting a quick victory. But Maherero has his men strategically placed, and the Namas rode unsuspectingly into the jaws of death. Hereros held fire until the last moment, and with their first shots mowed down the front line of Nama leaders, including Christian Afrikander, his brother David, his uncles Jager and Jonas, and his councillor Timothy. Still the battle raged until the Hereros charged and the Namas fled, picking up the unhorsed when possible. One leader, Oasib (q.v.), barely survived by jumping behind a Nama horseman. Some horses carried three men. The Hereros continued to chase the Namas for many miles, killing the stragglers. More than 200 Namas died, while the Hereros lost about 60, including Philip Katjimune and some of Maherero's close relatives. The end result of the attack was a new balance of power between the Namas and Hereros.

OTJIMBINGWE, SIEGE OF. During World War I the South African forces working as allies of Great Britain, invaded German-ruled Southwest Africa. A force led by General Louis Botha encircled the town of Otjimbingwe and laid siege to it. German soldiers there eventually broke through the South African forces, but with great loss of life. They fled with the South Africans in pursuit. The battle at Otjimbingwe occurred on April 30, 1915, a little over two months before the Germans surrendered at Korab.

OTTO, JOHN G. *See* YA-OTTO, JOHN G.

OUB RIVER. *See* FISH RIVER.

/OUNIN (variant: OUNI). The original name of the people called the Topnaar Namas (q.v.). Topnaar is actually a translation of this word.

OUTJO. A town in the northwestern quadrant of Namibia, it still has the appearance of a pioneer town. It is seventy-three kilometers northwest of Otjiwarongo. There is an airfield and a rail terminal there. Its population of about 3800 is mostly Herero, but a white community is also firmly established. The first white man to settle there, Thomas Lambert, arrived by wagon in 1880. A German military post was established in 1895 for the purpose of controlling rinderpest (q.v.). The garrison attacked and defeated the rebellious Swartbooi Namas at Grootberg in February 1898. Outjo is a convenient stopping point on the road north to Okaukuejo and to the Etosha National Park, which is 102 kilometers from Outjo. The Paresis Mountain is near Outjo, which reputedly means "the place of the cone-shaped mountains."

OVAHIMBA. See HIMBA.

OVAMBO (variants: AMBO; WAMBO). While more properly called the Wambos today, these people have been most commonly known by Europeans as the Ovambos. Regardless, it is the collective name for eight matrilineal societies of Bantu-speaking people: the Kwanyama, Kwambi, Kwaluudhi, Eunda, Ndonga, Ngandjera, Mbalantu (qq.v.), and Nkolonkati. These groups compose by far the largest ethnic subdivision of Namibia. One estimate indicates their numbers in 1989 to be 641,000. In keeping with their large population, they are the dominant people in SWAPO, the ruling party of Namibia at independence.

The home of the Ovambos was generally referred to as Ovamboland, but is today called Owambo (q.v.). It is in the extreme north of Namibia. One advantage of this location is that they were freer from German colonial interference than the Hereros and Namas to their south. Likewise their missionaries were not from the Germany-based RMS, but were from the Finnish Mission Church (q.v.). The missionaries provided a fairly good educational base for the people, although the large population did place a strain on the Finnish resources.

Meanwhile some of the Ovambos retained their traditional chieftainships, especially the Ndonga, Kwambi, Ngandjera, and Kwaluudhi. The other four accomplished tribal governance through councils of headmen. The four groups with chiefs retained a hierarchy down through senior headmen and headmen. In all instances, however, South African administrators came in during the second and third decades of the twentieth century and set up their own administration, often by integrating it with the traditional leaders.

The Ovambos both practiced agriculture and raised livestock, but cattle were kept more for milk than for slaughter. To some extent this reflects the quality of the land on which they live, which is suitable for farming. Millet, sorghum, and beans are popular crops. A beer is brewed from a mixture of the millet and sorghum. Chickens and pigs are also kept to provide meat.

The Ovambos came into Namibia from the north, probably from Angola, where related people still live. Indeed their clans are found on both sides of the Namibia/Angola border. They arrived in Namibia about the seventeenth century. They are clearly related to the Kavango people, who are their neighbors to the east, and some oral traditions also link them as directly related to the Hereros, through an ancestor named Nangombe Ya Mangundu (q.v.). The Ovambos believe in a Supreme Being, who was traditionally called Kalunga (q.v.). An important part of their tradition involved the holy or sacred fire (*see* FIRE, SACRED), a practice or belief that is common through many of the peoples of Namibia.

Many of the customs and traditions have fallen away under the influence of Christianity. Another modern influence, forced in part by the coming of Europeans, has been wage employment. Large masses of Ovambo men went south to work in mines, either in Namibia or in South Africa. Some went as far as Cape Town to work under contract (*see* LABOR, AFRICAN). This situation curiously gave rise to modern political nationalism, as an important predecessor to SWAPO was the Ovamboland People's Congress (q.v.), many of whose founders in Cape Town in 1958 were still actively engaged in politics in 1989. Some of them are top government officials in Namibia today.

OVAMBO-KAVANGO CHURCH. *See* EVANGELICAL LUTHERAN OVAMBOKAVANGO CHURCH (ELOK).

OVAMBOLAND. *See* OWAMBO.

OVAMBOLAND CONSTITUTION PROCLAMATION No. R104 (1973). This government proclamation of April 27, 1973, was the legal basis for Owambo being declared a self-governing territory on May 1, 1973. A cabinet was sworn in on that day, and Chief Councillor Philemon Elfias (q.v.) became chief minister. The proclamation also provided for the dismissal of the old Legislative Council and called for new elections in Owambo, to be held in mid-January 1975.

OVAMBOLAND INDEPENDENT CHURCH. Founded in 1971 by Rev. Peter Kalangula (q.v.), it is a breakaway church from the Anglican Church in Namibia. It was founded because of disagreements between members of the Anglican Mission in Owambo and Bishop Colin Winter (q.v.), then head of the Synod of Damaraland. The discord involved practices, not theology, such as whether English or Wambo languages should be used in services (Kalangula favored the vernacular), and whether the Anglican Mission there should retain that status or gain the semi-autonomous status of an archdeaconship. By 1974 the new church claimed 13,000 members in 8 separate congregations. However Kalangula's leadership was always questioned by some Wambos, who felt he was too solicitous of South Africa. This was in contrast to the more courageous leadership of another Wambo church leader, Bishop Leonard Auala (q.v.).

OVAMBOLAND PEOPLE'S CONGRESS (OPC). The first "modern" nationalist political group founded by Namibians, it was organized under the leadership of Herman (Andimba) Toivo Ya Toivo in 1958 in Cape Town, South Africa. About thirty or forty Namibian students plus another two hundred laborers met in a barber shop there, motivated in part by the injustice of the contract labor system. Aside from Ya Toivo its key members, most of whom are still active politically more than thirty years later, were Andreas Shipanga, F. J. Kozonguizi, Jacob Kulangua, Solomon Mifima, Emil Appolus, Peter Mueshihange, Maxton Joseph Mutongulume, and working in sympathy and keeping in touch while in the United States, Mburumba Kerina (qq.v.).

A railway employee who occasionally got to Cape Town, Sam Nujoma (q.v.), visited the group on several occasions and decided to organize a similar group in Windhoek. At the time the OPC was strongly influenced by South African nationalist groups, especially the African National Congress, and some of its members were communists and even Maoists. A corp of its members decided that the group should strive for independence from South Africa, and thus wanted a broad-based political group. However when it changed its name in 1959 it called itself the Ovamboland People's Organization (q.v.). A year later it again changed, this time to South West Africa People's Organization (q.v.), better known as SWAPO.

OVAMBOLAND PEOPLE'S ORGANIZATION (OPO). Founded originally as the Ovamboland People's Congress (q.v.) in Cape Town in 1958, it was reorganized in Windhoek on April 19, 1959, as the Ovamboland People's Organization.

The Cape Town leader of the OPC, Herman Toivo Ya Toivo, had been harassed by police, so leadership fell to its leading activists in Windhoek, Sam Nujoma, who became the OPO's first president, and Louis Nelengani its first vice-president. Ya Toivo returned to Owambo to organize the OPO there, and likewise was active in Walvis Bay, where a slowdown strike was successfully operated as a means of political protest. When the riots occurred at the Windhoek "Old Location" (q.v.) in December 1959, the OPO and its leaders were accused by the government of being major instigators.

Meanwhile, the South West Africa National Union (q.v.) had been organized as a territory-wide nationalist group, albeit with a heavy Herero leadership. To broaden its base

SWANU added Nujoma, Nelengani, and Ya Toivo onto its executive committee in September 1959. The Windhoek riots spurred the government to arrest or ban many of the young nationalists from both SWANU and OPO. Jacob Kuhangua, the OPO secretary-general, was even deported to Angola. Fearing retribution, many others fled into exile, including Sam Nujoma. He fled to New York, where he could join Mburumba Kerina (q.v.) in appealing to the United Nations.

However a split developed in the nationalist ranks. Kerina had a disagreement with the Herero Chief's Council and also with its New York spokesman, J. T. Kozonguizi (q.v.), the president of SWANU. Kerina then urged Nujoma to convert the OPO into a truly national organization that could compete with SWANU. He recommended that the word Ovamboland be replaced by South West Africa. This was done in June 1960, and SWAPO was thus born. (*See* SOUTH WEST AFRICA PEOPLE'S ORGANIZATION.)

During its time as the OPO, this group's focus was on the welfare of contract workers from the north, especially Owambo and the Kavango area. However, it clearly stated that its objectives included attaining national independence.

OVENSTONE INVESTMENTS. Founding company of the Walvis Bay Canning Company in 1943, it also daringly began the pilchard industry in Namibia in 1948. Owned by the Ovenstone family, it has been one of the more prosperous and innovative companies involved in Namibia's fishing industry (q.v.).

OWAMBO. Probably better known in many sources as Ovamboland, this region in the north-central section of Namibia was set apart as a territory for the Wambo or Ovambo people by Proclamation No. 27 of 1929. No portion of it could thus be expropriated except by act of the South African Parliament. The area so designated was 4,200,000 hectares, but with additions it is now 5,600,000 hectares or 56,000 square kilometers. A vast plain, the greater portion of it was originally heavily timbered with mopani, teak, thorn, and other trees. It is intersected by omurambas (dry watercourses) which descend from Angola, converge below On-dangwa, and ultimately feed (when rains allow) the Etosha Pan. Owambo is bordered on the north by Angola, on the west by Kaokoveld, on the east by the Kavango area, and on the south by the Etosha National Park.

The region derives its name from its inhabitants, Wambos or Ovambos, who are themselves divided into eight sub-groups (*see* OVAMBO). These people constitute the largest single ethnic group in the country, an estimated 641,000 in 1989, easily 50 percent of the entire population of Namibia. It was obvious to South Africa that this should be its first "Homeland" to be given self-government. Thus a Legislative Council was formed on October 17, 1968. Its first chief councillor was Ushma Shiima (q.v.).

As the home of the Wambos, some of whom have been top leaders of SWAPO, Owambo was the site of numerous early clashes between this nationalist party and the "collaborators" who were active in the Legislative Council. As SWAPO became active militarily, Owambo became a battle-ground for SWAPO guerrillas and the increasingly large body of police and, eventually the South African Defence Force. From 1966 to 1989 it was a dangerous place for civilians as well as the opposing forces. Even after independence there has been trouble in parts of Owambo, as fighting in neighboring Angola spills over the border. Through its heavy representation in SWAPO, Owambo is well-represented in Namibia's National Assembly. If anything there is the danger that the rest of the country will resent the strength of Owambo in the governing bodies of independent Namibia.

- P -

PACKAGE PLAN OF THE WESTERN FIVE CONTACT GROUP. The Western Five Contact Group (Great Britain, France, Canada, West Germany, and the United States), seeking a satisfactory solution to the Namibian conflict after the Turnhalle Conference (q.v.), released a "package plan" in early April 1978. It suggested a major UN military and civilian presence in Namibia during a period of transition up to independence. It also called for the cessation of violence, a phased withdrawal of South African troops, and a special representative of the UN secretary general to work with South African-appointed administrator-general in setting up free elections. The Walvis Bay question was to be set aside and dealt with by South Africa and the new government of Namibia. South Africa surprised everyone by announcing later in the month that it would accept the package plan. SWAPO requested further clarification, but then suspended contact with the Western Five when South African forces made a surprise attack on SWAPO bases in Angola. Negotiations resumed in July 1978, this time with the added participation of the African "Front Line States," who encouraged SWAPO's Sam Nujoma to agree to the package plan. On July 12 he accepted the plan. It called for UN supervised elections and the establishment of a UN transitional group (UNTAG) of 5000 troops and 1000 civilian administrators. South African troops were to be reduced drastically and confined to a couple of camps. SWAPO was to end its military activities and return its fighters to bases. Prisoners were to be released and refugees allowed to return. South Africa was surprised, however, to learn that the Western Group had made a private promise to SWAPO regarding the status of Walvis Bay (q.v.), supporting SWAPO's position that Walvis Bay is an integral part of Namibia. This was affirmed by a vote of the UN Security Council. South Africa's cabinet kept its options open by neither rejecting nor endorsing the implementation of the plan. It rejected the UN position on Walvis Bay, however. A visit by UN commissioner for Namibia, Martti Ahtisaari (q.v.), occurred in August, and he reported that political differences were not insoluble. SWAPO then began another guerrilla attack, however, and South African forces entered Zambia in hot pursuit. As a result of Ahtisaari's report, the size of the UNTAG force was to be increased, and Dr. Waldheim, the UN secretary general, proposed a plan that included elections in seven months. On September 20, 1978, however, South African Prime Minister J. Vorster resigned, claiming ill health, and announced that the cabinet had decided to go ahead with sponsoring internal elections in Namibia. The elected body could then decide for itself what to do about accepting any settlement plan. This left the situation unresolved.

PADRÃO. Portuguese word for the stone marker, typically a pillar with a cross, used to mark the advancing frontiers of the Christian world. The Portuguese navigator, Diego Cão (q.v.) was the first European to reach the coast of Namibia, and in 1482 left padrãos at the mouth of the Congo River and at Cape Santa Maria in Angola. He returned to the area in 1485 and planted a marker at Cape Cross, 130 kilometers north of Swakopmund. This remained there until the Germans took it to the Kiel Museum in 1893. It then went to a Berlin museum, and is now in Berlin. In July 1488 a similar marker was placed at Lüderitz Bay by another Portuguese navigator, Bartholomeu Dias. The present granite cross there (at "Dias Point") was erected by South African authorities in 1929. The original had seriously deteriorated already by 1786, according to the report of Captain T. B. Thompson. Fragments of the Dias padrão are in Lisbon, Berlin, and Auckland, New Zealand.

PALGRAVE, DR. WILLIAM COATES (1833–1897). Born in Berkshire, England, of an old family, he studied law and medicine and then moved to South Africa about 1860. In 1869 he was appointed to the Cape Civil Service in the position of sub-inspector of the Frontier Armed and Mounted Police. Two years later he became a magistrate on the Griqualand West Diamond fields. A few years later several African leaders (notably Maherero, Jan Jonker Afrikander, and Hermanus Van Wijk, qq.v.) were concerned about the advance of Boers into Namibia, especially the "Thirstland Trekkers" (q.v.), and petitioned the British governor at the Cape for protection (June 21, 1874). Palgrave was sent as special commissioner to South West Africa in 1876 (a post he held until 1880) to set up a protectorate for the Hereros, as he had previously hunted and traded in Namibia and was even a friend of Maherero. The treaty was signed on September 9, 1876, in Okahandja, Palgrave's headquarters.

Palgrave then travelled the region extensively and recommended to the Cape government that much of the territory be annexed, saying that everyone (Black and white) favored protection. He also recommended that Walvis Bay be annexed along with the surrounding area, which was done in 1878. Palgrave returned to Cape Town on several occasions, once with two of Maherero's sons, Wilhelm and Samuel. He began a new pact in 1880, serving as magistrate of Walvis Bay and Hereroland, but he lacked the physical support of the Cape government to enforce order. It refused to send police or military help. He was negotiating with the Namas when a Herero-Nama conflict broke out. His appeals to the British government to help protect life and property went unheeded, so he fled to Walvis Bay, which remained a Cape protectorate. Palgrave served as a magistrate for four years in the Cape, while the Germans were becoming increasingly active in Namibia. By 1884 Namibia was under German protection, but Palgrave was sent back in November 1884 on a fruitless mission to try to consolidate his old Herero contacts. Palgrave's efforts between 1876 and 1880 to encourage Great Britain (via the Cape government) to annex the territory had failed primarily because of lack of interest in London, not in Cape Town. The pleadings of Adolf Lüderitz (q.v.) to the German government were answered, however.

PAN. A sheet of standing water formed during the rainy season in depressions in otherwise level country. Also known as a vlei (q.v.), the largest in Namibia is Etosha Pan (q.v.), but the "Sassusvlei" (q.v.) is also a well-known attraction.

PARENTS' COMMITTEE (variant: THE COMMITTEE OF PARENTS). This highly vocal group, founded in 1985, demanded to know the whereabouts of their family members who had joined SWAPO's guerrilla movement, were detained by SWAPO, and then seemingly vanished. Rumors of torture and killings were rife. SWAPO responded in 1986 that it was holding 100 "spies" working for South Africa. Amnesty International confirmed that SWAPO had committed human rights abuses. The Parents Committee continued to put public pressure on SWAPO (even after independence) and some members joined the Patriotic Unity Movement (q.v.). In April 1989, SWAPO released more than 200 detainees, but several hundred more are still unaccounted for.

PASS LAWS. A series of laws, but primarily the Native Administration Proclamation of 1922 (q.v.), which regulated the movement of Africans in and out of most areas or communities of the country. A "liberation" reform movement included the repeal of the pass laws by Judge Steyn on October 20, 1977. The obligation to carry passes at all times was abolished, but total freedom of movement around the country did not accompany it.

The pass laws were a maze of official permits that were required of all adult male Blacks, especially the workers who wished to work and live in the Police Zone (q.v.). Those not carrying appropriate passes risked arrest by the police or even labor inspectors. The basic law, the 1922 Native Administration Proclamation, required that a native African found outside certain areas had to show a proper pass when required by police. Fines, forced labor, or deportation were the main penalties. The Native (Urban Areas) Proclamation of 1924 (q.v.) imposed stricter controls on the towns and mines, and the Mines and Works Proclamation of 1917 and the Masters and Servants Proclamation of 1920 (qq.v.) placed additional restrictions in the areas of mining and farming respectively. The general assumption of all the laws was that indigenous Africans only had rights in an area if they were gainfully employed by whites and had all the technical papers in proper order. While the general pass laws were repealed in 1977, influx controls still existed.

PATRIOTIC UNITY MOVEMENT (PUM). A direct result of the peace plan and schedule for elections was the return home to Namibia of many of ex-SWAPO detainees and exiles who wanted to create an alternative to SWAPO. This movement was led by Eric Biwa, a former member of the SWAPO Youth League (q.v.) in the 1970s, and a member of SWAPO's Central Committee in the mid-1980s, who was later detained by SWAPO in Angola. On July 20, 1989, in Windhoek, Biwa and a group of colleagues created the PUM.

They felt that although the constitutional ideas of SWAPO were irreproachable, its leadership had become autocratic and tyrannical. The new country of Namibia needed leadership that believed in democracy and justice, Biwa claimed. The PUM received support from such non-party groups as the Parents Committee and the Political Consultative Council (qq.v.), both of which were working for the release of ex-SWAPO detainees, many of whom seemed to have vanished. For the 1989 elections, the Patriotic Unity Movement aligned itself in August with the United Democratic Front of Namibia (q.v.), which won four seats in the Assembly. No seats are held by PUM leaders.

PAULINEUM COLLEGE. A seminary located at Otjimbingwe, it received this name in 1963 when the independent Evangeliese Lutherese Owambokavangokerk (ELOK) combined its theological students with those of the Evangeliese Lutherse Kerk (ELK) at the latter's seminary. This cooperation between two leading Black churches is said to have been a symbol and an inspiration to the formation of a national consciousness.

PEGMATITE. A coarse, crystalized kind of granite. Such minerals as tin, tungsten, lithium, beryl, fluorspar, bismuth, tantalite, mica, and others occur in pegmatites and are produced primarily in the districts of Swakopmund, Warmbad, Otjiwarongo, Omaruru, and Karabib. Semi-precious stones, such as topaz, amazonite, amethyst, aquamarine, smoky quartz, and rose quartz are produced from pegmatites in the Swakopmund, Omaruru, and Karibib districts.

PELAGIC FISHING. Fishing along the surface of the open seas, as distinct from demersal or deep sea fishing. In the case of Namibia, pelagic fishing concentrates on pilchards (q.v.), anchovies and cape horse mackerel.

PENGUIN ISLANDS (variant: GUANO ISLANDS). A series of islands off Namibia's southern coast, they extend 180 nautical miles between 24°38' and 27°40' south latitude. From north to south they are named: Hollams Bird, Merker, Ichabo, Seal Penguin, Halifax, Long (actually two, North and South),

Possession, Albatross, Pomona, Plumpudding, and Sinclair (also called Roast Beef). The middle eight are just a little north and south of Lüderitz Bay. All the islands are partially submerged ridges or rocks formerly part of the mainland. They are small, uninhabited, and virtually barren. Some sand has been deposited by ocean currents. As breeding places for birds they are deep and rich in deposits of guano as well. Rainfall is minimal, but mists and fog allow sparse grasses to grow. The nearby waters have been rich in fish, until recent years, and some whaling and seal capturing has been done nearby.

Holland was the first country to claim the islands, linking them to its sovereignty over Angra Pequeña (now Lüderitz). The Cape changed European rulers several times until the Cape of Good Hope Colony was formally ceded to the United Kingdom in 1814. British subjects were exploiting the fish and guano of the islands commercially as early as 1842, but no attempt to take formal possession occurred until 1861, when the governor of the Cape Colony proclaimed that the Penguin Islands were under British dominion. Since there was uncertainty that annexation by proclamation was legal, Captain Charles Codrington Forsyth, captain of Her Majesty's Frigate *Victorious* stepped ashore Penguin Island on May 5, 1866, and declared Queen Victoria's sovereignty over the islands. On February 27, 1867, the British Crown issued Royal Letters Patent that formally appointed the governor of Cape Colony to govern the islands and authorized the Cape Parliament to request annexation of the islands. Due to some parliamentary confusion over the Letters Patent, the request for annexation was not passed by the Cape Colony Parliament and approved by the governor until July 6, 1874.

German officials soon became involved, and in 1884 Baron von Plessen, German chargé d'affaires in London, notified the British foreign minister that the islands would be regarded as belonging to the mainland. This position was not accepted by the British, and in March 1885, Chancellor Bismarck instructed his negotiator that British sovereignty over the islands was not to be questioned. However, other islands off the Namibian coast were acknowledged by the British as being under German sovereignty.

The islands have been considered to be part of South Africa

since it became a British dominion in 1910, and the islands were not included by the League of Nations as part of the mandate of South West Africa. Their status with an independent Namibia will not be quickly determined. They could be important to South Africa for the water rights (and thus mineral and fishing rights) they confer, but also could be used for bargaining power by South Africa in negotiating political and economic treaties with an independent Namibia.

The specific island called Penguin Island in the chain is one of the larger ones, covering about thirty-six hectares.

PEOPLE'S LIBERATION ARMY OF NAMIBIA (PLAN). The military wing of SWAPO, it was formed in 1970 when SWAPO leaders announced that it would be necessary to place primary emphasis on armed struggle (which had actually begun in 1966) in the attempt to gain Namibian independence. PLAN was set up to coordinate and lead the military efforts. Guerrilla activities spread in northern Namibia and advanced southward to Tsumeb and Grootfontein. PLAN had four operational zones in the country: the northeastern zone (the Caprivi strip), the central (Grootfontein district), the northern (Okavango and Owambo) and the northwestern (Kaokoveld). All these zones lie in the northern part of the territory, both because the largest number of Africans are there, and because the greater vegetation made the land more suitable to guerrilla operations than the more barren south or open central parts of Namibia. Nevertheless, PLAN moved into those latter regions between 1974 and 1980, attacking military installations near Windhoek. The underground PLAN units outside the north concentrated more on organizational work and training.

Geographical considerations generally required PLAN units to be small and mobile. They utilized tactics such as ambushes, sabotage, and land mines, the latter being especially effective on the network of roads used by military vehicles. In the late 1970's PLAN stepped up its battle, establishing semi-liberated zones and becoming bolder in striking further south. A major offensive occurred in Owambo in 1975–76, and a rainy season offensive in 1978–79 surprised the South African Defence Force, some units of which found their areas of movement restricted. SWAPO claimed that PLAN was an army of several thousand, well-armed soldiers with rockets, bazookas, and anti-aircraft guns, and organized in groups of 80 to 100. As with most guerrilla groups, the PLAN forces lived off its supporters in the citizenry, but later it attempted to raise food for its own troops. Women served equally with men in PLAN, and duties were reportedly shared. In "liberated areas," PLAN set up hospitals, schools, and even garages to repair the equipment. Its agricultural production includes wheat, maize, and millet. PLAN hoped to keep South African forces limited to certain parts of the territory and then to wear down the will of the South African electorate to continue the battle. In fact, however, South African counterattacks in the early 1980s generally pushed PLAN forces north of the Namibian border into Angola where South African troops and aircraft continued to attack them.

The first commander of PLAN was Tobias Hanyeko. He was killed in 1967 by South African forces on the Kwando River in Caprivi. His successor, Dimo Hamaambo, continued to lead the organization until independence. The deputy commander was Salomon Hawala (Auala), who was also chief of security. The latter has been accused by members of the Political Consultative Council (q.v.) of the arrest and abduction of many members of both SWAPO and PLAN.

With the coming of Namibian independence, some members of PLAN have been integrated into the Namibian Defence Force, police units, or even into the presidential guard. The overall commander of the Namibian Defence Force is the former PLAN leader, Dimo Hamaambo.

PEREZ DE CUELLAR, DR. JAVIER. United Nations' secretary general since December 1981, he listed the Namibia issue as one of the areas that continued to threaten international stability. He visited the country in late August 1983, and on August 25 met in Windhoek with representatives of SWAPO and several other Namibian political parties. When he reported to the UN Security Council on August 31, he announced that he had secured South African acceptance of several of the provisions needed for a settlement, for example, the composition of the multinational peacekeeping force (UNTAG). A diplomat since 1944, he was the Peruvian ambassador to Switzerland and in 1969 became Peru's first ambassador to the Soviet Union. He first led Peru's delegation to the United Nations in 1971. In 1975 he was appointed the secretary general's special representative to strife-torn Cyprus, and in 1979 was appointed the UN under-secretary general for special political affairs.

During the last five years leading toward Namibia's independence, the secretary general worked hard to develop an agreement among the various sides for a strong United Nations contingent. He reluctantly agreed to an American insistence upon reducing the number of UN troops from 7500 to 4650. He appointed his special representative, Martti Ahtisaari (q.v.), to supervise the UNTAG forces during the election period. When independence came in March 1990, the secretary general was in Windhoek assisting in the transfer of power.

PERMANENT MANDATES COMMISSION. The body within the League of Nations (q.v.) charged with the responsibility for supervising the mandate system (q.v.), it functioned from about 1920 to the beginning of World War II in 1939. It was composed of five members from non-mandate states and four from the mandate states, chosen as experts on colonial affairs, not as representatives of their countries. The commission's task was to review the annual reports which the mandatories were required to compile and to uncover information that was being concealed. The commission was not reluctant to criticize the mandatories, and it found ample and repeated cause to do so. Nevertheless, possessing no sanctions for enforcement, its criticisms were ineffective and were treated with disdain by the South African leadership.

Resolutions under consideration by the commission required unanimous agreement for passage. Thus any mandatory could prevent the adoption of a resolution critical of its own administration of a mandate. South Africa was the most criticized of all the mandatories, and drew the ire of the commission for its delinquency. The early reports filed by South Africa were very weak and carelessly prepared. A series of South African officials were called to Geneva to explain themselves to the commission. They were frequently required to explain their attitudes toward the Africans, as South Africa was the most reluctant mandatory in arranging for the political progress of the Africans. The commission specifically forbade South Africa from expropriating the Namibian railway system and from ceding the Caprivi Strip to British administrators. South Africa had to back away from both of these positions. Its spokesmen also had to explain the frequent statements by South African officials that they expected to incorporate Namibia into the Union. The commission chastised the South Africans, warning that incorporation could not take place as long as Namibia was still a mandate. The penalty for such a transgression would be forfeit of the mandate and the granting of immediate self-government.

One of the major questions before the commission over the nearly two decades was: who in Namibia should pay for progress? The commission regularly urged the territory's administration to find more money to spend on the Africans. The administration complained that it was not fair to make the whites pay more to improve conditions for the Blacks. One of the commission's several responses to this was that South Africa was granted the mandate in 1920 because it had the necessary resources to help the territory stand on its own feet. A major meeting of the League on South Africa's administration of its mandate was the last meeting it held before World War II. Perhaps the major weakness of the Permanent Mandates Commission was that the question of final authority over mandate matters was ambiguously handled in Article 22 of the League of Nations' Covenant. The League itself lacked sovereignty. Near the end the Mandates Commission, while still probing, seemed frustrated by its lack of power, and resigned itself to it.

PERSIAN LAMB. Popular name for the fabric made from the wood of karakul (q.v.) sheep.

PETRIFIED FOREST. Located at Franzfontein (q.v.) in the Outjo district, the trees were blown over by a seismic disaster perhaps two hundred million years ago and were silicified by the sand that accumulated on them over millions of years. When the sand eventually wore away again, the fossil trees were exposed. Some of the fallen trunks measure as large as thirty meters in length and three meters in diameter. While some are almost perfectly preserved, others lie in broken segments, like the pillars on the Athenian Acropolis. The seventy-hectare site has been declared a national monument and is a popular tourist attraction. It is a rare example of the petrification of an entire forest.

PHILIPP'S CAVE (variant: PHILIPP CAVE). Located in the Erongo Mountains near the Ameib Mine and about twenty miles northeast of Usakos, this cave is the site of probably the second most significant (after Brandberg) collection of rock art in Namibia. There are several similar caves in the vicinity, but none as important as Philipp's Cave. It was named after Emil Philipp, a German karakul sheep breeder who had owned the property and discovered the cave while out hunting. The cave itself is large, about twenty meters deep and about fifty meters across the mouth. The paintings have stylistic similarities to those of the Brandberg, about ninety miles to the northwest along the Ugab River. For example, there is a white elephant similar to the "White Lady" of the Brandberg. The cave was studied in 1950 by the noted French archaeologist, Abbé Henri Breuil, who published a book called *Philipp Cave* in 1957. The cave's large low mouth resembles an open oyster, and overlooks a wide valley. The rock is granite. Tools found in the region indicate that the inhabitants for a long time were Stone Age people. Abbé Breuil did not believe the artists were Bushmen, but found many similarities (in his view) to the art of Nilotic peoples. Carbon 14 tests from charcoal found in the cave dates the charcoal—but not necessarily the paintings— at about 141 BC (+ or − 200 years), but radio carbon work on other materials provide a date of 1670 AD. The subject matter in the cave varies. One scene shows nine people, three of them helmeted and guarding five unarmed figures. The figures are generally stylized. Other subjects include animals (elephants, antelopes, birds, ostriches, springboks), handprints, bows and a quiver, a waterbag, and perhaps helmets. Colors used include red, pink, orange-yellow, orange-red, reddish brown, and yellow, along with white and black. While the identity of the painters is not known, the human figures do not resemble present-day indigenous Namibians. Abbé Breuil felt that the more recent artistic effort on the wall could probably be related to the Bushmen.

PIENAAR, LOUIS (1926–   ). Namibia's last administrator-general, he assumed that post July 1, 1985, and turned over his authority to President Sam Nujoma at independence, March 21, 1990. Born in Stellenbosch in the Cape Province of South Africa, he received a BA in law from Stellenbosch University in 1945, and an LLB from the University of South Africa in 1952. When he was appointed Namibia's adminis-trator-general in 1985, he knew he would be working toward an independent status for Namibia, although what group would be leading the country was still unclear. At one point in 1986 he pursued the possibility of political parties and groups inside Namibia to negotiate independence directly with South Africa. by mid-1987, however, he was working closely with the UN's Martti Ahtisaari on an internationally supervised independence process. Nevertheless, as late as January 1988, he was proposing elections for the Second Tier and Third Tier governments in order to strengthen the hand of the Transitional Government of National Unity.

PIENAAR, PIETER. A Dutch hunter and explorer, he accompa-nied Col. R. J. Gordon (q.v.) and Lt. William Paterson on an expedition to the mouth of the Orange River, which they reached on August 17, 1779, the first Europeans to reach that spot. They crossed into Namibia and followed the river east for a while before returning. Another man in that party, Sebastian Van Reenen (q.v.), in 1793 was traveling with Pienaar on the *Meermin* (q.v.) on a mission of the Dutch East India Company to lay claim to all the harbors on the west coast up to Walvis Bay to prevent them from falling into foreign hands. Pienaar and Van Reenen were on their own private pursuit of copper and gold mines in Namibia. They also hoped to make contact with the cattle-herding Hereros.

The ship stayed at Walvis Bay for about a month, until the end of February, as Pieneer and Van Reenen traveled inland. Pienaar went on a hunting trip, accompanied by ten armed Namas and three horses. They were desperate for water when several Bergdamas helped them, taking them to the Swakop River bed. (Pienaar is given credit for "discovering" it.) He travelled for twelve days in the Swakop valley, and encountered five African settlements, where he traded for some copper trinkets, which had been made from metal found to the south. Pienaar saw great quantities of game, and killed twenty-one rhinoceroses, three elephants, and other game. He returned to the boat at Walvis Bay and reported the discovery of the river bed. Pienaar and Van Reenen then travelled to the mouth of the Swakop, but heavy surf prevented them from landing. They sent other men to the mouth by land who reported back that there was no good landing spot, but that the valley was fantastically rich in game and trees. The *Meermin* left Walvis Bay on March 3, and returned to Cape Town on April 10, 1793. Pienaar had experienced one life-threatening situation when he became ill after having been bitten by a poisonous spider. Pienaar then settled down to farming in the northwestern Cape. He was said to be a particularly cruel, avaricious, and licentious man. He got into an argument with several Africans over wages they were receiving as farm servants. One of these servants, Titus Afrikander, shot and killed Pienaar c. 1796, and then fled with his followers into Namibia.

PILCHARDS. The *Sardinops ocellata,* known commonly as pilchards, are a type of sardine, small (about eight inches) surface-swimming fish formerly found in great numbers in the Atlantic off Walvis Bay. The cold Benguela Current (q.v.) sweeping north from the Cape made it one of the world's richest feeding grounds, especially in the quarter of a century after World War II. The pilchards are caught in the high seas in boatloads of up to 600,000 and brought to Walvis Bay, where they are the heart of a fish-canning industry.

The fishing industry began at Walvis Bay in 1859 when Barry Munnik of Cape Town established a fishery there. World War II brought a shortage of food and a new interest in

Namibia's fishing potential. The Walvis Bay Canning Company was established in 1943 by Russell Ovenstone (q.v.) and was canning pilchards in 1949. Three other companies began in 1949, 1950, and 1953. The control of canning became the responsibility of the Bureau of Standards. In the late 1940s a policy of limiting the fishing catch was sensibly initiated, but this was replaced later by a much more reckless approach. The production of fish-meal and canning pilchards increased greatly during the 1950s. In 1959 about 40,000,000 cans of sardines were produced. Six licensed pilchard factories caught 312,000 tons of pilchards in 1960, worth R17 million. That figure was more than doubled by 1970. The beginning of the downturn probably began when South Africa granted concessions to two factory ships to work the Namibian coast. Soon quotas and other restrictions became necessary. Foreign fishing fleets were blamed in part, but a Commission of Enquiry into the Fishing Industry said that a definite yearly maximum was needed for pelagic fishing (q.v.). A pilchard quota of 90,000 tons per year/per factory was considerably reduced in stages. The quota was periodically revised. The drop in fishing in the late 1960s reversed, however, and record catches were again made in 1974. But again the fish catch quickly dropped as the pilchards were brought close to extinction. A catch of 545,000 tons in 1975 dropped to only 325,000 tons in 1979 and 241,000 tons in 1980. The canneries formerly canned the best pilchards and processed the rest into fish-meal (high protein for South African livestock), with the fish-oil a useful byproduct for manufacturing varnishes, pressed board, linoleum, and other products. The canneries closed, but were reopened in 1982. Pelagic fish catches for 1983 were up 50 percent over those in 1982. The catches have remained between 42,000 and 63,000 tons in the 1980s, with 59,260 tons recorded in 1988. The government controlled total allowable catch (TAC) for pilchards in 1991 was 60,000 tons. This is allocated in the form of quotas for each of the six companies that were awarded pilchard concessions.

POHAMBA, LUCAS HIFIKEPUNYA (1935–). An early leader in SWAPO, he was born in northern Owambo. He was educated at the Holy Cross Mission School at Onamunama, barely south of the Angolan border. He worked in the Tsumeb copper mines and joined SWAPO in April 1959. In 1961 he fled the country to work with Sam Nujoma at the Dar es Salaam provision headquarters. From 1962 to 1964 he was back doing recruiting work inside Namibia. In exile since 1963, he ran the SWAPO office in Lusaka, Zambia, from 1966 to 1970, when he was appointed as SWAPO's representative in Algeria. He later represented SWAPO at various international conferences. He returned briefly to the country in March 1966, when he and Nujoma flew into Windhoek to challenge South Africa's claim that nationalist leaders could move freely into and out of the country. They were detained at Windhoek and quickly sent back to Zambia.

In 1969 he was appointed SWAPO's deputy administrative secretary on the Central Committee, and six years later he was promoted to SWAPO's Politbureau as secretary for finance and administration in Lusaka, Zambia. In 1979 the headquarters were at Luanda, Angola, where he became chief of operations. He returned home in June 1989. In the elections that year he was ranked eighth on SWAPO's list and easily procured a seat in the Assembly. He has since been appointed minister of home affairs.

POLICE ZONE. Namibia's own version of the Group Areas Act or Grand Apartheid, this is a method of dividing the land into two distinct regions. In 1906, after battles with the Africans, the German administrators restricted whites from crossing north of a specific boundary, and from shipping guns, horses, and alcohol there. In 1919, the South African administrator of the territory issued Proclamation 15 of 1919, whereby the general public was forbidden beyond a line (usually drawn on the map in red ink, thus the ''Red Line'') that set the outer limit of the Police Zone. The Red Line (q.v.) began at the mouth of the Omaruru River, followed the river east a distance and then shot north to the Etosha Pan along the Omuramba Ovambo, then it turned south again to Epukiro, and finally east to Beacon No. 19 on the Botswana border. This northern border of the Police Zone was shifted to the north on November 23, 1928, by Proclamation 26 of 1928, and perhaps another dozen times in subsequent years as more European settlers wanted to expand their land holdings or acquire new ones.

Thus the land designated for the Africans to the north of that line (generally the Ovambo, Kavango, and Caprivi peoples) gradually shrank from the one-third of Namibia that was once outside the Police Zone. That name had a very practical origin, as the Germans and later the South Africans limited police protection to the area south of the Red Line, and had police posts at various spots along it, primarily to prohibit unauthorized Africans from entering the Police Zone. In addition, the Germans administered the "Polizei-Zone" directly, and left the northern areas to traditional leaders of the Ovambos and others. Agreements were held with Ovambo chiefs, however, regarding the supply of manpower for work in mines in the Police Zone. In later years the South African government sent officials north of the line to administer the region, which was designated by the Odendaal Commission (q.v.) for several Bantustans. The contract labor system did not apply to those living inside the Police Zone, but Africans there found their lives limited by the need for permits and the Pass Laws (q.v.). The Police Zone contained the country's best agricultural land and mineral reserves. Africans were not allowed to own farm land or stock there, except in several Reserves, which are little more than dust bowls. This whole concept was abandoned after independence.

POLITICAL CONSULTATIVE COUNCIL (PCC). A highly vocal organization during the 1989 Assembly election campaign, this group was formed on July 4, 1989, to work for the release of SWAPO detainees. Under the leadership of its chairman, Riundja Kaakunga, this group of 153 ex-SWAPO detainees issued a list of more than 500 names of people still missing in Angola or elsewhere, and said that there may be another 1800 or more others in SWAPO camps. The work of the PCC led to the appointment of a special UN team to investigate the charges. That team reduced the number but agreed with the premise. SWAPO leaders eventually admitted that some unfortunate excesses had occurred, including torture and brutalities against these people. The group agreed to disband after the November 1989 elections, during which it worked with the Patriotic Unity Movement, which was affiliated with the United Democratic Front (qq.v.).

POMONA. Now a ghost town, located nine kilometers from the coast and about eighty kilometers south of Lüderitz, it was in the heart of the diamond mining district in the 1910s. The largest diamonds were found in the Idatal (q.v.) near Pomona. The town was founded in 1910 as the headquarters of the Südwest-Minengesellschaft and abandoned in 1930.

POPULATION. A new census for Namibia was held in October, 1991. Provisional results became available early in 1992, and showed a total population of 1,401,700, close to the projections of the last South African officials, and much less than the United Nations' estimate of 1.7 million. (With some exceptions more specific figures for many towns were not available at the time of publication.)

The population of Namibia falls into a large number of ethnic categories. It is quite difficult to subdivide them all accurately and to everyone's satisfaction. For example, there are the Black Africans (Ovambos, Hereros, Kavangos, among others); the people of African origin but who are physically not obviously like other indigenous Africans (such as the San and the Nama); people of European origin (South Africans, Germans, and British), plus people of mixed race (the Coloureds and the Rehoboth Basters). The facing table gives some available figures for several dates in Namibia's history. Increases in numbers can sometimes be attributed to better census techniques. Some discrepancies and lack of information are due to official changes in designating groups. The great decrease in Hereros was due to a major war and its aftermath.

PORTUGAL. There are at least three periods when Portugal played a major role in Namibian history. First, Portugal's Prince Henry the Navigator encouraged Portuguese seamen to explore the west coast of Africa. Thus Diego Cão (q.v.) reached the area near today's Swakopmund in 1485 and

NAMIBIAN POPULATION 1877–1988

	1877	1894	1904	1921	1936	1960	1970	1982	1988(*)	% of pop.
Ovambos	98,000	100,000	(**)	91,500	151,973	239,363	352,640	516,600	623,000	49.8%
Kavangos	N.A.	N.A.	N.A.	20,000	19,150	27,871	49,512	98,000	117,000	9.3%
East Caprivians	N.A.	N.A.	N.A.	4,249	11,708	15,840	25,580	39,500	47,000	3.8%
Hereros	85,000	80,000	80,000	31,063	30,720	35,354	50,589	77,600	94,000	8.0%
Kaokolanders	N.A.	N.A.	N.A.	1,500	4,200	9,234	6,547	N.A.	N.A.	N.A.
Damaras	N.A.	N.A.	N.A.	20,883	26,042	44,353	66,291	76,800	94,000	7.5%
Tswanas	N.A.	N.A.	N.A.	OTHERS	OTHERS	OTHERS	4,407	6,800	7,000	0.6%
Bushmen	3,000	(***)	N.A.	3,931	6,724	11,762	22,830	30,000	36,000	2.9%
Berg Damaras	30,000	40,000	N.A.	N.A.	N.A.	N.A.	N.A.	N.A.	N.A.	N.A.
Coloureds	N.A.	N.A.	N.A.	3,438	5,818	12,708	28,512	43,500	51,000	4.1%
Namas/Hottentots	18,350	20,000	20,000	20,968	26,250	34,806	32,935	49,700	60,000	4.8%
Rehobothers	1,500	4,000	4,000	5,719	7,000	11,257	16,649	25,800	31,000	2.5%
Others	N.A.	N.A.	N.A.	200	3,852	9,992	15,089	12,400	12,000	1.0%
Whites	N.A.	N.A.	N.A.	19,714	31,200	73,464	90,583	75,600	80,000	6.4%
Total	235,850	244,000	(****)	223,165	320,457	526,004	762,184	1,039,900	1,252,000	100.0%

(*)   estimated population for 1988 with corresponding percentages of the total population
(**) the Ovambo population in 1904 is estimated between 100,000 and 150,000
(***) in 1894, the Bushman population is included with the Berg Damara population
(****) the total population in 1904 is not calculable

POPULATION OF LARGEST TOWNS IN NAMIBIA*

	Census 1981	Estimate 1988
Windhoek	96,057	114,500
Swakopmund	12,219	15,500
Rehoboth	12,378	15,000
Rundu	12,307	15,000
Keetmanshoop	11,502	14,000
Tsumeb	11,269	13,500
Otjiwarongo	9,087	11,000
Grootfontein	7,536	9,000
Okahandja	6,721	8,000
Mariental	5,367	6,500
Gobabis	5,528	6,500
Khorixas	5,349	6,500
Luderitz	4,748	6,000
Oshakati	3,684	4,000
Karasburg	3,484	4,000
Usakos	2,852	3,500
Otjimbingwe	2,465	3,000
Aranos	1,725	2,000
Maltahohe	1,842	2,000
Karibib	1,608	2,000
Odangua	1,049	1,500

*Namibia has 74 towns, cities, and settlements, each with its own form of local management. There are 15 municipalities, 20 peri-urban areas, 34 towns and settlements in communal areas, and 5 village management boards.

planted a pillar of stone, a padrão (q.v.) in the name of his majesty, King John II. Two years later Bartholomeu Dias (q.v.) commanded another expedition that reached Namibia's shores. This time the padrão was placed at Lüderitz. Second, though the Portuguese never made a significant attempt to control Namibia, they did dominate Angola to the north. In 1915 a war broke out between the Portuguese and the Kwanyama (q.v.), the second largest group of Ovambos, and many Africans died. In 1917 South Africa intervened, as the conflict affected the Namibian border. South Africa then accepted the border as drawn by Portugal, which split the Ovambo people, especially the tribal land of the Kwanyama. Third, in the 1970s the Portuguese completed a major dam on the Kunene River, with great potential for both irrigation and hydro-electric power in northern Namibia. But in the mid-1970s the Portuguese ended their futile attempt to hold on to Angola by military means. When it allowed a fragmented nationalist movement to take control of the underdeveloped territory, Portugal set the stage for both a continuing conflict among the nationalists and for a political vacuum that attracted the major world powers as well as Cuban and South African troops. This latter result had a direct negative effect on the hopes of Namibians to achieve a quick and peaceful independence.

PRETORIUS, JACOBUS W. F. (1935–   ). Popularly known as Kosie, he is the leader of the National Party in Namibia. He was born in Swakopmund. He became a political activist in college at the University of the Orange Free State in South Africa, from which he received both an AB and MA in political science. He entered politics in Namibia at the age of twenty-four as assistant secretary of the National Party. He became chief secretary in 1961 and was elected to the Gobabis seat in the Legislative Assembly. He held the seat for a record twenty-eight years. He was also on the Executive Council from 1969 to 1981, when he was named chairman of the Executive Council of the new Second Tier White Legislative Assembly. He was the leader of AKTUR (q.v.) in 1977, and a member of the National Assembly in 1980 and 1981. He worked on the Constitutional Council in 1985–87, an appropriate assignment, as his masters' thesis was on the constitutional development of South West Africa. On the Constitutional Conference he fought to retain separate group rights, especially in areas such as education. When the council submitted its final report, he submitted a minority report.

When the 1989 elections were scheduled, Pretorius led the National Party into a new political alliance called the Action Christian National (q.v.). It won three seats in the Assembly, and he holds one of them.

Married and father of four children, Pretorius lives in Windhoek. He has owned a farm since 1959 and has been a director (and now chairman) of Die Suidwes Drukkery since 1965.

PRITCHARD, MAJOR S. M. A South African military man in the early twentieth century, he was in command of an expedition sent to Ovamboland in 1915. His purpose was to establish good relations with the various chiefs and to announce that South Africa was taking over control from the Germans. In the process Pritchard received two specific requests for protection. Chief Martin of the Ndonga asked him to grant British protection to the Ndonga area, and Mandume (q.v.), chief of the Kwanyama, sought South African protection from the Portuguese, who had just defeated his troops in battle. This latter request resulted in Pritchard arranging a meeting with Portuguese officials in Mandume's village. This meeting produced a tentative border between Namibia and Angola, one which left two-thirds of the Kwanyama people in Angola. In his report on the expedition, Pritchard recommended that South Africa take advantage of the instability in Ovamboland by instituting administrative control over the region. The absence there of any general form of government administration and the anxiety of the Africans caused by the Portuguese combined to create a uniquely receptive attitude where resistance might well have been anticipated, Pritchard reported. His recommendations were accepted and officials were sent that year to Ondangwa and Namakunde.

PROCLAMATION R17 OF 4 FEBRUARY 1972. As a result of the labor upheaval among Namibia's workers (but especially among Ovambo laborers throughout the country) and the subsequent violence against chiefs and official buildings, Resolution 17 was proclaimed on February 4, 1972. This resolution and the subsequent Proclamation 26 ten days later resulted in the ruling of Ovamboland in a near state of emergency. They stated that all meetings, gatherings, and assemblies, with some exceptions (entertainment, church services, sporting events, etc.), were prohibited unless pre-authorized in writing by the Native commissioner. Certain individuals could be prohibited even from attending gatherings that were otherwise legal. It was also an offense to say or do anything likely to "undermine the authority" of a chief or headman, the Ovambo government, or the state, or even to boycott a meeting called by a headman, chief, or government official. The minister of justice could prohibit any person from "entering, being in, or leaving Ovambo or any part of it." One could be arrested and detained for questioning without right to legal advice and without a warrant, only on the suspicion that the individual might have knowledge of an offense. These and other provisions of these proclamations resulted in the arrest of hundreds of Ovambos. (Even tighter controls were imposed in May 1976.) These proclamations were designed to weaken the ability of SWAPO to organize politically, and thus it was SWAPO that fought them most. John Ya-Otto (q.v.) and Johannes Nangutuuala were among those SWAPO leaders accused of trying to subvert state security by issuing political statements and holding an illegal political meeting. Others tried to evade the law by gathering in stores for political discussions. SWAPO and DEMCOP (q.v.) used these proclamations to justify their unwillingness to participate in Ovambo elections, and SWAPO continued to protest Proclamation R17 in international circles, citing it as one of the elements of the system that had to be changed if a peaceful resolution was to come in Namibia.

PROCLAMATION R104 OF 27 APRIL 1973. The Ovamboland Constitution Proclamation, it declared that on May 1, 1973 Ovamboland would become a self-governing territory. It also required that, for certain purposes, Oshidonga was to be recognized as the official language of Ovamboland. It also set down a series of constitutional provisions.

PROCLAMATION R291 OF 1968. This proclamation provided for the establishment of a Legislative Council in Ovamboland. It stated that the Ovambo people had been duly consulted on the matter, which presumably meant that the traditional leaders had been "consulted." The entire Legislative Council was to consist of nominated members, up to six from each of the seven officially recognized Ovambo tribes. The various tribal authorities were to appoint the members according to their own customs. An Executive Council would also exist, with each of the seven tribes having the right to nominate one member. The Legislative Council would select one of the seven members as chief councillor, who could be dismissed by the state president at the request of the council. The duties of the Executive Council were also set out, and seven administrative departments were designated. In no way did the proclamation provide for "one person, one vote" franchise rights, or for the participation of modernizing political groups.

- Q -

QUEEN ADELAIDE'S BATHS. A name given to the Windhoek (and Klein Windhoek) area by the early British explorer, Sir James Alexander (q.v.), because of the natural hot springs in the vicinity.

QUIVER TREE. Another name for the koker tree or koker baum (q.v.). It is scientifically known as the *Aloe dichotoma*. The name comes from the fact that Nama and San hunters used its hollowed branches as quivers for their poisoned arrows. The densest stand of these trees anywhere in the world is a forest thirteen kilometers northeast of Keetmanshoop.

- R -

RAAD. A council of representatives, such as that chosen by the residents of the Rehoboth Gebiet.

RAILWAYS IN NAMIBIA. The forerunner of the Namibian railway was the attempt of a German officer, Lieutenant Troast, to solve the problem of transporting equipment through the Namib Desert. In 1897 he imported a steam tractor, which carried a few loads before getting stuck in the sand a few miles outside Swakopmund. It is today a National Monument and is nicknamed "Martin Luther" (q.v.). With rinderpest (q.v.) devastating the territory's cattle, a railway running inland from the coast became essential. The first such move was a two-foot, six-inch wide line running from Walvis Bay toward Husab. This eleven-mile stretch was built

in 1897–98 to connect with a transport road from Swakopmund to the interior.

The rights to build railways were given by the German
government to major companies, first the Deutsche Koloni-
algeseilschaft (q.v.), and later the South West Africa Company (q.v.) and the Otavi Minen und Eisenbahn Gesellschaft
(q.v.), known as OMEG. The Northern State Railway Line
was begun in 1897 and took five years to complete. It was
designed to connect the seaport, Swakopmund, with the
capital, Windhoek. It traversed a total of 238 miles, 121 from
Swakopmund to Karibib, and 117 from there to Windhoek.
There was also a ten-mile branch from Jakalswater. This
main line was built with a narrow gauge; it was widened (at
least the Karibib-Windhoek segment) in less than a decade to
three feet, six inches to allow linkage with the Cape railway,
which came toward Windhoek from the south. Meanwhile
the Swakopmund-Karibib segment was abandoned, as a
parallel line built by OMEG became the main route. This line
was begun at Swakopmund in 1903 and was completed to the
Otavi mines by 1906. It branched off at Karibib and headed
north to Otavi and Tsumeb, the latter a trip of about 356
miles (565 kilometers). The rich copper ore in the north
justified the expense of construction. Another 57-mile segment went from Otavi to Grootfontein. The protectorate
government bought all of these narrow gauge OMEG lines in
1910, while the mining company retained the rolling stock
and ran it on a lease.

Curiously, Cecil Rhodes was interested at one point in
building a line from Grootfontein to Rhodesia, but this did
not occur, nor did the proposal to build from Otavi to
Ovamboland. Two rail stations were built in Swakopmund,
one by the State Railway and the other by OMEG. They both
still exist, with the latter being the present station. The
invasion of troops from the Union of South Africa in 1915
produced further changes. Retreating German troops had
torn up the old narrow-gauge line, and the invading South
Africans rebuilt it as far as Usakos with their own three-foot,
six-inch gauge. The Union government also laid its line from
Walvis Bay to Swakopmund in 1915. Other early lines of
importance were the North-South Railway that linked Wind-

hoek to Keetmanshoop in the south, which began in 1910. The main line of 317 miles was set to the Cape (or Union) gauge. A Southern Railway was begun in 1905 from Lüderitz Bay to Aus (88 miles), but was extended to Keetmanshoop and later to Kalkfontein. When South Africa invaded the German Protectorate in 1915, it added a link from Upington in the Union to Kalkfontein. The invasion north from there to Windhoek was easier because that line (via Keetmanshoop) was all of the wider gauge.

The South African Railway Administration took over the system on August 1, 1915. It converted some of the remaining narrow-gauge track by 1924, but the line from Usakos to Tsumeb remained narrow until January 30, 1961, when the last of the old German line was replaced with the standard gauge. Old coaches were dismantled in 1962, and 145 old railway bridges the next year.

While the narrow-gauge line had been a masterpiece for its era, it lacked comfort. The benches were hard, and no sleeping compartments were possible due to the narrow width. Thus trains had to stop at night so passengers could sleep at little terminal hotels. The old trains ran on wood, so stops were frequent to gather fuel. Passengers rested under trees and some even went hunting until notified to return.

A South African Act (No. 20 of 1922) placed the Namibian railways and harbors under South African administration. Improvements were aimed mainly at the export of ore and transportation between centers of European settlements. A significant new line extends east from Windhoek to Gobabis. Other small lines have been added. Recent figures show 2300 kilometers of railway in Namibia. The railways use diesel-electric power. There are five depots, the largest located at Windhoek.

RAUTANEN, REV. MARTTI (1845–1926). One of the most devoted of the early Christian missionaries, he was born in Novasolka, Finland. At the age of twenty-five he arrived in South West Africa, where he and six other colleagues from the Finnish Mission Society stayed for a while with Rev. Hugo Hahn (q.v.). He learned Herero from Hahn at Otjimbingwe. He then traveled to Ongandjero where he set up a mission station which he called Rehoboth (later Okahao). This was north of the Etosha Pan and has no relation to the other site called Rehoboth (q.v.). This station had to be abandoned as the local chief opposed it. Rautanen went south to the other Rehoboth in Namaland, where on September 11, 1872, he married Frieda Kleinschmidt. He returned to Ovamboland and worked at Ondonga until June 1880. His final mission was at Olukonda, where he worked for forty-six years until his death in 1926. For many years he was the bishop of the area, and when he died there were Ovambo pastors at his grave. He served in many roles, advising chiefs, writing articles about the Ovambo people (and especially the Ondonga), and translating the New Testament into their language. His work in northern Namibia has been compared to noted missionaries such as Hahn among the Hereros and Robert Moffat among the Tswanas.

RED LINE. The northern boundaries of the Police Zone (q.v.) were always marked with a red line on maps; thus the term became a quick reference to the area. The actual location of the boundaries (and thus of the Red Line) was shifted at least a dozen times over the years. Beyond the Red Line, there were no police stations and one travelled at one's own risk.

RED NATION. Prior to the eighteenth century, many groups of Nama lived in the Western Cape, south of the Orange River. The lack of sufficient water and grazing land led some of them to cross into Namibia. The first major group to do this, which became a power in southern Namibia for more than 150 years, was known as the Red Nation ("Rode Natie"). They called themselves "Awa-khoin" or "Red People," as they are described as having dull red complexions under a "pale-yellow" base. They seem to be distinct from the many Bantu peoples of Africa. The Red Nation is also called in various places the Geikous, Gei-//khaun, the Kouben, and the //Khauben. The root of all of these is the Nama word "Kou," which when spoken in a high tone means "to defend," thus describing them as "the defenders." The Red Nation, including its allies and those who chose to leave the original base at Hoachanas (q.v.), would ultimately claim all the southern half of Namibia, between the Swakop and Orange Rivers. As strong as they were at times, the risk of making that claim was not to be taken lightly. The land had been inhabited by rather loose bands of San and Damas.

As the first Namas in the area, the Red Nation could declare hegemony there and require subsequent groups to pay tribute. Ultimately five other Nama groups allied with the //Khauben, including those who became known as the Franschmännsche (Frenchmen) Hottentots, the Feldschuträgers, the Groot-doden, the Kara-oan, and the //Khan-/goan or Zwartbooi Hottentots (qq.v.). Leadership for the six allied groups was under the chief at Hoachanas. The San and Damas either fled, hid in the mountains or Namib Desert, or were captured as servants for the Nama. Not all Nama groups allied with the Red Nation. Two that did not were the Topnaars and the Bondelswarts (qq.v.).

The first true chief of the Red Nation is said to have been named Hab. He ruled firmly, convincing the various clans of the necessity of cooperating. It is said that "Hab made the Nama a nation." Hab's son, Hanab, succeeded him, and one of the sons of Hanab, Gao-karib was next to take charge. The latter has been described as benevolent and peaceful. A treaty he secured with San leaders on the Waterberg gave him credibility in extending his sovereignty north to the Waterberg, Herero claims notwithstanding. Gao-karib died without leaving a male successor, and a wealthy cattle-owner named Haromab was selected as chief. His thirty-year reign was filled with dissension and civil war. He was arrogant and cruel to his people. His death brought a plea for the return of the royal line of Hab. From this family Nanieb I was chosen. During his reign late in the eighteenth century, the Namas had some minor skirmishes with northern tribes such as the Herero, whom they encountered north of Windhoek and Okahandja. His successor, Nanieb II, ruled briefly. When the latter's son Oasib was too young to rule, the Red Nation turned to Games, sister of Nanieb I. This remarkable leader ruled the Red Nation for about the first third of the nineteenth century. During that period the Red Nation received and granted requests from five Orlam (q.v.) groups to cross the Orange River into Namaland. As the decades passed and the

Herero became an increasing threat in the north, Games called on Jonker Afrikander (q.v.), leader of an Orlam group near the Orange River, to provide military assistance. His small but superior force turned the tide against the Hereros, and his stature rose. He even set up his capital at Klein Windhoek. Meanwhile Games retired as regent, and Oasib became leader of the Red Nation. But Jonker Afrikander's military exploits overshadowed Oasib, and attacks in the name of the Red Nation can be better attributed to Jonker than Oasib.

Other Nama groups began to flex their muscles in their areas, the Zwartboois and Witboois among them. The various groups found themselves competing with each other for land and influence. Jonker was prepared to concede Oasib's leadership only of the early Namas. An attempt by Oasib and the Zwartboois at Rehoboth to weaken Jonker's influence met defeat in 1854. A peace treaty was signed by all Nama leaders (including Jonker) except the Bondelswarts (whose territory was not involved in the conflicts) on January 9, 1838 at Hoachanas, the traditional capital of the Red Nation. It was designed to resolve all areas of disagreement. Yet less than ten years later the conflicts were renewed. An attack upon the Witboois and Bersebas in 1866–67 by Oasib resulted in his own devastating defeat in July 1867. He died soon after, and his son Barnabas agreed to a peace treaty on March 18, 1868, ending all claims by the Red Nation to hegemony over the other Nama tribes.

REGIONS. At the time that the Constituent Assembly was creating a new constitution for Namibia in 1990 it was understood by all the participants that new arrangements would be needed in order to create second tier (regions) and third tier (local) authorities. (These new regions would replace the old Districts created by the South African Government under the Odendaal Plan and Proclamation AG8/1980.) One of the reasons for the change was that the constitution provides that new regional councils are to select two members each to a second national government chamber, the National Council. To establish the regions and the voting rolls, however, a new census was needed. When that was completed in 1991, a Delimitation Commission was appointed. The three member commission, chaired by Judge Strydom, published its recommendations in October, 1991. The goal was to establish regions based on geographic considerations rather than ethnic ones, so as to reverse the divisive trends created by the previous districts. It recommended thirteen regions, based on the ideas heard at about forty public meetings, and on suggestions made by the various political parties. About six months later President Sam Nujoma issued a proclamation on the 13 new regions and 45 local authorities, with the regional boundaries identical to the commission's recommendations. Regional and local elections were held in November, 1992. (A map of the regions and some results from the election are to be found in the Appendix.)

REHOBOTH. The word has different implications depending on its context. For example, it is a town of approximately 25,000 inhabitants located 88 kilometers south of Windhoek on the Great North Road that leads to South Africa. It has been the administrative center of the Rehoboth district (q.v.). But the term Rehoboth Gebiet (q.v.) refers to a smaller unit that is considered a Reserve or Homeland for a specific ethnic group, the Basters (q.v.). In this connection it becomes part of the name of a wide range of political and economic organizations.

While linked closely today with the Basters, the Rehoboth area was once the home of various Nama groups. Jonker Afrikander (q.v.) was living in the high country there in 1837. The Zwartbooi (q.v.) Namas arrived, however, and lived there for over two decades until Jan Jonker Afrikander defeated them in battle there in 1864. Meanwhile the Rhenish missionary Frans Kleinschmidt (q.v.) went to serve the Zwartboois (or Swartboois), arriving at Rehoboth (called Anis by the Namas) on May 11, 1845. He gave it its current Biblical name. Although not there continuously, Rev. Kleinschmidt and his family did not leave Rehoboth until the Zwartboois abandoned the town in July 1864 when Jan Jonker's forces approached. Jonker's forces caught up with the fleeing peoples at the Kuiseb River (q.v.) on August 18, 1864.

The Basters (q.v.), a mixed race group then living in the Western Cape Colony, had despaired at the combination of drought and prejudice there and decided to move north of the Orange River. In February 1868, the decision was made to move, and about ninety families led by Hermanus Van Wyck (q.v.) and accompanied by Rev. Johann Heidmann began their trek. Jan Jonker Afrikander would have welcomed them in Windhoek, but only if Van Wyck resigned and they accepted his authority. They rejected this condition and decided to settle at Rehoboth, where there was a church and mission house vacated six years earlier in 1864 by Kleinschmidt. This move did not go unchallenged, however, as the Basters discovered after settling in. Van Wyck had to cope with claims by Jan Jonker, the Zwartboois, and even the Hereros. At a peace conference in Okahandja he met with Willem, chief of those Zwartboois who had lived at Rehoboth, and requested permission to remain there. It was granted at the fee of one horse per year. (A later "sale" price was much higher.)

While this ended the Basters wandering, it did not end conflict over the territorial rights. (*See* VAN WYCK, HERMANUS.) These conflicts continued until the Basters received protection by the Germans in a treaty formalized on September 15, 1885. This treaty of "protection" allowed internal affairs to remain in the hands of the Baster Council (Raad), but relations with other tribes and countries would be under German control. Despite this treaty, the Rehobothers retained a great deal of independence down to the present. After World War I the Basters negotiated a similar treaty with South Africa, again placing internal authority in the Baster Council (Raad) under a written constitution known as the "Vaderlike Wette" or patriarchal laws. These rules had been followed by the Basters since long before the treaty with the Germans. The agreement with South Africa was reached in 1923, but the next year a newly elected council declared independence. A rebellion on April 4, 1925, was met by the arrival of South African police and soldiers who put a stop to this rebellion.

The 14,182 square kilometers of the Rehoboth Gebiet (q.v.) is a reserve, and the sale of land to whites is forbidden.

The approximately 30,000 inhabitants are industrious and enterprising, and their pastoral territory and livestock are well-tended. The South African government created a ministry for Rehoboth affairs in the South African Parliament; and following the report of the Odendaal Commission (q.v.) enlarged the *Gebiet* by adding some white farms. However, the *district* had considerable territory removed from it and added to the neighboring white-ruled districts. Until December 4, 1970, the Rehoboth district had consisted of 29,614 square kilometers, so it was reduced to almost half its earlier size. The people of Rehoboth have remained active politically, some supporting SWAPO, some working within the Democratic Turnhalle Alliance, and some taking a middle road. Those positions would be represented by Dr. F. S. Stellmacher, Dr. B. J. Africa, and Mrs. Otillie Abrahams, respectively. The current Baster Kaptein (q.v.) (''Chief''), Johannes (''Hans'') Diergaardt, refused to accept the dissolution of the Second Tier Governments that allowed Rehoboth Basters to have self-government. Two days before Namibia became independent, he challenged the new government by declaring a unilateral Declaration of Independence for the Rehoboth Gebiet.

The town of Rehoboth is located along the dry bed of the Rehoboth River, and has primary schools and a secondary school. The water supply comes from its hot water mineral springs.

REHOBOTH BASTERS. A non-pejorative phrase used to refer to the multiracial inhabitants of the Rehoboth area who are more commonly called Basters (q.v.).

REHOBOTH BASTER VERENIGING (ASSOCIATION). Formed in 1971 by Dr. B. J. Africa, it was successful in gaining four of the seven seats in the Basterraad during the April 1975 election. The party opposed the nationalist movement led by SWAPO, and has been supportive of separate development according to individual groups. This position would support the autonomy of the Basters within a larger Namibia. Dr. Africa supported the positions of Dirk Mudge and Clemens Kapuuo at the Turnhalle Conference. When Mudge formed the Democratic Turnhalle Alliance

(DTA) in 1977, the Baster Vereniging became one of its constituent member organizations. The chairman of the Baster Vereniging, Petrus Junius (q.v.) was elected to the National Assembly in December 1978, and was chosen the Assembly's vice-president. Dr. Africa, meanwhile, remained the party leader and also was chosen vice-president of the DTA. Also a member of the 1979–83 National Assembly, he was chosen to the Council of Ministers in July 1980. With the formation of the Government of National Unity in June 1985, Junius was named deputy minister.

The party has experienced two major splits. The first occurred in 1977 when several of its members in the Basterraad resigned and formed the Rehoboth Democratic Party (*see* LIBERATED DEMOCRATIC PARTY). A more serious split occurred in 1986 when Junius and twenty-five other members were expelled by Dr. Africa because they stated that they had no confidence in him. Junius had been the party chairman. He led the others into a new group, the Progressive People's Party. In doing so Junius cost the party its last seat in the Raad, as it was his. Meanwhile the PPP was also granted membership in the DTA. In the 1989 Assembly elections both Junius and Dr. Africa received DTA seats in the new Assembly. Since November 1986 it has been called the Rehoboth DTA Party.

REHOBOTH BURGERS' ASSOCIATION (variant: BASTERSRAAD). A semi-political association to which all citizens of Rehoboth automatically belong. At the time in the late 1950s when political parties were just starting to develop in the territory, the Burgers' Association was already recognized as an organization committed to opposing apartheid.

REHOBOTH DEMOCRATIC PARTY. *See* LIBERATED DEMOCRATIC PARTY.

REHOBOTH DTA PARTY. *See* REHOBOTH BASTER VERENIGING.

REHOBOTH DISTRICT. As early as 1890 the Germans subdivided their territory into Bezirksämter (regions) and Distriksämter (districts). The Bezirk Rehoboth contained the Rehoboth Gebiet (q.v.) in its center but was about double the size of the Gebiet, extending both to the west and east of it. Under South African administration in 1921, the Rehoboth district was very similar in size except for a wing in the northwest that was added to the Windhoek district. This administrative pattern remained static until the implementation of the Odendaal Plan in December 1970, when Rehoboth was reduced to little more than the traditional area of the Gebiet or "Reserve." It went from 29,614 square kilometers to 14,182 square kilometers. The remaining land areas were added to the Windhoek, Maltahöhe, and Mariental districts. The old district had at one time reached as far south as the village of Schlip, as far southeast as Hoachanas.

REHOBOTH GEBIET. Located south of Windhoek and almost in the geographical center of Namibia, this "Reserve" for the Rehoboth people of Basters (q.v.) consists of 1,312,000 hectares. Under the leadership of Hermanus van Wyck (q.v.), these "Coloureds" from South Africa had settled in the Rehoboth district in 1879. Previously the Zwartbooi Namas had lived there. A treaty with the Germans in 1885 promised friendship and protection, but after World War I a new treaty was needed. Thus an agreement was signed in 1923 with South Africa concerning the administration of the Gebiet. A Baster Council (Basterraad) would regulate the affairs of the area. The Gebiet's 14,180 square kilometers contain about 30,000 people, plus some excellent pastoral land. The major settlement in the district is also called Rehoboth (q.v.). (*See also* REHOBOTH DISTRICT.)

REHOBOTH LIBERATION PARTY/FRONT. *See* LIBERATED DEMOCRATIC PARTY.

REHOBOTH VOLKSPARTEI (variant: PEOPLE'S PARTY). For years the most popular political organization in Rehoboth, it was led by Dr. D. J. Izaaks and Mr. J. G. A. (Hans) Diergaardt (qq.v.). The latter was the chairman at the organizational meeting of the National Convention of Freedom Parties when it formed in November 1971. Volkspartei was strongly antigovernment, and until 1974 held all seven elected seats in the Basterraad. When the National Convention split in 1974–75, the Volkspartei also split. One group, led by Dr. F. S. Stellmacher and Mrs. Martha Ford, retained the party name, supported SWAPO, and joined the Namibia National Convention. D. J. Izaaks and Hans Diergaardt formed the Rehoboth Liberation Party (*see* LIBERATED DEMOCRATIC PARTY), a more conservative group. At elections for the Basterraad in April 1975, the Volkspartei retained only one of its seven seats (that of its leader, Dr. Stellmacher), and the Liberation Party won two. The Rehoboth Bastervereniging won the other four. In November 1976, Dr. Stellmacher announced the dissolution of the Volkspartei, and that its members would join SWAPO. Instead, however, some joined the Federal Party (q.v.), and the party died except for a small "study group." In 1989 the latter few formed the core of a group called the Rehoboth Volksparty. Its leaders are Arrie Smith and Berend de Klerk. For election purposes they joined the Namibia National Front (q.v.). Neither won an Assembly seat.

REHOBOTHERS. *See* BASTERS.

REITERDENKMAL. Officially known as "Der Reiter von Südwest," this "Cavalryman Memorial" is silhouetted on a hillside in Windhoek with the Alte Feste (Old Fort) in the background. The attractive equestrian statue was suggested by Col. Ludwig von Estorff (q.v.), commanding officer of the Schutztruppe who wanted a monument erected to honor the German troopers killed battling the Hereros and Namas from 1903 to 1907. The sculptor, Adolf Kürle, was from Berlin, who (curiously) only won third prize with his design. The winning statue was not popular in Windhoek and so was shipped to Swakopmund; the second-prize winner was considered inappropriately gory. Thus Kürle's design was cast and finally unveiled by the governor, Dr. Seitz, on January 27, 1912.

REPUBLICAN PARTY. An important part of the Democratic Turnhalle Alliance (q.v.), it was formed on September 28,

1977, by Dirk Mudge (q.v.) after he lost a leadership fight within the National Party (q.v.) to more conservative elements. This all-white party became the chosen ally of South Africa, although most settlers in Namibia remained in the National Party. It was Mudge's position that multiracial elections and meetings were inevitable, and so a multiracial political alliance had to be created. In this spirit he created the Democratic Turnhalle Alliance (DTA), a coalition of political parties and groups, with Clemens Kapuuo (q.v.). Mudge became its first chairman and Kapuuo its first president. Mudge and his party members consider themselves "verligte" or enlightened, but also pragmatic. Yet the National Party (N.P.) has been more successful among white voters, such as in the November 1980 Second Tier elections where the Republican Party was overwhelmed by the N.P.

In 1985 it opened its membership to all races. Through its leader it has taken part in the Multi-Party Conference, and in the Transitional Government of National Unity (qq.v.). In the 1989 Assembly elections, the DTA won 21 seats, of which two went to members of the Republican Party, Mudge, and Party Chairman "Hans" Staby. With the adoption of the new unitary form of the DTA of Namibia in November, 1991, the Republican Party ceased to be a separate entity and was absorbed into the DTA.

RESERVES. Set up by South African administrators even before the mandate was given by the League of Nations, the "reserves" were limited geographical areas set aside for African settlement, but designed to serve as labor reservoirs for mining companies or white settlers. This limited the number of Africans in "white" areas, and gave them a place for the old and infirm Africans as well as their livestock. The reserve system was first recommended by an administrator's report in 1920. While a particular tribe would usually dominate a specific reserve, minority groups would often coexist there. A local magistrate was arbiter for the area, and a reserve board represented different groups. The magistrate also issued the permits needed to leave the reserve. Housing was mostly traditionally built huts, and agricultural production was not overly successful. The recommendations of the

Odendaal Commission (q.v.) led to the proposal in 1964 that transformed the Reserves into ten tribal "homelands." A system of Reserves was not unusual in areas of Africa where white settlers came in any significant numbers, but this fact did not make the policy any more just or humane. South Africans like to compare the Reserves to American Indian reservations. (*See also* BANTUSTANS.)

RESOLUTION 385. A UN Security Council resolution passed January 30, 1976, it set out the principles and conditions to be observed in a transition to Namibian independence. Passed unanimously, the resolution condemned South Africa's illegal occupation of Namibia, the brutal oppression of the people, and the military build-up by South Africa, and demanded free elections for the country as a single entity, under UN supervision. This led to activity by the Western Five Contact Group (q.v.) in an effort to get a negotiated settlement with South Africa. These negotiations ultimately led to Resolution 435 (q.v.).

RESOLUTION 431. Passed by the UN Security Council in 1978, this resolution called on the secretary general to appoint a special representative for Namibia, with the goal being Namibia's early independence through free elections supervised by the UN. The secretary general then appointed Mr. Martti Ahtisaari.

RESOLUTION 432. A UN Security Council resolution passed unanimously in 1978, it stated that for the sake of Namibia's territorial integrity, Walvis Bay (q.v.) must be reintegrated into Namibia, and that South Africa must not use Walvis Bay in any way prejudicial to Namibia's independence or its economic viability.

RESOLUTION 435. Passed by the UN Security Council on September 29, 1978, this resolution endorsed the report issued a month earlier by Secretary General Kurt Waldheim concerning Namibia's independence. Dr. Waldheim's report was based on the results of negotiations initiated by the Western Five Contact Group, and it had the support of

SWAPO. The report would require a three-stage sequence: (1) cessation of all hostile acts by all parties, and the withdrawal of all armed forces; (2) free and fair elections to a Constituent Assembly would be held, *after* restrictive laws were repealed, political prisoners were released, exiles were allowed to return, and the United Nations had monitored an appropriate campaign period; (3) the adoption of a constitution by the elected Assembly, followed by its entry into force and national independence. Waldheim reported that for all three stages to occur, there must be established a UN Transition Assistance Group (UNTAG) in Namibia, consisting of both a civilian component of 2260 UN officials and police, plus a military component of 7500 soldiers.

In response to Resolution 435, the South African government defiantly announced that it would hold its own elections in December for a Namibian Assembly, in direct contravention of Resolution 435. Nevertheless further efforts were made to implement Resolution 435, and indeed international meetings and agreements in 1988 led to the process by which implementation of 435 began in 1989, with independence in 1990.

RHENISH MISSIONARY SOCIETY (RMS). The dominant missionary society in Namibia for more than a century, its history from the 1840s to the 1940s could include reference to almost every significant resident of the territory (outside Ovamboland) in that period. (This essay can only skim the surface; more information will be found in the entries devoted to specific RMS missionaries, such as C. H. Hahn, H. Vedder, F. H. Kleinschmidt, J. Roth, and others mentioned here.)

The RMS was founded in 1828 as the Vereinigte Rheinische Missions Gesellschaft. It was a merger of four small Lutheran mission agencies, Elberfeld, Barmen, Wesel, and Köln. The next year they sent their first missionaries to the Eastern Cape in South Africa. More than a decade passed before they moved into Namibia. The London Missionary Society (q.v.) was already there, and the Wesleyan Missionary Society (q.v.) was also about to enter the territory.

The London Society (LMS) had experienced setbacks

working among the Namas, and in 1840 transferred its rights to the RMS. Rev. J. H. Schmelen (q.v.) of the LMS urged the RMS to send enough missionaries to work with the Orlams of Jonker Afrikander, other Nama groups, and the Hereros. Capt. James Alexander (q.v.) also urged the RMS to send missionaries north of the Orange, in response to which the society sent Rev. Carl Hugo Hahn and Rev. F. H. Kleinschmidt (qq.v.).

In 1842 Hahn and Kleinschmidt arrived in Namibia, under instructions to see what could be done among the Hereros. They arrived in Windhoek on December 9, 1842. They left there in 1844 as Jonker Afrikander suggested that the Wesleyans should work there. They first went to work among the Hereros at Okahandja (q.v.), but when a drought forced the Africans to move their herds, the missionaries followed to a place called Otjikango. This they renamed Barmen (q.v.), honoring the German town where they began their missionary training. The mission was established October 31, 1844. When things appeared stable, Kleinschmidt went to Anis (now Rehoboth, q.v.) to work among the Zwartboois. He arrived May 11, 1845.

Meanwhile in 1842 H. C. Knudsen, another RMS missionary, had followed the Hahn-Kleinschmidt route, but remained at Bethanie (q.v.) in Schmelen's old LMS station. Knudsen left for his Norwegian home of Bergen in 1847 to be married, and returned two years later to Bethanie with unfortunate results.

More RMS men came. Rev. J. Rath and Rev. Scheppmann landed at Walvis Bay in 1844. Rath set up a station among the Hereros at Otjimbingwe, while Scheppmann worked among the Topnaars at Rooibank. The latter died a few years later of an accident. Rev. F. W. Kolbe came in 1848, and set up a station at Okahandja the next year. Rev. J. S. Hahn came the same year to Bethanie to succeed Knudsen, but two years later set up a station among the Orlams at Berseba, only to return to Germany because of ill health the next year. When the Wesleyans returned to England for lack of missionaries and money, the field was left to the RMS. It in turn invited the Finnish (Lutheran) Mission Society (q.v.) to join them in Namibia, suggesting that the newcomers work among the

Ovambos in the far north of the territory. Hugo Hahn (who became the senior missionary, serving at Barmen for decades) felt that the RMS would be spread too thin if it attempted to work among the Ovambos as well.

As the RMS stations took hold, there were a number of effects. The very presence of the missionaries opened the area for trade, as newcomers found the mission stations havens for rest and renewal and also sources of travel advice. Dr. H. Vedder (q.v.), also an RMS missionary, claims that the stations (and their churches and schools) helped to encourage the different tribal groups to settle down, adopting the mission location as their spiritual and intellectual "capital." When the Augustineum (q.v.) was constructed at Otjimbingwe by the RMS in 1866, Maherero was so pleased that he sent his sons to be its first pupils.

The missionaries provided a number of services, some of them far removed from church work. For example, the need to travel between missions resulted directly in the establishment of some new roads. A postal system was encouraged by missionaries so their letters from and to Europe would reach their destinations more quickly. Rev. Knudsen helped the Namas at Bethanie to codify their traditional tribal regulations in a book. Indeed it is in the area of literature and linguistics that the RMS probably had its greatest impact. Various missionaries worked diligently on setting down the spoken languages of the Africans in written form. They then put together grammars for teaching, and of course translated the Bible—as well as traditional European tales—into the languages. The Revs. Knudsen, Krönlein, Olpp, Vedder, and Rust all worked among the Namas and wrote in their language, while Roth, C. H. Hahn, Irle, Kuhlmann, and again Vedder wrote in the Herero language.

Not everyone sees the RMS role as being a positive force. Some claim that by encouraging the Africans to use the station as a tribal center and thus settle down, they disrupted the important migrating patterns of the pastoralists and thus their economies. The missionaries also set up trading outlets at the mission stations, thus "indoctrinating" the Africans into a foreign culture and inducing a dependence on imported goods (and thus also a cash economy). Some argue also that the RMS preachers gained undue influence in tribal life, their authority surpassed only by the tribal leaders and the family heads. No one was truly accepted as a community leader if he were not a member of the faithful. It is said that Samuel Maharero was chosen to succeed his father as chief because RMS missionaries supported him over his non-Christian rivals. When the RMS closed its stations in Namaland, Hendrik Witbooi (q.v.), himself a convert, proclaimed undauntedly that *he* would be supreme bishop of the native church. Prior to that he justified attacks on neighboring tribes by claiming that he was an instrument of the Lord who was sent to punish other tribes for their sins.

While the RMS worked among many of the tribes, it could not prevent them from attacking each other, as in the case of Witbooi. When a war broke out in 1863 between Namas and Hereros, there were constant attacks upon the mission stations. In 1868 the RMS (supported by German Chancellor Bismarck) urged British intervention, even that Damaraland be declared British territory. This was not done, but a British warship did go to Walvis Bay, and the good offices of the governor of the Cape Colony was used to bring peace to the tribes in 1870.

Whether or not the RMS caused Namibian colonization, it is a fact that the missionaries agreed to it, and even facilitated it by serving as interpretors and advisors to the tribal leaders. After the German-Herero War in 1905, the Germans turned over three camps of surviving Hereros to the RMS men, who thereby helped to save about 12,000 Hereros from genocide. Nevertheless, Hereros generally resented the RMS support of the Germans and had to be won back.

But the RMS missionaries were ultimately successful in converting the Africans. Progress was slow at first, but by 1874 there were 2200 converts, and 3000 in 1888, especially among the Hereros in Damaraland. By 1909 there were 13 main stations of the RMS and 10 out-stations in Damaraland, plus 6 main stations among the Namas. At that time there were 11,000 converts.

In 1957 the RMS granted its Namibian church local autonomy as the Evangelical Lutheran Church (q.v.). Ten years later it became fully independent and today has a membership of about 150,000.

RINDERPEST. A lung disease, this cattle plague hit some of Namibia very hard, especially the cattle-raising Hereros. It also prevented travelers from moving about, as the wagon oxen were very vulnerable. It was one factor in the urgency to build a railway line from Swakopmund to Windhoek. The years 1896 and 1897 were especially bad disease years. In 1897 roughly 80 to 90 percent of Herero cattle were lost to the disease. Meanwhile, German settlers had initiated a timely inoculation program and their cattle fared much better, losing only about 25 percent. The disease swept southern African on other occasions, for example, it invaded Namibia in 1860 as well.

RIO TINTO ZINC (RTZ). Known now as RTZ, this British-based multinational group is the principal stockholder in Namibia's major uranium mine, the Rössing Uranium Mine (q.v.). It bought the rights to the huge deposits in 1966. It signed long-term contracts with the British government and others to supply them with uranium. Actual production of uranium ore from Rössing began in 1976. RTZ owns 46.5 percent of the equity shares in Rössing, but only 26.5 percent of the voting rights. South Africa's state-owned Industrial Development Corporation (IDC) with 13 percent, and Rio Algom, a Canadian subsidiary of RTZ with 20 percent, are among RTZ's partners.

One of RTZ's major contracts is with British Nuclear Fuels, providing the UK with a low-cost uranium oxide source. This contract was made in the face of United Nations pressures against further world investment in Namibian mines after the World Court decision (or "non-decision") of 1966. SWAPO maintains that all mining titles and prospecting rights granted after 1966 are illegal. Rössing is very important to RTZ. While in 1982 it was only 4.5 percent of the group's assets and only 5.5 percent of its sales, it provided RTZ with 40 percent of its pre-tax profits and 20 percent of its post-tax profits.

High profitability of the Rössing mine in 1980–82 was dependent on long-term sales contracts secured by RTZ. When the main contract for the sale of 7,500 tons of oxide to the UK ended in 1984, RTZ has had to attempt to sell more on the open market, which has consistently lower spot prices in the 1980s with low immediate prospects for increase in the future.

RIRUAKO, KUAIMA (1935–   ). A politician in both the traditional and the modern spheres, Riruako was born in the Aminuis Reserve for Hereros, a great-nephew of Maherero (q.v.). Educated in Windhoek at St. Barnabas School, he earned a diploma in printing. His teacher at the Anglican school was Clemens Kapuuo (q.v.), founder of the National Unity Democratic Organization, which Riruako joined in 1964. At the age of 28 he left the country as a refugee, seeking further education. He was arrested by British authorities in Botswana and was found guilty of "violating the Queen's laws." Soon released, however, he traveled to Ethiopia, where in 1965 he was appointed the envoy of Kapuuo's National Unity Democratic Organization (NUDO) to Nkrumah's Ghana. When Nkrumah was overthrown in 1966, Riruako returned to Zambia where SWAPO threatened him with jail unless he joined them. Committed to NUDO, he chose jail, which resulted in a year of solitary confinement in Pretoria. He ultimately ended up in a Lusaka refugee camp. He was eventually released to the care of Dr. Kenneth Abrahams, whose wife is related to Riruako.

With the aid of the UN deputy high commissioner for refugees and an American development officer, he was transported to New York, where he resumed his studies. He earned a BA in political science and philosophy at the City University of New York. Having maintained close ties with Kapuuo, he was named NUDO's representative at the United Nations in 1973. When Kapuuo (q.v.) was assassinated in 1978, Riruako was called home to Namibia. Having been the nephew of the noted Herero chief and apartheid opponent, Hosea Kutako (q.v.), and great-nephew of Maherero himself, Riruako was a strong candidate for Kapuuo's chieftainship of the Hereros. In June 1978, he was selected by the Herero Chief's Council. He also was chosen to replace Johannes Karuuihe, who was a temporary successor to Kapuuo in the Democratic Turnhalle Alliance. Assembly elections took place in December 1978, and Riruako was selected to the council of ministers. He was also selected vide-chairman of the Democratic Turnhalle Alliance, in which capacity he opposed a UN-sponsored plan for Namibian elections, fearing that SWAPO would win. In 1982 he was elected president of the DTA, after Rev. Peter Kalangula (q.v.) left the position and the DTA in February 1982. Riruako also became a leader of the Multi-Party Conference. Despite his position Chief Riruako did not gain a seat in the National Assembly. He purportedly refused to have his name on the DTA electoral list because he had not been given the top position. It was announced at a DTA meeting in March, 1990 that Chief Riruako had resigned as President of the DTA.

RIVERS OF NAMIBIA. There are only three perennial streams in the country, each helping to form a boundary with its neighbors. The Orange River (q.v.) on the south separates Namibia from South Africa. The Kunene River (q.v.) is on the northwest boundary with Angola, while the Okavango River separates the same two countries in the northeast. All other rivers in Namibia are intermittent streams, which flow only during the rare periods of heavy rainfall. However, potable water can sometimes be found flowing beneath the dry riverbeds of these streams.

A number of rivers flowing westward toward the Atlantic Ocean are stopped by the Namib Desert and are absorbed into the same or evaporate. One of the few westward-flowing rivers to reach the Atlantic is the Kuiseb River, which is important as the water supply for the town of Walvis Bay and sometimes Swakopmund. The Swakop River, a little to the north, only reaches the Atlantic in the heaviest rainy seasons, as it is normally a dry bed. During the 1934 extraordinary rainfall and floods, the Swakop flowed steadily for three months. The southward flowing Fish River (q.v.) is another significant intermittent river, as are the Omaruru and Ugab Rivers, which are north of the Swakop.

ROCK ART. There are few subjects on Namibia about which as much has been written, yet so little known for certain. Some facts are easy. There are tremendous quantities of visual art that can be found on walls and in caves throughout the country. Some consist of engravings, others are painted images. The subjects include animals, human figures, and geometric shapes. Beyond this, little else is certain.

The dates of the origin of the rock art varies, naturally, from site to site. A rock shelter in southern Namibia contained six slabs of granite, each the size of a hand, and a pebble. All had traces of paint and shapes of humans, animals, or lines. They have been dated to the beginning of the Late Stone Age, or about 30,000 years ago. These finds are credited to W. E. Wendt. On the other extreme, some of the art is clearly the work of nineteenth-century Africans. Observations by Europeans and statements by living Africans confirm this.

The art is often conveniently lumped together as "Bushman Art." While indeed much of it can be attributed to these people (as is also the case in Zambia, Zimbabwe, Swaziland, and so on) the identity of much of the art is not that simply resolved. The origin of the inhabitants 30,000 years ago is certainly in question. Similarities are frequently noted between some of the art and works in caves in Spain. Others see signs of Egyptian influence. Some of the questions of origin are simply the result of Europeans being unable to acknowledge that African peoples could have been that creative. Some of the major sites for rock art are treated elsewhere in this book. Certainly the "White Lady of the Brandberg" (q.v.) is the most famous, followed probably by the large collection of art found in the Philipp's Cave (q.v.) at Ameib. And Twyfelfontein (q.v.) is the site of beautiful engravings.

Unique to Namibia is the fact that petroglyphs (engravings) and paintings are found in about equal quantity and even in the same locations. Neither is true of other southern African countries. The petroglyphs tend to be inferior in quality to the paintings, perhaps because they are usually older. Often they are seriously weathered. Yet some of them had once been polished and painted. As one might expect, the engravings are generally found in the mountainous areas along the north-south spine of the country, between the Namib and Kalahari deserts. For many millennia these areas were populated by herds of animals and their human hunters.

This story is recorded in the numerous petroglyphs and paintings in the rock shelters. The art is generally found near the sites of water holes.

The engravings are equally divided between humans and animals, usually single figures, outlined in a continuous line (not dotted). The whole figure is chiseled in, not just outlined. A mallet and chisel were probably used, probably a knob-kerrie and a quartz fragment. Giraffes and zebras are found most often, but virtually all the animals (shown in profile) still exist in Namibia today. Humans are not as well depicted as animals. In some areas nonrepresentational geometric designs are found. They may represent some things symbolically, for example, a hut.

Some of the most beautiful of the engravings are 1000 to 4000 years old and fully patinized. The identity of the engravers is unknown, although Bushmen (now called the San) are given the credit, and the motivation is also unclear. They apparently were not doing it for a pastime or for decoration of the caves, nor were they creating landmarks, for the hunters would know the terrain well.

The rock paintings are much more detailed than the engravings. Earth colors are most popular, especially brown, red, and maroon, but yellow, black, and white are also frequently found. Iron oxide was probably the main pigment; it was pulverized and then mixed with egg whites and animal blood. The ''brush'' was sometimes feathers or stocks or fingers, or even the tail hairs of gnus.

Most of the paintings were monochromatic, but polychromatic works are also found frequently. Paintings tend to be fresco scenes that include a number of figures in groups. In fact, some analysts note that the unified composition of large scenes is given precedence by the artists over naturalistic detail. The largest collection of the paintings is at the great mountain, the Brandberg (q.v.), which may have more than 1000 individual sites.

ROCK LOBSTER. *See* LOBSTER, SOUTH AFRICAN ROCK.

RODE NATIE. *See* RED NATION.

ROMAN CATHOLIC MISSION. The first Roman Catholic missionaries came to the territory in 1878, but they withdrew when the chief at Omaruru opposed them. A new attempt took place in 1896 when the Oblates of Mary Immaculate successfully established a mission among the Hereros. In 1899 Catholic missionaries set up a station at Klein Wind-hoek. (A winery established there became extremely successful.) German administrators who wanted Namibia for the Rhenish (Lutheran) Church, placed major restrictions on Catholic missions until 1905. By 1910 they had at least thirteen mission stations and sixty-four missionaries, twenty-five of them priests. A Kwanyama chief allowed the first Catholic mission to be established in Ovamboland in 1923. Government restrictions the next year required all missions to stay within their appointed areas, and also to encourage the Africans to cooperate with official policy, including labor migration. Educational programs came under government supervision.

Catholic missionaries maintained their rigid standards for seminarians, which made it difficult for Africans to enter the priesthood. The first two African priests to be ordained there was a Herero in 1948 and a Kavango in 1951. It was 1980 before the first black Namibian Catholic bishop was consecrated. The predominantly German priests were generally paternalistic in their approach, yet the Catholics were also very liberal in integrating traditional customs into their doctrines. Animism was not regarded as incompatible with Catholic value-systems. In recent decades the Catholic priests have shifted from their position of benevolent neutrality on political issues to a more activist role in union with other Namibian churches such as the Ovambokavango Church, the Anglican, Methodist, and Evangelical Lutheran Churches. Still, most of the Catholic missionaries are white expatriates, some of whom are afraid to become too active on political matters lest they be deported (as several were). They have stuck to education and medical care for the Namibians. Nevertheless, in recent years the Bishop of Windhoek and his close associates have become increasingly vocal on political matters. The Catholic population of Namibia is around

140,000, of whom about 40,000 are in Ovamboland. The Catholic Cathedral in Windhoek was built in 1931.

ROSH PINAH MINE. One of the country's more important mines, it is located in the extreme southeast, about fifteen kilometers north of the Orange River and fifty kilometers east of the ocean. A community has now grown up around it. the mine owes its existence to an intrepid prospector, a German-born Jew named Mose Kohan. The name "Rosh Pinah" is the Hebrew term for "cornerstone," and is a biblical reference. He discovered the zinc there in the Hunz Mountains in 1963. Later prospecting also found lead, copper, and even some silver. An agreement with Iscor, the South African parastatal, was drawn up by Mose only hours before his death. His son George concluded the deal, which places ownership in Imcor Zinc (51 percent) and Moly Copper Mining & Exploration Company (49 percent). But Imcor is totally owned by Iscor, which has first call on the production for South Africa's industries. Moly Copper has major American investors.

By 1967 a 1000-foot tunnel had been blasted into one of the Hunz Mountains, and a 70-mile gravel road north to Aus had been constructed. From there ore was trucked to Pretoria. By 1969 an ore reserve of more than 4 million tons was proved, with a zinc content of 5.78 percent. Rapid development of the mine took place, water was pumped 17 miles from the Orange River, a power station was built, and a heavily automated plant would produce up to 200 tons of zinc concentrate a day. Rosh Pinah and Berg Aukas (q.v.) fill South Africa's zinc needs. Fully opened in 1971, Rosh Pinah's reserves have been estimated recently at 12 million tons. In 1986 production increased 25 percent, from 4,000 to 5,700 tons per month, due to a new R3.7 m processing plant built by Iscor. Production of zinc concentrate was about 60,000 tons in 1988.

RÖSSING MOUNTAIN. Rising tall above the Namib Desert, fifty-five kilometers east of Swakopmund, this impressive mass is visible even from the sea. It had been given the name Mt. Colquahoun by earlier explorers. While uranium ore was discovered there as early as 1914, extensive prospecting did not begin until 1955. (See RÖSSING URANIUM MINE.)

RÖSSING URANIUM MINE. The largest uranium mine in the world, it has produced about 4000 tons of uranium oxide a year. Sixty million tons of rock is moved to obtain that amount. The mine uses about 26,000 cubic meters of water a day to produce its uranium oxide or "yellow cake" (q.v.). Unique for uranium deposits, it is found in granite. The mine employs 2300 Blacks and about 900 whites. It is located in the Rössing Mountains in the Namib Desert, and about seventy kilometers east of Swakopmund.

The existence of uranium at the site has been known since at least 1914, but intensive prospecting only began in 1955. 46.5 percent of the mining enterprise is owned by Rio-Tinto Zinc Corporation, and South Africa's parastatal Industrial Development Corporation (IDC) owns 13 percent. There are at least a half dozen other companies that own the remaining 40.5 percent.

The mine was opened in 1976 at a cost of $350 million. Many at the United Nations denounced the owners for both exploiting the workers and stripping the territory of its valuable resources. The company countered by saying it spends $3 million a year on training programs and literacy classes for its workers, and that it has done everything possible to eliminate discrimination in hiring, housing, pay, pension, and medical care. At current rates of production the mine can produce until about the year 2020.

Among the effects of the mine is the large investment in staff housing in Swakopmund, Tamariskia, and Arandis. The latter is a new town, about twelve kilometers from the mine. Potentially one of the largest population centers in Namibia, it is being developed as an "open" town, and shopping, recreational, and educational facilities have been built, along with a forty-one-bed hospital. Medical care for its residents is free, and the workers are tested regularly for signs of radiation exposure. Workers ride a fleet of about forty buses daily to the mine.

Higher-level employees, most of them white, have access to a beautiful golf course and clubhouse in the Namib Desert, from which the Rössing Mountains can be clearly seen in the distance. The lush green of the golf course stands out brilliantly against the contrasting desert soil. Nevertheless, attempting to prepare for a Black-ruled Namibia, Rössing attempted to establish a good image in the country. The Rössing Foundation set up educational centers in several cities and proposed rural development programs. Some scholarships to overseas universities have been established for potential mine management staff members. Dr. Zedekia Ngavirue (q.v.), an early nationalist political activist, is presently the Rössing chairman.

In the mid-1980s, Rössing began to experience difficulty getting new contracts, and began operating at only 80% of capacity. With world demand for uranium weakening further, Rössing announced in early 1991 that it would reduce production to 60% of capacity for about three years. But a further cut in production occurred on September 26, 1991, and a third of its workforce was laid off. The company's leadership expects to see production pick up again in 1994, as a new contract with France will become effective in 1995. Nevertheless, Rössing also began new explorations, including the evaluation of a graphite deposit near Otjiwarongo. They began a pilot plant there in June, 1991.

RUACANA FALLS AND HYDRO-ELECTRIC SCHEME. Part of Namibia's international border, this cataract on the Kunene River (q.v.) is ranked as the world's tenth-largest waterfall. As the result of a 1926 agreement by a South African and Portuguese joint commission, Kunene River waters that flow south to the falls are in Angola. They turn west for twenty-two miles of foamy rapids before plunging 400 feet or so over the falls. The commission agreed that at that point the river becomes the international boundary between Angola and Namibia. (Further border adjustments were made in 1928 and 1964.) The main falls are on the Angola side of the border, especially in the dry season when the flow divides into two separate falls along the gorge. At its peak flow the river is about 700 meters from bank to bank.

The falls' name is reputedly derived from a Otjiherero phrase ''Oruka Hahakana'' (''the place of the hurrying water''), which the Portuguese corrupted to Ruacano. Some German maps show it as the Kambele Falls.

A major hydroelectric scheme was built at the falls in the 1970s. The power house is in Namibia, but the key water control works are at Calueque in Angola. The dam headquarters became a target for SWAPO guerillas who periodically damaged it and blew up power lines, notably in 1978. However most of the power-station activities occur in two 100-meter long tunnels bored through rock. The capacity of the Ruacana hydroelectric project is 240 megawatts with a water capacity of 219 meters cubed per second.

RUKORO, VEKUII REINHARD (1954–   ). A Namibian political figure since the mid-1970s, he was born in Otjiwarongo in 1954. His education was in Swakopmund and Karibib. In 1974 he graduated with distinction from the Döbra Training College in Windhoek. In 1975 he became president of the Namibia Black Students Organization. He also joined SWANU in 1975 and was quickly appointed deputy secretary-general. He worked for the Christian Centre from 1976 to 1978 and for the next two years he was the secretary for information and publicity for the Namibia National Front. He was chosen SWANU's secretary-general in 1976, a post he resigned four years later. He was also a law clerk in Windhoek in 1975 and 1976.

In 1980 he went to England to study law; he was called to the bar four years later. He then returned to Windhoek to lead the legal aid and community advice bureau. Also in 1984 he was chosen SWANU secretary-general after the party had split. In 1986 he was its delegate to the /Ai//gams Conference (q.v.). He then travelled to the United States, where he worked for the International Human Rights Law Group, as well as at the UN. He was elected president of SWANU-NNF in 1988, and was elected president of the Namibia National Front (NNF) in 1989. Rukoro takes an ideologically Socialist position on most issues, and wants Namibia to become a "Socialist state," in which all means of production and natural resources are owned by the people. He says that is merely a revival of Namibian traditions. The NNF won only one seat in the 1989 elections, and Rukoro is filling it in the National Assembly.

He was then appointed Deputy Minister of Justice in the new Government. In party affairs, however, he led his SWANU delegation out of a meeting of the NNF in mid 1990 when the NNF central committee voted to merge with the DTA. This merger did not occur, and in October, 1991 the NNF voted to disband and merge with Rukoro's branch of SWANU. He then suggested that his party might consider allying itself with SWAPO.

RUNDU (variant: RUNTU). A town of about 20,000 people, located on the border with Angola along the Okavango River, it is the capital of the Kavango district. Originally spelled "Runtu," it has been corrected to suit the Kwangala language, in which it means "high place." It sits on a high sand dune that overlooks the river, it was originally spotted as a potential site for a German government station in 1911 by an old German medical officer, Doctor Graf. The same site was noted in June 1932 by a South African official, Harold Eedes, and the government station was completed by September 1936. Located about 235 miles northeast of Grootfontein, to which it is connected by a major road, it soon developed into a prospering community with a trading store and even a radio station. The trading store was run by the South West Africa Native Labour Association in the 1940s on a nonprofit, concession basis. The government controlled the wages and prices. A state-run hospital for Africans was also begun there in 1948. In later years a power station was built there, as well as an air base. The population of the town was only 1600 in 1970, but tripled in the next decade. It is the business center for a large rural area. The white population is probably less than five hundred, as Kavangos make up over 80 percent of its population. When the guerrilla war began in northern Namibia in the 1960s, it became a station for South African troops, a refugee center for fleeing Angolans, and a base for UNITA forces fighting in Angola.

- S -

SAAN. *See* SAN.

SACRED FIRE. *See* FIRE, SACRED.

SACRED TRUST. A phrase that has become almost a slogan, it is part of Article 22 of the Covenant of the League of Nations (q.v.). It is this article that set up the mandate system that included "South West Africa" as a mandate assigned to the Union of South Africa. Article 22 begins by referring to the former German and Turkish colonies as "not yet able to stand by themselves under the strenuous conditions of the modern world" and states that their well-being constitutes "a sacred trust of civilization." This term has been frequently used to signify the obligation of the countries accepting supervision of a mandate territory.

SALT. Great salt pans line Namibia's coast, so salt has been a major export for the country. In 1988 it mined almost 125,000 tons of salt, of which a large percentage was exported. Natural salt deposits occur north of Swakopmund, at Cape Cross, and at Etosha (once a great salt lake). The reserves are tremendously large. Coastal lagoons are mined; the supply is naturally replenished after removal, the sea water fills the holes, and the water evaporates, leaving the salt. It is so abundant that salt is used as the base for roads in the desert. Prior to the coming of Europeans to Namibia, the Wambo people mined salt at Etosha and traded it to peoples to the north.

SAMBJU (variant: SAMDYU). One of the five tribal subgroups of the Kavango people (q.v.). Historically they are all offshoots of the Wambo.

SAN (variant: SAAN). A Nama word for the people who are often called "Bushmen." In fact, San and bushmen may well have once been two separate peoples. In any case, the San were among the very first people in Southern Africa. They were nomadic by inclination but also by necessity, as the Bantu were pushing them out of areas they previously had lived in. Thus we see remnants of their language among peoples throughout southern Africa. Rock art (sometimes called "Bushman art") can be found as far away as Swaziland.

Most San in Namibia were driven away or killed by Namas. Many of them settled in western Botswana. The most notable group of San still living in Namibia is the Hei//om or Heikom. The typical San has a distinctive physical appearance that includes a lighter skin (almost a tanned yellow) and a short stature. But the Heikom are moderately tall and blacker than other San. They may have mixed with other ethnic subdivisions somewhere back in time.

San traditionally lived off the land, being neither farmers nor cattle raisers, a situation rapidly in a state of change. The men were hunters, while the women gathered tubers, berries, and other veldkos (field food). A San group may only have fifteen to twenty members or as many as fifty. The group had to be mobile to follow the game. Thus they had no permanent dwellings. The men in the small group met regularly to make the group's important decisions (such as when to move to a new area) and served as a court for disputes. One of their important ceremonies involves extinguishing and then re-lighting the holy fire. Part of their "first fruits" celebration, it involves one of the group's elders who blesses the first fruits and then kneels to start the fire by spinning a stick between his hands. The stick will glow and, if properly done, a good fire will result. Fine grass is added for fuel and it flares to life. The San also believe in a Supreme Being who will listen to their pleas.

San can be found in Angola, Namibia (an estimated 32,000 in 1990), and especially in Botswana. Many of the latter consider the Kalahari Desert to be their home. There they are generally called by the name Basarwa. About a quarter of the San currently in Namibia fled there from Angola after Portuguese rule ended in 1975. They had been supporters of Portuguese colonialists and feared retribution at the hands of the new African government. It was from these refugees that Battalion 202 was formed by the South Africans in 1976. It was one of two San battalions in the South African military forces in Namibia. Most of the officers, however, were white South Africans. Most San today are no longer nomads, and younger ones attend schools where they are available. San elders continue to teach them their traditions, however.

SAND DUNES. *See* DUNES, SAND.

SANDER, WILLI (1860–1930). Born Wilhelm Sander in Berlin on December 10, 1860, he was the son of a master-smith, W. J. Sander, and his wife. When he was twenty-two years old he was studying architecture at the "Baugewerkschule" in Hoexter, Westphalia. In 1886 he received his degree, and after working for three years he married Paula Eck of Berlin. Of their five children, only two survived their youth. (One, a son, lived in Lüderitz for many years.) In 1891 the young architect was sent by the Deutsche Kolonialgesellschaft (q.v.) to Namibia, the first qualified architect to come to the country. His efforts retain their visual impact on independent Namibia. His first projects were the railway station and the lighthouse at Swakopmund. He then was sent to Windhoek where he planned the beautiful government buildings, such as the Tintenpalast (q.v.). He is also responsible for the three wonderful "German castles" overlooking Windhoek, Sperlingslust (which he renovated as Schwerinburg), Heynitzburg, and Sanderburg. The last of the three was his own home, where he lived from 1917 to 1924. He remarried during this time, as his wife Paula died in Potsdam in 1910, never having seen Namibia. Sander also designed a castle called Duwisib (q.v.), far to the south of Windhoek. Sander designed numerous other private and public buildings in Namibia, most of them still standing. They include everything from churches to farmhouses. His hobbies included photography and horse-riding. Sander became ill in 1924 and went to live with his son Hans at Lüderitz. He died of a heart ailment there on November 27, 1930, and was buried in Windhoek.

SANDFONTEIN. There are two sites called Sandfontein. First, a German police station was established at the Botswana border seventy-four miles east of Gobabis. The site was called Sandfontein, but today it is known as Buitepos. The road from there to Ghanzi in Botswana is best suited to four wheel drive vehicles. Second, a battlefield located in the Warmbad district of south-central Namibia, barely twenty kilometers north of the Orange River. It was the site of a clash between Bondelswart rebels and the Germans, October 20–22, 1903. Eleven years later the Germans had a different opponent there. A fierce battle took place there on September 26, 1914, early in World War I. Colonel Grant of the South Africa Defence Force and his battalion had dug themselves in, prepared for battle. German troops under Colonel von Heydebreck spent the night of September 25 advancing from different positions. At dawn Grant found his forces surrounded. After a valiant battle Grant surrendered and von Heydebreck took the 250 prisoners plus considerable arms. This had a domino effect, in that General Lukin, who was leading another force from the south, retreated back across the Orange River.

SANDVELD. A word found on maps of the early nineteenth century and used loosely to refer to the area northeast of Windhoek and Gobabis, extending to Lake Ngami in today's Botswana. The land is either desert or near-desert, and its main human inhabitants were the San.

SANDWICH BAY AND HARBOUR (variant: SANDFISH BAY). The Dutch called the area Sandvisbaai when they visited it several times in the seventeenth century. Located about sixty kilometers south of the town of Walvis Bay, it was at the mouth of what was once the course of the Kuiseb River (q.v.). The *Grundel* (q.v.) in May 1670 and the *Bode* in March 1677 visited the bay for the Dutch East India Company. The area has always been noted for excellent fishing. Today a lagoon there is home to both fish and colonies of flamingos and many other aquatic species that live in the shadow of giant sand dunes in the adjacent Namib Desert. German ships used Sandwich Harbour extensively in the nineteenth century as a port of entry after the British claimed Walvis Bay. But a dispute over land and water rights persuaded the Germans to switch their shipping north to Swakopmund (q.v.).

SCHAMBOCKBERGE (variant: SAMBOCK HILLS). The site of a conflict in 1904 between German forces and Jacob Marengo and his men. It is located about 50 kilometers from the eastern border with South Africa, and about 130 kilometers north of the Orange River. A German force of thirty-two men, led by Lieutenant Stempel was trying to locate Marengo's fortified camp in the mountains near the eastern border. Stempel and his men were on a farm owned by a Boer named Freyer when they were ambushed by Marengo. Four Germans were killed, including Stempel, and four others wounded. This occurred on either August 29 or 30, 1904. The Germans suspected the complicity of Freyer and his two mixed-race sons. A firing squad executed the sons immediately, and Freyer was taken to a court in Keetmanshoop. Marengo and his men had been unharmed and moved into the nearby Karras Mountains.

SCHEIBE, DR. A German geologist, he gave up his job prospecting for the Gibeon Schürf-und Handelsgesellschaft to join with August Stauch (q.v.) in a private venture to find diamonds in Namibia.

SCHMELEN, JOHANN HEINRICH (1777–1848). A missionary who served in Namibia for about fifteen years, he was a pioneer among the Christian missionaries. He also devoted himself to the study of the Nama language and how to reduce it to writing. His accomplishments include translating the four gospels into the Nama language and distributing printed copies of them to the Namas.

   Born in Germany at Casselbruck near Bremen, Heinrich had middle-class parents who provided him with a good education. He avoided service in the Napoleonic wars by traveling to London in 1804. Influenced by a German pastor, Dr. Steinkopf, and after meeting a missionary and several Africans in London, he decided to become a missionary himself. He studied at a seminary in Berlin for four years and then was accepted by the London Missionary Society (q.v.), which sent him to South Africa in 1811. His first station was at Pella, just south of the Orange River, where he worked with J. C. Albrecht (q.v.). While there he married a Nama woman, which did not please the LMS nor some of the other missionaries. In 1814 he was assigned the task of exploring the mouth of the Orange River for use as a port and to explore further north as well. He did this and travelled as far north as Okahandja, becoming the first European to penetrate the heart of Herero country. Returning to Pella, he found a drought had devastated some of his people, so he led 150 Orlams to the north of the Orange River. They settled about 150 kilometers north of the Orange, and he called the site Bethanie (or Bethany). His home there, called Schmelenhaus (q.v.), still stands and is the oldest building in Namibia. Travelling to the port at Angra Pequeña for supplies, he pioneered the cutting of the road for later travellers. Other paths he took also became the basis for important roads. His work took him to the Cape periodically.

Problems among Nama leaders forced him to leave Bethanie in 1822. He tried to reestablish the mission several times in the next six years, but the drought and locusts were additional factors in his failure. After leaving Bethanie he explored other areas, including Walvis Bay, Rehoboth, and even the Auas Mountains near Windhoek, where he met Jonker Afrikander. After his final failure to reestablish Bethanie in 1828 he decided to return south of the Orange River. He established a mission at Komaggas in the Cape Colony in 1829. His wife died the next year, but he remarried in 1832. Eight years later the RMS granted his request and took over the station at Komaggas. He died there, July 26, 1848. Future missionaries remained greatly in debt to him for his work in recording the language of the Namas and writing a grammar, a dictionary, a catechism, and other books in the language. His first wife, Anna, was a big help in this work, being a Nama herself.

SCHMELENHAUS. Built by the missionary Heinrich Schmelen (q.v.) in Bethanie in 1814, it is the oldest house in Namibia. The simple, flat-roofed building has been declared a national monument and houses a small museum today.

SCHRECKLICHKEIT. See EXTERMINATION ORDER.

SCHUCKMANN, BRUNO VON (1857–1919). The governor of German South West Africa (Namibia) from 1907 to 1910, he was born in Rohrbeck, Germany. He was the owner of a large estate before entering the German consular service. One of his consular assignments was in the United States. From his base in Chicago (beginning in 1880), he studied the immigration of peoples into the Midwest USA. He then served as acting governor of Kamerun and as consul-general in Cape Town (1896–99). He returned to Germany and became active in the Deutsch-Konservative Partei. He was then elected to the Prussian Landtag from 1904 to 1907. All these experiences were valuable for preparing him to be governor of the territory. He was a strong promoter of colonization. He prepared government land for farms and houses, had boreholes drilled for water, and had dams built. Good stud stock was brought in from Germany. The white population of Namibia doubled in his three years as governor. He also promoted local government, establishing municipal councils and appointing mayors. The construction of railways inland from the ports was begun. Income from the copper mine at Tsumeb and the diamond discoveries enabled him to balance the budget. In his term he regularly disagreed with Bernhard Dernburg, the secretary of state for colonies. The latter was particularly concerned with reforming the civil service and limiting the bureaucracy. He thought that it was the duty of the civil service to work for the progress of the colony and to encourage economic development through private initiative. But he rejected Schuckmann's appeals to allow more self-government. As a result of his inability to get along with Dernburg, Schuckmann resigned in 1910 and returned to Germany. He resumed his seat in the legislature and also served as executive member of the Deutschnationaler Kolonialverein. In 1909 a German officer on patrol in the Eastern Caprivi Strip named a town Schuckmannsburg. It is on the Zambesi River, about thirty kilometers from the east end of Caprivi.

SCHUTZGEBIET. Translated as "protectorate," this German word was used frequently by German administrators to refer to the whole territory known today as Namibia.

SCHUTZTRUPPE. The German word is translatable as "colonial troops." The first arrival of the Schutztruppe was in July

1889, when Captain Curt von Francois (q.v.) landed with a small force of twenty-one men. They first established a fort at Wilhelmsfeste and then moved on to Windhoek. The foundation stone for what is now known as the Alte Feste (q.v.) was laid on October 18, 1890. At this point it was uncertain that the territory would remain a German colony, in part because of its poverty. A major change occurred when the German Chancellor von Caprivi announced on March 1, 1893, that South West Africa would definitely remain a German colony, and that ''we wish to become masters of the country.'' This step would require a greater commitment in troops. Reinforcements for the original garrison were sent. A larger force was sent in 1894 when Major Theodor von Leutwein (q.v.) arrived. In March he was made commander of the Schutztruppe, replacing von Francois. Conflict was occurring at this time with the great Nama leader, Hendrik Witbooi (q.v.), which was resolved in September 1894 by a peace treaty.

Conflict with a group of Hereros, the Mbanderus (q.v.), took place in 1897, and again the Schutztruppe was called upon. The biggest challenge came in the 1903–07 period when first the Bondelswarts (q.v.) revolted, then the Hereros under Samuel Maharero (q.v.), which culminated in the Battle of Waterberg (q.v.). Barely was that over when Hendrik Witbooi (q.v.) declared war on the Germans on October 4, 1904. Earlier that year General Lothar von Trotha took over from Leutwein. The Witbooi conflict ended after the death of their leader on October 29, 1905, but other Nama leaders continued a long and successful guerrilla campaign against the Germans into early 1907. The notable Nama leaders were Simon Koper and Jacob Marengo (qq.v.). Many of these battles were very costly to the Schutztruppe.

Despite earlier problems, the full number of German military men on active duty in the territory in January 1904 was 766. About a third of these were serving in local police capacities or as administrators. The other 500 or so were divided into four companies of mounted infantry and one artillery company. These were stationed at Windhoek, Keetmanshoop, Omaruru, Outjo, and Okahandja (the artillery). Even these were further divided between the main post and external posts. In addition 764 trained men belonged to the reserves, many of them former members of the Schutztruppe who had been persuaded to stay in the territory after their discharge. (Some other untrained reserves and reliable African supporters also were available.)

The Herero War tested the Schutztruppe to the limit, and large groups of reinforcements arrived during 1904. In February and March alone 1576 officers and men arrived by ship, along with artillery pieces and 1000 fresh horses. Nevertheless, through March and April the Schutztruppe were regularly defeated or outsmarted by the Hereros. Late in April another 1200 officers and men arrived from Germany. By then more than two hundred members of the Schutztruppe had been killed in major engagements.

Five troop transports left Hamburg for Namibia between May 20 and June 17, 1904. On board were 2354 officers and men and 2000 horses, bringing the total Schutztruppe strength to nearly 5000 men. Eventually the German colonial troops in the territory would reach almost 20,000. In time the Hereros were defeated, and the subsequent revolts with Namas in the southern part of the territory were also put down by the troops. On March 31, 1907, the German government announced that the territory had been pacified and ordered the Schutztruppe there to be reduced to 4000 men under the command of Major von Estorff. From January 1904 to March 1907, the Schutztruppe suffered 2348 casualties: 676 killed in battle, 689 dead from disease, 76 missing in action, and 907 wounded.

By August 1914 the Schutztruppe in Namibia was down to 1603 men. When World War I broke out, however, reserves were called up (some formerly in the Schutztruppe) to bring the total number in uniform to about 6000. They were not able to hold off the South African forces that invaded in a multipronged attack, and on July 9, 1915, the German forces handed over the colony to the South African forces at the Peace of Korab.

SCHWERINSBURG. A castle-like home in the hills overlooking Windhoek, it was commissioned in 1913 by a government official, Hans Bogislaw Graf von Schwerin. The famous architect, Willi Sander (q.v.), who was responsible for several nearby castles, was hired to convert "Sperlingslust" (q.v.), formerly a tower built by German soldiers and later a restaurant, into a home for von Schwerin.

SCOTT, REV. MICHAEL (c. 1907–1983). An Anglican priest and a champion of the rights of the oppressed, Rev. Scott became almost a legendary figure, especially in the 1940s and 1950s. A number of books were written either by him or about him. Scott went to South Africa in 1926 at the age of nineteen because of pulmonary tuberculosis. His work there in a leper colony helped him develop a strong interest in the welfare of Africans. He was ordained there in 1930. He also worked in India before World War II. In the war he returned to England to serve in the Royal Air Force, but in 1943 he received a medical discharge. He then returned to work in the Province of the (Anglican) Church in South Africa. He became an outspoken champion of the rights of the deprived in South Africa. He drew international attention to the squalid Black towns around the beautiful white cities. In 1946 he participated in a passive resistance campaign on behalf of land tenure rights of Indians in South Africa. For this he was sentenced to three months in jail and then expelled from the country.

Scott has been described as a zealot and a fighting idealist, and as "stubborn and tenacious in defending what he believes to be right." In 1947 he was contacted by Herero chiefs including Hosea Kutako (q.v.) and members of the Chief's Council to plead their cause at the United Nations. He visited Namibia to see for himself the injustices against the Hereros, and indeed against all black Namibians. He then personally took the petition of the chiefs to the UN and presented it to the 1947 session. Over the next fifteen years he fought for the prevention of South African annexation of Namibia and for inclusion of it under the trusteeship system. His lobbying efforts paid dividends in several UN resolutions. In later years he turned his interest to the Rhodesias and Nyasaland.

SEALS AND SEALING INDUSTRY. The hunting of seals off the southwestern coast of Africa has been going on since at least the early seventeenth century, when the French were active there. The best location for sealing in Namibia is at Cape Cross, but there is another large colony about twenty miles south of Lüderitz. The Seal Reserve at Cape Cross usually has from 100,000 to 150,000 seals, the largest colony on any mainland. Many thousands of seals are killed there every year, some for their pelts but others to thin the colony, as they consume a huge amount of fish. In 1969 the South African government took control of sealing operations in Namibia, replacing the private concessionaires. Guidelines made the annual seal slaughter at least somewhat more humane than in earlier days.

SECOND TIER. A system of legislatures governing eleven ethnic groups (including the whites), this unwieldy and expensive system (considering the country's small population) completed a tripartite plan of government. The first tier was the national government, and the third tier was municipal government. This system has multiple parents. It is an obvious extension of South Africa's "separate development," as well as the Odendaal Commission plan for Namibia; it also was recommended by the Turnhalle Conference (qq.v.). Specifically, however, it was spelled out in AG8 (q.v.), a proclamation in 1980. In 1989, during the implementation of the plans for Namibian independence, Administrator-General Louis Pienaar replaced AG8 (1980) with AG8 (1989). This transferred the executive and legislative powers of ethnic ("second tier") authorities to the administrator general, but left the administrative structures intact, such as schools and other services. After independence this system has been replaced by new regions (q.v.).

SECURITY COUNCIL (SC). The United Nations Security Council is one of the most important of the UN constituent organs, commanded by the UN Charter with the "responsibility of maintaining international peace and security." Its membership consists of five permanent members (US, UK, Russia, France, and China), each of which has an absolute veto power over any resolution before the SC, plus additional member states selected for two-year terms. Originally there were six of these, but that number was expanded to ten in the 1960s. A majority vote of the Security Council is enough to pass any resolution, as long as none of the five permanent members vetoes it.

While other UN bodies, notably the General Assembly and the International Court of Justice (qq.v.), were concerned with the status of South West Africa/Namibia for more than two decades, the Security Council generally ignored the issue until the late 1960s. In part their indifference was due to the fact that the ICJ was still hearing cases involving the territory, but also because the UK and US were not eager to become involved. When the major ICJ judgment of July 1966 left Namibia's status in doubt, the General Assembly met on October 27, 1966, and, acting independently, passed a resolution that terminated the mandate of South Africa (from the days of the League of Nations). The Security Council then gave both tacit and explicit support to that resolution, although South Africa rejected it.

In 1967 South Africa brought to trial thirty-seven Namibians under the Terrorism Act (q.v.). The Security Council responded with Resolution 245 (1968), which both condemned South Africa and demanded that it discontinue the trial and release the Namibians. The SC followed up with later demands when the trial ended, but South Africa was unmoved.

A series of SC resolutions (264, 269, 276, 283, and 284) in 1969 and 1970 declared South Africa had no legal right to occupy or administer Namibia, and Resolution 284 called for an advisory opinion of the ICJ. The opinion was handed down June 1971, and the SC agreed with it in Resolution 301 (October 1971). In 1972 and 1973 the SC requested that the secretary-general of the UN begin negotiations to secure Namibia's independence, but nothing was achieved. In December 1974 the SC demanded that South Africa withdraw from Namibia by May 1975 (Resolution 366). In January 1976 it repeated the demand and declared that the UN would organize and supervise elections for a free Namibia (Resolution 385).

Meanwhile in both 1975 and 1976 the SC tried to impose mandatory sanctions against South Africa, but these were triple-vetoed by the US, UK, and France. In 1977 the Western Five Contact Group (q.v.) tried to seek a resolution of the Namibian question through diplomacy. However, following the incidents in Soweto (in South Africa) in 1977, the SC did impose a mandatory arms embargo against South Africa (Resolution 418).

In July 1978 the Security Council requested that the secretary-general (S-G) try to implement the proposals of the Western Five Contact Group and appoint a special representative for Namibia (Resolution 432). This was done, and in September the major resolution was passed by the SC. Resolution 435 (q.v.) approved the S-G's report and established a United Nations Transition Assistance Group (UN-TAG) to assist in implementing a plan for independence through free elections under the supervision and control of the UN. This resolution would be the key step, and all subsequent activities related to it. When Independence came in 1990 it was under these arrangements. Two months later (November 1978) the SC condemned South Africa's plan to hold elections outside this framework (Resolution 439).

The next several years consisted of diplomatic moves by the S-G and the Western Five Contact Group, countered by actions by South Africa. SC attempts to impose sanctions were regularly vetoed by the US, UK, and France. In 1983 the gap seemed to narrow. The S-G told the SC that relatively few issues remained unresolved. The SC then called upon South Africa to firmly commit to comply with Resolution 435 (in Resolution 532). However, further actions by South Africa led to a SC resolution (Resolution 539) calling for determination of the electoral system before the implementation of Resolution 435. South Africa refused to agree to this. In 1984 the SC condemned South Africa for its occupation of Angola and using Namibia as a springboard for attacks on Angola (Resolution 546). In 1985 South Africa established an interim government in Namibia, but the SC declared it to be null and void.

By 1986 the issue of Namibia was clearly winding down, but not without some problems. For example, South Africa agreed to abide by Resolution 435, but on condition of the withdrawal of all Cuban forces from Angola. This condition had been an issue for four years, but South Africa claimed that it was the only remaining obstacle. Thus, potentially, diplomatic negotiations would be sufficient and further direct SC action might not be necessary. But little progress was made in 1986, and the General Assembly made a new call for mandatory sanctions against South Africa. The US and UK vetoed a SC resolution on this in 1987. The US continued to try diplomatic efforts to achieve an Angolan cease-fire, obviously now a prerequisite for solution of the Namibian issue. Moreover, on October 30, 1987 the SC authorized the S-G to arrange a cease-fire between South Africa and SWAPO, as the S-G reported to it that all other obstacles to the implementation of Resolution 435 had been settled. In 1988 all matters fell into place, as the Angolan cease-fire and troop withdrawal was arranged. Resolution 435 then came into full play and actual implementation under UN supervision began on April 1, 1989. This was formalized in the Security Council through Resolution 632, adopted February 16, 1989.

SEITZ, DR. THEODOR (1863–1949). The last governor of German South West Africa, he replaced Governor Bruno von Schuckmann in 1910 and served until the military victory by South Africa in 1915. This period included both the peak of the diamond prospecting frenzy and the war effort against South Africa. He was also responsible for completing several railways and the telegraph system. Dams were constructed to aid agriculture, and stud animals were imported, especially for the breeding of karakul sheep. Born in Seckenheim, Germany, he became one of the most respected and competent members of the German Colonial Office. He had served as governor of the Kamerun from 1907 to 1910 (and as government secretary there from 1895) before being sent to Namibia. In regard to race relations, he favored a system of ethnic separation for the African peoples. After being forced to surrender the territory in 1915, he returned to Germany where he was president of the Deutsche Kolonialgesellschaft from 1920 to 1930. He wrote two books in the 1920s.

SEOPOSENGWE PARTY. Now merged into the new unitary DTA of Namibia, it became a constituent part of the

Democratic Turnhalle Alliance when it was formed in 1980. Its membership has been Tswanas, and its founder a Tswana Paramount Chief, Constance Kgosiemang (q.v.). Prior to its existence the Tswanas were represented in the DTA by a group called the Tswana Council (q.v.) or Tswana Alliance. When Second Tier elections were scheduled for 1980 to select regional Tswana authorities, Chief Kgosiemang organized the Seoposengwe ("Unity") Party. It won all the seats in the Second Tier Legislative Assembly without opposition. The Tswana Council or Alliance members all joined the new party as well, and Seoposengwe assured their place in the DTA alliance. The holders of the National Assembly seats, Party Chairman Bernard Mukhatu, and Publicity Officer Matheus Lebereki continued until the National Assembly disbanded in 1983.

A split occurred early in the party, however, and in 1981 a new Tswana Party was formed, the Ipelegeng Democratic Party. A later split in Seoposengwe occurred in May 1986, when some members complained about the quality of party leadership and formed the Mmabatho People's Party.

Seoposengwe continued to follow the DTA political line, and joined the Transitional Government of National Unity from 1985 to 1989. Two of its members were highly placed: Andrew Matjila was minister of national education and Gregor Tibinyane (qq.v.) was deputy minister of transport. The latter has since died.

In the 1989 National Assembly elections Chief Kgosiemang was number ten on the DTA electoral list, and thus now sits in the Assembly of independent Namibia.

SEPARATE DEVELOPMENT. Another term for apartheid (q.v.). (*See also* HOMELANDS POLICY.)

SESFONTEIN (variant: ZESSFONTEIN). A small community in a picturesque setting in the Kaokoveld of northwestern Namibia, its name is derived from the six powerful springs that gush in a lush valley where giant sycamores grow. The white crumbling ruins of an old German fort sit among date palms and fig trees against the background of the "blue" Kaokoveld mountains. A road goes north to Opuwo and then further to the Ruacana Falls on the Angola border. Another road goes westward toward Rocky Point on the Skeleton Coast (q.v.).

The area around Sesfontein became the home of the Topnaar Namas and the Zwartboois (qq.v.). These people owned both horses and guns and successfully controlled the region. In 1898 the Namas resisted the efforts of the Germans to administer the region and began an armed uprising. Both the Topnaars of Sesfontein and the Zwartboois at Fransfontein to the southeast were involved in the uprising. The Germans won a battle at Grootberg (almost exactly halfway between the two) on March 13, 1898.

SHEEP. *See* KARAKUL.

SHIIMI, USHONA (variants: OSHONA; SHIIMA; SHIMI; SHIMII; UUSHONA) (1919–1971). A leader of the Ngandjera group of the Wambo nation, he accepted the South African proposal to create a homeland within Namibia for the Wambos. When the first Owambo Legislative Council was established in 1968, he was appointed its chief councillor.

Growing up in the kraals of the Ngandjera chiefs, he eventually became a kind of secretary to his maternal uncle, Chief Shaanika Ipinge. He attended school sporadically, achieving a maximum of Standard II. In 1942 he joined the army, was stationed for a short time at Tsumeb, and then helped recruit Wambos to serve for the Union of South Africa. When Chief Ipinge died in 1948, Shiimi succeeded him.

As chief councillor, Shiimi was seen by many Wambos as one who had sold out to South Africa. He repeatedly preached its line, such as praising the progress of the Owambo Homeland, and complaining that the UN was meddling in domestic affairs. He felt that SWAPO should have no role in the territory's future, which would remain in the hands of traditional leaders. He maintained that the people of Owambo wished to remain under South African control. He died in an automobile accident, November, 14, 1971.

SHIPANGA, ANDREAS Z. (1931–). One of the earliest of the modern political activists in Namibia, he was part of the handful of Wambo workers who organized the Ovamboland People's Congress (q.v.) in Cape Town in 1958. It would soon evolve into SWAPO. He played an important role in Namibian politics for thirty-one years, until his SWAPO-D (q.v.) political faction failed to attract more than a few voters in the 1989 elections for the Constituent Assembly.

SIMBWAYE, BRENDAN KONGONGOLA (variant: BREDAN). Founder and president of the Caprivi African National Union (CANU) in late 1963 or early 1964, he was from the eastern part of the Caprivi Strip. In October 1964 he led CANU into a merger with SWAPO, of which he was elected vice-president. He was arrested by territorial authorities in July 1964 for organizing a political meeting. At first he was restricted to staying within his home area. (His work was assumed by his co-organizer, Mishake Muyongo.) Later he was moved to another part of the country. Stories in the late 1970s indicate that he may have been killed by either territorial authorities or South African police. The stories are unconfirmed, but he did vanish.

SINCLAIR MINE. Located in the Tsaris Mountains, it was a significant producer of copper as early as the mid-nineteenth century. It was named after the man who first achieved a treaty with the chief of Bethanie granting him the mineral rights. Actual production began in 1864. It was still being profitably worked in the early 1920s.

SKELETON COAST. The name is loosely applied to most of the Namibian coastline north of Swakopmund, but since the creation of the Skeleton Coast Park it is more specific to the area from the mouth of the Ugab River (q.v.) northward to the Kunene River (the border with Angola). About 80 percent of the area, which averages 30 kilometers deep from the coast, is composed of sand dunes. The coast and the dunes are whipped by ''Soo-oo-oop-wa,'' the relentless wind that whips through the dunes. In the process the wind has been known to uncover bones (''Skeleton''), both human and nautical. The latter refers to the rotted timbers or rusted hulls of ocean vessels that sank near the coast.

SMUTS, JAN CHRISTIAN (1870–1950). South African soldier and statesman. After earning a degree from the University of the Cape of Good Hope in 1891, he read law at Cambridge University for three years. He then practiced law in Cape Town but soon became involved in Afrikaner politics. After the 1896 Jameson Raid he moved to the Transvaal, where he became its state attorney. During the Anglo-Boer War he became a commando leader and finally rose to the rank of general. In 1901 he used the southern part of Namibia as a base for attacks upon the Cape Colony.

After the war he practiced law in Pretoria but stayed active in politics, forming an Afrikaner party called Het Volk in 1905. He then became minister of education in the Transvaal government. A few years later he was the major shaper of the Constitution of the Union of South Africa. At independence in 1910 he held three cabinet portfolios: mines, defence, and interior. When World War I began he and General Botha led forces into Namibia. Smuts occupied the southern part in April 1915. He then became an officer in the British Army and in 1916 directed the British campaign against the Germans in East Africa. After the Armistice that ended World War I, Smuts proposed an international organization, publishing in December 1918 *The League of Nations, A Practical Suggestion.* He then gained a great amount of recognition and acclaim at the Versailles Peace Conference, where he and Botha represented South Africa. He opposed the harshness of the peace treaty, fearing correctly that it would later destabilize Europe, and signed the treaty under protest.

Smuts' prestige and good standing at Versailles led to Namibia's being assigned as a mandate to South Africa under the League of Nations. Smuts planned ultimately to incorporate it into South Africa. Back in South Africa he served as prime minister from 1919 to 1924, during which he sent armed forces to Namibia to break up the Bondelswarts Rebellion (q.v.). His party lost in 1924, and he became leader of the opposition. He did join the "Fusion Government" in

1933, however. This broke up in 1939 over the issue of South Africa's participation in World War II. He was then re-elected prime minister of South Africa. This time he served two terms, 1939–1943 and 1943–1948. He participated in plans to set up the United Nations in 1945, although he disapproved of parts of the Charter. He also refused to allow Namibia to become a trusteeship territory of the United Nations. He unexpectedly lost the election of 1948—even his own seat—to the National Party. He died after several heart attacks, on September 11, 1950.

SORGHUM. Along with millet and maize, this grain is an important part of the diet of Namibians. Local production is best in the northern areas of Owambo and Kavango. Much of Namibia's grain needs must be met by importation. The generally arid condition of much of the country plus the periodic droughts that occur make grain production undependable. Mahango is the name of the grain sorghum that is popular in Namibia and which is produced on a relatively large scale for local consumption.

SOSSUSVLEI. Site of the world's highest shifting sand dunes (about 300 meters), the Sossusvlei is actually a large (12 hectares) dried-up clay pan or depression. The dunes tower over it. Shallow water covers the pan for several months each year, as water will flow into it from the Tsauchab River. In the wet season, it attracts a number of species of aquatic birds, and the rest of the year various game animals wander to the pan and feed on the sparse vegetation. Large camel-thorn trees grow near the edge of the pan. The dunes and the oasis-like pan—when there is water—makes it a singularly beautiful and unique spot. It is part of the Namib-Naukluft Park (q.v.) and about 240 kilometers southeast of Walvis Bay.

SOUTH AFRICA AND NAMIBIA. In many ways large segments of this book cover this topic. Eighteenth-century Dutch settlers were aware of the territory across the Orange River, and some attempted to explore it. The next two centuries saw numerous South Africans visit Namibia, work in it for a number of years, or permanently settle there. This includes people of many racial or ethnic origins. Most of the Africans in the southern half of Namibia have ancestors who migrated north across the Orange River. The Cape Colony was the starting point also for many of the traders, hunters, and missionaries recorded in these pages. A somewhat more direct involvement began in late 1914 when South African soldiers began to invade Namibia in order to defeat the Germans there, all part of the European war called World War I.

The peace conference that ended that war also provided for the establishment of a League of Nations (q.v.). On December 17, 1920, the Council of the League of Nations granted South Africa the right to govern Namibia as an integral part of its territory, subject to the terms of a class "C" mandate and the supervision of the Permanent Mandates Commission. Numerous acts of the South African Parliament or government proclamations were approved and subsequently applied to Namibia. Among these are the following:

1. Native Administration Proclamation (1922) (q.v.)
2. South West Africa Naturalization Act (1924)
3. South West Africa Constitution Act (1925) (q.v.)
4. Native Administration Act (1927) (q.v.)
5. Native Administration Proclamation (1928) (q.v.)
6. South West Africa Affairs Amendment Act (1949) (q.v.)
7. Development of Self-Government for Native Nations in South West Africa Act (1968) (q.v.)
8. South West Africa Affairs Act (1969)
9. South West Africa Constitution Amendment Act (1977) (q.v.)

Entries under administrator and administrator general are also relevant.

These entries barely scratch the surface. Military action ranges from the ruthless suppression of the Bondelswarts Rebellions (q.v.) in the 1920s, to the role of the South African Defence Force (q.v.) in the 1970s and 1980s. The Terrorism Act (q.v.) and the subsequent trial must be seen as just one part of South Africa's attempts to throttle the nationalist revolt against its rule. In the legal arena South Africa regularly fought all attempts by the United Nations to use the International Court of Justice (q.v.) to take away its Mandate. Even after Namibia's independence in 1990 South Africa claimed a legal right to sovereignty over Walvis Bay (q.v.) and nearby islands. However in 1991 the two countries began negotiations about those territories, and a resolution appears promising in the near future.

For many years South Africa used the fear of world communism as a justification of retaining a ring of protection that included Namibia. With the demise of the Soviet Union and the withdrawal of Cuban troops from Angola, South African President P. W. Botha agreed in 1989 to set in motion the final transition to Namibia's independence—although his government continued to subsidize political groups that opposed SWAPO (*see* NICO BASSON). Botha's successor, F. W. de Klerk was in Windhoek on March 21, 1990 to witness SWAPO's Sam Nujoma being sworn in as President of Namibia.

SOUTH AFRICAN DEFENCE FORCE (SADF). In 1914 and 1915, military forces of the Union of South Africa invaded the territory later to become Namibia by land and sea in order to defeat the German military stationed there. This invasion was in keeping with the goals of the British government in the early stages of World War I. While there were important South Africans who disapproved, Parliament accepted the idea by a large majority. The invasion was under the orders and leadership of Prime Minister (and General) Louis Botha, but other prongs of the attack were led by officers named McKenzie, Berrange, and Van Deventer, among others. Ultimately the Germans surrendered at Khorab (q.v.) on July 9, 1915.

After the war the SADF was periodically involved in quelling internal uprisings. The defeat of the Bondelswarts (q.v.) in 1922 was completed in part by attacks by airplanes connected to the SADF, in addition to the ground forces. Similarly the defeat of the Wambo Chief Ipumbu (q.v.) was due to a combination of SADF armored cars and airplanes.

Nevertheless the SADF did not have a high profile in

Namibia until the late 1960s. Previous to that most internal difficulties were resolved by the South African Police (q.v.). After the July 1966 ruling by the International Court of Justice, SWAPO leaders realized that military activity would have to replace diplomatic and legal efforts, and they announced that intention. The People's Liberation Army of Namibia (PLAN) was formed by SWAPO in 1970. Since SWAPO's strength was concentrated in Owambo and other northern areas, SADF's bases were mostly in the northern third of the country. There SADF units worked with units of the South Africa Police trying to contain and defeat SWAPO's guerrilla forces. In addition, however, they worked to coerce the northern Namibians to avoid, expose, and betray the guerrillas. Mass arrests of anyone suspected of SWAPO activity took place.

The big change in SADF involvement began in 1974. The Portuguese government had been an ally of the South African government, making policing of the northern borders easy. But in 1974 a coup occurred in Lisbon, and the new government was determined to withdraw from Angola in 1975, whether or not there was a unified and stable African government in charge. At that point there were an estimated 15,000 members of the SADF and counter-insurgency police in Namibia. But when a pro-SWAPO government controlled Angola's capital in 1976 the SADF expanded its forces and moved them increasingly north, even into Angola. Simultaneously, Angolan leaders invited the help of Cuban troops to counter the SADF. A South African invasion of Angola occurred and was only 100 miles from the capital (Luanda) before being thrown back.

The next years witnessed a see-saw movement of military forces, SADF, Angolan, and Cuban alike. Invasions of Angola by the SADF occurred periodically, as did subsequent withdrawals. The 15,000 troops *and* police reported in 1974 had multiplied to a Defence Force (excluding Police of 70,000 to 80,000 in September 1980. This occupation was in direct violation of both the League of Nations mandate and United Nations resolutions. South Africa's main bases were set up at Grootfontein, Ondangwa, Rundu, Mpacha, Ruacana, and Walvis Bay, but there were a dozen smaller military bases in northern Namibia also, virtually all in Owambo. Six sites had both army and air-force bases. In 1980 South Africa increased its military capacity by organizing the South West Africa Territorial Force (q.v.), known as SWATF, which recruited many thousands of Namibians, Black and white.

SADF had two separate missions. First, it attempted to control, contain, and if possible defeat the SWAPO forces, which were being forced northward into Angola. Second, it was charged with protecting both Namibia and South African borders from hostile armies to the north, be they Angolan or Cuban. If that meant attacking deep inside Angola or even attempting to destroy an oil refinery at the mouth of the Zaire (Congo) River on Cabinda, then so be it. To accomplish these goals there were unified or coordinated forces that included SADF, SWATF, the South African Police, the South West African Police, and a 3000-member counter-insurgency group called Koevoet (qq.v.). The coordinated forces also included an allied army of UNITA, a political movement in southern Angola that has been revolting against the Angolan government in Luanda virtually since independence in 1975. Both South African and American assistance assured UNITA of military supplies to fight their battles, which forced the Angolan and Cuban forces to fight a war on at least two fronts.

The SADF frequently attacked concentrations of refugees and SWAPO or PLAN members within Angola. While purportedly striking only guerrilla camps, the SADF frequently killed many noncombatants. The 1978 massacre at Cassinga (q.v.) is cited by SWAPO as one that was totally unjustified from a military standpoint.

The 1970s and 1980s was a tremendously costly period for the SADF, both in money and manpower. The war in northern Namibia and Angola required the SADF to expand the National Service requirement in 1982 to a 12-year active reserve period (up from 8), to include 720 days of training (from 240), an average of 60 days a year. Personnel in the reserve could be called to active duty at any time. Plans in South Africa called for an expansion of the SADF from 370,000 men in 1977 to an estimated 1,000,000 originally planned for 1990. Despite traditional opposition to the inclusion of black soldiers in the SADF, four new black battalions were formed in 1980. Some of these were used in northern Namibia, along with black units of SWATF.

Despite the fact that negotiations were taking place virtually throughout the 1980s, the SADF remained active, both in trying to weaken SWAPO and for the purpose of maintaining its bargaining position vis-à-vis Angola. The latter was accomplished through periodic raids by the SADF into Angola, sometimes attacking SWAPO (PLAN) bases, and other times destroying infrastructure vital to Angolan and Cuban troops. The use of the Casspir troop carrier was a particular advantage of the SADF, giving it high-speed mobility through mined areas.

Perhaps the most significant battle of the whole period took place at Calueque (q.v.) on the Namibian/Angolan border. The attack by a Cuban-Angolan force on June 27, 1988 seriously threatened the whole Ruacana Falls hydro-electric project. The huge buildup of Cuban troops (about 15,000) in the southwestern corner of Angola threatened the SADF to the point where a mass call-up of South African reserves might be necessary. The tremendous financial cost of the war had already made it unpopular in South Africa. Thus this battle seems to have forced South Africa to reconsider its use of the SADF in Namibia and Angola. (Also critical had been the loss of 40 SA Air Force planes in early 1988.) A little over a month later in Geneva, Switzerland, cease-fire negotiations were successful. On August 22, 1988, the treaty ratifying the cease-fire was signed at Ruacana, and SADF forces immediately began crossing back into Namibia. SWAPO leaders complained that the SADF used this withdrawal from Angola to provide more troops to clean up SWAPO guerrillas inside Namibia. However, with the negotiations concerning Cuban and South African troops reaching fruition, agreement on Namibian independence came quickly. The SADF chief of staff, General Jannie Geldenhuys, confirmed early in 1989 that SADF troops would be reduced to 1500 men by the time of elections in November 1989, and Koevoet would be "reintegrated" into the police force. Meanwhile, the 1500 SADF forces would be restricted to their bases. These remaining troops left Namibia within a week after the UN certified the election results. After Namibia's independence some senior officers of the SADF agreed to remain in the country for a short period in order to help train the new Namibian Defence Force.

SOUTH AFRICAN POLICE (SAP). In the thirty or so years prior to independence—roughly the period since SWAPO was founded—the South African Police have regularly worked to control or intimidate African political activists. Numerous examples are available. In 1963 SAP followed a group of political activists that included Andreas Shipanga, Dr. Kenneth Abrahams, and others into Botswana, where SAP arrested them and shipped them to jail in Namibia. After the assassination of Chief Elfias in 1975 the police arbitrarily arrested and detained nine leaders of SWAPO and the Namibia National Convention, including a minister who was head of the Paulineum College.

The South African Police were especially active in northern Namibia, particularly in Owambo where SWAPO had its greatest concentration of support. SWAPO accused it of practicing intimidation and violence against those whom the SAP suspected of SWAPO sympathies.

South African Police first assumed the "law and order" role in the territory in 1939, when a South West African Police Force was dissolved. SAP continued in this role until April 1, 1981, when the new South West African Police (q.v.) was formed. However, most Namibians felt that SAP was still functioning through a series of very close ties with SWAPOL in the nine years left until independence came.

SOUTH WEST AFRICA. In his book, *Lake Ngami,* published in English in 1856, the Swedish explorer C. J. Andersson (q.v.) is the first person known to have used the words South West Africa to refer to the territory bordered by the Orange River, the Kunene River, and the Atlantic Ocean. (It actually would be almost forty years later before the true boundaries would be set.) During the German period of rule it was of course called German South West Africa (or actually Deutsche Südwest-Afrika). After the defeat of the Germans by South

African troops in 1915 it was again called South West Africa. More casually, however, many have called it simply "South West." In 1969 the UN General Assembly proclaimed that henceforth it would be called Namibia, "in accordance with the desire of its people."

SOUTH WEST AFRICA AFFAIRS AMENDMENT ACT (1949). A law passed by the South African Parliament in 1949, it provided for representatives from Namibia to sit in the Union Parliament. Six MPs were to be elected to the House of Assembly, two senators were to be elected and two other senators were appointed. All of these received full rights and privileges in the Parliament. In fact, the law was a scheme by National Party leaders to add a greater margin to their insecure parliamentary majority. All the new members were expected to be supporters of that party, and their numbers were much larger than would be justified by the population of "South West." In a related development, in 1961 provision was made to appoint one of the six Assembly members to a newly created post of deputy minister for South West affairs. Later this position was dropped.

SOUTH WEST AFRICA COLOURED ADVISORY COUNCIL. The Coloured (q.v.) population of Namibia, like the Rehoboth Basters (q.v.), are of mixed ethnicity. Population projections indicate as many as 52,000 Coloureds in Namibia in 1989. In the early 1960s the government offered a Coloured Advisory Council, to be made up of appointed members. In 1974 the first elections to the Coloured Council were held. The Coloured Council had few powers, however, and only stirred the resentment of the Coloured community. In August 1976, Chairman A. J. F. Kloppers and the other members of the council voted to suspend their sessions and seek a hearing on this problem. However, it continued to exist. In 1978, one member called for the dissolution of all "ethnic councils" in the territory.

SOUTH WEST AFRICA COLOURED PEOPLE'S ORGANIZATION. Formed in 1959 under the original name of South West Africa Coloureds Organization, it regularly supported the position of the South African government. It accepted promises that the Coloureds would be considered partners in the development of the territory. In 1973 it changed its name to the Federal Coloured People's Party of SWA, and again in 1975 to the Labour Party (q.v.).

SOUTH WEST AFRICA COMPANY (SWACO). A company formed in London in 1892 as an Anglo-German venture, it remained active in mining and other activities until Gold Fields of South Africa absorbed it in the mid-1970s. A registered investment holding company, Gold Fields of Namibia, was then created in Windhoek to handle SWACO's assets.

On January 3, 1893, SWACO secured from the German government the three million acre Damaraland Concession. Its holding comprised freehold occupation of 4500 square miles within an area of 22,000 square miles over which it gained mining rights. It was also granted both freehold and mining rights over a strip of land six miles wide on either side of any rail line that it built north of the Tropic of Capricorn. Some of the latter was passed on to an offshoot of SWACO, the Otavi Minen und Eisenbahn-Gesellschaft (q.v.). Later, SWACO's right to build railroads was withdrawn by the German government in exchange for exclusive mining rights in part of Owambo.

The original Damaraland Concession contained all the known copper deposits in the Otavi area. Despite the fact that SWACO sent Dr. Matthew Rogers to begin intensive prospecting (with great success), there was little early payoff for the company. Unrest among the Africans plus a rinderpest epidemic hindered progress until 1900. It then sent a large group of men to prepare for development of its area. Many small companies were formed with SWACO involvement, most of which were eventually liquidated. Huge amounts of money were spent in exploring for minerals. The De Beers company added its involvement, purchasing a R200,000 interest in SWACO. Eventually a number of mines were opened. Vanadium was produced at the Abenab Mine near Grootfontein beginning in 1921, but that mine, once the largest vanadium producer in the world, is played out. The

Abenab West Mine also is exhausted of its lead, zinc, and vanadium. The Berg Aukas Mine produced the same three minerals, but in 1978 it was placed on a care and maintenance basis. The tin/tungsten mine at Brandberg West was dismantled more recently. SWACO also mined salt (q.v.) at the White Lady Salt Mine, and owned large herds of beef cattle in the Grootfontein area. As late as 1980 the company continued to advertise that it was still searching for new mineral deposits and was carrying out a diamond drilling and general prospecting program on its Otavi Mountain properties. It continued to show profit, in part by its small share of the Tsumeb Corporation (q.v.).

The South West Africa Company in its early years was a political concern for Germany. Its biggest investors were British, yet the territory was German. SWACO adjusted in part by including a number of Germans on its board of directors. One of its chief supporters was its manager in Berlin, Julius Scharlach, whose job description seemed to include constant lobbying of the German media and government.

SOUTH WEST AFRICA CONSTITUTION ACT (1925). An act passed by the South African Parliament in 1925, it granted a constitution to the territory, which gave the white residents (about 15,000 at the time) a measure of local autonomy. It allowed limited self-administration by a Legislative Assembly (q.v.) made up of eighteen members. Twelve of these were to be elected and six appointed by the administrator. Four of the eighteen were to be selected to serve as an executive cabinet. (In later years, all eighteen were elected by white voters, who had to be South African citizens.)

SOUTH WEST AFRICA CONSTITUTION AMENDMENT ACT (1977). An act passed by the South African Parliament which gave its state president full powers to administer Namibia through a presidential appointee known as the "Administrator General of South West Africa." The first AG was Justice M. T. Steyn (q.v.). The act also empowered the president to make, amend, repeal, or regulate by proclamation any law affecting Namibia. No authority in Namibia could make any law without the approval of the South African state president.

SOUTH WEST AFRICA DEMOCRATIC UNION (SWADU). One of the earliest of the anti-apartheid organizations to be formed in Namibia, it was founded among the Damaras in the late 1950s and still existed in the 1960s. Its leaders were Jeremiah Jager and Kephes Conradie. Eventually its membership drifted away, but Conradie formed Voice of the People (q.v.) in 1969 and considers it to be SWADU's successor organization.

SOUTH WEST AFRICA NATIONAL PARTY. See NATIONAL PARTY OF SOUTH WEST AFRICA.

SOUTH WEST AFRICA NATIONAL UNION (SWANU). The oldest Namibian nationalist party still functioning under the same name, SWANU was founded in August 1959 by a number of the young political leaders who had been active in the South West Africa Progressive Association and the Ovamboland People's Congress. These men had agreed with representatives of the Herero and Nama chiefs that a truly nationalist political organization was needed. Uatja Kaukeutu was named acting president at the organizational meeting, but in September a meeting attracted broader support and a major activist in the movement, Jariretundu Kozonguizi, was elected president. Other early activists included Sam Nujoma (q.v.) of the Ovamboland People's Organization and members of the Herero Chief's Council.

SWANU's claim to be the only nationwide organization lasted less than a year, as SWAPO was then formed by Nujoma and others. He had been encouraged to do this by Mburumba Kerina (q.v.) in New York and by the Herero Chief's Council. The latter group had been angered by SWANU's support for the claim of an independent chieftainship by the Mbanderu (eastern Herero), as well as SWANU's opposition to the selection of Clemens Kapuuo (q.v.) as deputy chief.

Despite this internal conflict, SWANU's first year also had some notable positive activity as well. Kozonguizi again visited the UN to petition for a reversal of South Africa's mandate. Also SWANU organized opposition (in the form of boycotts and demonstrations) to the removal of workers living in the Windhoek Old Location (q.v.) to a new, more distant, and more expensive area called Katutura. Rioting occurred in December 1959, and thirteen Africans were killed by police. Since SWANU's leaders were blamed by authorities, its organizers were banished. Kozonguizi left the country shortly after.

Once SWANU had a rival in SWAPO, SWANU's membership dipped to about seven thousand by September 1960. (Several attempts to merge the two groups failed.) However, Kozonguizi continued to visit the UN regularly but with a new approach. He rejected SWAPO's "constant petitioning" as a futile technique. He said that liberation could only come after all recent settlers from South Africa were removed from Namibia (although he assured older white families with a strong history in Namibia that they could stay). He also rejected a settlement that might be imposed by the UN and called for Namibians to write their own constitution at a conference they would organize.

In seeking aid wherever possible, Kozonguizi found friends in China. The 1960s were filled with recriminations as SWANU was supported by Mao Tse-Tung and SWAPO had the backing of the Soviet Union. There were numerous confrontations at the International meetings. SWAPO won support for its liberation activities from the Organization of African Unity, while SWANU was active in the Cairo-based Afro-Asian Peoples' Solidarity Organization. SWANU gained the reputation as being slightly more radical than SWAPO.

SWANU's leadership changed over the years. In July 1966 Kozonguizi submitted his resignation as president, in part because of a continuing dispute with leaders of SWANU's "External Council," a Stockholm-based group of Namibians. In 1968 he was replaced by H. Gerson Veii, who had been vice-president and a leader of the National Executive Committee. Veii had been arrested in 1967 and found guilty under South Africa's Suppression of Communism Act. After his release in 1972 he remained in Windhoek as an activist and led SWANU into membership in the National Convention (q.v.). He claimed in 1977 that SWANU had six thousand members. He also protested the UN's support of SWAPO as the only true nationalist party in Namibia. After the Turnhalle Conference he led SWANU into another political federation, the Namibia National Front (q.v.).

Meanwhile SWANU leaders in exile had formed their own leadership. The External Council was led in 1969 by Chairman Charles Kauraisa, Zed Ngavirue (secretary for finance), Tungura Huaraka (secretary for international relations, propaganda, and information), Nora Chase (secretary for education), Godfrey Gaoseb (secretary of the council), and Moses Katjiuongua (secretary for positive action). A 1971 reorganization moved Huaraka to chairman and Kauraisa to vice-chair (Ngavirue was replaced).

Moses Katjiuongua returned to Namibia and became its president. In 1983 he led SWANU into participation in the Multi-Party Conference (q.v.) and ultimately into the Transitional Government of National Unity (q.v.). This work angered a faction led by Kuzeeko Kangueehi in 1984, which claimed to have replaced him, but Katjiuongua won out over the dissidents. SWANU-P (q.v.) was then formed to unite the dissidents. Despite the party split, Katjiuongua continued to lead SWANU as the 1989 elections approached. He led his faction, sometimes referred to as SWANU (MPC) into a new federation of parties called the National Patriotic Front of Namibia (q.v.) in December 1988. There were rumors that he would be reconciled with SWANU-P, but that did not occur at that time. SWANU-P (q.v.) ran under the electoral banner of the Namibia National Front. Both Katjiuongua and SWANU-P's leader, Vekuii Rukoro, won seats in the Assembly in 1989.

SOUTH WEST AFRICA NATIONAL UNION—PROGRESSIVES (SWANU-P) (variant: SWANU-NNF). After SWANU's leader Moses Katjiuongua agreed to make the party a partner in the Multi-Party Conference (MPC) (q.v.), a group of dissidents declared in September 1984 that their leader Kuzeeko Kangueehi had replaced Katjiuongua as

SWANU's leader. They also said that the party would seek to merge with SWAPO. The revolt failed, however, and Katjiuongua retained the top position. Kangueehi then was described as the leader of the dissidents. This group then became known as SWANU-Progressives. New leadership emerged, and Vekuii Rukoro became president and Imbu Uirab vice-president. The faction denounced SWANU's participation in the Transitional Government of National Unity. SWANU-P advocated independence for Namibia after free elections supervised by the UN in accordance with Resolution 435 (q.v.). As elections approached in late 1988 and early 1989 several party coalitions were rumored. It ultimately became part of the Namibia National Front (q.v.). During the campaign Rukoro demanded that all Hereros who had fled to Botswana decades ago be repatriated to Namibia so they could vote in the elections. (Both SWANU and SWANU-P tend to be Herero parties.) In the election itself the NNF won one seat, and that was taken by Rukoro, leader of SWANU-P, as he was clearly the spokesman for the coalition during the campaign. In October, 1991 the NNF voted to disband and join with Rukoro's branch of SWANU, with the added possibility of SWANU-P working with SWAPO in later elections to oppose "enemies of the state."

SOUTH WEST AFRICA NATIVE LABOUR ASSOCIATION (PTY.) LTD. (SWANLA). Founded in 1943 by the amalgamation of the Southern Labour Recruiting Organization and the Northern Labour Recruiting Organization, it had the sole right to recruit workers in the territory until 1972. Its head office was established in Grootfontein. An employer would send a request for the number of workmen along with the type of employment to Grootfontein. There was a fee of £13–£15 per worker. The employees were then selected at the Grootfontein compounds and dispatched to the job by truck or train. The merger came about because employers, both farmers and mining interests, had experienced a terrible labor shortage. The cream of the crop had been skimmed off by the Witwatersrand Native Labour Association (WNLA), a much older organization that recruited for South African mines. By the creation of SWANLA, most of Namibia's workers were persuaded to stay home, especially when new recruiting offices were set up at Ondangwa (Owambo) and Rundu (Kavango). After workers arrived they were given physical examinations and classified to fitness for heavy, medium heavy, or light labor. The worker then stated his preference for mining, industry, or agriculture. The latter was least popular as pay was poor and working conditions sometimes very poor. In a good year about 30,000 workers were recruited by SWANLA, about a third to farms, another third to mines and industry, and the remainder to the mines of the Witwatersrand in South Africa. The latter was a concession to WNLA.

When major strikes occurred in Owambo in 1972 due to protests about pay and working conditions (*see* LABOR, AFRICAN), the new governments of Owambo and Kavango (under the Homeland policy) became responsible for recruitment. SWANLA then became defunct. Among the complaints of the workers were that the system dehumanized them by giving them no real choice of employer and by removing their ability to bargain for a better wage. They had to either accept the contract or stay in their Tribal Reserve. If they accepted it they were stuck with it for eighteen to twenty-four months.

SOUTH WEST AFRICA PEOPLES' DEMOCRATIC UNITED FRONT (SWAPDUF). Originally known as the Damara United Front, it changed its name in April 1976, in order to broaden its membership base. It never had the support of more than a minority of the Damaras. About that same time it was part of the National Convention of Namibia (q.v.). It later joined the Democratic Turnhalle Alliance (q.v.) and sometimes used the simpler designation of Damara-DTA. In the Second Tier elections to a Damara Legislative Assembly in 1977 it won all the seats, as the Damara Council boycotted the elections. However, when new elections were held December 3, 1982, the Damara Council won twenty-four of the forty seats and Damara-DTA won the other sixteen. SWAPDUF participated in both the Multi-Party Conference and the TGNU. Its president at the time of independence was Joseph "Max" Haraseb and the vice-president was Engelhardt Christy. Johannes Skrywer was Secretary-General. In November, 1991 SWAPDUF lost its separate identity as the DTA became a new unitary party, instead of an alliance of ethnic parties.

SOUTH WEST AFRICA PEOPLE'S ORGANISATION (SWAPO). The most renowned of the African nationalist organizations in Namibia, it was deservingly chosen in the 1989 elections to be the first ruling party of independent Namibia. SWAPO actually developed from at least two direct predecessors. The Ovambo People's Congress (q.v.) was founded in 1958 in Cape Town by young Wambo workers such as Solomon Mifima, Andreas Shipanga, and Herman Andimba Toivo Ya-Toivo. The latter was its principal organizer. When South African police ordered him to leave South Africa because of his political activities, he returned to Namibia and, with Jariretundu Kozonguizi, was determined to continue political organizing there. However, Kozonguizi was sent to talk to the UN in New York, so the Ovamboland People's Organization (q.v.) was founded in Windhoek in April 1959 by two young colleagues, Sam Nujoma and Jacob Kuhangua (qq.v.). The following month the South West Africa National Union (SWANU) (q.v.) was formed. While it was led by Hereros, it accepted Nujoma and other OPO leaders onto its board. Kozonguizi was president.

The December 1959 riots concerning the Windhoek "Old Location" (q.v.) removal plan radicalized large numbers of Namibians. In March 1960 Nujoma, the president of OPO, left Namibia to petition the UN and to set up an office in Tanzania. On April 19, 1960, the OPO was transformed into the South West Africa People's Organization (SWAPO), and Nujoma was named its president. Since its goal was "the liberation of the Namibian people from colonial oppression and exploitation," it had to be more than just a group of Wambos or Hereros. It had to be national in scope. Its early supporters were workers and the educated young people. One of those to encourage Nujoma to form SWAPO was a Namibian intellectual studying in New York, Mburumba Kerina (q.v.). He is said to have created the name and become its chairman. Two Namibian writers claim that

Kerima urged the formation of SWAPO out of a sense of personal rivalry with Kozonguizi, the SWANU leader. Both men spent a great deal of time in New York, petitioning the UN to act on the territory's independence from South Africa.

Inside Namibia SWAPO was getting support from such diverse sectors as the Herero Chiefs Council and Wambo contract workers who were being organized by Ya-Toivo. By 1961 SWAPO claimed a membership of fifty thousand in the territory, despite the fact that several hundred of its leaders and members had been arrested, deported, or fled into voluntary exile. SWAPO and SWANU competed for membership and international recognition, and both had offices in Dar es Salaam, virtually side-by-side in a row of store-front operations that also included ANC, PAC, FRELIMO, and others. At the same time there were several attempts in New York to bring them together. Various incipient groups were announced, usually by Kerina, such as the South West Africa National Liberation Front (1963), and the United Namib Independence People's Party (qq.v.) in 1964.

While SWAPO and SWANU had common goals, around 1962 SWAPO saw the need to organize for possible guerrilla action and began to send young men for training to sympathetic African, Asian, and Eastern European countries. This became especially critical after many SWAPO leaders were banned from political activity within Namibia. Extra-legal methods seemed all that was left.

SWAPO also concentrated its efforts on international groups. As early as 1960 it was calling for the UN to terminate South Africa's mandate, as well as for self-government immediately and independence no later than 1963. It requested a UN police force to maintain law and order and to disarm all South African military personnel. It also demanded freedom for all those detained and imprisoned for political reasons. With the territory still under South African rule in 1963 and the International Court of Justice puttering along on the road to a decision on South Africa's mandate, SWAPO re-emphasized the need for guerrilla training. It was supported in this by the Liberation Committee of the Organization of African Unity. When the ICJ dismissed the Namibia case on July 18, 1966, SWAPO sent its guerrillas into action, clashing several times with South African forces in 1966. However, it received a setback on August 26, 1966, when South African troops overran its Ongulumbashe training camp in Owambo. This forced SWAPO into different tactics, especially the organization of raiding forces from neighboring territories. The Botswana border in the east, the Zambian border along the Caprivi Strip, and the Angolan border just north of Owambo (Wambos also live in southern Angola) were crossed and recrossed repeatedly over the next decade, as SWAPO supporters fled Namibia to gain training abroad. Many then returned in guerrilla raids.

SWAPO maintained active political organizations both outside and inside Namibia. Its external leader was Sam Nujoma. (Kerina quit as party chairman in 1966, claiming SWAPO was only a Wambo tribal organization.) It had at least nine overseas offices, in New York, Cairo, Lusaka, Helsinki, Stockholm, London, Algiers, and Dar es Salaam (its provisional headquarters). Nujoma spent much of his time representing the party at the UN and at the various party offices. (Some dissidents accused him of liking to travel too much.)

Financial support came from many groups, including the government of Sweden and the World Council of Churches. The party paper, *Namibia News,* was published in London. SWAPO was officially recognized by the UN in 1973 as the spokesman for the Namibia people. Thus it worked closely with the UN Council for Namibia (q.v.). Extensive education and training was given to SWAPO members and others who hoped to fill important administrative positions in Namibia after independence. This was at the UN Institute for Namibia (q.v.) in Lusaka, Zambia.

In addition to its external leadership and its guerrilla forces (*see* PEOPLE'S LIBERATION ARMY OF NAMIBIA), the party had an internal organization and a youth wing and a Women's Council. Its chairman inside Namibia from 1964 to 1975 was David Meroro (q.v.). He left in 1975 after a wave of arrests. Others remained to lead the internal SWAPO, such as Daniel Tjongarero and Rev. Hendrik Witbooi (qq.v.), to name just two. While loosely knit and working under constant observation by the government, it kept the SWAPO spirit alive inside Namibia. It officially opposed all violence and appealed to the UN to intervene and force South Africa to withdraw. It also opposed the Turnhalle Conference, but was active in coalitions of parties. It was part of the National Convention of Freedom Parties (q.v.), from which it resigned in December 1974, and later in the Namibia National Convention (q.v.), which it helped to form.

The internal wing of SWAPO received a great deal of moral and physical support from various church leaders and their organizations in Namibia. Some have argued that this support from religious groups was a useful counterweight to the support SWAPO received from the communist bloc.

A more radical group within SWAPO formed itself as the SWAPO Youth League (q.v.). After calling for violence in a number of inflammatory speeches, some of its leaders were jailed. Other members of the Youth League retained a position of nonviolence, however.

While some conjectured that "external" and "internal" SWAPO may have difficulty reconciling their political stands and their leadership after independence, this does not seem to have been too much of a problem. both Meroro and Rev. Witbooi, for example, were rewarded with high places on the 1989 electoral list, right below Nujoma. While Tjongarero was not, he was given a deputy cabinet post and Witbooi was named minister of labour, public service and manpower development.

More significant was a split in SWAPO that involved some of its founding fathers. The rift became public in 1976 when people like Andreas Shipanga and Solomon Mifima (qq.v.), both SWAPO office-holders, accused Nujoma of corruption, mismanaging funds, and poor leadership. He had made himself a cult figure, they implied, and they called for new leadership. They ended up in protective custody in Zambia and jail in Tanzania. After their release they formed SWAPO-D (Democrats) (q.v.) in Sweden in June 1978. They later returned to Namibia and participated in the Multi-Party Conference and the Transitional Government.

While splits occurred, SWAPO also saw other groups fold in order to join ranks with SWAPO, for example, the Caprivi

African National Union in 1964, and the Rehoboth Volkspartei and the Namibia African Peoples' Democratic Organization, both in 1976.

In August 1975 SWAPO produced a "Discussion Paper on the Constitution of Independent Namibia." It had the tentative acceptance of both the internal and external wings of SWAPO. A very moderate document, it advocated parliamentary democracy, protection of minorities, and an independent judiciary. It guaranteed human rights and the rule of law, and opposed racialism. While SWAPO rhetoric was usually Marxist, the document left the question of socialism versus capitalism to an independent government. (Since independence SWAPO has opted for a mixed economy and seems to be working well with the major industries and their owners.) Whites were to be entitled to citizenship and welcome to remain as long as they supported an independent, free Namibia. It firmly rejected any kind of division of the country into ethnic-based subdivisions, while recognizing the need for some organizational level between the central government and the municipal governments. All of this has since found its way into the constitution of independent Namibia.

In 1978 SWAPO engaged in various talks with Western bloc leaders and UN officials concerning the future of Namibia. Although South Africa accepted in April 1978 the Western proposals for elections and Namibian independence, Nujoma refused to accept the same agreement. He demanded total withdrawal of all South African troops prior to an election and a guarantee that Walvis Bay would remain a part of an independent Namibia. (Over the next decade he eventually compromised on both of these demands.) However, the 1978 negotiations stalled when, in early May, a large South African force of paratroopers attacked a SWAPO camp at Cassinga (q.v.), 150 miles inside Angola. South Africa said it attacked guerrillas, while SWAPO claimed that only refugees lived at the camp, and many women and children were killed.

The decade from 1978 to 1988 echoed the themes just stated. International negotiations continued on a regular basis, but SWAPO and South Africa seemed to take turns in backing away from potential resolution, complicated further by the civil war in Angola itself and the involvement of Cuban troops. South African raids into Angola regularly destroyed or disrupted the efforts of SWAPO's army wing, the People's Liberation Army of Namibia.

Meanwhile South Africa sought various internal solutions to its own advantage, seeking always to keep SWAPO from having an opportunity to get a majority control of the government. The Turnhalle Conference and the Transitional Government of National United were two such attempts by South Africa, and SWAPO boycotted each, contending that they failed to allow national political parties to have their proper proportional representation.

When internationally supervised elections were finally agreed on, to be held in November 1989, SWAPO got its wish. Seventy-two seats were to be filled in the Constituent Assembly, later to become Namibia's first National Assembly. SWAPO won 384,567 votes (57.3 percent) and 41 of the seats. Its support was strongest in Owambo, but it received strong support in other areas also. After the constitution was written, Sam Nujoma was elected the country's first president.

The one major negative development for SWAPO in the few years approaching independence was the question of SWAPO members being tortured and even killed by SWAPO leaders. At first reported by Andreas Shipanga but confirmed as exiles returned from Angola in 1988 and 1989, SWAPO dissidents received severe discipline and were sometimes killed in the Angolan and Zambian camps. Some were accused of being South African spies (not an impossibility in some instances), but others had dared to dissent from the party line or challenge the leaders. Whatever the circumstances, many SWAPO members did not return to Namibia, and groups gathered lists of the names, challenging SWAPO to account for those missing. Hundreds were still unaccounted for when independence came in 1990.

SOUTH WEST AFRICA PEOPLE'S ORGANIZATION—DEMOCRATS (SWAPO-D). This faction of dissident members of SWAPO was organized as SWAPO-D in June 1978.

Its leadership included Andreas Shipanga and Solomon Mifima. They had been founders of the Ovamboland People's Organization, SWAPO's immediate predecessor. They and eleven other former SWAPO leaders had been just released from two years detention in Tanzania and made their way to Stockholm, Sweden, where they founded SWAPO-D. The detention had been imposed in Zambia because they were leaders of a group that attempted to oust Nujoma from the leadership of SWAPO, claiming among other things corruption and a nondemocratic leadership style. Shipanga claimed that about 1800 other SWAPO freedom fighters who supported him were being detained in camps by Zambian authorities. The principles of SWAPO-D at its organization were stated to be the original SWAPO program and principles, from which they felt Nujoma had deviated.

In July 1978 Shipanga had talks in Paris with leaders of the Namibia National Front (q.v.), and subsequently said he subscribed to its policies. In September the SWAPO-D leaders then returned to Windhoek, where they set up an office. Shipanga was president, Mifima was vice-president, and Emil Appolus (q.v.) was secretary of information. While the party was opposed to Nujoma's rule of SWAPO, it joined it in boycotting the December 1978 elections to the Constituent Assembly.

SWAPO-D operated for a long time on limited income. They charged a minimal fee for those who joined and claimed that they didn't hold mass meetings because they had no money for placards and posters. Others said that they did not hold mass meetings because their following was minimal. While SWAPO-D hoped to draw support away from Nujoma in Owambo, it was not exclusively a Wambo party. Appolus for one is Nama. (Later both Mifima and Appolus split from Shipanga, Mifima in about 1983 and Appolus in 1988. The latter claimed that he had discovered that Shipanga had been receiving kickbacks from the Consolidated Diamond Mines for several years.)

Without question Shipanga has been the driving force behind SWAPO-D, traveling to other countries and speaking out against Nujoma as a leader, but not against SWAPO and its cause. He was extremely upset with Nujoma when

SWAPO had captured a South African soldier, and instead of demanding the release of the venerable Herman Toivo Ya-Toivo (q.v.) in return for the soldier Nujoma had traded for the release of a Russian spy. At one point in 1980 there was an attempt to merge SWAPO-D with the NNF, but that came to naught as there was considerable squabbling over how much power Shipanga would have in the merged group. The other factions claimed much larger membership than could SWAPO-D.

Although South Africa originally saw Shipanga and his party as an alternative to SWAPO, his lack of support and his fence-straddling positions worked against that developing. However in 1983 Shipanga proceeded to join the government-sponsored Multi-Party Conference (q.v.). This moderate to conservative collection of parties included the Democratic Turnhalle Alliance. The MPC then became in April 1985 the basis for a new Transitional Government of National Unity (q.v.), which was supposed to lead the country to independence outside of UN Resolution 435 (q.v.). Shipanga represented SWAPO-D in this new government, serving as its minister of mining, commerce, nature conservation, and tourism. He was an especially vocal member of the cabinet. When negotiations for Namibia's independence resulted in a call for elections, he ensured SWAPO-D a place on the ballot as one of the ten competing groups. When final election results came in, however, SWAPO-D procured only 3161 votes nationwide, 35 percent of them in Owambo. It ranked eighth of the ten groups and received no seats in the Assembly.

SWAPO's first party congress to be held in Namibia took place December 6–10, 1991. It adopted a new party program and constitution and endorsed the policies of the party leaders since independence (despite the more pragmatic nature of the policies). President Nujoma said in his speech closing the congress that SWAPO had now made the change from a national liberation movement to a "mass political party." About 800 delegates participated in debates that approved a series of policy resolutions.

The party selected Moses Garoëb as Secretary General in place of the elderly Minister of Mines and Energy, Andimba (Herman) Toivo ya Toivo. Reverend Hendrik Witbooi was reelected Vice-President. Fifty-eight Central Committee members were elected, with the top vote-getters being Theo-Ben Gurirab, and Ben and Libertine Amathila. Others elected included two white members of the Government and leaders of trade unions. Aside from the elected members, others were appointed by President Nujoma.

In November, 1992 SWAPO competed in the various regional and local elections with great success. It won 56 of the 79 regional elections, giving it numerical control of 9 of the 13 new regions.

SWAPO YOUTH LEAGUE. Since many of SWAPO's early founders were young, it was not until the 1970s that a second wave of young leaders assumed a separate identity. The SWAPO Youth League came to political maturity in about 1973. It led protest meetings both in Owambo and in the south against the creation of a self-governing Owambo under the "homeland" (q.v.) concept. They begged Wambos to boycott the elections and criticized the traditional leaders for their opposition to SWAPO. It was clear from their actions that the youth were much more highly radicalized than SWAPO's older leaders. As some of them joined SWAPO's central committee, more senior members began to identify with the youth movement, thus increasing its influence within SWAPO. Some of the youth had also played a part in the 1971–72 strikes that shut down some of the mines.

Some of the Youth League members fled Namibia in 1974, and some of them became part of a power struggle within SWAPO. Andreas Shipanga identified with some of the Youth League and became a magnet for those who opposed Nujoma and other earlier leaders. SWAPO eventually reacted to the growing criticism, and in July 1976 held a meeting of an enlarged Central Committee outside Lusaka, Zambia. As a result of a restructuring the Youth League (and other groups like PLAN and the Women's Council) were made more accountable to SWAPO through the Central Committee on which they all had representatives.

SOUTH WEST AFRICA PROGRESSIVE ASSOCIATION (SWAPA). Formed in late 1955, it is sometimes—and inaccurately—called Namibia's first African political party. Despite a strong political orientation, the group was more culturally oriented; it focused on improving the educational situation for qualified Namibian students. SWAPA was really a spin-off (or even successor) of the South West Africa Student Body (q.v.). One goal was to find spots in South African schools for young Namibians. With such a narrow focus, its membership was heavily composed of teachers, clerical workers, and similarly educated people living in Windhoek. The group had substantial discussions on educational and cultural issues as well as national politics. It even published in 1959 the first black newspaper in Namibia, the *South West News,* which was quickly banned by the government. This increased political consciousness led at least indirectly to the formation of such groups as the Ovamboland People's Congress (q.v.), a predecessor of SWAPO. A young SWAPA activist, Uatja Kaukuetu, was a founder of SWANU in 1959.

SOUTH WEST AFRICA STUDENT BODY (SWASB). A predecessor of the major nationalist parties like SWAPO, it was formed in the early 1950s by a group of Namibian students enrolled in South African secondary and post-secondary schools. They had been inspired by the 1952 Defiance Campaign in South Africa. Many of the students had close links with the African National Congress in South Africa. When they later returned to Namibia, some of the young militants, seeking a broader nationalist base than their ethnic groups could provide, formed the South West Africa Progressive Association (q.v.). Some refer to this latter group as the first African political party formed in Namibia. With its formation, the South West Africa Student Body lost much of its leadership and eventually died. Among the more significant leaders of the SWASB were Jariretunda Kozonguizi, Mburumba Kerina, and Zedekia Ngavirue (qq.v.).

SOUTH WEST AFRICA TERRITORIAL FORCE (SWATF). During the 1970s South Africa was recruiting blacks into its military forces. The South African Defence Force (q.v.) formed ethnic units of Namibians recruited, trained, and paid to fight SWAPO. This was in preparation for the formation of a Namibian army to supplement the SADF. The planning for SWATF actually began in 1978. Thus when it was announced in September 1979 that SWATF would be formed the "tribal" battalions and a multiracial unit were ready to become part of it. In May 1980 the force was placed under the control of the administration in Windhoek, but its budget was funded by South Africa, and the administrator general was appointed by South Africa. Moreover, the conduct of the war against SWAPO guerrillas was being coordinated by the SADF, and South African troops could be seconded to the SWA Territorial Force.

At first only whites in Namibia were required to do service with the SADF. The "tribal" battalions were recruited as mercenaries. But in January 1981 blacks in Namibia within certain age groups were required to undergo compulsory military service with the SWATF. Many young Namibians crossed the borders rather than sign up. Others took it with this interesting pragmatic switch: "That's all right. We will let South Africans teach our young ones how to use their modern weapons of war. When the time comes we can use that knowledge against them to get our independence." In October 1984 it was announced that compulsory military service would be introduced for all males between the ages of 17 and 55, but compulsory service continued to be very unpopular and provoked a great amount of protest and resistance.

By 1982 SWATF had an estimated strength of 20,000, half of them white. Anticipating vigorous international action, South Africa announced that SWATF would remain a part of SADF until independence. Nevertheless SWATF and a new South West African Police force provided power for the political leaders in Namibia. By the end of 1984 SWATF boasted that virtually all SWATF guerrillas had been eliminated from the war zone. Yet this claim didn't mesh with SWATF's own statements that SWAPO acts of sabotage doubled in 1984 (over 1983). Furthermore, in 1984 SWATF formed a new "crack unit" to stop SWAPO's activities in the vicinity of white farms in northern Namibia, which also belied the claim that SWAPO guerrillas had been wiped out.

Nevertheless, the elimination of SWAPO remained the goal of SWATF, which freed the SADF to devote its efforts more to fighting Cubans and Angolans (and SWAPO bases) north of the Namibian border with Angola.

Recruitment for SWATF was done in various ways. The South West African Broadcasting corporation's local mouth-piece, Radio Wambo, would announce that recruitment was taking place. White schoolteachers used classrooms for war propaganda. And the perks were outstanding. A life-insurance policy left "fortunate" SWATF widows with large amounts of monetary compensation.

On the other hand, SWATF acquired a bad reputation for maltreatment of civilians. A SWATF spokesman in 1986 said it was a misunderstanding and that the civilians were merely being "screened" to detect SWAPO infiltrators. Ben Ulenga, a SWAPO leader, nevertheless called SWATF an army of occupation that committed atrocities against civilians.

In 1987 the SWATF, now numbering an estimated 23,000, went through a change of command when South African Major General Meiring was succeeded by Major General Willie Meyer on January 23. A year and a half later it was confirmed that under Meyer's direction SWATF had fought inside Angola, in contrast to its previous limitation to the war zone in northern Namibia. However, the accomplishment of a cease-fire in 1988, along with approval of plans for Namibian independence, made all this moot. The command structure of both the SADF and the SWATF were to be dismantled. SWAPO's main fear was that a slightly restruc-tured SWATF would be forced on it as the army for an independent Namibia.

In April 1989 SWATF saw its last formal action. When SWAPO guerrillas crossed into Namibia on April 1 (presum-ably misinterpreting the UN supervised agreement), six SWATF battalions were assigned to hunt for them and "stabilize" the situation. Reportedly 275 guerrillas were killed and 50 SWATF or SWAPOL members died in these final battles. SWATF was demobilized at the end of April 1989 in accordance with agreements, but some past SWATF members have become part of the Defence Force of indepen-dent Namibia, along with members of SWAPO's PLAN.

SOUTH WEST AFRICAN POLICE (SWAPOL). Formed in 1981 after a restructuring of the South African Police in Namibia, SWAPOL retained its links to the South African Police. SWAPOL units were heavily armed and operated with jeeps and helicopters, working closely in a paramilitary capacity with the South African Defence Force. Many of its members had been members of the South African Police. These units operated in the tribal areas, especially in Owambo where SWAPO had many supporters. In December 1988 there were 8,300 members of SWAPOL. South Africa informed the UN in January 1989 that it felt the size could be reduced to 6000. The much-feared special counter-insurgency unit within SWAPOL was known as Koevoet (q.v.).

There was an earlier version of the South West African Police that existed from 1919 to 1939, when the South African Police assumed the policing function.

SOUTH WEST PARTY. The counterpart in Namibia for the National Union, a South African party formed on February 10, 1960, by Japie Basson, a member of the South African legislature representing "South West Africa." He had been expelled from the National Party and began a new party with more liberal tendencies. It favored allowing Coloureds to elect their own people to parliament and stated the need to rapidly pursue political and economic development for Africans. On July 19, 1960, Basson formed the South West Party in Windhoek, with the same goals as the National Union. It specifically advocated that South West Africa be allowed self-government on the basis of a federal arrangement with South Africa, but with a goal that the territory achieve as much autonomy as the situation allowed. In the March 1961 Legislative Assembly elections it worked with the United National South West Party (q.v.) in contesting two seats. In both instances the National Party majority was noticeably reduced, as the new party attracted some voters, especially Germans, who did not fully approve of the Government policy. Events in the former Belgian Congo were played up by the National Party, which used fear tactics to discourage a more liberal party, and the South West Party soon faded from the scene.

SOUTHERN AFRICAN CUSTOMS UNION (SACU). A system by which South Africa has pooled external customs payments and shared a small portion with its land-locked neighbors, Swaziland, Botswana, and Lesotho according to a formula. Namibia has been a de facto member by nature of its relationships with South Africa prior to independence. Some British MPs contended that if an independent Namibia could formally join the Customs Union but renegotiate its fair share of the total pool, it could gain an additional R400 million a year in revenue from customs duties and mineral royalties. At independence the new government decided to stay a member of SACU for at least two years, and South Africa pledged an adjustment of Namibia's share. The increase of about R392 million is partly balanced by South Africa's cut in its past subsidy to Namibia by R228 million. Since independence, Namibia's income from SACU has been substantially greater than anticipated.

SOUTHERN LABOUR RECRUITING ORGANIZATION (SLO). *See* LABOR, AFRICAN.

SOUTHERN RAILWAY. With the uprising of the Namas in 1904 requiring German soldiers to get a better supply system, an 87.5-mile rail line was built from the port of Lüderitz across the sands of the Namib Desert to Aus. It was begun in December 1905 and completed the following year. This first section of what became the Southern Railway led to an extension of the line to Keetmanshoop, as much for economic reasons as military, which was finished in 1908. A branch from Seeheim south to Kalkfontein (now Karasburg) was finished by mid-1909. When the Union of South Africa invaded Namibia as part of World War I, it extended a rail line from Upington in the Union to Kalkfontein. The main line from Lüderitz to Keetmanshoop is 227 miles long, and the Seeheim to Karasburg link covers 112 miles. This is now all operated by the National Transport Corporation Ltd. under the name TransNamib.

SPECIAL COMMITTEE FOR SOUTH WEST AFRICA. When the Committee on South West Africa was dissolved by the

UN General Assembly in 1961, it created a successor, the Special Committee for South West Africa. It was to assume the functions of its predecessor plus achieve certain objectives, such as (1) a visit to the territory by May 1, 1962; (2) withdrawal of all South African troops from the territory; (3) the release of all political prisoners; (4) the repeal of all laws restricting freedom of movement for Africans (such as "Reserves"); (5) preparation for general elections to be supervised by the UN for a legislative body, and so on. The committee's chairman and vice-chairman visited Cape Town, the Carpio-DeAlva Mission, with negative results. The committee's final report said that South Africa rules Namibia in contradiction to all principles and purposes of the UN Charter, that South Africa had no intention of reforming its rule, and that the territory's population wanted the UN to assume control and prepare the country for independence. It recommended that South Africa be given a short time to comply with UN resolutions, and if it refused to do so the UN should revoke the mandate and assume control of Namibia. The General Assembly accepted the report, dissolved the special committee, and transferred its functions to the Decolonization Committee.

"SPERLINGSLUST." Meaning "Sparrow's Joy,"it was the name of a restaurant/tavern for German soldiers at the beginning of the twentieth century. It has since been expanded to become the lovely "castle" called "Schwerinsburg" (q.v.).

SPERRGEBIET. Translated as "the forbidden region," it is the area of the southern Namibian coast where the Consolidated Diamond Mines has exclusive mining concessions. Despite images to the contrary, there are no watchtowers, armed police, or savage dogs. The Namib Desert is enough to discourage undesirable people from trying to enter the area. There are some security personnel, however, and permission is needed to travel in the area.

SPITZKOPPE (variant: SPITZKOPJE). A set of huge granite rocks that rise high above the flat Namib plain like an island in a calm sea. They are 56 kilometers northwest of Usakos and 40 kilometers southwest of the Erongo Mountains. They are accessible by road from Swakopmund. The Great Spitzkop is an awesome sight, rising like a spire 700 meters above the plain. It has been called the "Matterhorn of Namibia," and was not scaled until 1956 when two climbers cut steps into the rock face. To its west is the Little Spitzkop, the site of spectacular findings of semiprecious stones, especially sparkling blue aquamarines. Numerous examples of rock art are found in the caves of the Spitzkoppe. Nearby in the Pontok Mountains is an area called "Bushman's Paradise," after the presumed artists. The Spitzkoppe are composed of granite variously called "pink" and "red-brown." Almost resembling a gigantic pyramid, the landmark attracts many visitors.

STATE MUSEUM. Originated by Governor Bruno von Schuckmann (q.v.), who in 1907 ordered collections for a museum to begin, it has become a treasure house of scientific artifacts in Windhoek. Despite its early beginnings, it made little progress until the founding of the Scientific Society of South West Africa in about 1926, which saw to the organization and collection of the materials. In 1957 it officially became the State Museum, when the administration decided to finance and run it. It moved into its modern building on Leutwein St. in 1959. It covers many scientific fields plus history and culture, but some of its greatest strengths are in archaeology, geology, natural history, and ethnology. Its displays are of very high quality. It sponsors research and a journal.

STATE RAILWAY. See NORTHERN RAILWAY; see also RAILWAYS IN NAMIBIA.

STAUCH, AUGUST (1878–1947). A true Cinderella story, but featuring diamonds instead of a glass slipper, is that of August Stauch. Born the son of the mayor of a village in Thuringia in Germany, Stauch lived in an old peasant house not far from Eisenach where J. S. Bach was born and Martin Luther was schooled. As Stauch matured he went to work for the Deutschen Kolonial-Eisenbau und Betriebsgesellschaft, an engineering firm that built railroads. One assignment was to Pomerania, where he met Ida Schwerin and married her in Franzborg, her home village. They set up a small home in a rented house in Neumark where they had the first of two children. Stauch had asthma, however, so when his company got a contract to build a railway in warm, dry, Namibia, he asked to work on that project.

In May 1907 Stauch arrived in Lüderitzbucht, where he was assigned to supervise the maintenance of a stretch of rail line. Fascinated by the countryside in general but the dunes in particular, he obtained a prospecting permit from the Deutsche Kolonial-Gesellschaft für Südwestafrica. He told the members of the railway gang he supervised to watch for any unusual stones, jokingly adding that they should especially watch for diamonds. (This was considered impossible, as diamonds were only found in "blue ground," everyone knew.) Two weeks later one of his workers saw a glittering object and took it to Stauch. Testing the hard stone on the glass face of his watch, Stauch realized it was indeed a diamond.

Without showing his excitement, he quickly pegged out his claims, quit his job, set up a tent, and began working the area. He explored to the south, whence the winds came, and soon found the first diamonds ever discovered in alluvial sand, free of blue ground. People in Lüderitzbucht doubted him, and there was no initial excitement. On June 20, 1908, he took his gems to Swakopmund, where the Deutsche Kolonial-Gesellschaft verified them. Geologists flocked to the area, and a stampede of prospectors came. In July German State Secretary Dernberg arrived to see "the diamond fields of Kolmanskop."

Stauch founded a syndicate with two partners and increased his prospecting. They formed a company called Die Koloniale Bergbaugesellschaft. With the arrival of Dr. Scheibe (q.v.), a geologist, Stauch had a knowledgeable assistant. After two failures they reached the Pomona area. Stauch named the valley Idatal (Ida Valley) after his wife. On Dec. 31, 1908, Stauch was surveying the area when he saw a young African boy. He told him to watch for diamonds, and the youth barely knelt in the sand before he found one. The boy quickly picked up hands full, while Stauch and Dr. Scheibe looked on in wonder. The diamonds in the sand were as abundant as fruit under a fruit tree. Despite the fact that other prospectors had tracked the two and soon made similar discoveries, the diamonds at Pomona made Stauch a millionaire.

He returned to his wife and Franzborg to a hero's welcome. They settled in a home at Eisenach, Germany, and had a third child. but he returned later to Namibia to settle his affairs and bought a farm near Mariental. He brought his wife and children from Germany to a beautiful house, complete with stables, sheep pens, and other buildings on his 70,000 hectares (the size of some small kingdoms near his birthplace). While Ida loved it, she was concerned about the children's education, so they returned to Berlin, and Stauch commuted periodically. A fourth child was born. Despite his wealth, Stauch fought for his country in World War I. He returned to Namibia in 1919 and two years later sold his diamond interests to Mr. Ernest Oppenheimer (q.v.), for fear his holdings would be confiscated by South Africa. He brought several farms near Windhoek and in the north and also became involved in tin mining. In Germany his money founded the Vox Haus (which became the German Broadcasting Co.), and was a pioneer in making gramophones and wax records. He also put a fortune into developing dictaphones. Unfortunately business collapsed in Germany, and he was forced into bankruptcy. He and his family lived in Windhoek, but his debts reached him there also. He retained only his lovely farm at Dordabis when the people of Windhoek conspired to remain silent as it was being auctioned; two of his older children thus bought it. In 1939 he was diagnosed with cancer, but that didn't slow him down. In 1945 he went to the University of Breslau to study mathematics and astronomy. He died of cancer in Eisenach in 1947. His ashes were returned to Namibia, where his wife and children lived for many more years.

STEYN, MARTHINUS T. A justice of the Free State Supreme Court, M. T. Steyn was appointed the first administrator general of Namibia on July 6, 1977. This move was part of the aftermath of the Turnhalle Conference; he was to help administer the territory toward autonomy under South African supervision.

The grandson of a Free State president (1896–1902), and son of a minister of justice under Jan Smuts, Steyn came from a family that had covered the South African political spectrum. A student of law at the University of Cape Town, he returned to the Free State to practice law. He was eventually appointed as a judge where he established a reputation for being fair and impartial. He was very surprised to be appointed administrator general, a post he assumed in September 1977.

The AG had almost dictatorial powers, and Steyn's first actions were to liberalize life in Namibia in preparation for elections in December 1978. He relaxed the Pass Laws (q.v.), opened many facilities to multiracial use by repealing much of the "petty apartheid," and withdrew both the Mixed Marriages Act and the Immorality Act (which banned sex across racial boundaries). None of these gave Africans real power, however. Even the Abolition of Racial Discrimination Act of 1979, which opened housing rights in "white" areas would only benefit a very few wealthy Africans. A ruling by the AG to liberalize the right to have political gatherings was also only slightly less restrictive. On the other hand, he instituted stringent emergency regulations in April 1978, which resulted in the arrest of many SWAPO members. Any person could be placed in custody for an indefinite period without trial. He replaced martial law in the north with a slightly less severe decree. However he reimposed martial law under Proclamation AG9 in the middle of 1979. On July 4, 1978, he amended an ordinance that resulted in Africans gaining—at least in theory—the right to join registered trade unions.

Justice Steyn also began a school-building program and declared a common school syllabus. He ordered the opening of the civil service to Black Africans. In June 1978 he issued a proclamation providing for the election of a Constituent Assembly, an election that SWAPO boycotted. When a group of church leaders in Namibia asked Steyn in a letter to investigate torture they claimed was being conducted by police officials, he not only refused but soon deported those signers who were foreign missionaries.

Despite Steyn's claim of neutrality, his support of the Democratic Turnhalle Alliance was very clear, as was his opposition to AKTUR (qq.v.). A backlash by white settlers resulted in Steyn's resignation in August 1979, and he returned to his position on the Free State Supreme Court. His successor as AG was Gerrit Viljoen.

STONE AGE. There are numerous remnants of Stone Age societies who lived in Namibia. Traces have been found near several rivers (the Fish River and Elephant River, among others) and at Sossusvlei and Gamsberg. Site ages range from 25,000 years old up to a suggested 250,000-year-old site. The oldest of the rock art (q.v.) in the country has been carbon-dated to about 25,000 BC. These are stone tablets found near Lüderitz by Dr. W. E. Wendt around 1970. The tablets contain depictions of animals. The other rock art in the country is similarly attributed to very early dwellers of Namibia, perhaps ancestors of today's San. Early missionaries in the nineteenth century reported that they saw some Africans still working with stone implements. The Tjimba people (q.v.), a branch of the Hereros, live in the northwestern corner of Namibia and were described as still being stone tool-makers when a museum expedition found them in 1964. The State Museum developed an extensive project to learn more about this group, perhaps Africa's last Stone Age people. Another Stone Age group, referred to by anthropologists as Strandlopers, appear to have died out about thirty years ago.

SUPREME COURT OF NAMIBIA. Established February 1, 1982, it replaced the old South West Africa Division of the Supreme Court of South Africa. Judicial authority is exercised independently of the legislative and executive authority. Roman Dutch law is the traditional base of the legal system. The Supreme Court of Namibia now functions independently from that of South Africa. Until independence, however, the right of final appeal to the Appeal Court of the Republic of South Africa still existed. The Supreme Court sits in Windhoek and consists of a judge-president and four judges.

SWAKARA. A commercial word that was adopted in 1965 to indicate garments made from karakul that originated in Namibia (SWA = South West Africa) or South Africa. Public relations and advertising campaigns promoted use of the word. The karakul (also known in fashion as "Persian lamb") from Namibia today is lighter, flatter, softer, and more supple than early karakul pelts. Its texture is as rich as velvet, and the designer can do much more with the pelts that come from newer breeding stock. The Swakara designation is only applied to the top 20 to 40 percent of the area's total karakul production. An official stamp on the underside and a special sew-in label aids consumers in identifying true Swakara.

SWAKOP RIVER. One of Namibia's major intermittent rivers, it rises in the country's central highlands and flows westward through the Namib Desert to the Atlantic Ocean at Swakopmund. The main stem of the river begins in the Onjati Mountains northeast of Windhoek. Several smaller tributaries join it halfway to the ocean. One, the Omusema, joins it as it passes Otjimbingwe. The Khan joins it later. Another small tributary begins in the Khomas Highlands. Below Otjimbingwe the Swakop has cut a deep, narrow gorge in the escarpment mountains. Throughout its course there is often both ground and surface water, so its bed and banks are covered with trees and vegetation. Agriculture and gardening has been practiced in several places.

Historically, the river's mouth was visited by Sebastian van Reenen (q.v.) in the late eighteenth century, as he searched for copper and gold, or at least the great cattle herds of the Hereros. A British ship reached the Swakop mouth in 1824, and the captain named it Somerset River. Later Europeans heard Namas call it "Tsoakhaub," which means "to push out." This refers to the sticks and mud that were pushed out to the ocean when the river was flowing. The whites tried to repeat the word and it became Swakop. When the Germans arrived there in 1892 they founded a town at its mouth ("mund" in German) and called it Swakopmund (q.v.) and built a harbor there. The river in full flow is large; early in the twentieth century a 350-foot-long bridge was built to span the river at Okahandja. One estimate is that the Swakop flows, on the average, twenty times a year, each time for a period of three or four days.

SWAKOPMUND. Literally translated from the German as the Swakop's mouth, this town of about 28,000 is located near the entrance of the Swakop River into the Atlantic Ocean. By rail it is 40 kilometers north of Walvis Bay, and 378 kilometers west of Windhoek. It was founded in 1892 when Capt. Curt von Francois (q.v.) landed with German troops late in the year; however, the first dwelling wasn't built until 1893. As Francois moved on to Windhoek, Swakopmund became the starting point for military, trading, and mining expeditions. Six commercial trading houses had already been established there by 1895. In 1897 the town was laid out and soon the construction of a rail line to Windhoek began. Rails also connected it to Walvis Bay and Tsumeb far in the interior. The latter was begun in 1903. Water mains were laid down in the town in 1899.

The first pier was built from 1899 to 1903, but its basin soon silted up and a jetty was erected. The present jetty (the second one) was started in 1911, but only 262 meters of the planned 640 meters were completed before World War I interrupted. This long walk "into the sea" is unparalleled in Africa. After the war Walvis Bay became the official Port of Entry. The town remained a commercial and educational center. The numerous buildings built at the turn of the century are all in a very charming Germanic style, called by one observer "wedding cake style." Architects claim that many of the buildings are in the then popular "Jugendstil" style. Among the major structures still to be seen are the railway station (1901) and light-house (1902), both designed and built by Willi Sander (q.v.). The Woermann House (1905) is perhaps the most beautiful, having been the headquarters of the powerful Woermann shipping company. The Alte Kazerne (1904) looks like a fortress but had entirely different usages over the years.

The city has created a museum for its early treasures and has proudly restored many of its older buildings for tourists. The marvelous beach makes it a very crowded town in the summer. It is also the best place for a tourist to begin a tour into the Namib Desert. For years the administrator of the territory made Swakopmund his summer (December–January) headquarters, and other governmental officials joined him.

With the coming of the Rössing Company and its uranium mine nearby (55 kilometers) in the 1970s the town has experienced a building boom. Many of the company's executives choose to live in Swakopmund. Other mines are or were active nearby as well, such as the Brandberg West (tin) and the Khan (copper). Salt is produced in great quantities northward along the coast. However, tourism and the holiday season remain as healthy industries as well. Hotels and bungalows near the beach cater to this element.

During World War I Swakopmund became a valuable target of South African forces wishing to dislodge the Germans and cut off their supplies at the port. Thus General Skinner landed at Walvis Bay in December 1914 and marched north to occupy Swakopmund. This battle occurred December 26, 1914. Gen. Botha arrived a month or more later and another battle took place on February 12, 1915. The British then occupied the port for the remainder of the war.

SWARTBOOI. *See* ZWARTBOOI NAMAS.

SWARTBOOI, WILLEM. This somewhat militaristic-minded chief of the Swartbooi people at Rehoboth in the 1840s and 1850s was actually named Frederick Willem Swartbooi, after the great Prussian rulers. He had been held in check by the local presence of Jonker Afrikander and his forces, but when they moved north to Windhoek, Willem increased his raids. For example, about 1841 he raided the Topnaars in the Walvis Bay area, leaving them with almost nothing. He was restrained somewhat over the next decade, however, by the presence and counsel of Rev. Kleinschmidt (q.v.) of the RMS. For example, he decided against joining Oasib, leader of the Red Nation, in uniting their forces against Jonker

Afrikander in 1846. In 1850 he again refused to join Oasib in a raid, against Hereros this time, thus defusing a potential conflict. However, in 1853 the aging Willem decided to reject the advice of Kleinschmidt and raid Jonker's camp at Windhoek. (His complaint was that other chiefs were busy acquiring property through raids, but Kleinschmidt prevented him from doing so.) When he did go to Windhoek finally there was no battle at all. Jonker made it a festive occasion, and he and Willem made peace. In subsequent years he was content to spend his time at a copper mine north of Rehoboth compelling the authorities to pay him a tax on their ore, as he claimed the mine was his. In 1856 he granted a mining concession at another location, at a charge of £12 for each ton of ore mined.

By the late 1850s Willem had alienated most of his Rehoboth followers, so he moved to the Walvis Bay area to live among the Topnaars whom he had raided almost twenty years earlier. His importance was still recognized, however, and in 1868 he was sought out by Hermanus van Wyk (q.v.), a Baster leader, about using the recently vacated Rehoboth area. Willem agreed at the price of one horse a year for rent. In 1870 Willem assisted his old ally Maherero, warning him that a large group of Namas camped near Windhoek were preparing to move on to attack Okahandja. Forewarned the Herero leader gathered his armed allies. Instead of a battle a peace was negotiated and signed.

- T -

TERRORISM ACT (1967) AND TERRORISM TRIAL. On June 21, 1967, the South African government promulgated the Terrorism Act passed by its Parliament. It was made retroactive to June 21, 1962. The act provided that the police could arrest and detain any person on suspicion of terrorist activities. Terrorism was defined in it to include, among other things, "prejudicing any industry or undertaking or production or distribution of commodities or foods," encouraging "social or economic change by force or violence," or "causing financial loss to any person or the state." Detention "on suspicion of terrorism" was for an indefinite period, and those detained could be held incommunicado.

The act and its retroactivity were specifically written to allow the arrest and trial of a group of Namibian political activists, some of whom had already been placed under detention prior to the passage of the act. Within five days thirty-seven Namibians were served with a very long indictment and brought to a judge. The indictment had been prepared long before the act was passed. (An example of an ex post facto law.) The actual trial began in Pretoria in August 1967. The Namibians were defended by Joel Carlson. The use of torture to obtain "confessions" was claimed by a number of them. Each of the thirty-seven was charged with specific violations of the newly written Act, and SWAPO members were charged with planning to overthrow South Africa's administration of Namibia by force.

The trial attracted international attention, in part due to Carlson's heroic efforts to contact the legal world abroad, and legal observers from around the world sat in on the trial. Nevertheless all were found guilty of some crime, which is not surprising, as the law was written to suit the charges. One elderly defendant, Ephraim Kaporo, died during the trial. Twenty of the accused were sent to prison for the rest of their natural lives; nine, including Hermann Toivo Ya-Toivo (q.v.), perhaps SWAPO's major leader at the time, were given twenty years in jail. The other seven received lighter sentences; among them SWAPO's E. G. Nathaniel Maxuilili, John Ya-Otto, and Jason Mutumbulwa each received five year sentences, all but one month of which was suspended.

While South Africa later suspended the Terrorism Act within South Africa, it retained it in Namibia. It was in force there as late as 1988, when a number of important SWAPO leaders were held in detention under its provisions.

THIRD TIER. As proposed by the Turnhalle Constitutional Conference in 1975, Namibia should have a three-tier governing system. At the top would be a central government that represented each ethnic group in a multiracial legislature. The second tier would be a series of regional "homelands" similar to the recommendations of the Odendaal Commission (q.v.). The third tier would be local authorities whose connection with the citizenry would be most immediate. The first elections of local authorities since independence were held in November, 1992.

THIRION COMMISSION. Appointed in 1982 to investigate alleged corruption and mismanagement of second-tier officials, its chairman was a Natal Supreme Court judge, P. W. Thirion. The investigation widened to include investigation of the mining industry. The commission's report, consisting of nine volumes of evidence and findings, was published in March 1986. The report strongly criticized the degree of foreign ownership of the mining industry and the inadequacy of Windhoek's power to regulate the industry. It focussed especially on alleged abuses of existing legal obligation on the companies concerning the declaration of taxable income, the rate of mineral exploitation, and the forms of exploration. Some of the allegations were contradicted by CDM or regarded as unsubstantiated by a committee that looked into the findings in 1987. Some of the Thirion Report's recommendations were included in a mining white paper published by the government in 1987, but no major changes were implemented. SWAPO then used the report as ammunition to demand changes in the mining industry after independence. Since independence the SWAPO-led government has vowed changes both within the industry and in regulation and enforcement.

THIRSTLAND TREKKERS (variants: ANGOLA BOERS; DORSTLAND TREKKERS). A mass movement of Transvaal Boers who decided to search for new land in the last quarter of the nineteenth century. Their route took them through Namibia, and many stopped there for several years. The name implies a more unified movement than actually existed. At least three or four distinct wagon trains started, and along the way many turned back, settled down, or deviated from the main routes.

Motivation for this pioneering movement also varied. Some were disturbed by the "liberal" (political and religious) practices of the Transvaal's President Burghers. Others were attracted by descriptions of the wonderful and productive land in central and northern Namibia. Still others were probably motivated by common feelings of wanderlust.

The first of the trekkers were actually two small groups led by Gerrit van der Merwe and Gert Alberts. Between them they had about fifty to sixty wagons. They negotiated with the Tswana Chief Khama for the right to pass through this Ngwato territory, which they did late in 1875. They successfully passed through the Kalahari Desert ("The Thirst"), past Lake Ngami with few losses, reached Ghanzi (where a few settled), and in late January 1876 moved on to Rietfontein in extreme east-central Namibia. That group settled there for awhile, with the approval of the Orlam leader Andries Lambert, the recognized chief in that area. Only fifteen families were there, but they stayed two years, hunting and tending their herds in anticipation of the arrival of larger groups.

A much larger group, led by Jan Greyling, consisted of 128 wagons, 480 people, and thousands of animals. Chief Khama had a harder time accepting such a large group as this, but the trek finally began in mid-1877. This party lost a tremendous number of animals en route and had to send word to Alberts for help. He sent 183 oxen and later met the party at Sebetwane's Drift in August. Thirty-seven people had died, some had turned back, and only a hundred wagons reached Lake Ngami. Ten families split off and reached Rietfontein in October 1877. The others, led by Greyling, went north to the area south of the Okavango River, where again some died and some turned back. All those at Rietfontein left there on January 28, 1878, to join the rest, reaching them near the Okavango in midyear. Here J. F. Botha was elected the leader, but eighteen families decided to return to the Transvaal by way of Rietfontein. The main body travelled along the Okavango to the west, but Greyling and four families took a separate route and vanished. Botha's group met Axel Eriksson (q.v.) at the Omuramba Ombongo and stayed a couple of months. In January 1879 they headed toward Namutoni (q.v.). Alberts scouted the area ahead and recommended against going to the Kaokoveld, so instead the group skirted the south shore of the Etosha Pan. They reached Sesfontein and spent many months there, well into 1880.

Meanwhile Alberts and a small party scouted the area near the Kunene River. There was a hostile attack, but they escaped with their lives. Portuguese traders befriended them. Also Eriksson had relayed word that the Trekkers needed supplies, and a committee in Cape Town gathered aid, which they sent to Walvis Bay. In early 1880 twenty wagons went south to Walvis Bay to bring the relief supplies donated in the Cape. At this point there were at Sesfontein about 352 trekkers and 70 wagons. Hearing attractive descriptions of southern Angola, most of the trekkers left for the Kunene River in late 1880 and set up farms at Humpata in early 1881. Two hundred seventy whites and 50 African servants settled there—a loss of about 300 whites due to death or defections from the original trekkers. However, Humpata also had problems, as many of the livestock died of disease. About half of the ''Angola Boers'' decided to return to the Transvaal. Hearing this, W. W. Jordan (q.v.) acquired land from two Wambo chiefs near Otavi and Grootfontein in Namibia. He divided the 1000 square miles into large farms and declared it to be the republic of Upingtonia (q.v.). About twenty-five families settled there in 1885. The rest stayed on in Angola. The Upingtonia scheme failed quickly, as the Hereros claimed the land. Jordan himself was murdered by Wambos on June 30, 1886. The Germans could not protect the settlers from African attacks, so some returned to Humpata and others headed back to the Transvaal.

A final trek of Transvaal Boers travelled by way of northern Namibia to Humpata in 1894.

THORER, PAUL ALBERT. A late-nineteenth-century German businessman who was involved in the fur processing industry in Leipzig, Germany, he had imported Bokhara sheep to Germany. They did not prosper in that climate, however, so he was encouraged to ship some to Namibia. Twenty-three rams and 255 ewes arrived at Swakopmund in 1909. Of these 40 were a gift from Thorer. These sheep plus another large shipment in 1913 became the basis of Namibia's karakul industry (q.v.).

THRELFALL, REV. WILLIAM (1799–1825). Considered by some to be one of the first Christian martyrs in Namibia, Threlfall was born in England in 1799 and ordained in 1821. He arrived as a Wesleyan Methodist Missionary at Cape Town in April 1822. He had periodic illnesses and was recuperating at Lilyfontein in South Africa when two Nama Christians, Jacob Links and Johannes Jager, recruited him to reopen the vacant mission church at Warmbad (q.v.). His superior agreed so the three left in June 1825. At Warmbad they picked up a San guide to help them investigate the area to the north. Four days later they were at Korasse when the guide and two accomplices waited until night to kill them in their sleep. The Namas were killed first with a gun, and Rev. Threlfall awoke. He knelt in prayer but the guide struck him on the head with a large stone. The murders, c. August 10, 1825, were evidently motivated only by robbery.

TIN. The first deposits of tin (in the form of cassiterite ore) were found south of the Erongo Mountains at Ameib in 1910. Later a thirty-eight-mile-wide belt of land from Otjimboyo to Uis was discovered to be rich in cassiterite. It is found in veins, large grains, and crystalline masses in pegmatite. When the latter disintegrates naturally the cassiterite is found as gravel and fragments. There have been three tin mines in Namibia: Tin Tan, Uis, and Brandberg West (q.v.). The latter has been closed for many years, and Uis closed in December, 1990. The Uis mine had been opened by South Africa's Iscor in 1958 and expanded in 1970. Its reserves are vast, but not of a high grade. Iscor exported its tin to South Africa in an unprocessed state. The low world price for tin made the mine lose a substantial amount of money. Although now closed it could be reopened if the world price rises. Iscor opened the Uis mine in 1958 and expanded it in the 1970s. Brandberg West (q.v.) is currently closed. The reserves at Uis are vast, but not of a high grade. Iscor exports its tin to South Africa in an unprocessed state. Namibia's tin production generally averages a little over one thousand tons per year.

"TINTENPALAST." Literally translated from the German as "The Ink Palace," this beautiful building, long, low and white, was the German Government's Administrative Headquarters for its final years. Built on a hill overlooking Windhoek in 1912–13, its plans were drawn by the government architect Gottlieb Redecker, and the contractor was the creator of Windhoek's picturesque "castles," Mr. Willi Sander. In 1932 beautiful gardens were laid out in front of the building and it has now become a popular stop for tourists.

After the Germans it continued to be used by later administrations and in the 1980s became the meeting place for the Council of Ministers. Also in recent years a new, modern administrative center has been built nearby. The historic importance of the venerable building has been assured, as it was chosen as the site for the formal adoption of Namibia's new constitution in February, 1990. It has since been renovated for use by the National Assembly.

TJAMUAHA (variant: TJAMUAKA) (c. 1770–1861). One of the renowned leaders of the Herero nation, he was the father of Maherero (q.v.). The grandson of Mutjise and son of Tjirue, Tjamuaha was born to the chieftaincy. As a young warrior he participated in the necessary battles against conflicting neighbors. Around 1819 he participated in the successful battle against the Tswanas near Lake Ngami (in today's Botswana), referred to as the battle of Etemba.

The date of his ascending to the chieftainship is not known, but was presumably prior to 1840. While today seen as a cherished leader, Tjamuaha was also notably divisive. He opposed many other Herero chiefs (over whom he had no direct influence) and attacked both their people and their cattle (which he took for himself). He acquired large herds in this manner, but alienated many other Hereros. He desired to be known as chief over all Hereros. At the same time it seems that this strong leader had accepted a position of subordination to the Nama leader, Jonker Afrikander (q.v.). Around 1840 Jonker sounded out Tjamuaha about moving his village to Windhoek. Although Herero lived near there, Tjamuaha allowed Jonker and his people to settle near Windhoek. (Later he lived to regret it, as Jonker broke the peace in 1846, attacking Hereros.) Tjamuaha lived a little to the north at Okahandja. Tjamuaha also placed two of his sons (*see*

MAHERERO) in the employ of Jonker at Windhoek, thinking they could return with new skills and knowledge. Instead they were sometimes tortured under orders from Jonker. But Tjamuaha tolerated the embarrassments because the Nama leader supplied the Hereros with guns. The building of his cattle herds through conquest was more important than his pride. In addition there was a period of relative peace. From 1840 to 1846 the Nama did not raid Herero cattle. This ended in March 1846 when Jonker attacked the kraal of a wealthy Herero named Kahena and stole four thousand oxen. Herero cattle seemed to be fair game for Namas again. Tjamuaha now feared for his own, especially after a supporter of Jonker killed one of Tjamuaha's sons and no justice was done. Raiding and plundering became rife, and the Herero leader lost some cattle to Nama raiders. Maherero's cattle were taken by some of Jonker's men. Finally on August 23, 1850, a large force of Namas led by Jonker attacked the kraals of an important Herero leader, Kahitjene (q.v.), massacred most of the men, mutilated the women for their copper jewelry, and then stole the cattle. This was at Okahandja. Tjamuaha lived on the east side of the town, at the base of a mountain. Only his village was left unharmed. Many other nearby Hereros also lost their cattle and their people were also killed. Many suspected Tjamuaha of having cooperated with Jonker in order to save his own herds. Jonker reputedly made Tjamuaha his vassal, supplied him with weapons and instructed him to raid other Hereros to supply Jonker with cattle. Many Hereros fled north to avoid contact with their own chief. The unholy alliance between Jonker Afrikander and Tjamuaha continued, sometimes Nama and Herero combined in attacking wealthy Herero. By now Maherero was playing a larger role as a chief in his own right, although still subject to his father, Tjamuaha. Peace in the area was finally restored in 1858 when a treaty was signed at Hoachanas (q.v.). Maherero agreed for his father, who was too ill to attend.

In mid-1861 both Jonker and Tjamuaha fell ill. Jonker died first. Still fond of Maherero, he told his heir Christian to give Maherero all of his personal belongings and called Maherero in. He told the two to live in peace, as brothers, and that they should rule the Namas and Hereros together. He died August 16, 1861. Tjamuaha heard of this and called his people together and told them, "Children, now I am ready to follow the man who was my friend. My friend is waiting for me." He then gave Maherero his blessing as his successor and keeper of the sacred fire (q.v.). Christian also visited him on his deathbed. However, Tjamuaha held on for several months, dying sometime in December 1861. (Curiously, the marker at his grave site says 1859.) The two tyrants were dead, and few Hereros or Namas mourned either one. However, peace did not last long, and on June 15, 1863, a battle between Maherero's supporters and the Namas at Otjimbingwe resulted in the death of Christian Afrikander, who was succeeded by his brother, Jan Jonker Afrikander. [Author's note: Several sources state that Tjamuaha died in 1859, and one indicates that the battle of Otjimbingwe occurred in 1860. I have chosen to use the dates that seem most probable.]

TJIMBA (variant: SHIMBA). A small group of Africans living near the Baynes Mountains and the Kunene River in Namibia's northwestern corner, they are probably of Herero ancestry. The name refers to the "ant-bear," an animal that literally scratches the ground for its food. The Tjimba are a relatively poor society that has survived by hunting and gathering and raising small livestock. Wambos have sarcastically called all Hereros "Shimbas" in the past, but Hereros only use the word for the poorer inhabitants of the Kaokoveld. The Tjimbas call themselves Hereros, whose customs and traditions they follow.

TJONGARERO, DANIEL (1947–). One of SWAPO's most visible members for many years because he stayed in Windhoek as a leader of the "internal SWAPO," Tjongarero has been rewarded at independence with the post of deputy minister for information and broadcasting. Born in 1947 in Omapato, his family later moved to Swakopmund. Tjongarero received a BA degree from South Africa's University of the North in 1973. Back in Windhoek he became an editor for African Lutheran churches, specifically editing *Imman-*

uel, their monthly journal. He has also held the post of director of the Institute for Social Advancement. In 1975 he helped organize the Namibia National Convention (q.v.). In 1976 he was named SWAPO's secretary for information and publicity, and as such was one of its principal spokesmen in Windhoek. In 1977 he became deputy national chairman, the title he held in 1978 when he received a number of death threats and fled the country. He later returned. Generally his was the voice of reason, explaining to whites that SWAPO would not take away any of their rights as citizens when it came to power. In February 1989 he was selected to SWAPO's Central Committee. However, when the 1989 elections were held, Tjongarero received an unexpectedly low placement on SWAPO's list of candidates. As a result he was not among those to get seats in the Constituent Assembly. Despite this oversight he was placed in the cabinet as deputy minister for information and broadcasting.

TOIVO, HERMAN ANDIMBA. *See* YA-TOIVO, HERMAN ANDIMBA TOIVO.

TOPNAAR. One of the eight identifiable subgroups of the Namas, the Topnaars are one of only two of these to remain independent when the other six federated into "The Red Nation" (q.v.). They are sometimes called the Topnaar Hottentots in older literature, and one branch is occasionally differentiated as the Topnaars of Sesfontein. The name Topnaar is said to have been given by Dutch traders at Walvis Bay who encountered them there. The word is Dutch for "the point," and refers to the fact that this was the northern-most group of Namas in the territory. Their Nama name is /Aunin, from /aub which also means "the point," as they had migrated to the seacoast near Walvis Bay by 1820. Some people use the term Aonin to mean the Kuiseb Topnaars, and the word Gomen (also "!Gomen") for the Sesfontein Topnaars. They have also been called !Naranir, referring to the nara fruit (q.v.) that was once an important part of their diet. However, that term is considered degrading, as it implies that they must scrounge for this food in the sand dunes because they have no money to buy other kinds of food. Topnaars are no longer hunters or livestock grazers, although some families keep goats. Today they generally work at Walvis Bay, in the fishing industry, or at the Rössing Mine.

While some Topnaars are to be found in Windhoek and other large towns, the two major divisions of Topnaars live either at Sesfontein in Namibia's far northwest (the major group), or in small villages along the Kuiseb River southeast of Walvis Bay. It was the latter group that had much interaction with Europeans in the nineteenth century. In the 1880s several Topnaar leaders, such as Chiefs Piet Haibib and Josef Frederiks, sold coastal land to German agents, while simultaneously securing treaties. In fact most of the land they "sold" did not belong to the Topnaars at all; much of it was claimed by the Hereros. Tribal principle also did not allow the chiefs to sell the land. In 1904, when many Namas revolted against the Germans, the Topnaars hesitated to do so. Before they could make a decision, alert German officials disarmed them.

TRANSGARIEP. A very early name for Namibia and one based on a South African perspective. The Nama people called the Orange River the Gariep. Thus some Europeans in South Africa called the area beyond that river "Transgariep," just as "Transvaal" also got its name from the Vaal River. It was sometimes called Great Namaqualand because of the large Nama population. This term could only properly be applied to the southern half of Namibia, however.

TRANSITIONAL GOVERNMENT OF NATIONAL UNITY (TGNU). A result of the work of the moderate to conservative Multi-Party Conference (q.v.), which sent a mission to Cape Town in April 1985. It received a pledge from South Africa that a transitional government would be established. Thus on June 17, 1985, the Republic of South Africa transferred to Namibia all governmental powers except constitutional status changes, national defense, and international relations. The Transitional Government of National Unity could exercise all other powers of local government, make laws, establish a budget, levy taxes, control its civil service, hire police, and so on. The leaders of the TGNU all came from the old Multi-Party Conference, mostly from the Democratic Turnhalle Alliance plus SWANU, SWAPO-D, the Labour Party, and the Rehoboth Free Democratic Party. It soon became clear that the TGNU planned to pursue a course leading to its eventual claim to be the independent government of Namibia, with no reference to the United Nations, participation by other parties (such as SWAPO) or world opinion. While it took several positive steps, such as declaring an end to educational segregation, it was clearly trying to establish credibility without having a true electoral mandate. Some of its efforts were pointed toward the preparation of a constitution for an independent Namibia. At one point in April 1988, South African President P. W. Botha travelled to Windhoek because he objected to some of the constitutional plans that were being considered, especially concerning the so-called "second-tier" authorities. When independence negotiations were finally successful later in 1988, the TGNU became superfluous. By common agreement, it transferred its authority on March 1, 1989, to Administrator General Louis Pienaar. The United Nations agreed to work with the AG beginning April 1, leading to elections later in the year, in accordance with UN Resolution 435.

TRANSNAMIB. A Namibian parastatal concentrating on transportation matters, TransNamib operates a number of separate entities: TransNamib Rail (the country's railway system), TransNamib Carriers (road haulage), Air Namibia (the national airlines), TransNamib Shipping, and Namibia Shipping Lines. Its purpose was to free the country of its reliance on South African Transport Services.

TREKBOERS. A "Boer" is a farmer of Afrikaner descent. A "Trekboer" has been described as a Boer with wanderlust, stubborn, romantic, and unable to adapt to the new commercial society. Some South African trekboers crossed the Orange River in the nineteenth and early twentieth centuries and settled in Namibia. Some of them got caught up in the diamond fever of the early twentieth century, and a few of them became wealthy.

The one most prominent group of trekboers to move into Namibia have been called the Thirstland Trekkers (q.v.).

TROTHA, GEN. LOTHAR VON (1848–1920). Born the son of an army colonel in Magdeburg, Germany, he seemed destined to be a professional soldier. His first service was in the wars of German unification in 1866 and 1870–71. In 1894 he was placed in command of German forces in East Africa (Tanganyika), where he suppressed an African war of resistance. Promoted to brigadier, he was the commander of a German detachment in the Boxer Rebellion in China in 1900.

When the Hereros began their war of resistance in 1904, Major Theodor von Leutwein (q.v.) was blamed for mishandling the situation. To regain control for the Germans, a strong leader was needed. Von Trotha was appointed to succeed von Leutwein in his capacity as military commander of the German Schutztruppe. He arrived June 11, 1904. He felt that he had instructions to defeat the Hereros as completely as possible. He was successful in organizing the Battle of Waterberg (*see* WATERBERG, BATTLE OF), in which the German troops shattered the Herero forces, in mid-August 1904. His techniques of cutting off retreat paths have since been studied by other nations. As the Hereros fled the battle scene, Trotha's forces pursued them relentlessly. On October 2, he issued his famous "Extermination Order," in which he said, "Within the German borders, every Herero, with or without a gun, with or without cattle, will be shot. I shall not accept any more women or children. I shall order shots to be fired at them." He also told his troops that while all male Hereros should be shot (no prisoners taken), they should fire over the heads of the women and children so they would flee (again, rather than waiting to be taken into custody as prisoners of war). However in practice the soldiers felt that the order meant to kill all Hereros, including women and children. This is what happened, and the Herero population was decimated. Some escaped, but many into the desert areas where they did not survive very long.

German public opinion was appalled at the massacre of the Hereros. Reichstag members vilified the policy, and the Kaiser even repudiated it. Nevertheless Trotha continued in his position. The Nama insurrection began on October 4, 1904, and General von Trotha took command of the German forces in Namaland six months later. He found the Namas had learned well from the Herero defeat and would not mass against the Germans in a single battle. The Namas had multiple leaders and fought guerrilla-type battles on many fronts. Trotha's tactics did not work against the likes of Jacob Marengo (q.v.). In one instance he sent his son, Lieutenant von Trotha (q.v.) to negotiate peace with the Nama leader, only to have his son killed in the African's camp. While Trotha did succeed finally in defeating some of the Namas, his repressive tactics resulted in his being called home on November 17, 1905. He retired from the army in 1906, and died fourteen years later in Bonn, Germany.

TROTHA, LIEUTENANT VON. The son of the German commander, General Lothar von Trotha (q.v.), he was sent by his father in June 1905 to conduct negotiations with Chief Cornelius (q.v.), with whom the young man had been well-acquainted. He had been the chief's commander in battles where the Namas joined the Germans against the Hereros. The lieutenant entered the Nama camp near dusk and the two men sat by the campfire to discuss a peaceful resolution of recent hostilities. While they were talking there was some distant gunfire. A German patrol, unaware of von Trotha's presence, was attacking the Nama camp. Cornelius told his young friend to stay with him to avoid harm. But an aide of the chief, thinking that von Trotha was part of a plot setting up this ambush, fired at the German and killed him instantly.

TRUSTEESHIP COUNCIL. *See* UNITED NATIONS TRUSTEESHIP COUNCIL.

TSAM, PEACE OF (variant: TSAMS). Signed September 15, 1894, between the Germans and the Witboois (led by Hendrik Witbooi, q.v.), it ended a long series of conflicts between the two sides. The Battle of Gams had occurred about two weeks earlier and the two forces had engaged in a continuous chase and ambush pattern after that. Both forces were exhausted. Witbooi finally established a camp at Tsam. While Gen. Leutwein was heading in that direction he received word from Witbooi that he was prepared to place himself and his followers under German authority. The peace and protection treaty acknowledged the sovereignty of the German emperor. The previous home of the Witboois at Gibeon was returned to them, along with as much land as they needed. Witbooi pledged in turn to keep peace and order in his territory. He would be given as remuneration an annual allowance of R200. In an unusual gesture, Leutwein allowed the Witboois to keep their guns so that they could use them to hunt game. Witbooi finally allowed the Germans to establish a military post at Gibeon, after having steadfastly refused this concession earlier. Perhaps he was persuaded by Leutwein's very civil manner during the negotiations and by the general's withdrawal of an earlier declaration that the Nama leader was an outlaw. In any case, the Peace of Tsam was very important. It concluded a fourteen-year conflict and allowed the Germans to extend civil administration to that part of the country. Witbooi was the last of the Nama leaders to accept German authority.

TSAMMAS. An example of veldkos ("field food") for the San and other nomadic desert people, the Tsammas is a type of watermelon. Growing in the eastern Namib Desert and in the Kalahari Desert, the Tsammas is technically known as *Citrullus lanatus*. For desert nomads it is one of the few sources of water, which is procured by poking a hole in one end of the melon (which looks like a small football) and punching at the pulp until it becomes watery and can be drunk. The thirsty must be sure they don't have one of its cousins, the *Citrullus ecirrhosus*, which is poisonous. The tsammas melon is plump and shiny; it resembles the coyote melon (or "buffalo gourd") of the American Southwest. Tsammas can also be used in other ways. Its rind can be used for pots, containers, and as resonators for musical instruments, and its seeds can be roasted and then pounded into meal.

TSAUB. Located about 150 kilometers west of Outjo in northwestern Namibia, it was the site of an attack by German troops in March 1898. Their opponents were the Swartboois, whose chief, Lazarus, surrendered to Gen. Leutwein's forces. The Germans took 550 Swartbooi men, women, and children to Windhoek where they were still engaged in public work at least eight years later.

TSISAB VALLEY. Meaning Leopard Valley, this ravine lies along the Brandberg massif in Namibia's northwestern quadrant. It was named by an early twentieth century German surveyor/soldier named Burfeindt, who claimed he had killed a leopard there and drunk its blood in order to survive. The lovely rock-strewn Tsisab Valley is also the site of Namibia's most famous work of rock art, the so-called "White Lady of the Brandberg" (q.v.). To reach it one must climb the beautiful Tsisab Ravine.

TSUI-//GOAB. A tribal hero in Nama tradition, he has achieved a godlike status and has been worshipped openly by those who follow a traditional religion. The name means "wounded knee," as he was wounded in a knee in a struggle with an enemy. One group of Nama (the Koranna) claim that he was once their chief. Some see him as the one to pray to for rain and for good harvests. A rain-making ritual has been used for this purpose.

TSUMEB (TOWN AND DISTRICT). Under South African administration the Tsumeb district consisted of an area 19,135 square kilometers in northeastern Namibia. It was south of the Owambo and Okavango districts. Most of the Etosha Game Park was in the westernmost part of the district, and the district's jagged southern border did not reach as far south as either Otavi or Grootfontein. The district is mostly flat country, with a few low hills. The savannah-type vegetation consists of bush and patches of thick grass. Only one significant river crosses the area; the Omurambo Ovambo, which flows into the Etosha Pan (q.v.). Rainfall is adequate in normal years, and there is underground water to be tapped. Several springs exist, as well as Lake Otjikoto (q.v.). Some grain is raised, and cattle have good grazing. Still, mining has been the big income generator for the area, notably at the Tsumeb Mine (q.v.), but it is scheduled to be closed in 1994.

The town of Tsumeb is essentially a mining town, with an estimated 1991 population of 15,000. This will change dramatically if the Tsumeb mine closes. However it will remain significant as it is on the main North-South road, and is the northern terminus of a major rail line from Swakopmund. Secondary industries could find it attractive as a link between Namibia and Angola.

The name "Tsumeb" ties in with its importance as a center for copper mining. The Herero called the area "Otjisume," which means "the place of green algae" or "frog place." This refers to the green rocks, indicative of the copper content. Other Africans eliminated the "Otji" prefix of the Herero word and added a "b" for a gender-specific ending. Aside from Hereros, other Africans who roamed the area on occasion were the Wambo, Bergdama, and San. Some of these came because of the readily available copper. The first European to spot the copper was Sir Francis Galton (q.v.) in 1851, but it took a surprising forty-one years before the South West Africa Company (q.v.) sent an expedition to investigate the mineral potential. In 1900 the mineral rights were acquired by the Otavi Minen-und-Eisenbahn-Gesellschaft (q.v.) for the purpose of mining the copper. Six years later a narrow-gauge railway connected Tsumeb with Swakopmund to transport the ore for export. Mission stations opened in 1905 (RMS) and 1913 (Roman Catholic). In 1947 the American Tsumeb Corporation acquired the mining rights and greatly increased the development of the mine and the town. It built separate communities for its white and African employees. Most of the residents are mine employees, business people, or civil servants.

The good rainfall in the area (400 millimeters per year) has made Tsumeb a beautiful garden city. It has good schools, a modern hospital, two hotels, a golf course, and even a small museum. In 1960 the rail-line was upgraded to standard size.

TSUMEB CORPORATION LTD. (TCL). During World War II South Africa expropriated the Tsumeb Mine from the German owners, and it was held by the custodian of enemy property. In 1946 an American-owned company, the Tsumeb Corporation, was formed to purchase it, and it took over January 6, 1947. The corporation is actually a consortium consisting of American Metal Climax, Selection Trust, Union Corporation, and Newmont Mining Co. It paid a ridiculously low R2 million for the mine, which it recovered in the first year. It then began a major development program there. For many years the mine was underworked. Two world wars and a depression had closed it down for long periods. The mining had been all open-cast, with no underground work, and copper was the only ore being mined. All this changed as the Tsumeb Corporation invested in modern machinery and in bringing to Namibia skilled mining technicians from Europe and North America. Tsumeb also began or developed other mines, such as Kombat and Matchless (qq.v.), Asis Ost and West, and Otjihase. Production includes copper, lead, zinc, silver, cadmium, pyrites, arsenic, and germanium. The corporation invested in new power plants, homes for its employees (Black and white, segregated), numerous community facilities (hospital, athletic fields, sewage systems, etc.), and an upgrade of the railway.

Until 1982 the corporation's principal owners were Newmont and American Metal Climax (AMAX), with British and South African companies holding the rest. However, in 1982 the Anglo American group took a major interest in Tsumeb through Gold Fields of South Africa, with Newmont and BP Minerals International (formerly Selection Trust) holding their strength but most others selling at least half of their holdings to Gold Fields of South Africa, which held 43 percent. AMAX sold all of its interests. Profits of the corporation have usually been extremely high—93 percent between 1974 and 1981—and nearly all of the profits are paid out as dividends to the shareholders. On January 1, 1987, Gold Fields of South Africa took over direct control of Tsumeb Corporation Ltd. Until then Newmont Mining Corp. managers had controlled the operations while owning only 30 percent of the corporate stock. In early 1988 Gold Fields of South Africa bought out the Newmont interests, increasing its equity to 78 percent. BP Minerals International with 14 percent was the only other significant shareholder. Later that year GFSA merged the Tsumeb Corp. with a previously unlisted subsidiary, Gold Fields Namibia, retroactive to the beginning of the year. It also wanted to buy out BP Minerals' share. Tsumeb became a wholly owned subsidiary of Gold Fields Namibia. The year 1988 was profitable for Tsumeb, with sales revenues at a record $160 million. Profits were a little lower because of a flooding disaster at Kombat Mine in November 1988, but both the Tsumeb and Otjihase Mines had higher output. However the next years were increasingly unkind to Gold Fields Namibia, with the Tsumeb Mine reserves running out, world copper prices depressed, and decreased supply for the smelters from outside sources. It was announced in mid-1991 by TCL that the Tsumeb copper and lead mine would be closed within three years.

TSUMEB MINE. As early as 1851 Sir Francis Galton (q.v.) reported in his journal that he had met caravans of "Bush-men" conveying copper ore from Tsumeb to the skilled metal workers of the Ondonga segment of the Wambo nation. But it was half a century later when the South West Africa company confirmed the value of the deposits by means of an exploratory expedition. Mineral rights were then transferred to the Otavi Minen- und Eisenbahn-Gesellschaft (q.v.), which began to mine the more and sent it to Swakopmund for export via a rail-line that it built. Copper was the only product of the mine for many decades, and this was procured by superficial extraction techniques. Also the mine was frequently closed during times of crisis, such as both world wars and the depression of the 1930s. After World War II, when the mine was in the hands of the custodian of enemy property, it was purchased by the Tsumeb Corporation Ltd. (q.v.). Large investments quickly paid off, and not only did copper production increase dramatically, but other minerals were also found.

The mine has owed its success in large part to a geological freak. It is a vertical, elliptical replacement deposit in dolomite country rock, having a longer axis of 600 feet and a shorter axis of 250 feet. The ore consists of lead, zinc, and copper sulphides and carbonates occurring in massive lens-shape bodies. In addition, cadmium, germanium, and silver are produced as by-products. By the late 1950s 50,000 tons of ore were mined each month, plus 40,000 tons of "country rock" from the so-called "Glory Hole." A smelting plant was erected at Tsumeb to do most of the refining. Tsumeb has an excellent supply of water, as about nine million liters are pumped daily from the lower parts of the mine. This is used for supplying power for the mine and the town, plus meeting other local needs.

Not everything ran perfectly, however, as wages for the Africans were very low, and strikes against the contract labor system broke out there in 1971. Even after reforms, however, Tsumeb workers were paid considerably below workers for CDM or Rössing. The South West Africa Mine Workers Union was recognized by management about 1982. In 1986 the Mine Workers Union of Namibia (led by SWAPO activists) was founded and began recruiting Tsumeb heavily. On July 26, 1987, more than 4000 workers at the three TCL mines went on strike for higher wages and better working conditions. It was the largest strike since 1971. However, it was only partly successful, as TCL reemployed fewer than one-third of the strikers. With the copper reserves of the mine rapidly being exhausted and the world price of copper very low, the owners of the Tsumeb Mine announced in mid-1991 that the mine would be closed within three years. (*See also* KOMBAT MINE; OTJIHASE MINE.)

TSUMKWE (variant: TSUMKWA). The capital of "Bush-manland" in the period before independence, the community is located in the extreme northeastern part of Namibia (not including the Caprivi Strip). It is about 50 kilometers west of the border with Botswana and about 180 kilometers south of Angola. There is a school there and a Dutch Reformed Church Mission.

TSWANA. The approximately 8000 Tswana (1989 projection) living in Namibia are closely related to the main body of Tswana who are the principal inhabitants of Botswana, Namibia's eastern neighbor. The Tswana (or Botswana) people are a Sotho-speaking people who generally live east of the Kalahari Desert. They extend into the Republic of

South Africa as well in areas both east and south of Botswana. Tswana tribal structure calls for local chiefs, but there is no one "King" of all Tswanas. Within Botswana there are at least eight separate subgroups of Tswanas (plus other non-Tswanas), most of whom fragmented from a few of the larger ones. It is not out of character, therefore, for some Tswanas to have moved west across the Namibian border. They generally live in the Aminius and Epukiro areas in east central Namibia. While some live in urban areas, many live on scattered farms or in small villages. They represent three different Tswana groups, the Bakgalagadi, the Batlhaping, and the Batlharo. They were represented at the Turnhalle Constitutional Conference by such men as Gregor Tibinyane. Later the Tswana Council, the Seoposengwe Party, and the Ipelegeng Democratic Party were formed (qq.v.).

TSWANA COUNCIL (variant: TSWANA ALLIANCE). The Tswana Council was the name given to the five-member delegation of Tswanas who attended the Turnhalle Constitutional Conference (q.v.). Its leader, G. Tibinyane, generally followed the Herero position at the conference, working closely with the National Convention of Namibia (q.v.). After the conference the group reorganized under the name Tswana Alliance and joined as a member of the Democratic Turnhalle Alliance in 1977. It was supplanted in the DTA in 1980 by the Seoposengwe Party (q.v.), led by a Tswana chief, Constance Kgosiemang.

TURNHALLE. A former German military gymnastic hall built in Windhoek in 1913. It has been the site of a variety of events over the years since World War I, but especially the Turnhalle Constitutional Conference (q.v.). Located at the corner of Leutwein and Bahnhof Streets, it has also served as the South West African Command Headquarters. The 1991 sessions of the National Assembly were also held at the Turnhalle as renovations were being made to the Tintenpalast (q.v.).

TURNHALLE (CONSTITUTIONAL) CONFERENCE. The first significant multiracial, multiethnic constitutional conference to be held in Namibia, it convened on September 1, 1975, and was formally dissolved by Administrator General Steyn on October 7, 1977. While its broad-based membership gave the appearance of representing all segments of Namibia's population, it really represented only the moderate to conservative elements. Members were chosen by ethnic group, not political affiliation, so no one from SWAPO was there, for example. On the other hand, some of its members were selected arbitrarily by the conference's founders to "represent" their ethnic group with no sign of any true popular mandate. Originally 156 people attended, but this was later reduced to 136.

The Turnhalle Conference was organized from the initiative of the South African government, operating through the National Party of South West Africa (q.v.). Two of its leading members in 1974 were Eben Van Zijl and Dirk Mudge (qq.v.). A split would develop between them and Mudge broke off to form his own party, but ultimately both were important leaders at the conference. The challenge for the conference was to find a constitutional arrangement that would lead to democratic elections yet avoid the strongly anti-apartheid "radicalism" of SWAPO. "One man—one vote" was not seriously considered. Voting by ethnic blocs (Basters, Wambo, Herero, etc.) seemed a safer option, and Mudge urged the "consensus" solution: all decisions would have to be unanimous. The National Party sought to ensure group privileges by installing second-tier authorities based on the "homelands" concept of the Odendaal Commission (q.v.) plus a third tier of local officials.

Preparations for and propaganda about the conference were begun at least a year in advance by its organizers. The key to a "moderate" result would be the selection of the black representatives. SWAPO, SWANU, and the Damara Council, among others, rejected the talks as unrepresentative and meaningless. The only African with a significant following to participate was Herero Chief Clemens Kapuuo (q.v.). But the price was to allow him a thirty-four-member Herero delegation (about 20 percent of the total) while Hereros represented only about 7 percent of the population. Much of the conference's major discussion was at the committee level, thus excluding mass participation. Open debates were not known, as the delegates were sworn by oath to secrecy, for some unexplained reason. Dissident delegates were not allowed to participate in the committee work. Charlie Hartung and N. Krohne of the National Independence Party resigned from the conference in March 1977, because they were unhappy with the way decisions were ramrodded by a few controlling leaders.

The delegates received a princely salary (for most of them) of R20,000 a year, and were housed in the best hotels in Windhoek, most of which would not have been open previously to those who were not white. In 1976 thirty-five were sent to the United States to try to persuade the US State Department that they truly represented all Namibians. Kapuuo threw a $40,000 party in New York, with unacknowledged backers paying the cost.

Finally on August 17, 1976, the Turnhalle Conference proposed that a multiracial interim government be formed by early 1977, with a provisional independence day set for December 31, 1978. While that exact scenario did not occur, elections were held on December 4, 1978, for a new Constituent Assembly (later "National Assembly"). It was controlled by a new political coalition called the Democratic Turnhalle Alliance (q.v.), which was in fact a restructuring of many of the partners at the Turnhalle Conference, especially Dirk Mudge and Chief Clemens Kapuuo.

TURNHALLE INTERIM GOVERNMENT. A proposal by the Turnhalle Constitutional Conference on August 17, 1976, stated that an interim government should be formed as soon as 1977, and that independence for Namibia should be set for December 31, 1978. The UN Council for Namibia totally rejected the plan, especially because the government was to be based on ethnicity. In 1977 the new American President, Jimmy Carter, sent his Vice President Walter Mondale to inform South African Prime Minister Vorster that the Turnhalle plan was unacceptable. The "Western Five" (q.v.) all put pressure on South Africa, and the plans for this interim government were put aside for the time being.

TWYFELFONTEIN. The site of some of Namibia's finest rock art, it is located in the northwest quadrant of Namibia. It is about seventy kilometers southwest of Khorixas and the same distance northwest of the Brandberg (q.v.). The rock engravings there represent the greatest and most interesting variety to be seen in the country. They depict animals and birds realistically, but also abstract designs. However the engravings are not in as good a condition as some others, as many of them have weathered badly or been damaged by fissures in the rock.

TYPHUS EPIDEMIC. At the end of the nineteenth century, a typhus epidemic swept parts of northern Namibia. An estimated 10,000 Hereros died in it.

- U -

UGAB RIVER. Starting in north-central Namibia, south of the Etosha Pan, this intermittent stream meanders in a southwest direction, emptying into the Atlantic west of the Brandberg. The Ugab only flows a couple of times per decade. Only in times of heavy rains is it known to flood. The Ugab Valley is very scenic and attractive to tourists. The deep-cut bed indicates that it was once a major river. Perhaps within the last several hundred years it was linked to the Kunene River or the Okavango. The area was once teeming with game, but most of the animals have retreated two hundred miles north to the Etosha area. One explanation for its scarcity of water is that the limestone of the Karstveld above Outjo absorbs most of the rainfall. The Ugab has no large tributaries in its three-hundred-mile course. Historically the Ugab has marked the northern boundary of Herero dominance and the southern boundary of the Kaokoveld. There are a number of major tin deposits near the Ugab. Reputedly the area from the mouth of the Ugab south to Walvis Bay is a fisherman's paradise.

UIS MINE. It is located in an area called Uis, 193 kilometers northeast of Swakopmund, east of the Brandberg and about

14 miles from the Ugab River. The deposit of minerals was discovered as early as 1911 by Germans, and some mining began soon after. A large mine was opened in 1951 by the Uis Tin Mining Co., which was acquired by the South African Iron and Steel Industrial Corporation (ISCOR) in 1958. They expanded it in the 1970s. In addition to tin, some zinc, wolfram, tantalite, and columbite has also been produced. Uis produced 60% of ISCOR's tinplate needs, and in 1982 employed between 400 and 500 workers, mostly black Namibians. Several million tons of rock were mined annually. The Uis was an open pit mine with vast reserves, but of a low grade. When the world price of tin dipped very low in 1990 all production there was stopped.

ULENGA, BEN (variant: UULENGA). The secretary general of the Mineworkers Union of Namibia (MUN), he is a member of SWAPO and was elected to the Assembly in 1989. A former Robben Island detainee, he organized the MUN in November 1986, with the encouragement of the SWAPO-led National Union of Namibian Workers. He went to London the following March to seek assistance in union organizing from the Trades Union Congress. Four months later a major strike occurred at Tsumeb Corp. mines, where Ulenga was recruiting members. In January 1988, Ulenga claimed membership had tripled during 1987, to 9000 members. In 1988 he led the MUN to agreements with two major mining companies, the Consolidated Diamond Mines and Rössing (qq.v.). The fourth congress of the MUN reelected him general secretary in April, 1990. On February 19, 1991 President Sam Nujoma announced that Ulenga would also serve as Deputy Minister of Wildlife.

UNION PARTY. A white party formed in 1924 to compete in the 1926 Legislative Assembly elections. It lost to the Deutscher Bund, however, and thus merged in 1927 with the equally unsuccessful National Party of South West Africa (q.v.). The new party was called the United National South West Party (q.v.), but that merger collapsed in 1939 and the National Party faction regained its old identity.

UNITED DEMOCRATIC FRONT OF NAMIBIA (UDF). An electoral coalition of minor parties, it began organizing in January 1989. Among the groups mentioned as being interested at first were the Labour party, the United Party, the National Independence Party, SWANU-P, the Damara Council, the Christian Democratic Action Party, the Namibia National Independence Party, and the Ipelegeng Party. The politicians wanted to create a group unaffiliated with either SWAPO or DTA. Ultimately it consisted of the Damara Council, the Labour Party, the Namibia National Independence Party, and the Original People's Party, and was founded February 25, 1989. Its president is Justus Garoëb, leader of the Damara Council. Garoëb (q.v.) accused the UN of being partial toward SWAPO during the campaign of 1989. The party chairman, Reggie Diergaardt (q.v.), a Labour Party leader, announced in July that the UDF advocated a unitary state for Namibia and pledged to protect individual rights including freedom of religion, a mixed economy, and a single educational system.

In August 1989 the Patriotic Unity Movement announced that it was joining the UDF, and at the end of the month the Workers Revolutionary Party also joined.

When election results were in, the UDF won 37,874 votes, the third highest total, and four seats in the Constituent Assembly. These are held by Garoëb, Diergaardt, Theophelus Soroseb, and Gabriel Siseho. In the second tier or regional elections of November, 1992, the UDF won a total of three seats, two of the five in the Kunene region and one in the Erongo region. In the third tier or local elections it received a fair number of votes but did best in its stronghold of the northwestern quadrant of the country. Its best percentage results came in Khorixas, Uis and Outjo, but its highest total was the 1720 votes it received in Windhoek.

UNITED DEMOCRATIC PARTY (UDP). Now merged into the unitary DTA of Namibia, the UDP first came into existence as a result of a merger in August, 1985. Its founders were Mishake Muyongo (q.v.) (then Vice President of CANU) and Patrick Limbo (then leader of the Caprivi Alliance Party). However, both CANU and CAP continued to exist, as opponents of the merger kept them functioning. Meanwhile the new UDP assumed the old CAP seats in the Caprivi Second Tier Legislative Assembly. The party also was represented in the Assembly of the TGNU from 1985 to its conclusion in 1989.

While avidly seeking independence for Namibia, the UDP sought to use negotiations as the most effective means. Also it believed that chiefs should be allowed their traditional roles but should not be involved in modern politics. The UDP leadership experienced a split in 1988 when co-founder Patrick Limbo was expelled (or broke away) and formed the National Progressive Party.

The UDP affiliated with the Democratic Turnhalle Alliance and participated in its electoral slate in 1989. Muyongo was first on the DTA slate, in respect for his title as DTA's "Senior Vice-President." This alienated the DTA President, Chief Riruako, who coveted the first spot. He resigned and Muyongo was named the DTA Acting President in March, 1990, and later was confirmed as President of the new unitary DTA of Namibia.

UNITED EVANGELICAL LUTHERAN CHURCH OF SOUTH WEST AFRICA (VELKSWA). A very important political and moral force in Namibia today, it was originally a federation of two large Black Lutheran churches, the Evangelical Lutheran Church (ELK) and the Evangelical Lutheran Ovambokavango Church (ELOK) (qq.v.). Its driving forces were Dr. J. L. de Vries and Bishop L. Auala (qq.v.), leaders of those two churches respectively. The two alternated in the top leadership positions of the 400,000-member church federation. As early as 1963 the two churches had combined their theological training at the ELK seminary in Otjimbingwe, which they renamed the Paulineum. By 1978 the German Evangelical Lutheran Church (DELK) joined VELKSWA in a union of three independent churches, backed by the Lutheran World Federation.

Both Dr. de Vries and Bishop Auala were outspoken critics of South Africa's rule in Namibia. They both repeatedly called for independence, condemned the government's treatment of Blacks, and protested the ethnic composition of

the Turnhalle Conference. Despite accusations of a link with
SWAPO (indeed some like Daniel Tjongarero, q.v., were
active in both), the federation proclaims itself unaligned with
any specific political party.

UNITED NATIONAL SOUTH WEST PARTY (UNSWP) (variant: VERENIGDE NASIONALE SUIDWES PARTY).
Formed on January 31, 1927, it was a merger of the National
Party led by F. J. Jooste and the Union Party of B. J. Smit
following the victory in the first (1926) Legislative Assembly elections by the German-speaking Deutsche Bund. Its
electoral support came from the Afrikaners and the few
English who realized that a united front was necessary to
protect themselves from the Germans controlling the political structure. At this point it was not affiliated with any South
African party. It did, however, generally support the policies
of Gen. J. B. Hertzog in South Africa. It alienated the
Germans by advocating that the territory be administered as
a fifth province of South Africa.

The party formed its own newspaper in May 1927, *Die
Suidwes-Afrikaner*. With aggressive campaigning the party
won elections on July 3, 1929, gaining eight of the twelve
seats. The Depression of the early 1930s caused the party to
work closer with the Germans to help the economy. In this
spirit of cooperation it passed a resolution in the Assembly
on April 27, 1932, recognizing German as the third official
language. On the other hand, when a Nazi Party (NSDAP-
SWA) emerged shortly after, the UNSWP was responsible
for an Assembly resolution banning it. In the 1934 elections
the UNSWP called for annexation by South Africa, a tactic
that won them two-thirds of the seats in the Legislative
Assembly. The Germans withdrew from all government
bodies in protest.

With the coming of the National Party of South West
Africa in the late 1930s, some Afrikaners switched loyalties
to the new party. Meanwhile, after 1939 the policy of the
UNSWP tended to follow Gen. Smuts instead of Gen.
Hertzog, in part because of the fear of a new German interest
in the territory. It continued to control the Legislative
Assembly until 1950, at which point it held fifteen of the

eighteen seats. But the National Party had won control in South Africa in 1948, and in 1950 elections in Namibia the National Party won sixteen seats while the UNSWP retained only two (which it lost in 1966).

After the 1950 electoral disaster, the party became much more conservative, attacking the National Party for helping the "Kaffirs"and neglecting the interests of whites. It also attacked the plan of the Odendaal Commission (q.v.) on those grounds. The party leader during most of this ultra-conservative period was J. Percy Niehaus, who held the post for almost twenty years, until 1974. The party failed to gain any political advantage with this policy, and in 1971 even gave up its independent status by becoming the South West Africa branch of South Africa's United Party, with which it amalgamated. The increased immigration of South Africans, especially Afrikaners, was a factor in the party's poor electoral showing.

A radical shift in the party occurred in 1974 when Niehaus was succeeded as Party Leader by Bryan O'Linn, his younger vice-chairman. In 1973 the party had accepted a plan drawn up by O'Linn which called for a federal system within the territory, with whites controlling the National Assembly at first, but with majority rule evolving along with economic and educational advances. A Bill of Rights would protect individuals and minorities. In the 1974 elections O'Linn's party won thirty percent of the votes despite its "verligte" (enlightened) policy. In October 1975, the party divorced itself from the United Party of South Africa and took the name "Federal Party" (q.v.), remaining under O'Linn's leadership.

UNITED NATIONS. Founded in the United States in 1945 by fifty-one founding member states, it has since become virtually the universal organization of world states envisioned by its founders. Despite this common vision, however, not every member state has seen its roles in the same way. Thus, for example, while most of its members saw it as a successor to the League of Nations, and therefore the Trusteeship Council as being the logical extension of the League's Permanent Mandates Commission (q.v.), South

Africa did not. Thus the administration of South West Africa/Namibia was a point of contention within the UN for forty years. Since 1946 the General Assembly sought to block Namibia's annexation. It even appointed a council and a commissioner. It also recognized SWAPO as the sole and authentic representative of the Namibian people. The International Court of Justice considered the issue on three separate occasions, and both the Security Council and the various secretaries general have repeatedly been involved with the Namibian issue. (For further information, see the following entries: INTERNATIONAL COURT OF JUSTICE; GENERAL ASSEMBLY; SECURITY COUNCIL; UNITED NATIONS COMMISSIONER FOR NAMIBIA; UNITED NATIONS COUNCIL FOR NAMIBIA; UNITED NATIONS INSTITUTE FOR NAMIBIA; UNITED NATIONS SPECIAL REPRESENTATIVE FOR NAMIBIA; UNITED NATIONS TRANSITION ASSISTANCE GROUP; UNITED NATIONS TRUSTEESHIP COUNCIL; WALDHEIM, KURT; PEREZ DE CUELLAR, JAVIER.)

UNITED NATIONS COMMISSIONER FOR NAMIBIA. In 1967 the UN General Assembly established a post of United Nations commissioner for South West Africa (changed to commissioner for Namibia in June 1968). The commissioner should be entrusted with whatever executive and administrative tasks as the Council for Namibia deems necessary. The commissioner "shall be responsible to the Council." Regional offices are maintained in Lusaka, Zambia, and in Gaborone, Botswana, for the sake of facilitating communications with Namibians. The commissioner is appointed on an annual basis. An acting commissioner, Constantin Stavropoulos of Greece, was named at first, and he was followed by another acting commissioner, Agha Abdul Hamid, in December 1969. On December 18, 1973, Ireland's Sean MacBride (q.v.) was chosen commissioner by the General Assembly, to assume office on January 1. He was then succeeded by a Finn, Mr. Martti Ahtisaari, on January 1, 1977. He in turn was succeeded by Brajesh Chandra Mishra on April 1, 1982. Ahtisaari was especially active in the process of trying to come up with workable plans for a transition to elections and independence in the late 1970s, when it appeared that a plan by the Western Five Contact Group might result in Namibian independence. Ahtisaari reported his recommendations to UN Secretary-General Kurt Waldheim.

UNITED NATIONS COUNCIL FOR NAMIBIA. On May 18, 1967, the representatives of Nigeria, Chile, and the Philippines presented a draft resolution to the UN General Assembly signed by seventy-nine member states, primarily in the Afro-Asian bloc and the Latin American bloc. It provided for the establishment of a UN Council for South West Africa. It was adopted the next day by a vote of eighty-five to two (South Africa and Portugal), with thirty abstentions. The latter group included the USA, USSR, UK, and France. The eleven-member council was elected on June 13, 1967, and included Chile, Colombia, Guyana, India, Indonesia, Nigeria, Pakistan, Turkey, United Arab Republic, Yugoslavia, and Zambia. It was to be aided by a United Nations commissioner for South West Africa (soon changed to Namibia), q.v. The council was declared to be the only legal authority to administer the Territory of South West Africa until independence, and until that time it was to work to prepare the territory for independence. The council was instructed to contact South Africa about the procedures for transferring control, to go to the territory to take over the administration, to see to the withdrawal of South African forces, to draw up a Constitution, and to arrange for independence. June 1968 was to be the goal for independence. A series of other resolutions were passed in subsequent months—and years—by the General Assembly (q.v.).

In April 1968, the council attempted to send a delegation into Namibia, but was thwarted by South Africa's refusal to comply with the UN authority. While in Africa, however, the delegation interviewed many Namibians, especially those in Zambia and Tanzania, and sought advice on what it could accomplish in the face of South African defiance. One major task clearly identified was to provide education and training for refugee Namibians so that an echelon of trained personnel would be available when independence came. The United Nations Institute for Namibia (q.v.) was created to assist in fulfilling this task. In June 1968 the General Assembly declared that, in keeping with the wishes of the people, the territory would be renamed Namibia, and the council became the UN Council for Namibia. In addition to organizing and funding educational projects, the council handled the issuance of travel documents (called by some ''UN passports''), and closely monitored developments in the country, reporting on them to both the General Assembly and Security Council (q.v.).

Membership on the Council was enlarged to eighteen in 1972, to twenty-five in 1974, and to thirty-one member nations in 1978. The council members ranged the ideological spectrum of the Afro-Asian bloc plus six Latin American states, four Warsaw Pact states, and three ''European'' states (Belgium, Finland, and Australia). The Soviet Union and China were the only significant larger powers represented. In addition, SWAPO participated actively in the Council's work. Some of this work involved promoting international compliance with UN resolutions on Namibia, exposing foreign economic interests that support South Africa's presence there, seeking means to apply pressure on South Africa, and raising funds for and administering the UN Fund for Namibia (q.v.). A major step was taken in 1974 when the Council for Namibia enacted Decree No. 1. Aimed at preserving Namibian natural resources and at applying pressure to both South Africa and major mining companies active in Namibia, it stated that resources exploited in Namibia without the permission of the Council are liable to seizure, and those who defy this will be subject to paying damages to the government after Namibian independence. At a meeting the previous year (1973) in Lusaka, the Council adopted the Lusaka Declaration, which declared its intention to increase support for SWAPO in its armed struggle for Namibia's independence. With independence in 1990, the Council played a role in the transition process and will now presumably cease to exist.

UNITED NATIONS COUNCIL FOR SOUTH WEST AFRICA. Established by the United Nations General Assembly in

1967, its name was soon changed (June 1968) to the United Nations Council for Namibia (q.v.).

UNITED NATIONS INSTITUTE FOR NAMIBIA (UNIN). Established in 1974 by the United Nations Council for Namibia, the institute began operating in a series of modest buildings near the center of Lusaka, Zambia, on August 26, 1976. Hage Geingob was its first director. UNIN's principal objective was to provide training and education for Namibians who will become the core of civil service and bureaucracy now that Namibia has achieved independence. In addition, it conducted research on the problems and potential of the country. Its seven subdivisions were: Constitutional; Legal and Judicial Affairs; Historical, Political, and Cultural; Economics; Agricultural and Land Resources; Social and Education; and the Information and Documentation Centre on Namibia. Most of the institute's $5 million (as of 1987) annual budget came from the UN and Western nations: Canada, France, the Netherlands, Norway, Sweden, West Germany, and the United States. (The Reagan Administration reduced its support in 1984 from $1 million to $250,000.) Its faculty came from more than a dozen countries in Africa, Asia, Europe, and North America. UN officials held eight of the sixteen seats on the senate (the top policymaking body), while SWAPO held three seats and most administrative posts.

Though students were required to pass an entrance exam, many came to the institute unprepared in skills such as English and mathematics. Though many students knew Afrikaans, it was not studied as it was seen as a symbol of South African apartheid. The students who came best prepared generally completed secondary school in SWAPO refugee camps. As a result, about 80 percent of its trainees were SWAPO supporters.

The institute's students prepared to be administrators, magistrates, secretaries, or teachers. Those who needed administrative experience to complete their education were seconded to the Economic Commission for Africa, to the OAU, or to governmental departments of other African countries.

With independence, the functions of the UNIN are being absorbed by the University of Namibia.

UNITED NATIONS SPECIAL REPRESENTATIVE FOR NAMIBIA. A term sometimes applied to the United Nations Commissioner for Namibia for diplomatic reasons when the commissioner is sent to Namibia or South Africa by the secretary-general of the UN.

UNITED NATIONS TRANSITION ASSISTANCE GROUP (UNTAG). The Security Council Resolution 435 of September 29, 1978, established a UN Transition Assistance Group for a period of up to twelve months. Its purpose was to assist the secretary-general's special representative to ensure the early independence of Namibia through fair and free elections under the control and supervision of the United Nations. UNTAG was to consist of between 5000 and 7500 troops from various states in a UN force, plus a corps of about 1500 civilians. UNTAG was to monitor the cease-fire and the reduction of South African troops over a three-month period following the beginning of the cease-fire. After four more months a free and fair election would take place. UNTAG was to be under the command of an Austrian, Major-General Hannes Philipp. These proposals came in large part because of the diplomatic efforts of the so-called Western Five Contact Group (q.v.). However, with the change of South African prime ministers (Botha succeeded Vorster), and the setting up of elections in December 1978 by the administrator general of Namibia (elections that did not include SWAPO), the tentative agreement that brought the planning of UNTAG quickly deteriorated. South Africa especially had a series of concerns about UNTAG (countries represented, size of forces, alleged partiality of UN toward SWAPO) which required further negotiation. Nevertheless UNTAG, in one form or another, continued to be considered by many to be a key factor in any peaceful settlement that would be eventually adopted.

As it turned out, the plan for UNTAG was followed almost precisely as set up, but eleven years later than first expected. When the agreements were reached leading to elections in

1989 and independence in 1990, the plans for UNTAG were put into effect. The man in charge of this UN operation was the secretary general's special representative, Mr. Martti Ahtisaari (q.v.). The major deviation from the original plan was the result of the United States urging a reduction in the number of troops used as a cost-cutting measure. The secretary-general reluctantly agreed to a deployment of 4650 troops, but insisted on leaving 7500 as a possible upper limit if needed. This became important when conflict erupted April 1, 1989, between SWAPO guerrillas crossing the Angolan border into Namibia and members of the South African Defence Force. There were not enough UN troops available to police the border area. Fortunately cool heads prevailed and the situation was resolved quickly. Full deployment of the 4650 troops only was achieved on May 1.

The commander of UNTAG forces was India's General Prem Chand and at least ten nations provided either troops or logistical support. The bureaucratic staff of UNTAG was truly international in background, including Americans, Soviets, Africans, South Americans, Asians, and Europeans. The large civilian corps of UNTAG (divided among ten regional offices) successfully handled the election period, and ultimately declared the election to be "free and fair." The UNTAG military force was scheduled to leave April 30, 1990, but with no new Namibian army in place some feared problems could develop. Thus Kenya agreed to let its contingent of 850 troops remain for three more months.

UNITED NATIONS TRUSTEESHIP COUNCIL. One of the six principal organs of the United Nations (q.v.), the trusteeship council was created by Chapters XII and XIII of the UN Charter. Intended as a successor to the Permanent Mandates Commission (q.v.) of the League of Nations, the council is implied under Article 75, which reads: "The United Nations shall establish under its authority an international trusteeship system for the Administration and supervision of such territories as may be placed thereunder by subsequent individual agreements. These territories are hereinafter referred to as trust territories." Article 76 identifies the trusteeship system's objectives as including: "To promote the political, economic, social, and educational advancement of the inhabitants of the trust territories, and their progressive development towards self-government or independence as may be appropriate to the particular circumstances . . . and the freely expressed wishes of the peoples concerned.'' Article 77 adds: ''1. The trusteeship system shall apply to such territories in the following categories as may be placed thereunder by means of trusteeship agreements: a) territories now held under mandate; . . . . 2. It will be a matter for subsequent agreement as to which territories in the foregoing categories will be brought under the trusteeship system and upon what terms.''

South Africa's position has been that the League of Nations dissolved, thus releasing South Africa from mandate obligations. Wishing to annex Namibia after World War II, South Africa refused to enter into trust agreements with the UN as provided for (but not required by) Articles 75, 77, 79 and other articles. It was the only country to defy world opinion in this manner.

UNITED PARTY. The United National South West Party (q.v.) was founded in 1927, but on November 16, 1971 it was merged with the United Party of the Republic of South Africa, becoming a provincial branch of the latter. Senator J. P. Niehaus was elected chairman of it, but he lost his bid for reelection to the Senate in April 1974 and the party began to deteriorate into factions. A ''verligte'' faction led by Bryan O'Linn defeated Niehaus for control of the party, and in 1975 renamed it the Federal Party (q.v.). Conservatives led by Niehaus formed a SWA Action Group and formed an alliance with AKTUR (q.v.).

UNITED PARTY OF NAMIBIA (UPN). As its name implies, this small group was formed (May 1986) with the purpose of bringing together a number of Namibian parties that would work toward independence under UN Resolution 435. Its founders, especially veteran politician L. J. (''Barney'') Barnes, favor a Christian-based, Western-style democracy for Namibia. Having received minimal public support the party joined with the Democratic Turnhalle Alliance in

January 1989. He was placed ninth in the DTA electoral list and won a seat in the Assembly. When the DTA became a unitary party in November, 1991 the UPN lost its separate identity. In March, 1992 Barnes resigned his position in the National Assembly, and the next month he also resigned from the DTA.

UNITED SOUTH WEST AFRICA PARTY. *See* UNITED NATIONAL SOUTH WEST PARTY.

UNITED STATES POLICY ON NAMIBIA. Inevitably US policy towards Namibia has been tied to its policy towards South Africa. During the Paris Peace Conference following World War I, the US originally supported the incorporation of a German South West Africa into the young Union of South Africa, primarily because so much of the land seemed destitute and unproductive. During World War II the Smuts government of South Africa joined with the West against fascism. South African troops fought in the North African campaign and in Italy, and the US even signed a lend-lease agreement with South Africa. Nevertheless, after the war the US tried not to encourage Prime Minister Smuts' idea of Pan-Africanism that would have put most of Eastern and Central Africa under South African leadership.

Under President Harry Truman, South Africa was just another friendly country that assisted us in both the Berlin airlift and the Korean War. At the UN, however, South Africa became a problem. The US supported only mildly worded resolutions on South Africa, aware that its own race record left much room for improvement. It was critical of South Africa's defiance of the UN trust plan for Namibia because it was clearly a "rule of law" issue. During the Eisenhower years (1952–1960), the US was more concerned with rising problems in Southeast Asia than with South Africa, standing finally on the old "we shouldn't intervene in the internal affairs of another sovereign state" argument. However in May 1958, recognizing the changes on the African continent, the US State Department realigned its subdivisions to separate the African assignment from the Middle Eastern bureau. Washington even backed a weak UN resolution expressing "regret and concern" over South African racial policies.

President Kennedy was more knowledgeable about Africa than any previous US President except Theodore Roosevelt. He opposed French colonialism in Africa and South Africa's racial policies, and he appointed a strong liberal as the first US assistant secretary of state for African affairs. In several ways the US administration let South Africa know that it would not support South African apartheid in any way. Yet the US military and the Defense Department practiced business as usual, cooperating with South Africa on several projects. President Johnson continued Kennedy's policy of opposition towards South Africa's policies, even voting for a UN resolution that would study the use of sanctions against South Africa. However, Vietnam distracted both Presidents Johnson and Nixon from spending too much time on African issues. The major exception was American support of the anti-South Africa position in the World Court case over control of Namibia. The US was equally active at the United Nations through its ambassador to the UN, Arthur Goldberg, who condemned South Africa for not allowing self-determination in Namibia.

Nixon's foreign policy advisor, Henry Kissinger, viewed US-African relations in the global context of US-USSR relations. In one notable study for the State Department, the conclusion was made that on the issue of Namibia there was "no solution in sight." Kissinger and Nixon concluded that the whites were in southern Africa to stay, and constructive change could only come through working with them. Black violence was futile, they felt. "Constructive communications" with South African leaders became the policy, and at the UN abstention on South African issues became more common as American diplomats stifled their previous condemnations of apartheid. As the Angolan revolution progressed, Kissinger, now President Ford's secretary of state, ignored the advice of his African experts by viewing the issue as one of the US against the USSR. Thus he supported covert actions that placed the US on the same side of the conflict as South Africa. Not only did this tactic result in thousands of Cuban troops flocking to Angola, but also in diplomatic isolation for the US. Kissinger then tried a different approach by using his unique form of "shuttle diplomacy" to attempt to resolve the Zimbabwe issue.

President Jimmy Carter executed a major reversal of US-African policies. First he viewed southern Africa from a regional perspective, not the previous global view. In addition, both his Secretary of State Cyrus Vance and his ambassador to the UN, Black activist Andrew Young, agreed that something must be done to fight racial injustices in southern Africa. African nationalism was viewed as a positive force, not a negative one, and in a day and a half of frank discussions, Vice President Mondale confronted South African Prime Minister Vorster on both the Zimbabwe and Namibia questions. Progress was required on those issues (and within South Africa itself) if American relations with South Africa were to improve. Of some importance was that the US joined the rest of the world states in voting at the United Nations for mandatory sanctions against arms transfers to South Africa.

In addition it was Carter's policy to try to solve the stalemate over Namibia by organizing the US, Britain, France, West Germany, and Canada into the Western Five Contact Group (q.v.). Since all of them had significant trade and investment ties with South Africa, it was assumed that the Western Five could apply pressure to bring about fulfillment of United Nations Resolution 385. The Contact Group did achieve at least one thing: it got the two sides (South Africa and SWAPO) to negotiate. At one point it looked like Namibian independence was just a signed document or two away.

When it became obvious that President Carter might be defeated in his reelection bid by a noted conservative politician, Ronald Reagan, South Africa began to stall in the Namibian negotiations. Indeed it was accurate. President Reagan's policies, if not pro-apartheid, worked for what he called greater balance and even-handedness in US dealings with South Africa. His undersecretary for African affairs, Dr. Chester Crocker, proposed a new approach (actually a more pragmatic form of Kissinger's constructive communication) called "constructive engagement." In essence it said that the

US should offer South Africa the carrot of understanding rather than the stick of confrontation. US abstentions and vetoes were frequent at the United Nations. Yet it apparently brought Namibia no closer to independence, especially when the Reagan administration insisted on linking the issue of Cuban troops in Angola with the negotiation of Namibia's freedom.

UNIVERSITY OF NAMIBIA. One of three units of the Academy (q.v.) founded in 1980, in its initial years it was closely associated with the University of South Africa. In 1985 it became a fully autonomous university. Its degree and diploma programs span a wide range through its faculties of arts, education, nursing, and medical sciences. Post-graduate programs are increasing in some of the areas. Its city campus in Windhoek is shared with the Technikon, another of the Academy's units. In 1990 the university had 1800 students, but with rapid growth it could easily double or triple in size. Its teaching faculty in 1990 consists of 128 teachers, but only 11 have received their doctorates.

UPINGTONIA, REPUBLIC OF. A short-lived republic, it was established by a party of Boers who were part of the Thirstland Trekkers (q.v.) who had settled in Angola. This dissatisfied segment followed the advice of a trader, W. W. Jordan (q.v.), who "purchased" a large area of land from the Ovambo Chief Kambonde for twenty-five muskets and some brandy. The area encompassed the region that today would include Otavi, Grootfontein, and Waterberg plus mineral rights at Tsumeb. (He had failed earlier to acquire land at Rehoboth.) While the transactions and settlement occurred in 1884, it did not officially declare itself a Boer republic (with a constitution) until October 20, 1885. It was named Upingtonia after Thomas Upington, prime minister of the Cape Colony, from whom they hoped to receive protection and aid. Meanwhile the German government of the territory, speaking through Dr. Goering, said it could not tolerate a Boer republic in its territory.

The president of the republic was G. D. Prinsloo. While its government allocated land to the forty-six trekkers, farms were not immediately worked, as most of the group stayed together near today's Grootfontein. They built huts there and worked small plots. Eleven families left for the Waterberg and others for the Transvaal when Chief Maherero (q.v.) requested them to leave the area (which he claimed to be part of his land). Those remaining renamed the area Lijdensrust. Jordan was murdered by brothers of Kambonde on June 30, 1886, presumably at the urging of Hereros. Severe medical problems, including fever, also hit the Boers, and in 1887 the remaining trekkers left the region.

URANIUM. Namibia has been one of the top producers of uranium in the world, producing as much as 4.5 thousand tons a year. However the Rössing Uranium Mine (q.v.) completed many of its contracts in the 1980s and the world market experienced a major drop. Production by Rössing was lowered to 2.5 thousand tons a year in 1991, and a third of its workforce was laid off, at least until a new contract with France restores some of the production in 1995.

Namibia's "reasonably assured reserves" are estimated to be the eighth largest in the world, and perhaps 10% of the world's total uranium reserves. Thus production of "yellowcake" could expand considerably, even tripling or quadrupling if the market justified it. It could even replace diamonds as the country's greatest revenue producer.

The major deposit is at Rössing in the Namib Desert, about twenty kilometers northeast of Swakopmund. At its peak production the Rössing complex boosted the economy of both Swakopmund and nearby Arandis. Other sites in Namibia have been explored for uranium deposits. The uranium at Rössing is found in granite, and similar rocks of the so-called "Damara Mobile Belt" underlie a sizeable part of Namibia.

USAKOS (translation: "HEAD IN HANDS"). Located in the Khan River Valley between the Nubib and Rooiberg mountains, this is a major town with a population in the 3,500 range. Near the Namib Desert, it is extremely dry (150 millimeters of rainfall per year) and hot. Although the ocean is 150 kilometers to the west, a sea breeze comes up to moderate afternoon temperatures. On a major road, Usakos is 150 kilometers northeast of Swakopmund, 30 kilometers west of Karibib, and 222 kilometers northwest of Windhoek. It is also located on the main rail line from Windhoek to Swakopmund, and in the 1920s the railway shops were moved from Karibib to Usakos, as it lies a few miles south of the junction of the main line (Swakopmund to Windhoek) and the rail line to the important mining areas in the north, notably Otavi and Tsumeb, not to mention population centers such as Omaruru, Kalkfeld and Otjiwarongo. The line from Usakos to Tsumeb covers 249 miles.

The town began in 1905 when a German copper-mining company purchased a farm called "Usakos" and built a railroad workshop and a narrow-gauge line on the farm. The line was to carry copper from Tsumeb to Walvis Bay via Swakopmund. The railroad workshops were closed in 1981 when the line was converted to standard gauge. The economy of Usakos received a major boost when it was announced in 1991 that a consortium of local and overseas investors planned to construct Namibia's first oil refinery there. The $100 million project, scheduled for completion by the end of 1992, would go a long way toward removing Namibia from the need to import refined petroleum products from South Africa and Angola.

UULENGA. Variant form of Ulenga (q.v.), the surname of a prominent labor leader and member of the government.

- V -

VAALGRAS (variant: FAHLGRAS). A site near Keetmanshoop in southern Namibia, it is the location where the great and elderly Nama leader, Hendrik Witbooi, met his death. Forced by German troops into the Kalahari, Witbooi led harassing attacks, including one at Vaalgras against a supply convoy for the German troops on October 29, 1905. He was wounded in the fight but escaped, only to die of his injuries on November 13.

VAN DER WATH, JOHANNES GERT HENDRIK (1903–). Born in Ladybrand in South Africa's Orange Free State, he was educated at Glen College, Norman College in Bloemfontein, and the University of Halle. He was elected an MP for Windhoek and became deputy minister for the territory from 1961 to 1968. He was also leader of the National Party in Namibia until 1968. He was appointed administrator of the territory by South Africa, serving from 1968 to 1971. He was a strong advocate of the South West Africa Affairs Bill in the South African House of Assembly in February 1969. It provided for tighter controls over the administration of the territory and permitted the state president to apply any South African law to Namibia, however amended, with the approval only of the cabinet, not Parliament.

VAN NIEKERK, DR. WILLIE. Administrator general of Namibia beginning February 1, 1983, van Niekerk was a medical doctor by profession. Raised in Pretoria, he attended the University of Pretoria, where he specialized in obstetrics and gynecology. From 1970 until his appointment he served as head of the Department of Obstetrics-Gynecology at Stellenbosch University in South Africa. He also studied at a medical institute in New York, and had been a doctor for twenty-three years before his appointment. His political experience included serving on the South Africa President's Council, where he headed the committee on cooperation. Among the priorities he listed when being named to the post in Namibia was the promotion of tourism with an eye toward new revenue for development in the territory. But in mid-1983 he announced the formation of a State Council, claiming that his mandate from South Africa was to get the political parties to work together toward independence. This led to the formation of the Multi-Party Conference (q.v.) in August 1983. With the announcement that the position of administrator general was being dropped, van Niekerk returned to South Africa after power was officially transferred to the Transitional Government of National Unity on June 17, 1985. He returned to South Africa where he became minister of national health and population development. In 1989 he was called back to Namibia to serve in a liaison role between the authorities in South Africa and Namibia in the period leading up to independence. His work involved dealing with the AG, the Transitional Government of National Unity, and the UN special representative for Namibia, Mr. Marti Ahtisaari.

VAN REENEN, SEBASTIAAN VALENTIJN (1760–1821). Among the earlier European visitors to Namibia, S. V. van Reenen and others sailed in 1793 on the Dutch ship, *Meermin,* with the goal of annexing a portion of the coast. They did that, claiming Dutch sovereignty over Walvis Bay, Halifax Island, and Angra Pequeña. The ship then traveled north to the mouth of the Swakop River, where he and several companions, including the hunter, Pieter Pienaar (q.v.), explored inland. Captain van Reenen's hope was to find copper mines (which he did not) or at least reach the Hereros and begin a cattle export trade to St. Helena. While he found Hereros in the Swakop Valley, no commercial tie was established, as the Hereros were unwilling to part with their cattle for useless "money" or European merchandise.

This was not S. V. van Reenen's first trip to Namibia. He reached the Orange River in 1778 with Lieut. William Paterson and others, and spent a few days hunting giraffes on the north side of the river. Three times in 1779 he and companions traveled to the Orange, crossing over briefly on each occasion. It was two years later when Paterson met van Reenen at the Cape and they discussed the possibility of finding a good harbor on the coast north of the Orange. This led to his trip on the *Meermin.* Also on that ship was his oldest brother Dirk Gijspert Van Reenen (1754–1828), who later traveled north of the Orange with Governor Janssens in 1803. Another brother to visit Namibia was Willem Van Reenen (q.v.).

VAN REENEN, WILLEM (1756–1806). One of four brothers, Sebastiaan V. (q.v.), Dirk (see in Sebastiaan's entry) and Jacob Van Reenen III, he lived at Rondebosch in the Cape. He received permission from Dutch authorities to seek gold in Great Namaqualand and left Cape Town on September 17, 1791, adding several others to his party along the way. They crossed the Orange River at Raman's Drift on October 30. Three days later the party reached Warmbad, where they were joined by Barend Freyn and Pieter Brand, still following the trail taken by Hendrik Hop (q.v.). They next reached Modderfontein (now Keetmanshoop) where they were assisted by G. Visagie. They then hired a local guide, Jan Sieberd, to assist them as they moved north. The party left Modderfontein on December 28, and crossed both the Fish and Leber Rivers, where they killed rhinos, giraffes, and buffaloes for food. They reached the "Rhenius Mts." (perhaps the Aus Mts.) on January 23, 1792, where they found "valuable mineral springs," and in the vicinity, a copper mine. It is probable that they were actually near Rehoboth, where the hot springs belonged to the Nama chief of the Red Nation (q.v.). Van Reenen set up camp there and sent Pieter Brand north with seven Namas. Instead of reaching the cattle-rich Hereros whom they sought, they evidently encountered the Bergdamas, presumably near Windhoek. Brand returned to the hot springs camp and Van Reenen led his party south on February 14, 1792. They reached Van Reenen's farm on the Olifants River on June 20. Van Reenen's vivid stories inspired many other adventurers to travel into Namibia.

VAN WYK, HERMANUS. Nineteenth-century leader of the Basters (q.v.), he was elected in 1868 to lead them from their home in the northern part of South Africa's Cape Province, an area being overrun by diamond prospectors, into a new homeland in Namibia. Van Wyk was in the advance party that reached Warmbad on July 13, 1868. The full party left for Bethanie shortly after Christmas, searching for an unoccupied area to set up their homes. They stayed several months before moving on. Van Wyk discovered that Rehoboth had been unoccupied since 1864, when Willem Swartbooi left. However, they could not simply move in and take over, as the Red Nation claimed the area by right of conquest, and Maherero also maintained that it was his. At a conference in Okahandja, van Wyk was encouraged to deal with Abraham Swartbooi, who then agreed to let the Basters use the area until he needed it, for the payment of only one horse a year. Payment of a horse to several other African leaders settled the issue temporarily. A few years later Jan Jonker Afrikander wanted to move into the area of Rehoboth, just as the Basters were beginning to develop the area. To avoid further dispute, van Wyk went back to Swartbooi and reached a purchase agreement. The land around Rehoboth was bought for 120 horses and 5 wagons.

This sale did not end conflicts. In 1876 van Wyk had to stand up to several European traders who claimed rights in the area, and he evicted two of them. Various groups of Namas and Damaras drove off Baster cattle, Hereros took their cattle to wells sunk by the Basters, and added insult to injury by stealing some of their stock. And Jan Jonker continued to try to force the Basters out of Rehoboth. Van Wyk was therefore happy to encourage W. C. Palgrave's (q.v.) mission in October 1876. Palgrave simultaneously tried to encourage the Namas to stop their thievery and to persuade van Wyk that the Cape government would assist him if the matter became worse. One problem was resolved when Maherero agreed to a peace with van Wyk on February 15, 1882. This was important because almost four months later (June 13) Maherero signed a treaty with many of his other opponents. That treaty contained a provision that the Basters would be allowed to stay at Rehoboth. Jan Jonker Afrikander was not a signee, however, and was unhappy that van Wyk had made a separate peace with Maherero. Afrikander then attacked Rehoboth and burned half of it. Abraham Swartbooi was fatally wounded in the attack. As battles in the area continued (notably between the Hereros and Hendrik Witbooi), van Wyk turned to the new Europeans in the area, and on October 11, 1884, gave a letter to Dr. C. Hopfner requesting protection from the German Kaiser. Internal affairs would remain in control of the Baster Council (q.v.), but relations with other chiefs and foreign nations would be managed by the Germans. The treaty was formalized on September 15, 1885. In 1892 and 1893 van Wyk tried to serve as a mediator between Hendrik Witbooi and Samuel Maharero on the latter's request. He met little success, as

Witbooi didn't trust him. In the 1904 war van Wyk remained loyal to the Germans.

VAN ZIJL, EBENEZER ("EBEN") (1931–). One of Namibia's leading conservative politicians, Van Zijl was born in Keetmanshoop. He attended Stellenbosch University, where he received a BA in 1953 and an LLB in 1955. He then became an advocate, but has also been a farmer for over twenty years. He joined the National Party of South West Africa (q.v.), and was chosen its vice-chairman in 1975. In 1964 he was elected to represent Klein Windhoek in the SWA Legislative Assembly. From 1966 to 1980 he was a member of the Executive Council and held several different portfolios. Van Zijl and Dirk Mudge (q.v.), a much more liberal member of the NP, were chosen to help organize the Turnhalle Conference (q.v.), and he was a member of its white delegation throughout the conference (1975–77). However, a party split occurred and Mudge formed a new party. Van Zijl remained working under NP leader A. H. de Plessis (q.v.), and was expected to succeed him.

Van Zijl was elected in 1978 to the National Assembly, serving from 1979 to 1981, and from 1980 to 1981 he was also on the Second Tier White Representative Authority. He was also a leading member of AKTUR (q.v.), a political alliance, from 1977 to 1981. In 1981 he was not chosen to succeed du Plessis as NP leader, and retired from politics for two years. He reemerged as delegate of the NP to the Multi-Party Conference (q.v.) in 1973 and subsequently joined the Transitional Government of National Unity. He was its minister of agriculture, water affairs and sea fisheries from 1985 to 1987.

Ironically by 1987 Van Zijl found himself among the more liberal elements of the NP and split with it to form the Action National Settlement (q.v.) and became its chairman. He led it into an alliance, the National Patriotic Front of Namibia (q.v.) for the 1989 elections. He was chosen its vice-chairman. However, it only won one seat in the Assembly, and he did not get it. In February 1990, he led his party out of the NPF, saying the ANS would be a nonpolitical interest group.

VAN ZYL COMMISSION OF 1935. Hendrik S. Van Zyl, a distinguished South African jurist, was named head of a three-man commission in 1935. The commission was appointed by the South African government to quiet demands by Afrikaners in Namibia who wanted the territory incorporated into the Union as a fifth province. German-speaking residents were opposed to incorporation, seeing it as a threat to their right to their own German culture. The existence of some Nazi support among this element was also investigated by the commission but to no effect. The commission also spent time studying the Ovambo tribal system and the "indirect rule" by South Africa. While the commissioners decided that the current system worked well and should be continued, it recommended increased spending by the Union of South Africa on the tribal areas, noted that the system tended to suppress individualism, and warned South African officials to be wary of the way their policies could have disruptive effects in traditional societies.

All the commissioners agreed that the existing constitution of the territory should be abandoned, but the three totally disagreed on the best alternative. Van Zyl favored the administration of the territory as an integral part of South Africa, or better yet as a fifth province. A second commissioner strongly opposed that view, and a third said that the time was not yet ripe for incorporation.

There was a second "Van Zyl Commission" in Namibia. This one (in 1958) investigated the status of "non-White" education in the territory.

VEDDER, DR. HEINRICH (1876–1972). Described by most as Namibia's greatest historian and ethnologist, the much honored missionary was born in Westerenger in the German state of Westphalia on July 3, 1876. He was sent to Namibia in 1903 by the Rhenish Missionary Society (RMS), which had trained him at their German seminary. Quick with languages, after only two years at mission stations at Otjimbingwe, Karibib, and Scheppmannsdorf, he was fluent in the Herero, Nama, and Ovambo languages. He opened a new mission station at Swakopmund and also began writing the first of his books, these being religious books in the Nama and Herero languages.

In 1911 he opened a training school for African teachers and lay preachers and also learned the language of the San, while simultaneously ministering to the German Lutherans at Gaub. During World War I he began intense study of the Damaras and later wrote a book on them. He was repatriated for several years in Germany, but returned in 1922 to Namibia. He spent twenty years training teachers and lay preachers at the Augustineum (q.v.), which he founded in Okahandja, and indeed spent most of the rest of his life there.

In 1934 Vedder published his *magnum opus, Das Alte Südwestafrika,* which has been translated into other languages. In English it is called *South West Africa in Early Times.* Not without flaws (a pro-German missionary prejudice, and a disputed view of Damaras historically, for example), it is still a phenomenally thorough study of the territory up to 1890. In addition his *Introduction to the History of South West Africa* supplements the main work by dealing with the German period. But those two books are only the tip of the iceberg, as his production includes countless items in African languages, Biblical interpretations, hymns and sacred songs, numerous historical, philological, and ethnological studies, and much more published, in both religious and popular magazines and newspapers.

Vedder served as Präses of the Rhenish Mission in the territory from 1937 to 1943, and during World War II, also as moderator of the Lutheran Church in Namibia. One who sought to bridge the gulf between all peoples, his scholarship and humanitarianism were honored by the University of Tübingen with an honorary doctorate in the 1920s; he was similarly honored in 1948 by the University of Stellenbosch. He served in the South African Parliament as an appointed senator for Namibia's African people from 1950 until his resignation in 1958. A brief autobiography was published in 1953. He died nearing his 96th birthday, on April 26, 1972, in Okahandja.

VEII, HITJEVI GERSON (1939–). Leader of the South West Africa National Union (SWANU) from 1968 to the mid-1980s, Veii has a Herero mother and a German grandfather. A product of the excellent Augustineum School in Okahandja, he failed to matriculate when his essay on the Afrikaner pioneers was decidedly negative. While there he was a founder of the South West Africa Student Body (q.v.). He found a job in Windhoek, and his many travels made him conscious of the discrimination faced by black Africans in his country. Thus he became involved in the formation of the South West African Progressive Association, a very left-wing organization. When SWANU was formed in 1959 he was at first overlooked for membership in its executive, but he soon came to the attention of its leaders and was appointed its vice-secretary-general in 1960. His speeches got him into trouble with the territory's government, and he was charged with incitement to riot. In 1967 he began a term on Robben Island under the Suppression of Communism Act. In 1968, while still on the island, he was chosen the party's president. He was released in 1972 and continued his party activity in Windhoek. He led SWANU into membership in the National Convention (q.v.), a group that soon split up. Veii busied himself with party organization (claiming 6000 members in 1977) and with protesting to the UN that SWAPO was not the only significant party in Namibia. After the Turnhalle Conference left out many of Namibia's political parties, Veii led SWANU in 1977 into another grouping, the Namibian National Front (q.v.), an alliance of the protesting parties. He served as its vice-president 1978–80. SWANU split in 1984, and the faction led initially by Kuzeeko Kangueehi became known as SWANU-P (for Progressives) or SWANU-NNF. Veii was elected its vice-president, a post he still holds. When the NNF was revived as an electoral coalition in 1989 he became its national organizer. In the election the NNF only won one seat in the Assembly, and Veii did not get that seat. Nevertheless he remains one of the country's more active political figures.

VELDKOST (variant: VELDKOS). Literally "field food," the word is used in several languages and depicts a phenomenon common to most of the Africans in Namibia. While the gathering of nature's own vegetable and fruit products is most widely practiced among the San and Damaras, it has been seen even in the heart of Windhoek, as edible foods are found growing on open lots. Generally the gathering of veldkost is done by the females of the family, especially when the men are hunting or watching cattle, but men will also pick the fruits of the earth. The women are careful not to pick a source clean, so that there will be more remaining when they return, also to avoid providing an unbalanced diet by serving only one item, regardless of its availability.

Veldkost are even found in the Namib and Kalahari deserts if one knows where to look. Certainly the San of the Kalahari are familiar with every square foot of their territory. Their menu can be quite varied. Ants and their eggs ("Bushman rice"), snakes, field mice, and lizards are found in the Kalahari, as is a real delicacy, wild honey. Vegetarian products include a wide variety of tubers, bulbs, roots, nuts, wild figs, melons, and leaves of certain plants. In good rainy seasons, for example, large quantities of truffles can be found in one region. A species of termitomyces (related to mushroom) grow near ant mounds and are very edible. Walleriamitons are tubers very similar to potatoes. Several roots or tubers are noted for emitting a water substitute when chewed raw, such as the Fockea or waterroot. Tsammas (q.v.) serves the same purpose. There are other plants in the pumpkin and cucumber families growing wild, such as the naras (q.v.). Some of these even grow among the sand dunes, with roots comfortably reaching an underground water supply.

A number of trees provide fruits and seeds that are edible, including the baobob and the marula. The latter provides fruits suitable for juice or jelly, or if allowed to become overripe, for fermenting into alcoholic beverages. Baboons and elephants are fond of them and have become inebriated. The *Phylogeiton discolor* produces a delicious wild date (although it is not in the palm family). The fibrous pulp of the palm apple of the makalani (*Hyphaena ventricosa*) is a very sweet-tasting food. Berries grow abundantly on bushes in good rainy seasons, and they can be dried and preserved for months. This list provides only a small portion of the veldkost available in Namibia.

VELDSKENDRAERS. This group is referred to under many variants, including Veldschoendragers, Velskoendraers, and Feldschuhträgers (q.v.).

VERSAILLES PEACE CONFERENCE AND TREATY. Following World War I, the victorious countries met at the Palace of Versailles outside Paris in 1919 to forge a peace. In regard to Namibia its major result was to put an end to German colonial rule (worldwide, not just in Namibia). Thus the spoils of war were divided, and Namibia was awarded to the Union of South Africa as a "Class C" mandate, to be administered as an integral part of South Africa, subject only to the duty "to promote to the utmost the material and moral well-being and the social progress of the inhabitants of the territory." The conference did reject, however, General Smuts' plea that South Africa should be allowed to incorporate it as a fifth province. South Africa was also obligated to submit an annual report on the progress of the territory to the Permanent Mandates Commission (q.v.) of the League of Nations. The territory also became officially known as South West Africa.

VILJOEN, DANN T. DU P. Administrator of Namibia in the early 1950s, this South African civil servant was a noted nature conservationist. When he was administrator, there was considerable pressure to have the former Aukeigas Reserve for Damaras (who had been moved to a larger Reserve) made available for white farming settlements. Viljoen resisted these efforts and insisted that it be declared a nature conservation area and game park. The area has since been named after him, and the Dann Viljoen Game Park is a delightful outdoor haven for residents of Windhoek. Located only fifteen miles (twenty-four kilometers) west of the city, it is on the road to the Khomas Highlands. There are rondavels and camping sites under shady trees and picnic spots along the dam. A restaurant and swimming pool are added pleasures for both tourists and Namibians. The game trails can be driven for several miles, but drought has made the animals harder to find. Most of the game consists of kudu, gemsbok, wildebeest, zebra, impala, springbok, and small game.

VILJOEN, DR. GERRIT. Appointed administrator general of Namibia on August 13, 1979, Viljoen took charge with the reputation of being perhaps the second most powerful man in South Africa. A professor by profession, and former rector of Rand Afrikaans University, he was also head of the Broederbond, a secret society of elite Afrikaners that served virtually as an executive council for the National Party of South Africa. Yet Viljoen was reputedly more liberal than most in the Broederbond, and his appointment was expected to defuse the ultraright political element in Namibia. A "reformist," he believed in making accommodations to urban Africans within the context of apartheid. During his brief tenure as administrator general he indeed worked to eliminate some of the "petty apartheid" in Namibia and encouraged the political involvement of moderate Africans. He also proposed second-tier elections for the white community. A pragmatist, he seemed to recognize that South Africa could not hang on to the territory indefinitely. He thus encouraged a moderate multiracial coalition, hoping it would attract support away from SWAPO. On August 26, 1980, South African Prime Minister Pieter Botha shuffled his cabinet and called Viljoen home to become minister of national education.

VISAGIE, GUILLIAM (variant: GIDEON). Called the first white farmer and settler in Namibia. It is uncertain whether Guilliam and Gideon are the same person or if the former is perhaps father to the latter. In any case, Guilliam was born about 1751 at the Cape and became a farmer there near the Olifants River. In 1780 he and J. Joubert were found guilty of killing one Nama and wounding two others. Defying his punishment by authorities, Visagie moved north of the Orange River with his wife. In 1791 he was living at Swartmodder (Keetmanshoop today), farming and trading firearms to the Namas for cattle. Willem van Reenen's (q.v.) party stopped there in both 1791 and on their return in 1792, receiving assistance each time from Visagie. About 1820 a Visagie aided the Bondelswarts in raiding the Hereros. In turn, however, he and his son (perhaps grandson of the first) helped his Nama neighbors fight off an attack by Jager Afrikander and his men. The Visagie family was still living at Swartmodder about 1830.

VLEY (variant: VLEI). Also known as a pan, the vley is a sheet of standing water that forms during the rainy season in depressions in otherwise level country. Vleys are very shallow and salty. They are most numerous in Damaraland and in the eastern part of the country near the Kalahari Desert. The Etosha Pan, on the border of Ovamboland, is the largest in the country. Ovambos begin their planting after the onset of the rainy season when the vleys begin to collect water. If rainfall and river runoff is especially heavy, large expanses are covered with shallow water, with only scattered "islands" breaking the watery landscape.

VOGELSANG, HEINRICH CHRISTIAN (1862–1914). Born in Bremen, Germany, this son of a German tobacco merchant was only a teenager when he visited South Africa in 1877 and worked two years for a Cape trader. He then went to West Africa for several years, representing a German trading company. There in the Gold Coast (today's Ghana) he met Adolf Lüderitz (q.v.), and informed him of trade possibilities on the Namibian coast. Working together, they planned a trade venture. Vogelsang went ahead and landed in Cape Town on January 6, 1883 to plan the trip. When Lüderitz' ship the *Tilly* arrived two months later, Vogelsang was prepared, having gained much information from Dr. Theophilus Hahn, who had spent many years among the Namas. The *Tilly* arrived at Angra Pequeña (q.v.) on April 10, where it was unloaded into a hut, erected by the crew, which they called "Fort Vogelsang." Travelling to Bethanie with two colleagues, Vogelsang negotiated an agreement with the Nama leader, Josef Fredericks, on May 1, 1883. It gained Angra Pequeña and the surrounding area for Lüderitz in exchange for £100 and 200 rifles. A German flag was hoisted at Angra Pequeña on May 12, and soon a second hut (filled with merchandise) was set up at Bethanie. On August 25, Vogelsang concluded a second deal with the same Chief Fredericks, "purchasing" the whole coast area from the Orange River north to the 26th latitude, to an inland depth of 20 miles. This cost only £100 and 60 rifles, and the area was called Lüderitzland. The purchase was greeted with surprise by other traders, especially De Pass, Spence & Co. (q.v.), which was working in the area and claimed that the chief had no right to sell the land, as it had been purchased twenty years earlier by De Pass. Chief Fredericks informed Lüderitz that he had sold De Pass only a mining concession. Vogelsang then turned eagerly to handling weapons trade in the area.

Further negotiations involving Dr. Gustav Nachtigal (q.v.) placed Nama tribes under German protection. Vogelsang was left in Walvis Bay as the provisional consul to watch over German interests in the territory. He traveled to Okahandja in late December 1884, but despite the support of missionaries there he was unable to persuade Kamaherero to agree to a treaty of protection. The next month he went to Rehoboth, where the Basters wanted protection, but he encountered conflicts over existing land rights. He was more successful at Hoachanas, where Manasse and the Red Nation Council signed the protection agreement on January 14, 1885, and likewise at Berseba where Jacobus Izaak agreed to the treaty on January 29. In August Vogelsang was replaced by Dr. H. E. Goering (q.v.). While he returned for awhile to Germany, he came back to Namibia from 1888 to 1890, representing the Deutsche Kolonial-Gesellschaft.

VOICE OF THE PEOPLE. A successor to the South West Africa Democratic Union (formerly led by Kephes Conradie and J.W. Skrywer), it was founded by them and Jeremiah Jagger. It is a town-oriented organization of Namas and Damaras, with headquarters in Windhoek. Founded in the late 1960s, it joined five other parties in the National Convention in 1972, which was weakened by the defection of SWAPO in 1975. Meanwhile, the Voice of the People had worked closely with SWANUF (q.v.), with which there were signs of amalgamation in 1973. While favoring independence and rejecting all forms of apartheid and homeland creation, its leaders also rejected SWAPO's claim to be the territory's sole leader. Its leadership split over the Turnhalle Conference issue, as Jagger attended but Conradie and the organization opposed the conference.

In 1977 Conradie led the organization into a new alliance, the Namibia National Front (q.v.). The next year, however, he helped form another new alliance, the Namibia People's Liberation Front (q.v.), and Conradie became its life president. Meanwhile the Voice of the People has consistently favored a unitary independent Namibia. When elections came in 1989, the NPLF Alliance (led by Conradie) joined the Federal Convention of Namibia for an election bloc, and Conradie served on its executive. The FCN won only one seat, however, and no one from the Voice of the People received it.

VOIGTS, ALBERT (1869–1938). The first karakul farmer in Namibia, he and his three brothers built up a farming and trading dynasty. Born in Germany in 1869 at Meerdorf, he travelled to South Africa where he worked for the trader Fritz Wecke in 1891. His trade included cattle from the Herero sold as slaughtered stock in Johannesburg. He and his brother Gustav moved to Namibia, starting trading communities in both Okahandja and Windhoek, especially supplying provisions to German soldiers and settlers. While Gustav continued trading, Albert ran a 100,000-hectare estate (called Voigtsgrund), which became a model farm. He built a large dam, developed an extensive irrigation system, and bred excellent stud cattle there, between Gibeon and Maltahohe. In 1907 Governor Von Lindequist gave him several of the new karakul sheep he had imported, and from this stock he literally began Namibia's great karakul industry.

Voigts became active in politics, heading the German Bund in the 1930s, representing German colonists in the Legislative Assembly and in the Executive Committee. In these positions he fought for equal rights for the Germans in Namibia, including the right to their own schools. Illness forced him to return to Germany for medical treatment, where he died November 18, 1938. He was buried back at Voigtsgrund.

VOLKSRAAD. An elected council, the term is used primarily in regard to the community at Rehoboth. A variant of Raad (q.v.).

- W -

WALVIS BAY (variants: WALFISHBAAI; WALVICH BAY; WALVIS BAAI). These variants are just some of the alternate spellings and names for this important and controversial port. One Portuguese navigator described it as "a shallow bay teeming with fish of all kinds, including whales." Thus an early Portuguese sailor called it "Bahia das Baleas" or "Bay of Whales." Ultimately a Dutch version "Walvis" survived over the German spelling of Walfisch. Bartholomew Dias called it Golfo de Santa Maria de Conceicao after the feast day on which he anchored there, December 8, 1487. It is believed that no European had been there previously. Two years later a mapmaker using Dias' charts called it Praia dos Sardinha (Sardine Coast). Another Portuguese ship landed there in 1506, and the Dutch sailors of the seventeenth century knew the bay. Captain Duminy, piloting the *Meermin* (q.v.), proclaimed Dutch sovereignty over Walvis Bay and several nearby area in February 1793. In the long period between 1506 and 1793 it is known that many anonymous seal and whale hunters visited the bay. It is reputed that the infamous pirate Capt. Kidd once stopped there. In 1795 the British also claimed it while extending their control over the whole Cape. The vessel *Star* carried the British flag to Walvis Bay. Despite this activity by British sailors, the British government itself refused to recognize this annexation. Other ships visited the bay, including one notable stop by Capt. Benjamin Morrell (q.v.) in 1828, who discovered guano deposits nearby. In 1836 Sir James E. Alexander entered Namibia by ox-wagon and took a route that went from Warmbad to Windhoek and then to Walvis Bay, pioneering the important Walvis Bay–Windhoek road. His expedition was sponsored by the Royal Geographical Society in London.

The first permanent claim of sovereignty over Walvis Bay came on March 6, 1878, when Commander Richard C. Dyer (q.v.) annexed Walvis Bay and surrounding areas in the name of Queen Victoria. However, six years later, July 25, 1884, sovereignty over the area was passed to the Cape government. When the Union of South Africa was established in 1910, the

Cape colony brought Walvis Bay and its environs into the Union. It is clear that even when the Germans controlled Namibia, Walvis Bay was excluded from their jurisdiction. That is why they prepared a new port for their use at Swakopmund, although the harbor at Walvis Bay was much better.

Throughout the nineteenth century Walvis Bay was one of the preferred landing spots for traders, adventurers, and missionaries, not to mention fishermen. The fishing industry truly began there in 1859 when Barry Munnik of Cape Town began a fishery there and exported dried fish. Others followed. Even in the twentieth century, after the whales were hunted almost to extinction in the area, a whaling station at Walvis Bay operated from 1923 to 1930. And in 1946 the Walvis Bay Canning Company began to explore the likelihood of processing pilchards there. Production began in 1948. It remains the center of Namibia's fishing industry today (despite South Africa's claims of sovereignty). Seven processing factories and a smokery are situated there. Most of the canned fish, fish oil, and fishmeal is sent to South Africa. However, the rock lobster industry is based at Lüderitz (q.v.).

Some of this progress is due to tremendous physical improvements to the harbor after World War II. The quay was tripled in length to 1400 meters, warehouses were added, many new cranes were brought in, and better means of handling bulk items were developed. A giant platform with twenty-two synchronized winches was finished in 1973 allowing ships to be hoisted ashore for repair. The port is now the major location for exporting mineral ores produced in Namibia.

Walvis Bay had not had a large African population prior to the coming of Europeans in the nineteenth century. There had been only a small group of Topnaar Namas there. However, industry brought both white managers and Black workers. Many of the latter came from northern Namibia on work contracts. The census of 1970 counted whites: 7353; Coloureds: 3762; Namas: 185; and Bantu: 10,423. This made it the second largest community in Namibia. A 1982 estimate states there are about 10,000 whites and 15,000 Blacks in the enclave of 969 square kilometers.

As Namibia began to move toward independence, the question of the status of its best port became more important. After South West Africa became a mandate under the League of Nations, the Union of South Africa chose to make Walvis Bay administratively a part of that territory. Walvis Bay became an integral part of it economically. Logic suggested that this is where it belonged. Nevertheless South Africa's claims to the enclave are as sound as Great Britain's claim to Hong Kong or Portuguese claims were to Goa and Macao. The Turnhalle Conference (q.v.), which consisted exclusively of conservatives and moderates, agreed that Walvis Bay would remain South African. Thus with pressure increasing at the UN and elsewhere for Namibia to be independent, South African Prime Minister Vorster in 1977 proclaimed the formal annexation of Walvis Bay and the offshore islands by South Africa. At the same time the UN, SWAPO, and the Western Contact Group (q.v.) had all taken the stance that Walvis Bay must remain part of Namibia. A historic occasion took place in the Security Council on July 27, 1978, when all fifteen members approved a resolution that called for the "early re-integration of Walvis Bay into Namibia." Nevertheless, there is no specific mention of Walvis Bay in Resolution 435 (q.v.), the major UN resolution that incorporates the plan for Namibian independence drawn up by the West. American diplomats insisted that this was an issue to be negotiated by an independent Namibian government and South Africa. At the time of Namibian independence in 1990 that is where the matter stood. South Africa claimed Walvis Bay and used it as a military and naval base, while the Namibian Government claimed Walvis Bay was an integral part of Namibia and must be recognized as such by South Africa.

Later in the year, however, it became clear that negotiation was possible. Formal talks on the status of Walvis Bay and the offshore "Penguin Islands" (q.v.) began in Cape Town on March 14, 1991. Namibia's foreign Minister, Theo-Ben Gurirab met with South Africa's Roloef Botha. Gurirab suggested a period of Dual Administration; Foreign Minister Botha was willing to discuss sharing use of the port but not sacrificing South Africa's claim of sovereignty.

A second round of talks two months later had better results. Gurirab switched his position and accepted a period of joint administration without requiring a timetable for South Africa's withdrawal (a previous stand). Both sides agreed that this period would last while the sovereignty issue was being resolved. This led to the formation of a Namibia/South Africa joint technical committee, which met in December, 1991 and March, 1992. While it announced at the latter meeting that proposals for joint administration had been submitted to each government, several significant obstacles remained. In June Gurirab suggested that the United Nations Security Council might decide the issue, as South Africa was not truly negotiating a transfer of the enclave and islands. Meanwhile the South African Government of F. W. de Klerk stated that the status of the areas should be determined by a more representative South African Government in the future (presumably one with black membership).

The Walvis Bay enclave has a population of about 31,000 and about 90% of Namibia's sea trade is handled at the harbor.

WAMBO. A more contemporary form of the older and very commonly used word, Ovambo (q.v.). Another valid form of the word is Ambo.

WAR OF THE BOUNDARY. A conflict lasting several weeks in March 1896, it involved the Germans and Hereros. It was precipitated by General T. von Leutwein's persuading Samuel Maharero (q.v.) to agree to a southern boundary for Herero land. Anything below this line, from Otjimbingwe east to Gobabis, could be sold by the German government to new German settlers. Profits would be divided between the government and Maharero. Not only does no Herero chief have the power to "sell" his people's land, but some eastern Herero chiefs, especially Nikodemus and Kakimena had long claimed and used this southern land. They thus began an uprising which the Germans suppressed in a few weeks. Nikodemus and Kakimena were executed.

WARMBAD. The village or town of Warmbad was the first white settlement in Namibia. LMS missionaries Christian and Abraham Albrecht (q.v.) founded a mission station there in 1905 which they called Blyde Uitkomst ("happy deliverance"). Because of the hot water spring there, the local Namas called it /Ai-//gams (or Gei-ous), which means "large fountain." Early explorers used the same hot spring to call it Warm Bath or Warmbad. The site became a popular first stop for people traveling north from South Africa, as it is only eighty-four kilometers north of the border at Goodhouse. The Albrechts' mission station only lasted from 1805 to 1811, as Jager Afrikander (q.v.) destroyed it. The legendary missionary Robert Moffatt reopened it in 1818, and it was given to the Wesleyan Missionary Society in 1834. Edward Cook of the WMS renamed it Nisbet's Bath after a financial backer of the mission work. That effort did not last either, and in 1867 the station was given to the Rhenish Mission Society (RMS) (q.v.). Meanwhile the Dutch name Warmbad seemed to stick. In 1894 a German fort was built there, and it was especially under attack at the time of the Bondelswart Rebellion of 1906.

Despite the importance of Warmbad in the nineteenth century, it has not grown into a major community. In fact the seat of the Warmbad magistrate district was moved in 1935 to Karasburg, which lies fifty kilometers north of Warmbad. One important reason is that the town is not on any major road from the south or east. It does have access by road to Karasburg, however. Warmbad sits along the Hom River, which flows into the Orange River. The town is in the center of a karakul breeding area, as the area gets adequate rainfall for excellent grazing. The Warmbad district covers 37,438 square kilometers and its borders are the Fish River on the west, the Orange on the south, the South African border on the east, and as far north as Keetmanshoop. Much of the district is mountainous and has sparse vegetation, despite several rivers.

WATERBERG, BATTLE OF. The decisive battle in the conflict between the Hereros and the Germans in 1904, the bulk of the fighting occurred on August 11. German General Lothar von Trotha (q.v.) had about five thousand soldiers available, including 25 companies of mounted troops, 36 artillery pieces, and 14 machine guns, along with 10,000 horses. On the Herero side were 6,000 fighting men but only 2,500 rifles and limited ammunition. There were 40,000 Herero women and children encamped in the area south of the Waterberg, but of little use in the battle. During the two months prior to the battle the Germans carefully surveyed the area and moved their men and supplies into striking position. While Samuel Maharero, the Herero leader, appeared to welcome the impending battle, it is not clear whether he thought he could win it or just inflict great damage on the Germans. The fact is that the battle would be closely contested and, according to one excellent analyst, with a little luck the Hereros might have defeated the Germans there, as they had repeatedly done early in the year. The Hereros might also have had a better chance had Samuel Maharero moved his people further to the north, which would have put great pressure on the German supply lines, but he made no move to escape the obvious German troop positioning. He did set up field fortifications using thorn bushes around his warriors. A German report called the bushes their "worst enemy," as the Hereros were used to them and made good use of them, almost like barbed wire fences. The German soldiers were not used to African fighting conditions, and Maharero evidently counted on that to be an advantage for the Hereros.

On the evening of August 10, a German patrol reached to the top of Great Waterberg and set up a signal station. From this viewpoint they could watch the battle unfold and signal General von Trotha. Before the next dawn the six German fighting sections moved into their battle positions. The German troops were led by Colonel Deimling, Lieut. Colonel Mueller, Major von Estorff, Major von der Heyde, and Majors von Lengerke, Meister, and von Wahlen. The latter three led battalions under Deimling, while von Estorff and von der Heyde served under Mueller. As the battle raged, Deimling's forces took the village of Waterberg and generally met little opposition. However, the Mueller and von der Heyde sections had furious battles, and their survival was long in question. Mueller's forces fought at the Hamakari (q.v.) riverbed, where they were surrounded, outnumbered, and outfought. Von der Heyde's section also received extensive casualties.

But German artillery had battered not only Herero warriors but the camp of women, children, and cattle. The Herero wagons were filled with their blankets, jewelry, feathers, and household items. At nightfall Samuel Maharero and his advisers decided they could not win and called for a hasty flight to the southeast. Von Trotha saw this and ordered his men to stop fighting and allow the retreat to the east, into the desert. Moreover, he ordered that women and children should not be harmed as they moved, but that all armed men who were captured were to be killed. Despite these orders, German troops broke into Herero camps and killed indiscriminately. Elderly blind women were burned alive in their huts. Seventy Herero prisoners of war were all killed. Evidently many thousands of fleeing Hereros were slaughtered. Also as an aftermath, those who escaped into the desert didn't fare much better, as they lacked water. Some, including Samuel Maharero, managed to arrive safely in British Bechuanaland (Botswana), but the Herero population was decimated by the defeat and its aftermath.

WATERBERG, THE GREAT. More properly a plateau than either a mountain or mountain range, it is often just called the Waterberg. Klein (or Little) Waterberg is a smaller plateau separated from it by a gap. The Great Waterberg is 64 kilometers (44 miles) long by 15 kilometers (9 miles) wide, and its highest point is about 1860 meters (6300 feet) above sea level. It is composed of stratified red sandstone and has a brilliant escarpment that lies about 150 meters above the surrounding countryside. Its name was given to it because of the unusually high number of streams that it contains. It also has a varied and unusual collection of subtropical flora and fauna. The Great Waterberg is the southern section of the much larger Waterberg Plateau Park (q.v.). In 1904 it was the scene of the conflict between Germans and Hereros. (*See* WATERBERG, BATTLE OF.)

WATERBERG PLATEAU PARK. Covering an area of 40,549 hectares, this rugged area is home to a wide variety of exotic animals and unusual and interesting vegetation. Near the fountains and springs the land is especially lush. The park is forty-eight kilometers in length and ranges from a very narrow southern "tail" to a width of sixteen kilometers much further north. Rock engravings and dinosaur tracks are among other interesting features on the plateau. The park extends to the northeast from the Great Waterberg. In 1989 construction work was completed on the luxurious "Otjahewita" Game Reserve, at a cost of R4 million. It is owned by a Swiss businessman, Mr. Werner Egger.

WELWITSCH, FRIEDRICH MARTIN JOSEF (1806–1872). An Austrian botanist and explorer born in Carinthia, he moved to Portugal where he became curator of the Coimbra Botanical Gardens in 1839. He built it into a world-famous herbarium. In the period 1853–1861 he made several expeditions to Angola on behalf of the Portuguese government. On one of these trips he discovered a plant later named after him, *Welwitschia mirabilis* (q.v.). On his trips he collected a fantastic number of plants and animals, bringing thousands of each back to Europe for identification. He lived from 1863 until his death in London, cataloguing and identifying his collection and writing about his discoveries.

WELWITSCHIA. 1. The simplified name of the famous plant found in Namibia, the *Welwitschia mirabilis* (q.v.). 2. A village in the northwest quadrant of Namibia within the Welwitschia Plains. It is the administrative center of the Damara people. The village is in the Outjo district, about 158 kilometers west of Outjo. Founded in 1954, it was named after the numerous *Welwitschia mirabilis* plants nearby. The village management board, established in 1957, provides services for the numerous farms in the region.

WELWITSCHIA BAINESII. The same remarkable plant that is called *Welwitschia mirabilis* (q.v.), it was first discovered in Angola in 1859. When the great artist Thomas Baines (q.v.) discovered the plant in 1861 in the Namib Desert, he sketched it and wrote about it. Scientists saw this description first and honored him by calling the plant *Tumboa Bainesii*. It was soon found that Dr. Friedrich Welwitsch (q.v.) had discovered it first in 1859, so it was renamed *Welwitschia mirabilis*. Eventually a compromise was made and it has been given the alternate name of *Welwitschia bainesii*.

WELWITSCHIA MIRABILIS. Also known as the *Welwitschia bainesii* (q.v.), this unique desert plant is only found in a narrow band of northern and western Namibia and south-western Angola. The first European to discover it, in 1859, was the famous botanist Dr. Friederich Welwitsch (q.v.). Of course Africans have long known of its existence, using it for fuel and making stools from its seedy stems. Also it is said that the explorer C. J. Andersson (q.v.) discovered the plant in 1857, two years before Dr. Welwitsch, and sent two samples back to England. However, they never arrived. In 1861 the plant was captured in sketches by the artist Thomas Baines (q.v.).

The plant belongs to the Gymnosperm family, producing both male and female plants. It is a living coniferous fossil and is related to the pine family. A kind of dwarf tree, it can grow as tall as six feet. Each year in May the seeds ripen in the cones and are blown away by the wind. Those that are moistened by rain or heavy ocean mist will germinate. The body of the plant stands in the middle of a tangled mass of narrow "leaves" and dried out leaf-tips. It appears that many leaves are hanging strap-like from the top of the plant, but there are actually only two. They have been whipped so much by desert winds that they have been torn into numerous narrow ribbons, some as long as nine meters. However these ribbons then catch the mist from the desert fog and the droplets roll down the leaves to feed a fine network of small surface roots. The mature tap root looks like a giant carrot that thrusts downwards as much as nine feet into the desert soil, looking for any subterranean moisture it can find. The plant is slow to mature and is thought to have a fantastic life span. A "young" plant was accurately dated at about five hundred years old, while others are thought to predate Jesus Christ. A plant photographed in 1885 was rephotographed in

1975 and it had not changed in appearance. Even nearby rocks were unmoved in the barren scene. The *Welwitschia mirabilis* is now a protected species in Namibia. Its common name in Afrikaans is "tweeblaarkanniedod," which means "the two-lobed die hard."

WERF (variant: WERFT). A small village of Africans who are all members of a family, the term has been used to describe both Herero and Wambo life styles. The word is from the Afrikaans language and more specifically refers to the dwelling place on a farm with all of its surrounding buildings and the space in between them. In the context of the Africans this might mean a number of dwelling places belonging to different members of an extended family, especially if it belongs to a chief or a headman. A werf may range from 2.5 to 5 acres and consist of a circle of round dome-shaped huts (at least among the Hereros). The village leader has a hut of his own, for he lives in the house of his "Great Woman." In the center of the circle of huts of "pantoks" would be the kraal for calves. In the center of the entire werf was the "sacred fire" (*see* FIRE, SACRED).

WESLEYAN MISSIONARY SOCIETY (WMS). Formed in Great Britain in 1813, the Wesleyan Missionary Society had men in South Africa as early as 1815. The first to enter Namibia was Rev. Barnabas Shaw who accepted the invitation of LMS missionary J. H. Schmelen (q.v.) to visit him at Bethanie, which he did in 1820. The visit led to an attempt by Rev. James Archbell to reopen the Warmbad mission station soon thereafter. Local warfare interfered, however, so Archbell turned back. Similarly Rev. William Threlfall (q.v.) tried to reopen the Warmbad station in 1825, but he was murdered by his African guide. One of the most successful WMS missionaries was Rev. Edward Cook, who did reopen Warmbad in 1834 and eventually made many conversions. Cook did not limit himself to Warmbad, but made visits to Walvis Bay, Windhoek, and set up several out-stations. One was even called "Wesleyville," and is thought to be today's Rehoboth. Poor health hindered his efforts, however, and he died in 1843. He is buried at Warmbad. WMS missionaries were not equal to the demand, so no reinforcements could be sent from England. Mission funds were also insufficient. As the Rhenish Mission Society (RMS) occupied the territory in force, both the WMS and the London Missionary Society (LMS) turned their stations over to the RMS. The Wesleyans did this in 1867.

WESTERN CAPRIVI. The Caprivi Strip (q.v.) is the long arm that stretches from the main body of Namibia from the northern border east across the top of Botswana. It is frequently divided into eastern and western sections for various reasons. The western segment is that which lies to the west of the Kwando River, which cuts the strip in two as it passes from north to south. It has few large communities, one of which is Andara, where a Catholic mission station was established in 1913. It is on the Okavango River, and technically in the Kavango area just across the river from the Western Caprivi. The Okavango also slices through the Caprivi Strip from north to south. The Western Caprivi is generally dry, sandy, and without much development potential. The San people live in the area, hunting amidst the dense bush.

WESTERN CONTACT GROUP. This term refers to a group of diplomatic representatives from the five Western countries on the UN Security Council in 1977: US, UK, Canada, France, and West Germany. The five formed the group to promote dialogue among the major parties involved in the process of negotiating Namibian independence, especially SWAPO, South Africa, and the six Front Line States (q.v.). The American representative during the Carter years was our UN Ambassador, Donald McHenry. Under President Reagan the US representative was usually Chester Crocker, the assistant secretary of state for African affairs. After its formation in 1977 the group held periodic negotiations in a number of cities. Sometimes they were ''proximity talks,'' not face-to-face negotiations between the opposing sides. The group spent most of its time trying to overcome South African objections to various UN and Contact Group proposals. It also had to deal with SWAPO fears of the South

African military might. The Western Five did not stay united all the time either, especially in the Reagan years when the US and UK seemed to be the only ones who were working together. While many factors could be cited for the eventual success of the negotiations that have led to an independent Namibia, the persistence of the team led by Chester Crocker must be given some credit.

WHALING. While the fishing industry is important to contemporary Namibia, whaling today is of minimal importance. Yet in the seventeenth and eighteenth centuries the southwest African coast was swarming with whales to the point that one area was named for the giant mammals: Walvis Bay (literally, Whale Fish Bay). The whales followed their food fish along the Benguela Current (q.v.) and up the coast past Namibia. Walvis Ridge was reportedly the popular area for whales to mate. American, British, and French whaling ships plied the waters, and even landed briefly in Namibian bays. When the British took control of the Cape in 1795 it forbade any whaling ships other than British ships to hunt whales in the region; however, whaling did flourish there under British control until about 1825. As the numbers of whales declined, the fishing industry concentrated on other fish, such as sardines, anchovies, and hake, and of course the rock lobster (q.v.). In 1923 the whaling station at Walvis Bay was opened again on an experimental basis, and 296 whales were caught. However, it was closed down again in 1930 when the coming of "factory ships" had decimated the whale population.

"WHITE LADY OF THE BRANDBERG." The most written-about sample of all the Namibian rock art (q.v.), it was first seen by a European in 1917 when a surveyor, Dr. Reinhardt Maack, and a companion scaled "Königstein," the highest peak in Namibia. Maack spent the night in a cave, and when he awoke he discovered the art work. The cave or rock shelter is fairly small, eighteen feet long and seven feet wide. But it is filled with rock art from a number of different periods and artists. Some are more badly weathered than others. Maack made a crude sketch of the main figure, the "White Lady." A watercolor copy appeared in a book on rock paintings in

1930, and another artist's rendering appeared in 1931. The famous authority on prehistoric art, Abbé Henri Breuil (q.v.), saw "the White Lady" in 1947 and spent ten days copying all the figures on the frieze. He revisited it again in 1948 and 1950 before publishing his classic *The White Lady of the Brandberg* in 1955.

The key figure is a 15.75 inch painting of a figure that has been called a woman. She is in the midst of a ceremonial procession that passes in profile between two rows of oryx (antelopes) as it moves toward a group of musicians (two of whom are playing on a musical bow). The "White Lady" (the coloring distinguishes the central figure) is dressed in a fancy garment and carries a goblet and also a bow and arrows. Seventeen of the twenty-five figures in the procession have red hair, and their features suggest different ethnic types. All wear shoes and perhaps helmets.

The theories about the "White Lady" are as varied as the appreciation of the art is unified. Rock painting is notoriously difficult to date, even using Carbon 14 testing. Some suggest it could be as new as 300 years old, while others believe it could date back 20,000 years. One recent archaeologist found the Brandberg caves to be between six and eight thousand years old. "The White Lady" figure is explained in one theory as a European woman who survived a shipwreck off the Namibia coast and was made the "white queen" of the San. Perhaps equally fanciful, but more important because it came from the highly respected Abbé Breuil, is that she is the product of sailors from the island of Crete in the Mediterranean who sailed the west coast of Africa about 2000 BC. He compared her to goddesses like Diana and Isis. He also suggests that visitors from the Nile (or Crete) travelled through Africa and reached Namibia. Thus he saw aspects of Egyptian mythology (Isis) in the work. Finally others saw the work as possibly stemming from the civilization that built the great kingdom of Zimbabwe.

Revisionists explain the figures differently. Unlike Breuil they see no Nilotic or European types in the cave at all. The "White Lady" is possibly a young boy going off to an initiation ceremony, or perhaps the figures are those of African hunters (they have the steatopygia common among the San and Nama) who followed the widespread African practice of smearing their bodies and lower limbs with white clay or ashes. The reason that the latter theories came so late is that many scholars, especially those in southern Africa, found it difficult to believe that such sophisticated art could have been produced by an African.

WHITE NOSSOB RIVER. Along with the Black Nossob River, the White Nossob is one of the two source rivers for the Nossob River (q.v.) that eventually flows to the southeast and into Botswana. The Nossob forms the boundary between Botswana and the Republic of South Africa. The White Nossob rises in the highlands east of Windhoek. It has three tributaries, one rising just northeast of Windhoek and combining with a second near Omitara. They join a third slightly west of Witvlei and form the full White Nossob as it flows southward to its merger with the Black Nossob at Aais.

WIKAR, HENDRIK JACOB. Born in Gothenburg, Sweden, in the mid-eighteenth century, Wikar came to Cape Town in 1773 as an employee of the Dutch East India Company. As a result of large gambling debts he deserted his job and fled north to the area of the Orange River, where he survived by hunting game along its banks. He lived in the area just to the north and south of the river for four years and kept a detailed journal, especially about the African people there and further north. His journals even make references to groups we now know as the Herero and Wambo, far to the north. In 1779 he asked the governor for a pardon for deserting his job, and was granted it if he would write a thorough report on the area, about which little was then known. His published journals were surprisingly accurate, considering his lack of training for such a task, and his treatment of the different African groups along the river and to its north provided later historians with an excellent basis for understanding the origins of the peoples of Namibia and the northern Cape.

WILHELM II, KAISER. The Emperor of Germany at the time that Namibia was taken over by the Germans as German South West Africa (Deutsche Südwestafrika). He did not intervene frequently in the administration of the territory, leaving that to his chancellors, such as Otto von Bismarck. Nevertheless he was consulted on major issues, such as the suppression of the Hereros, in which he showed considerable support of Gen. Lothar von Trotha (q.v.) even while many Germans were appalled by the massacre. Kaiser Strasse, the main business street in Windhoek, is named after Wilhelm II.

WILHELMSTAL INCIDENT. One of the earliest examples of labor activity in Namibia, it occurred during the construction of the rail line in 1911. At that time about 6500 workers, many from the Cape, were employed on the rail project or in mines. Some of the young workers from the Cape protested conditions on the rail construction project and went on strike. The troops were called in, and they fired on the strikers, killing an undetermined number. Recruiting of workers from South Africa was reduced later that year.

WILTON DEPOSITS. Wilton is the name given to a culture of the Late Stone Age that is characterized by small stone implements (including small tools, scrapers, grindstones, ostrich-egg-shell beads, bone points, bored stones, etc.) along with some wooden implements, pottery, and rock paintings. Some sites may be as much as 250,000 years old. Found in many parts of southern Africa, these remnants of a vanished people are evidence of industrious and intelligent humans. Some experts say that these people have not vanished and are obviously the ancestors of the San (q.v.). In Namibia the artifacts are found in a number of locations, but notably in the Brandberg region and near Lüderitz. Radio-carbon dating pinpoints sites from 5800 BC to 730 AD. Wilton people in Namibia were hunters and gatherers who used poison arrows and animal traps to catch their prey. Many of their cultural characteristics are similar to those of the nineteenth-century San.

WINDHOEK. The capital of independent Namibia, it is by far the largest city. The 1991 census indicated that Windhoek and its surrounding areas had a population of 159,000 of whom 140,000 lived in the urban areas of Windhoek, Kalutuia, and

Khomasdal. No other town had a population exceeding 16,000. It is a physically attractive city with both beautiful modern buildings and striking structures with strong Germanic influence from the beginning of the twentieth century. It is located in the temperate central highlands region of the country and is very near to the geographic center of the country. Its average high summer temperature is 85 degrees Fahrenheit, while its annual rainfall is about 13 inches. It is situated between the Auas Mountains (to the south) and the Eros Mountains (to the northeast). The Khomas Highlands lie to the west. Windhoek is 1700 meters (5534 feet) above sea level. The major north-south road and rail line run through Windhoek, and roads connect it to both the Botswana border and the Atlantic Ocean. It is served by an international airport.

The location has had many names over the years. Namas called it !Ai-//gams (Ai-gams or Aighams), which means "hot water," and Hereros called it Otjimuise, which means "the place of smoke." Both refer to the nearby hot springs that attracted the indigenous peoples. Captain James Alexander (q.v.) in 1837 called it Queen Adelaide's Bath; German missionaries in 1842 called it Elbersfeld; and Wesleyan missionaries in 1844 called it Concordiaville. The name Windhoek means "windy corner," an appropriate name because the gaps in the surrounding mountains present paths for the winds to penetrate. Nevertheless the name is considered a corruption of Winterhoek, a similarly mountainous region near Tulbaugh in the Cape Province and the early home of the great Nama leader Jonker Afrikander (q.v.). He set up his capital at Windhoek, and presumably named it after his South African farm.

There were evidently Hereros living in the vicinity of Windhoek at the beginning of the nineteenth century, as they expanded their cattle-grazing land ever southward. The further south of Windhoek they went, the more the Hereros ran into conflict with various Nama groups, especially during the drought of 1829–30. Thus Jonker Afrikander, an Orlam chief, was encouraged by other Namas to force the Hereros to retreat. In the early 1930s Jonker did this, pushing them to an area just north of today's Windhoek. But not feeling strong enough to possess the valley at the time, he didn't occupy it yet. When Capt. James Alexander visited the location in 1837 there were virtually no inhabitants of "this beautiful oasis, the constantly watered and evergreen plain round the Baths" (the hot springs).

Jonker did make his home there in 1840, however, at which time he called it Winterhoek. The area became a war zone for decades, as Herero and Nama leaders fought over it. An RMS mission station was set up there in 1842, originally run by Rev. C. H. Hahn (q.v.); however, two years later Jonker requested that he move on and leave the mission to Rev. Haddy of the Wesleyans. Jonker died in 1861, after decades of conflict between his people and the Hereros throughout the central part of Namibia. His son and successor, Jan Jonker, also lived at Windhoek. When peace returned to the region by about 1870 the Rhenish Mission Society was invited back and set up a mission at today's Klein Windhoek, a suburb. However in 1880 the Hereros attacked Windhoek, defeated the Namas, and partly destroyed the mission station.

Thus the area was again virtually uninhabited when the Herero leader, Maherero, signed a protection treaty with the Germans in 1885. In October 1890, a German commander, Curt von Francois, entered Windhoek and laid the foundation for the first European building, a fort now called the Alte Feste (q.v.). His contingent consisted of only 32 men. They also repaired the mission station. Settlement was encouraged in Germany, and by 1893 Windhoek had a population of 127. A school was then built, a civil administration set up, a street plan established, and little by little both settlers and traders came. The main street was named Kaiserstrasse. In 1903 the rail link to the port of Swakopmund was finished, and the first passengers arrived June 19, 1903. Rebellions by both Namas and Hereros from 1903 to 1907 threatened the German future there. German victory stabilized the colony, however, at least until World War I broke out in 1914, and the South African forces took Windhoek in 1915. These forces controlled the city until 1920, when municipal governments were established in the territory. On July 9, 1920, Peter Müller, who had been mayor in 1915, was unanimously elected mayor of Windhoek.

From 1890 to 1915 a great amount of construction work took place, governmental, commercial, and private. The Christkirche, the Tintenpalast, the "castles" overlooking the town, and even seven hotels and three breweries were built. Windhoek's appearance is owed heavily to the government architect, Gottlieb Redeker, and a private architect, Willi Sander. On March 31, 1920, there were 716 taxpayers in Windhoek and Klein Windhoek, and the city employed 23 white and 155 Black workers. The dramatic population growth is shown by the statistics: 10,000 in 1939, 17,000 in 1949, and about 36,000 in 1959, of whom 20,000 were whites. In 1959 a new section of Windhoek was opened called Katutura (q.v.), part of the government plan to force Blacks out of Windhoek proper and into a segregated community. Similarly construction was begun in 1960 on a residential area for the Coloured community of Windhoek called Khomasdal (q.v.). The J. G. Strijdom airport (for international service) was opened to flights on October 1, 1965. It is 29 miles east of the city. In the 1980s the University of Namibia was established in Windhoek.

In the late 1980s, as independence became imminent, a new building boom began. Prices of land and real estate jumped as the need arose for such buildings as embassies and offices for international agencies, not to mention dwellings for the influx of foreigners.

Windhoek has long been a center for the arts, in part due to the German influence. A choral society began in Windhoek in 1907, which soon evolved into a series of musical groups. A public library was founded in 1924, the same year as the South West African Scientific Society. The Arts Association began in 1947, a German theater group in 1961, and the Shakespeare Society in 1964. The first school of dancing was opened in Windhoek in 1928, and the National School of Ballet twenty years later.

WINDHOEK "OLD LOCATION" RIOT. In the late 1950s the South African regime was forcibly removing Africans to new areas, as part of their separate development philosophy. Damaras were moved from their community at Aukeigas, and Namas were to be moved from Hoachanas. However, the major effort was to move people from the Old Location in Windhoek to a newly created township known as Katutura (q.v.). Sixteen thousand Africans lived in this shanty town on land claimed by the Windhoek municipality, to whom they paid a rental fee. Water and sanitation were not adequate. While the government claimed that the newly built community at Katutura was much better, it was five miles outside Windhoek, and both rents and bus fare would be much larger. Even worse, in keeping with the apartheid philosophy, the community would be divided into separate sections for each ethnic ("tribal") group. Opposition to the plan swelled throughout 1959, and public meetings stirred up the anger. On December 4, 1959, hundreds of African women marched on the municipal headquarters in protest against the impending forced removal. The next day a highly effective boycott of municipal services (buses and beer halls) occurred. On December 10, 1959, protesters outside the beer hall were arrested and a crowd of 2000 angry Africans burned buildings and cars and then protested at the municipal headquarters. Police reinforcements fired into the crowd and killed eleven people. Two others died of injuries the next day. Fifty-four others were injured. The shootings became an issue at the United Nations, with South Africa blamed by some, and South Africa blaming the rioters. A number of the principal African nationalists were implicated in the riots, such as Herman Toivo Ya-Toivo, Sam Nujoma, and Clemens Kapuuo (qq.v.).

WINTER, BISHOP COLIN O'BRIEN (1928–1981). Born at Stoke-on-Trent in England and educated at Oxford and Ely Theological College, he was ordained in 1956 as an Anglican priest. He served as rector of a parish near Cape Town from 1959 to 1964, and then at St. George's Cathedral in Windhoek from 1964 to 1969. The politically conscious priest was a strong supporter of racial integration and also a pacifist. As such he stirred controversy. When the Bishop of Damaraland, Robert Mize, was deported for his political activity late in 1968, Winter was the next man chosen to be bishop of this diocese that includes most of the country. An outspoken critic of the government's racial policies, Bishop Winter became an easy target when Wambo workers conducted a general strike late in 1971. The various churches had supported the strike, provided the international media with information, and helped provide for the defense of strikers in court. Thus in March 1972 Bishop Winter and three assistants were deported to England. He held his title in exile, however, until his health failed in 1981. During these nine years in exile he travelled and spoke widely, including appearances at the United Nations in support of racial justice in Namibia. He also set up two centers for southern African refugees in England, and wrote three books, perhaps the best titled simply *Namibia,* published in 1977. He died in London after his third heart attack, in November 1981.

WINTERHOEK. An early form of the word "Windhoek," it was given to that area by Jonker Afrikander (q.v.). Encased by mountains, the area reminded Jonker of his earlier home near Tulbaugh and a mountain named Winterhoek there. The name gradually took the form of Windhuk before finally acquiring its current spelling.

WITBOOI, CHIEF HENDRIK (c. 1838–1905). The greatest of the Witbooi chiefs, he serves as a fascinating link to Namibian history. His grandfather, Kido Witbooi (q.v.), led his people into the country from South Africa at the beginning of the nineteenth century; and his great-grandson and namesake, Rev. Hendrik Witbooi (q.v.) is a leader of SWAPO and a minister in Namibia's first cabinet after independence, near the end of the twentieth century.

Educated for years at the mission school in Pella (just south of the Orange River), Hendrik was very bright and also a fervent student of the Bible. He also learned to read and write the High Dutch language. In his biblical readings he saw many parallels with life in Namibia, and saw himself ultimately as the "chosen one" who would lead his people to correct injustices. One of these injustices involved the Herero practice of raiding Nama villages and stealing all the cattle. This man of very small stature saw himself to be the instrument of the Lord.

By the mid-1860s Hendrik was old enough to be a leader

of his people, but his father, Moses Witbooi (q.v.), was still alive and active, as indeed was his grandfather, Kido. He had fought in battles against the Afrikanders and even lost his right thumb to an enemy's bullet. When peace with the Red Nation (q.v.) came, Hendrick settled down. He married and ultimately had seven sons and five daughters. In 1868 he finally became a baptized Christian. Four years later he was unanimously elected the church elder. He was very supportive of Rev. Johannes Olpp, the RMS missionary who baptized him.

In 1880, with his father now the chief of the Witboois, a series of events occurred. His father, Moses had lost a battle against the Hereros, and he and his followers barely returned with their lives. Along with other earlier embarrassments, there were increasing doubts among the Witboois about the leadership of Moses. In the same year Hendrik was visited by a young man who seemed to tell him that he was divinely ordained to lead his people to a wonderful country in the north. He meditated extensively at his grandfather's grave, and finally concluded that he had been chosen to defeat the hated Hereros. Of course this conviction led to greater hostility with Moses, who was becoming less rational in his rule of the tribe. Moses accused Hendrik of trying to anoint himself as chief of the Witboois. In 1884 he led a large army north to take on Maherero. At a site called Onguheva, the two sides clashed for a day, June 24, 1884, and while neither side was superior, Maherero chose to seek peace. Negotiations were successful, especially after Hendrik rounded up a large herd of Herero cattle that had been stolen by some of his reinforcements and returned them to the Herero chief. The peace was agreed upon, and Hendrik returned to Gibeon as a conquering hero. Many accepted him as de facto chief of the Witboois, as Moses had virtually gone into seclusion.

In July 1885 Hendrik led all his supporters on a march northward to the "promised land" in the north. It was a peaceful journey until Maherero let Hendrik know that he was not pleased that all other Namas had not agreed to the peace at Onguheva. However, he advised the Witboois to camp at Osona, not far from Okahandja, the Herero capital. They arrived there on October 14, 1885. While the two leaders appeared to be at peace, the Witbooi camp was adjacent to a large group of Hereros and a scuffle broke out over rights to the water supply. This led to a major battle between the two sides. Hendrik felt that he had been treacherously set up by Maherero for defeat. When the Witboois ran out of ammunition they fled south, leaving all their belongings behind. Two of Hendrik's sons were killed and a third had his arm shattered. On October 19 Hendrik sent Maherero a letter that said, in short, "I came in peace but you deceived me, and murdered my people. We fled because we ran out of ammunition, but we will return again prepared for war." Maherero decided to sign a treaty of protection with the Germans.

Hendrik then set up his camp at Nauas, where he gathered supporters from many of the other Nama groups, including Topnaars, Boois, Grootdodens, and even some Basters. His next attack occurred against Okahandja, April 17, 1888. While surprised, the Hereros had established good fortifications and beat off the large Nama force. They then followed the fleeing Namas and even took all the goods at the camp at Nauas. Hendrik and his followers fled into the Gansberg Mountains. From here he conducted a number of guerrilla-style raids against the Hereros, stealing large numbers of cattle and horses.

In February 1888 Moses Witbooi had been killed by his brother-in-law, Paul Visser, who then claimed the leadership at Gibeon. Five months later Hendrik pursued Visser and killed him, avenging his father's death and leaving no doubt as to the leadership of the Witboois. In December 1888, Hendrik's followers captured 4000 Herero cattle and sold them to traders for huge quantities of ammunition. They then established a new camp at Hoornkranz, a mountainous area west of Rehoboth.

Throughout the late 1880s the German representative, Dr. H. Goering, repeatedly tried to get the Witboois to agree to German "protection." Hendrik defiantly held out, saying that the people he needed to be protected from were the Germans themselves. Meanwhile Hendrik was solidifying his leadership among Namas in general. Jan Jonker Afrikander (q.v.), who had supported Visser, had lost many of his followers to Witbooi, including his illegitimate son, Phanuel. Jan Jonker fled north in August 1889, hoping to escape Hendrik's wrath. On August 10 the Witbooi force caught up to him. Hendrik offered him the chance to discuss their problems, but as Jan Jonker approached and set down his gun, Phanuel killed his father. The Witbooi forces then returned to their camp at Hoornkranz.

By 1892 German troops had arrived in Namibia and established a military presence. Their leader, Curt von Francois, visited Hendrik at Hoornkranz on June 9, 1892, seeking to persuade him to accept German protection. Hendrik refused, saying that that would make him subject to the Germans and no longer independent. The German agreed, but said that it was a better alternative than to have all supplies of arms and ammunition cut off. Hendrik replied, undaunted, that a peace that comes from cutting off supplies is no real peace. True peace comes only from the heart. Nevertheless Hendrik knew the danger posed by the Germans and decided to eliminate one source of problems by making peace with the Hereros. This he accomplished by agreeing with Maherero's son and successor, Samuel Maharero, to the Peace of Rehoboth later the same year.

This step didn't protect him from the Germans, however, and on April 12, 1893, a large force of Germans made a surprise attack at daybreak on Hoornkranz. They killed at least 150 Namas, of whom only 60 were warriors. This became known as the Hoornkranz Massacre. Hendrik and most of his fighting men had escaped into the mountains. The massacre shocked some people back in Germany, and early in 1894 von Francois was called back home and replaced by Major Theodore von Leutwein (q.v.). Witbooi and his forces had retreated into the Naukluft mountains and recruited other Namas to rebuild his forces. Some diplomatic letters were exchanged between Leutwein and Witbooi, but to no avail. In September 1894 the Germans attacked. Both sides suffered severe casualties, but Witbooi realized the futility of further resistance. He agreed to sign a treaty with the Germans. The treaty generously allowed Hendrik and his forces to retain their arms and ammunition. Leutwein later confided that he had to be generous, as he didn't have the manpower to stop Hendrik from another mountain-based guerrilla war. In turn Witbooi abided by the agreement which pledged him to help the Germans against other Africans when the need arose. Hendrik kept the agreement for ten years. When an uprising of Namas and eastern Hereros took place near Gobabis in 1897 Witbooi and his followers helped the Germans put it down, as did Samuel Maharero as well. The same thing occurred when small uprisings occurred among Swartboois and, later, Basters. Witbooi and Leutwein trusted one another and developed a friendship. Hendrik meanwhile had returned to Gibeon with his followers, happy to no longer be on the run.

When the Bondelswarts (q.v.) began an uprising in 1903, Leutwein was instructed to disarm all Namas. He refused to do this to Hendrik, because he both needed him and trusted him. But Leutwein's superiors opposed his leniency, and when the Hereros revolted in 1904 Leutwein was stripped of his command (May 4, 1904) and replaced as military commander by Gen. L. von Trotha.

With his friend no longer in charge of the German army, Witbooi felt free to break the peace. This he did on October 1, 1904. It is said that Hendrik also had come under the influence of a man named Stuurman, who was preaching "Africa for the Africans" as in itinerant preacher. This revolt surprised the Germans, as Hendrik had even sent a hundred men to help put down the Herero revolt. On the other hand, southern Namas under Jacob Marengo (q.v.) had continued a very successful guerrilla war against the Germans. When nineteen of the men who fought against the Hereros returned home to Gibeon, they told Witbooi of the horrible massacres the Germans had committed against the Hereros. This news may also have contributed to his decision to revolt. In calling for a revolt Hendrik quickly found allied among many southern Nama leaders. He had about 850 warriors himself, and the others supplied about 500 more. German settlers were the early targets. However, German forces also had early victories, including driving Hendrik from Rietmond. But guerrilla warfare continued for another year. On October 29, 1905, the Witboois attacked a German supply convoy near Vaalgras. The sixty-seven-year-old Hendrik Witbooi suffered a serious wound in this battle near Keetmanshoop. Without medical aid he soon died.

WITBOOI, REV. HENDRIK (1934–). Rev. Witbooi has been an active member of SWAPO for many years. A great-grandson of the famous Nama chief after whom he was named, Rev. Witbooi has been a leader of the African Methodist Episcopal (AME) church in Namibia and is a former teacher and principal. Paster Witbooi has made his residence in Gibeon and stayed there during the period that many SWAPO leaders went into exile. In 1976 he made a public statement with several others in which they specifically chose SWAPO over collaboration with the Turnhalle Conference. Eventually he was named vice-president of SWAPO. In this capacity as a leader of ''internal'' SWAPO he made numerous public statements and appearances in the 1980s. In the 1989 elections for the Constituent Assembly, Rev. Witbooi was placed second on SWAPO's list of candidates, thus assuring him of a seat in the Assembly. At independence he joined the President's cabinet as minister of labour, public service, and manpower development. At SWAPO's first congress held inside Namibia, in December, 1991, Rev. Witbooi was reelected as party Vice President unopposed. Prime Minister Hage Geingob had been proposed for the position but declined to compete for it so as to avoid dividing the party.

WITBOOI, KIDO (c. 1780–1875). The hereditary chief of an Orlam (q.v.) tribe in the northern Cape Province, he was determined to lead his people to freedom north of the Orange River. His people had been called the /Khowesin (q.v.), but because of his long reign as their leader they became known in Namibia as the Witboois. Kido and his people lived at the missionary station at Pella, just south of the Orange River, for many years. By 1810 they had crossed into the Fish River area of Namibia, but lived a somewhat nomadic existence. In the 1840s they even moved into southern Botswana. The large group of people attracted the attention of another Orlam leader, Jonker Afrikander (q.v.), who sought an alliance with Kido in the 1850s (by which time the Witboois were back in Namibia). Kido was ready to settle down, and Jonker was eager to find a strong ally against tribes to the north. Meanwhile the various Nama groups were frequently at odds with each other, and at one point in 1857 Kido served as a neutral peacemaker. His efforts were partly responsible for the signing of the Peace of Hoachanas, January 9, 1858.

Finally in 1863 Kido and his people settled at what is now Gibeon in south central Namibia, and shortly after, a Rhenish Mission station was established there. (Kido became a Christian before he died.) The neutrality of Witbooi did not afford his people protection from attack, as the Red Nation (q.v.) raided them in both 1864 and 1865. In the first instance, December 3, 1864, a three-day battle left Gibeon in ruins, the crops destroyed, and the stock stolen. Witbooi got help from his son and successor, Moses Witbooi (q.v.), and other allies, who provided livestock and other food to live on. Scarcely had the help arrived when Oasib's Red Nation and allies attacked again in late January 1865. Again they stole the livestock. This time Kido got his allies from Bethanie and Berseba to help him and they pursued the raiders to Hoachanas and Rehoboth and recovered all that had been stolen. The rivalry continued in September 1866 when Kido was visiting his son Moses at Goa-mus. He had many men with him. Gibeon was left with only thirty or so men plus the women and children. Oasib and his allies threatened to attack Gibeon, but then feigned a peaceful intent. Oasib used treachery to deceive the residents and then killed all the men and abducted the women and children. Kido and Moses heard of the third attack on Gibeon and pursued Oasib, who moved his people from Hoachanas into the Fish River Valley. Kido got help from his Berseba allies and they followed Oasib. The Witboois spotted Oasib's camp and attacked it. The Gibeon women and children escaped, so Kido stopped the battle until the escapees could reach safety. As Oasib and his followers fled, Kido resumed the pursuit, finally catching up to them at Rehoboth sometime in about April 1867. The Witbooi forces overwhelmed the Red Nation and its allies, killing many of the men, but Oasib and his son Barnabas hid and escaped the slaughter. All Oasib's cattle and other stock (some originally from Gibeon) were captured. A few milk cows were left with the women and children. Kido and his main ally, Paul Goliath (q.v.), returned to their homes at Gibeon and Berseba. Oasib returned to Hoachanas, where he soon took ill and died. Kido lived about another eight years, but the very elderly man turned over most of his duties to his son, Moses Witbooi (q.v.). He died December 31, 1875, in his ninety-fourth year.

WITBOOI, MOSES (c. 1808–1888). The son of Kido Witbooi (q.v.), he was sometimes called Klein Kido ("Little Kido"). Since his father lived well into his nineties, Moses was left as a frustrated heir apparent. Yet he had his own followers and even set up his own village at Goa-mus, away from the main tribal center at Gibeon. In the 1860s, when Gibeon was attacked several times by Oasib and the Red Nation, Moses and his people were safe at Goa-mus. In fact Kido was visiting there at the time of the third attack and Moses and his men joined his father in pursuit of Oasib. They ultimately caught him (for details *see* WITBOOI, KIDO) and destroyed his forces in 1867. Moses was now gray-haired like his father and about fifty-nine years old. Kido began to give him more authority. But on his first major mission he disappointed his father and his supporters. Instead of joining his father's allies in a peaceful mission to meet Maherero at Okahandja, he went directly there by himself and told the Herero leader that an armed force of Namas was preparing to attack Okahandja. The grateful Maherero told Moses that he would give him Windhoek as a reward. Moses wrote home only about Windhoek and concealed his treachery. The people at Gibeon were thrilled because Windhoek had much better hunting and grazing. Moses returned to Gibeon in January 1870 to great rejoicing, but his deception soon became known and he was scorned by his father and even most of his followers.

Kido Witbooi died on December 31, 1875, and Moses became his successor. When Jan Jonker Afrikander requested that Moses join him in attacking the Herero, Moses turned him down, saying that Gibeon could not march alone and would have to have the support of his allies at Berseba and Bethanie. However in 1880 he did join in an attack on the Hereros, working in coordination with Jan Jonker. But

Moses and his forces could never quite catch up to the Herero forces, and in one case was surprised by a Herero counterattack. The men from Gibeon barely escaped with their lives. Without horses and ammunition, they returned to Gibeon on oxen. In the remaining eight years of his life Moses feuded with just about everyone. His ambitious son, Hendrik Witbooi (q.v.) was alienated and had his own following. His brother-in-law, Paul Visser, was also a rival and even had himself "anointed" as chief. Moses had a feud with several of his counselors and had them tied up for several days. At one point he disappeared for a while to a small outpost. He even sold his finest farm, Goa-mus, to raise money for arms and ammunition. (He actually sold it three times to different buyers!) Moses even refused to confer with his old allies.

Finally a showdown came between Moses and Paul Visser, his sister's husband, over leadership of Gibeon. There was a declaration of war between then; a fierce battle ensued in 1887. Moses was captured and resigned his chieftainship in favor of Visser. He was then released. Visser then was confronted by Moses' son Hendrik. A series of battles between them ensued. Although generally victorious, Visser felt that Moses had sent his son after him, so he declared Moses guilty of treason. He captured Moses and a counsellor at Gibeon in February 1888. After a brief trial they were both shot to death. Moses was buried next to his father, Kido. Hendrik heard of this and decided to avenge his father. In July of the same year, he ambushed Visser's force and personally shot him dead. He returned to Gibeon, held a funeral for his father and declared himself chief.

WITBOOI, REV. SAMUEL H. A twentieth-century chief of the Witboois, he had also fought against the Germans in the wars of resistance from 1904 to 1907. In succeeding decades he and other traditional African leaders, such as Hosea Kutako (q.v.), continued to resist foreign rule. Although a Nama, he worked with Kutako in the Herero Chief's Council (q.v.), which petitioned the United Nations repeatedly to hear the cause of Namibia's Africans. In 1960 they worked together with the fledgling SWAPO organization in another plea to the UN. In 1964 Witbooi, Kutako, and Chief Clemens

Kapuuo helped to organize the National Unity Democratic Organization (NUDO) (q.v.). Unfortunately it was unable to truly unify the liberation forces, as both SWAPO and SWANU retained their separate status.

WITBOOI TRIBE. One of five Orlam (q.v.) tribes to enter Namibia from South Africa, they crossed the Orange River near the beginning of the nineteenth century under the leadership of Kido Witbooi (q.v.), from whom they took their name. The word Witboois came from a white band Kido wore around his head. Like other Orlams, Witboois are mostly of Nama origin, but may have some Dutch ancestors. The Witboois eventually settled in Gibeon in 1862. They are also known as the /Khowesin. Over the years the Witbooi were set upon frequently by the forces of the Red Nation (q.v.), but this was reversed late in the nineteenth century because of the leadership of Hendrik Witbooi (q.v.). His great-grandson, Rev. Hendrik Witbooi (q.v.) was unanimously elected chief of the Witboois in 1976, a post he still holds.

WITWATERSRAND NATIVE LABOUR ASSOCIATION (WNLA). "Wenela" was a nineteenth-century product of the spectacular gold and diamond discoveries in South Africa. With workers in great demand, this employment association was formed by the big mining companies to recruit and hire Africans from most of south Africa, as far north as Angola and Tanzania. Herero, Dama, Damara, and Wambo workers were among those to go to South African mines. They were transported through Botswana to either Kimberley or the Rand. After fifty years, however, WNLA was faced with a new competitor, the South West Africa Native Labor Association (q.v.). SWANLA's creation in 1934 ensured that most of Namibia's available African labor pool would remain to work in the Namibian mines. (*See also* LABOR, AFRICAN.)

WOBMA, CAPT. C. T. Captain of the *Bode* in which he explored the Namibian coast with a goal of surveying and mapping it and the Angolan coast to the north. His charge included the goal of finding sources of food products and reporting about the African inhabitants and their way of life. The "Bode" sailed on January 20, 1677, from Cape Town and on February 17 it weighed anchor in a small sandy bay along Namibia's coast.

WOERMANN LINIE (variant: LINE). Under German rule, most of Namibia's trade was limited to German companies. Adolf Woermann, a shipping magnate in Hamburg, founded the Damara und Namaqualand-Handelgesellschaft in 1894. He opened a branch in Swakopmund under the first manager, Georg Schluckwerder. The Woermann Company was soon granted a monopoly of the landing and shipping business of both German ports, Swakopmund and Lüderitz Bay. The monopoly was renewed in 1912 with the provision that in the interests of national defense the government could expropriate the tugs, lighters, and landing appliances of the Woermann-Linie. The company cooperated with other shipping companies on longer voyages, for example the Deutsche Ost-Afrika Linie and the Hamburg-Amerika Afrikadienst. Both passengers and freight were carried.

One of Swakopmund's landmarks today is Woermann Haus, which was built in 1905 as the head office of the Woermann Linie in Namibia. A more modern byproduct of the great shipping business is the import and retail firm Woermann and Brock, which has its main store in Swakopmund.

WOOD, BISHOP RICHARD JAMES. Born in England in 1920, Anglican Bishop Wood studied for the ministry at Wells Theological College in Somerset. He and his wife went to South Africa in 1955 to serve his church there. He was appointed to serve in Keetmanshoop, Namibia, in 1971, and was made Canon of St. George's Cathedral in Windhoek in 1972. In 1973 he was named Suffragan Bishop of the Damaraland Diocese. He was one of several ministers (Bishop Leonard Auala, q.v., was another) who became outspoken on the subject of government persecution and torture of political activists. They challenged the actions in the Supreme Court of Namibia and won a temporary stay.

Eventually the South African Supreme Court in Bloemfontein agreed that floggings of people suspected of SWAPO membership must be stopped. Nevertheless Bishop Wood was told to leave the country by authorities, one of several Anglican churchmen who were so treated.

- Y -

YA MUNGUNDU, NANGOMBE. Reputedly the common father of two great nations of Namibia, the Wambo and the Herero. Known also as Amangundu, he is referred to in several folk narratives. It is presumed that he lived near the upper stretches of the Zambezi River. His two sons came south, according to the tales. One, named Nangombe, founded the Wambo nation. The other Kathu, traveled further and is the ancestral father of the Hereros.

YA-OTTO, JOHN G. (1938–). A SWAPO activist for thirty years, his activism was rewarded when he was elected to Namibia's Constituent Assembly in 1989. As a baby in 1938 he was smuggled by an aunt from his home area near Ondangwa in Owambo to further south in order to improve his educational opportunities. Growing up in Aus, a small railway town on the edge of the Namib Desert, he learned to speak Nama and Herero as well as his native Ovambo. As a youth he did farm work, but his intelligence and skill at school led him to become a teacher. Always concerned about politics as well, he became involved with SWAPO after witnessing the Windhoek "Old Location" (q.v.) massacre in 1959. He soon became part of the recognized leadership of SWAPO. A detailed study of Owambo in the early 1970s showed that people there ranked him as the fourth most important person in Owambo. Two who preceded him were Bishop Leonard Auala and Chief Elfias. Ya-Otto was the leader of SWAPO in Owambo at that time and was chairman of the Teachers' Association in 1973.

He didn't reach this reputation easily, however. He served for several years as a SWAPO organizer on the local level in the 1960s. He had worked his way up to acting secretary-general of SWAPO in 1961. Five years later he and thirty-six others were arrested and tried under the Terrorism Act (q.v.). He was one of the lucky few, however, as he was sentenced to only five years, and all but one month of that was suspended. As indicated above, however, he continued working for SWAPO, mostly in Owambo. On April 30, 1973, he was arrested again and charged with addressing an illegal meeting. Finally he fled the country in 1974, He remained active while in exile, and was declared to be SWAPO's "shadow" secretary of labor in 1976. In 1980 he and two co-authors published his autobiography, called *Battlefront Namibia.* He has continued to be the SWAPO spokesman on labor affairs, and was also the general secretary of the National Union of Namibian Workers. Gaining a seat in the Assembly gives him a platform for espousing workers' rights and the improvement of industrial relations.

YA-TOIVO, HERMAN ANDIMBA TOIVO (variant: JA TOIVO) (1924–). Considered by many the true father of African nationalism in Namibia, and the most universally venerated of all the SWAPO leaders, he was born in 1924 at Umungundu and educated at St. Mary's Mission School (Anglican) at Odibo in Owambo. In World War II he served as a corporal in the Native Military Corps, serving as a guard at an ammunition dump. He then returned to school and completed Standard Eight. Later he worked in the mines on the Witwatersrand and subsequently found work as a contract laborer in a white grocery business in a Cape Town suburb. He became the leader of a group of contract workers in Cape Town, organizing them politically in a barber shop he chose for his headquarters. In 1958 he and a number of other early SWAPO stalwarts, including Andreas Shipanga, Emil Appolus, and Solomon Mifima (qq.v.), formed the Ovamboland People's Organization (OPO) (q.v.). The group discussed common problems and began taking political stands.

Ya-Toivo sent a petition on tape concerning Namibia's status to a colleague, Mburumba Kerina (q.v.) in New York to present to the United Nations. It received a favorable reaction there, and South Africa subsequently deported him from Cape Town. He returned to Namibia and worked fulltime as an organizer for a new national organization soon to be known as SWAPO. His base was Owambo and his activities so successful that he was placed under house arrest at the home of Chief Shihepo until 1961. He nevertheless found ways to continue his work for SWAPO, despite police harassment. His leadership and organization were at the heart of SWAPO's work until he was arrested in 1966 and tried under the ex post facto Terrorism Act (q.v.).

The thirty-seven arrested men were accused at the Terrorism Trial of attempting to overthrow the existing government of Namibia and install in its place a SWAPO-led government. Before the judgment was given, Ya-Toivo made a brilliant and stirring long statement in the court. It then became virtually the political credo of SWAPO. It was the classic appeal of a nationalist fighting for his freedom and for self-rule against an alien, colonial government. Nevertheless, Ya-Toivo and most of the others received a sentence of twenty years at Robben Island.

Ya-Toivo's stay in prison was difficult, as he was the father of four children, but he was in good company; Nelson Mandela and other leading South African activists were also there. He was finally released March 1, 1984. Then sixty-nine years old, he had served almost sixteen years in detention. When he returned to Windhoek thousands of Africans poured into the streets of Katutura (q.v.) to welcome him. While no one was sure why he was released early, it was conjectured that his freedom might post a challenge to Nujoma for the leadership of SWAPO. Such a conflict did not develop, however, and Ya-Toivo chose to keep a fairly low profile during the next five years. He was given the title of secretary-general of the party in 1986.

Ya-Toivo's place of respect in the party is emphasized by his placement as number four on SWAPO's 1989 electoral list. Now a member of the National Assembly, he was chosen to hold the critical cabinet post of minister of mines and energy. Within the party he has been outspoken in his demand for an investigation concerning the disappearance of SWAPO members in detainee camps. At the SWAPO congress in December 1991, Ya-toivo stepped down from his position as Secretary General in order to devote more time to his important cabinet post. Moses Garoëb was elected in his place.

YELLOW CAKE (variant: YELLOWCAKE). The common name for uranium oxide. It is extracted from large quantities of ore at the Rössing Mine (q.v.), and did not reach its full rated capacity of 5,000 short tons per year until 1980.

- Z -

ZAMBIA. This south-central African country became independent in 1964. Formerly known as Northern Rhodesia, it is surrounded by Angola, Zaire, Tanzania, Malawi, Mozambique, Zimbabwe, Botswana (at one small point), and Namibia's Caprivi Strip. Historically some of the ethnic groups currently in Namibia migrated there through Zambia. The Ovambo and Kavango peoples, for example, are said to have taken that route. In the nineteenth century there was considerable movement of people across the Caprivi Strip into western Zambia, and vice versa. The Makololo, Lozi and Subia all saw both sides of the Zambezi River that separates Zambia from Namibia today. In recent decades a number of people have fled fighting in Namibia to take refuge in Zambia, notably Ovambos and Caprivians. Some went to Lusaka for education there at the United Nations Institute for Namibia (q.v.). Others used part of southwestern Zambia as a SWAPO military base. Not everyone found security there. An estimated 1800 dissident members of SWAPO, led by Andreas Shipanga, were held by the Zambian government in "protective custody" and later jailed in Tanzania.

ZERAUA, CHIEF WILLEM. One of the most powerful of the Herero chiefs in the second half of the nineteenth century, his centers of influence were primarily in and near Otjimbingwe and Omaruru. He was especially effective in forming into a community the Hereros who worked at the mine near Otjimbingwe run by the Walfisch Bay Mining Co. in the

1850s. In mid-1850, Zeraua's nephew Maherero was in Windhoek and facing frequent harassment and punishment by Jonker Afrikander. Zeraua sent a group of warriors to free Maherero, but before that occurred, Maherero and his family and followers made their own way to Otjimbingwe (by way of Barmen). All of the Herero chiefs seemed to be linked by either family ties or marital connections. For example, Maherero's mother was a younger sister of Zeraua's principal wife at Otjimbingwe. Zeraua was not a "paramount chief," and indeed didn't even have the true sacred fire (q.v.) (as Maherero did). He was however, a chief, an influential man, and rich. Part of his strength came from his good relations with the Europeans at the mission and at the Otjimbingwe mines. In 1863, however, with the threat of another Nama attack imminent, Zeraua, as the oldest Herero chief, was chosen paramount chief. Although still energetic, he turned down the position and proposed Maherero, who was elected. In 1874, the elderly Zeraua, despite an illness, joined with two other Herero chiefs in petitioning the governor at the Cape to prevent more Boers from entering their territory. This was interpreted as a request for British "protection," so W. C. Palgrave (q.v.) was sent from England as a special commissioner for Hereroland and Namaland. Palgrave was merely investigating the problem. At a meeting with Zeraua and many of the other Herero chiefs, Palgrave was chosen by the Hereros as the territory's magistrate, in effect placing Hereroland under the protection of the Cape government. Zeraua was one of the signatories on September 9, 1876.

ZINC. Not as significant to Namibia's economy as uranium and diamonds, nevertheless the zinc reserves of the country represent about 1 percent of the world's known reserves. Zinc is found at the Tsumeb Mine as well as at Kombat, Berg Aukas, Otjihase, Rosh Pinah, Elbe, and Uis (qq.v.). Over 50,000 tons of zinc in the form of sulfide and oxide concentrates have been produced in just three of the mines. Annual production could easily exceed 100,000 tons, especially as several of the mines are fairly young, but in 1983 production was barely half that total. Rosh Pinah opened in mid-1970, for example. It is managed by South Africa's ISCOR, and sends its output to the Zinc Corporation of South Africa, Ltd. (ZINCOR), for processing. The huge ore body at Tsumeb contains zinc among its many minerals. At one time it was Namibia's largest base metal mine, and was Africa's largest producer of lead and zinc. Both the Otjihase and the Berg Aukas mines had produced zinc, but were put on a care and maintenance basis in the 1970s. The Kombat Mine continues to produce well, however. The value of zinc mined in Namibia rose from R28 million in 1985 to R69 million in 1988 and R99 million in 1990. While some of this represents an increase of production, most of it is price related.

ZWARTBOOI HOTTENTOTS (variant: SWARTBOOI). One of the many subgroups of the Nama (q.v.) population of Namibia, their name means literally "black boys." They are also called //Khan-goan, that is, children of the tribe of the //Khauben. About 1700 AD many Namas crossed north of the Orange River into Namibia. During the eighteenth century at least eight identifiable Nama groups made this trip. Six of them, including the Zwartboois, formed a confederation under the leadership of the //Khauben or Red Nation (q.v.). The Zwartboois lived in the Rehoboth area until they were defeated in a battle by Jan Jonker Afrikander in 1864. The survivors fled north to Salem. Meanwhile in 1871 a large group of Basters (q.v.) under Hermanus van Wijk (q.v.) arrived at Rehoboth and bought the land from the Zwartbooi chief for 5 wagons and 120 horses. Then the Zwartboois left Salem and trekked north to Amieb in the Erongo Mountains, Herero country. The Herero Chief, Maherero, decided not to confront them with battle, concluding a treaty of peace with them on March 3, 1882, instead, on condition that they trek north of Franzfontein in southern Kaokoland. A settlement there was thriving by 1890. In 1896 the Zwartbooi rose in rebellion against the Germans because of a leadership dispute. The Germans had sided with Lazarus Swartbooi against the legitimate "kaptein," David Swartbooi, who was deposed by Major Leutwein and taken to Windhoek. But problems arose again in 1898 and Leutwein sent troops to

Franzfontein. The kaptein surrendered and 550 of the Zwartboois were taken to Windhoek to work on plots. When other Namas revolted in 1904, the Zwartboois hesitated to rise again, and German officials at Franzfontein disarmed them.

APPENDICES

NAMIBIAN REGIONAL ELECTIONS NOVEMBER 1992

Caprivi (D-4, S-2)
1=SWAPO
2=DTA
3=DTA
4=DTA
5=DTA
6=SWAPO

Erongo (S-4, D-1, U-1)
1=SWAPO
2=SWAPO
3=UDF
4=SWAPO
5=DTA
6=SWAPO

Hardap (D-4, S-2)
1=DTA
2=DTA
3=DTA
4=DTA
5=SWAPO
6=SWAPO

Karas (S-4)
1=SWAPO
2=SWAPO
3=SWAPO
4=SWAPO

Khomas (S-6, D-3)
1=SWAPO
2=SWAPO
3=SWAPO
4=SWAPO
5=SWAPO
6=SWAPO
7=DTA
8=DTA
9=DTA

Ohangwena (S=7)
1=SWAPO
2=SWAPO
3=SWAPO
4=SWAPO
5=SWAPO
6=SWAPO
7=SWAPO

Kunene (U-2, S-2, D-1)
1=DTA
2-UDF
3=UDF
4=SWAPO
5=SWAPO

Okavango (S-6)
1=SWAPO
2=SWAPO
3=SWAPO
4=SWAPO
5=SWAPO
6=SWAPO

Omaheke (D-5, S-1)
1=DTA
2=DTA
3=DTA
4=SWAPO
5=DTA
6=DTA

Omusati (S-6)
1=SWAPO
2=SWAPO
3=SWAPO
4=SWAPO
5=SWAPO
6=SWAPO

Oshana (S-8)
1=SWAPO
2=SWAPO
3=SWAPO
4=SWAPO
5=SWAPO
6=SWAPO
7=SWAPO
8=SWAPO

Oshikoto (S-4)
1=SWAPO
2=SWAPO
3=SWAPO
4=SWAPO

Otjozondjupa (S-4, D-2)
1=SWAPO
2=SWAPO
3=DTA
4=SWAPO
5=SWAPO
6=DTA

1989 CONSTITUENT ASSEMBLY ELECTION RESULTS BY DISTRICT

	ACN	CDA	DTA	FCN	NNDP	NNF	NPF	SWAPO-D	SWAPO	UDF
Bethanie	258	30	1153	51	2	6	8	15	398	69
Maltahohe	355	13	579	128	12	8	10	7	758	334
Karibib	344	20	1637	47	2	45	139	12	1932	1289
Mariental	1319	72	6584	307	18	59	78	24	2411	878
Omaruru	198	38	2538	30	3	152	280	18	1022	499
Tsumeb	848	32	3452	78	7	41	45	44	6476	1085
Hereroland	44	74	8440	147	23	486	1573	26	1835	58
Outjo	719	32	2658	73	2	21	39	9	984	1186
Okahandja	611	41	3672	30	8	45	283	20	3256	993
Luderitz	453	15	1890	56	7	204	56	21	5422	342
Keetmanshoop	1312	92	8229	284	44	404	192	103	4778	1314
Kaokoland	33	71	6699	83	51	31	2152	20	1025	41
Rehoboth	96	58	6590	4499	68	252	196	38	2460	326
Damaraland	140	23	2040	26	4	73	39	19	3407	6944
Caprivi	86	154	12782	411	40	38	649	80	9350	514
Karasburg	3588	39	7727	323	26	26	111	35	1830	651
Gobabis	1801	151	10539	137	41	289	320	52	2119	374
Swakopmund	1020	24	4998	318	4	207	119	49	11479	1400
Otjiwarongo	626	38	4274	56	10	99	79	16	3194	1540
Grootfontein	1418	93	7226	198	22	45	323	41	6336	1094
Windhoek	4153	194	30475	1208	65	1574	1554	287	39060	6147
Kavango	407	413	22046	356	156	134	455	284	27256	1202
Ovambo	247	449	9200	107	186	73	428	1172	197100.	4674
Grand Total	23728	2495	191532.	10452	984	5344	10693	3151	384567.	7874
Number of seats	3	0	21	1	0	1	1	0	41	4

- A total of 670 830 votes were cast
- There were 8 532 spoilt ballot papers
- Each party needed a quota of 9 317 votes to gain a seat in the Constituent Assembly
- Tendered Votes: A Total of 96 281 Tendered Ballots were counted
- Elections were held 7-11 November 1989

1990 NATIONAL ASSEMBLY

SWAPO

Rev. M. Amadhila
B. Amathila
Dr. L. Amathila
N. Angula
N. Bessinger
W. Biwa
D. P. Botha
J. Ekandjo
M. Garoëb
H. G. Geingob
T. B. Gurirab
H. Hamutenya
H. Haufiku
M. M. Hausiku
H. T. Hishongwa
J. Hoebeb
M. M. E. K. H. Huebschle
P. Ithana
Dr. N. Iyambo
Dr. Z. Kameeta

R. Kapelwa
Dr. P. Katjavivi
Rev. W. Konjore
Dr. K. Mbuende
P. Mweshihange
K. N. Nauyula*
I. G. Nathaniel
S. Nujoma**
L. Pohamba
H. Ruppel
P. Shoombe
Dr. N. Tjiriange
Dr. M. Tjitendero
B. U. Ulenga
J. W. Wentworth
A. von Wietersheim
Rev. H. Witbooi
S. P. Wohler
J. Ya Otto
A. Toivo Ya Toivo

DTA

Dr. B. Africa
L. J. Barnes
M. Barnes
G. Dan
J. Gaseb
A. Fwnsw
J. M. Haraseb
J. Jagger
P. M. Junius
G. Kashe
N. K. Kaura

C. Kgosiemang
F. J. Kozonguizi
D. Luipert
A. Majavero
A. Matjila
S. D. Mudge
M. Muyongo
A. Nuule
H. F. Staby
C. A. C. van Wyk

UDF

R. R. Diergaardt
J. Garoëb
G. Siseho
T. Soroseb

ACN	W. O. Aston
	J. W. F. Pretorius
	J. M. de Wet
FCN	J. G. A. Diergaardt***
NNF	V. Rukoro
NPF	M. K. Katjiuongua

President Nujoma appointed six non-voting members as well: Otto Herrigel, Gerhard Hanekom, and four Deputy Ministers.

*Peter Tsheema replaced the late Mr. Nicki Nauyala of SWAPO.
**Helmut Angula took over the seat vacated by President Nujoma.
***Mburumba Kerina replaced Hans Diergaardt, who stepped down due to poor health.

NAMIBIAN GOVERNMENT JUNE 1, 1990

President:	Sam Shafilshuna Nujoma

Prime Minister,
  in charge of public service
  personnel:
	Hage Gottfried Feingob

Ministers:

foreign affairs:	Theo-Ben Gurirab
Deputy:	Netumbo Mdaitwah
defence:	Peter Mueshihange
Deputy:	Phillemon Malima
finance:	Otto Herrigel
information & broadcasting:	Hidipo Hamutenya
Deputy:	Daniel Tjongarero
home affairs:	Hifikepunye Pohamba
Deputy:	Nangolo Ithete
trade & industry:	Ben Amadhila
Deputy:	Reggie Diergaardt
mines & energy:	Andimba Toivo ya Toivo
Deputy:	Helmut Angula
works, transport, & **communications:**	Richard Kapelwa Kabajani
Deputy:	Klaus Dierks
labour & manpower **development:**	Hendrik Witbooi
Deputy:	Hadino Hishongwa
agriculture, fisheries, water, **& rural development:**	Gerard Hanekom
Deputy:	Kaire Mbuenoe
wildlife, conservation, & **tourism:**	Nico Bessinger
Deputy:	Pendukeni Ithana
education, culture, youth, & **sport:**	Nahas Angula
Deputy:	Buddy Wentworth
health & social services:	Nicky Iyambo
local government & housing:	Libertine Amathila
Deputy:	Jerry Ekandjo

lands, resettlement, & rehabilitation:	Marco Hausiku
Deputy:	Marcus Shivute
justice:	Ngankutuke Tjiriange
Deputy:	Reinhard Rukoro

NONCABINET:

Intelligence chief:	Johan Mauritz
National Planning Commission:	Zedekia Ngavirue (Director-General)
Minister of State for Security in the President's office:	Peter Tsheehama
Attorney General:	Hartmut Ruppel
Auditor General:	Jan Jordaan
Chief Justice:	Hans Berker

GERMAN RULERS OF SOUTH WEST AFRICA

Landeshauptmänner

1885–1890	Heinrich Ernst Goering
1891–1894	Curt Von Francois
1894–1899	Theodor Leutwein

Governors

1899–1905	Theodore Leutwein
1905–1907	Friedrich Von Lindequist
1907–1910	Bruno Von Schuckmann
1910–1915	Theodor Seitz

SOUTH AFRICAN ADMINISTRATORS

Administrators

1915–1920	Howard Gorges
1920–1926	G. R. Hofmeyr
1926–1933	A. J. Werth
1933–1943	D. G. Conradie
1943–1951	P. I. Hoogenhout
1951–1953	A. J. R. van Rhijn
1953–1963	D. T. du P. Viljoen
1963–1968	Wenzel C. du Plessis
1968–1971	J. F. H. van der Wath
1971–1977	B. J. van der Walt

Administrators-General

1977–1979	M. T. Steyn
1979–1980	Gerrit Viljoen
1980–1983	Danie Hough
1983–1985	W. van Niekerk
1985–1990	Louis Pienaar

Mayors of Windhoek

1908–1911	Houtermans
1920–1921	Peter Müller
1921–1923	J. Rautenbach
1923–1924	J. D. Lardner-Burke

1924–1925	J. Hebenstreit
1925–1926	A. Menmuir
1926–1927	J. Hebenstreit
1927–1929	Rev. J. Wood
1929–1938	John Meinert
1938–1941	Edgar Sander
1941–1946	Marie Elizabeth May Bell
1946–1949	G. Van Schalkwyk
1949–1951	E. Sander
1951–1952	H. J. Steyn
1952–1953	S. Frank
1953–1954	Peter Falk
1954–1955	W. H. Immelman
1955–1957	H. J. Steyn
1957–1961	Jaap v. D. Snyman
1961–1963	S. J. Spies
1963–1965	J. L. Levinson
1965–1966	San Davis
1966–1967	J. Labuschange
1967–1968	S. W. Berger
1968–1969	C. E. Katzke
1969–1971	J. B. H. Von Prittwitz und Gaffron
1971–1973	J. J. Botha
1973–1974	J. H. L. Nel
1974–1976	E. G. E. Kaschik
1976–1978	A. G. C. Yssel
1978–1979	M. J. Van Taak
1979–1982	S. G. Beukes
1982–1984	A. G. C. Yssel
1984–1987	J. S. Olivier
1987–1988	E. Joubert
1988–	A. B. May

ELECTION RESULTS AUGUST 30, 1950

Electoral Division	Candidates	Votes polled	Major- ity	% poll
Aroab	C. J. Lotter (N)	585	57	96
	J. A. Louw (U)	528		
Gobabis	H. J. Steyn (N)	692	98	98
	C. P. Michau (U)	594		
Grootfontein ..	H. Lombard (N)	918	331	92
	C. J. B. Uys (U) ..	587		
Keetmanshoop .	H. J. Nell (N)	627	87	97.6
	J. H. Jooste (U)	540		
Luderitz	J. H. Cloete (N)	684	135	95
	P. J. Castle (U) ..	549		
Maltahohe ..	P. C. Roux (N)	608	139	95.6
	J. L. van Zyl (U)	469		
Mariental	D. J. van Niekerk (N) ..	587	11	90
	D. J. Visser (U)	576		
Okahandja ..	A. Nel (N) ..	698	175	95.7
	D. J. Pretorius (U) ..	523		
Otjikondo ..	J. G. van der Wath (N) ..	786	405	93.7
	P. J. Hamman (U).. ..	381		
Otjiwarongo ..	P. J. Pretorius (N)	661	182	95.7
	A. J. Bester (U)	479		
Outjo..	J. D. Herholdt (N).. ..	828	340	92.5
	W. F. E. Meyer (U) ..	488		
Rehoboth	W. J. G. Lategan (U) ..	650	112	97
	J. Forrer (N)	538		
Swakopmund ..	M. C. E. McDonald (U).	625	2	95
	J. J. M. van Zyl (N) ..	623		
Usakos	A. H. du Plessis (N) ..	707	236	95
	S. J. van Pletsen (U) ..	471		
Warmbad ..	J. D. de Villiers (N) ..	572	36	98
	C. H. B. Oberholzer (U).	536		
Windhoek East..	S. J. de Villiers (U) ..	751	75	94
	A. C. J. van Rensburg (N)	676		
Windhoek North	E. A. Nel (N)	713	87	94.3
	N. C. Fraser (U)	626		
Windhoek West.	W. H. Weder (N)	846	171	95
	A. O. E. Sander (U) ..	675		

Out of a total possible of 23,794 votes, 22,467 votes were cast of which 12,434 (55.3 per cent.) were in favour of the Nationalist Party and 10,033 (44.7 per cent.) in favour of the United S.W. Party).

Electoral Division	Candidates	Votes polled	Major. ity	% Poll
Etosha	A. J. van Niekerk (N) ..	2,412	846	93
	Dr. H. R. Meintjes (U)..	1,566		
Karas	J. von S. von Molkte (N)	1,731	67	96.5
	L. C. F. Taljaard (U) ..	1,664		
Midlands	A. Webster (N)	1,966	229	96
	F. A. Venter (U)	1,737		
Namib	J. D. du P. Basson (N) ..	1,963	441	97
	M. J. Kritzinger (U) ..	1,522		
Omaruru	R. le Riche (N)	2,096	584	94
	J. P. de M. Niehaus (U) ..	1,512		
Windhoek ..	J. H. Visser (N)	2,266	234	94
	J. D. Lardner Burke (U)	2,032		

BIBLIOGRAPHY: TABLE OF CONTENTS

INTRODUCTION   613

1. GENERAL
   A. General Information and Guides   617
   B. Demographic Statistics   619
   C. Travel and Description   620
   D. Bibliographies   623

2. CULTURAL
   A. Archaeology   629
   B. Fine Arts   631
      1. Rock Art   631
      2. Other Fine Arts   634
   C. Linguistics   635
      1. General   635
      2. San (Bushman)   636
      3. Damara   636
      4. Herero   637
      5. Nama   638
      6. Ovambo   639
   D. Literature   640
      1. General   640
      2. San (Bushman)   640
      3. Herero   641
      4. Nama   642
      5. Ovambo   642
      6. German   643

3. ECONOMIC
   A. General Economy and Development, pre-1960   643
   B. General Economy and Development, post-1960   644
   C. Agriculture   646
   D. Mining   647

E. Furs   649
F. Fishing   649
G. Miscellaneous Industry and Development   650
H. Water Development   650
I. Labor, Contracts, and Strikes   651
J. Foreign Investment   653

4. HISTORIC
A. General   654
B. Pre-Colonial   656
C. The German Period   659
    1. General Colonial History and Biography   659
    2. Military Action   663
D. 1915–1945   665
E. At the United Nations   670
F. The International Court of Justice   674
G. Since 1945   680

5. POLITICAL
A. Constitution, Law, and Government   682
B. Politics and Political Parties   687
C. Race Relations   690
D. For and Against South African Control   692
E. Foreign Affairs and Diplomacy   698

6. SCIENTIFIC
A. Geography   702
B. Geology   703
C. Medicine   704
D. Botany   705
E. Zoology   706

7. SOCIAL
A. Anthropology and Ethnology   707
    1. General   707
    2. The San and Bushmen   709
    3. Nama (Hottentot)   713
    4. Herero   714
    5. Ovambo   716
    6. Damara and Bergdama   717
    7. Kavango and Caprivi People   718

　　　8. Basters　　　　　　　　　　　　718
　　　9. Others　　　　　　　　　　　　　718
　B. Education　　　　　　　　　　　　719
　C. Religion and Missions　　　　　　720
　D. Sociology　　　　　　　　　　　　723

About the Author　　　　　　　　　　725

BIBLIOGRAPHY

Introduction

Compared to many other African countries, there is an unusually large amount of printed material on Namibia. There are at least two reasons for this. First, the country has had the misfortune of living under two different colonial "mothers." Thus, both German and South African authors have devoted considerable effort to writing about it. Second, as a major international issue, Namibia has generated a great deal of output from scholars in academic and political centers in Great Britain and the United States, not to mention at least half a dozen other countries. The United Nations and several other international agencies also have turned out a significant amount of literature.

While it would be desirable to make this a comprehensive bibliography, that is just not practical, especially within the goals and guidelines of this series of books. It is hoped that interested parties would turn to some of the bibliographies identified in these pages for additional information concerning the literature on Namibia.

It must also be mentioned here that a great deal of the research for this bibliography was done by Professor Robert Bradford, Ph.D., of Susquehanna University. Without his years of diligent bibliographic work on two continents, this bibliography would be much shorter. He cannot be held responsible, however, for any omissions or errors in citation that may occur here, as this must be the responsibility of the author.

A few words are necessary on how works were selected for inclusion here. The decision was made not to include many works other than those in English and some in German. Thus, a large body of South African publications in Afrikaans has been omitted. Also most brief works have been omitted, as have those published in relatively obscure journals. Unless a work seems to be reasonably accessible it has not been included. Exceptions were made if the item was especially significant and/or original. Many of the official publications of the South African government have been intentionally omitted, as have some of the briefer United Nations publications.

The remainder of this introduction is designed to point the reader to a few classics in a number of categories. These works might be seen as the basics for a core collection of Namibia. A starting point in the category of bibliography itself should be the works by Eckhard Strohmeyer that are a part of a projected multivolume Namibian National Bibliography, published by the Basel African Bibliography in Switzerland. Also from Switzerland is Micheline Fontoliett's *Bibliography of Namibia,* which tends toward political and economic subjects. Less than comprehensive but extremely valuable is Elna Schoeman's *The Namibian Issue, 1920–1980: A Select and Annotated Bibliography.* Numerous bibliographies, on a wide variety of topics, have been published by the School of Librarianship at the University of Cape Town. An annotated bibliography on Namibian history and political economy by Tore Linne Eriksen and Richard Moorsom, *The Political Economy of Namibia,* is also very useful.

The standard introduction to the people of Namibia is *The Native Tribes of South West Africa,* which contains separate chapters by C. Hahn, H. Vedder, and L. Fourie. It was first published in 1928, so most readers will want to follow it with more recent items by anthropologists and sociologists who may be less encumbered by the prejudices or viewpoints of this group of early writers.

There is really no one good history of Namibia that covers its entire existence. *A History of South West Africa* by I. Goldblatt published in 1971 is limited to the nineteenth and twentieth centuries. Even within that scope it is somewhat cursory. A "History of Namibia" popular with some scholars is *South West Africa and Its Human Issues* (1967), written by a geographer, John H. Wellington. It has good scope and depth, but with a generally pro–South African slant. Also it is over twenty years old, and thus contains little on SWAPO, the guerrilla movement, and modern political activity. A remarkable book for those wanting a quick introduction to the broad scope of Namibian history is Olga Levinson's *Story of Namibia,* published in 1978 in Cape Town by

Tafelberg. A thin volume, it is packed with information by a lady who loved her country and all its people dearly. If one could read only one book on Namibia, this should be the choice.

It is a little easier to find books in depth on specific periods of the country's history. First in line must be Heinrich Vedder's classic, *South West Africa in Early Times*. Vedder was a German missionary and certainly had a number of prejudices, but this volume (which stops in 1890) contains a wealth of facts about life in the territory. He mentioned many obscure traders, missionaries, and settlers, in addition to his survey of the indigenous Africans. He is something of an apologist for both the missionaries and the Germans in general. His prejudices against the Damara peoples result in a particularly distorted treatment of them. Nevertheless, Vedder is considered the pioneer on the early history of Namibia.

The German period has been covered by many volumes. Among those available in English, three that stand out are Horst Drechsler's *Let Us Die Fighting* (1980), *South West Africa, 1880–1894*, by J. H. Esterhuyse (1968), and Jon Bridgman's *The Revolt of the Hereros* (1981). But many scholars think the best work on this period is Helmut Bley's *South West Africa Under German Rule, 1884–1914* (1971). A unique and valuable original source is general T. Leutwein's *Elf Jahre Gouverneur in Deutsch-Südwestafrika*, an autobiography by the most significant of the German administrators of the territory.

A substantial work on Namibia's mandate period is Gail Maryse Cockram's *South West African Mandate*. It continues through the period of ICJ decisions up to the book's publication in 1976. The same time span is covered in even greater depth by the South African legal expert, John Dugard, the *The South West Africa/Namibia Dispute*. Dugard is especially thorough in his coverage of the cases before the International Court of Justice. Perhaps the best brief survey of Namibian history through the early 1960s is Ruth First's *South West Africa*. Her scholarship is excellent, despite her strong leftist views which show through occasionally. Likewise tainted by obvious political bias, but extremely valuable at times, is *To Be Born a Nation*, written by members of SWAPO's Department of Information and Publicity.

A truly unique book that must be seen to be fully appreciated is *National Atlas of South West Africa (Namibia)*, edited by J. H. van der Merwe. Its ninety-two maps provide a phenomenal amount of information that covers everything from geography to demographics to history and politics to infrastructure.

Volumes on modern Namibia generally leave a lot to be desired. One of the better ones, especially on political matters, is J. H. P. Serfontein's *Namibia?*, but also strong is Gerhard Tötemeyer's *South West Africa/Namibia: Facts, Attitudes, Assessments, and Prospects*. Tötemeyer's *Namibia Old and New* is also excellent, but the title is deceptive. It is a study of the development of Owambo from a traditional society to a modern one. While Wambos constitute almost half of the country's population, the scope is limited.

In the economic sphere most people would start with *Economic Development in Namibia* by Wolfgang H. Thomas. It includes both a survey of Namibia's past and an assessment of various strategies for future economic development. Useful in a similar vein is *Namibia, the Last Colony*, edited by R. H. Green, K. Kiljunen and M-L. Kiljunen.

Among the more recent books on Namibia, David Soggot's *Namibia, the Violent Heritage* covers most of the guerrilla warfare period (1967–1986) very well. Alfred Moleah does much of the same in *Namibia, the Struggle for Liberation*. Peter Katjavivi, Ph.D., a scholar as well as a high-ranking member of SWAPO, has provided a very useful book, *A History of Resistance in Namibia* (1988). Somewhat more slanted but also a useful volume on recent Namibian history is *The Devils Are Among Us: The War for Namibia* (1989) by Denis Herbstein and John Evenson.

An excellent book on Namibia was produced by the United Nations Institute for Namibia in 1987, but *Namibia, A Direct United Nations Responsibility* focuses heavily on the international organizations. Finally a whole series of excellent books on various subtopics under the heading ''A Future for Namibia'' were produced throughout the 1980s by the London-based Catholic Institute for International Relations.

An absolutely essential book on Namibian politics is a book published right before the 1989 elections, *Namibia Handbook and Political Who's Who*. It was compiled by J. Pütz, H. von Egidy, and P. Caplan and published in Namibia. This is actually a much improved second edition of a similar volume published in 1987. It will probably be updated regularly. It is a reference book rather than a narrative.

Keeping in mind the problem of subjectivity in all newspapers, the reader might find valuable material in the *Allgemeine Zeitung, Windhoek Advertiser,* and *The Namibian,* all Windhoek dailies, and the *Johannesburg Star.*

It is a truism that one will never get all the facts and a totally balanced perspective from just reading one book on a subject. If forced to choose just one as an introduction to Namibia, however, one might find Olga Levinson's *Story of Namibia* to be the best beginning point.

1. GENERAL

A. General Information and Guides

Afrikaans-Deutsche Kulturgemeinschaft (SWA) [A.D.K.]. *A.D.K. Facts and Figures* (six booklets): No. 1. "What One Should Know about South West Africa," No. 2. "The Population Groups of South West Africa (Part 1)," No. 3. "The Population Groups of South West Africa (Part 2,)" No. 4. "My Country South West Africa (History and Stories)," No. 5. "The Leaders of South West Africa (Part 1)," No. 6. "The Leaders of South West Africa (Part 2)." Windhoek: A.D.K., 1978–80.

Bannister, Anthony, and Peter Johnson. *Namibia: Africa's Harsh Paradise.* Chicago: Domus Books, 1979.

Bruwer, J. P. Van S. *South West Africa: The Disputed Land.* Cape Town: Nasional Boekhandel Bpk., 1966.

Catholic Institute for International Relations and British Council of Churches. *Namibia in the 1980s.* London: CIIR/BCC, 1982.

Cubitt, Gerald, and Johann Richter. *South West.* Cape Town: C. Struik, 1976.

Desjeunes, Christian. *Namibia.* Outlooks on Africa Series. Paris: C.C.L.S., 1984.

Great Britain. Ministry of Foreign Affairs. *South-West Africa.* Foreign Office Peace Handbook No. 112. London: H. M. Stationery Office, 1920.

Green, Lawrence G. *Lords of the Last Frontier: The Story of South West Africa and Its People of All Races.* London: Stanley Paul, 1953.

Horrell, Muriel. *South-West Africa.* Johannesburg: South African Institute of Race Relations, 1967.

International Defense and Aid Fund. *Namibia: The Facts.* London: IDAF, 1980.

Knappert, Jan. *Namibia, Land and Peoples, Myths and Fables.* Leiden: E. J. Brill, 1981.

Levinson, Olga. *The Story of Namibia.* Cape Town: Tafelberg Publishers, 1978.

Metzges, J. *Otjimbingwe.* Windhoek: 1962.

Mossolow, N. *Windhoek Today.* Windhoek: John Meinert, 1967.

Putz, J., H. von Egidy, and P. Caplan. *Namibia Handbook and Who's Who.* Windhoek: The Magus Company, 1989.

Selle, Rianne, ed. Amy Schoeman, trans. *Namibia Today.* Windhoek: Liaison Services of the Department of Government Affairs, March 1988.

Serfontein, J. H. P. *Namibia?* Randberg: Fokus Suid Publishers, 1976.

Shell Tourist Guide. *SWA/Namibia.* Windhoek: Shell Oil South West Africa, 1985.

South Africa, Department of Foreign Affairs. *South West Africa Survey 1967.* Pretoria: The Government Printer, 1968.

South Africa, Department of Foreign Affairs. *South West Africa Survey 1974.* Pretoria and Cape Town: The Government Printer, 1975.

South Africa, Department of Information. *South West Africa: The Land, Its Peoples and Their Future.* Johannesburg: Dagbreek, [c. 1965].

South-West Africa Administration. *South West Africa, Its Attractions and Potentialities.* Windhoek: SWA Administration, 1937.

————. *South-West Africa—Its Possibilities.* Windhoek: SWA Administration, 1925.

Steward, Alexander. *South West Africa: The Sacred Trust,* Johannesburg: DaGama Publications, 1963.

Tötemeyer, Gerhard. *South West Africa/Namibia Facts, Attitudes, Assessment and Prospects.* Randburg: Fokus Suid, 1977.

Van der Merwe, ed. *National Atlas of South West Africa.* Goodwood, Cape, South Africa: National Book Printers, 1983.

B. Demographic Statistics

International Defense and Aid Fund for Southern Africa. *Apartheid in Namibia Today: Recent Data on Poverty, Living Conditions and Racial Segregation.* London: International Defense and Aid Fund for Southern Africa, 1982.

South Africa. *First Results of the Population Census 6 September 1960 . . . geographical distribution of the population.* Part I: "Union of South Africa"; Part II: "Territory of S.W.A.," Pretoria, 1961.

C. Travel and Description

Alexander, Sir James Edward. *An Expedition of Discovery into the Interior of Africa* . . . . London: Henry Colburn, Publisher, 1838.

Alexander, Capt. J. E. "Report of an Expedition of Discovery, through the countries of the Great Namáquas, Boschmans, and the Hill Dámaras, in South Africa." *Papers Read before the Royal Geographical Society* VIII (1838): 1–28.

Andersson, Charles John. "Explorations in South Africa, 1855," *Journal of the Royal Geographical Society* XXV (1855): 79–107.

————. *Lake Ngami* or, *Explorations and Discoveries during Four Years' Wanderings in the Wilds of South Western Africa.* New York: Harper & Brothers, London: Hurst and Blackett, 1856. (German edition as *Reisen in Südwestafrika biszum Ngami in den Jahren 1850–1854.* Leipzig, 1857.)

————. *Notes of Travel in South Africa.* Edited by L. Lloyd, London: Hurst and Blackett, Publishers, 1875. (Facsimile reprint by C. Struik (Pty) Ltd., Cape Town, 1969. American edition *Notes of Travel in South-Western Africa,* New York: G. P. Putnam's Sons, 1875.)

————. *The Okavango River: A Narrative of Travel, Exploration, and Adventure.* New York: Harper & Bros., 1861. (Facsimile reprint, 1968 by C. Struik (Pty) Ltd., Cape Town.)

Axelson, Eric. *South African Explorers.* London, New York, Cape Town: Oxford University Press, 1954.

Baines, Thomas. *Explorations in South-West Africa* . . . . London: Longman, Roberts, & Green, 1864.

Becker, Peter. *Trails and Tribes in Southern Africa.* London: Hart-Davis, MacGibbon, 1975.

Brown, John. *The Thirsty Land.* London: Hodder and Stoughton, 1954.

Chadwick, Douglas H. "Etosha: Namibia's Kingdom of Animals." *National Geographic* 163, No. 3, (March 1983): 344–385.

Chapman, James. *Travels in the Interior of South Africa 1849–1863: . . . .* Edited from the original manuscripts by Edward C. Tabler, 2 volumes, Cape Town: A. A. Balkema, 1971.

Coetzee, Cora. *Cora Coetzee's Namibia.* Cape Town: C. Struik, 1979.

Cornell, Lt. Fred C. *The Glamour of Prospecting: Wanderings of a South African Prospector in Search of Copper, Gold, Emeralds and Diamonds.* London: T. Fisher Unwin Ltd., 1920.

———. *A Rip van Winkle of the Kalahari and Other Tales of South-West Africa.* London: T. Fisher Unwin Ltd., [n.d.]

Galton, Sir Francis. *Narrative of an Explorer in Tropical South Africa, being an Account of a Visit to Damaraland in 1851.* London: John Murray, 1853.

———. "Recent Expedition into the Interior of South-Western Africa." *Journal of the Royal Geographical Society* 22 (1852): 140–163.

Gibson, Alan G. S. *Between Capetown and Loanda: A Record of Two Journeys in South West Africa.* London: Wells, Gardner, Darton & Co., 1905.

Green, Lawrence G. *The Coast of Treasure.* Cape Town and London: Howard B. Timmons, 1932.

———. *At Daybreak for the Isles.* Cape Town: Howard B. Timmons, 1950.

———. *Old Africa Untamed.* London: Stanley Paul & Co., 1940.

———. *On Winds of Fire.* Cape Town: Howard B. Timmons, 1967.

———. *Panther Head: The Full Story of the Bird Islands off the Southern Coast of Africa.* London: Stanley Paul & Co., 1955.

Hardinge, Rex. *South African Cinderella: A Trek through ex–German West Africa [sic].* London: Herbert Jenkins, 1937.

Hartmann, Georg. *Meine Expedition 1900 ins Nördliche Kaokoveld und 1901 durch das Amboland.* Berlin: Wilhelm Süsserott, 1905.

Holub, Dr. Emil. *Seven Years in South Africa: Travels, Researches, and Hunting Adventures, Between the Diamond Fields and the Zambesi (1872–1879).* Translated by Ellen E. Frewer, 2 volumes. London: Sampson, Low, Marston, Searle, & Rivington, 1881.

Legendre, Sidney J. *Okavango, Desert River.* New York: Julian Messner, 1939. Reprinted: Negro Universities Press, 1971.

LeVaillant, Francois. *New Travels into the Interior Parts of Africa.* 3 volumes. London: G. G. and J. Robinson, 1796.

Martin, Henno. *The Sheltering Desert.* Translated from the German by Edward Fitzgerald. London: W. Kimber, 1957.

Mertens, Alice. *Namib: Photographs of the Namib Desert—South West Africa.* Johannesburg: Hugh Keartland Publishers, 1971.

———. *Kavango.* Cape Town (etc.): Purnell, 1974.

———. *South West Africa and Its Indigenous Peoples.* London: Collins, 1966.

Morrell, Capt. Benjamin, Jr. *Narrative of a Voyage to the South and West Coast of Africa . . . .* London: Whittaker and Company, 1844.

Oldevig, Margareta. *The Sunny Land.* London: Hodder and Stoughton, 1944.

Parker, Bill. *Via SWA.* Cape Town: South African Universities Press, 1979.

Paterson, William. *A Narrative of Four Journeys into the Country of the Hottentots and Caffraria in the Years 1777, 1778, 1779.* London: Johnson, 1790.

Ridsdale, Rev. Benjamin. *Scenes and Adventures in Great Namaqualand.* London: T. Woolmer, 1883.

Serton, Petrus, ed. *The Narrative and Journal of Gerald McKiernan in South West Africa, 1874–1879.* Cape Town: Van Riebeeck Society, 1954.

White, Jon Eubank Manchip. *The Land God Made in Anger: Reflections on a Journey through South West Africa.* Chicago: Rand McNally, 1969.

Zur Strassen, Helmut. *Game Trails in S.W.A.* [Schwabish Gmund:] Africa Verlag der Kreis, 1963.

————. *South West Africa.* Cape Town, London: Purnell & Sons, 1976.

————. *Land Between Two Deserts—South West Africa.* Cape Town: Purnell & Sons, 1971.

————. *Namib: Portrait of a Desert.* Cape Town, Johannesburg, London, New York: Purnell & Sons, 1973.

————. *South West Africa.* Cape Town: Purnell & Sons, 1976.

————. *Windhoek.* Cape Town: Purnell & Sons, 1975.

D. Bibliographies

Anderson, Irene. *Rock Paintings and Petroglyphs of South and Central Africa, 1959–1970: A Bibliography.* Johannesberg: University of Witwatersrand, 1971.

Archibald, Jane Erica. *The Works of Isaac Schapera: A Selective Bibliography.* Johannesburg: University of Witwatersrand, 1969.

Ball, Richard W. *The Earlier Stone Age in Southern Africa: A Bibliography.* Cape Town: University of Cape Town, 1964.

Bielschowsky, Ludwig. *List of Books in German on South Africa and South West Africa Published up to 1914 in the South Africa Public Library.* Cape Town: University of Cape Town, 1949.

Both, Ellen Lisa Marianne. *Catalogue of Books and Pamphlets published in German relating to South Africa and South West Africa as found in the South African Public Library published between 1950–1964.* Cape Town: University of Cape Town, 1969.

Botha, Laurette Isabella. *The Namib Desert: A Bibliography.* Cape Town: University of Cape Town Libraries, 1970.

Brownlee, Margaret. *The Lives and Work of South African Missionaries: A Bibliography.* Cape Town: University of Cape Town, 1952.

Craig, Barbara June. *Rock Paintings and Petroglyphs of South and Central Africa: Bibliography of Prehistoric Art.* Cape Town: University of Cape Town, 1947.

Cross, Sholto. *Namibian documents collection, prepared for the United Nations Institute for Namibia.* [Lusaka: United Nations Institute for Namibia], 1977.

Decalo, Samuel. *South West Africa 1960–1968: An Introductory Bibliography.* (Occasional Papers in Political Science No. 5), Kingston, R.I.: University of Rhode Island, 1968.

DeJager, Theo, comp., Brigitte Klaas, ed. *South West Africa/ Suidwes Afrika.* Pretoria: State Library, Bibliographies (No. 7), 1964.

De Lange, E. J. Roukens. *South West Africa, 1946–1960: A Selective Bibliography.* Cape Town: University of Cape Town, 1961.

Dugard, John. *The South West Africa/Namibia Dispute.* Berkeley and Los Angeles: University of California Press, 1973, 543–562.

Eriksen, Tore Linne. *The Political Economy of Namibia: An Annotated, Critical Bibliography.* Uppsala: The Scandinavian Institute of African Studies, 1985.

————. Revised, second edition, 1989.

Evborokhai, A. O., comp. *A descriptive list of United Nations reference documents on Namibia (1946–1978).* Lusaka: United Nations Institute for Namibia, 1978.

Fontoliett, Micheline, comp. *Bibliography on Namibia.* [Geneva]: Lutheran World Federation, 1976–1977. 4 volumes.

Hillebrecht, Werner. *Namibia in Theses and Dissertations.* Basel: Basler Afrika Bibliographien, 1985.

Kahn, Evelyn Ruth. *Karakul Sheep in South West Africa and South Africa: A Bibliography.* Cape Town: University of Cape Town, 1959.

Köhler, Jochen. *Deutsche Dissertation über Afrika: Ein Verzeichnis für die Jahre 1918–1959.* Bonn: Schroeder, 1962.

League of Nations, Library. *List of Works relating to the Mandate System and Territories under Mandate catalogued in the Library of the League of Nations.* Geneva: League of Nations, 1930.

Loening, Louise S. E. *A Bibliography of the Status of South-West Africa up to June 30th, 1951.* Cape Town: University of Cape Town, 1951.

Logan, Richard F. *Bibliography of South West Africa: Geography and Related Fields.* Scientific Research in South West Africa (8th Series). Windhoek: The committee of the S.W.A. Scientific Society, 1969.

Malan, Jocelyn Eleanor. *The Physical Anthropology of the Bushmen: Bibliography 1930–1962.* Cape Town: University of Cape Town, 1962.

Malan, Stephanus I. *Union Catalogue of theses and dissertations of the South African Universities 1942–1958.* Potchefstroom: University of Potchefstroom, 1959.

Martin, Henno. *A Bibliography of Geology and Allied Subjects, South West Africa.* Bulletin (I). Cape Town: University of Cape Town, Chamber of Mines Precambian Research Unit, 1965.

Minter, William. "Namibia: More than Diplomacy." (bibliographic essay) *Africa News* XVIII, No. 19 (May 10, 1982): 8–11.

Mokobane, Simon Rapule. *A Select Bibliography on South West Africa—Namibia.* Johannesburg: South African Institute of Race Relations, 1980.

Plaat, A. F. *List of Books and Pamphlets in German on South Africa and South West Africa published after 1914 as found in the South African Public Library, Cape Town.* Cape Town: University of Cape Town, 1951.

Pollak, Oliver B. and Karen Pollak. *Theses and Dissertations on Southern Africa: An International Bibliography.* Boston: G. K. Hall, 1976.

Poller, Robert Manfred. *Swakopmund and Walvis Bay: A Bibliography.* Cape Town; University of Cape Town, 1964.

Rogers, Barbara L. "Namibia" in El-Khawas, Mohamed and Francis A. Kornegay, eds. *American–Southern African Relations: Bibliographic Essays.* African Bibliographic Center,

Special Bibliographic Series, New Series, No. 1. Westport, CT: Greenwood Press, 1975.

Rosenkranz, Ingrid. *Rock Paintings and Petroglyphs of South and Central Africa 1947–1958: Bibliography.* Cape Town: University of Cape Town, 1958.

Roukens de Lange, E. J., comp. *South West Africa, 1946–1960: a selective bibliography.* Cape Town: University of Cape Town, School of Librarianship, 1961.

Schapera, I. "The Present State and Future Development of Ethnographical Research in South Africa: Select Bibliography," *Bantu Studies: A Journal devoted to the Scientific Study of Bantu, Hottentot and Bushmen* 8, No. 3 (September 1934): 280–342.

Schlettwein, Carl. "Bibliographie Südwest-afrika (Namibia), 1971." *Mitteilungen der Basler Afrika bibliographien* Communications from the Basel Africa Bibliography, 2/3. Basel: Basler Africa Bibliography, 1972, 17–74.

Schoeman, Elna. *The Namibian Issue, 1920–1980.* Boston: G. K. Hall, 1982.

———. *South West Africa/Namibia: An International Issue 1920–1977. A Select Bibliography.* Braamfontein: South African Institute of International Affairs, 1978.

Schoeman, Stanley, and Elna Schoeman. *Namibia.* Santa Barbara, CA, and Oxford: Clio Press, 1984.

Spohr, Otto Hartung. *Catalogue of Books, Pamphlets and Periodicals published in German relating to South Africa and South-West Africa, as Found in the Jagger Library, University of Cape Town.* Cape Town: University of Cape Town, 1948.

Spohr, Otto H., and Manfred R. Poller, comps. *German Africana: German Publications on South and South West Africa.* Pretoria: The State Library, 1968.

Stich, H. *South West Africa: List of Books in German and English published up to 1918.* Cape Town: University of Cape Town, 1955.

Strohmeyer, Eckhard. "Namibische National Bibliographie 1971–1975/Namibian National Bibliography 1971–1975." *Mitteilungen der Basler Afrika Bibliographien/Communications from the Basel Africa Bibliography* 20. Basel: Basler Afrika Bibliographien, 1978.

———. *NNB: Namibische National Bibliographie—Namibian National Bibliography, 1976–1977—* Basel: Basler Afrika Bibliographien, 1979 (Appears Annually).

———. *Umfassende Bibliographie der Volker Namibiens (Südwestafrikas) und Südwestangolas = Comprehensive Bibliography of the Peoples of Namibia (South West Africa) and Southwestern Angola.* Band 2 (vol. 2). Karben: Strohmeyer, 1982.

Strohmeyer, Eckhard and Walter Moritz. *Comprehensive Bibliography of the Peoples of Namibia (South West Africa) and Southwestern Angola.* Starnberg, Germany: Max Planck-Institut, 1975. (Originally published in German in Kampala, Uganda.)

———, comps. *Umfassende Bibliographie der Völker Namibiens (Südwestafrikas) und Südwestangolas.* Starnberg: Max Planck-Institute, 1975.

Tötemeyer, Gerhard. *Südafrika, Südwestafrika/South Africa, South West Africa: Eine Bibliographie/A Bibliography 1945–1963.* Freiburg im Breisgau: Arnold Bergstrasser Institut fur Kulturwissenschaftliche Forschung, 1964.

Vogt, Martin. "Bibliographical Aids for Studies on South West Africa." *Mitteilungen der Basler Afrika Bibliographien/ Communications from the Basel Africa Bibliography* 13. Basel: Basler Afrika Bibliographien, 1975.

Voigts, Barbara Hedwig Luise. *South West African Imprints: A Bibliography*. Cape Town: University of Cape Town, 1963.

Welch, Floretta J. *South-West Africa: A Bibliography*, Cape Town: University of Cape Town, 1967.

Willet, Shelagh M. *The Bushman: A Select Bibliography 1652–1962*. Johannesburg: University of Witwatersrand, 1965.

2. CULTURAL

A. Archaeology

Clark, J. D. "Reflections on the Significance of Prehistoric Cultural Influences in S.W.A." *South African Museum Association Bulletin* (Sept. 1959): 37–45.

Clark, J. Desmond and James Walton. "A Late Stone Age Site in the Erongo Mountains, South West Africa." *Prehistoric Society, Proceedings* (New Series), 28 (1962): 1–16.

Fock, G. J. "Survey of Archaeological Research in South West Africa." *South African Archaeological Bulletin* 14, No. 53 (March 1959): 9–17.

Gevers, T. W. "Ice Ages in South West Africa," *Journal of the S.W.A. Wissenschaftlichen Gesellschaft* Band V, 1929–1931.

Kinahan, John. *Pastoral Nomads of the Central Namib Desert*. Windhoek: Namibia Archaeological Trust, New Namibia Books, 1991.

Korn, H. and H. Martin. "The Pleistocene in South West Africa." *Pan-African Congress on Prehistory* 3 (1955): 14–22.

MacCalman, H. R. "Carbon 14 Dates from South West Africa." *South African Archaeological Bulletin* 20 (1965): 215.

———. "The Otjinungwa Valley Site: A Middle Stone Age

Occurrence on the South West Africa/Angola Border."
Cimbebasia/SWA Research. Series B, Vol. 2, No. 2 (1
October 1972): 65–80.

Rudner, I. "The Brandberg and Its Archaeological Remains."
Journal of The South West African Scientific Society 12
(1956–1957): 7–44.

―――. "Some Stone Implements from Northern S.W.A.," *South
African Archaeological Bulletin* (Dec. 1952): 155–161.

Sandelowsky, B. H. and A. Viereck. "Supplementary Report on
the Archaeological Expedition of 1962 to the Erongo Mountains of South West Africa." *Cimbebasia* Series B, Vol. 1,
No. 1 (March 26, 1969): 1–43.

―――. "Archaeology in Namibia." *American Scientist* 71
(1983): 606–615.

Sydow, W. "Erongo Expedition," *SWA Scientific Society News-
letter/Mitteilungen* 38 (1962).

Viereck, Albert. "The Archaeology of Neuhof-Kowas, South
West Africa." *South African Archaeological Bulletin* 12,
No. 45 (March 1957): 32–36.

―――. "Erongo Expedition der S.W.A. Wissengesellschaftli-
chen Gesellschaft." *Journal of the SWA Scientific Society.*
Special Publication 2 (June 1962).

―――. "Some Relics from South West Africa." *South African
Archaeological Bulletin* 14, No. 55 (Sept. 1959).

Wadley, L. "Radiocarbon dates from Big Elephant Shelter,
Erongo Mountains, South West Africa." *South African
Archaeological Bulletin* 31, No. 123/124 (Dec. 1976): 146.

Wayland, E. J. "From an Archaeological Notebook," *South
African Archaeological Bulletin* 5, No. 17 (March 1950):
4–14.

Wendt, W. E. "Notes on Some Unusual Artifacts from South West Africa." *Cimbebasia* Ser 3, Vol. 2, No. 6 (29 August 1975): 179–186.

──────. "Preliminary Report on an Archaeological Research Programme in South West Africa." *Cimbebasia: S.W.A. Research* Ser. B, Vol. 2, No. 1 (31 July 1972): 1–61.

B. Fine Arts

1. Rock Art

Baard, Eline. "The 'White Lady' of Kalkoenkrans." *South African Journal of Science* 66 (5) (May 1970): 151–154.

Battiss, Walter W. *The Artists of the Rocks.* Pretoria: Red fawn Press, 1948.

──────. "New Art and Old Art in South Africa." *The Studio* 144, No. 714 (1952): 66–75.

Boyle, Mary E. "The Redhaired People in the Rock Paintings of South-West Africa," *Journal of the S.W.A. Scientific Society* 8: 5–10.

Breuil, Henri. "The Age and the Authors of the Painted Rocks of Austrial Africa." *South African Archaeological Bulletin* 4, No. 13 (1949): 19–27.

──────. "Carbon Tests and South West African Paintings." *South African Archaeological Bulletin* 9, No. 34 (1954): 48.

──────. "Further Details of Rock Paintings and Other Discoveries." *South African Archaeological Bulletin* 6, No. 22 (1951): 46–50.

──────. "The Influence of Classical Civilisations on the Cave Paintings of South Africa." pp. 234–347. In Leakey, L. S. B., *Proceedings of the Pan-African Congress on Prehistory, Nairobi, 1947.* Oxford: Blackwell, 1952.

————. "Remains of Large Animals Paintings in South-West Africa, Older than All the Other Frescoes." *South African Archaeological Bulletin* 4, No. 13 (1949): 14–18.

————. "Rock Paintings: South West Africa. Translation by Mary Boyle; Ed. by C. van Riet Lowe. Johannesburg: Archaeological Survey, 1949.

————. "Rock Paintings of South Africa." *Anthropological Quarterly (1954): 31–42.*

————. *The Rock Paintings of Southern Africa.* 6 vols. Paris: Trianon (1966–1975).

————. "The So-Called Bushman Art: Paintings and Engravings on Rock in South Africa and the Problems They Suggest," *Man* 46 (1946): 84.

————. "Some Foreigners in the Frescoes on Rocks in Southern Africa." *The South African Archaeological Bulletin* 4, No. 14 (1949): 39–49.

————. "What Secret Does the 'White Lady' Hold?" *South West Africa Annual,* 1948.

————. "The White Lady of the Brandberg (S. W. Africa), Her Companions and Her Guards." *The South African Archaeological Bulletin* III, No. 9 (1948): 2–11.

Fritsch, G. "Rock Paintings Existing near Ameib in Damaraland, South Africa." *Cape Monthly Magazine* Vol. 18 (1879): 198–204.

Harding, J. R. "Interpreting the 'White Lady' Rock Painting of South West Africa: Some Considerations." *South African Archaeological Bulletin* 23, No. 90 (August 1968): 31–34.

Holub, Dr. Emil. *Felsgravierungen der Südafrikanischen Buschmänner.* Leipzig: F. A. Brockhaus, 1925.

Johnson, R. Townley. *Major Rock Paintings of Southern Africa.* Edited by Tim Maggs. Bloomington: Indiana University Press, 1980.

Levinson, Olga. "Cave Walls Were their Canvases (Rock Paintings in S.W.A.)." *Outspan* 50, No. 1294 (Dec. 14, 1951): 57+.

Maack, Reinhard. "Die 'Weisse Dame' vom Brandberg: Bemerkungen zu den Felsmalereien des paläolithischen Kulturkreises in Südwest-Afrika." *Ethnologica N.F.* 3 (1966): 1–84.

Mason, Revil. "New Prehistoric Paintings in the Brandberg, South West Africa, and the Waterberg, Northern Transvaal." In *Lantern* [Journal of Knowledge and Culture, Pretoria] VII, No. 4 (June 1958): 357–368.

Obermaier, Hugo and Herbert Kühn. *Bushman Art: Rock Paintings of South-West Africa,* Based on the photographic material collected by Reinhard Maack. London, New York, Toronto, Melbourne, Cape Town, Bombay: Humphrey Milford/Oxford University Press, 1930.

Rudner, I., and J. Rudner. "Who Were the Artists? archaeological notes from South-West Africa." *The South African Archaeological Bulletin* No. 55 (1959): 106–108.

Rudner, Jalmar, and Ione Rudner. *The Hunter and His Art: A Survey of Rock Art in Southern Africa.* Pasadena, CA: Munger Africana Library, Cape Town, 1970.

Scheben, L. H. D. "Sites and Engravings in Namaqualand, South-West Africa," *South African Archaeological Bulletin* 3, No. 10 (1948): 31–32.

South African National Gallery. *Art in South West Africa/Kuns in Suidwes-Afrika.* Cape Town: South African National Gallery, n.d. [c. 1963].

Tongue, M. Helen. *Bushman Paintings.* Oxford: Clarendon Press, 1909.

Viereck, A. and Jalmer Rudner. "Twyfelfontein—A Centre of Praehistoric Art in South-West Africa." *South African Archaeological Bulletin* 12, No. 45 (1957): 15–26.

Walton, James. "South-West African Rock Paintings and the Triple-Curved Bow." *South African Archaeological Bulletin* 9, No. 36 (1954): 131–134.

Weyersberg, Maria. "Bushman Paintings in South-West." *Journal of the South West Africa Scientific Society* V (1929–1931): 55–63.

2. Other Fine Arts

Arnott, B. *John Muafangejo: Linocuts, Woodcuts and Etchings.* Cape Town: C. Struik, 1977.

England, N. M. "Bushmen Counterpoint." *International Folk Music Council Journal* 19 (1967): 58–66.

Jentsch, Adolpf. *Südwestafrikanische Aquarelle/Suidwest Afrikaanse Waterverftekeninge/South West African Watercolours.* Ed. by Otto Schröder. Swakopmund: Ferdinand Stich, 1959.

Le Vaillant, Francois. *Francois le Vaillant: Traveller in South Africa; and His Collection of 165 Water-colour Paintings, 1781–1784.* 2 Vols. Cape Town: Library of Parliament, 1973.

Levinson, Olga. *Adolph Jentsch.* Cape Town: Human and Rousseau, 1974, second edition 1982.

———. "Art Through the Ages." In *Story of Namibia.* Cape Town: Tafelberg Publishers (1978): 129–136.

————. *Our First Thirty Years: The History of the South African Association of Arts (S.W.A.).* S.A. Association of Arts, S.W.A., 1979.

Loeb, Edwin. "Courtship and the Lovesong." *Anthropos* 45 (1950): 821–851.

Rudner, Jalmar. "Three Carved Stone Heads." *South African Archaeological Bulletin* 101 (1971).

Sandelowsky, Erwin. *Anekdoten, Lieder mit Noten und die alten Geschichten von Deutsch-Südwestafrika.* 6th Ed. Windhoek: John Meinert, 1973.

Sydow, W. *The Pre-European Pottery of South West Africa.* Cimbebasia Memoir No. 1. Windhoek: State Museum, 1967.

Volger, Hans. "Bauten: Architektur gestern—heute—morgen und Zeitgemasser Wohnungsbau'." *Journal of the S.W.A. Scientific Society* IV (1928–1929): 29–49.

C. Linguistics

1. General

Baucom, K. L. "More on the Indigenous Languages of South West Africa." *Anthropological Linguistics* 12, No. 9 (1970): 343–348.

Bleek, W. H. I. *A Comparative Grammar of South African Languages.* 2 Vol. London: Trübner, 1862/1869.

Stanley, George E. "The Indigenous Languages of South West Africa." *Anthropological Linguistics* 10, No. 3 (1968): 5–18.

2. San

Bleek, Dorothea Francis. *A Bushman Dictionary.* New Haven: American Oriental Society, 1956.

———. "Bushman Terms of Relationship." *Bantu Studies* (1924).

———. *Comparative Vocabularies of Bushman Languages.* Cambridge: Cambridge University Press, 1929.

———. *The Distribution of Bushman Languages in South Africa.* Hamburg und Glückstadt: Festschrift Meinhof, 1927.

Doke, Clement Martyn. "An Outline of the Phonetics of the Language of the Chu Bushmen of Northwest Kalahari." *Bantu Studies* 2 (1925): 129–166.

Snyman, J. W. *An Introduction to the !Xu (!Kung) language.* Cape Town: Balkema, 1970.

South West Africa. Department of Education. *!Xu* (a Bushman language). Orthography No. 1, 1969.

Traill, A., ed. *Bushman and Hottentot Linguistic Studies.* Johannesburg: University of Witwatersrand, African Studies Institute, 1978.

———, ed. *Khoisan Linguistic Studies 3.* Johannesburg: University of Witwatersrand, African Studies Institute, 1977.

3. Damara

Klein, H. E. M. "Tense and Aspect in the Damara Verbal System." *African Studies* 35, No. 3/4 (1976): 207–227.

South West Africa. Department of Education. *Nama/Damara Orthography.* No. 1, [Windhoek]: Department of Education, 1970.

Vedder, Heinrich. *Die Spruchweisheit der Bergdama.* Barmen Rhenisch Missionary Society, 1921.

4. Herero

Brincker, Peter Heinrich. *Wörterbuch und Kurzgefasste Grammatik des Otji-Hérero.* Leipzig: Weigel, 1886.

Gestwicki, Rev. and Mrs. Ronald (comp.). *An English-Herero, Herero-English Dictionary.* Windhoek: Anglican Church, 1966.

Hahn, Carl Hugo L. *Grundzüge einer grammatik des Hereró (im westlichen Afrika) nebst einem Wörtebuche.* Berlin: Wilhelm Hertz, 1857.

Irle, J. *Deutsch-Herero-Wörterbuch.* Hamburg: Friederichsen, 1917.

Kolbe, F. W. *An English-Herero Dictionary.* Cape Town: Junta, 1883. Also London: 1883.

South West Africa. Department of Education. *Herero Orthography.* No. 1, [Windhoek]: Department of Education, 1968.

Vedder, Heinrich. *Die Spruchweisheit der Herero.* Barmen: Rhenisch Missionary Society, 1921.

Viehe, G. *Unter den Hereros.* Barmen: Rhenisch Missionary Society, 1890.

————. *Grammatik des Otjiherero*, Vol. 16 of *Lehrbücher der Seminars für orientalische Sprachen zu Berlin*. Stuttgart: 1897.

————. *Grammatik der Otjiherero, nebst Wörterbuch*. Berlin: G. Reimer, 1897.

5. Nama

Hahn, Theophilus. *Die Sprache der Nama, nebst einen Anhange enthaltend Sprachproben aus dem Munde des Volkes*. Leipzig: Barth, 1870.

Jeffreys, M. D. W. "Origin of the Name Hottentot." *African Affairs* (July 1947): 163–165.

Krönlein, J. G. *Nama Worterbuch*. Rev. and Ed. by F. Rust. Pietermaritzburg: University of Natal Press, 1969.

————. *Wortschatz der Khoi-Khoin*. Berlin: 1889.

Maingard, L. F. "The Origin of the Word 'Hottentot'." *Bantu Studies* 9, No. 1 (March 1935): 63–67.

Nienaber, G. S. "The Origin of the Name 'Hottentot'." *African Studies* 22, No. 2, (1963): 65–90.

Olpp, Johannes. *Nama-deutsches Wörterbuch*. Elberfeld: Friederichs, 1888.

Planert, Wilhelm. *Handbuch der Nama-Sprache in Deutsch-Südwestafrika*. Berlin: Reimer, 1905.

Rust, Friederich. *Praktische Namagramma tik: Auf Grund der*

Namagrammatiken von H. Vedder und J. Olpp. Cape Town, Amsterdam: A. A. Balkema, 1965.

Tindall, Rev. Henry. *A Grammar and Vocabulary of the Namaqua-Hottentot Language.* Cape Town: 1857.

Vedder, Heinrich. *Semitische Lehnworte in der Namasprache.* Swakopmund: 1909.

————. *Die Wortbildungsgesetze der Namasprache.* Swakopmund: 1909.

————. *Versuch einer Grammatik der Namasprache.* Swakopmund: 1909.

6. Ovambo

Baucom, K. L. "The Phonology of Proto-Wambo." *African Studies* 34 (1975): 165–184.

South West Africa. Department of Education. *Kwanyama Orthography.* No. 1, Windhoek: Department of Education, 1966.

South West Africa. Department of Education. *Ndonga Orthography.* No. 1, Windhoek: Department of Education.

Tobias, G. W. R., and B. H. C. Turvey. *English-Kwanyama Dictionary.* Johannesburg: Witwatersrand University Press, 1954.

Turvey, B. H. C., comp. *Kwanyama-English Dictionary.* Ed. by W. Zimmermann and G. B. Taapopi. Johannesburg: Witwatersrand University Press, 1977.

D. Literature

1. General

Held, Toni von. *Märchen und Sagen der Afrikanischen Neger.* Jena: 1904.

Melber, Henning, ed. *It Is No More a Cry: Namibia Poetry in Exile.* Basel: Basler Afrika Bibliographien, 1982.

St. Lys, Odette, comp. *From a Vanished German Colony: A Collection of Folklore, Folk Tales and Proverbs from South-West Africa.* London: Gypsy Press, n.d. [c. 1916].

2. San

Biesele, M. *!Kung Folklore.* Cambridge, MA: Harvard University Press.

Bleek, Dorothea. *The Naron, A Bushman Tribe on the Central Kalahari.* Cambridge: Cambridge University Press, 1928.

―――. "Bushman Folklore." *Africa* II, No. 3 (July 1929): 302–313.

―――. "!Kung Mythology," *Zeitschrift für Eingeborenen-Sprachen* XXV (1934–1935): 261–283.

―――, ed. *The Mantis and His Friends: Bushman Folklore.* Collected by the late Dr. W. H. I. Bleek and the late Dr. Lucy C. Lloyd. Cape Town: T. Maskero Miller. London and Oxford: Basil Blackwell Ltd., [1923].

Bleek, W. H. I., and L. C. Lloyd. *Specimens of Bushman Folklore.* London: George Allen and Company, 1911.

Bleek, W. H. I. *A Brief Account of Bushman Folk-lore and other Texts.* Cape Town: J. C. Juta; London: Trübner & Co.; Leipzig: F. A. Brockhaus, 1875.

————. *Reynard the Fox in South Africa; or Hottentot Fables and Tales.* London: Trübner & Co., 1864.

Burton, William Frederick Padwich. "Bushman Folklore." *Folk-Lore Journal* II, No. 3 (May 1880): 39–43.

Helfman, Elizabeth S. *The Bushmen and Their Stories.* New York: Seabury, 1971.

Seed, Jenny. *The Bushman's Dream: African Tales of Creation.* Scarsdale, NY: Bradbury Press, 1974.

Thomas, Elizabeth Marshall. *Bushman Stories.* Cape Town and London: 1950.

3. Herero

Beiderbecke, H. "A Herero Legend, The Fleeing Girls and the Rock." *Folk-Lore Journal* II, No. 5 (Sept. 1880): 76–85.

Buttner, Carl Gotthilf. "Märchen der Obaherero." *Zeitschrift für Afrikanische Sprachen* I (1887–1888): 206ff.

Hahn, C. H. "Herero Sayings or Proverbs." *Folk-Lore Journal* I, No. 6 (Nov. 1879): 146–147.

For a bibliography of items in the Herero language, see Vedder's bibliography in Hahn, et al., *The Native Tribes of South West Africa.* Cape Town: Cape Times Ltd., 1928, p. 211.

4. Nama

Baumann, C. "Nama-Texte." *Zeitschrift für Kolonialsprachen* VI (1915): 55–78.

Bain, Thomas. "The Lion and the Jackal, A Hottentot Story." *Folk-Lore Journal* II, No. 4 (July 1880): 53–57.

Hahn, C. H. *Tsuni-Goam.* London: 1882.

Marais, Josef. *Koos the Hottentot.* New York: 1945.

For a selection of items in the Nama language, see Vedder's bibliography of the Nama in Hahn, et al., *The Native Tribes of South West Africa.* Cape Town: Cape Times Ltd., 1928, pp. 151–152.

5. Ovambo

Dammann, E., and T. E. Tirronen. *Ndonga-Anthologie.* Berlin: Reimer, 1975.

Kuusi, M. *Ovambo Riddles: With comments and vocabularies.* Helsinki: Suomalainen Tiedeak atemia Academia Scientarium Fennica, 1974.

Larson, Thomas J. "Epic Tales of the Mbukushu." *African Studies* 22 (1964): 176–189.

Loeb, Edwin Meyer. "Kuanyama Ambo Folklore." *Anthropological Records* 13, No. 4 (1951): 289–335.

Stefaniszyn, B. "Clan Jest of the Ambo." *NADA, Native Affairs Department Annual* No. 28 (1951): 94–107.

————. "The Hunting Songs of the Ambo." *African Studies* 10, No. 1 (March 1951): 1–12.

6. German

Holst, Meno. *Dieter und Hans im Amboland: Erzählung aus Deutsch-Südwest.* Potsdam: Ludwig Voggenreiter Verlag, 1943.

Kaempffer, Adolf. *Kitt gen Mitternacht: Roman aus Deutsch-Südwest-Afrika.* Braunsschweig, Berlin, Hamburg: George Westermann, 1939.

————. *Robert und der Hottentott.* Bad Godesberg: Voggenreiter Verlag, 1951.

————. *Roiland der Wanderer: Geschichte eines afrikanischen Treckochsen.* Bad Godesberg: Voggenreiter Verlag, 1950.

Schönhoff, Heinz-Oskar. *Mit Planwagen durch Deutsch-Südwest.* Stuttgart: Kosmos, 1940.

Spiesser, Fritz. *Schicksal Afrika: ein Kolonialroman.* München: Zentralverlag der NSDAP, 3 Auflage, 1942.

Voigt, Bernhard. *Das Herz der Wildnis: Ein Roman aus Deutsch-Südwest-Afrikas ersten Tagen.* Berlin: Safari-Verlag, 1940.

3. ECONOMIC

A. General Economy and Development, pre-1960

Dernburg, Bernhard. *Südwestafrikanische Eindrücke. Industrielle Fortschritte in den Kolonien.* Berlin: Ernst Siegfried Mittler und Sohn, 1909.

Great Britain, Department of Overseas Trade. *Report on the Conditions and Prospects of Trade in the Protectorate of*

South-West Africa. By J. L. Wilson Goode, H. M. Trade Commissioner at Cape Town, Command Paper 842, London: H. M. Stationery Office, 1920.

Krogh, D. C. "The Economic Relations between the Union of South Africa and South West Africa, with Special Reference to the Implications of Complete Integration." *Finance and Trade Review* 3, No. 5 (1959): 294–304.

————. "The National Income and Expenditure of South-West-Africa, 1920–1950," *South African Journal of Economics* 28, No. 1 (March 1960): 3–22.

Leistner. G. M. E. "Public Finance in South West Africa, 1945/46 to 1969/70." *South African Journal of Economics* 40 (1972): 1–32.

South West Africa. *Accounts of the Administration of South West Africa for the Financial Year . . . , Together with the Report of the Controller and Auditor-General Thereon.* Windhoek: John Meinert Limited, Government Printers, Annual.

Valentin, Viet. "The Germans in South-West Africa, 1883–1914: Civil Administration and Economic Conditions." Pp. 702–709. In A. P. Newton and E. A. Benians, eds. *The Cambridge History of the British Empire.* Vol. VIII, *South Africa, Rhodesia and the Protectorates.* Cambridge: Cambridge University Press, 1936.

B. General Economy and Development, post–1960

Collett, Sue. *The Economy of South West Africa: Current Conditions and Some Future Prospects.* Johannesburg: n.p., 1978.

————. "The Human Factor in the Economic Development of Namibia." *Optima* 28, No. 4 (1979): 190–219.

Green, Reginald Herbold. *From Südwestafrika to Namibia: The*

Political Economy of Transition. Research Report No. 58. Uppsala: Scandinavian Institute of African Studies, 1981.

—————. *Manpower Estimates and Development Implications for Namibia.* Ed. by N. K. Duggal. Lusaka: United Nations Institute for Namibia, 1978.

—————. *Namibia: A Political Economic Survey.* (Institute of Development Studies Discussion Paper No. 144). Brighton: University of Sussex, 1979.

—————, Marja-Lisa Kiljunen, Kimmo Kiljunen. *Namibia—The Last Colony.* Burnt Mill, Harlow, Essex: Longman, 1982.

Krough. D. C. "S.W.A.: Economic Change and Political Deadlock." *Africa* (Johannesburg) 1, No. 1 (May/July 1965): 48–68.

Leistner, G. M. E. "South West Africa's Economic Bonds with South Africa." *Africa Institute Bulletin* 9 (1971): 111–122.

Moorsom, R. *Walvis Bay: Namibia's Port.* London: IDAF, 1984.

Morna, Colleen Lowe. "Bridging the Gap." *Africa Report* 36, No. 3 (May–June 1991): 24–27.

—————. "The Development Challenge." *Africa Report* 35, No. 1, (March–April, 1990): 29–31.

"Namibia's Political Economy, 1978/9," Africa Bureau *Fact Sheet,* No. 60 (July/August 1979), entire issue.

Rogers, Barbara. "Namibia: economic and Other Aspects." *Southern Africa* 2 (1973): 117–136.

Rotberg, Robert I., ed. *Namibia: Political and Economic Prospects.* Lexington, MA: D.C. Heath/Lexington Books, 1982.

Schneider-Barthold, Wolfgang. *Namibia's Economic Potential and Existing Economic Ties with the Republic of South Africa.* Berlin: German Development Institute, 1977.

Setai, Bethuel. *A Statement on the Development Strategy for Namibia: A Preliminary Report.* Lusaka: United Nations Institute for Namibia, 1978.

Sparks, Donald L., and Roger Murray. *Namibia's Future: The Economy at Independence.* (E.I.U. Special Report, No. 197). London: The Economist Intelligence Unit, 1985.

Thomas, Wolfgang H. *Economic Development in Namibia.* München: Kaiser Verlag. Mainz: Grunewald, 1978.

————. *The Economic Implications of Independence for South West Africa.* Bellville: University of the Western Cape, Institute for Social Development, 1976.

Transforming a Wasted Land. A Future for Namibia Series. London: CIIR, 1982.

Weigend, Guido G. "Economic Activity Patterns in White Namibia.C *Geographical Review* 75, No. 4 (1985): 462–481.

C. Agriculture

Boetticher, Gerhard. *Die Landwirtschaftlichen Produktions—und Siedlungsverhältnisse in Südwestafrika vor und nach dem Weltkrieg.* Breslau: Hochschul-Verlag Breslau, 1930.

Holstein, Christine. *Deutsche Frau in Südwest: Den Erlebnissen einer Farmersfrau im heutigen Afrika nächerzahlt.* Leipzig: Kohler & Amelang, [1937].

Karow, Marie. *Wo sonst der Fuss des Kriegers trat: Farmerleben in Südwest nach dem Kriege.* Berlin: Ernst Siegfried Mittler und Sohn, 1909.

Mshonga, S. *Toward Agrarian Reform: Policy Options for Namibia.* Lusaka: United Nations Institute for Namibia, 1979.

Schlettwein, Carl. *Der Farmer in Deutsch-Sudwest-Afrika.* Wismar: Hintstorff, 1907.

Schmokel, Wolfe W. "The Myth of the White Farmer: Commercial Agriculture in Namibia, 1900–1983." *International Journal of African Historical Studies* 18, No. 1 (?): 93–108.

D. Mining

Dabreo, S. "South West Africa's Mineral Boom." *African Development* (December 1971).

DeVilliers, Cas., ed. *Southern Africa: The Politics of Raw Materials: A Selection of Papers Delivered at a Conference of the Foreign Affairs Assoc., Hamburg, June 1977.* Pretoria: Foreign Affairs Assoc., 1977.

Diamonds from the Desert. Johannesburg: Consolidated Diamond Mines of South West Africa, Ltd., 1956.

Die Deutschen Diamanten und ihre Gewinnung. Berlin: Dietrich Reimer, Ernst Vohsen, 1914.

Duggal, N. K., ed. *Namibia: Legal Framework and Development Strategy Options for the Mining Industry.* Lusaka, Zambia: United Nations Institute for Namibia, 1987.

Fischer, Jean. "Rössing—Namib Desert Mining Giant," *South West Africa Annual* (1970): 145–149.

Jepson, Trevor B. *Rio Tinto-Zinc in Namibia.* London: Christian Concern for Southern Africa, 1976.

Kaiser, Erich, ed. *Die Diamantenwüste Südwestafrikas.* 2 Vols. Berlin: Reimer, 1926.

Leutwein, Paul. *Die Leistungen der Regierung in der Sudwestafrikanischen Land und Minenfrage.* Cothen: Paul Dunnhaupt, 1911.

Levinson, Olga. *Diamonds in the Desert: The Story of August Stauch and His Times.* Cape Town: Tafelberg, 1983.

Mines and Independence. A Future for Namibia Series. CIIR, 1983.

Murray, Roger. *The Mineral Industry and Namibia: Perspectives for Independence.* London: HMSO, 1978.

————. *Namibia: An Initial Survey of the Pattern of Expropriation of the Mineral Resources of Namibia by the South African Government and Overseas Companies.* London: Africa Bureau, 1971.

Roberts, Alun. *The Rössing File: The Inside Story of Britain's Secret Contract for Namibian Uranium.* London: Campaign against the Namibian Uranium Contract, 1980.

Rohrback, Paul. *Dernburg und Die Südwest Afrikaner: Diamantenfrage, Selbstverwaltung, Landeshilfe.* Berlin: Deutscher Kolonialverlag (G. Meinecke), 1911.

Seeger, Gerd. "Gemstones of Namibia." *Rössing* (June 1980).

Sohnge, G. *Tsumeb: A Historical Sketch.* Windhoek: S.W.A. Scientific Society, 1967.

South Africa (Republic), Commission of Enquiry into the Diamond Industry of the Republic of South Africa and the Territory of South West Africa. *Report.* Pretoria: Government Printer, 1973.

"Tantalite Mining" [Tantalite Valley Minerals (Pty) Ltd.], *Mining Magazine* 117 (December 1967): 443+.

Voeltz, Richard A. *German Colonialism and the South West Africa Company, 1894–1914.* Athens, OH: Ohio University Center for International Studies, 1988.

Wagner, Percy Albert. *The Diamond Fields of Southern Africa.* Cape Town: C. Struik, 1971.

Williams, Alpheus F. *Some Dreams Come True.* Cape Town: Howard B. Timmins, [1948].

E. Furs

Krogh, D. C. "Economic Aspects of the Karakul Industry in South West Africa," *Southern African Journal of Economics* 23 (1955): 99–113.

————. *The Karakul Industry in S.W.A. with Special Reference to the Marketing of Karakul Pelts.* Windhoek: S.W.A. Karakul Advisory Industry Board in conjunction with the S.W.A. Scientific Society, [1954].

Nobbs, Eric Arthur. "A Note on the History of the Karakul Breed of Sheep in South-West Africa," *Archives Year Book for South Africa* 5, Pt. 2 (1943): 267–272.

Zur Strassen, Helmut. *The Fur Seal of Southern Africa.* [Cape Town]: Howard Timmins, 1971.

F. Fishing

Bull, O. E. "When Walvis Was Whaling," *South West Africa Annual* (1968): 77, 79, 81.

Exploiting the Sea. A Future for Namibia Series. Catholic Institute for International Relations, 1984.

Schultze, Dr. Leonhard. *Die Fischerei an der Westküste Süd-Afrikas*. Berlin: Salle, 1907.

South West Africa Administration, Marine Research Laboratory. *Investigational Reports*. Windhoek: No. 1–16, 1960–1969.

Sparks, Donald L. "Namibia's Coastal and Marine Resources Potential." African Affairs, the Journal of the Royal African Society, 334 (January, 1985): 477–496.

G. Miscellaneous Industry and Development

Gill, Fraser, ed. *Cohen of South West Africa: Dedicated to the 50th Anniversary of the Sam Cohen Enterprise in South West Africa*. Windhoek: South West Africa Commercial Holdings, Ltd., 1956.

Moir, S. M., and H. T. Crittenden. *Namib Narrow Gauge*. Chicago: Owen Davies, [1967].

Seymour, John. "Hunters, Herder, and Farmers in South-West Africa." *The Geographical Magazine* 23, No. 10 (February 1951): 470–482.

H. Water Development

Murray, Roger. "Cunene Scheme: A Focus for Confrontation." *African Development* 9, No. 11 (November 1975): 31–33.

South Africa, Department of Bantu Administration and Development. "South West Africa and Some Water Schemes, Past and Present." *BaNtu* 7 (1960): 637–645.

South West Africa, Department of Water Affairs. *Underground Water in South West Africa*. Windhoek: The Department, 1978.

World Council of Churches, Programme to Combat Racism.

Cunene Dam Scheme and the struggle for liberation of Southern Africa. Geneva: The Council, 1971.

I. Labor, Contracts, and Strikes

Anderson, Neil and Shula Marks. "Work and Health in Namibia's Preliminary Notes." *Journal of South African Studies* 13 (1987): 274–292.

Cronje, Gillian, and Suzanne Cronje. *The Workers of Namibia.* London: International Defense and Aid Fund for Southern Africa, 1979.

Dekker, L. Douwes, et al. "Case Studies in African Labour Action in South and South west Africa." *African Review* 4 (1974): 205–236.

Gebhardt, F. B. "The Socio-economic Status of Farm Labourers in Namibia." *South African Labour Bulletin* 4, Nos. 1/2 (Jan–Feb 1978): 145–173.

Gordon, Robert J. *Mines, Masters and Migrants: Life in a Namibian Mine Compound.* Johannesburg: Raven Press, 1977.

———. "A Note on the History of Labour Action in Namibia." *South African Labour Bulletin* 1, No. 10 (April 1975): 7–17.

———. "A Rite of Worker Solidarity in a Colonial Mine Compound: An Analysis of a Namibian 'Tribal Fight'." Pp. 51–70. In Robert J. Gordon and Brett Williams, eds. *Exploring Total Institutions.* Champaign, IL: 1977.

———. "Some Organisational Aspects of Labour Protest amongst Contract Workers in Namibia." *South African Labour Bulletin (Durban)* 4, Nos. 1/2 (Jan–Feb 1978): 116–123.

———. "Variations in Migration Rates: The Ovambo Case," *Journal of Southern African Affairs* 3, No. 3 (July 1978): 261–294.

Gottschalk, Keith. "South African Labour Policy in Namibia 1915–1975." *South African Labour Bulletin* 4, Nos. 1/2 (Jan–Feb 1978): 75–106.

International Labour Office. *Labour and Discrimination in Namibia.* Geneva: ILO, 1977.

Kane-Berman, John Stuart. *Contract Labour in South West Africa.* Johannesburg: South African Institute of Race Relations, [1972].

Kooy, Marcelle. "The Contract Labour System and the Ovambo Crisis of 1971 in South West Africa." *African Studies Review* 16, No. 1 (April 1973): 83–105.

Melber, Henning. "The National Union of Namibian Workers: Background and Formation," *The Journal of Modern African Studies* 21, No. 1 (1983): 151–158.

Moorsom, Richard. "Labour Consciousness and the 1971–1972 Contract Workers Strike in Namibia," *Development and Change* 10, No. 2 (1979): 205–231.

————. "Underdevelopment, Contract Labor and Worker Consciousness in Namibia, 1915–1972," *Journal of Southern African Studies* 4, No. 1 (October 1977): 52–87.

————. "Worker Consciousness and the 1971–1972 Contract Worker's Strike." *South African Labour Bulletin* 4, Nos. 1/2 (Jan–Feb 1978): 124–139.

Rogers, Barbara L. "Namibia's General Strike." *Africa Today* 19, No. 2 (Spring 1972): 3–8.

South West Africa, Native Labourer's Commission. *Report . . . 1945–1948.* Windhoek: 1948.

Working Under South African Occupation: Labour in Namibia. London: International Defense Aid Fund, 1987.

J. Foreign Investment

Church Investments, Corporations and Southern Africa. New York: National Council of Churches, Corporate Information Center, 1973.

Cooper, Allan D. *Allies in Apartheid: Western Capitalism in Occupied Namibia.* London: Macmillan Press. New York: St. Martin's Press, 1988.

Courtney, Winifred, and Jennifer Davis. *Namibia: U.S. Corporate Involvement.* New York: The Africa Fund/World Council of Churches, 1972.

Ferreira, E. "International Capital in Namibia, Tsumeb and the CDM." *UFAHAMU* 3, No. 2 (Fall 1972): 49–64.

Hovey, Gail. *Namibia's Stolen Wealth: North American Investment and South African Occupation.* New York: The Africa Fund, November 1981.

Hultman, Tami, and Reed Kramer. *Tsumeb—A Profile of the U.S. Contribution to Underdevelopment in Namibia.* New York: National Council of Churches, Corporate Information Center, 1973.

Murray, Roger, Jo Morris, John Dugard, Neville Rubin. *The Role of Foreign Firms in Namibia: Studies on External Investments and Black Workers' Conditions in Namibia.* London: Africa Publications Trust, 1974.

Rogers, Barbara. *White Wealth and Black Poverty: The American Investments in Southern Africa.* Westport, CT: Greenwood Press, 1976.

Seidman, Ann and Neva. *South Africa and U.S. Multinational Corporations.* Westport, CT: Lawrence Hill and Co., 1978.

United Nations. General Assembly. *Implications of the Activities of the Mining Industry and Other International Companies Having Investments in South West Africa.* UN.A/5840, 5 January 1965.

4. HISTORIC

A. General

Dundas, Sir Charles. *South-West Africa: The Factual Background.* Johannesburg: The South African Institute of International Affairs, 1946.

Eveleigh, William. *South-West Africa.* Cape Town: T. Maskew Miller. London: T. Fisher Unwin Ltd., [1915].

First, Ruth. *South West Africa.* Harmondsworth and Baltimore: Penguin Books, 1963.

Freyer, E. P. W. *Chronik von Otavi und Umgebung 1906–1966.* Windhoek: S.W.A. Wissenschaftlichen Gesellschaft, [1966].

Gaerdes, Fritz. *Geschichte und Entwicklung der Stadt Okahandja.* Windhoek: S.W.A. Wissenschaftlichen Gesellschaft, [1970].

Goldblatt, I. *History of South West Africa from the Beginning of the Nineteenth Century.* Cape Town: Juta and Company Ltd., 1971.

Hubrich, H. G. and H. Melber. *Namibia: Geschichte und Gegenwart.* Bonn: Issa, 1977.

International Conference on South West Africa. *South West Africa: Travesty of Trust.* Ed. by Ronald Segal and Ruth First. London: Andre Deutsch, 1967.

Jenny, Hans. *Südwestafrika: Land Zwischen den Extemen.* Stuttgart, Berlin, Köln, Mainz: K. Kohlhammer Verlag, 1966. (English translation: *South West Africa: Land of Extremes.* Windhoek: South West African Scientific Society, 1976.)

Kerina, Mburumba. *Namibia: The Making of a Nation.* New York: Books in Focus, 1981.

Kozonguizi, F. Jariretundu. "Historical Background and Current Problems." Pp. 45–58. In John A. David and James K. Baker, eds. *Southern African in Transition.* New York: Praeger, 1966.

Levinson, Olga. *The Ageless Land: The Story of South West Africa.* Cape Town: Tafelberg-Uitgewers (edms.) Bpk., 1961. Revised 1964.

————. *South West Africa.* Cape Town: Tafelberg Publishers Ltd., 1976.

————. *Story of Namibia.* Cape Town: Tafelberg Publishers Ltd., 1978.

Louw, Walter. *Owambo.* Standton, S.A.: Southern African Freedom Foundation, [1976].

Mbumba, Nangola, and Norbert Noisser. *Namibia in History.* London: Zed Books, 1988.

Melber, Henning. *Our Namibia: A Social Studies Textbook.* London: Zed Books, 1986.

Miller, W. B., ed. *A History of South West Africa.* Cape Town: Maskew Miller Ltd., [c. 1960].

Moleah, Alfred T. *Namibia: The Struggle for Liberation.* Wilmington, DE: Disa Press, Inc., 1983.

Mossolow, Nikolai. *The History of Namutoni, South West Africa.* Windhoek: 1971.

————. *This Was Old Windhoek.* Windhoek: John Meinert, 1965.

————. *Windhoek: Three Historical Landmarks.* Windhoek: John Meinert, 1972.

Saunders, Christopher, ed. *Perspective on Namibia: Past and Present.* Formally known as Occasional Paper No. 4/1983.

Cape Town: Centre for African Studies at the University of Cape Town, 1983.

Soggott, David. *Namibia: The Violent Heritage.* New York: St. Martin's Press, 1986.

Totemeyer, Gerhard, Vezera Kandetu, and Wolfgang Werner, eds. *Namibia in Perspective.* Windhoek: Council of Churches of Namibia, 1987.

Vedder, Dr. Heinrich. *Am Lagerfeuer: Geschichten aus Busch und Weft, von Pad und Landschaft, Menschen und Schicksalen in Sudwestafrika.* Herausgegeben von A. Wackwitz, Windhoek: Meinert, 1938.

————. *Einfurüng in die Geschichte Südwestafrikas.* Windhoek: 1953.

————. *Kurze Geschichten aus einem langen Leben.* Wuppertal-Barmen: Rheinischen Missions-Gesellschaft, 1958.

Vedder, Heinrich, and E. Meier. *Quellen zur Geschichte von Südwestafrika.* 28 volumes, manuscript. Parliamentary Library, Windhoek.

Walker, Eric Anderson. *A History of Southern Africa.* London: Longmans, Green & Co. Ltd., 1957.

Wellington, John H. *South West Africa and Its Human Issues.* Oxford: The Clarendon Press, 1967.

Woods, Brian, ed. *Namibia: 1884–1894; Readings on Namibian History and Society.* London: Namibia Support Committe and United Nations Institute for Namibia, 1988.

B. Pre-Colonial

Bell, Colin Earl. *South West Pioneer: A Memorial Tribute to James Frank Bassingthwaighte—First Permanent White Settler in South West Africa.* Sea Point, RSA: Bennu Books, 1977.

Birkby, Carel. *Thirstland Treks*. London: Faber and Faber, 1936.

Cape of Good Hope, Ministerial Department of Native Affairs. *Report of W. Coates Palgrave, Esq., Special Commissioner to the Tribes North of the Orange River, of His Mission to Damaraland and Great Namaqualand in 1876*. Cape Town: Saul Solomon & Co., Steam Printing Office, 1877.

Chilvers, Hedley Arthur. *The Seven Lost Trails of Africa* . . . . London, Toronto, Melbourne, Sydney: Cassell and Co., 1930.

Davies, Joan. "Palgrave and Damaraland." Pp. 92–203. In *Archives Year Book for South African History 1942*. Part II (1943).

DuPlessis, J. "the Name 'Hottentot' in the Records of Early Travelers." *South African Journal of Science* 29 (October 1932): 660–667.

Forrest, D. W. *Francis Galton: The Life and Work of a Victorian Genius*. London: Paul Elek, 1974.

Galton, Sir Francis. *Memories of My Life*. London: Methuen & Co., 1909.

Hodge, Amelia Lawrence. *Angra Pequeña*. München: B. Heller, 1936.

Kienetz, Alvin. "The Key Role of the Orlam Migrations in the Early Europeanization of South-West Africa." *Int. J. Afr. Hist. Stud* 10, No. 4 (1977): 553–572.

Lau, Brigitte. *Namibia in Jonker Afrikaner's Time*. Windhoek: Windhoek Archives, 1987.

Mossop, Dr. E. E., ed. *The Journal of Hendrick Jacob Wiker (1779); The Journals of Jacobus Coetse Jansz (1760) and Willem van Reenen (1791)*, Dutch with an English translation, Cape Town: Van Riebeeck Society, 1935.

———. *The Journals of Brink and Rhenius, being the Journal of Carel Frederik Brink of the Journey into Great Namaqualand (1761–2) made by Captain Hendrik Hop and the Journal of Ensign Johannes Tobias Rhenius (1742).* Vol. 28. Cape Town: The Van Riebeeck Society, 1947.

Sclater, W. L. "Note on Portions of the Cross of Memorial Pillar Erected by Bartholomew Diaz near Angra Pequeña in South-West Africa." *Transactions of the South African Philosophical Society* (1898): 295ff.

Snyder, Louis L. "The Role of Herbert Bismark in the Angra Pequeña Negotiations, 1880–1885." *Journal of Negro History (1950): 435–452.*

Tabler, Edward C. *Pioneers of South West Africa and Ngamiland, 1738–1880.* Cape Town: A. A. Balkema, 1973.

Theal, George McCall. *History and Ethnography of South Africa Before 1795.* 3 Vols. London, 1907–1910.

————. *History of South Africa Since September 1795.* 6 Vols. London: Swan Sonnenschein & Co., 1908.

Vedder, Heinrich. *South West Africa in Early Times, Being the Story of South West Africa up to the Date of Maherero's Death in 1890.* London: Oxford University Press, 1938.

————. "Über die Vorgeschichte der Völkerschaften von Südwestafrika, I: Buschmänner." *Journal of the South West Africa Scientific Society* I (1925–26): 5–16.

————. "Über die Vorgeschichte der Völkerschaften von Südwestafrika, II: Die Hottentotten." *Journal of the South West Africa Scientific Society* I, (1925–26): 37–48.

————. "Zur Vorgeschichte der Völker Südwestafrikas, III: Die Bergdama." *Journal of the South West Africa Scientific Society* II (1926–27): 35–48.

Wallis, John Peter Richard. *Fortune My Foe: The Story of Charles John Andersson, African Explorer (1827–1867).* London: Jonathan Cape, 1936.

————. *Thomas Baines of King's Lynn, Explorer and Artist, 1820–1875.* London: Jonathan Cape, 1941.

C. The German Period

1. General Colonial History and Biography

Aydelotte, William Osgood. *Bismarck and British Colonial Policy: The Problem of South West Africa 1883–1885.* Philadelphia: University of Pennsylvania Press, 1937.

————. "The First German Colony and Its Diplomatic Consequences." *Cambridge Historical Journal* V, No. 3 (1937): 291–313.

Bayer, Maximilian Gustav Stephan. *Die Helden der Naukluft: Eine Erzählung aus deutsch-Südwest.* Potsdam: L. Voggenreiter, [1943].

Bixler, Raymond Walter. *Anglo-German Imperialism in South Africa 1880–1900.* Baltimore: Warwick & York, 1932.

Bley, Helmut. "German South West Africa After the Conquest, 1904–1914." In R. Segal and R. First, eds. *South West Africa: Travesty of Trust.* London: Deutsch, 1967.

————. *South West Africa Under German Rule, 1894–1914.* Translated and edited by Hugh Ridley. London: Heinemann, 1971. Evanston: Northwestern University Press, 1971.

————. "Social Discord in South West Africa, 1894–1904." Pp. 607–620. In P. Gifford and W. R. Louis, eds. *Britain and Germany in Africa.* New Haven: Yale University Press, 1967.

Bülow, Franz Joseph von. *Deutsch-Südwestafrika: Drei Jahre im Lande Hendrik Witboois.* Berlin: Ernst Siegfried Mittler und Sohn, 1896.

Calvert, Albert Frederick. *The German African Empire.* London: T. W. Laurie, 1916.

————. *South-West Africa During the German Occupation 1884–1914.* London: T. Werner Laurie, 1915.

Deutsches Kolonial-Lexikon, Herausgegeben von Dr. Heinrich Schnee, Gouvenor, 3 vols. Leipzig: Verlag von Quelle & Meyer, 1920.

Esterhuyse, J. H. *South West Africa 1880–1894: The Establishment of German Authority in South West Africa.* Cape Town: C. Struik, 1968.

Falkenhausen, Helene von. *Ansiedlerschicksale: Elf Jahre in Deutsch-Südwestafrika 1893–1904.* Berlin: Dietrich Reimer/ Ernst Vohsen, 1905.

Francois, Curt von. *Deutsch-Südwest-Afrika: Geschichte der Kolonialisation bis zum Ausbruch des Krieges mit Witbooi, April 1893.* Berlin: Dietrich Reimer/Ernst Vohsen, 1899.

Freyor, C. "Jonker Afrikaner and His Time." *Journal of the S.W.A. Scientific Society* I (1925–26): 17–36.

Gann, Lewis H., and Peter Duignan. *The Rulers of German Africa 1884–1914.* Stanford: Stanford University Press, 1977.

Great Britain. *Union of South Africa: Report on the Natives of South-West Africa and Their Treatment by Germany; Prepared in the Administrator's Office, Windhoek, South-West Africa, January, 1918.* London: HMSO, 1918. (Command Paper 9146.)

Grimm, Hans. *Gustav Voigts, Ein Leben in Deutsch-Südwest.* Gütersloh: C. Bertelsmann, 1942.

Hartmann, G. *Karte des Nördl.: Teiles von Deutsch-Südwest-Afrika.* London: South West Africa Co., 1904.

Henoch, H. *Adolf Lüderitz: eine biographische Skizze.* Berlin: 1909.

Joelson, F. S. *Germany's Claim to Colonies.* London: Hurst & Blackett, 1939.

Johannsen, G. Kurt, and H. H. Kraft. *Germany's Colonial Problem.* London: Thornton Butterworth, 1937.

Lenssen, H. E. *Chronik von Deutsch-Südwestafrika: Eine Kurz gefasste Aufzählung geschichtlicher Ereignisse aus der Deutschen Kolonialzeit von 1883–1915.* Windhoek: S.W.A. Wissenschaftlichen Gesellschaft, 1966.

Leutwein, Theodor. *Elf Jahfre Gouverneur in Deutsch-Südwestafrika.* Berlin: Ernst Siegfried Mittler und Sohn, 1908.

Lewin, Percy Evans. *The Germans and Africa: Their Aims on the Dark Continent and How They Acquired their African Colonies.* London: Cassell, 1915.

Lüderitz, C. A., ed. *Akten, briefe und denkschriften zur erschliessung von Deutsch-Südwest-Afrika durch Adolf Lüderitz.* Bremen: 1943.

————. *Die Erschliessung von Deutsch-Südwest-Afrika durch Adolf Lüderitz.* Oldenburg: Gerhard Stalling Verlag, 1945.

Rautenberg, Hulda. *Das alte Swakopmund 1892–1915: Swakopmund zum 75 Geburtstag.* Neumünster: Karl Wachholtz, 1967.

Rohrbach. Dr. Paul. *Aus Südwest-Afrikas schweren Tagen.* Berlin: Wilhelm Weicher, 1909.

Sander, Ludwig, ed. *Geschichte der deutschen Kolonial-Gesellschaft für Südwest Afrika von ihrer Gründung bis zum Jahre 1910; nach den Akten bearb u dargestellt.* 2 vols. Berlin: Dietrich Reimer (Ernst Vohsen), 1912.

Schmokel, Wolfe W. *Dream of Empire: German Colonialism, 1919–1945.* New Haven and London: Yale University Press, 1964.

Schnee, Albert Hermann Heinrich. *German Colonization Past and Future: The Truth About the German Colonies.* London: George Allen & Unwin, 1926.

Schöllenbach, Dr. Hans Oelhafen von. *Die Besiedelung Deutsch-Südwestafrikas Bis Zum Weltkriege.* Berlin: Dietrich Reimer (Ernst Vohsen) Verlag, 1926.

Schönhoff, Heinz-Oskar. *Peter Klaussen trekkt durch Südwest.* No. 2 in the series *Deutsche in aller Welt: Packende Schicksale aus der Geschichte der deutschen Kolonisation.* [Dresden: Neuer Buchverlag, c. 1935].

Simon, John Marie. *Bishop for the Hottentots: African Memories 1882–1909.* Translated by A. Bouchard. New York: 1959.

Smith, Woodruff D. *The German Colonial Empire.* Chapel Hill, NC: University of North Carolina Press, 1978.

South Africa. *Report on the Natives of South-West Africa and Their Treatment by Germany; Prepared in the Administrator's Office, Windhoek, South-West Africa, January 1918.* London: HMSO, 1918. (Command Paper 9146.)

Sudholt, Gert. *Die deutsche Eingeborenenpolitik in Südwestafrika: Von den Anfängen bis 1904.* Hildesheim: Georg Olms, 1975.

Taylor, Alan John P. *Germany's First Bid for Colonies, 1884–1885: A Move in Bismarck's European Policy.* London: Macmillan and Co., 1938. Hamden, CT: Archon Books, 1967.

Townsend, Mary Evelyn. *Origins of German Colonialism 1871–1885.* New York: Columbia University Press, 1921.

———. *The Rise and Fall of Germany's Colonial Empire 1884–1918.* New York: Macmillan, 1930.

Voeltz, Richard A. *German Colonialism and the South West Africa Company, 1884–1914.* Athens, OH: Ohio University Center for International Studies, 1988.

Voigts, Gustav. *Hans Grimm: Ein Leben in Deutsch-Süwest.* Gütersloh: C. Bertelsman, 1942.

Weber, Otto von. *Geschichte des Schutzgebietes Deutsch-Südwest-Afrika.* Windhoek: John Meinert, [c. 1973].

Witbooi, Hendrik. *Die Dagboek van Hendrik Witbooi.* Cape Town: Van Riebeeck Society, 1929.

————. *Afrika den Afrikanern! Aufzeichnungen eines Nama-Häuptlings aus der Zeit der deutschen Eroberung Südwestafrikas 1884 bis 1894.* Ed. by Wolfgang Reinhard. Berlin and Bonn: Verlag J. H. W. Dietz Nachf., 1982.

2. Military Action

Alexander, Neville. "Jacob Marengo and Namibian History." *Social Dynamics,* 7, No. 1 (1981).

————. "Responses to German Rule in Namibia or the Enigma of the Khowesin." In *Three Essays on Namibian History.* Namibian Review Publications, No. 1, 1983.

————. "The Namibian War of Anti-Colonial Resistance 1904–1907." In *Three Essays on Namibian History.* Namibian Review Publications, No. 1, 1983.

Bridgman, Jon. *The Revolt of the Hereros.* Berkeley: University of California Press, 1981.

Carow, Richard. *Die Kaiserliche Schutztruppe in Deutsch-Südwest-Afrika unter Major Leutwein.* Leipzig: Eg. Freund, 1898.

Deimling, Berthold Karl Adolf von. *Südwestafrika: Land und Leute, Unsere Kämpfe, Wert der Kolonie.* Berlin: R. Eissenschmidt, 1906.

Dreschler, Horst. *Südwestafrika unter Deutscher Kolonialherrschaft: Der Kampf der Herero und Nama gegen den Deutschen Imperialismus (1884–1915).* Berlin: Akademie Verlag, 1966. English translation titled *"Let Us Die Fighting": The Struggle of the Herero and Nama against German Imperialism (1884–1915).* London: Zed Press, 1980.

Francois, Curt von. *Der Hottentottenaufstand: Studie über die Vorgänge im Namalande vom Januar 1904 bis zum Januar 1905.* Berlin: 1905.

Frenssen, Gustav. *Peter Moor's Journey to Southwest Africa: A Narrative of the German Campaign.* Trans. by Margaret May Ward. London: Archibald Constable & Co.; Boston and New York: Houghton Mifflin, 1908.

German General Staff, Military History Section. *Die Kämpfe der deutschen Truppen in Südwestafrika.* 2 vols. Berlin: Ernst Siegfried Mittler und Sohn, 1906–1907.

Leutwein, Paul. *Afrikanerschicksal: Gouverneur Leutwein und seine Zeit.* Stuttgart, Berlin, Leipzig: Union Deutsche Verlagsgesellschaft, 1929.

––––––. *Meine Erlebnisse im Kampf gegen die Herero.* Minden: 1905.

Leutwein, Theodor. "Der Aufstand in Deutsch-Südwestafrika." *Deutsche Revue* (1907).

––––––. *Die Kämpfe der Kaiserlichen Schultztruppe in Deutsch-Südwestafrika in den Jahren 1894–1896 sowie die sich hieraus für uns ergebenden Lehren.* Berlin: Ernst Siegfried Mittler und Sohn, 1899.

Park, Sir Maitland Hall. "German South-West Africa Campaign." *Journal of the African Society* 15, No. 58 (January 1916): 113–132.

Salzmann, Erich von. *Im Kampfe gegen die Herero.* Berlin: Dietrich Reimer/Ernst Vohsen, 1905. 3rd edition, Berlin: Globus Verlag GMBH, 1912.

Schüssler, Wilhelm. *Adolf Lüderitz: Ein Deutschen Kampf um Südafrika 1883–1886: Geschichte des ersten Kolonialpioniers im Zeitalter Bismarks.* Bremen: Carl Schünemann, 1936.

Seitz, Dr. Theodor. *Südafrika im Weltkriege: Der Zusammenbruch in Deutsch-Südwestafrika Die Politik der Südafrikanischen Union Während des Grossen Krieges, Weltfriede?* Berlin: Dietrich Reimer (Ernst Vohsen), 1920.

Stals, E. L. P. *Die Rol Van Viktor Franke in Suidwes-Afrika 1896–1915.* Johannesburg: Randse Afrikaanse Universiteit, 1972.

Vedder, Heinrich. "The Germans in South-West Africa, 1883–1914: The Military Occupation, 1883–1907." Pp. 694–702. In A. P. Newton and E. A. Benians, eds. *The Cambridge History of the British Empire,* Vol. VIII, *South Africa, Rhodesia and the Protectorates.* Cambridge: Cambridge University Press, 1936.

D. 1915–1945

Barron, L. Smythe. *The Nazis in Africa. Secret Documents on the Nazi Movement in Southwest Africa and Tanganyika before World War II.* Salisbury, NC: Documentary Publications, 1978.

Beer, George Louis. *African Questions at the Paris Peace Conference.* New York: Macmillan, 1923.

Blumhagen, Hans Ernst. *Die Doppelstaatigkeit der Deutschen im Mandatsgebeit Südwestafrika und ihre völkerrechtlicher Auswirkungen.* Berlin: 1938.

"The Bondelzwarts Affair." *Round Table* 14, No. 53 (December 1923): 171–175.

Braum, Robert Love, ed. *Southwest Africa Under Mandate.* Salisbury, NC: Documentary Publications, 1976.

Cockram, Gail-Maryse. *South West African Mandate.* Cape Town, Wynberg, Johannesburg: Juta & Co., 1976.

Cooper, Allan D. *The Occupation of Namibia: Afrikanerdom's Attack on the British Empire.* Landam, MD: University Press of America, 1991.

Dale, Richard. "The Ambiguities of Self-Determination for South West Africa, 1918–1939: A Concept or a Symbol of Decolonization?" *Plural Societies* 5, No. 1 (Spring 1974): 29–57.

Dalta, Ansu Kumar. "South-west Africa Under the Mandatory System." *Africa Quarterly* 2 (1962): 155–172.

Davey, Arthur M. *The Bondelzwarts Affair: A Study of the Repercussions, 1922–1959.* Pretoria: University of South Africa, 1961.

Dewaldt, Franz, ed. *Native Uprisings in South West Africa.* Documents on the Armed Uprising of the Bondelzwart Tribe (1922) and the Bloodless Revolt of the Rehoboth Bastaards (1925) in ex-German Southwest Africa, Administered by the Union of South Africa under Mandate. Salisbury, NC: Documentary Publications, 1976.

Dore, Isaak I. *The International Mandate System and Namibia.* Boulder, CO: Westview Press, 1984.

Duignan, Peter, and L. H. Gann. *South West Africa—Namibia.* New York: American African Affairs Association, 1978.

Emmett, Tony. "Popular Resistance in Namibia, 1920–1925." Pp. 6–48. In *Resistance and Ideology in Settler Societies*. Ed. by Tom Lodge. Johannesburg: Ravan Press, 1986.

Ewing, John. "South Africa and the World War." Pp. 710–733. In A. P. Newton and E. A. Benians, eds. *The Cambridge History of the British Empire*, Vol. VIII, *South Africa, Rhodesia and the Protectorates*. Cambridge: Cambridge University Press, 1936.

Freislich, Richard. *The Last Tribal War: A History of the Bondelswart Uprising Which Took Place in South West Africa in 1922*. Cape Town: C. Struik, 1964.

Germany's Claim to Colonies. Information Department Papers, No. 23. London: Royal Institute of International Affairs. New York: Oxford University Press, 1938.

Hailey, Malcolm. "South West Africa." *African Affairs* No. 183 (April 1947): 77–85.

Hofmeyr, Gysbert Reitz. *The Mandated Territory of South-West Africa*. London: Empire Parliamentary Association (United Kingdom Branch), 1924.

Jinadu, L. Adele. "South West Africa: A Study in the Sacred Trust Thesis." *African Studies Review* XIV, No. 3 (December 1971): 369–388.

Louis, William Roger. "African Origins of the Mandates Idea." *International Organization* XIX, No. 1 (Winter 1965): 20–36.

— —. "The South West African Origins of the 'Sacred Trust', 1914–1919." *African Affairs* 66, No. 262 (1967): 20–39.

Marsh, John H. *Skeleton Coast*. London: Hodder & Stoughton Ltd., 1944.

Pearson, Patrick. "The Rehoboth Rebellion." In Phillip Bonner, ed. *Working Papers in Southern African Studies.* Vol. 2. Johannesburg: Ravan press, 1981.

Rayner, W. S., and W. W. O'Shaughnessy. *How Botha and Smuts Conquered German South West.* London: Simpkin, Marshall, Hamilton, Kent & Co., 1916.

Reitz, Deneys. *No Outspan.* London: Faber and Faber, 1943.

————. *Trekking On.* London: Faber and Faber, 1933.

Ritchie, Eric Moore. *With Botha in the Field.* London: Allen & Unwin, 1915.

Robinson, J. P. Kay. *With Botha's Army.* London: G. Allen & Unwin, 1916.

Schnee, Dr. Heinrich. *The German Colonies under the Mandates.* Berlin: 1922.

South Africa. *Memorandum by the Administration of South-west Africa on the Report of the Commission appointed to enquire into the rebellion of the Bondelzwarts.* Cape Town: Cape Times Ltd., 1923.

————. *The Union of South Africa and the Great War, 1914– 1918: Official History.* Pretoria: 1924.

————. Commission to Enquire into the Rebellion of the Bondelzwarts. *Report of the [Roberts] Commission Appointed to Enquire into the Rebellion of the Bondelzwarts.* Cape Town: Cape Times Limited, Government Printers, 1923.

————. South West Africa Commission. *Report of the South West Africa [van Zyl] Commission.* Pretoria: Government Printer, 1936.

————. South-West Africa Territory. *Report of the Administrator on the Bondelzwarts Rising, 1922.* Cape Town: Cape Times Limited, Government Printers, 1922.

————. South West Protectorate. *Report of the Administrator for the Year . . . [date].* Presented to both Houses of Parliament, Cape Town: Cape Times Ltd., Government Printers, [date]. Published annually for the years 1918 to 1946, with publication dates normally one year after the year covered. Later years are published by the Government Printers in Pretoria.

————. State Information Office. *S.W.A. and the Union of S.A.: The History of a Mandate.* New York: South African Information Service, 1946.

"Southern Africa: South West Africa." *Round Table* 23, No. 89 (December 1932): 207–211.

"The South-West Africa Commission." *Round Table* 26, No. 104 (1936): 772–783.

"The South West Africa Mandate." *Round Table* 15, No. 59 (June 1925): 610–616.

Toynbee, Arnold Joseph. "The Delimitation of the Frontier Between the Mandated Territory of South-West Africa and the Portuguese Colony of Angola, 1925–6." Pp. 275–284. In *Survey of International Affairs, 1929.* Oxford: Oxford University Press, 1930.

————. "The Administration of the Mandate for South-West Africa." Pp. 243–272. In *Survey of International Affairs, 1929.* Oxford: Oxford University Press, 1930.

————. "The Administration of the Mandate for South-West Africa." In *Survey of International Affairs 1920–23.* Oxford: Oxford University Press, 1925.

Union of South Africa. *Report presented by the Government of the Union of South Africa to the Council of the League of Nations concerning the Administration of South West Africa for the Year . . . [date].* Pretoria: The Government Printer, [date]. Published annually for the years 1928 to 1939, with publication dates normally one year after the dates covered.

This was not published again until 1946 with the title slightly changed.

Wilken, J. J. J., and G. J. Fox. *The History of the Port and Settlement of Walvis Bay.* Johannesburg: Perskor Pub., 1978.

Wright, Quincy. *Mandates Under the League of Nations.* Chicago: University of Chicago Press, 1930.

Xuma, Dr. Alfred Bitini. *A Mandate that Failed.* New York: 1946.

———. *South West Africa—Annexation or United Nations Trusteeship.* New York: H. A. Naidoo and Sorabjee Rustomjee, 1946.

E. At the United Nations

American Committee on Africa. *South West Africa: The UN's Stepchild.* 2nd ed. New York: American Committee on Africa, 1960.

Arden-Clarke, Sir Charles Noble. "South-West Africa, The Union and the United Nations." *African Affairs* 59 (1960): 26–35.

Booysen, H., and Stephan. G. E. J. "Decree No. 1 of the United Nations Council for South West Africa." *South African Yearbook of International Law.* Vol. 1 (1975): 63–86.

Carroll, Faye. *South West Africa and the United Nations.* Lexington, KY: University of Kentucky Press, 1967.

Coker, Christopher. "Peacekeeping in Southern Africa: The United Nations and Namibia." *The Journal of Commonwealth and Comparative Politics* 19, No. 2 (July 1981): 174–186.

Dugard, John, ed. *The South West Africa/Namibia Dispute.*

Documents and Scholarly Writings on the Controversy Between South Africa and the United Nations. Berkeley: University of California Press, 1973.

du Pisani, Andre. "Namibia: On Brinkmanship, Conflict, and Self-Interest—The Collapse of the UN Plan." *Politikon* 8, No. 1 (June 1981): 1–16.

Evenson, John A. "The Transition Timetable." *Africa Report* 34, No. 2 (?): 26–30.

Goldblatt, I. *The Mandated Territory of South West Africa in Relation to the United Nations.* Cape Town: C. Struik, 1961.

Hall, H. D. "The Trusteeship System and the Case of South West Africa." *British Yearbook of International Law* 24 (1974): 33–71.

Herman, L. L. "The Legal Status of Namibia and of the United Nations Council for Namibia." *Canadian Yearbook of International Law* 17 (1975): 306–22.

Kerina, Mburumba A. "South West Africa and the United Nations." *Africa South* 3, No. 1 (Oct.–Dec. 1958): 8–15.

———. "South-West Africa, the United Nations, and the International Court of Justice." *African Forum* 2, No. 2 (Fall 1966): 5–22.

Lawrie, G. G. *South West Africa and the United Nations.* Johannesburg: South African Institute of Race Relations, 1965.

Mishra, Brajesh. "Ending the Impasse." *Africa Report* 30, No. 5, 65–69.

Possony, Stefan T. "South Africa, the Hague Decision and the United Nations." *Reports on the State of South Africa* 31 (1967).

Rocha, Geisa Maria. *In Search of Namibian Independence: The Limitations of the United Nations.* Boulder, CO: Westview Press, 1984.

Saxena, Suresh Chandra. *Namibia: Challenge to the United Nations.* Delhi: Sundeep Prakashan, 1978.

———. "Namibia and the United Nations." *Indian Journal of Political Science* 36 (1975): 274–96.

———. "Role of the United Nations Council for Namibia." *African Quarterly* 17 (1978): 5–31.

Scott, Michael. "The International Status of South West Africa." *International Affairs* 34 (July 1958): 318ff.

———. *The Orphan's Heritage: The Story of the South West African Mandate.* London: The Africa Bureau, 1958.

———. "The Sacred Trust of South West Africa." *Africa South* 5, No. 1 (1960): 46–49.

———. *Shadow Over Africa.* London: The Union of Democratic Control, 1950.

———. *A Time to Speak.* London: Faber & Faber, 1958; Garden City, NY: Doubleday, 1958.

Slonim, Solomon. *South West Africa and the United Nations: An International Mandate in Dispute.* Baltimore: Johns Hopkins University Press, 1973.

"South West Africa: A New Approach." *United Nations Review* 1 (Jan. 1955): 44–51.

"South West Africa Before the United Nations." *World Today* 16 (1960): 334–345.

Toussaint, Charmian Edwards. *The Trusteeship of the United Nations.* London: Stevens and Sons, 1956.

United Nations. Committee on South West Africa. *Reports.* New York: United Nations, 1953–1961.

United Nations. Council for Namibia. *Nationhood Programme for Namibia.* New York: Office of the United Nations Commissioner for Namibia, 1981.

————. *Reports,* 1967– , New York: United Nations, 1967– ; Published in United Nations General Assembly. *Official Records. Supplements.*

United Nations. Department of Public Information. *Namibia: A Unique Responsibility. Highlights of UN Action in Support of Freedom and Independence for Namibia.* New York: UN Department of Information, 1981.

United Nations. General Assembly. *Documents Relating to the Consideration . . . of the Statement by the Government of S.A. on . . . Their Consultations with the People of S.W.A. as to the Future Status of the Mandated Territory.* Cape Town: 1947.

————. *Report of the Special Committee on the Situation with Regard to the Implementation of the Declaration on the Granting of Independence to Colonial Countries and Peoples.* [committee of 24] 31 October 1967.

————. Committee on South West Africa. *Report,* 1st+ New York, 1954+. Issued as Supplements to the Official Records of the General Assembly.

————. Committee on South West Africa. *Information and Documentation in Respect of the Territory of South West Africa.* New York: United Nations, 1955.

————. Committee on South West Africa. *Petitions and Communication Relating to South West Africa Dealt with by the committee . . . in Its Report on Conditions in the Territory Submitted to the General Assembly at Its Sixteenth Session.* New York: United Nations, 1961.

———. Committee on South West Africa. *Report . . . Concerning the Implementation of General Assembly Resolution 1568 (XV) and 1956 (XV).* New York: United Nations, 1962.

United Nations. Office of Public Information. *A Principle in Torment, III. The United Nations and Namibia.* New York: United Nations, 1971.

———. *A Trust Betrayed: Namibia.* New York: United Nations, 1974. (A reissue of *A Principle in Torment* (1971) with one new section added on the ICJ advisory opinion of 1971.)

UNTAG in Namibia: A New Nation is Born. New York: United Nations Publications, 1990.

Van Wyk, Jacques Theodore. *The United Nations, South West Africa, and the Law.* Cape Town: University of Cape Town Press, 1968.

F. The International Court of Justice

Ballinger, Ronald B. "South West Africa after the Judgement," *Optima* 14 (1964): 142–154.

———. "The International Court of Justice and the South West Africa Cases: Judgement of 21st December 1962." *South Africa Law Journal* 81 (1964): 35–62.

Bishop, W. M. "Juridical Decisions: International Status of South West Africa." *American Journal of International Law* 44 (1950): 757–70.

Cheng, B. "The 1966 South-West Africa Judgement of the World Court." *Current Legal Problems* 20 (1967): 181–212.

Dugard, John. "The South West Africa Cases, Second Phase, 1966." *The South African Law Journal* 83 (1966).

———. "Namibia (South West Africa): The Court's Opinion,

South Africa's Response and Prospects for the Future." *Columbia Journal of Transnational Law* 11 (1972): 14–49.

Falk, Richard A. "The South West African Case: An Appraisal." *International Organization* 21 (1967): 1–23.

Friedmann, W. G. "The Jurisprudential Implications of the South West Africa Case." *Columbia Journal of Transnational Law* 6 (1967): 1–17.

Green, L. C. "South West Africa and the World Court." *International Journal* 22, No. 1 (winter 1966): 39–67.

Gross, Ernest A., et al. *Ethiopia and Liberia versus South Africa: The Southwest Africa Cases.* Los Angeles: University of California at Los Angeles, African Studies Center (Occasional Paper No. 5), 1968.

Gross, Ernest A. "The South West Africa Case: What Happened?" *Foreign Affairs* 45, No. 1 (October 1966): 36–48.

Hevener, N. K. "The 1971 South West Africa Opinion: A New International Legal Philosophy." *International and Comparative Law Quarterly* 24 (1975): 791–810.

Hidayatullah, M. *The South-West Africa Case.* New York: Asia Publishing House, 1967.

Higgins, Rosalyn. "The International Court and South West Africa: The Implications of the Judgment." *International Affairs* 42, No. 4 (Oct. 1966): 573–599.

———. "The International Court and South West Africa." *International Commission of Jurist Journal* (Summer 1967).

Indian Society of International Law. *The Question of South-West Africa (Documents and Comments).* New Delhi: The Indian Society of International Law, 1966.

International Commission of Jurists. *South West Africa: The Court's Judgment.* Geneva: ICJ, [1967].

International Court of Justice. *Admissibility of Hearings of Petitioners by the Committee on South West Africa (Advisory Opinion of June 1st, 1956).* Hague, ICJ, 1956.

————. *Counter-memorial filed by the Government of the Republic of South Africa.* Cape Town: Cape and Transvaal Printers, 1963–1964.

————. *Ethiopia and Liberia versus South Africa: An Official Account of the Contentious Proceedings on South-West Africa . . . 1960–1966.* 2nd ed. Pretoria: 1966.

————. *International Status of South-West Africa, Advisory Opinion of July 11, 1950: Pleadings, Oral Arguments, Documents.* Hague: ICJ, 1950.

————. *International Status of South West Africa (Reports of Judgements, Advisory Opinions and Orders. Order Dec. 30, 1949 and Advisory Opinion July 11, 1950).* 2 vols. bound in one vol. Leyden: 1949–1950.

————. *Judgement of the International Court of Justice in the South-West Africa Case, Dissenting Opinion: Judge Phillip C. Jessup.* New York: Reproduced and distributed by the African-American Institute, 1966.

————. *Legal Consequences for States of the Continued Presence of South Africa in Namibia (South West Africa) Notwithstanding Security Council Resolution 276 (1970).* 2 vols. Vol. I, *Request for Advisory Opinion, Documents, Written Statements.* Vol. II, *Oral Statements and Correspondence.* Hague: International Court of Justice, 1971.

————. *Legal Consequences for States of the Continued Presence of South Africa in Namibia (South West Africa) Notwithstanding Security Council Resolution 276 (1970), Advi-*

sory Opinion of 21 June 1971. Hague: International Court of Justice, [1971].

————. *Noting Procedure of Questions Relating to Reports and Petitions concerning the Territory of South West Africa (Advisory Opinion of June 7th, 1955).* Hague: ICJ, 1955.

————. *Pleadings, Oral Arguments, Documents (concerning the) International Status of S.W.A.* Hague: ICJ, 1950.

————. *Rejoinder Filed by the Government of the Republic of South Africa.* 2 vols. Cape Town: Cape and Transvaal Printers, 1964.

————. *Reports of Judgements, Advisory Opinions and Orders. South West Africa Cases (Ethiopia v. South Africa; Liberia v. South Africa), Second Phase, Judgement of 18 July 1966.* The Hague: ICJ, 1966.

————. *Reports of Judgements, Advisory Opinions and Orders: Advisory Opinion of 21 June 1971.* The Hague: ICJ, 1971.

————. *South West Africa Cases (Ethiopia v. South Africa; Liberia v. South Africa). Pleadings, Oral Arguments, Documents.* 12 vols. Hague: ICJ, 1966.

————. *South West Africa Cases (Ethiopia v. South Africa; Liberia v. South Africa). Second Phase, Judgement of 8 July 1966.* Hague: ICJ, 1966.

————. *South West Africa Cases: Its Pleadings, Oral Arguments, Documents.* Vols. 4–12. Leiden: A. W. Sijthoff, 1967–1970.

————. *South West Africa Cases (Ethiopia and Liberia and the Republic of South Africa). Preliminary Objections Filed by the Government of the Republic of South Africa.* Hague: ICJ, 1961.

————. *Verbatim Record (CR71/1 and on) South West Africa Pleadings.* The Hague: ICJ, 1971.

―――――. *Voting Procedure on Questions Relating to Reports and Petitions Concerning the Territory of South-West Africa, Advisory Opinion of June 7th, 1955*, [n.d.].

Kahn, E. "The International Court's Advisory Opinion on the International Status of South West Africa." *International Law Quarterly* 4 (1951): 78ff.

Kozonguizi. Jariretundu. "South West African Nationalism and the International Court of Justice." *African Forum* II, No. 2 (Fall 1966): 23–32.

Landis, Elizabeth S. "South West Africa in the International Court: Act II, Scene I." *Cornell Law Quarterly* 49 (1964): 179–227.

―――――. *South West Africa Cases: Remand to the United Nations.* New York: American Committee on Africa, [n.d.].

Lejeune, Anthony, comp. *The Case for South West Africa.* London: Tom Stacey, 1971.

Lissitzyn, O. J. "International Law and the Advisory Opinion on Namibia." *Columbia Journal of Transnational Law* 11 (1972): 50–73.

McKay, Vernon. "South African Propaganda on the International Court's Decision," *African Forum* 2, No. 2 (1966): 51–64.

Mockford, Julian. *South-West Africa and the International Court.* London: Diplomatic Press, 1950.

Nisot, J. "The Advisory Opinion of the International Court of Justice on the International Status of South West Africa." *South African Law Journal* 68 (1951): 274–85.

Obozuwa, Augustine Ukiomogbe. *The Namibian Question: Legal and Political Aspects.* Benin City, Nigeria: Ethiope Publishing Corp., 1973.

Persaud, Motee. "Namibia and the International Court of Justice." *Current History* (May 1975): 220–225.

Pisani, Andre du. "On Law and Politics—Review of the International Dispute over Namibia." *Politeia* 1, No. 2 (1982): 32–45.

Pollock, A. J. "The South West Africa Cases and the Jurisprudence of International Law." *International Organization* 23 (1969): 767–787.

Reisman, W. M. "Revision of the South West Africa Cases: An Analysis of the Grounds of Nullity in the Decision of July 18th, 1966, and Methods of Revision." *Virginia Journal of International Law* 7 (1966): 1–90.

Rubin, Neville. "South West Africa: From Courtroom to Political Arena." *Africa Report* XI, No. 9 (December 1966): 12–15.

Scott, M. "The International Status of South West Africa." *International Affairs* 34 (1958): 318–329.

Scrivner, Robert W. "The South-West Africa Case: 1962 Revisited." *African Forum* 2, No. 2 (1966): 35–50.

South Africa. *Memorandum on the South West Africa Cases: Ethiopia and Liberia vs. the Republic of South Africa.* Pretoria: The Government Printer [c. 1965].

South Africa, Department of Foreign Affairs. *South West Africa Advisory Opinion 1971: A Study in International Adjudication.* Pretoria: The Government Printer, 1972. Cape Town: Printed by Cape and Transvaal Printers for the Department of Foreign Affairs, RSA, 1972.

South Africa, Department of Information. *Ethiopia and Liberia versus South Africa (Official Account of the Proceedings on South West Africa before the International Court of Justice at the Hague, 1960–1966).* 2nd ed. Pretoria: Department of Information, 1966.

Trachtman, J. "The South-West Africa Cases and the Development of International Law." *Millennium: Journal of International Studies* 5, No. 3 (Winter 1976–1977): 292–302.

Umozurike, U. O. "The Namibia (South-West Africa) Cases 1950–1971," *Africa Quarterly* 12 (1972): 41–58.

Wiechers, Marinus. "South West Africa and the World Court," *Africa Institute Bulletin* 9 (1971): 449–461.

———. *South West Africa/Namibia: Review of the International Dispute.* Johannesburg: South African Institute of Race Relations, 1973.

Weichers, Marinus, and A. J. van Wyk. "The S.W.A. Case." *Africa Institute Bulletin* 4 (1966): 189–210.

G. Since 1945

Abrahams, Kenneth. "Present Imperfect, Future Indefinite; Namibia in Early 1983." *The Namibian Review* 7 (Jan.–March 1983): 1–15.

Centre for Extra-Mural Studies, University of Cape Town. *South West Africa: Problems and Alternatives.* Cape Town: University of Cape Town, 1975.

DuBois, S. G. (Mrs. W. E. B. Dubois). "The Rise of Namibia." *Africa and the World* 4, No. 45 (August 1968): 24–27.

First, Ruth and Ronald Segal, eds. *South West Africa: Travesty of Trust.* London: Andre Deutsch, 1967.

Hall, Richard, ed. *South-West Africa (Namibia): Proposals for Action.* London: The Africa Bureau, 1970.

Kelly, Sean. "Constructing a New Nation." *Africa Report* 35, No. 3 (1990): 28–30.

Konrat, Georg Von. *Passport to Truth: Inside South West Africa: An Astonishing Story of Oppression.* London: W. H. Allen, 1972.

Landis, Elizabeth S. "Namibia: Impending Independence?" Pp. 163–199. In Gwendolen M. Carter and Patrick O'Meara, eds. *Southern Africa in Crisis.* Bloomington: Indiana University Press, 1977.

Landis, Elizabeth S., and Michael I. Davis. "Namibia: Impending Independence?" Pp. 141–174. In Gwendolen M. Carter and Patrick O'Meara, eds. *Southern Africa: The Continuing Crisis.* Bloomington: Indiana University Press, 1979.

Leistner, G. M. E., P. Esterhuysen, and T. Malan. *Namibia/SWA Prospectus.* Pretoria: African Institute of South Africa, 1980.

Munger, Edwin S. *South-West Africa: Evolution or Revolution?* American Universities Field Staff Reports, Central and Southern Africa Series, Vol. IX, No. 6 (ESM-6-'61). New York: American Universities Field Staff, July 1961.

Murray, Roger. "Namibia: No Easy Path to Independence." *Africa Report* 22, No. 3 (May–June 1977): 17–20, 37–40.

South Africa. Commission of Enquiry into the Occurrences in the Windhoek Location . . . . *Report of the Commission of Enquiry . . . .* Pretoria: Cape Times, Ltd. for the Government Printer, 1960.

South Africa's Homelands: Two African Views—Chief Cedric Phatudi of Lebowa and Chief Clemens Kapuuo of South West Africa/Namibia. Pasadena, CA: Munger Africana Library, Volume IV/1973/74, Number 22.

South West Africa: Problems & Alternatives. Cape Town: The University of Cape Town, Center for Extra-Mural Studies, 1975.

Troup, Freda. *In Face of Fear: Michael Scott's Challenge to South Africa.* London: Faber & Faber, 1950.

United States Congress. House of Representatives Committee on Foreign Affairs, Subcommittee on Africa. *Critical Developments in Namibia.* Hearings before the Subcommittee on Africa of the Committee on Foreign Affairs, House of Representatives, 93rd Congress, 2nd Session, February 21 and April 4, 1974. Washington: USGPO, 1974.

Van der Merwe, Paul S. "South Africa and South West Africa." Pp. 69–84. In C. P. Potholm and Richard Dale, eds. *Southern Africa in Perspective.* New York: Free Press, 1972.

Van Pittius, E. F. W. Gey. "Whither South-West Africa." *International Affairs* 23 (1947): 202–212.

5. POLITICAL

A. Constitution, Law and Government

Abrahams, Kenneth. "Second-Tier Authorities." *The Namibian Review* No. 16 (April 1980): 3–6, 15–16.

————. "Representative Authorities and Ethnic Elections." *The Namibian Review* No. 18 (July/August 1980): 3–14.

Amnesty International. *Amnesty International Briefing: Namibia.* London: Amnesty International, 1977.

Amnesty International, Campaign for the Abolition of Torture. *Flogging in Namibia: Extracts of Affidavits.* London: Amnesty International, 1974.

Benson, Mary, ed. *The Sun Will Rise: Statements from the Dock by Southern African Political Prisoners.* London: International Defence and Aid Fund, 1974.

Bomani, M. D., and C. Ushewokunze. *Constitutional Options for Namibia: A Historical Perspective.* Ed. by N. K. Duggal. Lusaka: United Nations Institute for Namibia, 1979.

Brooks, Pierre, E. J. "The Legal Status of Walvis Bay." *South African Yearbook of International Law* 2 (1976): 187–191.

Carlson, Joel. *No Neutral Ground.* New York: Thomas Y. Crowell Co., 1973.

Clark, Roger S. "The International League for Human Rights and South West Africa, 1945–1957: The Human Rights NGO as Catalyst in the International Legal Process." *Human Rights Quarterly* (Winter 1981).

Cleary, Sean. "The Utility of Bills of Rights in Culturally Heterogeneous Societies: A Preliminary Examination of the Namibian Model." *South Africa International* 16, No. 4 (1986): 175–190.

Dale, Richard. "Ovamboland: Bantustan without Tears?" *Africa Report* 14, No. 2 (February 1969): 16–23.

D'Amato, Anthony A. "The Bantustan Proposals for South West Africa." *Journal of Modern African Studies* 4, No. 2 (1966): 172–192.

Dugard, Christopher John Robert. "South West Africa and the Supremacy of the South African Parliament." *South African Law Journal* 86 (1969): 194–204.

———. "South West Africa and the 'Terrorist Trial.' " *American Journal of International Law* 64 (1970): 19–41.

———. "SWAPO: The Jus ad Bellum and the Jus in Bello." *South African Law Journal* 93, No. 2 (May 1976): 144–158.

Duggal, N. K., ed. *Constitutional Options for Namibia: A Historical Perspective, Based on the Work of M. D. Bomani and C. Ushewokunze.* Lusaka: United Nations Institute for Namibia, 1979.

DuPisani, Andre. "Namibia: A New Transitional Government." *South Africa International* 16, No. 2 (1985): 66–73.

———. *SWA/Namibia: The Politics of Continuity and Change.* Johannesburg: J. Bell Publishers, 1985.

Evenson, John A. "The Transition Timetable." *Africa Report* 34 (March–April 1989): 26–30.

Faris, J. A. "The Administration of Walvis Bay." *South African Yearbook of International Law* 5 (1979): 63–81.

———. "The Western Proposal and Elections in South West Africa/Namibia: A Summary of Events for 1978." *South African Yearbook of International Law* 4 (1978): 90–108.

International Defence and Aid Fund. *All Options or None: The Constitutional Talks in Namibia.* Fact Paper on Southern Africa No. 3. London: International Defence and Aid Fund, 1976.

———. *Namibia: The Constitutional Fraud.* Briefing Paper on Southern Africa No. 2. London: IDAF, 1981.

Jones, John David Rheinallt. "Administration of South West Africa: Welfare of the Indigenous Population." *Race Relations* XIX, No. 1 (1952): 3–21.

Landis, Elizabeth S. "Human Rights in Namibia." *Human Rights Journal* 9 (1976).

———. "Namibia: Legal Aspects." *Southern Africa* 2 (1973): 107–116.

———. "The Turnhalle Constitution: An Analysis." *Africa Today* 24, No. 3 (July–September 1977): 12–23.

Lawrie, Gordon. "New Light on South West Africa: Some Extracts from and Comments on the Odendaal Report." *African Studies* 23, Nos. 3–4 (1964): 105–119.

Matthews, E. L. "The Grant of a Constitution to the Mandated Territory of South-West Africa." *Journal of Comparative Legislation and International Law.* 3rd ser. VIII, Part IV (1926): 161–183.

Moolman, J. "South West Africa: Self-determination, Majority

Rule, Democracy and Independence." *African Institute Bulletin* 14, No. 4 (1976): 103–115.

"Namibia Adopts a New constitution—Hailed as Most Democratic in Africa." *Africa Report* 35, No. 2 (March–April, 1990): 8–9.

O'Linn, Bryan. *The Priority for Namibia Today: An Honourable Peace.* Windhoek: Namibia Publications, 1985.

Remember Kassinga, And Other Papers on Political Prisoners and Detainees in Namibia. Fact Paper on Southern Africa No. 9. London: International Defence and Aid Fund for Southern Africa, 1981.

Richardson, H. J. III, "Constitutive Questions in the Negotiations for Namibian Independence." *American Journal of International Law* 78 (1984): 76–120.

Robertson, Elizabeth, comp. *Subject List and Index of the Laws of South West Africa, from 1915, in force in 1969.* Johannesburg: University of the Witwatersrand Department of Bibliography, Librarianship and Typography, 1973.

Schermers, H. G. "The Namibia Decree in National Courts." *International & Comporative Law Quarterly* 26, No. 1 (Jan. 1977): 81–96.

Sagey, Itsejuwa. *The Legal Aspects of the Namibian Dispute.* Ile Ife, Nigeria: University of Ife Press, 1975.

Sinclair, M. "Namibian Constitutional Proposals: The Fleeting Options and Implications for S.A." *South Africa International,* 12 (1982): 508–516.

South Africa. *Report of the Commission of Enquiry into the Language Rights of the German-speaking Section in South West Africa.* Windhoek: 1956.

South Africa. Commission of Enquiry into South West African Affairs. *Report of the Commission of Inquiry into South West*

African Affairs 1962–1963. (Odendaal Commission Report). Pretoria: The Government Printer, 1964.

South Africa. Commission of the Future Form of Government in the South-West Africa Protectorate. *Interim and Final Reports of the Commission appointed to enquire into the question of the Future form of Government in the South-West Africa Protectorate.* Cape Town: Cape Times Limited, Government Printers, 1921.

South Africa. Department of Foreign Affairs. *Ovambo.* [Pretoria]: Cape & Transvaal Printers, 1971.

South African Law Reports. *South-West Africa: Decisions of the High Court of South-West Africa 1920–[Annual].* Capetown and Johannesburg: Juta & Co., 1921– [Annual].

South West Africa. Administration. *White Paper on the Activities of the Different Branches.* Windhoek: Clerk of the Legislative Assembly, [Annual].

South West Africa People's Organization of Namibia. *Discussion paper on the constitution of independent Namibia.* London: SWAPO, 1975.

South West Africa. Statutes. *The Laws of South West Africa: Ordinances Issued in South West Africa during . . . [date],* 1915/1922– . Vol I– . Annual.

Sparks, Donald, and December Green. *Namibia: The Nation After Independence.* Boulder, CO: Westview Press, 1992.

Tauber, L. "Legal Pitfalls on the Road to Namibian Independence." *New York University Journal of International Law and Politics* 12, (1979), 375–410.

Verbaan, Mark. "Opening a New Chapter." *Africa Report* 35, No. 2, (May–June 1990): 25–28.

Verbaan, Mark. "The Road to Independence." *Africa Report* 34, No. 6, 13–16.

Woldring, Klaas. "Namibia: Reflections on Alternative Plans for Independence." *Australian Outlook* 35 (1981): 295–306.

B. Politics and Political Parties

Abrahams, Kenneth. "The Reverend Peter Kalangula and the Failure of Reformism." *The Namibian Review* No. 24 (May 1982): 1–19.

———. "A Review of the Geneva Conference." *The Namibia Review* No. 21 (January–March 1981): 1–14.

Abrahams, Ottillie. "An Interview with the Rev. P. T. Kalangula." *The Namibian Review* No. 24 (May 1982): 19–22.

Action Front for the Retention of the Turnhalle Principles (ACTUR). *The Differences: ACTUR-DTA.* Windhoek: ACTUR, 1978.

Cowley, Clive. "Political Parties in SWA/Namibia." *Bulletin of the Africa Institute of South Africa* 16, No. 4 and 5, (1978).

Democratic Turnhalle Alliance. *Guidelines for a Socio-Economic Policy for SWA/Namibia.* Windhoek: Liaison Department, DTA, [n.d.].

DuPisani, A. "Reflections on the Role of Ethnicity in the Politics of Namibia." *Plural Societies* 8, No. 3/4 (Autumn/Winter 1977): 79–95.

Evenson, John A. "The Question Still Stands." *Africa Report* 31, No. 5 (1986): 62–65.

Gibson, Richard. *African Liberation Movements: Contemporary Struggles against White Minority Rule.* New York and London: Oxford University Press, 1972.

Grotpeter, John J. "African Politics in Settler States: A Comparative study with Implications for Namibia." Paper presented to the conference on "Namibia, Africa's Last Colony." Burlington, Vermont, April 5 and 6, 1982.

Grundy, Kenneth W. *Soldiers Without Politics*. Berkeley and Los Angeles, California: University of California Press, 1983.

Gurirab, Theo-Ben. *Namibia: For Freedom and Independence (Voices for Liberation)*. New York: The Africa Fund in Association with the American Committee on Africa, 1981.

Hamutenya, Hidipo L., and Gottfried H. Geingob. "Africa Nationalism in Namibia." Pp. 85–94. In C. P. Potholm and Richard Dale, eds. *Southern Africa in Perspective*. New York: Free Press, 1972.

Hendrik, Colleen. "Sam Nujoma: Profile of SWAPO's Leader." *Munger Africana Library Notes* Issue 61 (September, 1981): 11–16.

Kelso, B. J., "A Legacy of Inequity." *Africa Report* 37, No. 6 (November–December 1992): 34–37.

Kerina, Mburumba K. "Nationalist Leadership and Responsibility." *Freedomways* 2 (1962): 455–462.

Morris, Michael. *Armed Conflict in Southern Africa*. Cape Town: Jeremy Spence, 1974.

————. *Terrorism: The First Full Account in Detail of Terrorism and Insurgency in Southern Africa*. Cape Town: Howard Timmins, 1971.

Namibia National Front. *Policy Manifesto and Alternatives*. Windhoek: Secretary General, NNF, 1978.

The Namibian Review No. 15 (October 1978). This entire issue of the journal is devoted to articles on forthcoming elections.

"Nazism in South-West Africa." *Round Table* 25, No. 98 (1935): 425–432.

Ndadi, Vinnia. *Breaking Contract: The Story of Vinnia Ndadi.* Recorded and ed. by Dennis Mercer. Richmond, British Columbia: LSM Press, 1974.

Ngavirue, Z. *Political Parties and Interest Groups in South West Africa: A Study of a Plural Society.* Unpublished Oxford D. Phil. thesis, 1972.

Nujoma, Sam. "Interview with Sam Nujoma." *Africa Report* 20, No. 2 (March/April 1975): 12–13.

———. "Namibians Want Immediate End to South Africa's Rule." *Objective: Justice* 4, No. 1 (January/March 1972): 6–8.

———. "South Africa's Bantustanization of Namibia." *Objective: Justice* 7, No. 3 (July/September 1975): 9–13.

Pütz, Joachim, Heidi Von Egidy, and Perri Caplan. *Namibia Handbook and Political Who's Who.* Windhoek: The Magus Company, 1989.

———. *Political Who's Who of Namibia* (Namibia Series Vol. 1). Windhoek: The Magus Company, 1987.

Shipanga, Andreas. *Interview with Andreas Shipanga.* Richmond, British Columbia: LSM Press, 1973.

Shipanga, Andreas, as told to Sue Armstrong. *In Search of Freedom: The Andreas Shipanga Story.* Gibraltar: Ashanti Publishing, 1989.

Shityuwete, Helao. *Never Follow the Wolf.* London: Kliptown Books, 1990.

South West Africa People's Organization. "Do Not Let the People of Namibia Down." *Southern Africa* 2 (1973): 97–106.

SWAPO. "Namibia; People's Resistance, 1960–1970." *Race and Class* (Summer 1980): 23–46.

SWAPO Department of Information and Publicity. *To Be Born a Nation: The Liberation Struggle for Namibia.* London: Zed Press, 1981.

Theodoropoulos, C. "Support for SWAPO's War of Liberation in International Law." *Africa Today* 26 (1978): 39–48.

Totemeyer, Gerhard Karl Hans. *Namibia, Old and New: Traditional and Modern Leaders in Ovamboland.* London: C. Hurst, 1978.

———. "Political Groupings in Namibia—Their Role and Chances." *International Affairs Bulletin* 2, No. 1 (1978): 3–31.

———. "The Potential Role of Political Parties in the Political Development of South West Africa." *South African Journal of African Affairs* 6, No. 1/2 (1976): 151–161.

Uys, Stanley. "Namibia: The Socialist Dilemma." *African Affairs* 81, No. 325 (October 1982): 569–576.

Verbaan, Mark. "Born in Blood." *Africa Report* 34, No. 5 (September–October 1989): 27–29.

———. "Namibia: Making it Work." *Africa Report* 36, No. 2 (March–April 1991): 38–40.

Vigne, Randolph. "SWAPO Congress." *Africa Report* XV, No. 3 (March 1970): 8–9.

Ya-Otto, John, with Ole Gjerstad and Michael Mercer. *Battle-Front Namibia: An Autobiography.* Westport, CT: Lawrence Hill, 1981.

C. Race Relations

Anti-Apartheid Movement. *Racism and Apartheid in Southern Africa: South Africa and Namibia.* Paris: The Unesco Press, 1974.

Bunting, Brian. "Windhoek Diary." *Africa South* 4, No. 3 (April–June 1960): 76–83.

D'Amato, Anthony A. "Apartheid in South West Africa: Five Claims of Equality." *Portia Law Journal* 1 (1966): 59–76.

Dewaldt, F., ed. *Native Uprisings in South West Africa: Documents on the Armed Uprising of the Bondelzwart Tribe (1922) and the Bloodless Revolt of the Rehoboth Baastards (1925) in Ex-German Southwest Africa Administered by the Union of South Africa under Mandate.* Salisbury, NC: Documentary Pubs., 1976.

Grundy, Kenneth W. *Soldiers Without Politics: Blacks in the South African Armed Forces.* Berkeley, Los Angeles, and London: University of California Press, 1983.

Hoogenhout, Petrus Imker. "The Strandlopers of South-west Africa." *Race Relations* 16, No. 2 (1949): 38–41.

International Commission of Jurists. "Apartheid in Namibia." *Objective: Justice* 6, No. 1 (1974): 16–24.

———. *Apartheid in South Africa and South West Africa.* Geneva: International Commission of Jurists, 1967.

Jones, John David Rheinallt. *The Administration of South West Africa: Welfare of the Indigenous Population.* Johannesburg: South African Institute of Race Relations, [n.c. (c. 1952 or 1953)].

———. *The Future of South-West Africa.* Johannesburg: South African Institute of Race Relations, 1946.

———. *The South West Africa Question.* Johannesburg: South African Institute of Race Relations, 1949.

Kozonguizi, Jariretundu. "Background to Violence." *Africa South* 4, No. 3 (April–June 1960): 71–75.

Mason, Philip. "Separate Development and South West Africa: Some Aspects of the Odendaal Report." *Race* 5, No. 4 (1964): 83–97.

Munger, Edwin S. *South West Africa: Key German Minority.* New York: American Universities Field Staff, September 1955.

Olivier, M. J. "Ethnic Relations in South West Africa." *Plural Societies* 2 (1971): 31–42.

Racism and Apartheid in Southern Africa: South Africa and Namibia. Paris: The UNESCO Press, 1974.

South Africa. Department of Coloured Relations and Rehoboth Affairs. *Annual Report of the Department of Coloured and Rehoboth Affairs.* Pretoria: The Government Printer, [Annual].

D. For and Against South African Control

Abdul-Rahim, Salih. "End Game or Old Game?" *Africa Report* 30 (1985): 14–18.

Apartheid's Army in Namibia: South Africa's Illegal Military Occupation. Fact Paper on Southern Africa No. 10. London: International Defence and Aid Fund for Southern Africa, 1982.

Auala, Bishop Leonard N. *The Ovambo: Our Problems and Hopes.* Munger Africana Library Notes No. 17. Pasadena: California Institute of Technology, 1973.

————. "SWA in Desperate Struggle: An Interview." *Pro Veritate* 12, No. 11 (March 15, 1974): 11–12.

Ballinger, Ronald B. *South West Africa: The Case Against the Union.* Johannesburg: The South African Institute of Race Relations, 1961.

Political / 693

Belfiglio, Valentine J. "The Issue of Namibian Independence." *African Affairs* 78, No. 313 (October 1979): 507–522.

Berat, Lynn. *Walvis Bay: Decolonization and International Law.* New Haven, CT: Yale University Press, 1990.

Brandt, H., et al. *Perspectives of Independent Development in Southern Africa: The Cases of Zimbabwe and Namibia.* Berlin: German Development Institute, 1980.

Bruckner de Villiers Research (Southern Africa). *Recent Political and Constitutional Developments in South West Africa: A Survey of the Namibian Impasse.* Johannesburg: Bruckner de Villiers Research (Southern Africa), 1976.

Carter, Gwendolen and Patrick O'Meara, eds. *Southern Africa: International Issues and Responses.* Bloomington: Indiana University Press, 1982.

Cowley, Clive. "South West Africa: Its Problems and Prospects." *Optima* 25, No. 3 (1975): 171–196.

Dale, Richard. "The Armed Forces as an Instrument of South African Policy in Namibia." *Journal of Modern African Studies* 18, No. 1 (1980): 57–71.

———. "South Africa and Namibia." *Current History* (December 1977): 290–313, 226–227.

Diescho, Joseph. "Freedom Around the Corner?" *Africa Report* 34, No. 1 (1989): 25–27.

Dreyer, Ronald. "Dispute over Walvis Bay—Origins and Implications for Namibian Independence." *African Affairs* 83 (1984): 497–510.

Fraenkel, Peter. *The Namibians of South West Africa.* London: Minority Rights Group, Report No. 19, 1974.

Goeckner, G. P., and Gunning, I. R. "Namibia, South Africa, and the Walvis Bay Dispute." *Yale Law Journal* 80 (1980): 903–922.

Green, R. H. "Transition to What? Some Issues of Freedom and Necessity in Namibia." *Development and Change* (July 1980): 419–453.

Grotpeter, John J. "Changing South Africa." *Current History* (March, 1980): 119–123, 134–136.

Herbstein, Denis. "The Propaganda War." *Africa Report* 32, No. 5 (1987): 35–38.

Herbstein, Denis, and John Evenson. *The Devils Are Among Us: The War for Namibia.* Atlantic Highlands, NJ: Zed Books, 1989.

Hunton, William Alphaeus. *Stop—South Africa's Crimes: No Annexation of South West Africa.* New York: Council on African Affairs, 1946.

Hurlich, S., and Richard Lee. "Colonialism, Apartheid and Liberation: A Namibian Example." Pp. 353–371. In G. Smith and D. Turner, eds. *Challenging Anthropology.* Toronto: McGraw-Hill-Ryerson, 1978.

Imishue, R. W. *South West Africa: An International Problem.* London: Pall Mall Press for the Institute of Race Relations, 1965.

Innes, D. "Imperialism and the National Struggle in Namibia." *Review of African Political Economy* 9 (May/Aug. 1978): 44–59.

International Defence and Aid Fund for Southern Africa. *Apartheid's Army in Namibia: South Africa's Illegal Military Occupation.* London: IDAF, 1982.

Jaster, Robert S. *South Africa in Namibia: The Botha Strategy.* New York: University Press of America, 1985.

Jinadu, L. Adele. "South West Africa: A Study in the 'Sacred Trust' Thesis." *African Studies Review* 14, No. 3 (Dec. 1971): 369–388.

Johnston, William. "Namibia: A 'Sacred Trust of Civilization.' " *Africa Today* 23, No. 3 (July/September 1976): 46–54.

Jowitt, H. "The Case against Incorporation." *Race Relations Journal*, XXIII, No. 1 (1956).

Katjavivi, Peter H. *A History of Resistance in Namibia.* London, Paris: UNESCO Press, 1988.

Konig, Barbara. *Namibia: The Ravages of War.* International Defence and Aid Fund, 1983.

Kozonguizi, Jariretundi. "South West Africa: Herero's Plea for Severing Relations with the Union." *Africa South* 2 (Oct.– Dec. 1957): 64–72.

Landis, Elizabeth. *Namibia: The Beginning of Disengagement* (Studies in Race and Nations). Denver: University of Denver Center on International Race Relations, 1971, (Vol. 2, No. 1), 1970–1971.

Lee, Richard. "The Gods Must Be Crazy, But the State Has a Plan: Government Policies Towards the San in Namibia." *Canadian Journal of African Studies* 20 (1986): 91–98.

Lowenstein, Allard K. *Brutal Mandate: A Journey to South West Africa.* New York: Macmillan, 1962.

Mbuende, Kaire. *Namibia, The Broken Shield: Anatomy of Imperialism and Revolution.* Uppsala: Nordiska Afrikainstitutet, Scandinavian Institute of African Studies, 1986.

Molnar, Thomas. *South West Africa: The Last Pioneer Country.* New York: Fleet Publishing Corp., 1966.

————. *Spotlight on South West Africa.* New York: American-African Affairs Association, Inc., 1966.

Murray, R. "Namibia's Elusive Independence: A Contrast between African Nationalism and South African Interests." *Round Table* No. 265 (January 1977): 42–49.

"Namibia: Dispute over Walvis Bay." *Africa* No. 59 (July 1976): 26–29.

Namibia in the 1980's. London: Catholic Institute for International Relations and British Council of Churches, 1981.

O'Linn, Bryan. *Die Zukunft Sudwestafrikas in realistischer Sicht.* Windhoek: John Meinert, 1976.

Prinsloo, Daan S. *SWA/Namibia: Towards a Negotiated Settlement.* Pretoria: Foreign Affairs Association, 1977.

————. *SWA: The Turnhalle and Independence.* Foreign Affairs Study Report No. 4. Pretoria: Foreign Affairs Association, 1976.

————. *Walvis Bay and the Penguin Islands: Background and Status.* Foreign Affairs Study Report No. 8. Pretoria: Foreign Affairs Association, 1977.

Rhoodie, Eschel Mostert. *The Paper Curtain.* Johannesburg: Voortrekkerpers, 1969.

————. *South West Africa: The Last Frontier in Africa.* New York: Twin Circle Publishers, 1967.

Roberts, Alun R. "The South African Strategy." *Africa Report* 34, No. 1 (1989): 29–30.

Seiler, John. "South Africa in Namibia: Persistence, Misconception, and Ultimate Failure," *Journal of Modern African Studies* 20, No. 4 (1982): 689–712.

Shepherd, George W. "Breaking the Namibian Impasse." *Africa Today* 29, No. 1 (1982): 21–35.

Simon, David. "Decolonization and Local Government in Namibia: The Neo-Apartheid Plan, 1977–1983." *Journal of Modern African Studies* 23 (1985): 507–526.

Smith, Suzanne. *Namibia: Violation of Trust.* Oxford, UK: Oxfam, 1986.

Streek, Barry. "South Africa's Stakes in the Border War." *Africa Report* 29, No. 2 (1984): 57–60.

Totemeyer, Gerhard, and John Seiler. "South West Africa/ Namibia: A Study in Polarisation and Confrontation." In John Seiler, ed. *Southern Africa Since the Portuguese Coup.* Boulder, CO: Westview Press, 1980.

Verbaan, Mark. "Peace on Pretoria's Terms?" *Africa Report* 34, No. 3 (1989): 13–16.

Vigne, Randolph. *A Dwelling Place of Our Own: The Story of the Namibian Nation.* London: International Defence and Aid Fund, 1973. 2nd ed., 1975.

———. "The Namibia File (Political Developments and Attempts to Resolve the Question of Independence for the Territory)." *Third World Quarterly* 5 (1983): 345–360.

Wellington, John H. "South West Africa: The Facts about the Disputed Territory." *Optima* 15 (March 1965): 40–54.

Winter, Colin O'Brien. *Namibia.* Grand Rapids, MI: William B. Eerdmans Publishing Co., 1977.

World Council of Churches. Program to Combat Racism. *Namibia: Background Paper.* Geneva: World Council of Churches, 1977.

———. *Namibia: The Struggle for Liberation.* Geneva: World Council of Churches, 1971.

E. Foreign Affairs and Diplomacy

Abrahams, Kenneth. "Namibian Independence Negotiations." *The Namibian Review* No. 25 (July/August 1982): 1–14.

Acheson, Dean. "United States' Involvement in South West Africa." *South Africa International* I, No. 4 (April 1971): 207–212.

American Committee on Africa. *U.S. Complicity in Underdevelopment in Namibia: The Issues Involved.* New York: Namibia Support Group, [c. 1972].

Cooper, Allan D. *U.S. Economic Power and Political Influence in Namibia, 1700–1982.* Boulder, CO: Westview Press, 1982.

———. *Allies in Apartheid.* New York: St. Martin's Press, 1988.

Crocker, Chester A., and Penelope Hartland-Thunberg. *Namibia at the Crossroads.* Washington, D.C.: Georgetown University Center for Strategic and International Studies, 1978.

Dale, Richard. "Walvis Bay: A Naval Gateway, an Economic Turnstile, or a Diplomatic Bargaining Chip for the Future of Namibia?" *RUSI: Journal of the Royal United Services Institute for Defence Studies* 127, No. 1 (March 1982): 31–36.

———. "The Politics of Namibian Immobilism: Conflict, Diplomacy and Guerilla Warfare in Southern Africa." *Conflict Quarterly* VI, No. 3 (1986): 26–38.

DuPisani, Andre. *Namibia: On Brinkmanship, Conflict and Self-Interest—The Collapse of the U.N. Plan." Politikon* 8, No. 1 (June 1981).

———. *A Review of the Diplomatic Efforts of the Western Contact Group on Namibia, 1976–1980.* Braamfontein: South African Institute of International Affairs, 1980.

Freeman, Charles W. "Anglo/Namibian Accords." *Foreign Affairs* 68, No. 3 (Summer 1989): 126–141.

Great Britain. *Angra Pequeña: Correspondence Respecting the Settlement at Angra Pequeña, on the S.W. Coast of Africa.* Presented to both Houses of Parliament by Command of Her Majesty, August 1884, Command Paper 4190. London: Eyre and Spottiswoode (printer), 1884.

————. *Angra Pequeña: Copy of a Dispatch from the Right Honourable the Earl of Derby, K.G., to Her Majesty's High Commissioner in South Africa . . . .* Command Paper 4265, London: Eyre and Spottiswoode, 1884.

————. *Angra Pequeña: Further Correspondence Respecting the Settlement at Angra Pequeña on the South-West coast of Africa.* Command Paper 4262, London: Eyre and Spottiswoode, 1884.

————. *Cape Colony: Further Correspondence Respecting the Claims of British Subjects in the German Protectorate of the South-West Coast of Africa . . . .* Command Paper 5180. London: Eyre and Spottiswoode, 1887.

————. *Correspondence Respecting the Anglo-German Agreement Relative to Africa and Heligoland.* Command Paper 6046. London: Her Majesty's Stationery Office, 1890.

Great Britain. Foreign and Commonwealth Office. *Namibia, Background to Independence Negotiations.* London: HMSO, 1980.

————. *Namibia (South West Africa): Independence Proposals.* London: HMSO, 1978.

Great Britain. Ministry of Foreign Affairs. *Agreement between the Government of the Union of South Africa and the Government of the Republic of Portugal in relation to the Boundary . . . .* Command Paper 2777. London: HMSO, 1926.

————. *Exchange of Notes between His Majesty's Government in the Union of South Africa and the Portuguese Government.* . . . Command Paper 3896. London: HMSO, 1931.

Grundy, Kenneth W. "Namibia in International Politics." *Current History* (March 1982): 101–105, 131–132.

Jabri, Vivienne. *Mediating Conflict: Decision-Making and Western Intervention in Namibia.* New York: St. Martin's for Manchester University Press.

Karns, Margaret P. "Ad Hoc Multilateral Diplomacy: The United States, the Contact Group, and Namibia." *International Organization* 41 (1987): 93–123.

Koroma, David S. M. "Namibia: The Case of a Betrayal of Sacred Trust." *Journal of African Studies* 12, No. 3 (1985): 141–153.

Landis, Elizabeth S. "American Obligations towards Namibia." *Issue* 1 (Fall 1971): 15–19.

————. "American Responsibilities towards Namibia: Law and Policy." *Africa Today* 18, No. 4 (1972): 38–48.

Leu, Christopher A. "The End of the Waldheim Initiative." *Africa Today* 21, No. 2 (1974): 43–59.

Levy, Marc A. "Mediation of Prisoners' Dilemma Conflicts and the Importance of the Cooperation Threshold: The Case of Namibia." *Journal of Conflict Resolution* 29, No. 4 (1985): 581–603.

Minter, William. "With All Deliberate Delay: National Security Action memorandum 295 and U.S. Policy Toward South West Africa." *The African Studies Review* 27, No. 3 (1984): 93–110.

Richardson, Henry J., III. "Constitutive Questions in Negotiations for Namibian Independence." *American Journal of International Law* 78, No. 1 (1984): 74–120.

Sano, Hans-Otto, et al. *Namibia and the Nordic Countries.* Uppsala: The Scandinavian Institute of African Studies, 1981.

Schroeder, Patricia. "A New Namibian Policy for the United States: Why It's Needed; What It Can Do." *Africa Today* 33, Nos. 2 & 3 (1986): 25–46.

Shepard, George W., Jr. "Breaking the Namibia Impasse." *Africa Today* 29, No. 1 (1982): 21–35.

Seiler, John. "Has Constructive Engagement Failed? An Assessment of Reagan's Southern African Policy." *South Africa International* 13, No. 3 (January 1982): 420–433.

———. "Reagan and Africa: Which Way in Southern Africa? (Emphasis on the Problem of Namibia)." *Africa Report* 26 (May–June 1981): 17–22.

Sinclair, Michael. "Namibian Constitutional Proposals: The Fleeting Options and Implications for South Africa." *South Africa International* 12, No. 4 (April 1982): 508–516.

Umozurike, Umozurike Oji. "International Law and Self-Determination in Namibia," *Journal of Modern African Studies* 8, No. 4 (December 1970): 585–603.

———. *Self-Determination and International Law.* Hamden, CT: Archon Books, 1972.

United States. Congress. House of Representatives Committee on Foreign Affairs. *Critical Developments in Namibia.* Washington, DC: Government Printing Office, 1974.

United States. Congress. House of Representatives Committee on International Relations, Subcommittee on International Organizations. *Namibia: The United Nations and U.S. Policy.* Washington, DC: Government Printing Office, 1976.

U.S. Policy Toward Namibia: Spring 1981. Washington, DC: Government Printing Office, 1981.

Wood, Brian. "Preventing the Vacuum: Determinants of the Namibia Settlement." *Journal of South African Studies,* 17, No. 4 (December 1991: 742–769.

Yankson, J. Ackah. *South-West Africa in the International Scene.* London: William Blackwood and Sons, 1953.

A. Geography

Bjerre, Jens. *Kalahari.* London: Michael Joseph, 1960. New York: Hill and Wang, 1960. (Originally published as *Kalahari atomtidens stenalder.* Copenhagen: 1958.)

Deutscher Kolonial-Atlas für den amtlichen Gebrauch in den Schutzgebieten. Text von J. Partsch. Berlin, [c. 1893].

Frey, Dr. C., and Ansley Watts. *A Regional Geography of South-West Africa.* Windhoek: John Meinert, 1924.

Hamilton, William J. III, "The Living Sands of the Namib." *National Geographic* (September, 1983): 364–377.

Jäger, Fritz. *Geographische Landschaften Südwestafrikas.* Windhoek: SWA Wissenschaftlichen Gesellschaft, 1965.

Leser, Dr. Hartmut. *Sudwestafrika: Eine Geographische Landskunde.* (Wissenschaftlichen Forschung in SWA, 14 Folge). Windhoek: SWA Wissenschaften Gesellschaft, 1976.

Logan, Richard Fink. *The Central Namib Desert, South West Africa.* Washington: National Academy of Sciences—National Research Council, 1960.

Schlichter, Henry. *Geography of South-West Africa.* 1891.

Wellington, J. H. *Southern Africa: A Geographical Study.* 2 Vols. Cambridge: Cambridge University Press, 1955.

B. Geology

Basler Geomethodischen Colloquiums. *Methodisch-geomorphologische Probleme der ariden und semiariden Zone Südwestafrikas.* Vol. 15 of Mitteilungen der Basler Bibliographien/ Communications from the Basel Africa Bibliography, Basel: Basel Afrika Bibliographien, 1976.

Cock, Gilbert. "The Composition of some Water Supplies in South West Africa." *Journal of the S.W.A. Scientific Society* II (1926–1927): 63–70.

Gevers, T. W. "Ice Ages in South-West Africa." *Journal of the S.W.A. Scientific Society* V (1929–1931): 77–88.

Kock, W. P. de. "Lithium—Its Distribution, Uses, Metallurgy and Chemistry with Reference to Its Deposits of the Karibib District." *Journal of the S.W.A. Scientific Society* VI (1931–1932): 95–100.

Martin, Henno. *The Precambrian Geology of South West Africa and Namaqualand.* Cape Town: Precambrian Research Unit, University of Cape Town, 1965.

Rogers, A. W. "Pioneers of South African Geology." *Transactions of the Geological Society of South Africa.* Annexure to Vol. 39 (1937).

South Africa. Department of Mines. *Geology of the Warmbad District, S.W. Africa* by S. H. Haughton and H. F. Frommurze. Memoir II. Windhoek: SA Dept of Mines, 1936.

————. *The Geology and Mineral Deposits of the Omaruru Area* by S. H. Haughton, H. F. Frommurze, T. W. Gevers, C. M.

2

Schwellnus, P. J. Rossouw. Pretoria: The Government
Printer, 1939.

Uranium Deposits in Africa: Geology and Exploration. Proceedings of a Regional Advisory Group Meeting, Lusaka, Zambia, 14–18 November 1977. Vienna: International Atomic Energy Agency, 1979.

Wager, Percy Albert. *Geological Survey: The Geology and Mineral Industry of South West Africa.* (Geological Survey Report No. 7.) Pretoria: Govt. Printing and Stationery Office, 1961.

C. Medicine

McRoberts, Dr. "The Influence of the Climate of South West Africa on the Nervous System of Europeans." *Journal of the S.W.A. Scientific Society,* IV (1928–1929): 5–10.

Proell, F. "Zahndeformation und Haartrachten in Südwestafrika." *Zeitschrift für Ethnologie* 64 (1932): 1–8.

Schultze, L. *Zur Kenntnis des Körpers der Hottentotten und Buschmänner.* Bd. 5, Lfg 3. Jena: Fischer, 1928.

Walker, Dr. H. F. B. *A Doctor's Diary in Damaraland.* London: Edward Arnold, 1917.

Weinberg, Con. *Fragments of a Desert Land: Memoirs of a South West African Doctor.* Cape Town: Howard Timmins, 1975.

Whitby, Jonathan Montague F. *Bundu Doctor.* London: Robert Hale, 1961.

Wilmsen, E. *Diet and Fertility Among Kalahari Bushmen.* Working Papers, No. 14. Boston: Boston University, African Studies Center, 1979.

D. Botany

Boss, Georg. *Aus dem Pflanzenleben Südwestafrika.* Windhoek: Meinert, 1934.

Craven, Patricia, and Christine Marais. *Namib Flora.* [Windhoek]?: Gamsberg, 1986.

Dinter, Kurt. *Deutsch-Südwest-Afrika: Flora-, Forst- underland wirtschaftliche Fragmente.* Leipzig: Weigel, 1909.

————. *Diagnosen neuer südwestafrikanischen Pflanzen. Kurzer Bericht über meine Reise 1929 in die Küstenwüste.* S.W.-Afrikas, spez. die Buchaberge. Sep.–Abdr. aus Fedde, Repertorium. Bd. XXIX: 253–272; Bd. XXX: 180–208.

————. *Neue und wenig bekannte Pflanzen Deutsch-Südwest-Afrikas, unter besonderer Berücksichtigung der Succulenten.* Okahandja: Selbstverlag, 1914.

————. *Vegetabilische Veldkost in Südwest Afrika.* Okahandja: Selbstverlag, 1912.

Giess, W. "Vledkost in Sudwest Afrika." *South West Africa Scientific Journal* 20, (1965/1966).

Herre, H. "The Age of 'Welwitschia bainesii'." *Journal of South African Botany* 27 (1961): 39.

————. *Die Narapflanze in Namib und Meer.* Swakopmund: Gesellschaft für Wissenschaftliche Entwicklung und Museum Swakopmund, 1974/1975.

Malan, J. S., and G. L. Owen-Smith. "The Ethnobotany of Kaokoland." *Cimbebasia/SWA Research* 2, Ser. B, No. 5 (18 September 1974): 131–178.

Marloth, Rudolf. *Vegetation of the Southern Namib.* 1910.

————. *The Flora of South Africa.* Vol. I, 1914.

Pearson, H. H. W. "Travels of a Botanist in S.W. Africa." *Geographical Journal* 35 (May 1910).

Shaw, E. M. "Bushman Arrow Poisons." *Cimbebasia: Journal of the South West African Scientific Society* 1, No. 1 (1963): 1–35.

Story, R. "Plant Lore of the Bushmen." In D. H. S. Davis, ed. *Ecological Studies in Southern Africa.* Hague: Junk, 1964.

————. *Some Plants used by the Bushmen in Obtaining Food and Water.* Botanical Survey of South Africa, Memoir No. 30. Pretoria: Government Printers, 1958.

E. Zoology

Barnard, K. H. "The Non-Marine Crustacea of South West Africa." *Journal of the S.W.A. Scientific Society* III (1927–1928): 61–68.

Coaton, W. G. H., and J. L. Sheasby. *Preliminary Report on a Survey of the Termites (Isoptera) of South West Africa.* Cimbebasia Memoir No. 2. Windhoek: State Museum, 1972.

Gill, E. L. "Biological Surveys." *Journal of the S.W.A. Scientific Society* II (1926–1927): 29–34.

Hesse, A. J. "Impressions of Insect Life in South West Africa." *Journal of the S.W.A. Scientific Society* III (1927–1928): 49–60.

Laurence, R. F. "The Reptiles of South West Africa." *Journal of the S.W.A. Scientific Society* II (1926–1927): 13–28.

Macdonald, J. D. *Contribution to the Ornithology of Western South Africa: Results of the British Museum (Natural His-*

tory) South West African Expedition, 1948–1950. London: Trustees of the British Museum, 1957.

Penrith, Mary-Louise. *the Zophosini (Coleoptera: Tenebrionidae) of Western Southern Africa.* Cimbebasia Memoir No. 3. Windhoek: State Museum, 1977.

Shortridge, Guy Chester. "Game Protection." *Journal of the S.W.A. Scientific Society* III (1927–1928): 69–76.

————. *The Mammals of South West Africa: A Biological Account of the Forms Occurring in that Region.* 2 Vols. London: Heinemann, 1934.

————. "Field Notes on the Northern Distribution of the Antelopes of South West Africa." *Journal of the S.W.A. Scientific Society* II (1926–1927): 5–12.

For information on many scientific subjects, see the *Journal of the South West Africa Scientific Society.* Volume I (1925–1926) was published in 1927, and it became an annual publication.

7. SOCIAL

A. Anthropology and Ethnology

1. General

Drury, J. "Preliminary Report on the Anthropological Researches carried out by Mr. Drury in S.W.A." *Annals of the South African Museum* 24, Part 2 and 5 (1935).

Estermann, Carlos. *The Ethnography of Southwestern Angola.* 3 volumes. Vol. 1. *The Non-Bantu Peoples: The Ambo Ethnic Group.* Vol. 2. *The Nyaneka-Nkumbi People.* Vol. 3. *The Herero People.* Ed. by Gordon D. Gibson. New York: Africana Publishing Co. (Holmes & Meier), 1976, 1979, 1981.

Die Ethnischen Gruppen in Südwestafrika. Windhoek: SWA Wissenschaftliche Gesellschaft, 1965.

Hahn, Carl Hugo Linsingen, Heinrich Vedder, and L. Fourie. *The Native Tribes of South West Africa.* Cape Town: Cape Times, Ltd., 1928, reprinted in London: Cass, 1966.

Hoernlé, A. "South-West Africa as a Primitive Culture Area." *South African Geographical Journal* 6 (1923): 14–28.

Jenkins, T., and C. K. Brain. "The People of the Lower Kuiseb Valley, S.W.A." *Scientific Papers of the Namib Desert Research Station* 35 (1967).

Levinson, Olga. "South West Africa and Its Indigenous People." *South Africa International* III, No. 1 (July 1972): 19–27.

Namibiana, Communications of the ethno-historical study group III, (2). Windhoek: SWA Scientific Society, 1981.

Norton, W. A. "The South-West Protectorate and Its Native Population." *Report of the South African Association for the Advancement of Science* 16, No. 5 (1920): 453–465.

Schmidt, Max. "Die Nama, Bergdama und Namib-Buschleute." Pp. 269–397. Vol. II (*Togo, Kamerun, Südwestafrika, die Südseekolonien*) of E. Schultz-Ewerth and L. Adam, eds. *Das Eingeborenenrecht.* Stuttgart: Strecker & Schröder, 1930.

Schwarz, E. H. L. *The Kalahari and Its Native Races.* London: H. F. & G. Witherby, 1928.

South Africa. Department of Bantu Administration and Development. *Ethnographic Survey of South West Africa,* by G. Wagner. Unpublished manuscript in the Department of Bantu Administration and Development, Ethnological Section. Windhoek, 1951.

————. *A Study of Otjiwarongo District (South West Africa)*. Ethnological Publication No. 44 by O. Köhler. Pretoria: The Government Printer, 1959.

Theal, George McCall. *Ethnography and Condition of South Africa before A.D. 1505*. London: George Allen & Unwin, 1919. A second edition with minor changes of Theal's *The Yellow and Dark-Skinned People of Africa South of the Zambesi*.

————. *History and Ethnography of Africa South of the Zambesi*. 3 vols. London: Swan Sonnenschein & Co., 1907–1910.

————. *The Yellow and Dark-Skinned People of Africa South of the Zambesi*. London: Swan Sonnenschein & Co., Ltd., 1910. Reproduced, New York: Negro Universities Press, 1969.

Vedder, Heinrich. *South-West Africa in Early Times; Being the Story of South-West Africa up to the Date of Maharero's Death in 1890*. Trans. and ed. by Cyril G. Hall. London: Oxford University Press, 1938.

Wissenschaftliche Forschung in Südwestafrika. Die Ethnischen Gruppen in Sudwestafrika. Windhoek: Wissenschaftlichen Gesellschaft von Vorstand, 1965.

2. The San and Bushmen

Bleek, Dorothea Frances. *The Naron: A Bushmen Tribe of the Central Kalahari*. Cambridge: Cambridge University Press, 1928.

Brownlee, Frank. "The Social Organization of the Kung (!Un) Bushmen of the North-western Kalahari." *Africa* 14 (July 1943): 124–129.

Crosby, Oscar T. "Notes on Bushmen and Ovambo in South West Africa." *Journal of The African Society* 30 (Oct. 1931): 344–360.

Dart, R. A. "A Note on Jan, the Bushman." *Bantu Studies* (1924).

Draper, P. "!Kung Women: Contrasts in Sexual Egalitarianism in the Foraging and Sedentary Contexts." Pp. 77–109. In R. Reiter, ed. *Toward an Anthropology of Women*. New York: Monthly Review Press, 1975.

———. "The Learning Environment for Aggression and Antisocial Behavior among the !Kung." Pp. 31–53. In A. Montagu, ed. *Teaching Non-Aggression*. New York: Oxford University Press, 1978.

Dunn, Edward John. *The Bushman*. London: Charles Griffin & Co., 1931.

Eriksen, H. "Facial Features of Kuanyama Ovambo and Heikum Bushmen." *South African Journal of Science* 51 (August 1954): 18–29.

Fourie, L. "Preliminary Notes on Certain Customs of the Hei-// om Bushmen." *Journal of the S.W.A. Scientific Society* I (1925–1926): 49–63.

———. "Preliminary Notes on Certain Customs of the Hel//Om [sic] Bushmen." *Journal of the South West African Scientific Society* (1951): 65–80.

Gordon, Robert J. *The Bushman Myth: The Making of a Namibian Underclass*. Boulder, CO: Westview Press, 1992.

Hahn, Theophilus. "Die Buschmänner." *Globus* XVIII (1870): 65–68, 81–85, 102–105, 120–123, 140–143, 153–155.

Jordaan, K. "The Bushmen of Southern Africa: Anthropology and Historical Materialism." *Race and Class* 17, No. 2 (1975): 141–160.

Konner, M. "Infancy among the Kalahari Desert San." In P. H. Leiderman, et al., eds. *Culture and Infancy.* New York: Academic Press, 1977.

Lee, Richard B. *The !Kung San: Men, Women, and Work in a Foraging Society.* Cambridge: Cambridge University Press, 1979.

Lee, Richard Borshay and I. DeVore, eds. *Kalahari Hunter-Gatherers: Studies of the !Kung San and their Neighbours.* Cambridge, MA: Harvard University Press, 1976.

Marshall, John. "Hunting Among the Kalahari Bushmen." *Natural History* 67 (1958): 291–309, 376–395.

Marshall, Lorna. "The Kin Terminology System of the !Kung Bushmen." *Africa* 27 (1957): 1–25.

———. "!Kung Bushman Bands." *Africa* 30, No. 4 (October 1960): 325–355.

———. "The !Kung Bushmen of the Kalahari Desert." In James Gibbs, ed. *Peoples of Africa.* New York: Holt, Rinehart and Winston, 1965.

———. *The !Kung of Nyae Nyae.* Cambridge, MA: Harvard University Press, 1976.

———. *Marriage among !Kung Bushmen."* *Africa* 29, No. 4 (October 1959): 335–365.

———. "The Medicine Dance of the !Kung Bushmen." *Africa* 39 (1969): 347–381.

———. "Sharing, Talking, and Giving: Relief of Social Tensions among !Kung Bushmen." *Africa* 31, No. 3 (July 1961): 231–249.

Metzger, Fritz. *Narro and His Clan.* Windhoek: John Meinert Ltd., 1950.

Perkins, Carol Morse, and Marlin Perkins. *"I Saw You from Afar": A Visit to the Bushmen of the Kalahari Desert.* New York: Atheneum, 1965.

Schapera, Isaac. *The Khoisan Peoples of South Africa: Bushmen and Hottentots.* London: George Routledge & Sons, 1930.

———. "A Preliminary Consideration of the Relationship between the Hottentots and the Bushmen." *South African Journal of Science* 23 (1926): 833–866.

———. "A Survey of the Bushman Question." *Race Relations* 6, No. 2 (1939): 68–83.

Shaw, E. M. *Man in Southern Africa: The Bushmen (Die Boesmans).* Cape Town: South African Museum, [c. 1971].

Shostak, Marjorie. *Nisa: The Life and Words of a !Kung Woman.* Cambridge, MA: Harvard University Press, 1981.

South Africa. Department of Bantu Administration. *A Study of Grootfontein District (South West Africa).* Ethnological Publication No. 45 by O. Köhler. Pretoria: The Government Printer, 1959.

Tanaka, J. "The Ecology and Social Structure of Central Kalahari Bushmen." In T. Umesao, ed. *African Studies.* Vol. 3. Kyoto: Kyoto University Press, 1969.

Thomas, Elizabeth Marshall. *The Harmless People.* New York: Alfred A. Knopf, 1959; London: Secker & Warburg, 1959.

Tobias, Phillip Vallentine. "Bushmen Hunter-Gatherers: A Study in Human Ecology." Pp. 67–86. In D. H. S. Davis, ed. *Ecological Studies in Southern Africa.* The Hague: 1964.

———, ed. *The Bushmen: San Hunters and Herders of Southern Africa.* Cape Town: Human and Rousseau, 1978.

————. "On the Survival of the Bushmen." *Africa* 26, No. 2 (April 1956): 174–186.

————. "Physique of a Desert Folk: Genes, not Habitat, Shaped the Bushmen." *Natural History* 170, No. 2 (1961): 16–24.

Van der Post, Laurens. *The Heart of the Hunter.* London: The Hogarth Press, 1961; New York: Morrow, 1961.

————. *The Lost World of the Kalahari.* New York: William Morrow & Co., 1958.

Vedder, Heinrich. "Die Buschmänner Südwestafrikas und ihr Weltanschauung." *South African Journal of Science* 34 (Nov. 1937): 416–436.

3. Nama (Hottentot)

Carstens, Peter. "The Inheritance of Private Property Among the Nama of Southern Africa Reconsidered." *Africa* 53, No. 2 (1983): 58–69.

Elphick, Richard. *Kraal and Castle: Khoikhoi and the Founding of White South Africa.* New Haven: Yale University Press, 1977.

————. *Khoikhoi and the Founding of White South Africa.* Johannesburg: Ravan Press, 1985.

Francois, Hugo von. *Nama und Damara: Deutsch-Süd-Westafrika.* Magdeburg: E. Baensch, 1896.

Hahn, Theophilus. "Die Nama-Hottentoten: Ein Beitrag zur Südafrikanischen Ethnographie." *Globus* XII (1867): 238sqq.

Hoernlé, Agnes Winifred. "Certain Rites of Transition and the Conception of Nau among the Hottentots." *Harvard African Studies* 2 (1918): 65–82.

———. "The Expression of the Social Value of Water among the Naman of South-West Africa." *South African Journal of Science* XX, No. 2 (December 1923): 514–526.

———. "The Social Organization of the Nama Hottentots of South West Africa." *American Anthropologist* (New Series) XXVII, No. 1 (January-March 1925): 1–24.

Hoernlé, Winifred. *The Social Organization of the Nama.* Johannesburg: Witwatersrand University Press, 1985.

Ross, Edward S. "The Kuiseb's Topnaar Hottentots." *South West Africa Annual* 27 (1971): 170–175.

Schapera, I. "A Preliminary Consideration of the Relationship between the Hottentots and the Bushmen." *South African Journal of Science* 23 (1926): 833–866.

Shaw, E. M. *Man in Southern Africa: The Hottentots/Die Hottentotten.* Cape Town: South African Museum, 1972.

Vedder, H. "The Nama." Pp. 109–152. In *The Native Tribes of South West Africa.* Cape Town: Cape Times, 1928.

4. Herero

Büttner, C. G. "Die Herero und ihre Toten." *Ausland* LVII (1884).

———. "Märchen der Ova-Herero." *Journal of the African Society* 1 (1888).

Gibson, Gordon D. "Bridewealth and Other Forms of Exchange among the Herero." In Paul Bohannon and George Dalton, eds. *Markets in Africa.* Evanston: Northwestern University Press, 1962.

————. "Herero Marriage." *Rhodes-Livingston Journal* No. 24 (1958): 1–37.

Irle, J. *Die Herero: Ein Beitrag zur Landes-, Volks-, & Missions-kunde.* Gütersloh: Druck and Verlag von C. Bertelsman, 1906.

————. "Die Religion der Herero." *Archiv für Anthropologie* XLIII, N.F., XV, (1917): 337ff.

Luttig, H. G. *The Religious System and Social Organisation of the Herero: A Study in Bantu Culture.* Utrecht: Keminken Zoon N.V., [1932].

Poewe, Karla. *The Namibia Herero.* Lewiston, ME: Edwin Mellen Press, 1985.

Schapera, I. *Notes on Some Herero Genealogies.* Cape Town: University of Cape Town, October 1945.

————. "Notes on Some Herero Genealogies." *Africa Studies* 38, No. 1 (1979): 17–42.

South Africa. Department of Bantu Administration. *Notes on the Kaokoveld (South West Africa) and Its People.* Ethnological Publications No. 26 by N. J. van Warmelo, Government Ethnologist. Pretoria: The Government Printer, 1951.

————. Department of Bantu Administration and Development. *A Study of Gobabis District (South West Africa).* Ethnological Publications No. 42 by O. Köhler. Pretoria: The Government Printer, 1959.

————. Department of Native Affairs. *A Study of Okahandja District (South West Africa).* Ethnological Publications No. 38 by Günter Wagner. Revised and edited by O. Köhler. Pretoria: The Government Printer, 1957.

Stuchlik, Milan. "Social Stratification of the Herero." Pp. 151–166. In *Social Stratification in Tribal Africa*. Prague: 1968.

Vedder, Heinrich. "Maherero und seine Zeit im Lichte der Dokumente seines Nachlasses." *Journal of the SWA Scientific Society* V (1929–1931): 5–31.

Vivelo, F. R. "The Entry of the Herero into Botswana." *Botswana Notes and Records* 8 (1976): 39–46.

Wagner, Günter. "Some Economic Aspects of Herero Life." *African Studies* 13 (1954): 117–130.

5. Ovambo

Eriksen, H. "Facial Features of Kwanyama Ovambo and Heikum Bushmen." *South African Journal of Science* 51 (August 1954): 18–29.

Galloway, A. "A Contribution to the Physical Anthropology of the Ovambo." *South African Journal of Science* 34 (1937): 351–364.

Hahn, C. H. L. "Preliminary Notes on Certain Customs of the Ovambo." *Journal of the South West Africa Scientific Society* 3 (1927–1928): 5–33.

Loeb, Edwin Meyer. *In Feudal Africa* [Kuanyama]. Indiana University Research Center in Anthropology, Folklore and Linguistics Publication No. 23. Bloomington, IN: University of Indiana Press, 1962.

———. "The Kwanyama Ambo." *Scientific American* 183, No. 4 (1950): 52–55.

———. *Kuanyama Ambo Magic*. Berkeley: University of California Press, 1951.

————. "Transition Rites of the Kuanyame Ambo." *African Studies* 7 (1948): 16–28, 71–84.

Tötemeyer, G. K. H. *Namibia Old and New: Traditional and Modern Leaders in Ovamboland.* London: C. Hurst, 1978.

Tuupainen, Maija. "Marriage in a Matrilineal African Tribe: A Social Anthropological Study of Marriage in the Ondonga Tribe in Ovamboland." *Transactions of The Westermarck Society* 18 (1970).

6. Damara and Bergdama

Eisinger, A. *In Damaraland und Kaoko-Feld.* Bühl (Baden): 1913.

Francois, Hugo von. *Nama und Damara: Deutsch-Süd-Westafrika.* Magdeburg: E. Baensch, 1896.

Gordon, R. J. "Towards an Ethnography of Bergdama Gossip." *Namib und Meer* Band 2 (November 1971): 45–57.

South Africa. Department of Bantu Administration and Development. *A Study of Omaruru District (South West Africa).* Ethnological Publications No. 43 by O. Köhler. Pretoria: The Government Printer, 1959.

South Africa. Department of Native Affairs. *A Study of Karibib District (South West Africa).* Ethnological Publications No. 40 by O. Köhler. Pretoria: The Government Printer, 1958.

Vedder, Heinrich. *Die Bergdama.* 2 vols. in one. Hamburg: L. Friederichsen & Co., 1923.

Viereck, A. "The Damaraland Culture." *Journal of the South West Africa Scientific Society* 21 (1967): 13–31.

7. Kavango and Caprivi People

Gibson, Gordon D., Thomas J. Larson, and Cecilia R. McGurk. *The Kavango Peoples.* Studien zur Kulturkunde 56. Wiesbaden: Franz Steiner Verlag, 1981.

Larson, Thomas J. "The Significance of Rainmaking for the Mbukushu." *African Studies* 25, No. 1 (1966): 23–36.

Nurse, G. T., and T. Jenkins. "The Kavango Peoples." *Journal of the South West Africa Scientific Society* XXX (1975/76): 55–58.

Streitwolf. *Der Caprivizipfel.* Berlin: Süsserot, 1911.

8. Basters

Bayer, Maxmilian (Hauptmann im grossen Generalstabe). *Die Nation der Bastards.* Berlin: 1907.

DeVilliers, J. *Report of the Rehoboth Commission.* Cape Town: Cape Times Ltd., 1927.

Fischer, Eugen. *Die Rehobother Bastards und das Bastardierungsproblem beim Menschen: Anthropologische und ethnographische Studien am Rehobother Bastard-volk in Deutsch-Südwest-Afrika.* Granz, Austria: Akademische Druck- U. Verlags-anstalt, 1961.

United Nations Secretariat. "The Rehoboth Community of South West Africa." *African Studies* 14, No.4 (1955): 175–200.

9. Others

Gibson, G. D. "Himba Epochs." *History in Africa* 4 (1977): 67–121.

Hitzeroth, H. W. "On the Identity of the Stone-Working Tjimba of South West Africa: A Comparative Multi-variate Anthropometric Analysis.'' In *Cimbebasia* Series B, Vol. 2, No. 9 (17 December 1976): 209–226.

―――. ''On the Identity of the Stone-Working Tjimba, South West Africa: A Comparative Study based on Fingerprint Pattern Frequencies.'' *Cimbebasia* Series B, Vol. 2, No. 7 (27 February 1976): 187–202.

―――. ''Peoples of the Kaokoveld.'' *Bulletin of the Africa Institute of South Africa.* 9, 5 (June 1971): 192–200.

MacCalman, H. R., and B. J. Grobbelaar. ''Preliminary Report of Two Stone-working OvaTjimba Groups in the Northern Kaokoveld of South West Africa.'' In *Cimbebasia: SWA Research* No. 13 (1965): 1–39 (entire issue).

Malan, J. S. ''Double Descent among the Himba of South West Africa.'' *Cimbebasia/SWA Research* Ser. B, Vol. 2, No. 3 (12 October 1973): 81–112.

―――. ''The Herero-Speaking peoples of Kaokoland.'' *Cimbebasia/SWA Research,* Ser. B, Vol. 2, No. 4 (21 June 1974): 113–129.

Wilhelm, Joachim H. ''Die Hukwe.'' *Stadtisches Museums für Völkerkunde Jahrbuch* 13 (1954–1955): 8–44.

B. Education

Doyle, M. V. ''Adult Literacy Education in Namibia.'' *Community Development Journal* 14, No. 2 (April 1979): 91–97.

Education, Repression & Liberation. A Future for Namibia Series. London: Catholic Institute for International Relations, 1984.

Lewis-Jones, Helen. *Report on the Survey of the Educational Situation & Needs of Namibians in Independent African*

720 / The Bibliography

Countries. London: International University Exchange Fund, [1973].

Mugomba, Agrippah, and Mougo Nyaggah (eds.). *Independence without Freedom: The Political Economy of Colonial Education in Southern Africa.* Santa Barbara and Oxford: Clio Press, 1980.

O'Callaghan, Marion. *Namibia: The Effects of Apartheid on Culture and Education.* Paris: UNESCO, 1977.

Rogerson, Christian M. "A Future 'University of Namibia'? The Role of the United Nations Institute in Namibia." *The Journal of Modern African Studies* 18, No. 4 (1980): 675–683.

South West Africa Administration. Commission of Inquiry into Non-European Education in South West Africa. *Report of the Commission of Inquiry into Non-European Education in South West Africa.* Windhoek: South West Africa Administration, 1958. 2 vols. Part I. *Native Education.* Part II. *Coloured Education.*

C. Religion and Missions

Andrew, Veronica. *Ovamboland.* London: The Society for the Propagation of the Gospel in Foreign Parts, 1953.

Baumann, Julius. *Mission und Ökumene in Südwestafrika: Dargestellt am Lebenswerk von Hermann Heinrich Vedder.* Vol. VII of *Ökumenische Studien.* Leiden/Köln: E. J. Brill, 1965.

Bonn, A. *Ein Jahrhundert Rheinische Mission.* Barmen: RMS, 1928.

Brincker, Peter Heinrich. *Aus dem Hererolande: Erinnerungen an Kriegswirren und missionarische Friedensarbeit.* Barmen: Missionhaus, 1896.

———. *Unsere Ovambo-Mission.* Barmen: RMS, 1900.

Broadbent, Rev. Samuel. *The Missionary Martyr of Namaqualand: Memorials of the Rev. William Threlfall, Late Wesleyan Missionary in South Africa* .... London: J. Mason, 1857.

Büttner, C. G. *Kolonialpolitik und Christentum, betrachtet mit Einblick auf die deutschen Unternehmungen in Südwestafrika.* Heidelberg: Carl Winter's Universitätsbuchhandlung, 1885.

Cook, Rev. Edward (comp. John Cook). *The Modern Missionary.* Liverpool: Thomas Kaye, 1849.

Drascher, W., and H. J. Rust (eds.). *Festschrift: Dr. H. C. Heinrich Vedder, Ein leben für Südwestafrika.* 2 inhaltlich unveränderte Auflage. Windhoek: SWA Wissenschaftliche Gesellschaft, 1961.

Dymond, G. W. "The Idea of God in Ovamboland, South-West Africa." Pp. 135–155. In Edwin William Smith, ed. *African Ideas of God: A Symposium.* London: Edinburgh House Press, 1950.

Engel, L. *Kolonialismus und Nationalismus im deutschen Protestanismus in Namibia 1907 bis 1945* .... Bern: Herbert Lang, 1976.

Evangelische Akademie. *Die Zukunft Namibias und die Kirchen: Bericht einer Tagung vom 3 bis 5 Oktober 1975.* Bad Boll: Evangelische Akademie, [1976].

The Finnish Missionary Society and Evangelical Lutheran Ovambokavango Church 1859–1959. Windhoek Library, 1960.

Groth, Siegfried. "The Condemnation of Apartheid by the Churches of South West Africa." *International Review of Missions* 61, No. 242 (April 1972): 183–193.

Hahn, Theophilus. *Tsuni-//Goam: The Supreme Being of the Khoi-Khoi.* London: Trübner & Co., 1881.

Holmio, Armas Kustaa Ensio. *The Finnish Missionary Society, 1859–1950*. Hancock, Michigan: 1950.

Loth, Heinrich. *Die Christliche Mission in Südwestafrika: Zur Destruktiven Rolle der Rheinischen Missiongesellschaft* . . . . Berlin: Akademie-Verlag, 1963.

Marshall, Lorna. "!Kung Bushmen Religious Beliefs." *Africa* 32 (1962): 221–252.

Moister, Rev. William. *Barnabas Shaw: The Story of His Life and Missionary Labours in Southern Africa*. London: Wesleyan Conference Office, 1877.

Mossolow, N. *Otjikango oder Gross Barmen: Ortsgeschichte der erster Rheinischen Herero-Missionsstation in Südwestafrika, 1844–1904*. Windhoek: John Meinert (Pty) Ltd., 1968.

"Octocentenary of the Church of Finland: A Church that Has Pioneered in S.W.A." *South African Outlook* (August 1955): 124.

Olpp, Johannes. *Deutsche Missions- und Segensstätten in Südwest beim Uebergang der Kolonie in andre Hände*. Barmen: Missionshauses, Rheinische Missions Gesellschaft, 1922.

Rohden, L. von. *Geschichte der Rheinische Missionsgesellschaft*. Barmen: Missionhaus, 1888.

Schlosser, Katesa. *Eingeborenenkirchen in Süd- und Südwestafrika, ihre Geschichte und Sozialstruktur*. Kiel: Walter G. Mülau, 1958.

Shejavali, A. *The Ovambo-Kavango Church*. Helsinki: Suomen Lähetysseura, 1970.

Strassberger, Elfriede. *The Rhenish Mission Society in South Africa 1830–1950*. Cape Town: C. Struik (Pty.) Ltd., 1969.

Tindall, Benjamin Arthur. *The Journal of Joseph Tindall, Missionary in South West Africa 1839–1855.* Cape Town: The Van Riebeeck Society, 1959.

Winter, Colin O'Brien. "Church and State in South West Africa." *South African Outlook* 102, No. 1210 (March 1972): 38–40.

———. "Cracks in the Granite Wall." *Pro Veritate* (December 1971): 10–12.

Wood, Joseph, *Methodism in South West Africa.* Rondebosch: 1956.

D. Sociology

Abrahams, Kenneth. "The Waserauta Phenomenon: Additional Notes on The Namibian Elite." *The Namibian Review* No. 25 (July/August 1982): 21–31.

Becker, Peter. *Tribe to Township.* St. Albans: Panther, 1974.

Clarence-Smith, W. G., and Richard Moorsom. "Underdevelopment and Class formation in Ovamboland, 1845–1915." *Journal of African History* 16, No. 3 (1975): 365–381.

Collins, Carole. "SWAPO Images of a Future Society: Women in Namibia." *Issue* 7, No. 4 (1977): 39–45.

Draper, P. "!Kung Women: Contrasts in Sexual Egalitarianism in the Foraging and Sedentary Contexts." Pp. 77–109. In R. Reiter, ed. *Toward an Anthropology of Women.* New York: Monthly Review Press, 1975.

———. "The Learning Environment for Aggression and Antisocial Behavior among the !Kung." Pp. 31–53. In A. Montagu, ed. *Teaching Non-Aggression.* New York: Oxford University Press, 1978.

Gordon, Robert J. "Variations in Migration Rates: The Ovambo Case." *Journal of Southern African Affairs* 3, No. 3 (July 1978): 261–294.

Hishongwa, Ndeutala Selma. *Women of Namibia*. Stockholm: By and Bygd, 1983.

Köhler, O. "The Stage of Acculturation in South West Africa." *Sociologus* 6 (1956).

Morna, Colleen Lowe. "Women's New Equality." *Africa Report* 35, No. 3 (1990): 31–33.

Pendleton, Wade C. *Katutura: A Place Where We Do Not Stay*. San Diego: San Diego State University Press, 1974.

————. "Social Categorization and Language Use in Windhoek, South West Africa." Pp. 63–80. In Kileff, C. et al., eds. *Urban Man in Southern Africa*. Gwelo: Mambo Press, 1975.

Steenkamp, Dr. W. P. *Is the South-West African Herero Committing Race Suicide?* Cape Town: Unie-Volkspers Bpk., [n.d., c. 1944].

ABOUT THE AUTHOR

JOHN J. GROTPETER (B.S., St. Louis University; M.A., Duke University; Ph.D., Washington University—St. Louis) was Professor of Political Science at the St. Louis College of Pharmacy, where he also held an endowed chair as the William S. and Edith C. Bucke Professor of Liberal Arts. He was the founder and, for 25 years, director of the college's Liberal Arts Division. His doctoral dissertation, completed in 1965, was on the early political history of Swaziland, Basutoland, and Bechuanaland. His first book, *The Pattern of African Decolonization: A New Interpretation* (1973), was co-authored with Warren Weinstein, and dealt with those countries as well as Rwanda and Burundi. His *Historical Dictionary of Swaziland* was published by Scarecrow Press in 1975, and his *Historical Dictionary of Zambia* (Scarecrow Press) followed in 1979. He visited Namibia for research purposes in both 1982 and 1991. He has written many articles, book reviews, and conference papers on southern African topics. In addition he has worked in the area of general education, forming the Liberal Education Special Interest Group in the American Association of Colleges of Pharmacy, and served as a member of the AACP Focus Group on the Liberalization of the Professional Curriculum.